Social Media Listening and Monitoring for Business Applications

N. Raghavendra Rao
FINAIT Consultancy Services, India

A volume in the Advances in E–Business Research
(AEBR) Book Series

www.igi-global.com

Published in the United States of America by
IGI Global
Business Science Reference (an imprint of IGI Global)
701 E. Chocolate Avenue
Hershey PA, USA 17033
Tel: 717-533-8845
Fax: 717-533-8661
E-mail: cust@igi-global.com
Web site: http://www.igi-global.com

Library of Congress Cataloging-in-Publication Data

Names: Rao, N. Raghavendra, 1939- editor.
Title: Social media listening and monitoring for business applications / N.
   Raghavendra Rao, editor.
Description: Hershey : Business Science Reference, 2016. | Series: Advances
   in e-business research | Includes bibliographical references and index.
Identifiers: LCCN 2016023650| ISBN 9781522508465 (hardcover) | ISBN
   9781522508472 (ebook)
Subjects: LCSH: Electronic commerce--Computer programs. | Electronic
   commerce--Computer networks. | Social media. | Information
   technology--Management.
Classification: LCC HF5548.32 .S6336 2016 | DDC 658.8/72--dc23 LC record available at https://lccn.loc.gov/2016023650

This book is published in the IGI Global book series Advances in E-Business Research (AEBR) (ISSN: 1935-2700; eISSN: 1935-2719)

British Cataloguing in Publication Data
A Cataloguing in Publication record for this book is available from the British Library.

For electronic access to this publication, please contact: eresources@igi-global.com.

Advances in E-Business Research (AEBR) Book Series

In Lee
Western Illinois University, USA

ISSN: 1935-2700
EISSN: 1935-2719

MISSION

Technology has played a vital role in the emergence of e-business and its applications incorporate strategies. These processes have aided in the use of electronic transactions via telecommunications networks for collaborating with business partners, buying and selling of goods and services, and customer service. Research in this field continues to develop into a wide range of topics, including marketing, psychology, information systems, accounting, economics, and computer science.

The **Advances in E-Business Research (AEBR) Book Series** provides multidisciplinary references for researchers and practitioners in this area. Instructors, researchers, and professionals interested in the most up-to-date research on the concepts, issues, applications, and trends in the e-business field will find this collection, or individual books, extremely useful. This collection contains the highest quality academic books that advance understanding of e-business and addresses the challenges faced by researchers and practitioners.

COVERAGE

- Economics of e-business
- E-procurement methods
- Web advertising
- Online consumer behavior
- B2B e-marketplaces
- Social network
- Electronic Supply Chain Management
- E-Marketing
- E-business standardizations
- Semantic Web

IGI Global is currently accepting manuscripts for publication within this series. To submit a proposal for a volume in this series, please contact our Acquisition Editors at Acquisitions@igi-global.com or visit: http://www.igi-global.com/publish/.

Titles in this Series

For a list of additional titles in this series, please visit: www.igi-global.com

Securing Transactions and Payment Systems for M-Commerce
Sushila Madan (University of Delhi, India) and Jyoti Batra Arora (Banasthali Vidyapeeth University, India)
Business Science Reference • copyright 2016 • 349pp • H/C (ISBN: 9781522502364) • US $205.00 (our price)

E-Retailing Challenges and Opportunities in the Global Marketplace
Shailja Dixit (Amity University, India) and Amit Kumar Sinha (Amity University, India)
Business Science Reference • copyright 2016 • 358pp • H/C (ISBN: 9781466699212) • US $215.00 (our price)

Successful Technological Integration for Competitive Advantage in Retail Settings
Eleonora Pantano (Middlesex University London, UK)
Business Science Reference • copyright 2015 • 405pp • H/C (ISBN: 9781466682979) • US $200.00 (our price)

Strategic E-Commerce Systems and Tools for Competing in the Digital Marketplace
Mehdi Khosrow-Pour (Information Resources Management Association, USA)
Business Science Reference • copyright 2015 • 315pp • H/C (ISBN: 9781466681330) • US $185.00 (our price)

The Evolution of the Internet in the Business Sector Web 1.0 to Web 3.0
Pedro Isaías (Universidade Aberta (Portuguese Open University), Portugal) Piet Kommers (University of Twente, The Netherlands) and Tomayess Issa (Curtin University, Australia)
Business Science Reference • copyright 2015 • 407pp • H/C (ISBN: 9781466672628) • US $235.00 (our price)

RFID Technology Integration for Business Performance Improvement
In Lee (Western Illinois University, USA)
Business Science Reference • copyright 2015 • 317pp • H/C (ISBN: 9781466663084) • US $225.00 (our price)

Integrating Social Media into Business Practice, Applications, Management, and Models
In Lee (Western Illinois University, USA)
Business Science Reference • copyright 2014 • 325pp • H/C (ISBN: 9781466661820) • US $225.00 (our price)

Electronic Payment Systems for Competitive Advantage in E-Commerce
Francisco Liébana-Cabanillas (University of Granada, Spain) Francisco Muñoz-Leiva (University of Granada, Spain) Juan Sánchez-Fernández (University of Granada, Spain) and Myriam Martínez-Fiestas (ESAN University, Perú)
Business Science Reference • copyright 2014 • 393pp • H/C (ISBN: 9781466651906) • US $215.00 (our price)

www.igi-global.com

701 E. Chocolate Ave., Hershey, PA 17033
Order online at www.igi-global.com or call 717-533-8845 x100
To place a standing order for titles released in this series, contact: cust@igi-global.com
Mon-Fri 8:00 am - 5:00 pm (est) or fax 24 hours a day 717-533-8661

Table of Contents

Section 1
Business in Social Media Environment

Section 2
Big Data and Knowledge Management Concepts in Social Media

Section 3
Social Media Metrics

Section 4
Conceptual Business Models in Social Media Environment

Section 5
Software Tools for Analysis and Research in Social Media Sites

Detailed Table of Contents

Section 1
Business in Social Media Environment

Chapter 1

R. Venkatesh, VIT Business School Chennai, India
Sudarsan Jayasingh, VIT Business School Chennai, India

Social media are widely used in regular operations of many companies, including start-ups, small, medium and large organizations. The Social media are fundamentally changing the way we communicate, consume, collaborate and create. It creates one of the most transformative impacts on business. The most significant consequence of social media has been the shift of power from the institution to the individual. These shifts in the consumer-brand relationship have thrown up new challenges and opportunities for business organization. Social media have transformed the ways businesses from marketing and operations to finance and human resource management. Increasingly, social media are also transforming the way businesses relate to workers, allowing them to build flexible relationships with remote talent, to crowdsource new ideas, or to engage in micro outsourcing. Social media are increasingly being used in organizations to improve relationships among employees and nurture collaboration and the sharing culture. The purpose of this research is to explore the major changes which have taken place in organization because of social media.

Chapter 2

Kijpokin Kasemsap, Suan Sunandha Rajabhat University, Thailand

This chapter explains the overview of social media; the perspectives of social media marketing; social media and communication management; social media competence and knowledge sharing in modern business; social media applications in the tourism industry; social media applications in the health care industry; the multifaceted applications of social media platforms in modern business; and the importance of social media in the modern business world. The implementation of social media is required for modern organizations that seek to serve suppliers and customers, increase business performance, strengthen competitiveness, and achieve continuous success in the modern business world. The chapter argues that applying social media has the potential to enhance organizational performance and reach strategic goals in the social media age.

Chapter 3

Neus Soler-Labajos, Open University of Catalonia, Spain
Ana Isabel Jiménez-Zarco, Open University of Catalonia, Spain

Companies gain competitive advantage when they are in a better position than its competitors to keep customers, so for providing the greatest value, become a captivating option, generate satisfaction and achieve the loyalty of consumers, it is necessary that they know the market and enter into a profitable relationship with the customer. In order to get closer to the public, the social media presence stands as a very attractive option for the companies, but these wonder if the effort will offset the result obtained. In this chapter, we will define the concept of enterprise 2.0, and will explain the main benefits that a company can get with the adoption of social media, in relation to its brand image and reputation, communication with the public and the increase of traffic that it can get to the corporate website. Then, and after pointing out the most popular social software tools, we will focus on social media metrics, defining the different types of metrics, designing a framework of social analysis and highlighting those that prove to be of greater business value.

Section 2
Big Data and Knowledge Management Concepts in Social Media

Chapter 4

Matilda S., IFET College of Engineering, India

Information technology has reached its pinnacle, with the era being dominated by two hi-tech driving forces - Big data and Social media. Big data encompasses a wide array of data mining workloads, extracted through various sources, the results of which are of keen interest to business leaders and analysts across every industry segment. Data from the social media is exploding at an exponential rate and is being hailed as the key, to crucial insights into human behavior. Extracting intelligent information from such immense volume, variety and velocity of data, in context to the business requirement is the need of the hour. Therefore, new tools and methods specialized for big data analytics is crucial, along with the architectures for managing and processing such data. Big data complemented with Social Media offers a new horizon to take management practice to an advanced level.

Chapter 5

Srinivasan Vaidyanathan, VIT Business School, Chennai, India
Sudarsanam S. K., VIT Business School, Chennai, India

This chapter discusses in detail about Knowledge Management and how Social Media tools and platforms can be used for Knowledge Management and how they can be integrated into Knowledge Management system. This chapter explains the key aspects of Knowledge Management and Social Media and how

Social media can be used to capture both tacit and explicit knowledge and also to share knowledge among the communities of practice both within organizations and also outside the organizations. The chapter provides an overview of using social media to enhance knowledge management and collaboration in a corporate context and gives an insight on how firms get the most value from social media tools like wikis, blogs, microblogging, social tagging and some such similar tools in Knowledge Management. Further research directions based on the review of the literature are proposed.

Section 3
Social Media Metrics

Social media is perhaps responsible for largest share of traffic on the Internet. It is one of the largest online activities with people from all over the globe making its use for some sort of activity. The behaviour of these networks, important actors and groups and the way individual actors influence an idea or activity on these networks, etc. can be measured using social network analysis metrics. These metrics can be as simple as number of likes on Facebook or number of views on YouTube or as complex as clustering co-efficient which determines future collaborations on the basis of present status of the network. This chapter explores and discusses various social network metrics which can be used to analyse and explain important questions related to different types of networks. It also tries to explain the basic mathematics behind the working of these metrics. The use of these metrics for analysis of collaboration networks in an academic setup has been explored and results presented. A new metric called "Average Degree of Collaboration" has been defined to quantify collaborations within institutions.

This chapter talks about what is social media, theories developed in social media, frameworks of social media, how organizations can build into the social media framework the business objectives. This chapter also discusses about the key social media metrics, their definitions, and guidelines on choosing the right metrics to address the key social media objectives for campaigns or product launches. This Chapter would help organizations identify the key social media metrics they need to track and monitor to measure the performance of their brands, products and services in the social media channels. Once the key social media metrics are identified, Organizations can choose the right tool to measure the metrics defined. This chapter provides a list of more than twenty different tools which could be used across social media channels like facebook, twitter, pinterest, LinkedIn, Google+ etc. Dashboards of various social media channels and also some customized dashboards are mentioned in this chapter. These dashboards will provide an overview of the performance of the social media metrics over a period of time. This would help Organizations to improve or enhance their marketing and operational business strategies by leveraging the power and reach of the social media channels. This Chapter highlights the limitations and the cost of performance reporting in social media. The future directions for research and the references provided would be of great help to researchers in the area of social media metrics.

Section 4
Conceptual Business Models in Social Media Environment

Chapter 8

Social Media is becoming increasingly important in society and culture; making people to join together on common interests and share opinions through internet. Most of the business organizations have been using social media as a communication tool for public relations and marketing. It is high time government departments should engage citizens of their country for interaction through social media. There are many schemes and programs initiated by the government need the attention of their citizens in a country. Government departments are required to form strategies to involve their citizens for making use of their schemes and programs. This chapter stresses the need for making use of social media by a government creating awareness of the schemes and programs to their citizens. Further it explains the importance of the interaction with their citizens through social media for good governance.

Chapter 9

Rapid changes are taking place in global business scenario. It has become a necessity for enterprises to adapt to these changes. Social media facilitates business enterprises to make use of the opportunities in the global market. Social media has become an important source of information for the stakeholders of business enterprises. Structured, semi-structured, and unstructured data from social media provide a good scope for developing business models for enterprises. This chapter mainly talks about developing the conceptual business models in the sectors such as automobiles, textiles and software developing companies. Further, this chapter explains making use of the concepts such as virtual reality, multimedia and cloud computing with the data from social media in developing conceptual business models.

Section 5
Software Tools for Analysis and Research in Social Media Sites

Chapter 10

Sentiment analysis has been used to assess people's feelings, attitudes, and beliefs, ranging from positive to negative, on a variety of phenomena. Several new autocoding features in NVivo 11 Plus enable the capturing of sentiment analysis and extraction of themes from text datasets. This chapter describes eight scenarios in which these tools may be applied to social media data, to (1) profile egos and entities, (2) analyze groups, (3) explore metadata for latent public conceptualizations, (4) examine trending public issues, (5) delve into public concepts, (6) observe public events, (7) analyze brand reputation, and (8) inspect text corpora for emergent insights.

Chapter 11
Shalin Hai-Jew, Kansas State University, USA

To introduce how related tags networks may be extracted from Flickr® and used for "gist" and other analysis, this chapter describes the related tag networks associated with some of the cities of the People's Republic of China (used as seeding terms). The software used for the data extractions (from the Flickr® API) and the creation of various graph visualizations is the free and open-source Network Overview, Discovery and Exploration for Excel (NodeXL Basic), available on Microsoft's CodePlex platform.

Chapter 12
Shalin Hai-Jew, Kansas State University, USA

For social media to work as a "human sensor network" or a relevant source for "eventgraphing" for some fast-moving events, it is important to be capture real-time and locational information. It may help to not only capture information from a particular social media platform but from across the Web. In such a context, Maltego Carbon 3.5.3/Chlorine 3.6.0's Tweet Analyser "machine" (with AlchemyAPI built-in) and used in combination with other "transforms," may serve the purpose—at least for initial and iterated sampling of the related messaging. This tool may be used to capture information from social media accounts.. social media accounts, linked URLs, geolocational information, and other information of research value. Maltego is an open-access tool with a community version and a proprietary commercial version available by subscription. Maltego Chlorine's Tweet Analyzer has a built-in sentiment analysis feature.

Chapter 13
Shalin Hai-Jew, Kansas State University, USA

There has been little work done on American emigration abroad and even less done on the formal renunciation of American citizenship. This chapter provides an overview of both phenomena in the research literature and then provides some methods for using the extraction of social media data and their visualization as a way of tapping into the public mindsets about these social phenomena. The software tools used include the following: Network Overview, Discovery and Exploration for Excel (NodeXL Basic), NVivo, and Maltego Carbon; the social media platforms used include the following: Wikipedia, YouTube, Twitter, and Flickr.

Chapter 14
Shalin Hai-Jew, Kansas State University, USA

Various research findings suggest that humans often mistake social robot ('bot) accounts for human in a microblogging context. The core research question here asks whether the use of social network analysis may help identify whether a social media account is fully automated, semi-automated, or fully human (embodied personhood)—in the contexts of Twitter and Wikipedia. Three hypotheses are considered: that automated social media account networks will have less diversity and less heterophily; that automated social media accounts will tend to have a botnet social structure, and that cyborg accounts will have select features of human- and robot- social media accounts. The findings suggest limited ability to differentiate the levels of automation in a social media account based solely on social network analysis alone in the face of a determined and semi-sophisticated adversary given the ease of network account sock-puppetry but does suggest some effective detection approaches in combination with other information streams.

Preface

Staying in touch with friends, family members and professionals from any part of the world has become possible under the different social networking sites through internet. The sites such as Facebook, Twitter, LinkedIn and numerous similar sites are facilitating people to form groups. These groups express and exchange their views, tastes, preferences and experiences among themselves. Online communication of the above groups is termed as social media. Now business enterprises make use of social media channels for their business activities. Social Media has also started gaining importance in business enterprises. This channel is mainly being used in the functional areas such as marketing and public relations by some business enterprises. This approach is known as social media marketing. The concept of social media marketing basically refers to the process of promoting business in websites through social media channels. This is an extremely useful tool for information, products description, promotion of products or services and all integrated in the chain of networking world. Many organizations have started adopting this method. It is mainly considered for a low cost promotional method.

A social media program is required to be designed before enterprises decide to make use of social media for their business. Implementation of process of social media program in an enterprise has four stages. The first stage is to understand the potential of various social media tools. The second stage is to identify business activities which need social media. The third stage is to choose and map various social media tools with the business activities and also with the relevant content strategies. Finally, an enterprise needs to measure social media effectiveness through predefined measurement metrics.

One of the most challenging tasks for social media strategist is convincing the management of the business enterprises on their return of investment from social media programs. Most of the activities of social media have no direct financial impact on website visitors, impressions, customer complaints, positive responses, re tweets, YouTube views, Face Book friends, Social mention, Blog comments, visitors to brick and mortar stores, delivered e-mails and other related activities. It is necessary to identify these activities for the business benefits. Business benefits will become baseline metrics before the launch of social media program. This process will also provide a proof that the concept of social media is working.

Data and information generated from the customers and prospective customers of an enterprise through their social media channels are available in the form of structured, semi structured and unstructured. Every business needs data and information from its social media sites for analysis and developing business models. The required data and information are already available in the social media channels created by the business enterprises. Many business enterprises are yet to make use of this source for their business purposes. There is a good scope for developing business models using the concepts of collaborative technology with the inputs form social media channels. Adapting to new methods is needed not only to survive but also thrive in the new business environment.

Information technology provides access to vast amount of structured, semi structured and unstructured data in Big Data. The users in enterprises need to master integrating that information and those technology capabilities to create relevant context. Cloud environment is preferred for processing because of the nature of data being big. The above two concepts are more useful for data in social media. The reason is because of volume, velocity and variety. Emerging concepts such as social media intelligence, social media analytics and social media metrics can be applied in making use of the information in Big Data for business strategy and decisions.

In the present business scenario success is no longer guaranteed for enterprises that have financial resources and size on their side. Smaller enterprises that are flexible can provide products or services at a faster pace and lower cost. Social media are facilitating them to achieve this. As boundaries are shrinking the level of competition is going up. Enterprises need to plan their business in both domestic and international markets. The better strategy will be integrating business with the knowledge of domain experts and making use of software and management tools. This will help them to gain competitive advantage in the present global market scenario. Social media facilitate to achieve the above strategy.

Social media is also useful for social cause. When disaster strikes, communication is often interrupted. In order to get assistance and aid for the affected area, an open on line of communication is critical in a crisis. Social media is being utilized more frequently for the relief effort. Friends and loved ones of victims who frantically search for information are now using wireless technology and social networking such as twitter, face book, flicker and you tube for information and assistance. It is interesting to note forester analyst Jererniah Owyang has used his blog to bring attention to the situation in China during the devastating earthquake occurred in that country. Jereniah used his blog as a platform to inspire people to donate money to the Red Cross.

FOCUS OF THE BOOK

Many new concepts have been emerging in information and communication technology discipline. Close analysis of these concepts indicate many of these concepts are the extension of the existing concepts. Every new concept has an advantage over the previous concept. Sometimes two or more concepts or technologies are combined to evolve a new concept. Social media is one among them. Further social media is changing business landscape across the borders of countries. This book mainly talks about transformation and managing business, making use of the concepts such as Big Data, Knowledge Management, and metrics under the social media environment. This book gives an idea of developing conceptual business models with the data from social media sites. This book stresses the importance of making use of software tools in the social media sites for the purpose of analysis and research.

BENEFITS FROM SOCIAL MEDIA

Social media tools empower all the stake holders of business enterprise to integrate most of the functional areas in the business enterprises for business processes and decisions. Mainly research, marketing, sales customer services and product development functions in organizations can be included within the social media programs. There is a scope for carrying out research activities for developing business models for manufacturing, education, and government sectors under social media programs.

TARGET AUDIENCE

This book offers comprehensive view of social media for business applications. This book would be useful as reference for research scholars, research and development departments in the corporate and education sectors. It is also a course supplement to the students pursuing business management and information technology related subjects. This is also a good resource for software professionals who are involved in developing business application models under social media environment. This will be useful for the corporate executives who want to update themselves in emerging trends in business.

GIST OF CHAPTERS

This book is broadly divided under five sections covering, Business in social media environment. Big data and Knowledge management concepts in social media, Social Media Metrics, Conceptual Business Models under social media environment, and Software tools for analysis and research in social media sites.

The contributors of this book are from academics and professionals who are involved in research related to the concept of social media and developing business models using this concept.

In introduction the editor observes that information and communication technology is the major stimulus for change in the various sectors in the business. Rapid advances in the internet have made the concept of social media popular. This concept is also gaining importance in business. Social media are nothing more than special class of web sites. These websites are considered as second generation web sites. The first generation websites are those created by organizations or an authority. Second generation websites such as social media websites by contrast are platforms that provide users for making use of tools to create their own mini websites or web pages. Social media sites have three distinctive characteristics. The first characteristic talks about the content being generated by the users themselves. The second characteristic allows integrating easily with other sites. The third characteristic is related to high degree of participation and interaction among users.

The editor indicates the role of social media in business functions and the importance of implementation of social media programs in business organizations. Further the editor talks about the various aspects in social media from the business perspective.

R. Venkatesh and Sudarsan Jayasing in their chapter "Transformation of Business through Social Media" talk about the dynamics of business are changing. Social media marketing is the result of changes taking place in traditional marketing. The authors feel that social media marketing is becoming very important due to the changes of the behavior of customers. Customers are adapting to new technologies and getting familiar with world business environment. The authors indicate the need for change of approach in customer relationship management by organizations in the present social media environment. Further they stress handling of risks and monitoring of business activities in the new business scenario. This indicates the importance of strong relationship with customers through engagement on social media platforms. They also explain HR practices, recruitment approach and knowledge management in social media environment for business purposes.

Kijpokin Kasemsap in his chapter "Mastering Social Media in the Modern Business World" explains the theoretical and practical overview of social media. While talking about the communication management, he observes that social media facilitates to build and maintain positive responses with the stake holders of the organizations. Social media has become an essential tool in the tourism sector for accessing various sources for tourist information. Healthcare professionals are able to share case studies and professional knowledge through Social Media sites. The author feels that social media facilitate to innovate on the basis of user generated ideas. Social media give ideas for the adoption of new business practices for the benefit of good governance.

Neus Soler Labajus and Ana Isabel Jimenez-Zarco in the chapter "Productivity on Social Media Web: Use of Social Media Expectations Response" talk about the parameters for calculation of return of investment in social media. The authors explain the various variables are to be considered from the angle of impact of relationship in social media sites. They mention about return on engagement in social media. They emphasize the importance of key performance indicators for implementation of social media plan in organizations. Further they relate the objectives in social media with key performance indicators with initiatives. They also make a mention about prediction markets in social media environment.

S. Matilda in her chapter "Big Data in Social Media Environment: A Business Perspective" observes that the concept of Big Data is more useful for the data in social media sites. The author talks about the significance of Big Data in the social media environment for the sectors such as banking and finance, healthcare, manufacturing, retail marketing, government, education and research. The author feels that big data is less about the data itself and more about one does with the data. While discussing about the types of big data analytics, the author explains the importance of predictive analytics and prescriptive analytics. The author makes a mention of dynamics and limitations of Big Data in social media. Further the author talks about the future prospects of Big Data in social media.

Srinivasan Vaidyanathan observes in his chapter "Social Media in Knowledge Management" that the integration of social media tools into knowledge management programs in corporate is gaining importance. Adoption of social media by business enterprises has been steadily increasing with its applications extending to various corporate functions besides marketing and customer management. This approach may be considered as a corporate strategy. He feels that social media can be helpful for tacit knowledge sharing through interaction and collaborative technology in business organizations. He discusses about the implementation approaches, opportunities and challenges of social media in the global business management scenario.

Tasleem Arif and Rashid Ali in their chapter "Social Media Metrics in an Academic Setup" say that the computational power of computers and their ability to store large amounts of data has provided the much needed impetus to the analysis and understanding of large scale complex social networks. While explaining the social networks, they say a network in simple terms is an organized collection of nodes or actors and their inter connections or relationships. Networks can be as simple as blood relations between two individuals or as complex as the World Wide Web. The relationships between actors have some sort of social bearing. They are called as social networks. They discuss about the levels and metrics of social network analysis. Further they have explained a new metric called "Average Degree of Collaboration" for quantifying collaborations within academic institutions.

Sudarsanam S. K. in his chapter "Social Media Metrics" explains the difference between traditional media and social media. The author gives an overview of AMEC social media frame work. He explains AMEC social media metrics model. He also gives an idea of AMEC channel metrics frame work. He discusses the guide lines for defining the key performance indicators. He says that social media metrics and bench marking of metrics should be based on the key objectives of organizations. He gives a list of various social media analytical tools for analyzing data in the social media sites. He feels that leveraging the power of social media will help business organizations to be competitive in the present business scenario.

N. Ragavendra Rao in his chapter "Social Media: An Enabler for Governance" talks about a conceptual business model for governance. This model mainly concentrates the need for interaction with citizens in a country through social media channels by governments. He suggests that a government should create an exclusive social media channel for citizen's articulation of their interests and explanations. He feels that it would be better that the government indicates their tentative plans and policies pertaining to such as deforestation of forests preserving wild animals, use of pesticides, disposal of waste materials and other related issues on the social media channels created exclusively for their citizens. Then only it will be possible for the citizens to take the part in the discussion and express their views on the proposed polices of the government. Their views will facilitate to frame proper policies by a government. The author mentions the discussion of professionals in their social media channels with regard to the rain and floods in Chennai (India). These discussions provide their professional views of the disaster management. The author narrates that several help groups in Chennai used the online media, as it was the only virtual communication room to get in touch with emergency numbers of ambulance during the disaster. The constant stream of whats app forwards and other social media channels extended help to the people stuck in the flood affected areas.

N. Ragavendra Rao in his chapter "Social Media: An Enabler in Developing Business Models for Enterprises" observes the existing ways of doing business are constantly changing. Opportunities in the in the present global markets are to be exploited at a rapid pace. Every business enterprise has unique challenges to face in its sector. It is high time business enterprises take advantages of making use of social media for their business. He feels that data from social media facilitates enterprises in developing conceptual business models for their products and services. Conceptual business models are nothing but identifying the relevant concepts in information and communication technology making use of them with the data from social media in developing business models appropriate to their business activities. He discusses three case illustrations in the sectors such as automobiles, textiles and management consultancy firms. Data and information generated in their social media channels from the interactions with their customers and prospective customers facilitate them to develop business models for their organizations. The author indicates social media channels can create an efficient frame work to leverage in business. Further he observes that technology does not drive change and it only enables change in enterprises.

Shalin Hai-Jew in the chapter "Employing the Sentiment Analysis Tool in NVivo11 Plus on Social Media Data: Eight Initial Case Types" says that sentiment analysis can be used to assess people's feelings, attitudes and beliefs ranging from positive to negative on a variety of phenomena from the data in social media. The author explains that several new auto coding features in NVivo11 plus tool facilitate to carry out sentiment analysis and extraction of themes from the text data sets. The author talks about the research approach in using NVivo11 tool for sentiment analysis with the social media data. The author explains about eight scenarios in which these tools have been applied to social media data.

The sentiment analysis tool enables asking questions about various types of social media data. The author explains from the eight types of targeted social media. They are (1) profiling the personalities of egos entities through related social media account, (2) describing the personalities of groups with interacting members (in ego neighborhoods, ad hoc networks, editing groups, and others) through network analysis and then sentiment analysis, (3) exploring meta data (folksonomic related tag networks and article networks) to surface latent public conceptualizations, (4) examining trending public issues through socially shared data and discourse sets, (5) delving into public concepts through socially shared data and discourse sets, (6) observing public events through socially shared data and discourse sets, (7) analyzing broad scale brand reputation through socially shared data and discourse sets, and (8) inspecting various individual texts and text corpuses for emergent insights. The author clearly explains the outcome of the above types of targeted social media by using the tool NVivo11 Plus for the sentimental analysis.

Shalin Hai-Jew in the chapter "Capturing the Gist(s) of Image Sets Associated with Chinese Cities through Related Tags Networks on Flickr[(R)]" talks about the related tags networks can be extracted from Flickr[(R)] and used for 'GIST' and other analysis's. The software tools used in data extractions and creation of various graphs visualization are Open Source Network Over View, Discovery and Exploration for Excel (NodeXL). These are available on Microsoft's Code Plex platform. The author introduced related tags networks and focused on a select list of cities in modern China as seeding terms. These networks have been extracted from Flickr[(R)] at I degree, 1.5 degree and 2 degrees, using NodeXL. This research work explores a case of the use metadata for information value, based on a limited use case. The author feels the research value of exploring related networks is only just beginning. It needs to be explored by further research. The author feels not much research is done in this area. The author's research work will be the base for further research in this area.

Shalin Hai-Jew in the chapter "Real Time Sentiment Analysis of Micro Blog Messages with the Maltego 'Tweet Analyzer' Machine" says twitter is one of the foremost micro blogging sites. The author also indicates twitter has been a favorite with the data mining researchers and general public. Twitter has enabled to have access of historical data, real time data and dynamic data with its application programming inter faces in the micro blogging sites. The author observes that Maltego is an open access tool with a community version. There is a proprietary commercial version available by subscription. This tool is more useful in micro blogging sites environment. The author talks about engaging public opinion of events and socio cultural phenomena through dynamic tweet extractions and sentiment analysis. Further the author explains Maltego tweet analyzer facilitates the process of extraction and analysis. The author has done an extensive research on the data in micro blogging sites by using the above tool. The author observes the tool Maltego Chlorine Tweet Analyzer provides some pretty capabilities.

Shalin Hai-Jew in the chapter "Exploring Public Perceptions of Native Born American Emigration Abroad and Renunciation of American Citizenship through Social Media" talks about the issues of American emigration and the renunciation of US citizenship. The author used the software tools such as Network Overview, Discovery and Exploration for Excel (NodeXL), NVivo and Maltego Carbon on the social media sites for understanding the public mindsets about this social phenomenon. The social media platforms selected for using the above tools are Wikipedia, YouTube, Twitter, and Flickr.

The author explores the relatively uncommon phenomena of American expatriation and the rare extreme cases of citizenship renunciation. The author has considered the sampling from an open and crowd sourced encyclopedia. The sources for sampling are from massive collection of videos on video content sharing sites, micro blogging sites and digital images and video sharing sites. The types of data extractions are article networks on Wikipedia, video networks on you tube, #hash tagged conversations on twitter. The author observes that the application of a range of techniques that could be applied to social media data for exploring something of the public mind (the broad conscious, subconscious, and unconscious mind) on a topic based on collective electronic spaces. The author feels these approaches are quite rudimentary. Further the author indicates that the potential for research in this area is enormous.

Shalin Hai-Jew in the chapter "Finding Automated (Bot, Sensor) or Semi-Automated (Cyborg) Social Media Accounts Using Network Analysis and NodeXL" observes that on a number of social media platforms today, there are accounts that are masks for algorithmic actors. They are robots and sensors, as well as cyborgs. Cyborgs represent human assisted robots or robot assisted humans. The author considers three hypotheses for the research. First hypothesis is in respect of purely automated social media accounts that will have a lot of less diversity and heterophily in their networks than non-automated (human) networks. The second hypothesis is the degree of the nodes in automated social media account's network that has one dominant account and a lot of other follower accounts. The third hypothesis is cyborg in social media platforms are popularly referred to as bot assisted humans or humans assisted bots. The author explains the results of the research in respect of the three hypotheses mentioned above.

IMPACT OF THIS BOOK

Social Media is growing at rapid pace. Now it has become a necessity for enterprises need to incorporate the concept of social media in their functional areas of their business. This book mainly focuses on the various aspects social media for business applications. Further this book highlights the importance of data in social media sites for business and research work.

N. Raghavendra Rao
FINAIT Consultancy Services, India

Acknowledgment

At the outset, I would like to thank all the chapter authors for their excellent contributions. I would like to offer my special thanks to IGI Global for giving me the opportunity to edit this publication. I would like to acknowledge the role of the reviewers and members of the editorial board for their support. Finally, I thank my wife Meera for her continuous encouragement and support in my scholastic pursuits.

N. Raghavendra Rao
FINAIT Consultancy Services, India

Introduction

Information and communication technologies are the major stimulus for changes in trade, commerce, governance in both corporate and government and every sector under the sun. Convergence of the above technologies has become possible due to rapid advancements made in the respective technology. This convergence is termed as information and communication technology (ICT) and considered as a separate discipline. ICT is advancing by delivering exponential increase in computing power and communications capabilities. This has resulted in the new concepts are being developed in this discipline.

COMMERCE IN ELECTRONIC ENVIRONMENT

Convergence of money, computing and networks has laid the foundation for electronic commerce. There have been various applications related to e-commerce. Many large organizations used to make electronic fund transfer by making use of the application of Electronic Fund Transfer known as EFT. Another application Electronic Data Interchange (EDI) has been used for direct exchange of documents from one business computer system to another. Communications through internet and emergence of websites during nineties have led the applications related electronic commerce to make rapid progress. The year 2000 has witnessed many dotcom companies going out of business. As a consequence to this electronic commerce was affected. Due to globalization policy followed by many countries across the globe the applications related to electronic commerce have started gaining momentum from the year 2003. Now many organizations have been making use of electronic commerce applications. In the present business scenario, it may be noted that e-commerce business models are being developed for various segments of business and industries. These models can be classified for the purposes such as organization purpose, people oriented and society purposes. The advancements in mobile communications have made mobile commerce (m-commerce) popular. Mobile commerce can be considered as one or more features in e-commerce. Mobile commerce is the result of PC based Commerce. Two more concepts have been becoming popular under electronic environment. They are Space commerce and Ubiquitous commerce. Commercial satellite systems are made use of developing business models in multiple domains such as health, education and business. Ubiquitous commerce focuses on the development of location based application software.

ORIGIN OF THE WEB

In the late 1970s Berner-Lee wrote software programs for D.G.N Ash limited. He joined CERN, the European particle physics laboratory in 1980. At CERN he wrote a program for his personal use, named 'ENQUIRE', that has become the conceptual start of title World Wide Web. 'Enquire' is a name from a book written in 1858 that inspired Berners-Lee: "Inquire within: anything you want to know". The program was put on the Internet. The following summer Berners-Lee continued his work on the web and created early specifications of universal resource locations, HTTP and HTML. He joined the Massachusetts Institute of Technology Lab for computer science in 1994 and formed the World Wide Web consortium. He preferred to work quietly in academia. His contribution has changed every business in the world. The use of internet is not restricted strictly to the selected few people. In fact many companies now owe their very existence to Berner-Lee's creation.

Berner-Lee's more memorable spare time projects happened when his boss refused to buy terminals in the temporary "Huts", where Berner-Lee and other contract workers sat. Berner-Lee has made a dummy out of a cardboard and it had a plastic sleeve in the place of the screen where he could slide in sheets of paper to "display" screen images. Many people who have visited his office noticed that he was typing on his card board terminal. Unfortunately even this was not enough to get his boss's approval for getting real terminals.

Berner-Lee used to avoid public eye and interviews. At an electronic commerce conference at Boston in the year 1998, he delivered a key note that provided some insight as to where he believed that the internet and the web were advancing. He believed that the web should be in two fold places for fluid communication and a tool for machines to analyze data. According to him this type of information processing would help people to focus on being creative.

Regarding the involvement of government in the development of the web and e-commerce, he said "my feeling is that when you have something common to everyone, it has to be run by people, for the people in a democratic way".

CLOUD COMPUTING AND WEB 2.0

Cloud computing and web 2.0 are the concepts among the number of other concepts provided by information and communication technology. The terms cloud computing and web 2.0 appeared at the same point of time. Both the concepts provide the same type of features to end users. Tim O'Reilly, the god father of Web 2.0 defines it as the network as platform, spanning all connected devices. According to Tim O'Reilly cloud computing is about computers, Web 2.0 is about people. According to Tim O'Reilly cloud computing refers specifically to the use of internet as computing platform. Further Tim O'Reilly defines that Web 2.0 is an attempt to explore and explain the business rules of that platform.

WEB 2.0 AND SOCIAL MEDIA

Web 2.0 coined by Tim O'Reilly at the WEB 2.0 conference held in San Francisco in 2004, refers to the second generation of internet based services that let people collaborate and share information online perceived in new ways. They are such as social networking sites, blogs, wikis and communication tools.

The hallmark of any buzzword is its ability to convey the appearance of meaning without conveying actual meaning. To many people the term social networking or social media has the feel of a buzz word. But Social Media is not a buzzword anymore. Social media is the evolution of a variety of technologies that are combined to alter an individual and an organization's approach to their needs and requirements (Bernal, 2010)

Many people want to be on social media. One of the main reasons is simple and free. Social media is a rare example of a true, modern and functional. In principle any node can speak as a peer to any other node as long it obeys the rules of TCP/IP protocols which are strictly technical not social.

SOCIAL MEDIA

Social media are nothing more than a special class of Web sites (Cornard Levinson & Gibson, 2010). It may be said that they are second generation websites. The first generation websites are those created by organizations or by an authority that upload information in the sites for anyone to read using a "top down". This is one too many providing information model. Second generation websites are such as social media web sites. These sites by contrast are platforms that provide users the ability using the software tools to create their own mini websites or web pages. The content on these sites is created by the participants from the "Bottom up" using a many-to-many model. The users of these sites, create, comment, give ratings and recommend the contents in these sites. Social media sites have generally three distinctive characteristics. They are 1-Majority of the content is generated by users 2-There will be high degree of participation and interaction among users and 3- It can integrate easily with other sites.

It can be said that social media platforms are blogs, social networking, social book marking, news and photo and video sharing sites. These are some examples. As time goes on, these categories will be on the increase.

FEATURES OF SOCIAL MEDIA

Social media sites mostly fall under at least any one of the five forms of activities.

1. Declaration of identity
2. Association-based information
3. User-initiated conversation
4. Provider-initiated conversation
5. In-person interaction

Declaration of Identity

Sites created by individuals, group of people or an organization provide more information about themselves. There will be very little interaction among the users of these sites.

Association-Based Information

Association based information provides an opportunity to the users of this site for associating with the sites.

User-Initiated Conversation

User initiated conversation gives an opportunity given to the users to create their own declarations or questions. There will be an opportunity for the site owner to respond questions.

Provider-Initiated Conversation

This will be mostly useful for marketing division in an organization. This site facilitates the marketing division in an organization to find out their customers thinking, feeling, likes and dislikes about their products/services.

In-Person Interaction

This will be the best form of interaction with their customers of an organization. Face to face interaction with the customers helps to build good relationship and facilitates better input, feedback, collaboration and communication.

COMPONENTS OF SOCIAL MEDIA

Social media use web based technology to disseminate knowledge and information to huge number of users. They allow creation and exchange of user generated content. Face Book, Twitter, Blog and other social networking sites are collectively referred to as social media.

SOCIAL MEDIA OPTIMIZATION

Social media optimization is a method of creating popularity for a website through social media like popular online communities or community websites. Social media optimization facilitates to get traffic to a website. This provides free access to a surfer. Social media optimization process is created in various ways by the use of networking in the social media sites.

SOCIAL NETWORK

A social network is a social structure made up of individuals or organizations called "nodes" which are connected by one to one or more specific types of interdependency. Interdependency means friendship, common interest, relationships of beliefs, and knowledge. Social network analyses the views of above relationships in terms of theory consisting of "nodes" and "connections". Nodes are the individual participants within the network. Connections are the relationships between the individuals. There may be many kinds of connections between the nodes. Research in a number of academic fields has shown that social network operates on many levels from individuals up to the level of nations. This plays an important role in deciding the method of solving problems. Further, it helps organizations to manage the business properly. It also facilitates individuals in achieving their goals. It may be said that a social network is a source of all the relevant connections between all the nodes. It will be useful for analysis. The network may be utilized to evaluate social capital.

BUSINESS APPLICATIONS

The use of social network services in business context provides a potential impact on the business scenario (Jacobson, 2012). The content in social network is available at a minimum cost. This will be beneficial for entrepreneurs and small business enterprises that have ideas to expand their business through social network environment. In the context of business, social network is considered to provide a management tool for business applications. In the present globalization scenario social network facilitates enterprises to keep in touch with contacts for their business purposes (Postman, 2009).

ENTERPRISE FUNCTIONS WITH SOCIAL MEDIA TOOLS

Enterprises need to identify their organization functions that can be integrated with the social media tools. Table 1 gives an idea of enterprise functions relating to social media tools.

SOCIAL MEDIA PROGRAMMES IMPLEMENTATION

Implementation of social media programs in enterprises generally has the following stages (Dentus Social Media Handbook, 2010).

Table 1. Enterprise functions and social media tools

Enterprise Functions	Objectives	Aims	Social Media Tools
Research	Understanding customers	To know customers knowledge about products, get ideas from competitor's products	Digital vision development.
Marketing	Promotion of Products	Making awareness of brands, changing perceptions of the brands.	Blog, Video Blog and Social network
Sales	Enhancement of Sales Prospects	To answer sales queries, to get ideas and suggestions from customers	Face Book, Twitter and Social network.
Customer Service	Providing Support to Customers	Understanding customer requirements	Creation of user community sites.
Product Development	Developing new products, increasing the features of the existing products	Getting ideas for product development, freezing development process.	Creation of user community sites.

1. Evaluating the potential of various social media tools.
2. Identifying the social media tools in relation to the business activities.
3. Selecting and mapping various social media tools with business activities are to be carried out by an enterprise with the relevant content strategy.
4. Effectiveness of social media tools need to be evaluated with predefined measurement metrics.

Training Programs

Orientation programs related to social media tools are required to be organized for executives in an enterprise.

Identification of Business Activities

An enterprise has to identify its business activity with its market share of its products and services. While selecting a particular social media tool, various business issues are to be considered.

Business Goals

Setting goals and bench marks are to be decided by an enterprise for their social media program.

Measurement

Social media program is to be reviewed with an enterprise's social media mix. Generally measurement details facilitate to know the transactions and traffic on to the web site of an enterprise (Poston, 2013).

Social Media Services

There are a variety of social media services. These are referred as social media channels. Some refer Web 2.0 as social Media Services. It is because Web 2.0 has interactive features. In fact Web 2.0 enables social media tools of social media for making use of social media channels.

Web Sites and Networking

Web sites and networking strategies that worked in the 1990's are no longer relevant to in the present day's context. The present day users expect instant reporting on everything from important news to insignificant messages.

Web Analytics

Web analytics is the process of analyzing the behavior of visitors to websites. Web analytics is often used as part of customer relationship management analytics. The objective of analysis is to promote specific products to those customers most likely to buy them. It is further to identify which products a specific customer is most likely to buy. Web analytics facilitate to identify the sites from which customers most often visit and communicate with other browsers. The results of web analytics are provided in the form of tables, charts and graphs. The results of web analytics will be beneficial for an enterprise to improve the ratio of revenue to marketing costs.

TWITTER

Twitter is an online service that allows users to share updates with other users by answering a one simple question. It is gaining a lot of importance in social media. It is not as functional as Face book. Twitter has become popular because of its simplicity Twitter allows friends, family and complete strangers to stay connected through quick updates. It takes a couple of seconds to write updates in Twitter. This is more useful for people who have limited time at their disposal.

MICRO BLOGGING

Micro Blogging is a web service that allows a subscriber to send short messages to other subscribers'. Micro posts can be made public on website. It can also be distributed specifically to a group of subscribers. Subscribers can read micro Blog posts online. They can request that updates may be sent to their e-mail Id's. They may also request that updates may be sent to their mobiles as short messages.

BLOG

A Blog is basically a journal that is available on the web. Blogs are generally updated almost daily. Updating and maintenance of a blog is considered to be as very simple process. Generally postings on blogs are mostly arranged in chronological order. The advantage in the blog is that the most recent updates will appear prominently in one's blog.

SOCIAL BOOK MARKING

Social book marking is considered to be an effective social media tool. This is mostly used in internet marketing service. This facilitates to increase the traffic and to generate more sales for online business. Social book marking allows the users to tag their websites with the relevant keywords. These keywords can be stored at a specific location for easy access. In the present global cyber village, social book marking plays an important role in the online business environment. The tag in the website is known to a sizeable number of users. This helps users to know more about products and services.

MOBILE SOCIAL NETWORKING

Mobile social networking has a combination of technologies and services. This is a segment of the mobile telecommunications industry. This is based on incessant media coverage provided to subscribers who have a real interest in this.

SOCIAL NETWORKING

Social networking is created by a specific group of people for a specific purpose or purposes. It is most popular online contact especially at the work place, universities, high schools; and colleges. Social networking websites function like an online community of internet users. Many of these online community members share common interests among themselves.

SOCIAL MEDIA MARKETING

Marketing tools of the past have become obsolete in the present globalization scenario. Enterprises who anticipate the changes are ready to adopt them quickly have better chances to stay ahead in the business. Social media marketing is one such great change that many business enterprises have been accepting in a big way (Haydon, 2014).

The concept of social media marketing basically refers to the process of promoting business on websites through social media channels (Meerman, 2012). It is an effective marketing process that explains the way people communicate. It is one of the effective promotional methods that provide business to large members of links. Business enterprises can expect to get good attention from customers. It really attracts the attention from customers. It really works in favor of business enterprises interest.

Social media is an extremely useful tool of information, product or service descriptions and promotions. It can be said that it is integrated in the chain of networking world. Many business enterprises have started designing innovative ways to develop their marketing plans. Social media marketing is a booming sector. This sector is redefining the way marketing strategies are to be formed for promoting products or services of an enterprise.

INTERNET PRIVACY AND CENSORSHIP

Privacy is becoming a big concern due to the increasing number of users making use of the internet. There are number of advertisers, stalkers and hackers on the internet. They are waiting for an opportunity to violate user's privacy over the internet.

Censorship of information on the internet has become a topic for discussion. Censorship is required to maintain a particular moral standard. During the past several years the internet has been expanding at a faster pace. It is because of the increase of internet users. It can be said that this has resulted in new issues of censorship and freedom of expression.

ESTABLISHING CONTACTS WITH CUSTOMERS

Social media is the best tool for brand image, online reputation management and online arbitration. Further it helps to establish good relationships with the customers (Zimmerman & Deborg, 2014).

BRAND IMAGE

Enterprises can talk more about the important features of their products and services. This promotes online conversation with their customers and prospective customers about their products and services.

PROFESSIONAL OUTLOOK

Enterprises can create forums and message boards for interaction with customers. Once enterprises answer the queries of the customers professionally, they can create a good reputation for themselves (Golden, 2011).

TOUCH OF MOUSE

In the earlier days, word of mouth has played an important role for brand image. Generally, people rely on the opinions expressed by their friends and relatives. In the present scenario people share their opinions online. Enterprises need to build strategies through social media for their products and services. Now word of mouth is replaced with touch of mouse.

ONLINE ARBITRATION

Some enterprises are hesitant to make use of social media for their business. It is because of negative comments they may get from their customers. In fact, social media helps enterprises to take measures for establishing positive outlook about their products or services. The result of these approaches enterprises will give an impression that they are concerned about their customers. In this context, social media plays a role of arbitration (Flynn, 2012).

FACEBOOK

The social networking site Face Book was launched in 2004 at Harvard University. It started out with the name "The Face Book" and was available only for Harvard students or anyone with a Harvard.edu e-mail address. The social network spread quickly because it was exclusive. Although it was originally launched as a network for Harvard students, Face Book was eventually made available to students at other universities and then finally to anyone with access to computer. Now it has become the largest social networking site for many people for communication.

ADVERTISEMENTS IN FACEBOOK

In the year 1950, the television started becoming popular in America. At first, there were black and white television sets and then towards the end of the decade, there were color television sets in the living rooms of American families. As more people started watching television instead of listening to the radio, marketers had to adopt their strategies to the new medium. Successful advertisement executives made an effort to understand television and its impact on American culture. Only after the survey conducted by them, they were able to create television advertisements. They learned to condense their advertisement messages to 30 seconds. In the same way, the present day advertisement executives have understood the new medium and making use of Face Book to market their brands.

Business enterprises have understood that paying for a full page advertisement in a national newspaper or buying 10-minute regional television time is not a cost effective way to reach targeted audience. In the present business scenario, Face Book provides an option such as likes and dislikes to their target audience. Face book is not about selling things or making them available at the lowest cost. Face book is relational. It is not transactional.

The concept of branding can be traced back in history to the early Romans. The practice among livestock farmers was to brand their cattle with branding icons so that they could be recognized by the farmer and his neighbors. When the animals wandered everyone would know who owned them. Branding is a way of distinguishing one's product from other product that looks very similar. Business enterprises can build awareness of their brand with their current and prospective customers through a Face Book page. Business enterprises notify people of an upcoming event and contact information. Further they show their new products, videos and other types of content. A face book page also allows for two-way interaction between the business enterprise and its customer, providing a customer to post messages. It is also a good feedback loop for enterprises to know more about the customers' needs. Face Book has an internal analytics system called Face Book insights to which one can gain a better understanding into visitors' behavior.

VISUAL SOCIAL MARKETING

Visuals are images and videos that are created to support visual social marketing. Some people are under the impression that visual social marketing is only relevant to businesses that offer highly visual products such as fashion design and food items. It is not the case that any business enterprise can benefit from participating in visual social marketing. Visual Social Marketing is a powerful way to make business presence felt on social networks (Neher, 2014). It is said that visual content is more powerful than text content. A video or an image allows for much more meaningful connection with customers than simply sharing text. If an enterprise has a unique product that performs better than people would expect, a product demo video can be a new way to generate new customers. Product demo videos are more useful to show a product in action. Video customer testimonials are dependable. It is because they have more visual impact than testimonials consisting text. People simply search for images online and use any image they find. Generally, the owner or creator of an image holds the copyright to that image. There are paid images sites. It would be better to select the images from these sites.

ONLINE MARKETING

Online Marketing is selling products or services over digital networks. Internet and cellular phone networks are considered to be digital networks. The art of online marketing involves finding the right online marketing mix of strategies. These strategies should be designed to address target market. These strategies should facilitate in resulting sales. Examples of online marketing are:

1. E-Commerce
2. Online Advertising
3. Search Engine Marketing
4. E-Mail Marketing
5. Social Media Marketing and
6. Article Marketing

The above list of online marketing is not exhaustive. More online marketing strategies are being developed.

SOCIAL MEDIA AND E-MAIL MARKETING

Social media gives public conversations a forum (Martin & Ericson, 2011). Anyone with an opinion, content or a link to share can join the conversation. It is timely and interactive. There is a difference between social media and e mail communication. The posts on social media websites generally get mixed up with all other messages. On the other hand, e-mail offers direct level of contact with the customers of a business enterprise. E-mail newsletters content is easily accessible because email account holders can it get it from there in boxes. The essence of social media is about sharing content and engaging in conversations. E-marketing interactions generally take to the next level of engagement. Some marketers feel the mix of e-mail and social media marketing can work together better for the benefit of their business.

DIGITAL MARKETING

Digital Marketing is the promotion of brands using all forms of digital advertising channels to reach consumers. It now includes television, radio, internet, mobile, social media marketing and any other form of digital media. While digital marketing does include many of the techniques and practices contained within the category of internet marketing, it extends beyond this by including other channels to reach people that do not require the use of internet.

E-COMMERCE

Electronic Commerce commonly known as E-Commerce consists of buying and selling of products or services over the internet and other computer networks. It is more than just buying and selling products online. It also includes the entire online process of developing, marketing, selling, delivering, servicing and paying for products and services. The amount of trade conducted electronically has grown extraordinarily with wide spread of internet usage.

SEARCH ENGINE MARKETING

Search Engine Marketing is a form of Internet marketing that seeks to promote websites by increasing their visibility. Search engine marketing is more as an art than science. Each search engine has its own formula for ranking search results. These algorithms change often, primarily to make results more relevant to the person who is searching.

INSTAGRAM

Instagram is an online mobile photo sharing, video sharing, and social networking services. This enables its users to take pictures and videos and share them on a variety of social media platform such as Face Book, Twitter, and Flicker. Instagram was created by Kevin Systrom and Mike Krieger. It was launched in October 2010 as a free mobile app. This service has gained popularity. Smart mobile devices such as i-phones, i-pads, kindle and similar internet enabled products are becoming more popular. The World Wide adoption of these websites enable tools in revolutionizing the online experience; including social media marketing.

SOCIAL BUSINESS INTELLIGENCE

The domains of business intelligence and social media are gaining importance in the present business scenario. Business Intelligence aims at supporting organization's decisions by providing relevant analytical data. Social media is a source of personal and individual knowledge, opinion and attitude of stake holders. Convergence of these two domains can result in a concept referred as social business intelligence. This convergence will provide a scope for research activities.

CONCLUSION

One of the most interesting opportunities in the present business scenario is the dynamic nature of the technological capabilities available for business. It is available in almost every sector that one could imagine.

The technology provides access to a vast amount of usage information. Enterprises need to integrate that information and those technology capabilities to create relevant context. The relevancy and context would help to transform enterprises' business.

Social media enables business executives to look forward for their market potential and their target market in the broader perspective (Safko & Brake, 2009). There is a good scope for making use of the concept of social media in the sectors such as health care, hospitality, manufacturing, academics, corporate and government governance and many other related sectors.

Return on investment of social media is to be measured to direct relation to the resource allocation investment into blogs, communities, face book and twitter (Blanchard, 2012). Then only it makes sound business sense.

N. Raghavendra Rao
FINAIT Consultancy Services, India

REFERENCES

Bernal, J. (2010). *Web 2.0 and social net working for the enterprise - Guidelines and examples for implementation and management within your organization*. New Delhi: Pearson.

Blanchard, O. (2012). *Social media ROI*. New Delhi: Pearson.

Cornard Levinson, J., & Gibson, S. (2010). *Guerrilla social media marketing*. New Delhi: Tata McGraw Hill Education Private Limited.

Dentus Social Media Handbook. (2010). Mumbai: Popular Prakashan Private Limited.

Haydon, J. (2014). *Facebook marketing for dummies*. New Delhi: Wiley India Private Limited.

Jacobson, J. L. (2012). *42 rules of social media for small business*. Prolibris Publishing Media Private Limited.

Martin, P., & Ericson, T. (2011). *Social media marketing*. New Delhi: Global Vision Publishing House.

Meerman, S. D. (2012). *The new rules of marketing and PR. New Delhi: Wiley India Private Limited. Golden, M. (2011). Social media: Strategies for professionals and their firms. Wiley and Sons. Flynn, N. (2012). The social media handbook*. New Delhi: Wiley India Private Limited.

Neher, K. (2014). *Visual social media marketing for dummies*. New Delhi: Wiley India Private Limited.

Postman, J. (2009). *Social corp: Social media goes corporate*. New Riders.

Poston, L. (2013). *Social media metrics for dummies*. New Delhi: Wiley India Private Limited.

Safko, L., & Brake, D. (2009). *The social media bible*. John Wiley.

Zimmerman, J., & Deborg, N. G. (2014). *Social media marketing all-in-one for dummies*. New Delhi: Wiley India Private Limited.

Section 1
Business in Social Media Environment

Chapter 1
Transformation of Business through Social Media

R. Venkatesh
VIT Business School Chennai, India

Sudarsan Jayasingh
VIT Business School Chennai, India

ABSTRACT

Social media are widely used in regular operations of many companies, including start-ups, small, medium and large organizations. The Social media are fundamentally changing the way we communicate, consume, collaborate and create. It creates one of the most transformative impacts on business. The most significant consequence of social media has been the shift of power from the institution to the individual. These shifts in the consumer-brand relationship have thrown up new challenges and opportunities for business organization. Social media have transformed the ways businesses from marketing and operations to finance and human resource management. Increasingly, social media are also transforming the way businesses relate to workers, allowing them to build flexible relationships with remote talent, to crowdsource new ideas, or to engage in micro outsourcing. Social media are increasingly being used in organizations to improve relationships among employees and nurture collaboration and the sharing culture. The purpose of this research is to explore the major changes which have taken place in organization because of social media.

INTRODUCTION

Social media are widely used in regular operations of many companies, including start-ups, small, medium and large organizations (Bell& Loane, 2010). The business environment in tandem with the technological developments has undergone an amazing transformation. Social media is a phenomenon that has transformed the interaction and communication of individuals throughout the world. It have transformed consumers, societies, and corporations with wide spread access to information, better social networking and enhanced communication abilities (Kucuk & Krishnamurthy, 2007). Social media is ''a group of internet based applications that builds on the ideological and technological foundations of

DOI: 10.4018/978-1-5225-0846-5.ch001

Web 2.0, and it allows the creation and exchange of user-generated content'' (Kaplan & Haenlein, 2010, p.61). Social networks are defined to be websites which link millions of users from all over the world with same interests, views and hobbies. Blogs, YouTube, MySpace, Facebook are examples of social media that are popular among all level of consumers (Sin, Nor & Agaga, 2012).

Worldwide, the social network user base is expected to increase from 1.47 billion in 2012 to 2.55 billion in 2017 (eMarketer, 2014). Social media usage in India as number of internet users in India reached 302 million users by December 2014 (EY, 2015). India is a key market for social media giants active as social media users in India grew to around 106 million and India is among the top three countries in terms of number of people using Facebook (100m+ users), whereas Twitter is seeing an increased user base of over 33 million (EY, 2015). The increased mobile web penetration is also seen as a key contributor to increased growth in active social media usage — 84% Facebook's 100 million users in India access it from their mobile devices. 81% of the brands surveyed considered Facebook to be the most important platform, while almost 48% of surveyed brands think that Twitter is the second-most important platform to be on, closely followed by YouTube (43% surveyed brands considered it to be the third–most important channel). Businesses are also establishing their own YouTube channels while actively producing, curating and distributing video content for promotional material and showcasing new developments for the brand. Meanwhile, Vine, the latest entrant in social media platforms, concentrates on short six second video snippets that can be shared using Facebook or Twitter.

The popularity of social media sites has also spread to companies and firms as part of their strategies. Research studies shows that 93% of Fortune 500 companies have accounts on social media sites (Barnes, Lescault & Holmes, 2015). 21 percent of Fortune 500 corporations had corporate blogs, 78% use twitter, 74% has Facebook, 84% has joined Glassdoor, 93% use LinkedIn and 13% use Instagram. More than 70 percent of organizations operating around the world are now active on social media (KPMG, 2011). Companies across variety of industries such as automobile, travel and tourism, banking and financial services, retailers, airlines fashion and education and many more using social media to tap opportunities in the market. The use it to build brands, promotions, product development, customer service, employee engagement and recruitments etc. In many organizations, the number of social media-specific roles is limited. Simply Measured survey of over 350 social media marketers found that 65% of teams have between 1 to 3 people dedicated specifically to social media (Simple Measured, 2015).

Now, ecommerce has come to occupy a centre stage in the way people transact business including shopping for clothing, accessories, fashion products, smart phones and consumer durables. It is clear that the mind set of an entire generation of shoppers (mostly young upwardly mobile people) is getting focused more on online purchases. Also, technology has made it easier for consumers to carry out financial transactions (netbanking, usage of credit & debit cards etc.). Web 2.0 is has transferred the Internet to a social environment by introducing social media, where individuals can interact and generate content online line (Lai & Turban, 2008). The aim of this research is to examine the role of Social Media (YouTube, Blogs, and Twitter etc.) and Social Networks (Facebook, Google, LinkedIn) and kind of business transformation takes place due to it.

E-COMMERCE TO SOCIAL MEDIA COMMERCE

The power of social networking is such that, the number of worldwide users is expected to reach some 2.5 billion by 2018, which is around a third of world's population (Statistic, 2015). An estimated half a billion of these users is expected to be from China alone and approximately a quarter of a million from India. The region with the highest penetration rate of social networks is North America, where around 60 percent of the population has at least one social account. As of 2015, over 70 percent of the United States population had a social networking profile (Statistia, 2015). Table 1 clearly shows that Facebook leads in number of active users, which is followed by YouTube.

The complete dynamics of eCommerce has changed over the last few years where people have started using the power of social computing. The ecommerce companies instead of mainly focusing on direct marketing and sales, retailers have started networking to reach out to a bigger mass, and using social connections to interact with people they would not have reached earlier (Bhattachary, 2015). Social media has brought in a huge change in the way businesses and customers interact. Customers have direct contact with merchants and can engage in real time with a retailer. The consumers can verify the authenticity of the brand, compare online with other similar products and then finally can make a decision. Retailers add social network plugins to their online applications to enable users to be interactive. In such cases, users have the option to login using their social networking credentials instead of creating a new profile which becomes cumbersome to maintain. Retailers start campaigns with incentives for sharing and referrals.

When shoppers make purchases, they are encouraged to share the name of the online store or their experience with their friends. In return they get loyalty points or rewards, which encourage repeat buying. When buyers share product or store related information or experience, their friends get to see it on social networks. This stirs interest among buyers' connections/friends to know more about the product and they can simply click on the link and visit the same store. Sites like Tumblr, Pinterest, Instagram, and Wanelo are becoming online catalogues for shopping ideas, fashion tips, and wish lists. Friends of buyers are also offered incentives or discounts to purchase, so they buy what they want and save some money. This expands customer base and creates awareness about the product among more people in the chain. In the whole process, retailers gain new customers, shoppers get rewards, and friends save money hence it's a win-win for everyone in the circle (Bhattacharya, 2015).

Pinterest and a handful of other platforms are started a phenomenon known as "social shopping"—a clever blend between typical social media and e-commerce experiences. The concept of social commerce was developed by David Beisel to denote user-generated advertorial content on e-commerce sites, and by Steve Rubelto include collaborative e-commerce tools that enable shoppers "to get advice from trusted individuals, find goods and services and then purchase them" (Cohen, 2011). Social commerce is defined as a form of Internet-based social media that allows people to actively participate in the marketing and selling of products and services in online marketplaces and communities (Stephen &Toubia, 2010).

Table 1. Social networking sites activity in November 2015

Social Networking Sites	No of Active Users (Millions)	Activity
Facebook	1,550	1001 Million daily active Facebook users
YouTube	1,000	300 Hours uploaded every minute and 1 Billion+ views each day
Instagram	400	70 Million Photos per Day
Twitter	316	500 Million Tweets per day
Tumblr	230	110.1 Billion Tumblr Posts
Pinterest	100	1 Billion boards created

Source: Statista, 2015

Social commerce is a part of ecommerce that involves social media, which supports social interactions and user contributions to assist online buying, and selling of products and services. The social commerce term was introduced in November 2005 by Yahoo, which describes collaborative shopping tools like shared pick lists, user ratings and other user-generated content-sharing of online product information and advice. According to survey it was found that 35 percent of online consumers have made a purchase based on an advertising they saw on a social network (Statista, 2014).

Social shopping sites integrate social aspects, such as product sharing and front-facing user engagement. Examples of Social commerce include photo-sharing social networks such as Pinterest or Polyvore, or highly curated e-commerce sites with strong social components such as Etsy, Fab or Fancy. Niche services such as Airbnb, which is a social platform providing individuals to rent living spaces short-term lodging have also taken advantage of social networking features. Social networks are moving towards social shopping, with nearly every major network implementing buy buttons. According to recent data from Addshoppers, Pinterest is pushing about one-quarter of social commerce for their retail clients (Knight, 2014). Pinterest allows brands to showcase product as well as increase organic reviews and conversation. Social media sites are trying to cash in on their users by directing them to online shopping, but Pinterest& Twitter are poised to allow people to buy items they see on the site, where people share images of art projects, recipes and fashion items. Instagram has its own social commerce, expanding its advertising platform to allow businesses to offer a number of options including "install app," "download," "learn more," "sign up" and "shop now," feature. Just clicking on the button will take the user to either a section of the advertiser's mobile website in Instagram's in-app browser, or the Google Play store or Apple App store in the case of 'install app.' Social login, buttons and pins are some of common features of social commerce and Table 2 lists the common features and its meaning.

The transition from retail commerce to e-commerce has been gradual, but from e-commerce to social commerce is happening at a rapid pace with more and more users getting comfortable to shop with their mobile phones and while catching up with friends. Nonetheless, the share of social commerce is still relatively small (less than 5% of total e-commerce sales) according to Morgan Stanley, indicating

Table 2. Common social commerce features

Social Commerce Features	Meaning
Social Login	Social login, also known as social sign-in, is a form of single sign-on using existing login information from a social networking service such as Facebook, Twitter or Google+ to sign into a third party website in lieu of creating a new login account specifically for that website.
Facebook Like Button	The Facebook "Like" button is a feature that allows users to show their support for specific comments, pictures, wall posts, statuses, or fan pages.
Pinterest Buyable Pins	Buyable Pins are a simple, secure way to buy products they discover on Pinterest. Using the new Buy it button, consumers that use Pinterest will soon be able to shop and securely checkout with the products they find on Pinterest - all without ever leaving the app.
Google Button	Google +1 button shows that you like or agree with something.
Rating and Review Button	A Review button has been added to certain types of Facebook Pages. Users have long been able to post recommendations on Facebook Pages known as Places Pages. A Places Page is one that includes a physical address and allows check-ins. These can be local businesses, entertainment and sports venues, restaurants, or any business that lists a physical location.
Product Recommendation	Recommendations feed displays the most recommended content on your site, using actions (such as likes) by your friends and other people.

huge scope for growth. In 2014, the estimated global social commerce revenue is projected to amount to 20 billion U.S. dollars and grow to 30 billion U.S. dollars in 2015 (Statista, 2015). Facebook is the top social commerce platform, driving more than two-thirds of mobile e-commerce traffic and boosting social media's quickly growing share of e-commerce web traffic. Facebook accounts for 50% of total social referrals and 64% of total social revenue (Smith, 2015). Despite the continued hype around social media, retailers are still figuring out how to best drive sustainable e-commerce purchases via social media. According to the Internet Retailer's Social Media 500 report, the top 500 retailers earned $3.3 billion from social shopping in 2014, a 26 percent increase over 2013, and well ahead of the average 16 percent growth rate for E-Commerce. The LoginRadius analytics research team has analyzed our 150,000+ customer websites 72% use Facebook login, 20% use google+ login and 3% use Twitter (LoginRadius, 2015). Social networks have become a vital component in the way people communicate. But this social networks will impact the way we as consumers currently shop and will have a big impact on the future of commerce.

SOCIAL MEDIA AND MARKETING PRACTICES

Marketing is essential to most businesses and is generally the most important aspect of any business strategy. Around 2 billion people worldwide use some form of social media which is around 28% of the world population (Simple Measured, 2015). Marketing via social is a priority for more companies than ever before. Social media may serve as a channel for many marketing activities including customer relationship management, customer service, buyer research, lead generation, sales promotion delivery channel, paid advertising channel, and branding. Today businesses realize that if they wish to reach their prospects and customers, their online presence in social media is a foundation of their overall marketing strategy. Social media marketing is the marketing strategies that organization employs in order to be a part of a network of people online. Social media has impacted and modified traditional marketing activities and communications. The unique aspects of social media and its immense popularity have revolutionized marketing practices such as advertising and promotion (Hanna, Rohan & Crittenden, 2011). Social Media applications like Facebook, LinkedIn, Twitter, WhatsApp&Viber are being increasingly used by both marketers and consumers to transact, build awareness of products & services and brand building. Online social networks (Facebook, MySpace, Twitter, YouTube, virtual communities, etc.), where individuals as members, construct public profiles to share their knowledge and their experiences, to post information about themselves and have contact with others who exchange and share similar interests (Cheung & Lee, 2010).

Customers are smarter than ever they are socially engaged and well informed. This new kind of buyer, Customer 2.0, develops opinions of our brands without ever viewing a single advertisement or listening to a sales pitch (Cognizant, 2014). Customer 2.0 can learn anything he/she wants to know about our products or services through social media. Social media websites provide an opportunity for businesses to engage and interact with potential consumers, encourage an increased sense of intimacy with consumers, and build all-important relationships with potential consumers (Mersey et al., 2010). Companies use these tools also for effective sales promotion and customer relationship management (CRM). Social media has also influenced consumer behavior from information acquisition to post purchase behavior such as dissatisfaction statements or behaviors about a product or a company (Mangold & Faulds, 2009). Social media has also influenced consumer behavior from information acquisition to post-purchase behavior such as dissatisfaction statements or behaviors (Mangold & Faulds, 2009) and patterns of Internet usage (Ross et al., 2009; Laroche et al., 2012).In the context of the digital era, the term "consumer engagement" typically includes the ways in which consumers and constituents engage with brands, companies or organizations through digital channels, such as the brand's website, blogs, social networking sites, and videos.

Marketing Communication on Social Media

Research studies showed that the communication by brands on social media positively affected brand equity and relationship equity (Kim & Ko, 2012). Brand's social media activities can be used to increase brand aware-ness and brand liking, promote customer engagement and loyalty, inspire consumer word-of-mouth communication about the brand, and potentially drive traffic to brand locations on and offline (Ashley & Tuten, 2015). Media propagation has changed the ways in which advertising messages are delivered and received. Due to the high costs incurred in delivering a mass audience, advertisers are moving away from television and investing in alternate media, such as social network sites, to reach their target customers. Advances in social media offer unprecedented opportunities to target consumers in increasingly personalized ways. The emergence of Internet-based social media has made it possible for one person to communicate with hundreds or even thousands of other people about products and the companies that provide them (Mangold & Faulds, 2009). Advertising and Brand Building using Social Media Social-network advertising enables brands to reach both mass markets and niche markets while targeting specific segments using the segmentation tools offered by sites (based on user behaviors and demographic data).

Today marketing communication is linked with the flow of communication through social media and traditional media. Figure 1. illustrates the new social media brand consumer communication model. The traditional media communication is mostly one way but social media communication is mostly two-way communication. The social media have both consumer generated and brand generated content. Facebook's

Figure 1. Social media brand- consumer communication

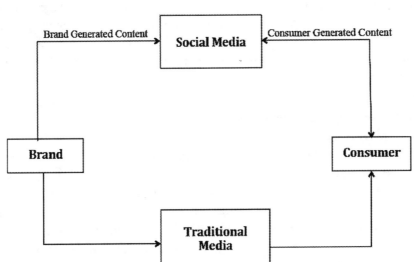

emergence as an important marketing channel has largely due to brand pages as they establish direct communication with their fans and customers. Facebook fan pages allow a brand to create an online community of brand users through the social networking site. Brand can post an item of content on its page, and reach is the number of people who receive an impression of a piece of content. Ninety-six percent of Interbrand Top 100 Global Brands have a dedicated Facebook accounts and 94% posted content in the month of April. 50 million businesses are now using Facebook Pages, up from 40 million in April 2015, and more than 2.5 billion comments are made on these Pages per month (Facebook, 2015). The number of social networks a brand is active on dependents on the brand's audience is actively participating. The monthly active users (the number of people who sign in each month) for each of these networks provide context into why brand interest is so high.

Many top brands now maintain a Facebook page from which they serve posts and messages to connected users. This is a form of free social media marketing that has increasingly become a popular and important channel for marketing. Jayasingh & Venkatesh conducted a research to find the Facebook brand page activities for Indian brands. They selected 134Facebook Indian Brand Pages, categorized into their respective industry and then monitored the daily interaction by fans based on the type of posts. The total number of posts of 134 selected brand pages is 12,925 and total interaction is 21,591,353 (Jayasingh & Venkatesh, 2015). Table 3. Facebook brand page interactions presents the total number of post, type of post and its overall interaction. The finding shows that average interaction is highest for offers and least for links. 89.5% of the posts are photos, which is followed by videos.

According to Cisco by 2017, video will account for 69% of all consumer Internet traffic. Videos are now making it into every interaction we're making online. From the launch of live video feeds on Twitter, the continued popularity of video on Facebook and Instagram, and the accessibility of high definition video on every mobile device. Video is the most powerful marketing tool being utilized now. People respond to the encapsulated storytelling modality of video on news and entertainment sites, as well as e-commerce sites of all kinds. Video can be used to convey corporate culture, introduce a new product, and even as a reputation management tool. YouTube is the leader in online video, and the premier destination to watch, share, and promote original videos online. YouTube is fully integrated with Google AdWords for video, leveling the playing field for businesses that want to reach new customers with online video.

Social media marketing has grown both in popularity and importance. Social media is no longer reactive function but it is integrated closely with many other marketing activities, and its share of attention, budget, and staffing needs is only continuing to grow (Simply Measured, 2015). Their survey of over 350 social media marketers found that 65% of teams have between 1-3 people dedicated specifically to social media. In 2015, there are an estimated 76,000 social media-marketing professionals in the workforce (Simply Measured, 2015). Social media activities can be difficult to quantify, and 60% of the marketers surveyed listed "Measuring ROI" as their top challenge (Simply Measured, 2015). The revolution of social media has a significant impact on the cooperation between organizations and consumers. The consumer's role has undergone a change from passive to co-creators of value.

Customer Relationship Management in Social Media Era

Web 2.0 tools reshaped the traditional CRM processes transforming them into CRM 2.0, by identifying and solving customer service issues, using forums, wikis and others (Schroeder, 2013). The social media influence the degree to which customers can engage with a company, and that the customer's level of engagement both affects and is affected by the company's approach to each of the three components of

Table 3. Facebook brand page interactions

No.	Brand	Total Fans	Total posts	Likes	Comments	Shares	Total Interactions	Average Interactions per post	Interactions per fan
1	Airlines	677920	479	229960	8515	9860	248334	519	0.37
2	Apparel	1333741	429	169248	2218	2314	173779	405	0.13
3	Automobile	2454462	692	1851019	22745	47118	1920881	2776	0.78
4	Consumer Electronics	2567726	733	683010	15875	27673	726557	992	0.28
5	Electronics - Phone	6505598	651	3693257	76582	72245	3842084	5898	0.59
6	Watches	752260	231	69615	2266	4161	76041	329	0.10
7	Bank	1721091	441	765545	15969	32128	813642	1845	0.47
8	Beverages - soft drinks	9882869	218	75478	17573	8281	101332	465	0.01
9	Beverages - Spirits	4340306	346	794128	14125	45432	853684	2464	0.20
10	FMCG Food	3445098	579	603364	109212	30577	743152	1284	0.22
11	Retail Food	4937737	1180	2812327	100337	55400	2968064	2516	0.60
12	Health	1251303	208	633432	7486	10573	651491	3129	0.52
13	Beauty	3404283	967	1015512	46313	45055	1106880	1145	0.33
14	Detergent	1392289	429	499102	14212	10501	523815	1222	0.38
15	eshop	3688091	2974	3050087	104897	55936	3210920	1080	0.87
16	Retail	4469225	614	682063	11081	8602	701746	1143	0.16
17	Sporting Goods	2697219	358	278605	3429	6104	288137	805	0.11
18	Telecom	6760033	564	2374288	62816	38653	2475757	4391	0.37
19	Travel	656665	833	149000	3930	12126	165056	198	0.25
Total		62937915	12925	20429040	639577	31257	21591353	1671	0.34

traditional CRM — acquisition, maintenance, and termination (Malthouse, Haenlein, Skiera, Wedge & Zhang, 2013). Social media and other new technologies have also enabled consumers to filter out advertising and compare prices with competitors from anywhere with mobile devices, and distribute positive or negative brand messages to a global audience. CRM must evolve if it is to survive in this marketplace, by producing contact points that engage the consumer and provide value to both the company and consumer (Malthouse et al., 2013). The technological developments and the growth of social media are also making possible innovative forms of business interaction and activity involving new types of business relationships. Social CRM integrates social media with CRM to optimize the social interactions with customers. Users, social media consumers and potential customers are demanding instant communication gateways. Social media will not replace CRM but bring forth a new generation of tools to support these social customers.

Customer service is undergoing a major evolution, with online communication moving away from private, anonymous, one-to-one channels toward public one-to-many channels that are mobile, social, and attached to real identity. Social customer service is rapidly becoming the new, critical channel to drive satisfaction and loyalty. Social media has already reached a high level of maturity as a communication channel. The business case for introducing social media customer service is supported by consumer research studies, which show that customers prefer using social media for its ease and speed of response when compared to traditional phone and email channels. Social care is different from traditional voice, email and chat support because social care conversations are public, often permanent and can easily go viral. The connection research showed that 37% of customers prefer using social media for customer service inquiries over traditional methods like telephone calls. Social listening is a study on real life social media conversations. The TCS research shows that companies spend an average of about$19 million on social media activities in 2013 and, on average, employ 56 people to plot their social strategy, listen and respond to consumer comments on public sites, and handle other tasks to stay in tune with social media discussions about their brands, products and practices (Tata Consultancy Services, 2015).

Social selling is when salespeople use social media to interact directly with their prospects. It is the process of developing relationships as part of the sales process. Today this often takes place via social networks such as LinkedIn, Twitter, Facebook, and Pinterest. Social Selling is gaining popularity in a variety of industries, though it is used primarily for B2B (business-to-business) selling. The main components of social selling are social prospecting, personal branding, employee advocacy and social relationship management. According to research findings, 75% of B2B buyers are influenced by information found on social channels, and 97% of the time cold calling is ineffective. Research has shown that the use of social media has a significant positive effect on sales. Salespeople using social media experience 78% greater sales than similarly situated salespeople not using social media. Social CRM is the new buzzword for businesses as they can reach out to customers online through social platforms like Twitter and Facebook and in turn, build loyalty and belief in their brands. The key advantage of social media is that it makes the businesses to respond quickly. Many companies today monitor online conversations about their brands and its competitors.

Risk and Monitoring Social Media

Although Social networks can help companies spread good news fast, it can also spread bad news just as quickly. Moreover, if customers want to vent their anger on your product or service, they can use your social network account. Managers need to understand how to handle those situations quickly and effectively. Also, as social media is not as widely moderated or censored as mainstream media, individuals can say anything they want about a company or brand, positive or negative. Today's customers act, and react, at lightning speed to your latest products, pricing plans and sales channels. They spread the word about their good and bad experiences with comments captured across a dizzying range of platforms. Social media command center is simply a dedicated area where a company's social media team can monitor and engage social conversation around their brand and market. The command center of the future is: valuable information that travels seamlessly between individuals, teams and locations. Contextual data that shows what is happening related to the brand and why its happening, allowing teams to make informed decisions. They demonstrate the work and results of your brand's social initiatives, then showcase these insights to other employees within the company.

But marketers need to quickly and cost-effectively collect social media data from various sources, analyze the data, and understand the results before sudden market changes undermine sales or damage their brands. This rapid response requires the discovery, extraction, cleansing and integration of a wider range of data than ever before. When rumors on social media threaten a product's reputation, or need detailed information immediately. They must be able to analyze and correlate many more types of customer data, sense danger and opportunity in their customers' experiences much more quickly, and response much more effectively than ever before. It also requires social media tracking and analytic tools, natural-language processing to draw insights from text, advanced predictive analytics to aid decision-making and easy-to-use dashboards and reports.

SOCIAL MEDIA AND HR PRACTICES

Social Media has changed the today's human resource practices. The Wipro research findings shows that social media can be used in three areas Internal Branding, Collaboration and Communication and Hiring were considered almost equally suited for use of social media, with Internal Branding favored the most (Wipro, 2012). Most jobs are currently being recruited through social media and many organizations now use active recruiting, essentially becoming their own headhunters to locate potential future employees (Wipro, 2012). For example, the website Glassdoor.com, an employee feedback and job seeker forum site, allows members to provide "inside" information on company cultures, employees and salaries. Members rate their own organizations on various characteristics, and these data are then searchable by other users on the site. Information posted can be seen by other employees, customers or competitors. Even if an organization has no official social media presence, its employees may be creating one (Ployhart, 2014). Social media allows HR executives to monitor the activities of their employees. If employees are posting to their personal social media accounts during the day and those posts do not relate to work, or relate in a negative way, then the company can enforce its social media policy. Some companies allow employees to use social media throughout the day so long as their posts relate to the company in a positive way (Vassallo, 2015).

Traditionally organization use break room suggestion boxes, employee hotlines and closed room meetings to record employee concerns. Due to social media, employees can now share their experiences and suggestions as well as the bad experience in social media sites. A survey by the Society for Human Resource Management (SHRM) mentions that 54% of HR professionals believe it is very important for job aspirants to be present on LinkedIn and 33% believe it is somewhat important (Ring, 2015). Human Resource Department in organization use social media for employee communication, corporate branding, background checks, emergency notification etc. Social networking can potentially be a great tool for resolving questions or problems. With a large network at your fingertips, chances are someone out there has the answer or an idea.

Social Media and Recruitments

Talent acquisition is one of key area within many companies to use the social media. In the past, to recruit employees, organizations advertise opportunities in the newspaper; engage a recruitment consultant or, post jobs online via the company website or on popular job boards. This 'passive approach', as many claim, is on the way out. One of the biggest advantages of human resource managers using social media on the job is that it makes the recruiting process easier and more successful for the company. HR managers can post job openings on all the company's social media sites, including links to the listings on the company website. This makes it easier for the company to get the notice out to the public when jobs become available and for candidates to apply for those open jobs. Companies are also seeing more success using social media to recruit new employees as they can browse the social media sites of potential candidates to determine if he or she will fit in with the company culture (Vassallo, 2015). 69 percent of HR departments now use social media channels such as LinkedIn, Twitter and Facebook to assist with the recruitment process (Bennett, 2013)

Cybervetting refers to the practice of viewing social networking sites such as Facebook and Myspace, blogs and microblogs like Twitter and using search engines like Google and Yahoo! to obtain information about job applicants or to monitor current employees. Science Daily Research study on cybervetting shows that the majority of the individuals conducted cybervetting as part of their evaluation of a job candidate. Over 90 percent of companies use social media to recruit (Perkins, 2015). Much of this recruiting (94 percent) is currently focused on LinkedIn. About two-thirds of recruiters utilize Facebook when looking for people to fill positions, and just over half of hiring managers use Twitter to recruit. Mostly, these recruiters use social media to support traditional hiring channels by searching for candidates, posting jobs, and vetting applicants. The data shows that 55% of Job Seekers use social media for job search purposes (among Recruiters, the percentage of use for HR professional purposes were around 73%). In this regard, LinkedIn is largely the most used social networking site (35%) followed by Facebook (17%) (Zanella & Pais, 2014).

Social Knowledge Management

The social media exponentially increasing these interactions, a new paradigm must be created to manage the explosive growth of knowledge associated with social interactions. The organization have shifted to social media that connect people, break down silos of information and reach beyond the boundaries of the office to enable to creation of innovative practices that re-ignite the collective intelligence. The primary goal of knowledge management is to "improve organizational performance by enabling individuals to capture, share, and apply their collective knowledge to make optimal decisions…in real time" (Smith & Farquhar, 2000, p. 17). The disruptive force of social media is forcing organizations to rethink their traditional knowledge management paradigms. Informal social networks have always existed in organisations but remained largely hidden. The emergence of social networking technologies makes the informal networks visible. Social networking websites can be one of the fastest ways to obtain information. Social networking websites provide an opportunity for management to have faster contact with their subordinates. If there is an issue that needs immediate attention, a manager can send a message through social networking websites and the internet to their employees to get the information they need to make a decision (Baker, Buoni, Fee & Vitale, 2015). "Organizations are actively leveraging the power of social networks to find new business opportunities, new groups of like-minded individuals and companies, and new sources of industry specific wisdom, advice and expertise" (Wilson, 2009). Social networks can act as an tool to help the company reach out to both potential employees and customers.

Another way social media has impacted human resources is that companies are now beginning to communicate with their employees using social media. Some companies will talk to employees on Twitter to discuss company events so the public can learn about them. Other companies use messaging apps such as Google Hangouts to talk with employees in one location or all over the world (Vassallo, 2015). CEOs who learn how to harness the power of social media can greatly improve the flow of information among their employees, while managing shared knowledge with their partners in unexpected new ways. This appealing outcome is fast becoming the norm for a new breed of cutting-edge Social CEOs (Drumwright, 2014). Social CEOs use internal crowdsourcing to identify knowledge assets or information resources from a distributed pool of contributors within their companies, or from their partners and suppliers. Crowdsourcing tools include open surveys and user-generated knowledge systems to aggregate and share the information (Drumwright, 2014). Employees can contribute, comment and vote on mutual ideas about how to improve business tasks and services. Through this application of collective intelligence, the best ideas soon bubble up to the top. Enterprise social networking tools offer community and collaboration features like profiles as a core component, blogging, bookmarking, RSS, wikis, and the creation of self-defined, self-managed online communities.

The importance of external contacts and networking was illustrated in a study by Cross & Kartzenbach, which found that around 90 percent of the information used for decision-making by senior company executives came from their informal networks rather than formal reports or databases (Cross & Katzenbach, 2012).Web 2.0 tools influence training processes since information is becoming user driven and companies face transitions toward shared data, user generated content, and user experience. As a result, training activities are not bound to a specific geographical location or time frame: webinars take place all over the world and blogs, RSS filters, forums, wikis, and podcasts may enhance the training experience (Smits & Mogos, 2014).HR Managers must recognize that social media important parts of their organization. The information no longer flows in one direction from the sender to the receiver; instead users now generate their own content. This has created new opportunities that can also add value for HR departments.

FUTURE RESEARCH DIRECTIONS

The usage of social media is evident from this study by both organization and consumers. Opportunities for further research include, continued study of social media adoption in various industries and how it transforms the traditional business processes. The future research need to be conducted to find out how businesses today adopting social media and measure its impact on customer and employee relationships. Researchers should also attempt to understand what types of social media initiatives work best for organizations of different industries and what business functional area is best suited for this new channel. Additionally, the social media communication channel should be tested in the field to check if it can deliver measurable business results for small, medium as well as large corporation.

CONCLUSION

Social media have fundamentally transformed the relationship among business, employees and consumers. The companies need to accept that today's business model is consumer driven and developing strong relationships with customers through engagement on social media platforms can help achieve business growth. The variety of social media touch-points provides greater opportunities to influence the consumers buying process at different stages. It's clear that social media have most significant impact on the day-today work for many customer-facing activities. It is necessary for today's organization to engage more employees, customers and external partners through social media, then achieving benefits and measuring them in a systematic way. It is clear that many more organizations will be adopting social media to achieve additional value from this new channel. Social media has not only opened new ways of communication and distribution throughout all industries, it also created new business models, which relay on participative communication in real time. As business functions are digitally transformed and new technologies become more fully integrated into everyone's jobs, it is increasingly important for all workers to have high degrees of digital literacy.

Keeping the customer engaged and managing them both emotional and physical, in term of time spent and the frequency of usage and interactions with organization are very important today. Social media has become an integral part of the consumer pre-purchase and purchase decision. The consumer now has convenient channel for expressing his views and also viewing others views in a public space. The social media has changed the world of technology as well as business, with the last few years. The revolution of social media has a significant impact on the cooperation between organizations and consumers. The consumer's role has undergone a change from passive to co-creators of value. It has become necessary for the business to understand this change and embrace this new technology.

REFERENCES

Ashley, C., & Tuten, T. (2015). Creative Strategies in Social Media Marketing: An Exploratory Study of Branded Social Content and Consumer Engagement. *Psychology and Marketing*, *32*(1), 15–27. doi:10.1002/mar.20761

Baker, D., Buoni, N., Fee, M., & Vitale, C. (2015). *Social Networking and its effects on companies and their employees*. Retrieved November 29, 2015, from https://www.neumann.edu/academics/divisions/business/journal/Review2011/SocialNetworking.pdf

Barnes, N. G., Lescault, A. M., & Holmes, G. (2015). *The 2015 Fortune 500 and Social Media: Instagram Gains, Blogs Lose*. UMass Dartmouth. Retrieved December 08, 2015, from http://www.umassd.edu/cmr/socialmediaresearch/2015fortune500andsocialmedia/

Bell, J., & Loane, S. (2010). "New Wave" Global Firms: Web 2.0 and SME Internationalisation. *Journal of Marketing Management*, *26*(3-4), 213–229. doi:10.1080/02672571003594648

Bennett, S. (2013). How does HR use Social Media. *Adweek*. Retrieved November 23, 2015, from http://www.adweek.com/socialtimes/hr-social-media/492469

Bhattacharya, R. (2015). *Social Commerce*. Retrieved November 06, 2015, fromhttp://www.happiest-minds.com/whitepapers/social_commerce.pdf

Cheung Christy, M. K., & Lee Matthew, K. O. (2010). A theoretical model of intentional social action in online social networks. *Decision Support Systems*, *49*(1), 24–30. doi:10.1016/j.dss.2009.12.006

Cognizant. (2014). *Customer Insight Command Center Speeds 'Just-in-Time' Marketing*. Retrieved December 04, 2015, from http://www.cognizant.com/InsightsWhitepapers/customer-insight-command-center-speeds-just-in-time-marketing-codex1015.pdf

Cohen, H. (2011). *What is Social Commerce?* Retrieved December 04, 2015, fromhttp://heidicohen.com/what-is-social-commerce

Cross, R., & Katzenbach, J. (2012). The right role for top teams. *Strategy & Leadership*. Retrieved November 29, 2015, from http://www.strategy-business.com/article/00103?gko=97c39

Drumwright, H. (2014). *How Social CEOs Harness Social Media for Knowledge Management*. Retrieved November 29, 2015, from http://www.kmworld.com/Articles/Editorial/ViewPoints/How-Social-CEOs-Harness-Social-Media-for-Knowledge-Management-99833.aspx

eMarketer. (2014). Social Networking Reaches Nearly One in Four around the World. *eMarketer*. Retrieved October 13, 2015, from http://www.emarketer.com/Article/Social-Networking-Reaches-Nearly-One-Four-Around-World/1009976

EY. (2015). *Social Media Marketing: India Trends Study*. Retrieved December 08, 2015, from http://www.ey.com/Publication/vwLUAssets/EY-social-media-marketing-india-trends-study-2014/$FILE/EY-social-media-marketing-india-trends-study-2014.pdf

Facebook. (2015). *New Tools for Managing Communication on Your Page*. Retrieved December 04, 2015, fromhttps://www.facebook.com/business/news/new-tools-for-managing-communication-on-your-page

Hanna, R., Rohm, A., & Crittenden, V. (2011). We're all connected: The power of the social media ecosystem. *Business Horizons*, *54*(3), 265–273. doi:10.1016/j.bushor.2011.01.007

Jayasingh, S., & Venkatesh, R. (2015). Consumer Engagement Factors in Facebook Brand Pages. *Asian Social Science*, *11*(26), 19–29. doi:10.5539/ass.v11n26p19

Kaplan, A. M., & Haenlein, M. (2010). Users of the world, unite! The challenges and opportunities of social media. *Business Horizons*, *53*(1), 59–68. doi:10.1016/j.bushor.2009.09.003

Kim, A. J., & Ko, E. (2012). Do Social Media Marketing Activites Enhance Customer Equity? An Empirical Study of Luxury Fashion Brand. *Journal of Business Research*, *65*(10), 1480–1486. doi:10.1016/j.jbusres.2011.10.014

Knight, K. (2014). How Pinterest is pushing social commerce. *BizReport*. Retrieved December 04, 2015, fromhttp://www.bizreport.com/2014/03/how-pinterest-is-pushing-social-commerce.html

KPMG. (2011). *Going Social How businesses are making the most of social media*. Retrieved November 21, 2015, from https://www.kpmg.com/FR/fr/IssuesAndInsights/ArticlesPublications/Documents/Going-social-how-business-are-making-the-most-of-social-media.pdf

Kucuk, S. U., & Krishnamurthy, S. (2007). An analysis of consumer power on the internet. *Technovation*, *27*(1-2), 47–56. doi:10.1016/j.technovation.2006.05.002

Lai, L. S. L., & Turban, E. (2008). Groups formation and operations in the Web 2.0 environment and social networks. *Group Decision and Negotiation*, *17*(5), 387–402. doi:10.1007/s10726-008-9113-2

Laroche, M., Habibi, M. R., Richard, M. O., & Sankaranarayanan, R. (2012). The effects of social media based brand communities on brand community markers, value creation practices, brand trust and brand loyalty. *Computers in Human Behavior*, *28*(5), 1755–1767. doi:10.1016/j.chb.2012.04.016

LoginRadius. (2015). *Social Login and Social Sharing*. Retrieved December 04, 2015, fromhttp://cdn2.hubspot.net/hubfs/436275/PDF/LoginRadius-Social-Login-Sharing-Trends-Q1-2015.pdf?t=1433972843555

Malthouse, E. C., Haenlein, M., Skiera, B., Wedge, E., & Zhang, M. (2013). Managing Customer Relationships in the Social Media Era: Introducing the Social CRM House. *Journal of Interactive Marketing*, *27*(4), 270–280. doi:10.1016/j.intmar.2013.09.008

Mangold, W. G., & Faulds, D. J. (2009). Social media: The new hybrid element of the promotion mix. *Business Horizons*, *52*(4), 357–365. doi:10.1016/j.bushor.2009.03.002

Measure, S. (2015). *State of Social Media*. Retrieved December 04, 2015, from http://get.simplymeasured.com/rs/801-IXO-022/images/2015StateOfSocialMedia.pdf

Measured, S. (2015). *The State of Social Marketing*. Retrieved December 08, 2015, from www.simplymeasured.com

Mersey, R. D., Malthouse, E. C., & Calder, B. J. (2010). Engagement with Online Media. *Journal of Media Business Studies*, *7*(2), 39–56. doi:10.1080/16522354.2010.11073506

Perkins, A. (2015). The Evolution of Social Media Recruiting. *Recruiter*. Retrieved December 04, 2015, from https://www.recruiter.com/i/the-evolution-of-social-media-recruiting/

Ployhart, R. E. (2014). *Social Media in the Workplace: Issues and Strategic Questions*. Retrieved December 03, 2015, from https://www.shrm.org/about/foundation/products/Documents/Social%20Media%20Briefing-%20FINAL.pdf

Qiao, Yu. (2014). *Customer Relationship using Social Media*. Retrieved December 04, 2015, from http://cse.tkk.fi/en/publications/B/1/papers/Qiao_final.pdf

Ring, D. (2015). *SHRM survey cites significance of social media in HR*. Retrieved November 29, 2015, from http://searchfinancialapplications.techtarget.com/news/4500253646/SHRM-survey-cites-significance-of-social-media-in-HR

Ross, C., Orr, E. S., Sisic, M., Arseneault, J. M., Simmering, M. G., & Orr, R. R. (2009). Personality and motivations associated with Facebook use. *Computers in Human Behavior*, *25*(2), 578–586. doi:10.1016/j.chb.2008.12.024

Schroeder H. (2013). The Art of Business Relationships Through Social Media. *Ivey Business Journal*. Retrieved December 06, 2015, from http://iveybusinessjournal.com/publication/the-art-of-business-relationships-through-social-media/

Sin, S., Nor, K. M., & Al-Agaga, A. M. (2012). Factors Affecting Malaysian young consumers' online purchase intention in social media websites. *Procedia: Social and Behavioral Sciences*, *40*, 326–333. doi:10.1016/j.sbspro.2012.03.195

Smith, C. (2015). Facebook is leading the way in social commerce. *Business Insider*. Available at: http://www.businessinsider.in/Facebook-is-leading-the-way-in-social-commerce/articleshow/48076273.cms

Smits M. & S. (2014). The impact of social media on business performance. *Proceedings of the 21st European conference on information systems*. Retrieved December 06, 2015, from http://www.staff.science.uu.nl/~vlaan107/ecis/files/ECIS2013-0713-paper.pdf

Statista. (2015). *Statistics & Facts*. Retrieved December 04, 2015, from http://www.statista.com/topics/1164/social-networks/

Stephen, A. T., & Toubia, O. (2010). Deriving Value from Social Commerce Networks. *JMR, Journal of Marketing Research*, 47(2), 215–228. doi:10.1509/jmkr.47.2.215

Tata Consultancy Services (TCS). (2013). *Mastering Digital Feedback: How the Best Consumer Companies Use Social Media*. A TCS 2013 Global Trend Study. Retrieved December 03, 2015, from http://www.tcs.com/SiteCollectionDocuments/Trends_Study/mastering-digital-feedback-with-social-media-2013.pdf

Vassallo, J. (2015). Social Media's Impact on the Human Resources Industry. *Business2community*. Retrieved November 23, 2015, from http://www.business2community.com/human-resources/social-medias-impact-on-the-human-resources-industry-01338454#ScJFrY7YSK6CIZ30.99

Wilson, J. (2009). Social networking: The business case. *Engineering & Technology.*, 4(10), 54–56. doi:10.1049/et.2009.1010

Wipro. (2012). *Social Media: Impact and Relevance in Managing Human Resources in India*. Retrieved December 03, 2015, from http://www.wipro.com/documents/Social_Media_Report_Feb_2012.pdf

Zanella, S., & Paris, I. (2014). Social Recruiting. *The Adecco*. Retrieved December 08, 2015, from http://www.adecco.com/en-US/Industry-Insights/Documents/social-recruiting/adecco-global-social-recruiting-survey-global-report.pdf

KEY TERMS AND DEFINITIONS

Customer Engagement: Consumer engagement is defined as the interactions between a brand and it's customer.

Customer Relationship Management: Customer relationship management (CRM) is a term that refers to practices, strategies and technologies that companies use to manage and analyze customer interactions and data throughout the customer lifecycle, with the goal of improving business relationships with customers, assisting in customer retention and driving sales growth.

Cybervetting: Cybervetting refers to the practice of viewing social networking sites such as Facebook and Myspace, blogs and microblogs like Twitter and using search engines like Google and Yahoo! to obtain information about job applicants or to monitor current employees.

E-Commerce: Is the buying and selling of goods and services, over an electronic network, primarily the Internet.

Internal Branding: Internal Branding is the set of strategic processes that align and empower employees to deliver the appropriate customer experience in a consistent fashion.

Social Commerce: Social commerce is a subset of electronic commerce that involves social media, which supports social interaction, and user contributions to assist online buying, and selling of products and services.

Social Media: It is a collection of online communications channels dedicated to community based input, interaction, content sharing and collaboration.

Social Media Marketing: Social media marketing (SMM) is a form of Internet marketing that utilizes social networking websites as a marketing tool.

Social Shopping: Social shopping is an e-commerce methodology in which the shopping experience is shared with a social network of friends and contacts.

Chapter 2
Mastering Social Media in the Modern Business World

Kijpokin Kasemsap
Suan Sunandha Rajabhat University, Thailand

ABSTRACT

This chapter explains the overview of social media; the perspectives of social media marketing; social media and communication management; social media competence and knowledge sharing in modern business; social media applications in the tourism industry; social media applications in the health care industry; the multifaceted applications of social media platforms in modern business; and the importance of social media in the modern business world. The implementation of social media is required for modern organizations that seek to serve suppliers and customers, increase business performance, strengthen competitiveness, and achieve continuous success in the modern business world. The chapter argues that applying social media has the potential to enhance organizational performance and reach strategic goals in the social media age.

INTRODUCTION

Social media has rapidly grown in modern business (Kim, Koh, Cha, & Lee, 2015). Social media technologies are a variety of networked tools that encourage collaboration, communication, and productivity among social media users (Dabbagh & Kitsantas, 2012). Social media can be categorized into microblogs (e.g., personal blogs and Twitter), online communities or social networking sites (SNSs) (e.g., Facebook), pictures or video sharing applications (e.g., Flickr and YouTube), and dictionary-type applications, such as Wikipedia (Leung, Law, van Hoof, & Buhalis, 2013). Social media is viewed as a group of Internet-based applications that enable Internet users from all over the world to share ideas, thoughts, experiences, perspectives, information, and forge relationships (Chan & Guillet, 2011). Social media is an electronic communication platform that conveys content generated by the networks of users (Suh, 2015).

Rapid diffusion of social media forms the landscape of communication in contemporary society, with deep impact in markets and the functioning of businesses (Boudreau & Lakhani, 2013). Social media business practices reach a significant business awareness among firms (Aral, Dellarocas, & Godes, 2013).

DOI: 10.4018/978-1-5225-0846-5.ch002

Braojos-Gomez et al. (2015) stated that social media can be leveraged to improve the firm's business activities to create value. Social media represents one of the most important platforms for electronic commerce (e-commerce) (Lee & Phang, 2015). Social media is considered as the quick, cheap, and interactive channels for reaching targeted audiences (Valentini, 2015). Companies use social media to communicate with consumers, and the content of social media affects consumer's decision making in modern business (Zhang, 2015).

Social media has expanded the boundary of mediated relationships that social media user can experience (Lim, Hwang, Kim, & Biocca, 2015). Consumers can interact with social media during multiple stages of the consumption process, including information search, decision making, word of mouth (WOM), and the acquisition, use, and disposal of products and services (Filo, Lock, & Karg, 2015). This chapter aims to bridge the gap in the literature on the thorough literature consolidation of social media in the modern business world. The extant literature of social media provides a contribution to practitioners and researchers by describing the challenges and implications of social media in order to maximize the business impact of social media in modern business.

BACKGROUND

Social media has grown exponentially over the last few years (Duggan & Smith, 2014). Many organizations have used social media as channels for marketing and promotion because of their potential to reach the broad and diverse population across the globe (Wang, Chen, & Wang, 2010). While prior studies have demonstrated various benefits, such as fostering the user engagement, participation, knowledge reuse, and collective innovation (Majchrzak, Wagner, & Yates, 2013) toward understanding the social media's impacts and potential implications of their adoption for organizations remains a fertile research ground for information systems (IS) researchers (Jarvenpaa & Majchrzak, 2010). Firms with the higher development of information technology (IT) infrastructure capability can develop more easily the social media competence due to its greater experience leveraging IT to acquire and provide the appropriate information (Braojos-Gomez et al., 2015).

Although more attention is being paid to the potential negative and unanticipated consequences of social media (Champoux, Durgee, & McGlynn, 2012) and its role in social change (Mohajerani, Baptista, & Nandhakumar, 2015), social media is recognized as a technological remedy for addressing communication and social interaction problems in modern business (Granados & Gupta, 2013). Conceptualizing the dyadic nature and potential of social media in delivering both positive and negative effects is still under-explored (Baptista, Newell, & Currie, 2010). The effects of social media within an organization is a growing area of research (Leonardi, 2014), but still relatively under-theorized (Majchrzak et al., 2013).

Social media is an interactive, collaborative, instant form of communication, which transcends geographical boundaries and social isolation (Lawson & Cowling, 2015). Social media users can quickly interact with geographically dispersed people through the social media, which is an emerging topic in social presence research (Schroeder, 2002). Social media use is an increasingly popular activity for Internet users (Filo et al., 2015). Studies examining social media-related phenomena primarily take a view from the community levels (Miller & Tucker, 2013) considering how organizations interact with customers (Aral et al., 2013) and other external stakeholders (Oestreicher-Singer & Zalmanson, 2013).

CHALLENGES AND IMPLICATIONS OF SOCIAL MEDIA PLATFORMS

This section emphasizes the overview of social media; the perspectives of social media marketing; social media and communication management; social media competence and knowledge sharing in modern business; social media applications in the tourism industry; social media applications in the health care industry; the multifaceted applications of social media platforms in modern business; and the importance of social media in the modern business world.

Overview of Social Media

Social media is broadly used across the globe as a platform for communication, sharing and connecting individuals with their networks in unprecedented ways (Kaplan & Haenlein, 2010). Social media is an alternative communication space embedded with opportunities for free and equal participation (Demirhan & Cakır-Demirhan, 2015). Life on social media has incorporated into many people's daily life (Mou, Miller, & Fu, 2015). The technological development from the World Wide Web to the Web 2.0 has created a new online communication environment (Linke & Oliveira, 2015). Web 2.0 represents an ensemble of technological platforms which allow the interaction of the users by creating and sharing information and other different online materials (Georgescu & Popescul, 2015).

Within the business disciplines, much research has been conducted on how businesses can leverage social media to increase exposure, profits, and other business goals (Brooks, 2015). There is a growing body of research on the social media role in the process of political change in both developed countries (Anstead & Chadwick, 2012) and developing countries, in particular the Middle East (including Iran) (Shirky, 2011), Pakistan (Shaheen, 2008), China (Yang, 2009), and Malaysia (Smeltzer & Keddy, 2010). Social media supports the creation of extensive networks that are capable of organizing business action (Howard & Hussain, 2011).

Social media tools (e.g., Facebook, Twitter, YouTube, and blogs) have played an influential role in political mobilization in the high-profile social movements (Karagiannopoulos, 2012). Kaplan and Haenlein (2010) considered social media as the Internet-based applications complex that build on the ideological and technological foundations of the Web 2.0, which allows its users to generate contents (e.g., articles, pictures, drawings, and videos) and build relationships via exchange material and ideas. Social media is viewed as a firm-specific capability that positively influences a firm's performance (Wu, 2010). Social media technologies allow user-generated content and provide new opportunities and challenges for firms to transform their business (Dong & Wu, 2015).

The utilization of social media (Deans, 2011), such as microblogging (Zhang, Qu, Cody, & Wu, 2010), blogs (Lee, Hwang, & Lee, 2006), wikis (Yates, Wagner, & Majchrzak, 2010), and social networking platforms (Richter & Riemer, 2009) has changed work processes, activities, and the patterns of communication (Luo, Zhang, & Duan, 2013). Huang et al. (2014) found that the adoption of enterprise microblogging improves operational performance by increasing the marketing capability. With the popularity of SNSs (e.g., Facebook) and content-sharing websites (e.g., Flickr and YouTube), images on SNSs or content-sharing websites, called social images, become the dominating multimedia objects on the Internet (Niu, Hua, Tian, & Gao, 2015).

The adoption of social media to support the internal communication effectively broadens participation (Denyer, Parry, & Flowers, 2011) and interactive dialogue (Miles & Mangold, 2014). Employees use social media in various ways and for different purposes, including building and maintaining social ties via Linkedin or Facebook, sharing stories through blogging and microblogging, collaborating through shared sites, and sharing pictures on Instagram and videos on YouTube (Ali-Hassan, Nevo, & Wade, 2015). Won et al. (2015) indicated that social media has the potential to facilitate the documentation of the design process from collaborative idea generation through the testing and refinement in the design-based learning environments.

For a successful implementation of social media, firms should execute strategies based on mindful adoption, community building, and absorptive capability (Culnan, McHugh, & Ubillaga, 2010). Kietzmann et al. (2011) suggested that a firm must develop strategies that are congruent with different social media functionalities and the goals of the firm. The development of social media affords the extensive connectivity and the easy information exchange concerning copyright infringement (Carpenter, 2012). Wu et al. (2015) proposed four perspectives to detect the creation of rumors in microblogging platforms (i.e., the combination of features from the topics of the original message, the sentiments that are communicated in the responses, the observed patterns of message propagation, and the profiles of the users who transmit the messages).

Social media helps organizations create new business models, improve demand predictions, enable management practices, and enhance innovation, knowledge sharing, collaboration, and communication in modern business (Aral et al., 2013). Social media becomes relevant to the whole spectrum of organizational interactions with the public, from brand promotion to complaints, queries, campaigning, and participation in policy making (Trainor, Andzulis, Rapp, & Agnihotri, 2014). Current work on social media in organizations focuses on business engagement, mainly relationships with customers (McCarthy, Rowley, Ashworth, & Pioch, 2014) and information management models (Aladwani, 2014).

Contributions outside business engagement have either mapped online interactions with public sector (Mergel, 2013) and cultural organizations (Padilla-Meléndez & del Águila-Obra, 2013) or explored how non-profit organizations use social media to engage with stakeholder groups (Lovejoy & Saxton, 2012). Kietzmann et al. (2011) explained that the relevance of social media in participation and interactivity is evident as their different functionalities enable organizations to share information, construct identities, and network according to their purposes. Panagiotopoulos et al. (2015) stated that modern organizations are expected to develop a social media presence in order to enable them to share information and engage with the networked public.

Perspectives of Social Media Marketing

Business literature has recognized social media from the marketing capabilities' point of view (Kim et al., 2015) because companies have adopted social media for an effective marketing strategy (Kim & Ko, 2012). Social media marketing efforts need to be congruent and aligned with the different needs of social media users (Zhu & Chen, 2015). Congruence of advertisement and website content will decrease the feelings of intrusiveness and increase positive reactions toward advertising (Newman, Stem, & Sprott, 2004). McCoy et al. (2007) indicated that consumers develop such a negative attitude toward the advertising that they avoid them whenever possible.

Social media helps firms to build a positive corporate image through improving transparency and accountability when various stakeholders actively communicate online (Jones, Temperley, & Lima, 2009). WOM generated in the right social media platform by the right social media users enhances brand loyalty and firm's revenues (Kumar & Mirchandani, 2012). Electronic word of mouth (eWOM) is a critical component of social media (Jeong & Jang, 2011). Online communication through social media websites can reduce information asymmetry because online contents (e.g., eWOM) include a wide range of information about firms, such as new product information and user experiences with products and services (Gu, Park, & Konana, 2012).

Trainor et al. (2014) stated that social media and customer relationship management (CRM) develop capabilities to better serve customer needs in modern business. Customer value, customer satisfaction, and brand loyalty have mediated positive effect on CRM performance (Kasemsap, 2014a). CRM becomes one of the most important business strategies in the digital age, thus involving organizational capability of managing business interactions with customers in an effective manner (Kasemsap, 2015a). The capability of social media in building brand in the global marketplace is practically important in modern advertising (Kasemsap, 2015b).

Social media activities generated by consumers in brand communities are claimed to have a game-changing impact on interaction among brand entities and brand building (Luo, Zhang, & Liu, 2015). Rishika et al. (2013) indicated that customer participation in social media increases customers' shopping visits and customer profitability. Regarding user and marketer-generated content, the indirect comments of informative and persuasive customers has a stronger effect on purchase than firm messages (Goh, Heng, & Lin, 2013).

Social Media and Communication Management

Computer-mediated communication (CMC) can bring together individuals from far and wide to the same online space (Pavelko & Myrick, 2015). The introduction of Web 2.0 technology and social media has dramatically impacted the day-to-day activities of public relations practitioners, who need to master the digital tools for effective communication (Taylor & Perry, 2005). Although it is recognized that the speed at which new technology is adopted by organizations and considerable research has focused on the specific use of a single platform (Waters & Jamal, 2011), more knowledge is required about the professional use of social media tools in public relations through empirical and cross-cultural studies. Task characteristics facilitate the usage of social communication technologies to increase the task performance (Koo, Wati, & Jung, 2011).

Following the approach of new institutionalism applied to communication management and public relations (Sandhu, 2009), most of the research about social media in communication management has approached from a meso-level perspective. The meso-level is above the individual and below the general societal system and allows studying organizations in a broad perspective. The meso-level is studied from normative perspectives and produced rational arguments about benefits and recommendations for the optimal use of new media and tools and for managing the impact on organization of empowered stakeholders (Moreno, Navarro, Tench, & Zerfass, 2015). The key aspect for explaining online communication is the micro level of communication practitioners' social media usage and their general attitudes toward digital platforms (Moreno et al., 2015).

To improve the firm's internal communication, social media tools should increase emotional capital (Huy & Shipilov, 2012). Emerging technologies, advances in social media, and new communication platforms represent powerful tools for enhancing public participation (Lovejoy, Waters, & Saxton, 2012), communicating with the public, bypassing traditional gatekeepers (Wright & Hinson, 2009), repairing the reputation and preventing potential boycotts in crisis situations (Schultz, Utz, & Göritz, 2011), achieving higher organizational credibility (Yang & Lim, 2009), and empowering practitioners by improving their productivity and managing issues better (Sallot, Porter, & Acosta-Alzuru, 2004).

Regarding stakeholders, social media has changed the landscape for communications and empowered publics, who are able to post, share, and republish information easily (Porter, Sweetser, & Chung, 2009). This perspective forces organizations to build and maintain the positive relationships with active consumers, bloggers, community managers, and other gatekeepers on the social web (Moreno et al., 2015). Citizens practically recognize social media as a credible source of information that is free from the organizational, marketing, and economic imperatives faced by traditional journalism (Banning & Sweetser, 2007).

Social Media Competence and Knowledge Sharing in Modern Business

Although an increasing number of organizations implement social media as the method to enhance internal knowledge exchange, employees are not motivated to make use of new technologies (Behringer & Sassenberg, 2015). Social media has the potential to contribute to knowledge exchange in the organizational context (Grace, 2009). Technology use is at the essence of many models explaining the acceptance, impact, and success of information systems (Ali-Hassan, 2015). IT infrastructure capability can enable the firm to develop the social media competence (Braojos-Gomez et al., 2015). Suh et al. (2013) stated that IT infrastructure refers to the set of shared technical and human IT resources in the firm that acquire and provide the foundation for utilizing various IT applications.

Technical IT resources include servers, computers, laptops, operating systems, software, electronic communication networks (e.g., e-mail, Intranet, Extranet, and wireless devices), and shared customer databases (Aral & Weill, 2007). Human IT resources refer to the technical and business skills of IT managers and employees (Wang, Chen, & Benitez-Amado, 2015). The firm's technical IT resources, such as computers, laptops, operating systems and electronic communication networks (e.g., wireless devices) are the base to early adopt social media and develop the social media competence through time and experience (Crossan, Maurer, & White, 2011).

The innovative firms search for experimentation and pursue to develop new products which can persuade them to early adopt social media practices to absorb customers' ideas on new products and product improvements (Camison & Villar-Lopez, 2012), which can enable the development of a social media competence through accumulated knowledge and experience (Real, Roldan, & Leal, 2014). Product innovation strategies and knowledge management efficiently support each other and together to achieve planned goals in modern business (Kasemsap, 2016a). Organizations should promote a culture of knowledge management and organizational innovation regarding the use of open communication, shared support, and collaboration (Kasemsap, 2016b).

Social media is significant in everyday life and in learning (Chantanarungpak, 2015). Firms with a higher innovation management capability have more innovative managers and employees, which are more open, proactive and pioneer in using social media (Nambisan, Agarwal, & Tanniru, 1999) to develop the social media competence. Trust in other bloggers, trust in the economic benefit of sharing knowledge, and trust in the blog service provider positively affect the knowledge sharing in blogs (Chai & Kim, 2010). Zhao et al. (2012) indicated that familiarity, trust, and perceived similarity positively affect the sense of belonging, which influence the intention to get and share knowledge in the virtual communities. Virtual user communities can foster the creation of knowledge for innovation projects at the firm level (Mahr & Lievens, 2012).

Social media technology can enhance the improved organizational productivity by fostering the communication and collaboration of employees which aids knowledge transfer and makes organizations more profitable (Kasemsap, 2014b). Social media enables the creation of knowledge value chain to customize information and delivery for a technological business growth (Kasemsap, 2014c). Social media marks a huge range of the personalized cloud computing platforms and functions of interaction on the Web 2.0 (Bianco, 2009). Many benefits are achieved through the utilization of technologies, such as cloud computing and virtualization (Kasemsap, 2015c). Researchers and practitioners should recognize the significance of cloud computing toward gaining sustainable competitive advantage in global supply chain (Kasemsap, 2015d).

Breschi and Lissoni (2001) indicated that the social media tools, based on personal knowledge coming from common professional experience, are the main channels for the distribution and the creation of knowledge. The employee's self-confidence to share knowledge with others, the perceived enjoyment, and the reward expectations affect the knowledge sharing via the firm's weblogs (Papadopoulos, Stamati, & Nopparuch, 2013). By providing a channel where collective action and communication is conducted in real time (Gallaugher & Ransbotham, 2010), social media facilitates the collaboration (Deans, 2011) and the transfer of both explicit and tacit knowledge (Begel et al., 2010).

Social Media Applications in the Tourism Industry

When faced with new technology for tourism purposes, travelers use information searches in the Internet and gain valuable travel information from various social media sources (Chung & Koo, 2015). In terms of travel information, social media becomes an external source of information where users combine what they know with what they have acquired (Chung, Lee, & Han, 2015). IT-enhanced social media (Choi, 2013) in the tourism industry has become an essential tool for accessing various sources of tourist information (Sigala, Christou, & Gretzel, 2011). In the field of tourism, social media on information sharing (Lee, Reid, & Kim, 2012), information searching (Xiang & Gretzel, 2010), intention of using (Yoo & Gretzel, 2011), and marketing (Chan & Guillet, 2011) have been extensively researched.

Many social media tools enable users to publically exchange information, opinions, and experiences, and are broadly recognized by potential tourists as external information sources (Kaplan & Haenlein, 2010). It is crucial to understand the changes in social media technologies and travelers' behaviors that impact the creation, distribution, and accessibility of travel information (Xiang & Gretzel, 2010). In the tourism industry, travelers have basic motivations to choose several valuable destinations to visit; therefore they pursue information reliability through an intensive information search via social media (Hwang & Fesenmaier, 2011). The characteristics of tourism products make travel information essential in reducing the risk of purchasing tourism products (Tan & Chen, 2012). The potential tourists become self-advisors by referencing their own experience and knowledge, but when the internal source does not provide enough information, they use the external sources of information, such as the Internet, books, travel agencies, and acquaintances (Kim, Lehto, & Morrison, 2007).

Through social media, potential tourists can express their opinions, share information about tourism destinations, attractions, and activities, and make decisions based on this knowledge exchange (Ku, 2012). Social media is essential for restructuring the tourism industry (Xiang, Wober, & Fesenmaier, 2008). Social media is directly related to tourist behaviors, such as planning in the pre-travel stage, sharing experience in the on-travel stage, and recommending tourism products in the after-travel stage (Chung & Buhalis, 2008). Huang et al. (2010) studied the factors that encourage and discourage travel information sharing on SNSs, such as Facebook. Kang and Schuett (2013) explored the factors in sharing travel experiences on travel websites, delving into how social factors affect perceived enjoyment, travel planning, and travel experiences through the utilization of social media.

Social Media Applications in the Health Care Industry

Thackeray et al. (2012) stated that heath agencies and organizations have proven to be no exception for the uses of online social media. With low cost and high reach, increasing numbers of public health promotion campaigns have been deployed through online social media platforms (Cugelman, Thelwall, & Dawes, 2011). An increasing number of health campaigns and programs will be deployed and implemented via online social media platforms (Abroms & Lefebvre, 2009). Health campaigns via online social media platforms open up the two-way communication routes through which audiences can engage and participate (Heldman, Schindelar, & Weaver, 2013).

Linking via social media encourages health care practitioners to share case studies, ask for advice, and contribute professional opinions (Kaufman, 2012). With the ever-growing uses of social media for health campaigns, scholarly attention is paid to understand how audiences respond to campaign messages on social media platforms (Korda & Itani, 2013). Syred et al. (2014) indicated that the majority of studies on health campaigns look at the application and feasibility of popular social media websites, such as Facebook and Twitter.

YouTube offers an alternative, cost-effective platform for health campaign videos (Dutta, 2015). With the option of posting comments and replies, YouTube provides a space for social interaction and audience engagement (Dynel, 2014). Postings on YouTube reflect audience attitudes and feedback (Shapiro & Park, 2015). Audience response presented and shared on a social media platform are important to study because they influence the subsequent viewers' attitudes and opinions (Paek, Hove, & Jeon, 2013). Social media users look for the responses of others and are swayed by their comments (Shi, Messaris, & Cappella, 2014). Audience comments practically set the context for social influence (Cialdini & Golstein, 2004).

Multifaceted Applications of Social Media Platforms in Modern Business

With the advances in IT, social media technologies support a large volume of user-generated content that provides opportunities and challenges for business transformation (Jarvenpaa & Tuunainen, 2013). As firms increasingly leverage IT in various innovation activities (Dong & Yang, 2015), they can use a particular social media technology, such as online user innovation communities (OUICs) for open innovation by crowdsourcing the ideas about new products, services, and processes (Di Gangi & Wasko, 2009).

OUICs are valuable for crowdsourcing by enabling firms to collect large amount of user-generated ideas (Bayus, 2013). A better understanding of the ways in which firms increase their business value through the strategic use of OUICs has important implications on the business value of social media technologies, as recent studies on the business value of IT have switched the focus to the IT enablement of innovation (Bardhan, Krishnan, & Lin, 2013). OUICs provide a social media platform for user-generated ideas on innovation (Nambisan, 2013). In OUICs, firms can assign the internal employees as the idea partners to evaluate and select the posts and comments (Dong & Wu, 2015).

If a firm is unable to gain access to enough new ideas, it results in missed opportunities (Hansen & Birkinshaw, 2007). Sourcing external ideas from customers is a solution to extend the scope of search because customers are able to expect the shift of demand (Nambisan, 2002). Dell Incorporation (i.e., an innovative firm) learned to leverage social media by creating a social media platform to enable the innovative customers to participate in the research and development (R&D) processes of the firm (Di Gangi, Wasko, & Hooker, 2010). OUIC-enabled ideation capability can therefore collect ideas from outside the company by tapping into the opinions of end users (Nambisan, 2013). For example, Dell Incorporation has gathered more than 22,000 posts and 100,000 comments on new ideas from its OUIC IdeaStorm, which are related to its desktops and laptops, mobile devices, servers and storage, software, printers and ink, accessories, broadband and mobility, advertising and marketing, retail, and service (Dong & Wu, 2015).

The role of social media in business and in the IT industry focuses on various researches, such as marketing strategies (Cachia, Compano, & Da Costa, 2007), the changing relationship between businesses and marketplaces (Aral et al., 2013), and the reshaping of industries, such as health care (Hawn, 2009), news and publishing (Hong, 2012), and education (Moran et al., 2011). The advancement in the IT sector is a new generation of entrepreneurs who are starting new businesses using social media, often challenging the business models of traditional companies (Mohajerani et al., 2015). For example, an individual software developer can use social media to collaborate with people to establish the new applications and software development (Begel, DeLine, & Zimmermann, 2010). Large firms from IT industries are more likely to adopt social media tools (Sinclaire & Vogus, 2011).

Kim et al. (2012) evaluated the determinants of continuance and WOM intention in Korea's social media. Wu et al. (2013) reported how four dimensions of perceived interactivity (i.e., control, synchronicity, surveillance, and social bandwidth) affect the users' bridging and bonding social capital in Taiwan. Zhang et al. (2013) explored how product attitudes form on online review sites with social networks in China. Chen et al. (2013) discovered the influence structure of users in online social networks through the application of the Bayesian model on data from China's social media website Douban allowing consumers to share reviews on books, movies, and music. Utilizing Douban data, Phang et al. (2013) inspected the types of online social network structure that may increase user participation and promote their tendency to purchase the niche cultural products.

Goh et al. (2013) conducted empirical research measuring the differential impacts of user-generated content and marketer-generated content in social media on consumer purchases in Singapore. Kim et al. (2014) considered the impacts of social media sentiments on stock prices in the Korean financial market. Using Twitter data, Pervin et al. (2014) found that retweetability is significantly affected by amplifiers and information starters. Regarding virtual communities, user identification and satisfaction with the community are related to the participation in the community and promotion to non-members, which in turn increase the member loyalty to the community (Casalo, Flavian, & Guinaliu, 2010).

Importance of Social Media in the Modern Business World

Social media has become an important area of exploration for researchers interested in online technologies and their impacts on customers and businesses (Lee & Phang, 2015). At corporate level, social media enables the firm's proficiency to seize business opportunities and the reconfiguration of business resources (Wagner & Wagner, 2013). At operational level, firms leverage social media to improve their relationships with customers (in terms of product, brand, engagement, and firm) toward increasing the brand trust to lead to a greater customer loyalty and business value (Laroche, Habibi, & Richard, 2013). Kiron et al. (2012) indicated that business managers are the most interested managers in the use of social media for business activities.

As social media use has developed, businesses and brands have evolved practices to communicate with consumers and generate revenue through interactive online tools (Filo et al., 2015). Due to its ease of use, speed, and reach, social media is fast changing the public discourse in society and setting trends and agendas in topics that range from the environment and politics, to technology and the entertainment industry (Asur & Huberman, 2010). Social media becomes the foundation for social interactions and a regular part of the social structure of communities and organizations (Baptista, 2009), adapting the arrangement of communication and interaction (Hoffman & Fodor, 2010). The adoption of social media within modern organizations shifts processes and practices (Subramaniam, Nandhakumar, & Baptista, 2013) as it becomes embedded in decision making and community building in modern business (Culnan et al., 2010).

Social media supports the informational capitalization by spreading the information about the organization and by acquiring the valuable information of employees, suppliers, and clients (Georgescu & Popescul, 2015). Social media and conventional media have a strong interaction effect on stock market performance (Yu, Duan, & Cao, 2013). Firm's corporate image strategies enabled by social media improve financial performance (Schniederjans, Cao, & Schniederjans, 2013). Luo et al. (2013) indicated that social media predicts firm equity value better, faster, and more accurately than conventional online media (e.g., Google search).

The more flexible and adaptive nature of smaller organizations allows them to more quickly and fully appropriate the participative features and practices of social media as a platform for communication (Meske & Stieglitz, 2013) and collaboration (Zeiller & Schauer, 2011). By using the capabilities of social media to access richer information, small and medium-sized enterprises (SMEs) are able to change how they interact with and manage customers (Stockdale, Ahmed, & Scheepers, 2012). The affordances of social media enable entrepreneurs to facilitate the adoption of new business practices (Djelic & Ainamo, 2005). Social media users are more willing to participate in social media from firms with greater corporate social responsibility (Lee, Oh, & Kim, 2013).

Practitioners with a high level of social media usage give more importance to social media channels, the influence of social media on the internal and external stakeholders, and the relevance of key stakeholders along with a better self-estimation of competences (Moreno et al., 2015). Concerning social media competitive analysis and text mining, the pizza manufacturing firms leverage Facebook and Twitter to engage customers and build online communities (He, Zha, & Li, 2013). Social media enable the relationships among customers, products, and companies, which in turn increase their brand loyalty (Laroche et al., 2013).

Social media builds a platform that instantly allows customers to report satisfaction or dissatisfaction with services or products (Kim et al., 2015). Lee et al. (2012) introduced Starbuck's practice that it uses social media not only as tools for direct communication with its customers, but also as windows to obtain the first-hand suggestions and criticisms from those customers. Many companies across industries assign employees who monitor customer reviews that are posted on social media in order to manage customer feedback (Huang, Chou, & Lin, 2010). Managing consumers' feedback in social media is crucial and it can even destroy the business when poorly managed (Gelb & Sundaram, 2002).

FUTURE RESEARCH DIRECTIONS

The classification of the extant literature in the domains of social media will provide the potential opportunities for future research. Social media platforms (e.g., Facebook and Twitter) allow organizations to improve communication and productivity by disseminating information among different groups of employees in a more efficient manner. Facebook is one of the most powerful social media platforms in modern business. Facebook has helped to create a personal brand for many individuals and for businesses. The Internet of Things (IoT) is a system where the Internet is connected to the physical world via ubiquitous sensors. Utilizing the IoT can save consumers and companies a lot of time and money.

Web 2.0 is a technology that is associated with the web applications, which enables interactive user-centered design, interoperability, information sharing, and collaboration on the World Wide Web. The applications developed using Web 2.0 can be shared among a number of users through Internet and can be simultaneously used by numerous users. Web search engines (e.g., Google and Yahoo!) utilize computer algorithms to search the Internet and identify items that match the characters and keywords entered by a user. The relationships among social media platforms, the IoT, and web search engines will be the beneficial topics for future research directions.

CONCLUSION

This chapter highlighted the overview of social media; the perspectives of social media marketing; social media and communication management; social media competence and knowledge sharing in modern business; social media applications in the tourism industry; social media applications in the health care industry; the multifaceted applications of social media platforms in modern business; and the importance of social media in the modern business world. Social media plays a growing role in business communication and becomes important platforms for marketing and advertising. Social media offers a chance to redefine the delivery of service to customers, thus changing the way they think about a company's brands while considerably lowering service costs.

Social media has many benefits, such as the increased awareness of the organization, the increased traffic to website, the greater favorable perceptions of the brand, the better understanding of customer perceptions of their brand, the improved insights into target markets, and the improved identification of new product opportunities in modern business. Social media allows organizations to improve communication and productivity by disseminating information among the different groups of employees in a more efficient manner. The most obvious opportunity of utilizing social media is to generate business revenue through building a business community and advertising products within social media platforms.

When considering social media campaigns, social media users can try to attract followers with promotions. Social media is an important approach to attracting new customers, enhancing brand management, and promoting knowledge management in modern organizations. Using social media allows customers to connect and interact with business on a more personal level. Applying social media has the potential to enhance organizational performance and reach strategic goals in modern business.

REFERENCES

Abroms, L. C., & Lefebvre, R. C. (2009). Obama's wired campaign: Lessons for public health communication. *Journal of Health Communication, 14*(5), 415–423. doi:10.1080/10810730903033000

Aladwani, A. M. (2014). The 6As model of social content management. *International Journal of Information Management, 34*(2), 133–138. doi:10.1016/j.ijinfomgt.2013.12.004

Ali-Hassan, H., Nevo, D., & Wade, M. (2015). Linking dimensions of social media use to job performance: The role of social capital. *The Journal of Strategic Information Systems, 24*(2), 65–89. doi:10.1016/j.jsis.2015.03.001

Anstead, N., & Chadwick, A. (2012). *Parties, election campaigning, and the Internet: Toward a comparative institutional approach.* London, UK: Routledge.

Aral, S., Dellarocas, C., & Godes, D. (2013). Social media and business transformation: A framework for research. *Information Systems Research, 24*(1), 3–13. doi:10.1287/isre.1120.0470

Aral, S., & Weill, P. (2007). IT assets, organizational capabilities, and firm performance: How resource allocations and organizational differences explain performance variation. *Organization Science, 18*(5), 763–780. doi:10.1287/orsc.1070.0306

Banning, S. A., & Sweetser, K. D. (2007). How much do they think it affects them and whom do they believe?: Comparing the third-person effect and credibility of blogs and traditional media. *Communication Quarterly, 55*(4), 451–466. doi:10.1080/01463370701665114

Baptista, J. (2009). Institutionalisation as a process of interplay between technology and its organisational context of use. *Journal of Information Technology, 24*(4), 305–319. doi:10.1057/jit.2009.15

Baptista, J., Newell, S., & Currie, W. (2010). Paradoxical effects of institutionalization on the strategic awareness of technology in organizations. *The Journal of Strategic Information Systems, 19*(3), 171–183. doi:10.1016/j.jsis.2010.07.001

Bardhan, I., Krishnan, V., & Lin, S. (2013). Business value of information technology: Testing the interaction effect of IT and R&D on Tobin's Q. *Information Systems Research, 24*(4), 1147–1161. doi:10.1287/isre.2013.0481

Bayus, B. L. (2013). Crowdsourcing new product ideas over time: An analysis of the Dell IdeaStorm community. *Management Science, 59*(1), 226–244. doi:10.1287/mnsc.1120.1599

Begel, A., DeLine, R., & Zimmermann, T. (2010). *Social media for software engineering.* Paper presented at the 2010 FSE/SDP Workshop on the Future of Software Engineering Research (FoSER), Santa Fe, NM.

Behringer, N., & Sassenberg, K. (2015). Introducing social media for knowledge management: Determinants of employees' intentions to adopt new tools. *Computers in Human Behavior, 48*, 290–296. doi:10.1016/j.chb.2015.01.069

Bianco, J. S.Jamie Skye Bianco. (2009). Social networking and cloud computing: Precarious affordances for the "prosumer." *WSQ:Women's Studies Quarterly, 37*(1/2), 303–312. doi:10.1353/wsq.0.0146

Boudreau, K. J., & Lakhani, K. R. (2013). Using the crowd as an innovation partner. *Harvard Business Review*, *91*(4), 60–69.

Braojos-Gomez, J., Benitez-Amado, J., & Llorens-Montes, F. J. (2015). How do small firms learn to develop a social media competence? *International Journal of Information Management*, *35*(4), 443–458. doi:10.1016/j.ijinfomgt.2015.04.003

Breschi, S., & Lissoni, F. (2001). Knowledge spillovers and local innovation systems: A critical survey. *Industrial and Corporate Change*, *10*(4), 975–1005. doi:10.1093/icc/10.4.975

Brooks, S. (2015). Does personal social media usage affect efficiency and well-being? *Computers in Human Behavior*, *46*, 26–37. doi:10.1016/j.chb.2014.12.053

Cachia, R., Compano, R., & Da Costa, O. (2007). Grasping the potential of online social networks for foresight. *Technological Forecasting and Social Change*, *74*(8), 1179–1203. doi:10.1016/j.techfore.2007.05.006

Camison, C., & Villar-Lopez, A. (2012). On how firms located in and industrial district profit from knowledge spillovers: Adoption of an organic structure and innovation capabilities. *British Journal of Management*, *23*(3), 361–382. doi: 10.1111/j.1467-8551.2011.00745.x

Carpenter, C. (2012). Copyright infringement and the second generation of social media websites: Why Pinterest users should be protected from copyright infringement by the fair use defense. *Journal of Internet Law*, *16*(7), 9–21. doi: 10.2139/ssrn.2131483

Casalo, L. V., Flavian, C., & Guinaliu, M. (2010). Relationship quality, community promotion and brand loyalty in virtual communities: Evidence from free software communities. *International Journal of Information Management*, *30*(4), 357–367. doi:10.1016/j.ijinfomgt.2010.01.004

Chai, S., & Kim, M. (2010). What makes bloggers share knowledge? An investigation on the role of trust. *International Journal of Information Management*, *30*(5), 408–415. doi:10.1016/j.ijinfomgt.2010.02.005

Champoux, V., Durgee, J., & McGlynn, L. (2012). Corporate Facebook pages: When "fans" attack. *The Journal of Business Strategy*, *33*(2), 22–30. doi:10.1108/02756661211206717

Chan, N. L., & Guillet, B. D. (2011). Investigation of social media marketing: How does the hotel industry in Hong Kong perform in marketing on social media websites? *Journal of Travel & Tourism Marketing*, *28*(4), 345–368. doi:10.1080/10548408.2011.571571

Chang, H. L., & Chou, C. Y. (2012). *Shaping proactivity for firm performance: Evaluating the role of IT-enabled collaboration in small and medium enterprises*. Paper presented at the 16th Pacific Asia Conference on Information Systems (PACIS 2012), Ho Chi Minh City, Vietnam.

Chantanarungpak, K. (2015). Using e-portfolio on social media. *Procedia: Social and Behavioral Sciences*, *186*, 1275–1281. doi:10.1016/j.sbspro.2015.04.063

Chen, X., Wang, C., & Zhang, X. (2013). *All online friends are not created equal: Discovering influence structure in online social networks*. Paper presented at the Pacific Asia Conference on Information Systems (PACIS 2013), Jeju Island, South Korea.

Choi, S. (2013). An empirical study of social network service (SNS) continuance: Incorporating the customer value-satisfaction-loyalty model into the IS continuance model. *Asia Pacific Journal of Information Systems*, *23*(4), 1–28. doi:10.14329/apjis.2013.23.4.001

Chung, J. E. (2015). Antismoking campaign videos on YouTube and audience response: Application of social media assessment metrics. *Computers in Human Behavior*, *51*, 114–121. doi:10.1016/j.chb.2015.04.061

Chung, J. Y., & Buhalis, D. (2008). *A study of online travel community and Web 2.0: Factors affecting participation and attitude*. Paper presented at the ENTER 2008 Conference on eTourism, Innsbruck, Austria. doi:10.1007/978-3-211-77280-5_7

Chung, N., & Koo, C. (2015). The use of social media in travel information search. *Telematics and Informatics*, *32*(2), 215–229. doi:10.1016/j.tele.2014.08.005

Chung, N., Lee, S., & Han, H. (2015). Understanding communication types on travel information sharing in social media: A transactive memory systems perspective. *Telematics and Informatics*, *32*(4), 564–575. doi:10.1016/j.tele.2015.02.002

Cialdini, R., & Golstein, N. (2004). Social influence: Compliance and conformity. *Annual Review of Psychology*, *55*(1), 591–621. doi:10.1146/annurev.psych.55.090902.142015

Crossan, M. M., Maurer, C. C., & White, R. E. (2011). Reflections on the 2009 AMR decade award: Do we have a theory of organizational learning? *Academy of Management Review*, *36*(3), 446–460. doi:10.5465/amr.2010.0544

Cugelman, B., Thelwall, M., & Dawes, P. (2011). Online interventions for social marketing health behavior change campaigns: A meta-analysis of psychological architectures and adherence factors. *Journal of Medical Internet Research*, *13*(1), 84–107. doi:10.2196/jmir.1367

Culnan, M., McHugh, P., & Zubillaga, J. (2010). How large US companies can use Twitter and other social media to gain business value. *MIS Quarterly Executive*, *9*(4), 243–259.

Deans, P. C. (2011). The impact of social media on C-level roles. *MIS Quarterly Executive*, *10*(4), 187–200.

Demirhan, K., & Cakır-Demirhan, D. (2015). Gender and politics: Patriarchal discourse on social media. *Public Relations Review*, *41*(1), 308–310. doi:10.1016/j.pubrev.2014.11.010

Denyer, D., Parry, E., & Flowers, P. (2011). "Social", "open" and "participative"? Exploring personal experiences and organizational effects of Enterprise 2.0 use. *Long Range Planning*, *44*(5/6), 375–396. doi:10.1016/j.lrp.2011.09.007

Di Gangi, P. M., & Wasko, M. (2009). Steal my idea! Organizational adoption of user innovations from a user innovation community: A case study of Dell IdeaStorm. *Decision Support Systems*, *48*(1), 303–312. doi:10.1016/j.dss.2009.04.004

Di Gangi, P. M., Wasko, M. M., & Hooker, R. E. (2010). Getting customers' ideas to work for you: Learning from Dell how to succeed with online user innovation communities. *MIS Quarterly Executive*, *9*(4), 213–228.

Djelic, M. L., & Ainamo, A. (2005). The telecom industry as cultural industry? The transposition of fashion logics into the field of mobile telephony. *Research in the Sociology of Organizations*, *23*(1), 45–82. doi:10.1016/S0733-558X(05)23002-1

Dong, J. Q., & Wu, W. (2015). Business value of social media technologies: Evidence from online user innovation communities. *The Journal of Strategic Information Systems*, *24*(2), 113–127. doi:10.1016/j. jsis.2015.04.003

Dong, J. Q., & Yang, C. H. (2015). Information technology and organizational learning in knowledge alliances and networks: Evidence from U.S. pharmaceutical industry. *Information & Management*, *52*(1), 111–122. doi:10.1016/j.im.2014.10.010

Duggan, M., & Smith, A. (2014). *Social media update 2013*. Washington, DC: Pew Research Center.

Dutta, M. J. (2015). New communication technologies, social media, and public health. In R. Detels, M. Gulliford, Q. Karim, & C. Tan (Eds.), *Oxford textbook of global public health* (pp. 388–399). Oxford, UK: Oxford University Press. doi:10.1093/med/9780199661756.003.0102

Dynel, M. (2014). Participation framework underlying YouTube interaction. *Journal of Pragmatics*, *73*, 37–52. doi:10.1016/j.pragma.2014.04.001

Filo, K., Lock, D., & Karg, A. (2015). Sport and social media research: A review. *Sport Management Review*, *18*(2), 166–181. doi:10.1016/j.smr.2014.11.001

Gallaugher, J., & Ransbotham, S. (2010). Social media and customer dialog management at Starbucks. *MIS Quarterly Executive*, *9*(4), 197–212.

Gelb, B. D., & Sundaram, S. (2002). Adapting to word of mouse. *Business Horizons*, *45*(4), 21–25. doi:10.1016/S0007-6813(02)00222-7

Georgescu, M., & Popescul, D. (2015). Social media: The new paradigm of collaboration and communication for business environment. *Procedia Economics and Finance*, *20*, 277–282. doi:10.1016/S2212-5671(15)00075-1

Goh, K. Y., Heng, C. S., & Lin, Z. (2013). Social media brand community and consumer behavior: Quantifying the relative impact of user- and marketer-generated content. *Information Systems Research*, *24*(1), 88–107. doi:10.1287/isre.1120.0469

Grace, T. P. L. (2009). Wikis as a knowledge management tool. *Journal of Knowledge Management*, *13*(4), 64–74. doi:10.1108/13673270910971833

Granados, N., & Gupta, A. (2013). Transparency strategy: Competing with information in a digital world. *Management Information Systems Quarterly*, *37*(2), 637–641.

Gu, B., Park, J., & Konana, P. (2012). The impact of external word-of-mouth sources on retailer sales of high-involvement products. *Information Systems Research*, *23*(1), 182–196. doi:10.1287/isre.1100.0343

Hansen, R., & Birkinshaw, J. (2007). The innovation value chain. *Harvard Business Review*, *85*(6), 121–135.

Hawn, C. (2009). Take two aspirin and tweet me in the morning: How Twitter, Facebook, and other social media are reshaping health care. *Health Affairs, 28*(2), 361–368. doi:10.1377/hlthaff.28.2.361

He, W., Zha, S., & Li, L. (2013). Social media competitive analysis and text mining: A case study in the pizza industry. *International Journal of Information Management, 33*(3), 464–472. doi:10.1016/j.ijinfomgt.2013.01.001

Heldman, A. B., Schindelar, J., & Weaver, J. B. (2013). Social media engagement and public health communication: Implications for public health organizations being truly "social". *Public Health Reviews, 35*(1), 1–18.

Hoffman, D. L., & Fodor, M. (2010). Can you measure the ROI of your social media marketing? *MIT Sloan Management Review, 52*(1), 41–49.

Hong, S. (2012). Online news on Twitter: Newspapers' social media adoption and their online readership. *Information Economics and Policy, 24*(1), 69–74. doi:10.1016/j.infoecopol.2012.01.004

Howard, P. N., & Hussain, M. M. (2011). The role of digital media. *Journal of Democracy, 22*(3), 35–48. doi:10.1353/jod.2011.0041

Huang, C. Y., Chou, C. J., & Lin, P. C. (2010). Involvement theory in constructing bloggers' intention to purchase travel products. *Tourism Management, 31*(4), 513–526. doi:10.1016/j.tourman.2009.06.003

Huang, J., Baptista, J., & Newell, S. (2015). Communicational ambidexterity as a new capability to manage social media communication within organizations. *The Journal of Strategic Information Systems, 24*(2), 49–64. doi:10.1016/j.jsis.2015.03.002

Huang, J., Zhang, J., Li, Y., & Lv, Z. (2014). Business value of enterprise micro-blogging: Empirical study from Weibo.com in Sina. *Journal of Global Information Management, 22*(3), 32–56. doi:10.4018/jgim.2014070102

Huang, Y., Basu, C., & Hsu, M. K. (2010). Exploring motivations of travel knowledge sharing on social network sites: An empirical investigation of U.S. college students. *Journal of Hospitality Marketing & Management, 19*(7), 717–734. doi:10.1080/19368623.2010.508002

Huy, Q., & Shipilov, A. (2012). The key to social media success within organizations. *MIT Sloan Management Review, 54*(1), 73–81.

Hwang, Y. H., & Fesenmaier, D. R. (2011). Unplanned tourist attraction visits by travellers. *Tourism Geographies: An International Journal of Tourism Space, Place and Environment, 13*(3), 398–416. doi:10.1080/14616688.2011.570777

Jarvenpaa, S. L., & Majchrzak, A. (2010). Vigilant interaction in knowledge collaboration: Challenges of online user participation under ambivalence. *Information Systems Research, 21*(4), 773–784. doi:10.1287/isre.1100.0320

Jarvenpaa, S. L., & Tuunainen, V. K. (2013). How Finnair socialized customers for service co-creation with social media. *MIS Quarterly Executive, 12*(3), 125–136.

Jeong, E., & Jang, S. C. (2011). Restaurant experiences triggering positive electronic word-of-mouth (eWOM) motivations. *International Journal of Hospitality Management, 30*(2), 356–366. doi:10.1016/j.ijhm.2010.08.005

Jones, J., Temperley, B., & Lima, A. (2009). Corporate reputation in the era of Web 2. 0: The case of Primark. *Journal of Marketing Management, 25*(9/10), 927–939. doi:10.1362/026725709X479309

Kang, M., & Schuett, M. A. (2013). Determinants of sharing travel experiences in social media. *Journal of Travel & Tourism Marketing, 30*(1/2), 93–107. doi:10.1080/10548408.2013.751237

Kaplan, A., & Haenlein, M. (2010). Users of the world, unite! The challenges and opportunities of social media. *Business Horizons, 53*(1), 59–68. doi:10.1016/j.bushor.2009.09.003

Karagiannopoulos, V. (2012). The role of the internet in political struggles: Some conclusions from Iran and Egypt. *New Political Science, 34*(2), 151–171. doi:10.1080/07393148.2012.676394

Kasemsap, K. (2014a). The role of brand loyalty on CRM performance: An innovative framework for smart manufacturing. In Z. Luo (Ed.), *Smart manufacturing innovation and transformation: Interconnection and intelligence* (pp. 252–284). Hershey, PA: IGI Global. doi:10.4018/978-1-4666-5836-3.ch010

Kasemsap, K. (2014b). The role of social networking in global business environments. In P. Smith & T. Cockburn (Eds.), *Impact of emerging digital technologies on leadership in global business* (pp. 183–201). Hershey, PA: IGI Global. doi:10.4018/978-1-4666-6134-9.ch010

Kasemsap, K. (2014c). The role of social media in the knowledge-based organizations. In I. Lee (Ed.), *Integrating social media into business practice, applications, management, and models* (pp. 254–275). Hershey, PA: IGI Global. doi:10.4018/978-1-4666-6182-0.ch013

Kasemsap, K. (2015a). The role of customer relationship management in the global business environments. In T. Tsiakis (Ed.), *Trends and innovations in marketing information systems* (pp. 130–156). Hershey, PA: IGI Global. doi:10.4018/978-1-4666-8459-1.ch007

Kasemsap, K. (2015b). The role of social media in international advertising. In N. Taşkıran & R. Yılmaz (Eds.), *Handbook of research on effective advertising strategies in the social media age* (pp. 171–196). Hershey, PA: IGI Global. doi:10.4018/978-1-4666-8125-5.ch010

Kasemsap, K. (2015c). The role of cloud computing adoption in global business. In V. Chang, R. Walters, & G. Wills (Eds.), *Delivery and adoption of cloud computing services in contemporary organizations* (pp. 26–55). Hershey, PA: IGI Global. doi:10.4018/978-1-4666-8210-8.ch002

Kasemsap, K. (2015d). The role of cloud computing in global supply chain. In N. Rao (Ed.), *Enterprise management strategies in the era of cloud computing* (pp. 192–219). Hershey, PA: IGI Global. doi:10.4018/978-1-4666-8339-6.ch009

Kasemsap, K. (2016a). Creating product innovation strategies through knowledge management in global business. In A. Goel & P. Singhal (Eds.), *Product innovation through knowledge management and social media strategies* (pp. 330–357). Hershey, PA: IGI Global. doi:10.4018/978-1-4666-9607-5.ch015

Kasemsap, K. (2016b). The roles of knowledge management and organizational innovation in global business. In G. Jamil, J. Poças-Rascão, F. Ribeiro, & A. Malheiro da Silva (Eds.), *Handbook of research on information architecture and management in modern organizations* (pp. 130–153). Hershey, PA: IGI Global. doi:10.4018/978-1-4666-8637-3.ch006

Kaufman, M. B. (2012). Online communities for healthcare professionals can help improve communication, collaboration. *Formulary (Cleveland, Ohio), 47*(4), 161.

Kietzmann, J. H., Hermkens, K., McCarthy, I. P., & Silvestre, B. S. (2011). Social media? Get serious! Understanding the functional building blocks of social media. *Business Horizons, 54*(3), 241–251. doi:10.1016/j.bushor.2011.01.005

Kim, A. J., & Ko, E. (2012). Do social media marketing activities enhance customer equity? An empirical study of luxury fashion brand. *Journal of Business Research, 65*(10), 1480–1486. doi:10.1016/j.jbusres.2011.10.014

Kim, D. Y., Lehto, X. Y., & Morrison, A. M. (2007). Gender differences in online travel information search: Implications for marketing communications on the Internet. *Tourism Management, 28*(2), 423–433. doi:10.1016/j.tourman.2006.04.001

Kim, H., Son, J., & Suh, K. (2012). Following firms on Twitter: Determinants of continuance and word-of-mouth intention. *Asia Pacific Journal of Information Systems, 22*(3), 1–27. doi:10.5859/KAIS.2012.21.2.1

Kim, S., Koh, Y., Cha, J., & Lee, S. (2015). Effects of social media on firm value for U.S. restaurant companies. *International Journal of Hospitality Management, 49*, 40–46. doi:10.1016/j.ijhm.2015.05.006

Kim, T., Jung, W. J., & Lee, S. Y. (2014). The analysis on the relationship between firms' exposures to SNS and stock prices in Korea. *Asia Pacific Journal of Information Systems, 24*(2), 233–253. doi:10.14329/apjis.2014.24.2.233

Kiron, D., Palmer, D., Phillips, A. N., & Kruschwitz, N. (2012). What managers really think about social business. *MIT Sloan Management Review, 53*(4), 51–60.

Koo, C., Wati, Y., & Jung, J. J. (2011). Examination of how social aspects moderate the relationship between task characteristics and usage of social communication technologies (SCTs) in organizations. *International Journal of Information Management, 31*(5), 445–459. doi:10.1016/j.ijinfomgt.2011.01.003

Korda, H., & Itani, Z. (2013). Harnessing social media for health promotion and behavior change. *Health Promotion Practice, 14*(1), 15–23. doi:10.1177/1524839911405850

Ku, E. (2012). Distributed fascinating knowledge over an online travel community. *International Journal of Tourism Research, 16*(1), 33–43. doi:10.1002/jtr.1895

Kumar, V., & Mirchandani, R. (2012). Increasing the ROI of social media marketing. *MIT Sloan Management Review, 54*(1), 55–61.

Laroche, M., Habibi, M. R., & Richard, M. O. (2013). To be or not to be in social media: How brand loyalty is affected by social media? *International Journal of Information Management, 33*(1), 76–82. doi:10.1016/j.ijinfomgt.2012.07.003

Lawson, C., & Cowling, C. (2015). Social media: The next frontier for professional development in radiography. *Radiography, 21*(2), e74–e80. doi:10.1016/j.radi.2014.11.006

Lee, H., Reid, E., & Kim, W. G. (2012). Understanding knowledge sharing in online travel communities: Antecedents and the moderating effects of interaction modes. *Journal of Hospitality & Tourism Research (Washington, D.C.), 38*(2), 222–242. doi:10.1177/1096348012451454

Lee, K., Oh, W. Y., & Kim, N. (2013). Social media for socially responsible firms: Analysis of Fortune 500's Twitter profiles and their CSR/CSIR ratings. *Journal of Business Ethics, 118*(4), 791–806. doi:10.1007/s10551-013-1961-2

Lee, S., Hwang, T., & Lee, H. H. (2006). Corporate blogging strategies of the Fortune 500 companies. *Management Decision, 44*(3), 316–334. doi:10.1108/00251740610656232

Lee, S. Y. T., & Phang, C. W. (2015). Leveraging social media for electronic commerce in Asia: Research areas and opportunities. *Electronic Commerce Research and Applications, 14*(3), 145–149. doi:10.1016/j.elerap.2015.02.001

Lee, W., Xiong, L., & Hu, C. (2012). The effect of Facebook users' arousal and valence on intention to go to the festival: Applying an extension of the technology acceptance model. *International Journal of Hospitality Management, 31*(3), 819–827. doi:10.1016/j.ijhm.2011.09.018

Leonardi, P. M. (2014). Social media, knowledge sharing, and innovation: Toward a theory of communication visibility. *Information Systems Research, 25*(4), 796–816. doi:10.1287/isre.2014.0536

Leung, D., Law, R., van Hoof, H., & Buhalis, D. (2013). Social media in tourism and hospitality: A literature review. *Journal of Travel & Tourism Marketing, 30*(1/2), 3–22. doi:10.1080/10548408.2013.750919

Lim, J. S., Hwang, Y. C., Kim, S., & Biocca, F. A. (2015). How social media engagement leads to sports channel loyalty: Mediating roles of social presence and channel commitment. *Computers in Human Behavior, 46*, 158–167. doi:10.1016/j.chb.2015.01.013

Linke, A., & Oliveira, E. (2015). Quantity or quality? The professionalization of social media communication in Portugal and Germany: A comparison. *Public Relations Review, 41*(2), 305–307. doi:10.1016/j.pubrev.2014.11.018

Lovejoy, K., & Saxton, G. D. (2012). Information, community, and action: How nonprofit organizations use social media. *Journal of Computer-Mediated Communication, 17*(3), 337–353. doi:10.1111/j.1083-6101.2012.01576.x

Lovejoy, K., Waters, R. D., & Saxton, G. D. (2012). Engaging stakeholders through Twitter: How nonprofit organizations are getting more out of 140 characters or less. *Public Relations Review, 38*(2), 313–318. doi:10.1016/j.pubrev.2012.01.005

Luo, N., Zhang, M., & Liu, W. (2015). The effects of value co-creation practices on building harmonious brand community and achieving brand loyalty on social media in China. *Computers in Human Behavior, 48*, 492–499. doi:10.1016/j.chb.2015.02.020

Luo, X., Zhang, J., & Duan, W. (2013). Social media and firm equity value. *Information Systems Research, 24*(1), 146–163. doi:10.1287/isre.1120.0462

Mahr, D., & Lievens, A. (2012). Virtual lead user communities: Drivers of knowledge creation for innovation. *Research Policy*, *41*(1), 167–177. doi:10.1016/j.respol.2011.08.006

Majchrzak, A., Wagner, C., & Yates, D. (2013). The impact of shaping on knowledge reuse for organizational improvement with wikis. *Management Information Systems Quarterly*, *37*(2), 455–469.

McCarthy, J., Rowley, J., Ashworth, C. J., & Pioch, E. (2014). Managing brand presence through social media: The case of UK football clubs. *Internet Research*, *24*(2), 181–204. doi:10.1108/IntR-08-2012-0154

McCoy, S., Everard, A., Polak, P., & Galletta, D. F. (2007). The effects of online advertising. *Communications of the ACM*, *50*(3), 84–88. doi:10.1145/1226736.1226740

Mergel, I. (2013). A framework for interpreting social media interactions in the public sector. *Government Information Quarterly*, *30*(4), 327–334. doi:10.1016/j.giq.2013.05.015

Meske, C., & Stieglitz, S. (2013). Adoption and use of social media in small and medium-sized enterprises. In F. Harmsen & H. Proper (Eds.), *Practice-driven research on enterprise transformation* (pp. 61–75). Heidelberg, Germany: Springer–Verlag. doi:10.1007/978-3-642-38774-6_5

Miles, S. J., & Mangold, W. G. (2014). Employee voice: Untapped resource or social media time bomb? *Business Horizons*, *57*(3), 401–411. doi:10.1016/j.bushor.2013.12.011

Miller, A. R., & Tucker, C. (2013). Active social media management: The case of health care. *Information Systems Research*, *24*(1), 52–70. doi:10.1287/isre.1120.0466

Mohajerani, A., Baptista, J., & Nandhakumar, J. (2015). Exploring the role of social media in importing logics across social contexts: The case of IT SMEs in Iran. *Technological Forecasting and Social Change*, *95*, 16–31. doi:10.1016/j.techfore.2014.06.008

Moreno, A., Navarro, C., Tench, R., & Zerfass, A. (2015). Does social media usage matter? An analysis of online practices and digital media perceptions of communication practitioners in Europe. *Public Relations Review*, *41*(2), 242–253. doi:10.1016/j.pubrev.2014.12.006

Mou, Y., Miller, M., & Fu, H. (2015). Evaluating a target on social media: From the self-categorization perspective. *Computers in Human Behavior*, *49*, 451–459. doi:10.1016/j.chb.2015.03.031

Nambisan, S. (2002). Designing virtual customer environments for new product development: Toward a theory. *Academy of Management Review*, *27*(3), 392–413. doi: 10.5465/AMR.2002.7389914

Nambisan, S. (2013). Information technology and product/service innovation: A brief assessment and some suggestions for future research. *Journal of the Association for Information Systems*, *14*(4), 215–226.

Nambisan, S., Agarwal, R., & Tanniru, M. (1999). Organizational mechanisms for enhancing user innovation in information technology. *Management Information Systems Quarterly*, *23*(3), 365–395. doi:10.2307/249468

Newman, E. F., Stem, D. E. Jr, & Sprott, D. E. (2004). Banner advertisement and web site congruity effects on consumer web site perceptions. *Industrial Management & Data Systems*, *104*(3), 273–281. doi:10.1108/02635570410525816

Niu, Z., Hua, G., Tian, Q., & Gao, X. (2015). Visual topic network: Building better image representations for images in social media. *Computer Vision and Image Understanding, 136*, 3–13. doi:10.1016/j.cviu.2015.01.010

Oestreicher-Singer, G., & Zalmanson, L. (2013). Content or community? A digital business strategy for content providers in the social age. *Management Information Systems Quarterly, 37*(2), 591–616.

Paek, H. J., Hove, T., & Jeon, J. (2013). Social media for message testing: A multilevel approach to linking favorable viewer responses with message, producer, and viewer influence on YouTube. *Health Communication, 28*(3), 226–236. doi:10.1080/10410236.2012.672912

Panagiotopoulos, P., Shan, L. C., Barnett, J., Regan, A., & McConnon, A. (2015). A framework of social media engagement: Case studies with food and consumer organisations in the UK and Ireland. *International Journal of Information Management, 35*(4), 394–402. doi:10.1016/j.ijinfomgt.2015.02.006

Papadopoulos, T., Stamati, T., & Nopparuch, P. (2013). Exploring the determinants of knowledge sharing via employee weblogs. *International Journal of Information Management, 33*(1), 133–146. doi:10.1016/j.ijinfomgt.2012.08.002

Pavelko, R. L., & Myrick, J. G. (2015). That's so OCD: The effects of disease trivialization via social media on user perceptions and impression formation. *Computers in Human Behavior, 49*, 251–258. doi:10.1016/j.chb.2015.02.061

Pervin, N., Takeda, H., & Toriumi, F. (2014). *Factors affecting retweetability: An event-centric analysis on Twitter.* Paper presented at the International Conference on Information Systems (ICIS 2014), Atlanta, GA.

Phang, C. W., Zhang, C., & Sutanto, J. (2013). The influence of user interaction and participation in social media on the consumption intention of niche products. *Information & Management, 50*(8), 661–672. doi:10.1016/j.im.2013.07.001

Porter, L. V., Sweetser, K. D., & Chung, D. (2009). The blogosphere and public relations: Investigating practitioners' roles and blog use. *Journal of Communication Management, 13*(3), 250–267. doi:10.1108/13632540910976699

Real, J. C., Roldan, J. L., & Leal, A. (2014). From entrepreneurial orientation and learning orientation to business performance: Analysing the mediating role of organizational learning and the moderating effects of organizational size. *British Journal of Management, 25*(2), 186–208. doi:10.1111/j.1467-8551.2012.00848.x

Richter, A., & Riemer, K. (2009). *Corporate social networking sites: Modes of use and appropriation through co-evolution.* Paper presented at the 20th Australasian Conference on Information Systems (ACIS 2009), Melbourne, Australia.

Rishika, R., Kumar, A., Janakiraman, R., & Bezawada, R. (2013). The effect of customers' social media participation on customer visit frequency and profitability: An empirical investigation. *Information Systems Research, 54*(1), 108–127. doi:10.1287/isre.1120.0460

Sallot, L. M., Porter, L. V., & Acosta-Alzuru, C. (2004). Practitioners' web use and perceptions of their own roles and power: A qualitative study. *Public Relations Review, 30*(3), 269–278. doi:10.1016/j.pubrev.2004.05.002

Sandhu, S. (2009). Strategic communication: An institutional perspective. *International Journal of Strategic Communication, 3*(2), 72–92. doi:10.1080/15531180902805429

Schniederjans, D., Cao, E. S., & Schniederjans, M. (2013). Enhancing financial performance with social media: An impression management perspective. *Decision Support Systems, 55*(4), 911–918. doi:10.1016/j.dss.2012.12.027

Schroeder, R. (2002). *Copresence and interaction in virtual environments: An overview of the range of issues.* Paper presented at the Fifth International Workshop on Presence, Porto, Portugal.

Schultz, F., Utz, S., & Göritz, A. (2011). Is the medium the message? Perceptions of and reactions to crisis communication via twitter, blogs and traditional media. *Public Relations Review, 37*(1), 20–27. doi:10.1016/j.pubrev.2010.12.001

Shaheen, M. A. (2008). Use of social networks and information seeking behavior of students during political crises in Pakistan: A case study. *The International Information & Library Review, 40*(3), 142–147. doi:10.1080/10572317.2008.10762774

Shapiro, M. A., & Park, H. W. (2015). More than entertainment: YouTube and public responses to the science of global warming and climate change. *Social Sciences Information. Information Sur les Sciences Sociales, 54*(1), 115–145. doi:10.1177/0539018414554730

Shi, R., Messaris, P., & Cappella, J. N. (2014). Effects of online comments on smokers' perception of antismoking public service announcements. *Journal of Computer-Mediated Communication, 19*(4), 975–990. doi:10.1111/jcc4.12057

Shirky, C. (2011). The political power of social media technology, the public sphere, and political change. *Foreign Affairs, 90*(1), 28–41.

Sigala, M., Christou, E., & Gretzel, U. (2011). *Web 2.0 in travel, tourism and hospitality: Theory, practice and cases.* Farnham, UK: Ashgate Publishing.

Sinclaire, J. K., & Vogus, C. E. (2011). Adoption of social networking sites: An exploratory adaptive structuration perspective for global organizations. *Information Technology & Management, 12*(4), 293–314. doi:10.1007/s10799-011-0086-5

Smeltzer, S., & Keddy, D. (2010). Won't you be my (political) friend? The changing Face(book) of socio-political contestation in Malaysia. *Canadian Journal of Development Studies, 30*(3/4), 421–440.

Stockdale, R., Ahmed, A., & Scheepers, H. (2012). *Identifying business value from the use of social media: An SME perspective.* Paper presented at the 16th Pacific Asia Conference on Information Systems (PACIS 2012), Ho Chi Minh City, Vietnam.

Subramaniam, N., Nandhakumar, J., & Baptista, J. (2013). Exploring social network interactions in enterprise systems: The role of virtual co-presence. *Information Systems Journal, 23*(6), 475–499. doi:10.1111/isj.12019

Suh, H., van Hillegersberg, J., Choi, J., & Chung, S. (2013). Effects of strategic alignment on IS success: The mediation role of IS investment in Korea. *Information Technology & Management, 14*(1), 7–27. doi:10.1007/s10799-012-0144-7

Suh, J. H. (2015). Forecasting the daily outbreak of topic-level political risk from social media using hidden Markov model-based techniques. *Technological Forecasting and Social Change, 94*(1), 115–132. doi:10.1016/j.techfore.2014.08.014

Syred, J., Naidoo, C., Woodhall, S. C., & Baraitser, P. (2014). Would you tell everyone this? Facebook conversations as health promotion interventions. *Journal of Medical Internet Research, 16*(4), 148–156. doi:10.2196/jmir.3231

Tan, W. K., & Chen, T. H. (2012). The usage of online tourist information sources in tourist information search: An exploratory study. *Service Industries Journal, 32*(3), 451–476. doi:10.1080/02642069 .2010.529130

Taylor, M., & Perry, D. (2005). Diffusion of traditional and new media tactics in crisis communication. *Public Relations Review, 31*(2), 209–217. doi:10.1016/j.pubrev.2005.02.018

Thackeray, R., Neiger, B. L., Smith, A. K., & van Wagenen, S. B. (2012). Adoption and use of social media among public health. *BMC Public Health, 12*(1), 242–247. doi:10.1186/1471-2458-12-242

Trainor, K. J., Andzulis, J., Rapp, A., & Agnihotri, R. (2014). Social media technology usage and customer relationship performance: A capabilities-based examination of social CRM. *Journal of Business Research, 67*(6), 1201–1208. doi:10.1016/j.jbusres.2013.05.002

Valentini, C. (2015). Is using social media "good" for the public relations profession? A critical reflection. *Public Relations Review, 41*(2), 170–177. doi:10.1016/j.pubrev.2014.11.009

Wagner, D., & Wagner, H. (2013). *Online communities and dynamic capabilities: Across-case examination of sensing, seizing, and reconfiguration.* Paper presented at the 19th Americas Conference on Information Systems (AMCIS 2013), Chicago, IL.

Wang, C., Chen, W., & Wang, Y. (2012). Scalable influence maximization for independent cascade model in large-scale social networks. *Data Mining and Knowledge Discovery, 25*(3), 545–576. doi:10.1007/ s10618-012-0262-1

Wang, Y., Chen, Y., & Benitez-Amado, J. (2015). How information technology influences environmental performance: Empirical evidence from China. *International Journal of Information Management, 35*(2), 160–170. doi:10.1016/j.ijinfomgt.2014.11.005

Waters, R. D., & Jamal, J. Y. (2011). Tweet, tweet, tweet: A content analysis of nonprofit organizations' Twitter updates. *Public Relations Review, 37*(3), 321–324. doi:10.1016/j.pubrev.2011.03.002

Won, S. G. L., Evans, M. A., Carey, C., & Schnittka, C. G. (2015). Youth appropriation of social media for collaborative and facilitated design-based learning. *Computers in Human Behavior, 50*, 385–391. doi:10.1016/j.chb.2015.04.017

Wright, D. K., & Hinson, M. D. (2009). An updated look at the impact of social media on public relations practice. *The Public Relations Journal, 3*(2), 1–33.

Wu, K., Yang, S., & Zhu, K. Q. (2015). *False rumors detection on Sina Weibo by propagation structures.* Paper presented at the International Conference on Data Engineering (ICDE 2015), Seoul, South Korea. doi:10.1109/ICDE.2015.7113322

Wu, L. (2010). Applicability of the resource-based and dynamic-capability views under environmental volatility. *Journal of Business Research, 63*(1), 27–31. doi:10.1016/j.jbusres.2009.01.007

Wu, L. L., Wang, Y. T., Su, Y. T., & Yeh, M. Y. (2013). *Cultivating social capital through interactivity on social network sites.* Paper presented at the Pacific Asia Conference on Information Systems (PACIS 2013), Jeju Island, South Korea.

Xiang, Z., & Gretzel, U. (2010). Role of social media in online travel information search. *Tourism Management, 31*(2), 179–188. doi:10.1016/j.tourman.2009.02.016

Xiang, Z., Wober, K., & Fesenmaier, D. R. (2008). Representation of the online tourism domain in search engines. *Journal of Travel Research, 47*(2), 137–150. doi:10.1177/0047287508321193

Yang, G. (2009). *The power of the Internet in China: Citizen activism online.* New York, NY: Columbia University Press.

Yang, S. U., & Lim, J. S. (2009). The effects of blog-mediated public relations (BMPR) on relational trust. *Journal of Public Relations Research, 21*(3), 341–359. doi:10.1080/10627260802640773

Yates, D., Wagner, C., & Majchrzak, A. (2010). Factors affecting shapers of organizational wikis. *Journal of the American Society for Information Science and Technology, 61*(3), 543–554. doi: 10.1002/asi.21266

Yoo, K. H., & Gretzel, U. (2011). Influence of personality on travel-related consumer-generated media creation. *Computers in Human Behavior, 27*(2), 609–621. doi:10.1016/j.chb.2010.05.002

Yu, Y., Duan, W., & Cao, Q. (2013). The impact of social and conventional media on firm equity value: A sentiment analysis approach. *Decision Support Systems, 55*(4), 919–926. doi:10.1016/j.dss.2012.12.028

Zeiller, M., & Schauer, B. (2011). *Adoption, motivation and success factors of social media for team collaboration in SMEs.* Paper presented at the 11th International Conference on Knowledge Management and Knowledge Technologies (i-KNOW 2011), Graz, Austria. doi:10.1145/2024288.2024294

Zhang, J. (2015). Voluntary information disclosure on social media. *Decision Support Systems, 73,* 28–36. doi:10.1016/j.dss.2015.02.018

Zhang, J., Qu, Y., Cody, J., & Wu, Y. (2010). *A case study of micro-blogging in the enterprise: Use, value, and related issues.* Paper presented at the 28th Annual ACM Conference on Human Factors in Computing Systems (CHI 2010), Atlanta, GA.

Zhang, K., Zhao, S. J., & Lee, M. K. O. (2013). *Product attitude formation on online review sites with social networks.* Paper presented at the Pacific Asia Conference on Information Systems (PACIS 2013), Jeju Island, South Korea.

Zhao, L., Lu, Y., Wang, B., Chau, P. Y. K., & Zhang, L. (2012). Cultivating the sense of belonging and motivating user participation in virtual communities: A social capital perspective. *International Journal of Information Management, 32*(6), 574–588. doi:10.1016/j.ijinfomgt.2012.02.006

Zhu, Y. Q., & Chen, H. G. (2015). Social media and human need satisfaction: Implications for social media marketing. *Business Horizons*, *58*(3), 335–345. doi:10.1016/j.bushor.2015.01.006

ADDITIONAL READING

Abril, P. S., Levin, A., & del Riego, A. (2012). Blurred boundaries: Social media privacy and the twenty-first century employee. *American Business Law Journal*, *49*(1), 63–124. doi:10.1111/j.1744-1714.2011.01127.x

Agerdal-Hjermind, A. (2014). Organizational blogging: A case study of a corporate weblog from an employee perspective. *Corporate Communications: An International Journal*, *19*(1), 34–51. doi:10.1108/CCIJ-09-2012-0066

Ali, H. (2011). Exchanging value within individuals' networks: Social support implications for health marketers. *Journal of Marketing Management*, *27*(3/4), 316–335. doi:10.1080/0267257X.2011.547075

Andre, P., Bernstein, M., & Luther, K. (2012). What makes a great tweet? *Harvard Business Review*, *90*(5), 36–37.

Babaesmailli, M., Arbabshirani, B., & Golmah, V. (2012). Integrating analytical network process and fuzzy logic to prioritize the strategies: A case study for tile manufacturing firm. *Expert Systems with Applications*, *39*(1), 925–935. doi:10.1016/j.eswa.2011.07.090

Baird, H. C., & Parasnis, G. (2011). From social media to social customer relationship management. *Strategy and Leadership*, *30*(5), 30–37. doi:10.1108/10878571111161507

Bertoni, M., & Chirumalla, K. (2011). Leveraging Web 2.0 in new product development: Lessons learned from a cross-company study. *Journal of Universal Computer Science*, *17*(4), 548–564. doi: 10.3217/jucs-017-04-0548

Brown, V. R., & Vaughn, E. D. (2012). The writing on the (Facebook) wall: The use of social network sites in hiring decisions. *Journal of Business and Psychology*, *26*(2), 219–225. doi:10.1007/s10869-011-9221-x

Chen, Y., Fay, S., & Wang, Q. (2011). The role of marketing in social media: How online consumer reviews evolve. *Journal of Interactive Marketing*, *25*(2), 85–94. doi:10.1016/j.intmar.2011.01.003

Chikandiwa, S. T., Contogiannis, E., & Jembere, E. (2013). The adoption of social media marketing in South African banks. *European Business Review*, *25*(4), 365–381. doi:10.1108/EBR-02-2013-0013

Gopsill, J. A., McAlpine, H. C., & Hicks, B. J. (2013). A social media framework to support engineering design communication. *Advanced Engineering Informatics*, *27*(4), 580–597. doi:10.1016/j.aei.2013.07.002

Green, E. (2011). Pushing the social media buttons. *Media Development*, *58*(1), 12–15.

Grieve, R., Indian, M., Witteveen, K., Tolan, G. A., & Marrington, J. (2013). Face-to-face or Facebook: Can social connectedness be derived online? *Computers in Human Behavior*, *29*(3), 604–609. doi:10.1016/j.chb.2012.11.017

Hall, R., & Lewis, S. (2014). Managing workplace bullying and social media policy: Implications for employee engagement. *Academy of Business Research Journal, 1,* 128–138.

Hansen, D. L., Shneiderman, B., & Smith, M. A. (2011). *Analyzing social media networks with Nodexl.* Burlington, MA: Elsevier.

Hsu, Y. H., & Tsou, H. T. (2011). Understanding customer experiences in online blog environments. *International Journal of Information Management, 31*(6), 510–523. doi:10.1016/j.ijinfomgt.2011.05.003

Hughes, D. J., Rowe, M., Batey, M., & Lee, A. (2011). A tale of two sites: Twitter vs. Facebook and the personality predictors. *Computers in Human Behavior, 28*(2), 561–569. doi:10.1016/j.chb.2011.11.001

Kietzmann, J. H., Silvestre, B. S., McCarthy, I. P., & Pitt, L. F. (2012). Unpacking the social media phenomenon: Towards a research agenda. *Journal of Public Affairs, 12*(2), 109–119. doi:10.1002/pa.1412

Kim, Y. A., & Ahmad, M. A. (2013). Trust, distrust and lack of confidence of users in online social media-sharing communities. *Knowledge-Based Systems, 37*(1), 438–450. doi:10.1016/j.knosys.2012.09.002

Kuksov, D., Shachar, R., & Kangkang, W. (2013). Advertising and consumers' communications. *Marketing Science, 32*(2), 294–309. doi:10.1287/mksc.1120.0753

Lau, R. Y. K., Xia, Y., & Ye, Y. (2014). A probabilistic generative model for mining cybercriminal networks from online social media. *IEEE Computational Intelligence Magazine, 9*(1), 31–43. doi:10.1109/MCI.2013.2291689

Lee, T. Y., & BradLow, E. T. (2011). Automated marketing research using online customer reviews. *JMR, Journal of Marketing Research, 48*(5), 881–894. doi:10.1509/jmkr.48.5.881

Moe, W. M., & Schweidel, D. A. (2012). Online product opinions: Incidence, evaluation, and evolution. *Marketing Science, 31*(3), 372–386. doi:10.1287/mksc.1110.0662

Oh, O., Agrawal, M., & Rao, H. R. (2013). Community intelligence and social media services: A rumor theoretic analysis of tweets during social crises. *Management Information Systems Quarterly, 37*(2), 407–426.

Okazaki, S., & Taylor, C. R. (2013). Social media and international advertising: Theoretical challenges and future directions. *International Marketing Review, 30*(1), 56–71. doi:10.1108/02651331311298573

Onishi, H., & Manchanda, P. (2012). Marketing activity, blogging and sales. *International Journal of Research in Marketing, 29*(3), 221–234. doi:10.1016/j.ijresmar.2011.11.003

Smock, A. D., Ellison, N. B., Lampe, C., & Wohn, D. Y. (2011). Facebook as a toolkit: A uses and gratification approach to unbundling feature use. *Computers in Human Behavior, 27*(6), 2322–2329. doi:10.1016/j.chb.2011.07.011

Sun, M., Chen, Z. Y., & Fan, Z. P. (2014). A multi-task multi-kernel transfer learning method for customer response modeling in social media. *Procedia Computer Science, 31,* 221–230. doi:10.1016/j.procs.2014.05.263

Wang, X., Yu, C., & Wei, Y. (2012). Social media peer communication and impacts on purchase intentions: A consumer socialization framework. *Journal of Interactive Marketing*, *26*(4), 198–208. doi:10.1016/j.intmar.2011.11.004

Yuan, Y., Zhao, X., Liao, Q., & Chi, C. (2013). The use of different information and communication technologies to support knowledge sharing in organizations: From e-mail to micro-blogging. *Journal of the American Society for Information Science and Technology*, *64*(8), 1659–1670. doi:10.1002/asi.22863

KEY TERMS AND DEFINITIONS

Blog: A website, similar to an online journal, that includes chronological entries made by individuals.

Business: The purchase and sale of goods in an attempt to make a profit.

Facebook: The name of a social networking service and website, launched in 2004.

Internet: A worldwide computer network that provides information on very many subjects and enables users to exchange messages.

Social Media: The website and application considered as collectively constituting a medium by which people share messages, photographs, and other information, especially in online communities or forums based on shared interests or backgrounds.

Technology: The use of scientific knowledge to solve practical problems, especially in industry and commerce.

Twitter: A website where people can post short messages about their current activities.

Website: The virtual location on World Wide Web, containing several subject-related web pages and data files accessible through a browser.

Chapter 3
Productivity on the Social Web:
The Use of Social Media and Expectation of Results

Neus Soler-Labajos
Open University of Catalonia, Spain

Ana Isabel Jiménez-Zarco
Open University of Catalonia, Spain

ABSTRACT

Companies gain competitive advantage when they are in a better position than its competitors to keep customers, so for providing the greatest value, become a captivating option, generate satisfaction and achieve the loyalty of consumers, it is necessary that they know the market and enter into a profitable relationship with the customer. In order to get closer to the public, the social media presence stands as a very attractive option for the companies, but these wonder if the effort will offset the result obtained. In this chapter, we will define the concept of enterprise 2.0, and will explain the main benefits that a company can get with the adoption of social media, in relation to its brand image and reputation, communication with the public and the increase of traffic that it can get to the corporate website. Then, and after pointing out the most popular social software tools, we will focus on social media metrics, defining the different types of metrics, designing a framework of social analysis and highlighting those that prove to be of greater business value.

INTRODUCTION

It is undeniable that Web 2.0 has become part of our lives.

Decades ago, technological development offered companies a series of digital tools; they could decide whether or not to use them. Over time, however, as technology has reached beyond business to society in general, digital is no longer an option but a necessary operational component.

The term 'digital natives' (Selwyn, 2009) refers to members of recent generations born into a digital environment. Unlike their parents, they love to share information (Prensky, 2004). They are younger than

DOI: 10.4018/978-1-5225-0846-5.ch003

'digital immigrants'—technology users from 35 to 50 years of age—who were born before the digital era but still use information and communication technology (ICT) intensively in their work (Bennett et al., 2008).

Web 2.0 is 'a label that marks the change described by the Internet to abandon its unidirectionality and move towards a more open system that maximizes the interaction between users, who relate among themselves through social networks, where they share content, generating knowledge' (O'Reilly, 2006). The main difference between the information society and the knowledge society is that the latter refers to the critical, and therefore selective, appropriation of information by people who know to use it. Users are no longer mere spectators; they are also actors. They write, create, share, review, disseminate, and exchange information. Companies must connect, converse, and empathize with them to engage them where they are: in social media. Firms need to understand how to structure strategies of brand and content in places in which customers communicate with not only the company but also one another, all in real time.

The 2.0 philosophy is an excellent way for companies to develop effective models of interaction and communication with clients (Preece et al., 2015). It allows them to meet and listen to their customers, know their needs and tastes, provide them with personalized attention, and even co-create with them. By being present on social networks, companies also can realize the long-term potential of 2.0 communication. Digital platforms allow the development of reciprocal feedback between the brand and the user; the use of such networks directly affects the reputations of companies, which is reflected in their income statements (Cornelissen, 2014).Many years after it was introduced, the thesis of the Cluetrain Manifesto, which invited companies to participate in an open, spontaneous and healthy forum—a conversation—remains valid (Levine et al., 1999).

1. ENTERPRISE 2.0

Traditionally, with the exception of a small group of technology enthusiasts ('early adopters') companies have pioneered the adoption of inbound technologies. However, Web 2.0 has disrupted this pattern. Users—eager to be able to express their views, participate in the World Wide Web, and communicate and share experiences with other people—have quickly adopted emerging Web 2.0 tools and left slower-moving businesses behind (McKenna & Bargh, 2000).

The vast numbers of users on Facebook, the largest social network in the world, illustrates this trend. As the popularity of social media tools has grown, companies have noted their social impact and begun to incorporate them into their business practices. They have realized that to be competitive, they must take advantage of opportunities and facilities that provide Web 2.0 tools to develop their transactions and conduct their daily activities.

The adaptation of 2.0 technologies, as well as the incorporation of citizen behavior in the network in the field of business, is known as 'Enterprise 2.0' (McAfee, 2009). Enterprise 2.0 uses Web 2.0 technologies to facilitate the sharing of knowledge and collaboration among employees, have close and direct contact with clients, and satisfy the needs and tastes of customers, suppliers, and other companies. It broadens communication, creating an image of transparency and increasing the level of trust in the brand.

Enterprise 2.0 fosters the development of a culture of participation, sharing, and networking, and it uses the tools of the social web both internally (employees) and externally (customers and stakeholders). The concept was developed by McAfee (2006) to refer to the use of the emerging platforms of social software within companies, between companies, and with customers and other third parties. The idea is closely linked to network organization based on knowledge.

This organizational model demonstrates that human resources are the most important resources in companies; creativity has no limits when technology is used to facilitate the interaction and contribution of groups (Oppong et al., 2005). The creation of value through digital technology requires the development of talent in the form of new perspectives. To realize the potential of digital, it is necessary to make sense of the business; the key to that effort is understanding how to contribute and obtain value.

2. SOCIAL MEDIA IN THE ENTERPRISE

The term 'social media' refers to applications, tools, platforms, and other media that facilitate the relationship, interaction, collaboration, and distribution of content between users. 'Social networks' are powerful 2.0 tools that bring significant benefits to the company, constitute a source of great opportunity (McAffee, 2009), and allow a greater diffusion of company news and announcements about products. Social networks promote interaction with customers, personalized customer attention, and greater visibility of the brand.In the internal environment of the company, the adoption of Web 2.0 and social media enhances the performance of all areas. It increases efficiency and drives enterprise integration, thereby improving productivity (Turban et al., 2011).

A study prepared by McKinsey & Co. (Bughin and Chui, 2010) reflects the tangible benefits obtained by the use of social media. Internally, it reduces operating costs and communication, provides easier access to knowledge, and contributes to greater employee satisfaction. Between the company or brand and the market, it increases the effectiveness of marketing actions, promotes greater client satisfaction, reduces marketing costs, and results in a greater number of successful innovations in products and services. In addition, the report concludes, the use of technologies of cooperation and interaction with the public improves the ability to add value to relationships, thereby increasing competitive advantage.

We detail below the factors that we believe are most improved by the adoption of social media and that therefore constitute the greatest benefits or advantages for the company.

2.1. Image and Brand Reputation

'Brand reputation' is the recognition or consolidated prestige that a trade mark achieves from its stakeholders by the degree of commitment to them and the actions developed over time (Schmidt & Ludlow, 2002). Prior to the development of social media, brand reputation could be controlled, but now 'it is only partially controllable by the brands and institutions, as it is created and recreated from perceptions that make up the climate of opinion' (del Fresno, 2012, p. 118). Thus, reputation management no longer depends on the communication of the brand as the main image, but on the prosumer (content producer and consumer) and the influencer (influential person in certain circles, whose opinions and recommendations are heard and credible in those circles).

Social media has transformed communication from one-way to two-way; companies no longer control the message or define an image in the mind of the consumer (Schmidt & Ludlow, 2002). Messages are shaped by the conversations of users; brands must promote participation to strengthen their relationship with consumers, increase customer confidence, and retain clients. Transparency in the relationship reinforces image.

According to Weber (2011), online reputation is generated by the perceptions of consumers in their social network deployment. To obtain reputation, the enterprise must:

- Consolidate an efficient and cohesive team.
- Establish, increase, and manage communication, internally and externally, with the interest groups with which it interacts.
- Innovate, focus effort, stand out from the competition, and advocate a strong message.
- Monitor constantly to detect unmet needs, generate leads (potential customers or prospects), evaluate feelings and brand image, and correct actions.
- Foresee possible crises and avoid improvisation. Discussion forums, blogs, and social networks host many free comments that the company must constantly manage to avoid unwanted situations or crises.

2.2. Communication

Various studies of social networks show the tendency of Internet users to use social networks on a daily basis, mainly to interact with their contacts (Wilson et al., 2009). Contacting customer care services, buying and selling, following a brand, talking about products, and commenting on advertising are some of the most popular activities on social networks. The main reason users start to follow a brand is that they are interested in it and want to be informed; they will continue to follow it if it continues to post relevant content. Therefore, for companies, a lack of social media presence or a lack of mechanisms to manage active social media participation is a failure to control what is thought about the brand and a missed opportunity to have a direct channel of communication with customers and potential customers through which to offer care and value. Such communication channels are new marketing tools that companies should know how to use and control to their advantage. With the use of social media, communication time is reduced, and satisfaction of both employees (who can now easily access the know-how of the company) and customers (whose needs are served in a more agile and personalized fashion) is increased (Strauss & Frost, 1999).

Furthermore, potential customers tend to use social media to find out about products and decide if they will make purchases. By taking advantage of the possibilities offered by social networks as a communications channel, companies can approach their targets and interact with them.

Various studies show that the confidence level generated by corporate information or advertisements is limited to 20%, whereas that created through contact networks exceeds 80%. The function of social media is not just to communicate, but also to influence (Strahilevitz, 2005).

As a result of more direct communication and active listening (understanding the message from the perspective of those who issue it and understanding what the consumer is conveying), companies have greater knowledge of clients and users; they can detect customer needs and preferences and improve the care or service dispensed to them. They can also use the knowledge to develop new products. Parallel information can adapt to the interest of the user, by being segmented and offered through preferred channels (e.g., RSS feeds, newsletters, social networking) (Bakshi, 2004). Suitable messages can be directed to the right people, when they want them. User contact with the company can occur when the user deems it most appropriate.

2.3. Traffic to the Corporate Website

Before the emergence of social networks, the positioning of a website in the search engines depended only on variables based on the optimization of web pages (SEO and SEM). However, we must now consider the opinions and comments of users about the brand or products as one of the main sources of quality traffic to company websites. This consideration requires social media optimization. According to Athey and Ellison (2009), to position a website optimally in search engines, we must understand the following distinctions:

- **Search Engine Optimization (SEO)** includes techniques of organic or natural positioning that achieve web page indexing in the top results of the search carried out by the search engine, a process that requires the following tasks:
  - Know the preferences of users, that is, what they look for, how often they look, how they come to a website, and what diverts them to competitors. The Google Trends tool provides specific information about the behavior of keywords in Internet searches, and Google Analytics provides a wide range of information about the operation of websites (e.g., number of visits and users, where they come from, how long they remain on the web).
  - Improve the choice of keywords by using the Google Adwords tool and studying the keywords used by competitors.
  - Use tags (title, description, keywords) that optimize the search.
  - Keep websites updated with quality content that search engines reward, with easy navigation between the pages. When content is linked to reference sites and further linked, commented on, featured, reviewed, and retweeted, online reputations grow.
  - Appear in professional directories and portals.
  - Intervene in specialized forums.
  - Try link building (to link with other websites, increase search engine relevancy, and achieve higher positioning) to increase page rank (i.e., the importance that Google assigns a page based on an algorithmic formula of its own creation).
- **Search Engine Marketing (SEM)** promotes websites by paying for search result visibility; it includes sponsored links in Google (the most prominent search engine), use of the Google Adwords tool, and the technique of pay-per-click (PPC), in which advertisers pay only when the user clicks on a designated link (Clifton, 2012).
- **Social Media Optimization (SMO)** attracts visits to and from the profiles of the major social networks and blogs. It includes content creation on company sites (e.g., fan Facebook pages, Twitter accounts, corporate blogs) and other platforms on which companies detect that their communities participate. The term was created by Bhargava (2006), who defined rules to achieve social media optimization, according to the use of links, tags, social bookmarking, and other tactics to facilitate access to content and promote its dissemination.

In contrast with SEO, SMO can generate web traffic more quickly (through wider dissemination of content and more attraction to the page) (Tang & Sampson, 2012), but if the technique is not applied continuously, its effect is less durable. In addition, results depend only on social networks and user proactivity.

3. SOCIAL SOFTWARE TOOLS

According to Kaplan and Haenlein (2010), social software is the set of applications that enable individuals to communicate and interact through the web. Today this concept refers not only to interaction through social groups but also to tools and services that enable sharing, labeling, and distributing digital objects (audio, video, images) and to applications of collaborative work such as blogs, wikis, and forums.

The constant development and continuous launch of 2.0 platforms and applications makes it impossible to mention all types of social software, but according to their most common characteristics, they can be classified as follows:

- *Instant messaging systems,* which are communication services in real time via text message, exchange files, video conferencing, or VoIP (technology that allows users to communicate voice over the Internet). The most popular systems are Messenger, Skype, Blackberry Messenger, and WhatsApp.
- *Blogs,* which are regularly updated web sites that collect articles from one or several authors in reverse chronological order. Strategic use of blogs improves relationships with customers and spreads corporate culture. They can be developed on company websites or on external publishing platforms, such as Blogger and Wordpress.
- *Systems for group work,* which include creation and content editing applications with no single management. They are suitable for cooperative work and the management of knowledge and include online services such as Google Docs. The undisputed leader in this category is the wiki (a web site edited in the browser by multiple users).
- *Social networks,* which are platforms and online channels that allow the creation of public profiles. They are classified into horizontal and general networks, with no subject defined or addressed to all types of users (e.g., Facebook, Tuenti, Google+, Twitter) or vertical and specialized networks, which are theme-defined and aimed at particular groups (e.g., hobbyists). The first category includes professional networks (e.g., LinkedIn, Xing, Viadeo) that aim to promote professional relationships between users.
- *Cooperative content classification,* which includes folksonomy or social tagging, in which users describe personal or outside resources (e.g., Delicious, Digg, YouTube, Flickr). These platforms establish non-hierarchical classifications that are shared with other users.

Aggregators and filtering systems, which use content syndication (RSS or forwarding of content from one original website to another destination, making available the content that was initially accessed by users of the source). These systems can distribute and share the information of a page so that other sites may reuse content and users can access the information quickly and easily.

4. METRICS IN SOCIAL MEDIA

Social monitoring tools are search engines that track the content generated by Internet users. They allow companies to track customer conversations about brands, products, and services, measure the reputation of the brand, check the response of consumers after launching an advertising campaign, analyze brand-related sentiment, identify opinion leaders (influencers), develop online strategies, and resolve crisis situations.Although the measurement of results obtained in social media is still being tested, there are certain parameters indicative of the success or failure of the actions carried out in social media (Sterne, 2010).

4.1. Measuring Social Media

We define information as a set of processed data that has significance (relevance, purpose, and context) and is useful for making decisions because it reduces uncertainty (Orlikowsky & Gash, 1994).

However, it is knowledge that allows us to act; knowledge integrates experience, values, and know-how, then uses them as the framework for the incorporation of new information and experiences. To gain knowledge and know whether the actions developed in social media are properly routed toward the goals we intend to achieve, it is necessary to measure and analyze information.Measurement allows us to know the results of the activities developed in social media, to check whether our objectives have been achieved and, above all, to value the performance of our strategies and the impact they have on the economic benefits to our companies. According to Sterne (2010), the main reasons to measure actions are to:

- Understand the feelings of users in relation to the trademark, to enhance feelings if they are positive and improve them if they are negative.
- Know the user community, offer interesting content, establish relations with it, and encourage engagement.
- Understand ways to improve user experiences.
- Obtain insights that help improve products and customer service and communicate with consumers according to what they feel and expect from the brand.
- Check positioning acquired by the brand in digital media with respect to competitors' positions.
- Assess the impact of social media marketing campaigns.
- Compare different periods and study the differences among them.
- Know the return on investment in social media (social media ROI).

Social media analysis measures, studies, and interprets information that is generated in social media by quantifying data extraction and identifying the feeling showed by the users when they talk (Dodds et al., 2011).

There are many types of metrics; the metrics chosen should provide value to the company and be analyzed within the company context. Only then will it be possible to correctly identify points of reference and determine whether projects are being developed optimally and in line with company objectives.

4.1.1. General Classification

In general, metrics used to assess the fulfillment of the objectives planned in social media are classified into three categories:

- *Quantitative metrics* measure numerical terms (e.g., number of visits to the company web page of the company, number of Twitter followers, number of views of YouTube videos).
- *Qualitative metrics* measure concepts related to perception, feeling, and the level of engagement of the users with the brand (e.g., the character of the mentions the brand receives, as positive, negative, or neutral).

- *Return on investment metrics* measure the benefits that social media delivers to the company (e.g., obtaining greater recognition of the brand, generation of business contacts, increase in sales).

The first two categories of metrics (qualitative and quantitative) are used to carry out the monitoring of actions to adjust them or correct them, if necessary, to achieve objectives and provide ROI. By applying these metrics to the context of the objectives that are part of the social analysis, we can know the behavior of network users. However, if the metrics are interpreted out of context, they lack sufficient basis for decision-making.

We address the third metrics category (ROI) in a later discussion.

4.1.2 Social Analytics Framework

Because the value of various metrics varies with the perspective of an enterprise, Lovett (2011), classifies digital metrics into the following types:

- *Counting metrics* are the most basic metrics associated with company social networks that quantify tactical performance (e.g., number of followers and fans, subscribers).
- *Business value metrics* are the most valued by the company managers because they reflect the success or failure of the social media (e.g., level of satisfaction of the customer, revenue).
- *Results metrics* quantify the effectiveness of social media, help correct actions that are being developed, and act as key performance indicators (KPI) (e.g., rates of interaction, conversion rates, average opinions).
- *Foundational metrics* contain the formula to create metrics that are customized and adapted to the needs of the company and allow an exponential increase in value and opportunities compared with general metrics (e.g., level of interaction, degree of commitment, influence, impact).

According to this classification of metrics, Lovett proposes a model of measurement known as the 'social analytics framework.' It is based on a strategy that is developed in an orderly manner and depends on the company's goals, social media objectives, KPI, and tactics used to achieve the planned objectives (Figure 1).

Figure 1. Alignment of goals, objectives, metrics and tactics in the social media strategy

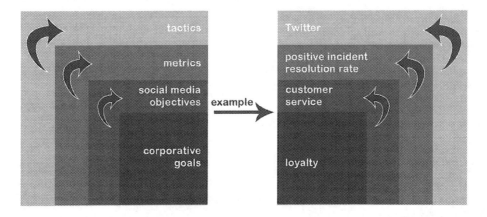

According to the established order in the development of the strategy, the social analytics framework is defined as a scheme of work to be followed to correctly define each data (goals, objectives, metrics, and tactics).

5. RETURN ON INVESTMENT (ROI)

Return on investment (ROI) indicates the benefit obtained by each dollar invested in social media and is calculated using the following formula:

$$\text{ROI} = \frac{\text{Investment Gain} - \text{Investment Cost}}{\text{Investment Cost}} \times 100$$

Therefore, ROI is a financial concept, measured in dollars, and reflects the profitability obtained from the activity carried out in social media (Hoffman & Fodor, 2010). The result is expressed in percentage, to evaluate its weight and determine whether profitability is positive or negative (e.g., how many dollars are earned for every $100 invested, what percentage of profit or loss the actions report).

Initially, this formula seems simple, but its components are highly variable; investment gain is particularly difficult to quantify, because most social activities do not involve a financial transaction.

To make it easier to identify the actions that create benefits, we must take the following steps:

- Identify the tangible benefits, defined as those that come from sales or commercial actions directly and are therefore not derived from the activities in social media.
- Calculate the cost reductions created by using social media (e.g., better customer service, more economical methods to investigate markets, designs obtained through co-creation, obtaining free content generated by users) to quantify them as a benefit.

To further determine the true benefits of social media (Hoffman & Fodor, 2010), we should:

- Segment the actions, measuring them separately, to calculate the benefits of each. If possible, actions should be undertaken at different periods of time, to make it easier to identify clearly the sources of social media–generated profits.
- Establish the relationship, if any, between soft indicators (engagement level, number of followers and fans) and financial indicators, to determine whether the growth of the first brings monetary benefits.
- Know the elements of cause and effect that have an impact on the results of the company, and determine whether actions in social media affect results, even in indirect ways. For example, if we launch a social media campaign at the same time we intensify sales team visits to customers, it is important to determine how each action affects sales. If we cannot affirm that the increase in sales comes from the social media campaign, we cannot determine its impact on the results of the company; we must know which element (campaign or commercial network) has caused the effect (increase in sales).

- Identify the intangible benefits, such as brand image and reputation; though these factors do not generate direct income, they do affect profit. To quantify their contribution to the benefit, we use measurement techniques such as 'avoided costs of marketing,' to tell us how much would have to be invested by other means (e.g., traditional marketing) to obtain the result (e.g., an increase in brand awareness) that has been achieved by social media.

The second part of the ROI formula (investment cost) includes variables that are difficult to measure. It is challenging to calculate the cost of time spent on social media activities, training of the social media team, implementation of the campaign, use of technological tools, and indirect costs. However, a solid understanding of all of these expenses is required to calculate ROI (Sterne, 2010).

Therefore, we define three types of essential metrics for ROI calculation:

- *Amount*, such as number of visits and number of committed users, which are not business value metrics but still help analyze the effectiveness of actions.
- *Cost,* such as costs of interaction or of compromised or satisfied visitors, which indicates expenditures incurred to develop actions and obtain income.
- *Conversion,* such as orders placed, users registered or subscribed, forms filled out, or content downloaded—that is, getting the actions the company seeks to achieve by using with social media. The term is used in reference to the conversion of users who complete the actions, by becoming customers, subscribers, or members. Conversion may or may not be an economic event (e.g., non-economic actions include filling in a form or downloading content), but it represents a quantifiable and monetary value that can be determined according to the objective of the conversion (e.g., the percentage of users who have completed forms that quality them as potential customers).

The ultimate goal is to determine whether the ROI justifies the company's use of social media. Different sets of metrics measure ROI directly and indirectly, recognizing both tangible benefits and intangible benefits. Although the metrics do not show causation, they indicate whether social media efforts have succeeded in having impact.

We measure the ROI in different ways depending on specific business objectives. Some common examples of measured results are the duration of emotional bonding (engagement), community size and degree of interaction, conversions (subscriptions, sales) or conversion opportunities, number and quality of mentions, and content virality.

Figure 2 illustrates the calculation of ROI.

6. IMPACT OF RELATIONSHIP (IOR)

The inability to insert a tracking code in conversations between brands and users in social media, as is done in other online activities, makes it difficult to calculate ROI. This challenge has led to the development of new ways to quantify the actions and relations of the brands in social media (Gilbert & Karahalios, 2009).

Impact of relationship (IOR) is a measurement that allows us to determine the values of various social media components in building the brand, that is, their success—or failure—in generating value.

Figure 2. ROI in practice

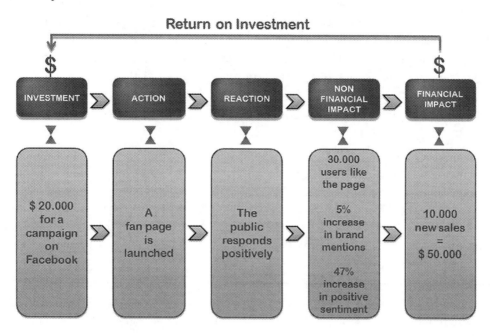

The measurement consists of four variables, determined by different ranges of values established according to the impact each has on company IOR, in accordance with the strategy and objectives of the brand:

- *Authority* of content that the brand shares in social media is related to the mentions the brand receives in external environments; such mentions reveal the quality of its presence. It is the variable that has the highest impact on relationships, because external references spread the online presence of a brand.
- *Influence* refers to the number of fans of the brand in various social media; it has the second highest impact on relationships.
- *Participation* reflects the reaction of the public to the strategy for the presence that the brand is developing in social media. Although it has less IOR value, it is the most important variable for calculating the success of the brand in social media.
- *Traffic* is the ability of the brand to drive its social media followers to the company website (its business environment). It has less IOR value, but it is important because high traffic values subtract from the relevance of the other variables.

When setting the ranges of values for each variable and considering the magnitude (impact) of company variables, we must keep in mind the weights of their various elements. That is, the values depend on the brand's social media objectives, so we must consider them for the purpose of calculating IOR.

For example, when calculating IOR, a mention of the brand in a blog must take into account the reference value of the blog, which may be of greater or lesser value. Similarly, an influencer who simply repeats the opinion of other users, or a retweet by someone with a few followers is less effective; the values must be weighed.

However, the IOR method of measurement recognizes that an overall multiplier effect occurs when one of the variables changes, such that an increase of IOR in a single variable affects all variables. The measurement of IOR thus demonstrates the impact of its variables—authority, influence, participation, and traffic—and allows us to identify the types of content and forms of communication that most appeal to the public. It tracks the evolution of the brand in social media and allows us to set numerical goals and check the success of our strategies.

Ultimately, by identifying relationships as a cost factor, IOR indicates ROI on the basis of relationships.

7. RETURN ON ENGAGEMENT (ROE)

Return on engagement (ROE) measures the global force that promotes the brand by the development of a particular action (Paine, 2011). This metric, considered essential by its advocates, analyzes the relationships and interactions that occur in the digital realm by converting them into quantitative data that is of interest to the company.

To understand this concept, we must first understand the meaning of 'engagement' in social media, that is, the emotional and cognitive connection to the public with the brand that generates or strengthens bonds and commitment. Engagement is achieved by building solid, mutual, and permanent relations with the public.

Thus, ROE first defines the various and significant types of commitment that occur in social media, and then it measures them. Modalities of engagement that can be measured include the following:

- *Authority,* such as portals of influence that link to the company website and retransmission of company content by users.
- *Influence,* such as the size of the base of registered users of company content and the ability of the brand to influence conversations.
- *Participation,* such as user reviews, messages, interactions, likes, retweets, and posts.
- *Sentiment,* such as perceptions that are inspired by the brand.

To achieve consistent measurements results, however, we must have a clear idea of what a company wants to achieve by using social media; we must focus on the information of interest and study it in the context of the company.Therefore, the nature of the return must be defined by the company itself, according to its own objectives (e.g., revenues earned, profit produced by achieving an increase in the reputation of the brand).From the perspective of engagement, the real value of social media investment comes from the number of fans of the brand who are committed to it in a way that can be aligned with the objectives of the company. Figure 3 illustrates the different grades of ROE that are generated by the actions carried out in social media, depending on the attitudes or behaviors adopted by users.

The work of Hoeffler and Keller (2002), shows how the concept of ROE detects the quality of the commitment adopted by the public with respect to the brand, through the analysis of customer behavior, interaction, and relationships. Monitoring, measuring, inspecting, and assessing such commitment will lead to a greater ROI.

The overall objective of this metric is to measure the company's time and money investment in social media to assess the anticipated benefits (especially financial), and ultimately, to achieve a good return.

Figure 3. ROE of social media actions

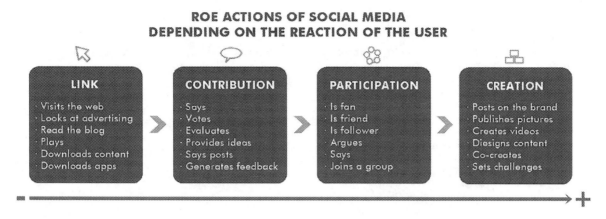

8. KEY PERFORMANCE INDICATORS (KPI)

Key performance indicators (KPI) are measurement elements that help the company measure its progress toward its goals (Cai et al., 2009). The indicators, selected according to the company's objectives, must be quantifiable; they are performance metrics that evaluate the success of an action. When they are correctly defined, KPI provide a context that allows companies to assess whether their progress and pace of actions toward the achievement of their objectives is successful or whether corrective actions are necessary to remedy a sub-optimal situation. The indicators are usually tied to long-term results and modified according to those results. If the objective is maintained, value is generated and a competitive advantage is established.

The main KPI of social media plans include the following: (Neiger et al., 2012):

- *Traffic* of visits to the web arriving from social networks (referrals) indicates the scope and influence of the brand in the networks according to the content of its publications and the engagement it generates. To add value to published content, the use of tactics such as interacting with customers and establishing relationships with opinion leaders (influencers) captures the attention of fans and direct visits to the website.
- *Search engine positioning* indicates the indexing rank of the web page resulting from searches; publishing quality content, promoting its dissemination, and optimizing the site increases page ranking.
- *Social media interaction* indicates the online visibility of the brand. Practicing active listening and encouraging feedback increases participation and engagement.
- *Newsletter subscriptions* lead to more active and committed subscribers, more shared content, and more product recommendations.
- *Blog content* provides information and encourages customer interaction; promotion of its existence and ease of access increases number of visits.
- *Mentions on websites, blogs, or social networks* reflect how often there are references to the brand; sharing news and disseminating relevant content increases the number of mentions.

- *Requests for information from bloggers and journalists* act as a free advertising channel and indicate positive public reaction to content. Regular posting of quality content creation and regular contact with professionals maintains brand interest.
- *Online sales (e-commerce components)* indicate the success of the marketing program. Calls to action, capturing the interest of users, and integrating various channels of marketing, both online and offline, increase conversion (goal attainment).

Table 1 summarizes the social media landmarks that companies want to achieve, KPI used to measure them, and initiatives that could be undertaken based on the results.

Table 1. Main objectives and KPI set out in social media

OBJECTIVES	INDICATORS (KPI)	INITIATIVES
REPUTATION	Mentions in online environments.	To influence the reputation using tactics of online communication or internal changes in the company.
	The positive or negative sentiment of mentions.	To prevent potential crises
AUTORITHY	Mentions in blogs, articles and news.	Developing actions that increase the authority.
	Links to our content.	To detect opinion leaders (influencers).
VISIBILITY POPULARITY	Number of fans on Facebook, followers on Twitter, subscriptions, clicks, retweets, bookmarks and inbound links.	To improve the policy of diffusion of the channels and know the kind of content that the public likes.
	The number of "likes".	
	Times that a content is shared (scope, dissemination).	
	Comments about our content.	
INTERACTION PARTICIPATION LOYALTY	Comments on the blog.	To assess the level of interaction and engagement and know what kind of content interest and generate more participation.
	Assessment of our content.	
	Participation in our channels (entries on our Facebook wall, mentions, replies and retweets on Twitter, comments on YouTube, likes, favorites, shared, etc.).	To encourage contact between users and strengthen the community.
		To achieve virality.
INFLUENCE	Increase followers and fans.	Enhancing the qualitative value of the community.
		To detect the brand evangelists.
	Number of subscribers on the blog and YouTube.	To get feedback.
	Number of times the web's URL is shared.	To detect the opinion leaders (influencers).
TRAFFIC	Visits to the corporate website.	Identifying areas for improvement to lead users to our goals.
	Traffic to the Facebook page.	
	Prints obtained by the activity on Twitter.	
	From where come the visits.	To discover sources of traffic.
CONVERSION	Generating leads and sales.	To make strategic decisions on the basis of the main objective.

9. WEB ANALYTICS

Web analytics allow us to measure accurately the nature of page views and apply corrective actions when necessary. Google Analytics offers multiple statistics and data on the operation of a website. The indicators we should consider include:

- Number of visits
- Number of unique users
- Origin of the visits (including the interconnection between the different areas where the brand is present)
- Entry page bounce rate (abandonment of the visit because what is being searched is not found) and other website pages (abandonment because the user does not like the content)
- Time spent on the page
- Tracked route when accessing the website
- Most visited content
- Most shared content
- Number of clicks to the buttons linking to social networks
- Number of responses to calls to action
- Rate of new visits
- Loading speed of the pages

Web performance optimization (WPO) (Souders, 2004) refers to the application of technological improvements related to web servers and elements of company sites, and to the connectivity of networks, to increase factors such as page loading speeds, loyalty and retention of the visitor, and user satisfaction.

We can use web analytics to improve our techniques of positioning, content, usability, and navigability. This information allows us to develop actions in channels of communication and initiate a process of trial and error to validate the assumptions we make.

9.1. Measurement for Results

Traditionally, brands calibrated the success of their marketing campaigns in financial terms that could be measured directly. In social media, however, benefits must be measured in both the short and long terms, whether or not they relate to the financial perspective (Harrison & Freeman, 1999).

According to Ray (2010), an effective 'Balanced Scorecard of Social Media Marketing' considers metrics from four different perspectives:

- *Financial,* in terms of increased revenues or decreased costs
- *Brand,* in terms of increasing the reputation of the brand
- *Risk management*, with regard to the company's preparations for dealing with issues that affect its brand reputation
- *Digital assets*, in terms of improving the online heritage of the company

One of the concerns of companies with regard to the use of social media is the measurement of ROI beyond the analytical quantitative metrics. Metrics such as number of Twitter followers, Facebook likes, and website bounce rates measure the performance of online marketing strategies but do not quantify the reported benefits. But it is these benefits that companies most care about; when they invest time and money in social networks, they want to be able to measure their progress toward tangible objectives. There are several metrics that matter from the perspective of business:

- *Sales level* reflects the number or volume of sales that have been made by actions carried out in social media.
- *Income level* determines whether the actions on social media affect the final balance sheet of the company; activities that achieve these revenues must be identified.
- *Increase in number of clients* shows how the actions carried out in social media influence the arrival of new customers.
- *Increase in the number of potential customers (leads)* identifies those who meet the profile of the target audience of the brand and show interest in it or its products, by measuring the growth of the company database.
- *Customer satisfaction levels* indicate possible loyalty to the brand and the potential for recurring sales. They reflect the earning ability of the company and indicate the percentage of retention of customers achieved by the company through social media.
- *Market share* reveals the organic positioning of the company online, in relation to the competition.

10. RESEARCH DIRECTIONS

Web 2.0 is a sociological phenomenon that has changed the ways people communicate, express themselves, and relate with others. It represents an important cultural change at the social level (Beer, 2008). For companies, it opens new channels of communication with both customers and suppliers, and it offers them the opportunity to improve internal employee relations and facilitate daily work through better communication and collaboration. To ensure their survival, companies must adopt a series of concepts and techniques.

10.1. Enterprise Mobility

Enterprise mobility is the concept of mobile enterprise in which employees have access to company information, wherever they are (Siau et al., 2001). New mobile devices, with a multitude of capabilities, including constant Internet connections, social applications, and cloud computing, maintain information and co-worker connectivity.

Cloud computing allows employees ubiquitous access to information from any computer; they no longer have to be sitting in an office (Sultan, 2011). Social media, in turn, enable them to communicate and collaborate from anywhere in the world. Through social networks and virtual worlds, employees can share information and attend courses and conferences without the need to be in one place. Mobile access even eliminates the need to carry a computer.

Cloud computing saves costs of maintenance and infrastructure improvement because employees can use less powerful computer equipment. Access to applications is fast; there is no need to wait for information to be downloaded. Information is always updated, so that everyone can have access to the latest versions. Social media such as blogs, wikis, podcasts, and social networks provide both employees and customers with constant connection to the company. Customers can contact the company, collaborate in the creation of products, or have the feeling of being part of a community, thereby increasing the commitment of users to brands.

Mobile applications help companies achieve information in real time and ensure that customer information is stored correctly in the company's systems. This leads to an improvement in effectiveness, thanks to accurate and relevant information provided by the consumers themselves.

The implementation of this type of employee–customer mobile architecture brings with it not only a number of technology challenges but also a multitude of benefits. The major benefit from the implementation of mobile enterprise is improvements in customer service, marketing, sales, and technological development.

Technological development departments benefit from applications that are cheaper, faster, and better able to adapt to organizational changes. Information obtained from social networks helps marketing departments improve their initiatives and campaigns, and sales departments find new revenue opportunities by increasing their knowledge of customer profiles.

The fusion of these elements—cloud computing, social media, and mobile applications—gives companies the opportunity to rethink their business strategies, create more intimate relationships, and improve existing ones.

At the internal level, companies that use these applications benefit from greater collaboration and faster expansion of knowledge (Skyrme, 2007).One of the greatest challenges to companies is the management of innovation. Constant change in our society requires constant company change; companies must adapt their structures to these changes to provide new products and services and adapt business models to be competitive and meet the needs of customers.

Because of the inherent vertical structure of business, employee talent is often wasted. Web 2.0 tools provide an opportunity to capture the talents and ideas of employees through multiple channels of collaboration and communication. The best of these ideas can be developed.

10.2. Prediction Markets

Prediction markets are speculative markets where bets are taken with the aim of making predictions. In this way, assets are created, with a final value linked to a particular event, such as the result of an election, or to a parameter, such as total sales from the next month. Market prices can be understood at a given time as the predictions of the probability of the event or the expected value of the parameter. Individuals who buy low and sell high are rewarded for improving the predictive power of the market, while those who buy high and sell low are punished for damaging the predictive capacity of the market. Prediction markets can help us obtain more precise models of results (Fama, 1998), for example, for sales, product delivery dates, manufacturing capacity requirements, product ideas, marketing campaigns, and competitive activities. However, if the number of bettors familiar with the technology is limited, or if results are easily predictable or can be determined by a small number of people, this technology does not help very much.

Prediction markets also allow us to obtain collective intelligence. They produce dynamic and objective probabilistic predictions of the results of future events by adding disparate information that companies provide when they agree on prices. Speculators then make their transactions based on the predictions. The value provided by a set of prediction markets consists of the precision provided by these markets in relation to other mechanisms of prediction (e.g., number of times the precision improves decisions, reduction of the costs of maintenance of those predictive markets). A set of prediction markets has little value if other predictive mechanisms can provide a similar prediction at a lower cost or if many substantial decisions are based on the accuracy of these predictions.

Currently, few companies are aware of this technology (Skyrme, 2007). Big companies, mainly pharmaceutical and technological businesses, have been the first to adopt it, but its extension to other vertical markets (as with most new technologies) has been slow. Although prediction markets have tended to produce disappointing results in early tests—probably because their precision has been underestimated—enterprises seeking to improve their forecasts in controversial areas in which users have differing but valid views will benefit from investments in prediction markets. Companies should strive to find the proper incentives to reward their more precise visionaries.

10.3. Web 3.0: The Semantic Web

The exponential increase in the amount of information that is housed on the web makes it difficult for consumers to find what they want. This will become an increasing problem if the level of success in search is not improved, especially in cases that are unusual (Hendler, 2009). The ranking systems of traditional search engines, such as Google, are based on criteria of use (e.g., number of links, number of visits) that make the top positions in any search those that have the most-used meanings—the concept of 'short head.' As Figure 4 illustrates, at first glance, this approach may seem positive, but the large amount of information that is in the 'long tail' zone to the left is often greater than the information in the head (though often more dispersed). Therefore, information with less relevance to the masses is more relevant to a small number of users. To find information in this area, it is necessary to search for different criteria to the traditional rankings; semantic technologies address this matter.

The Semantic Web is an extended web that gives greater meaning to the World Wide Web. It is also known as the 'web of data' or 'Web 3.0'. It is developed with universal languages that allow users to find answers to their questions in a faster and easier way, because of better structuring of information. It facilitates information sharing and integration and allows users to delegate tasks to web tools that process the information.

Figure 4. Positioning of information in searches

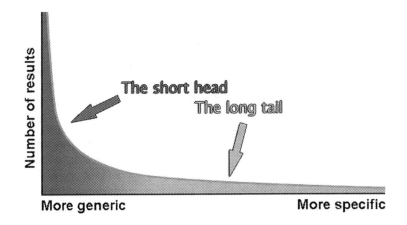

Semantic or Web 3.0 technologies can be defined as technologies capable of removing the explicit knowledge of the systems of information, storing that knowledge, and displaying it in a contextualized way as needed (Maass & Kowatsh, 2012). Web 3.0 does not create systems, products, or services under demand; it improves the user experience by giving the right information to the right person at the right time. The business application of semantic technology is based on knowledge management. Web 3.0 has an important role in the uptake of information, translation into knowledge, and contextualization to the different situations that may be required.

The first mission of semantic technology is to process information and 'understand' the content of this information. Semantic and syntactic analysis tools carry out this mission by storing information in company information systems while preserving the meaning through the use of a semantic database. From this knowledge base, contextual information is extracted to solve specific business problems, using semantic search engines or semantic contextualization. Semantic technologies can also be useful for broadcasting advertising and increasing the visibility of the company; with improvement in the meaning of searches comes improvement in the effectiveness of advertising.

CONCLUSION

Given that we are immersed in the economy of attention (Goldhaber, 1997), if a company competes to capture the attention of a user facing millions of stimuli, it must prove that it is worth looking at. Listening, talking, sharing, and generating content that interests the user is the premise of this new form of interactive relationship between the company and the public. Web 2.0 is the environment in which companies meet the opinions of brand users. Social media provide the most effective tools to meet customers, receive feedback, and disseminate information in an effective and efficient way. Social networks represent communities, much like ecosystems, of coexistence between people and brands, where the latter are 'humanized' while maintaining their business objectives.

Recommendations, critiques, reviews, and mentions are the tools that give power to the new consumer. A prosumer (Toffler, 1980) is any person who relates to a company with the ability to publish opinions about it. The consumer is no longer passive but someone who belongs to an interactive community and whose opinion influences the decision making of the company and others. Users generate advertising proposals, cause changes in services and products, and make their opinions count.

To profit from this new form of communication, companies must adapt to it, learn to use appropriate tools, and encourage the participation and interaction of the community. But above all, they must integrate the social element in their business processes by transforming the culture of their organizations. A strategic plan in social media should be developed according to the objectives of the business. It should ensure that the company's social media objectives align with business objectives. It should also ensure that the measurement of actions includes measures of the impact on relationships. Quantitative elements should not be analyzed solely from a financial perspective.

To convert information into knowledge and guide decision making, we use methods of measurement to determine whether objectives have been achieved and what value social media are contributing to the economic health of the company. To develop these measurements, we must choose optimal metrics, both quantitative and qualitative, that reflect the company context.

Web 2.0 is a sociological phenomenon that represents an important cultural change. Companies must not only adapt to this change but also pay attention to a new series of concepts and techniques that will help them advance even more, by making them mobile and able to predict the market using semantic web technologies. That is, 'Companies need connections to their markets to create long-term loyalty' (Li & Bernoff, 2009, pp. 278).

REFERENCES

Athey, S., & Ellison, G. (2009). *Position auctions with consumer search (No. w15253)*. National Bureau of Economic Research. doi:10.3386/w15253

Bakshi, K. (2004). *Tools for end-user creation and customization of interfaces for information management tasks*. (Doctoral dissertation). Massachusetts Institute of Technology.

Beer, D. D. (2008). Social network(ing) sites… revisiting the story so far: A response to Danah Boyd & Nicole Ellison. *Journal of Computer-Mediated Communication, 13*(2), 516–529. doi:10.1111/j.1083-6101.2008.00408.x

Bennett, S., Maton, K., & Kervin, L. (2008). The 'digital natives' debate: A critical review of the evidence. *British Journal of Educational Technology, 39*(5), 775–786. doi:10.1111/j.1467-8535.2007.00793.x

Bhargava, R. (2006). *5 Rules of Social Media Optimization (SMO)*. Retrieved from http://www.rohitbhargava.com/2006/08/5_rules_of_soci.html

Bughin, J., & Chui, M. (2010). *The rise of the networked enterprise: Web 2.0 finds its payday*. Retrieved from http://www.mckinsey.com/insights/high_tech_telecoms_internet/the_rise_of_the_networked_enterprise_web_20_finds_its_payday

Cai, J., Liu, X., Xiao, Z., & Liu, J. (2009). Improving supply chain performance management: A systematic approach to analyzing iterative KPI accomplishment. *Decision Support Systems, 46*(2), 512–521. doi:10.1016/j.dss.2008.09.004

Clifton, B. (2012). *Advanced web metrics with Google Analytics*. Hoboken, NJ: John Wiley & Sons.

Cornelissen, J. (2014). *Corporate communication: A guide to theory and practice*. London, UK: Sage Publications, Ltd.

del Fresno, M. (2012). *El consumidor social: Reputación online y social media*. Barcelona, B: Editorial UOC.

Dodds, P. S., Harris, K. D., Kloumann, I. M., Bliss, C. A., & Danforth, C. M. (2011). Temporal patterns of happiness and information in a global social network: Hedonometrics and Twitter. *PLoS ONE, 6*(12), e26752. PMID:22163266

Fama, E. F. (1998). Market efficiency, long-term returns, and behavioral finance. *Journal of Financial Economics, 49*(3), 283–306. doi:10.1016/S0304-405X(98)00026-9

Forrester. (2010). *The ROI of social media marketing*. Retrieved from https://frankdiana.files.wordpress.com/2011/04/roi-of-social-marketing-forrester-report.pdf

Gilbert, E., & Karahalios, K. (2009). Predicting tie strength with social media, In *Proceedings of the SIGCHI Conference on Human Factors in Computing Systems* (pp. 211-220). ACM.

Goldhaber, M. H. (1997). *The Attention Economy and the Net*. Retrieved from http://firstmonday.org/article/view/519/440

Harrison, J. S., & Freeman, R. E. (1999). Stakeholders, social responsibility, and performance: Empirical evidence and theoretical perspectives. *Academy of Management Journal*, *42*(5), 479–485. doi:10.2307/256971

Hendler, J. (2009). Web 3.0 emerging. *Computer*, *42*(1), 111–113. doi:10.1109/MC.2009.30

Hoeffler, S., & Keller, K. L. (2002). Building brand equity through corporate societal marketing. *Journal of Public Policy & Marketing*, *21*(1), 78–89. doi:10.1509/jppm.21.1.78.17600

Hoffman, D. L., & Fodor, M. (2010). Can you measure the ROI of your social media marketing? *MIT Sloan Management Review*, *52*(1), 41–49.

Kaplan, A. M., & Haenlein, M. (2010). Users of the world, unite! The challenges and opportunities of social media. *Business Horizons*, *53*(1), 59–68. doi:10.1016/j.bushor.2009.09.003

Levine, R., Locke, C., Searls, D., & Weinberger, D. (1999). *The Cluetrain Manifesto*. Retrieved from http://www.cluetrain.com/book/

Li, C., & Bernoff, J. (2011). *Groundswell: Winning in a World Transformed by Social Technologies*. Cambridge, MA: Forrester Research, Inc.

Lovett, J. (2011). *Social Media Metrics Secrets*. Indianapolis, IN: Wiley Publishing, Inc.

Maass, W., & Kowatsch, T. (2012). *Semantic Technologies in Content Management Systems: Trends, Applications and Evaluations*. Springer Science & Business Media. doi:10.1007/978-3-642-24960-0

McAfee, A. (2006). Enterprise 2.0: The Dawn of Emergent Collaboration. *MIT Sloan Management Review*. Retrieved from http://adamkcarson.files.wordpress.com/2006/12/enterprise_20_-_the_dawn_of_emergent_collaboration_by_andrew_mcafee.pdf

McAfee, A. (2009). *Enterprise 2.0: New collaborative tools for your organization's toughest challenges*. Boston, MA: Harvard Business School Publishing.

McKenna, K. Y., & Bargh, J. A. (2000). Plan 9 from cyberspace: The implications of the Internet for personality and social psychology. *Personality and Social Psychology Review*, *4*(1), 57–75. doi:10.1207/S15327957PSPR0401_6

Neiger, B. L., Thackeray, R., Van Wagenen, S. A., Hanson, C. L., West, J. H., Barnes, M. D., & Fagen, M. C. (2012). Use of social media in health promotion purposes, key performance indicators, and evaluation metrics. *Health Promotion Practice*, *13*(2), 159–164. doi:10.1177/1524839911433467 PMID:22382491

O'Reilly, T. (2006). *What is Web 2.0. Design patterns and business models for the next generation of software.* Retrieved from http://www.oreilly.com/pub/a/web2/archive/what-is-web-20.html

Oppong, S. A., Yen, D. C., & Merhout, J. W. (2005). A new strategy for harnessing knowledge management in e-commerce. *Technology in Society, 27*(3), 413–435. doi:10.1016/j.techsoc.2005.04.009

Orlikowski, W. J., & Gash, D. C. (1994). Technological frames: Making sense of information technology in organizations. *ACM Transactions on Information Systems, 12*(2), 174–207. doi:10.1145/196734.196745

Paine, K. D. (2011). *Measure what matters: Online tools for understanding customers, social media, engagement, and key relationships.* Hoboken, NJ: John Wiley & Sons.

Prensky, M. (2004). *The death of command and control.* Retrieved from http://www.marcprensky.com/writing/prensky-sns-01-20-04.pdf

Schmidt, K., & Ludlow, C. (2002). Inclusive branding: The why and how of a holistic approach to brands. Basingstoke, UK: Palgrave Macmillan. doi:10.1057/9780230513297

Selwyn, N. (2009). The digital native-myth and reality. *Aslib Proceedings, 61*(4), 364–379. doi:10.1108/00012530910973776

Siau, K., Ee-Peng, L., & Shen, Z. (2001). Mobile commerce: Promises, challenges, and research agenda. *Journal of Database Management, 12*(3), 4–13. doi:10.4018/jdm.2001070101

Skyrme, D. (2007). *Knowledge networking: Creating the collaborative enterprise.* London, UK: Routledge Publications.

Souders, S. (2007). *High performance web sites: Essential knowledge for front-end engineers.* Sebastopol, CA: O'Reilly Media, Inc.

Sterne, J. (2010). *Social media metrics: How to measure and optimize your marketing investment.* Hoboken, NJ: John Wiley & Sons.

Strahilevitz, L. J. (2005). A social networks theory of privacy. *The University of Chicago Law Review*, 919–988.

Strauss, J., & Frost, R. (1999). *Marketing on the Internet. Principles of online marketing.* Upper Saddle River, NJ: Prentice Hall.

Sultan, N. A. (2011). Reaching for the "cloud": How SMEs can manage. *International Journal of Information Management, 31*(3), 272–278. doi:10.1016/j.ijinfomgt.2010.08.001

Tang, L., & Sampson, H. (2012). The interaction between mass media and the Internet in non-democratic states: The case of China. *Media Culture & Society, 34*(4), 457–471. doi:10.1177/0163443711436358

Toffler, A. (1980). *The Third Wave.* New York, NY: William Morrow & Company.

Turban, E., Liang, T. P., & Wu, S. P. (2011). A framework for adopting collaboration 2.0 tools for virtual group decision making. *Group Decision and Negotiation, 20*(2), 137–154. doi:10.1007/s10726-010-9215-5

Weber, L. (2011). *Everywhere: comprehensive digital business strategy for the social media era*. Hoboken, NJ: John Wiley & Sons.

Wilson, C., Boe, B., Sala, A., Puttaswamy, K. P., & Zhao, B. Y. (2009). User interactions in social networks and their implications. In *Proceedings of the 4th ACM European conference on Computer systems* (pp. 205-218). ACM. doi:10.1145/1519065.1519089

ADDITIONAL READING

Atanda, D. (2013). *The Digitterian tsunami: Web 3.0 and the rise of the neo citizen (Volume 1: The 21 Principles driving the evolution of the Internet)*. Createspace.

Blanchard, O. (2011). *Social media ROI: Managing and measuring social media efforts in your organization*. New York, NY: Pearson Education, Inc.

Cavalcanti, J. (2012). ROI en Social – IOR Impact of Relationship. Retrieved from http://prezi.com/nc5xgqesitzt/roi-en-social-ior-impact-of-relationship/

Cook, N. (2008). *Enterprise 2.0: How social software will change the future of work*. Aldershot, UK: Gower Publishing Ltd.

Deans, P. C. (2010). *Social software and Web 2.0 technology trends*. Hershey, PA: IGI Global.

Glazier, A. (2011). *Searchial marketing: How social media drives search optimization in Web 3.0*. Bloomington, IN: AuthorHouse.

Kaushik, A. (2009). *Web analytics 2.0: The art of online accountability and science of customer centricity*. Indianapolis, IN: Wiley Publishing, Inc.

Kelly, N. (2012). *How to measure social media: A step-by-step guide to developing and assessing social media ROI*. New York, NY: Pearson Education, Inc.

McAfee, A. (2009). *Enterprise 2.0: New collaborative tools for your organization's toughest challenges*. Boston, MA: Harvard Business Press.

Paine, K. D. (2011). *Measure what matters: Online tools for understanding customers, social media, engagement, and key relationships*. Indianapolis, IN: Wiley Publishing, Inc.

Parmenter, D. (2010). *Key performance indicators (KPI): Developing, implementing, and using winning KPIs*. Hoboken, NJ: John Wiley and Sons, Inc.

Preece, J., Sharp, H., & Rogers, Y. (2015). *Interaction design: beyond human-computer interaction*. Hoboken, NJ: John Wiley & Sons, Inc.

Safko, L., & Brake, D. K. (2009). *The social media bible. Tactics, tools & strategies for business success*. Hoboken, NJ: John Wiley & Sons, Inc.

Shuen, A. (2008). *Web 2.0: A strategy guide: Business thinking and strategies behind successful Web 2.0 implementations*. Sebastopol, CA: O'Reilly Media, Inc.

Siegel, E. (2013). *Predictive analytics*. Hoboken, NJ: John Wiley and Sons, Inc.

Spitzer, D. R. (2007). *Transforming performance measurement: Rethinking the way we measure and drive organizational success*. Broadway, NY: AMACOM.

KEY TERMS AND DEFINITIONS

Enterprise 2.0: An organization that fosters the development of a culture of participation, sharing and networking, and uses the tools of the social web both internally (employees) and in its external relations with customers and stakeholders.

Social Software: A set of applications that enable individuals to communicate and interact through the web. Today, this concept not only refers to interaction through social groups, but also to tools and services that enable sharing, labeling, and distribution of digital objects (audio, video, images) and to applications of collaborative work such as blogs, wikis and forums. The concept is closely linked to collective intelligence.

Social Media: Applications, platforms, and online communication tools that facilitate relationships, interaction, collaboration, and content generation and distribution between users.

Social Media Metrics: Quantitative or qualitative indicators that allow companies to know the results of the actions carried out in social media, check that objectives have been achieved, and assess the performance of the strategy and its impact on economic benefits. Social media metrics are data analysis tools that convert data into information relevant to the company.

Web 2.0: Also known as the Social Web, a set of applications and tools that allow users to navigate and interact dynamically with information, share content, socialize opinions, and learn collectively.

Web 3.0: Also known as the Semantic Web, an extension of the World Wide Web in which a naturally understandable language is expressed. It is usable by software agents, thus permitting easy finding, sharing, and integrating of information.

Web Analytics: Activity designed to draw conclusions, define strategies, or set rules of business, on the basis of data collected in the web environments in which the company exercises control; consists of collecting information provided by users who interact with the company website, and analyzing the data with the aim of improving the user's browsing experience and the performance of the business.

Section 2
Big Data and Knowledge Management Concepts in Social Media

Chapter 4
Big Data in Social Media Environment:
A Business Perspective

Matilda S.
IFET College of Engineering, India

ABSTRACT

Information technology has reached its pinnacle, with the era being dominated by two hi-tech driving forces - Big data and Social media. Big data encompasses a wide array of data mining workloads, extracted through various sources, the results of which are of keen interest to business leaders and analysts across every industry segment. Data from the social media is exploding at an exponential rate and is being hailed as the key, to crucial insights into human behavior. Extracting intelligent information from such immense volume, variety and velocity of data, in context to the business requirement is the need of the hour. Therefore, new tools and methods specialized for big data analytics is crucial, along with the architectures for managing and processing such data. Big data complemented with Social Media offers a new horizon to take management practice to an advanced level.

INTRODUCTION

Today social media has become the most effective means of networking and hobby of any human being. With the proliferation of smart devices and services extended by social networks, it is gaining importance and attracts people in large numbers. The interaction between human beings via social media is a potential source of unstructured, finer-grained and larger-scale digital data. The term "Big data" is pervasive and includes huge quantities of data, social media analytics, next generation data management capabilities, real time data and much more. It is also the shorthand for advancing trends in technology that open the door to a new approach to understand the latest trends and making intelligent decisions (Schroeck, Shockley, Smart, Morales & Tufano, 2014). Most of the Big data surge is wild and contains words, images, video or a combination of these. It is exploding and is bound to grow at a faster pace in the years to come. Though only a few percentage of this data is used effectively, business leaders claim

DOI: 10.4018/978-1-5225-0846-5.ch004

that data obtained from social media is of immense support in making intelligent decisions. Tools are being developed to excerpt data derived from social media to gauge consumer behavior and turn it into active information. This chapter provides an insight into big data derived from social media, analytics and its consumption from a business perspective.

THE BIG DATA

Big data is the term which refers to a collection of data so large and complex that cannot be processed using existing database management tools or traditional data processing applications. The procedures and processes for capture, curation, storage, search, sharing, transfer, analysis, and visualization are different for big data (Fonseca & Boutaba, 2015). The term was coined to describe the exploding growth of data observed in the order of zetabytes, that may be analyzed computationally to reveal patterns, trends, and associations, especially relating to human behavior and interactions (Stawski, 2015).This data comes from everywhere: sensors used to gather information, posts and responses in social media sites, multimedia contents, online purchase transaction, and cell phone signals to name a few. The click of a mouse, a keystroke or a single touch on the mobile screen contributes to the big data. Therefore in the digital space, consumers, suppliers and organizations are creating and consuming vast amount of information. Gartner predicts that enterprise data in all forms will grow 650 percent over the next five years. IDC enterprise data growth stat envisages that the world's volume of data doubles every 18 months. This flood of big data is a golden goose for business leaders over which they can build their business architecture and marketing strategy. The real challenge lies in harnessing this data for various applications using advanced tools and techniques.

Gartner's definition of the 3V's is still widely used to define the characteristics of big data. Big data represents the information assets characterized by high Volume, Velocity and Variety (De Mauro, Greco & Grimaldi, 2015). The 3Vs can be expanded as:

- **Volume:** Data is available at a larger scale in the order of Terabytes or petabytes.
- **Velocity:** big data is often available in real-time and the rate at which it grows is very high.
- **Variety:** big data draws from text, images, audio, and video and completes missing pieces through data fusion (Hilbert, 2016).

The source of Big data can be broadly classified into three categories:

- **Data Streams:** Activity generated or process mediated data from Computers and mobiles such log files, sensor data, location tracking, data generated by processors etc.
- **Social Networks:** Human sourced information- Eg. Data from sites such as Google+, Facebook, YouTube, Twitter, LinkedIn, blogs, WhatsApp, Instagram, Pinterest etc.
- **Public Domains:** Data that is publicly available on the Web. Eg. Government portals, Wikipedia, The World Bank, SEC/Edgar, Microsoft Azure MarketPlace/ DataMarket.

Of these social media has become an addiction and the main communication network in the daily lives of people around the world. It generates insurmountable data that reflects the day-today emotions and is authentic and real-time. Big data from social media is a natural resource that comes in various types and forms, but unlike any other resource, it grows bigger by the minute. This makes it difficult to extract, refine or analyze as the data is fluctuating and unstructured. Unrefined data cannot be put into good use.

COMMON SOCIAL MEDIA PLATFORMS

Social networks offer free and fast communication with friends usually in multiple forms such as tweets, pictures, videos and texts. Another attractive feature is creation of groups for multicast communication with friends, colleagues or family members. The most popular social media platforms are given below.

- **Facebook:** A social networking website that makes it easy to connect and share with family and friends. For availing the services users have to create personal profiles. Interactions are in the form of 'posts' which may be text, images or videos, and users can indicate their preferences for the content, articles, products and services through a 'Like' function.
- **Google+:** It is a platform focused on bringing all the services of Google together for users to enjoy social networking. Features include the ability to post photos and status updates to interest based communities, group different types of relationships into Circles, multi-person instant messaging, text and video chat called Hangouts, events, location tagging, and the ability to edit and upload photos to private cloud-based albums (Gundotra, 2011; Lytle, 2013).
- **LinkedIn:** LinkedIn is a social networking forum designed specifically for professionals. The goal is to allow registered members to establish a network of people they know and trust professionally.
- **YouTube**: Allows users to upload, view and comment on videos.
- **Twitter**: It a microblogging service that allows users to broadcast their opinion on any subject and read 'tweets' of up to 140 characters.
- **Flickr:** It allows users to upload, view and comment on photos. Instagram and Pinterest are similar photo and image sharing sites.

Working of Big Data from Social Media Perspective

Social media is the richest source of big data on which organizations depend for forecasting their business requirement and development. Organizations set up pages on Facebook, Twitter and Google+ and start counting the likes, shares, tweets and comments which form the raw set of big data. The numbers may seem to be impressive, but it fails to provide details relating to sales, marketing campaigns, new customers or revenue generation. Organizing and storing big data is no more possible using the available database tools, due to the volume and velocity of data flowing in day-in and day-out. Strategies to select the required data and tools to process them are essential to acquire the required output. Intelligent businesses are capitalizing on this data to identify trends, detect patterns and glean other valuable findings through big data analytics. Big data analytics tools are software products that support predictive and prescriptive analytics applications running on big data computing platforms - typically, parallel processing systems based on clusters of servers, scalable distributed storage and technologies such as Hadoop and NoSQL databases. The tools are designed to enable users to rapidly analyze large amounts of data, often within a real-time window (Loshin, 2013). Well-planned analytical processes and people with the talent are required to unveil the essential information. Data scientists are Big data analysts with strong business acumen, who identify a pattern in the sea of data. The role requires: exploring, asking questions, doing "what if" analysis, questioning existing assumptions and processes. Big data analytics apply inductive statistics and concepts from nonlinear system identification to conclude laws of regressions, nonlinear relationships, and causal effects coming from large data sets to show relationships, dependencies as well as to perform predictions of outcomes and behaviors (Bowden, 2015). Armed with data and analytical results, the data scientist arrives at informed conclusions and recommends the same to the organization. Big data technology provides companies an insight into the consumer decision making and plays a major role, as to how an organization should approach a business challenge.

In short, big data is about deriving new insight from the ocean of data and integrating that insight into business operations, data warehouses, business processes and applications. The challenges in big data extracted from social media includes, inconsistency and complexity of the data, understanding the data pattern, limited time duration for data consumption, logical output design, security issues and familiarity with tools and techniques for data extraction and handling. Analyzing big data allows analysts, researchers, and business users to make better and faster decisions. Using advanced analytics techniques such as text analytics, machine learning, predictive analytics, data mining, statistics, and natural language processing, businesses can analyze previously untapped data sources to gain new insights resulting in significantly better and faster decisions. Patterson (2015) in his article "Social Media Demographics to Inform a Better Segmentation Strategy" gives a detailed statistics of various aspects of social media for creating a winning marketing strategy.

MAJOR SECTORS WHICH DEPLOY BIG DATA

Big data has the potential to make valid predictions by forecasting, business models and administrative systems based on the existing consumer experiences. According to IDC, the market for big data will reach $41.5 billion by 2018, growing at a 26% CAGR, six times faster than the overall IT market (Nadkarni & Vesset, 2014). Big data Analytics is a revolution in the IT sector and has a skyrocketing influence in all sectors. Right from booking a ticket for a theatre show to administrative architecture, big data has created a hockey stick curve, which is likely to zoom in the near future. Major sectors where big data has created a big impact are discussed below.

Education and Research

Big data serves as incremental information that can give a more complete picture of the learning process than traditional measures such as grades and test scores, which only measure outcomes. It can also help educators and researchers gain valuable insight into how to improve and personalize learning for students (Francisco, 2013).Educationalists armed with data-driven insight can make a significant changes on educational systems, quality of education, curriculum and research and development. By analyzing big data, they can identify student performance and progress regularly and modify the system based on the performance analysis and course outcomes. Better system for evaluation can be implemented to ensure fairness in competence. New academic disciplines such as learning analytics and educational data mining are emerging to make sense of this big data in education.

From scientific discovery to business intelligence, Big data is changing our world. Research on Big data is a massive work in itself. Research in all fields is made easy by the flow of data obtained from social networks saving the task of hunting and collecting data. All that is required of the researchers is to apply methods from statistics, computer science and machine learning to identify patterns and make predictions. The dissemination of nearly all information in digital form, the proliferation of sensors, breakthroughs in machine learning and visualization, and improvements in cost, bandwidth, and scalability together create enormous opportunity and saves a lot of time and money (Francisco, 2013).

Government

When government agencies harness and apply analytics to their big data, they gain significant ground to manage resources, create policies, managing calamities, dealing with traffic congestion, preventing crime, improving information technology and so on. But while there are many advantages to big data, governments must also address issues of transparency and privacy at the same time. The data obtained from census, feedback and complaints through government portals, transactions using identity cards and other statistical data provide a pool from which patterns can be identified for efficient governance, action plan in case of emergency and region-wise reforms and development.

Banking and Finance

With large amounts of raw information streaming in from social media, banks are finding new and innovative ways to improve their transactions and revenue. The onset of online banking and financial transactions through Internet has reduced personal contact considerably. To understand customers and boost their satisfaction it is essential to collect data through their online actions and transactions. This helps in implementing new schemes, improving security and elimination of fraud, while maintaining regulatory compliance. While Big data brings big insights into the customer behavior, but it also requires financial institutions to stay ahead with advanced analytics. The reasons for adopting big data solutions according to the survey conducted by IDC, are analysis of operations-related data and analysis of online customer behavior-related data.

Health Care

Standard medical practice is transforming from ad-hoc and subjective decision making to evidence -based healthcare. Healthcare industry is turning towards big data and analytics, to help them in understanding their patients and the contexts of the illnesses. The biggest concern in health care is that everything needs to be done quickly and accurately with adequate transparency to satisfy stringent industry regulations. Though social media plays a limited role in health care, electronic health records, treatment plans, prescription information and medical images serve as the major sources of big data. When big data is managed effectively, health care providers can uncover hidden insights that improve patient care. Effectively integrating and efficiently analyzing various forms of healthcare data over a period of time can answer many of the impending healthcare problems (Jensen, Jensen & Brunak, 2012).

Manufacturing Industry

The globalization of the world's economies is pushing the manufacturing sector to its next transformation – predictive manufacturing, for which manufacturers need to embrace emerging technologies, such as big data analytics (Lee, Lapira, & Bagheri, 2013). The analytics process, including the deployment and use of big data analytics tools, can help companies improve operational efficiency, drive new revenue and gain competitive advantages over business rivals. Armed with insight that big data can provide, manufacturers can improve quality and increase the production quantity of a particular product. This ensures wise investment which is crucial in today's highly competitive market. Manufacturers are moving towards this analytics-based culture, for solving problems and make business decisions faster. Big data expands the operational space for algorithms and machine-mediated analysis. At some manufacturers, algorithms analyze sensor data from production lines, creating self-regulating processes that cut waste, avoid costly (and sometimes dangerous) human interventions, and ultimately lift output (Brown, Chui & Manyika, 2011). Research results suggests that companies that use data and business analytics to guide decision making are more productive and experience higher returns on equity than competitors that don't (Brynjolfsson, Hitt, & Kim, 2011).

Retail Marketing

The retail market has changed in recent years as there has been a power shift over to consumers. Consumers have a choice of comparing products from different vendors or walk through a virtual store to shop for different products. Hence awareness of customer needs is critical for the retail industry. The best way to manage it is to analyze big data obtained from the customers through social media. Dealers need to know inventory and stock maintenance, marketing strategies, effective way to handle transactions and calculative techniques to bring back lapsed business. Big data remains at the heart of all these.

Big data technologies enable retailers to connect with customers through social media at an entirely new level by harnessing the vast volumes of data. Marketers scan social media or use location data from smartphones to understand teens' buying quirks. It helps retailers store, transform, integrate and analyze a wide variety of online and offline customer data in one central repository. Retailers can analyze this data to generate insights about individual consumer preferences and behaviors, and offer personalized recommendations in near real-time. The analysis offers the ability to optimize merchandise selections and pricing, that are tailored to a consumer's likes and dislikes. A next-generation retailer will be able to track the behavior of individual customers from Internet click streams, update their preferences, and model their likely behavior in real time (Brown, Chui & Manyika, 2011).

SOCIAL MEDIA: A BIG DATA INFLECTION POINT

The society continues to become more and more addicted with Social media which generates more information in a short duration than any other contemporary approaches. Data lies scattered across the Internet, while businesses, suppliers and customers are creating and consuming large amount of information. Understanding what it means for business and making intelligent decisions will give a competitive edge over one's peers in the global market. The quote on CNBC by Wilbad (2012), really exemplifies this "Data is the new Oil." which has the potential to turn business in any desired direction. Traditional approaches to large data are bound to break down soon under large exploding growth of data collected from social networks. This requires new technologies and techniques such as those used in big data. The ability to analyze and mine data from social networks and utilize the knowledge inside them will help in developing new business models, redesign business processes, accelerate ones business or control the direction of the business trend. The data analyzed can paint a picture of the needs and behavioral patterns of groups and individuals, of any product, on regional basis. Researchers and policymakers are beginning to realize the potential for converting these torrents of data into useful information that can be used to identify needs, develop new products, provide services, and predict and prevent crisis for the benefit of the organization. Better predictions can be made to target more-effective interventions, in areas that have been dominated by gut and intuition rather than by data. For this reason it has the potential to revolutionize management.

Big data has become a prominent area that business people are aware of. The attention it gets is as big as big data itself. The following are the excerpts from a few internationally recognised print media.

- **Wall Street Journal:** "Companies are being inundated with data"
- **Financial Times:** "Increasingly businesses are applying analytics to social media such as Facebook and Twitter,"
- **Forbes:** "big data has arrived at Seton Health Care Family."

Across all industries, including government, electronics, healthcare, media, food and production, data is becoming central to business operations. The volume and type of data available changes the way the businesses operate. Big data is already showing its potential in areas ranging from genetic mapping to personalized ecommerce. According to Erik Brynjolfsson, (2014), "big data backed by the exponential growth in processing power and software technologies such as Hadoop, are allowing organizations to handle all sorts of investment, production and marketing decisions".

The transformation will be both broad and deep, says Tsuneo Kawatsuma (2014), the CTO and CIO of global ICT Company Fujitsu. "Big data will have an impact on all industries and every process," he says. Its influence will be felt in business planning, research, sales, production and elsewhere. In Kawatsuma's view, this amounts to nothing less than new industrial revolution. Kenneth Cukier, (2010), in his interview to The Economist says "Facebook is a home to more than 40 billion photos, and Wal-Mart handles more than 1 million customer transactions every hour, feeding databases estimated at more than 2.5 petabytes. There are 4.6 billion mobile-phone subscriptions worldwide and almost two billion people use the internet". The right data sets can open doors to customer intelligence, insights on new trends and market needs. U.K. retail giant Argos uses social data to glean real-time insights on store performance, customer experience and brand reputation. James Finch customer and digital insight manager of Argos in an interview said that "Using social insights, we observe stores which are performing well and identify areas for improvement" (Newman, 2015).

The effective and economical way to harness massive data and collective intelligence across the globe is through social media. Social media allows data specialists to transcend time and space as it records every key stroke. There is a minute by minute flow of what is happening in the real world and in real time. Information derived from the data obtained throws light on spot trends and predicts happenings before they actually happen. Sentiment analysis, knowledge mining and aggregating conversations into trends are possible if the tools used are smart enough to tell what we ought to but that we don't know to ask for.

Key benefits of social media that add to the overall Big data analytics are:

- **Predicting Consumer Behavior:** Monitoring social activity can reveal where the source of future prospect lies. Analysis of such data could be utilized to select inventory levels and release new products. This is a way to predict consumer requirements and behavioral changes with respect to the market.

- **Reputation Management:** Another key contribution social media makes to the Big data is by identifying problems with products or services. Customers discuss opinions and feedback on products through their social media accounts. The data received can be analyzed to decide the future strategy of the company.

There are other ways Big data can combine with social media to help organizations provide better services to customers. According to International Data Corporation (IDC), the big data and analytics market will reach $125 billion worldwide in 2015. Rob Bearden (2013), CEO of Hortonworks, said that he expects see at least 60%, of enterprise data moving into Hadoop over the coming years, as it changes the economics of managing data, giving companies a sought-after "single platform that manages all data types and structures". Data-driven marketing is at an inflection point. The big picture of 2015 painted by Lewis (2014) predicts that

- 90% of existing data has been created in the last two years
- 64% of CMOs were interested in leveraging big data in 2014 – but only 8% have reached implementation stage
- 90% of fortune 500 companies have big data initiatives in place

Big data is less about the data itself and more about one does with the data. Big data analytics sees patterns where none exist and offer connections with an enormous quantity of data (Boyd & Crawford, 2012). Data obtained from social interactions forms an attractive set of information, particularly for marketing, sales and support functions. The diverse and unstructured forms, pose a challenge, when it comes to consumption and analysis. As social sites continue to generate torrents of data, organizations should not only turn the information generated into intelligent assessments, but also to measure the business value. Intelligent decisions can be arrived at, only if the data is current and decision is time-bound. The key aspect of big data analytics is integration wherein data of diverse types and patterns has a single platform for easy management. Analysts often struggle to determine which social data is suitable for a given business requirement. Therefore, there is a need for new tools and methods for big data analytics, as well as the required architectures for managing and processing such data. By deploying listening tools and sentiment analytics complemented with human intelligence, organizations can filter out noise and extract the critical and required data for business development. The emergence of big data has an effect on everything, right from the data itself, its collection, processing and the final extracted decisions. Analytics based on large data samples are more accurate and can influence business transformation.

Big data demands a different kind of business leadership and vision. Big data can power business innovation, if business leaders focus on fundamental questions and let the data discern the answers. The vision required to grow a company is not about having an elaborate plan, but about knowing the right questions to ask. An example of such vision is using the analytic power of Big data for innovative product development. Most companies have an unprecedented amount of information on the attitudes and behaviors of their customers. The question is to figure out what to do with heaps and heaps of data. Companies should use this to answer fundamental questions about their products, services and how can they continuously enhance their products, and create new ones. Ben Elowitz (2015), CEO of Wetpaint lists the five most important questions to ask for effective analysis. The remarks in parentheses indicate how these questions translate specifically to product development:

- What do my customers love? (Tapping into user passion)
- How do they want it? (How does the design, platform need to evolve?)
- How can I best relate? (Does the product experience project your brand personality?)
- What secret signals are my customers sharing? (Remain open to what the data shows)
- Where is the sweet spot? (What unmet customer need can be addressed in a way that best fits my ability to deliver?)

The investment community undoubtedly knows the power of this approach to product development that truly leverages big data. Companies need to change with the times and embrace innovation. Big data is a big deal only if business leaders use it to think big. Big data will help to create novel growth opportunities and totally new categories of companies, such as those that aggregate and analyze industry data. Many of these will be companies, that observe large information flows of data about products, services, buyers, suppliers, consumer preferences and intent, which can be captured and analyzed. Leaders with forward thought across all sectors should begin aggressively to build their organizations' big data capabilities. While online sales, social networking, and mobile applications have received most of the buzz when it comes to digital data, recent research finds that the greatest bottom-line impact may come where most companies are not looking—from cost savings and changes beyond the interface with customers. Across the industries examined by Olanrewaju & Willmott, (2013) of McKinsey and Company, the average bottom-line impact that can be realized from digital sales over the next five years is 20%. This is a significant opportunity, but much less than the bottom-line impact from cost reductions with an average of 36%. Pundits predict the failure of any organization that might ignore the opportunity that big data presents. Organizations are struggling with their approach, daunted by the ever-increasing torrent of data, high complexity and serious skills gap. Proper identification, design and deployment of strategies, processes, skills, systems and data that service providers will aid in evolving actionable intelligence resulting in increased business value for service providers both in traditional service markets, and also in new market roles (Rich, 2014).

TYPES OF BIG DATA ANALYTICS

With data in hand, one can begin doing analytics. But the daunting questions are, where do you begin? and which type of analytics is most appropriate for a given environment? When there is enough data, the data scientist starts to see patterns. Based on these patterns he builds a model of how these data work. Once a model is built, prediction can be done.

Descriptive analytics is the simplest type of analytics, which allows one to condense big data into smaller, more useful nuggets of information. It uses data aggregation and data mining techniques to provide insight into the past and answer "What has happened?" (Bertolucci, 2013). They are analytics that describe the past which may be any point of time that an event occurred, whether it is one minute ago, or one year ago. Descriptive analytics are useful because they allow us to learn details of past behaviors, and understand how they might influence future outcomes. More than 80% of business analytics especially social analytics are descriptive. For example, numbers of posts, mentions, fans, followers, page views, check-ins, pins, etc. are all just simple event counters. Descriptive statistics are useful to show things like, total stock in inventory, increase in sales after a particular advertisement or marketing strategy and changes in annual sales. Typically descriptive analytics are reports that provide historical insights regarding the organization's production, finance, operations, sales, inventory and customers. Descriptive statistics is used when organizations need to understand what is going on and to describe and review diverse facets of the business.

Predictive analytics is the next step up in data reduction with its roots in the ability to predict. It uses statistical models and forecasts techniques to understand the future and answer: "What could happen?" (Bertolucci, 2013). It utilizes a variety of statistical, modeling, data mining, and machine learning techniques to study recent and historical data, thereby allowing analysts to make predictions about the future. They combine historical data found in ERP, CRM, HR and POS systems to identify patterns in the data and apply statistical models and algorithms to capture relationships between various data sets. The purpose of predictive analytics is not to tell you what will happen in the future. Predictive analytics can only forecast what might happen in the future based on that data of what has happened earlier. All predictive analytics are probabilistic in nature. Predictive analytics provides companies with actionable insights based on data and estimates about the likelihood of a future outcome. It is important to remember that no statistical algorithm can "predict" the future with 100% certainty. Companies use these statistics to forecast what might happen in the future (Halo, 2014).

Predictive analytics can be used throughout the organization, from forecasting customer behavior and purchasing patterns to identifying trends in sales activities. Predictive analysis is used any time to know something about the future or fill in the information that is not available. They also help forecast demand for inputs from the supply chain, operations and inventory. One common application that most people are familiar with, is the use of predictive analytics to produce a credit score. These scores are used by financial services to determine the probability of customers making future credit payments on time. Typical business practices include, understanding how sales might close at the end of the year, predicting what items customers will purchase together, or forecasting inventory levels based upon a myriad of variables (Halo, 2014). Sentiment analysis is a common type of predictive analytics. The input to the model is plain text and the output of that model is a sentiment score, a value between +1 or -1.In this case, the model computes the score, but it is not necessarily predicting the future. It is predicting only the sentiment label, whether it is a positive or negative sentiment (Bertolucci, 2013).

Predictive Social Analytics is on the Horizon and most organizations are still maturing in their use. These companies need to understand how to monitor and listen to data on social media. More advanced businesses use the analysis in business intelligence. The most mature businesses integrate social media predictive analytics with other sources of information, such as CRM to provide social and nonsocial feedback. Big data in combination with high-powered analytics, can accomplish business-related tasks such as:

- Glean key insights
- Determine root causes of failures, issues and defects in near-real time.
- Enable cost reductions, time reductions, new product development and smart decision making.
- Generating coupons at the point of sale, based on the customer's buying habits.
- Recalculating entire risk portfolios within minutes.
- Detect fraudulent behavior before it takes its toll (DeLoatch, 2014).

Prescriptive analytics, the emerging technology, goes beyond descriptive and predictive models by recommending one or more courses of action and shows the prospective outcome of each decision. Prescriptive analytics prescribes an action which the business decision-maker can take and act. Predictive analytics does not predict one possible future, but rather "multiple futures" based on the decision-maker's actions. In addition, prescriptive analytics uses the predictive model with two additional components: actionable data and a feedback system that tracks the outcome produced by the action taken. It also recommends the best course of action for any pre-specified outcome. Prescriptive analytics use a combination of techniques and tools such as business rules, algorithms, machine learning and computational modelling procedures. These techniques are applied against input from different data sets including historical and transactional data, real-time data feeds and big data (Bertolucci, 2013).

Prescriptive analytics is relatively complex to implement and manage, and most companies are not yet using them in their daily course of work. When implemented correctly, it is bound to have a large impact on decision making and on the company's bottom line. Larger companies are successfully using prescriptive analytics to optimize production, scheduling and inventory in the supply chain to make sure that are delivering the right products at the right time and optimizing the customer experience.

TOOLS AND DATABASES USED IN BIG DATA ANALYTICS

In the past, analysis was delegated to the database software, which would use JOIN mechanism to compile tables, and add up the fields before handing off the subset of data to the reporting software. This is easier said than done, as complicated JOIN commands can lock up the database for hours and put all the other work on hold. Big data is much more complicated because the scale is much larger. Information is usually spread out over a number of servers and the work of compiling the data must be coordinated among them.

Hadoop is a popular tool for organizing the servers in racks and NoSQL databases are tools for storing data on these racks. This combination is more powerful than the old single machine. The terms "Hadoop" and "Big data" are used synonymously. Hadoop is an Apache distributed data processing open source software library that allows distributed processing of big data sets across clusters of computers using simple programming models. Built using Java, it is designed to scale up from single servers to thousands of machines, each offering local computation and storage. The Apache Foundation also sponsors a number of related projects that extend the capabilities of Hadoop supported by various platforms and operating systems. In addition, numerous vendors also offer supported versions of Hadoop and related technologies.

NoSQL commonly referred to as "Not Only SQL" represents a framework of databases that allows high-performance and quick processing of information at massive scale. It is a database infrastructure that adapts well to the heavy demands of big data. NoSQL databases are unstructured in nature, trading off stringent consistency requirements for agility and speed. NoSQL centers on the concept of distributed databases, where unstructured data may be stored across multiple processing nodes or multiple servers.

Originally developed by Google, MapReduce is a programming model and software framework for applications that rapidly process vast amounts of data in parallel on large clusters of compute nodes. It has been a game-changer in supporting the enormous processing needs of big data. For example a large data procedure which might take 20 hours of processing time on a centralized relational database system, may take 3 minutes using MapReduce.

GridGain, HPCC (high performance computing cluster) and Storm are tools which offer extended functionalities to Hadoop. GridGrain is an alternative to MapReduce that is compatible with the Hadoop Distributed File System. It offers in-memory processing for fast analysis of real-time data. Storm is owned by Twitter and is often described "Hadoop of real-time" as it supports distributed real-time computation capabilities (Harvey, 2012).

Cassandra, a NoSQL database was originally developed by Facebook and is now managed by the Apache Foundation. It is used by many organizations with large, active datasets, including Netflix, Twitter, Urban Airship, Constant Contact, Reddit, Cisco and Digg. HBase is the non-relational data store for Hadoop. MongoDB, Neo4j, CouchDB, OrientDB, Terrastore Hibari and Hypertable are other databases with varied features.

ANALYTICS SWEET SPOTS

For effective decision making, there are enough opportunities to try and understand market dynamics by crunching the data extracted from social networks. Social media, growth of internet users, growth of mobile devices has given the opportunity and opened up the eyes of many as a means to understand external factors in their decision making process. The challenge today is not the tools that need to be used for analyzing the different forms of data, but finding the Sweet Spot of information that would enable organizations to make the right decisions at the right time and give an edge over its competitors. According to Schefren (2015) strategic sweet spot in business is the intersection of all its uniqueness– it is the convergence of all its capabilities, and provides the best possible competitive outcome. For example, the current level of interest rates can be considered to be in a sweet spot if they keep inflationary pressures in check, but do not do so at the cost of the overall market. Similarly, if the current level of employment in an economy is enough to stimulate economic growth without leading to higher levels of inflation through wage pressures; it could be referred to as a sweet spot. However, a strategic sweet spot is never permanent and evolves over time, with change in markets, technologies, competitors, organizations, skill available etc. Hence, a business must continuously reassess and redefine its strategic sweet spot. In his article "Hitting the Sweet Spot", Paul O'Dea writes that: In business the strategic sweet spot is where a target customers' needs fit, with what is special about the business. For example in the proverbial 80:20 rule "20% of customers deliver 80% of the profit", the 20% is the sweet spot (Schefren, 2015).

To grow a business, energies must be focused on finding the sweet spot as it provides the clarity, focus, alignment that will propel business in the positive direction. However, if there is a rush to execute a business strategy before finding the right sweet spot, it is a waste of time and valuable resources on the wrong customers. Customers outside the sweet spot inhibit growth and should be considered off-strategy. In such cases effort is wasted on spots where there is little hope of being successful. Great companies know their sweet spot customers intimately and continuously deliver better value than their competitors. Their business is tailored around the sweet spot– that's when customers see themselves as self-select (Schefren, 2015). They also understand that finding the sweet spot is a continual battle driven by the top management which requires a systematic procedure and discipline. Sweet spot can be found by asking three simple questions:

- What is the business best at?
- What do the customers want the most?
- Where do competitors struggle?

These questions could be appropriately framed as a questionnaire and the response would be a rich repository to mine from. The business strategic sweet spot is the intersection of these three elements. Identifying this intersection provides clarity, creates opportunity, maximizes outcome which in turn, provide more efficient use of business resources, better focus, and greater cost-effectiveness. The final results are more potential customers, greater profitability and better return on investment. The key difference between business that identify their 'sweet spot' and those that do not is better positioning and optimal outcome. Sweet spots could be used to

- Identify and pursue the most profitable market segments
- Create new products and services
- Evaluate partnerships and alliances for maximizing business opportunities
- Focus to achieve higher return on investment (ROI) (Schefren, 2015)

ANALYTICS QUAGMIRES

One of the largest quagmires for big data analytics is sharing of social media data. Roski & McClellan (2011) found that a major reason big data analytics is not widely used is because of a sheer lack of real-time data, specifications for its collection, and lack of interconnection between all the sets of data. Groves, Kayyali, Knott, & Kuiken (2013) found that information is skewed because there is a lack of procedures for integrating data and communicating findings, as well as the security issues in sharing data. According to Hammond, Bailey, Boucher, Spohr & Whitaker (2010), the interoperability of information systems to organize data into a composite whole requires setting of standards. The 4 axioms of interoperability are

- Data should be available for multiple purposes, reusable, with auto collection preferable.
- Interoperability requires cooperation of stakeholders to ensure that the application is consistent with rules across domains (sensitive to legal, ethical, and societal requirements, including security, privacy, and confidentiality).
- A single global set of data elements with attributes must become building blocks of all systems with precise, unambiguous definitions..
- Interoperability among all/may diverse information systems.

Another issue in big data predictive analytics is siloed data. The difference with predictive analytics for social media is the immediacy of the information. Businesses that have real-time information can make timely offers, knowing that it is relevant to a customer's current interest and is more likely to be acted upon immediately. Using insights from today, to predict the future is not easy, as companies are unsure, whether the insights they have gathered are true indicators. They also struggle in translating the insights into an action plan. In addition, many companies have siloed departments and aggregating data and creating a strategy in unison is an obstacle. Social listening platforms scan the media, for specific text, images, keywords, and sentiments which has to be correlated with the nature of the person and period. For example, it would be useful to know if a person who posted negative comments about a product was a longtime customer or not. Connecting the sentiment through the company's customer relationship management (CRM) system would add context and value to the sentiments. If the CRM is a siloed department and is not integrated with social media listening platforms, complete prediction is not possible

(DeLoatch, 2014). Hence analysis using dual parameters for effective inference is impossible. Businesses often ask customers for their, address, mobile numbers and email-id, but it is time they ask for Twitter handles and other social media identification. Technical limitations which stem from mismanagement and commercial turf battles are other factors which act as a hurdle in implementing big data analytics.

ANALYTICS MATURITY

According to a study by IBM Institute of Business Value (IBV), 63% of organizations in 2014 realized a positive return on their analytics investments within a year. The study also noted that 74% of respondents anticipate that the speed at which executives expect new data-driven insights will continue to accelerate in the years to come. The reason behind this success is that big data and analytics maturity model considers not only the technology to lay out a path to success, but more importantly it also takes into account the business factors (Palmer, 2014). The maturity can be classified into six areas.

- **Information:** Use of data to manage the business is the base capability. However, highly mature organizations recognize that data is a business asset. Hence they seek for it not only from existing transactional records but also from personal records of individuals and external sources. Mature organizations provide governed access to data for effective utilization wherever it resides in the organization and are able to give it meaning and context.
- **Analytics:** Mature use of analytics optimizes the business. Organizations have reports to show their financial performance and demonstrate regulatory compliance, but analytics is necessary to understand why something has happened or to predict what is likely to happen. The resulting insight helps improve customer engagement and operational efficiency.
- **Architecture:** A coherent infrastructure and system is essential to establish durable capability in an organization. It enables ease of access by end users, agility in the capabilities to address current business needs and a managed approach to accessing required data. A mature architecture caters to all four characteristics of big data: volume, variety, velocity and veracity. It accommodates these big data characteristics through the creation and systematic reuse of architectural patterns, assets and standards including operational models to fulfill service levels and security requirements as well a consistent use of data models.
- **Implementation:** Access to data and using analytics to derive insight builds no business value in and of itself. The organization realizes benefits only when the system is implemented with the coordination of all those involved. All those involved in the implementation of the system should be able to visualize, share and provide feedback to learn and improve. A mature organization implements the architecture offered by the rich data and analytics services and evolves a mature business model which is optimized in all aspects.
- **Business Strategy:** Technology is required to acquire data and execute analytics but business expertise is necessary to derive meaningful insight and use it to differentiate outcomes. It demands the capacity to explore data for new opportunities and ability to construct quantified business cases. Mature organizations are able to harness sufficient data and apply analytics to it to innovate and create new business models.
- **Governance:** Information governance is a critical success factor for big data projects. Policies need to be established and enforced to a degree of confidence in information and so that resulting

insights are understood and reflected in decision-making efforts. Policies also need to span provenance, currency, data quality, master data and metadata, lifecycle management, security, privacy and ethical use. (Nott, 2015).

Good Practices for Effective use of Big Data

Installing big data software, hiring skilled personnel and setting up a framework will not meet the company's business needs. Certain practices which do not come with the rule book have to be adopted for the success of the system.

- **Data Analysis is Every Day Activity:** Data scientists should understand that data analysis is not a month end, quarterly or annual activity similar to balance sheets. If organizations are to recognize the market opportunity, understand their customer expectations and improve internal efficiency, analyzing data has to be given the required importance and has to be an integral part of the management day- today activities.
- **Making Full Use of Internal Data:** Success of data analysis, is about making the changes within the organization in response to new insights that emerge out of data analysis. Before investing heavily in big data analytics, organizations should understand how to make use of the data available within the organizations to support its operating decisions. It is a good practice to start with internal data before investing on analyzing data from external sources.
- **Administration of Data Analytics:** Organizations should have clearly defined people who are responsible and empowered in accessing and analyzing the data. Many times lack of clarity within the organization around the ownership of analytical systems leads to a miserable failure of the entire architecture. Organizations have started creating job roles like chief digital office and many chief executives are getting personally involved, which are signs that organization is giving importance to data analytics.
- **Deployment of Skilled Personnel:** The real value of data analytics comes from the human skill and intellect that is applied in questioning and analyzing the data. Experienced analysts are required for identifying the sweet spot for management recommendations. If the organization is not investing in this area there is no point in implementing in big data.
- **Prune Big Data as Soon as Possible:** There is a tendency for companies to store all of the incoming big data in raw form, until there is a requirement for analysis. Much of this data may never be used at all and will still remain stacked, occupying the memory for years together. The apprehension is that future queries might require old data, but there is an equally strong argument for sizing down the amount of data. Accumulating data is likely to create unwanted overhead, which in due time creates problems with respect to storage and organization. This makes mining and analytics difficult and slashes down the entire goal of implementing big data.
- **Know Your Customer:** Social media has emerged as a platform where people divulge a lot about their likes, personal tastes and opinions, unaware of the revelation. The buyer's persona can be understood based on the pages they like, or the posts they share. Based on this information, cookie-based ad of the products or service recommendations into social feed will induce the consumers to buy the product.
- **Promptness in Fixing Customer Issues:** Analyzing consumers' comments, obtaining feedback and interacting with them on social media can help organizations, detect and solve their problems

instantaneously. The resolution period is reduced as the data is readily available with the customer service representative. Individual attention aids in increasing customer satisfaction and loyalty. Social media is becoming one of the quickest avenues to get consumers answer questions in this regard. Most brands now understand the value of having a social media manager to address questions or concerns.

- **Learn from World's Experience:** The fine-grained, large-scale fresh record of people's actions, motivations and emotions from social networks is to be viewed as the opinion of the masses. Social media tells us about how people interact with the world and each other. The goal is to help people with their tasks and decisions by showing them what others have done in similar situations, why they did it, and how they felt afterwards. Experienced users say it is vital to gauge the potential business value that big data software can offer in alignment with the long-term objectives in mind as organizations move forward.

CASE STUDIES

BRAIN Initiative by White House

Brain Research through Advancing Innovative Neurotechnologies (BRAIN) was launched on April 2, 2013 by US President Barrack Obama to "accelerate the development and application of Big data technology that will enable researchers to produce dynamic pictures of the brain that shows the individual brain cells and complex neural circuits interact at the speed of thought." Launched with approximately $100 million in the President's Fiscal Year 2014 Budget, it aims to find new ways to treat, cure, and even prevent brain disorders such as Alzheimer's disease, epilepsy, and traumatic brain injury. The project is a joint effort by NSF, NIH, DARPA and uses advances in Big data to analyze the huge amounts of information that will be generated to understand how thoughts, emotions, actions and memories are represented in the brain. Data from social media is going to play a critical role (Insel, Landis & Collins, 2013).

Onset of Big Data Era at the Retailers

The top marketing executive at a retailer outlet was perplexed by the sales reports. A major competitor was steadily gaining market share across a range of profitable segments. Despite a counterpunch that combined online promotions with merchandizing improvements, the company kept losing ground. When the executive convened a group of senior leaders to dig into the competitor's practices, they found that the competitor had made efforts to collect, integrate, and analyze data from each store and every sales unit through the social networks. At the same time, it had linked this information to suppliers' databases, making it possible to adjust prices in real time, to reorder hot-selling items automatically, and to shift items from store to store easily. By constantly testing, bundling, synthesizing and making information instantly available across the organization—from the store floor to the CFO's office—the rival company had taken an advanced step to enhance their business. What this executive team had witnessed firsthand, was the game-changing effects of big data (Brown, Chui & Manyika, 2011).

Analysing Social Media Data for Sweet Spots

All businesses have strategic sweet spots– it's the business' energy source; it's where the business is most competent, in-sync, unique talent, predictable value, optimal outcomes. It is the intersection of the business– strengths, weaknesses, passions, differences. According to Peter Bregman a poll survey showed that 72% of workers admit to doing work they neither excel at nor enjoy. For a business to fulfill its purpose it must have an engaged workforce operating within its sweet spot and not outside of it. Represent the sweet spot for this case, using a Venn diagram and analyze how you would use social media for identifying the workforce to operate within its sweet spot.

Utilizing Big Data to Optimize Merchandise Displays

When it comes to product placement, stores have traditionally relied on historical sales trends, seasonal shopping patterns and gut instincts to determine inventory levels and merchandising strategies. However, merchants are taking a more scientific approach to how they stock everything, from the hottest items to evergreen basics- thanks to data and analytics. Dillard's, for example, turned to analytics to evaluate if the departmental store should merchandise Calvin Klein dresses in a separate section, away from the general sales floor. Tests in 11 stores determined it was a bad idea, revealing that sales of other brands' dresses dropped when Calvin Klein dresses were removed from the general floor, *The Wall Street Journal* reported. Overall, analytics gives retailers the ability to analyze store traffic in real-time to see which displays draw consumer interest and which layouts keep shoppers engaged for the maximum time. This information paired with predictions about optimal merchandise displays, can help retailers to be proactive with their visual displays and product placements (Thau, 2015).

DYNAMICS AND LIMITATIONS OF SOCIAL MEDIA BIG DATA

The flip side of big data is the erosion of privacy and security issues. We leave so many digital trails that, it is hard to remain private and anonymous. According to Ruths & Pfeffer (2014), many social forces that drive the formation and dynamics of human behavior and relations have been intensively studied. For instance, homophile - birds of the same feather flock together, transitivity – the friend of a friend is a friend and propinquity – those close by form a tie, have been used by designers to develop social media algorithms. Hence the data derived is a mixture of psychosocial and platform driven behavior. Limitations to data collected from Social media may be attributed to the following factors: Inconsistent human behavior, biased opinion, response of nonhumans (Spammers and bots masquerading as humans), proxy effect and data security. To fully utilize social media as a tool for arriving at intelligent decisions, the response should be proactive and obtained within a stipulated time-frame. The validity of the opinion, the correctness of the response, the accuracy of the content and the tone of voice are challenges which are yet to be resolved. Yet big data is largely going untapped.

Lack of Vision

Big data implementation is to be started by first gathering, analyzing and understanding the business requirements rather than gathering data. The analytics and architecture has to be then framed based on the initial research. Most of the organizations start in the reverse order and end up blaming the technology for their failure. The model followed by one organization for the same goal might not be suitable for another as the factors involved varies. Companies thriving on big data start with a targeted goal, but with passing time the focus gets shifted. Therefore the goal will not be achieved as the architecture and analytics has been designed as per the initial research.

User Data is Fundamentally Biased

The user-level data available from social media is only of individuals who have visited the page or viewed your online ads, which is typically not representative of the total target consumer base. Even within the pool of trackable cookies, the accuracy of the data obtained from the customer is mixed and unstable, as many consumers now operate across devices. Data collected from people who operate across multiple devices is likely to be from a different demography compared to those who only use a single device. User-level data is far from being accurate or complete and is subject to more noise, which means that there is inherent danger in assuming that insights can be applied to the consumer base at large. Accuracy tends to change when the same data is obtained from multiple sources and when the format of the data is changed. To make real impact big data analytics must deliver precise information, available almost immediately, in usable formats to generate visible results.

Lack of Infrastructure

The reason many organizations hesitate in implement big data is due to lack of resources which provide infrastructure support. A robust infrastructure is a key point for the successful operation and scalability of a big data project. Legacy systems and incompatible standards and formats prevent integration of data and the more sophisticated analytics that create value from big data. Big data storage and handling brings in new challenges that confront all organizations. Elastic data storage and massive parallel processing demanded by big data, requires cloud computing. Cloud storage can have a negative impact on both capacity and performance if it not designed properly. Creating highly virtualized cloud storage can be tricky since careful load balancing is required to maintain both capacity and performance. The infrastructure also extends to the consumer ends, who are generators of massive data. The mobile technology required for supporting big data at the consumer end has not proliferated to the required extent. The big problem for service provides is that details about the changes made in Big data is largely opaque to them and they do not get a complete picture.

Lack of Trained Personnel

The critical issue in big data market is the lack of trained personnel who can analyze data, build big data architecture and provide valuable insights. The worst part is that we are not creating them fast enough. The production, adoption, and adaptation of big data software are key ingredients for big data and require a properly trained workforce. Research firms paint a dire picture of a massive big data skills-gap that is bound to get worse with time. Trained personnel to look into the massive data and with skills to interpret the data are in demand.

Lack of Organizational Structure

The effectiveness of big data and data science is moderated by domain knowledge. According to Swink (2014) a company must not only collect information, it must decide how to use it effectively. For collected information to be useful for decision making, it must be available to managers who have relevant business knowledge. Organization leaders and policy makers will have to consider how industry structures could evolve in a big data world if they are to determine how to optimize value creation at the level of individual firms, sectors, and economies as a whole. Internal integration allows the information to flow quickly to the right decision-maker and aligns the information needs of the company with the business processes. Goals, role and responsibilities should be clearly defined at all levels. Administered access to data sources should be available to all those involved. The structure should facilitate the regular exchange of operational and tactical information between functional teams.

Even with the above challenges, there is still plenty of time to rise above, for a competitive advantage. According to Dr. Morgan Swink (2014) "Success requires a clear vision and business case coupled with complementary assets such as a supporting technological infrastructure (connectivity/visibility, mobile deployment, and systems for analysis and execution), analytics capabilities and supporting integrated organizational structure.

SOCIAL MEDIA'S BIG DATA FUTURE

Social media big data has been hailed as key to crucial insights into human behavior and extensively analyzed by scholars, corporations, politicians, journalists, and governments (Boyd & Crawford 2012). Social media promises to accelerate innovation, saves cost and popularize brands through mass collaboration. Organizations are using it to promote new products and services, and also monitor what people feel about their brand. Big data and Social Media promise to change management practice. Big, diverse data is opening opportunities in every industry. By tracking social data, companies can gauge recent trends and use the insights to evaluate marketing strategies and increase or reallocate advertising and outlets to maximize sales figures. Development of smart cities fostered by governments, 5G Communication technologies and success stories of organizations using Big data are bound to create an exponential increase in Big data implementation.

Customers value positive experiences, personal rapport and rapid response now, more than ever. Social media and big data analytics fuel the tools that help companies fulfill customers' expectations. According to a survey of 540 enterprise decision makers involved in big data purchases by Webopedia's parent company QuinStreet, about half of the respondents were applying big data and analytics to aid product development, improve customer retention and gain a competitive advantage. Whether an organization is looking to bring about major changes in sales, marketing, uncovering new revenue opportunities, improve customer service, optimize operational efficiency, reduce risk, or drive other business results, big data is the new oil which will fuel the fire.

As big data gathers momentum, big career opportunities are being created for IT professionals with the right skill set. According to a report published in 2011 by McKinsey & Co., the U.S. could face a shortage of 140,000 to 190,000 people by 2018, with analytical talent and of 1.5 million people capable of analyzing data in ways that enable business decisions. Companies are, and will continue look out for employees with a complex set of skills to tap big data's promise of competitive advantage, market watchers say.

FUTURE RESEARCH DIRECTIONS

Big data Analytics in its existing form is at an infant stage. Recognizing patterns, though an art, requires a framework and procedure for reducing errors in evaluation and preparing accurate reports. Pattern matching techniques opens up innumerable opportunities for research. Graphs are employed heavily in online social networks. The reason is that graphs offer a natural way of representing various kinds of relationships however complex they are. The friendship graph in Facebook, the follower graph in Twitter, endorsement graph in LinkedIn and product affinity graph in Amazon are some examples of social network and media graphs. The characteristics and properties of graphs vary significantly from one application to another. While MapReduce (MR) is a popular cluster computing paradigm, it is not well suited for graph analytics because many graph analytics tasks are iterative in nature. Despite these recent advances, scalable graph analytics is still challenging on multiple fronts and opens up avenues for research. More research is needed in this area, especially in regard to very large and distributed graphs, including the very large data sets (Miller, Ramaswamy, Kochut & Fard, 2015).

Linking data available and analytics with other systems already existing in the organizations is almost non-existent. To realize the big data advantage, suitable interfaces for linking with the existing computational models and frameworks are to be created. Research to address siloed working practices which inhibit the growth of big data is crucial, drawing immediate attention. This would lead to a single dashboard which provides big data analytics for each line of business. Storage Management and mining for required data is another avenue where research efforts are at an early stage. Cloud computing provides an apt platform for big data analytics in view of the storage and computing requirements of the latter. The immense popularity of data intensive applications like Facebook, LinkedIn, Twitter, Amazon, eBay and Google+ contributes to increasing requirement of storage and processing of data in the cloud environment. Schouten (2012) predicts that by the year 2016, half of the data will be on the cloud. This makes cloud-based analytics a viable research field. Security and privacy issues, web intelligence, Intelligent Management, data modelling for MIS are other major areas lacking research. Though progress in recent research activity in all aspects of big data has increased substantially, many challenges needs to be addressed.

CONCLUSION

Social media marketing and big data analytics are in the early stages. Developing countries are still far behind in the process, with organizational responsibility unclear. Though social media is a powerful addition, lack of technological infrastructure and personnel with data management and analysis skills tend to show slackness in progress. Still, organizations can channelize the information collected to their advantage by instilling the right company mindset, creating the right strategy and employing the right technology. By knowing how to effectively measure the business value of social activities, organizations can gain critical insights that allow them to improve and promote their products and services.

REFERENCES

Bertolucci, J. (2013). Big data Analytics: Descriptive Vs. Predictive Vs. Prescriptive. *Big data Analytics, Information Week*. Retrieved from: http://www.informationweek.com

Bowden, J. (2015). Reasons to Explore Big data with Social Media Analytics. *Social Media Today*. Retrieved from: http://www.socialmediatoday.com

Boyd, D., & Crawford, K. (2012). Critical questions for big data: Provocations for a cultural, technological, and scholarly phenomenon. *Information Communication and Society*, *15*(5), 662–679. doi:10.108 0/1369118X.2012.678878

Brown, B., Chui, M., & Manyika, J. (2011). Are you ready for the era of 'big data'. *The McKinsey Quarterly*, *4*, 24–35.

Brynjolfsson, E., Hitt, L. M., & Kim, H. H. (2011). *Strength in numbers: How does data-driven decisionmaking affect firm performance?*. Available at SSRN 1819486

De Mauro, A., Greco, M., & Grimaldi, M. (2015, February). What is big data? A consensual definition and a review of key research topics. In AIP Conference Proceedings (vol. 1644, pp. 97–104). doi:10.1063/1.4907823

DeLoatch, P. (2014). Predictive social analytics must clear data silo hurdles. *Content Management, TechTarget*. Retrieved from: http://www techtarget.com

Fonseca, N., & Boutaba, R. (2015). *Cloud Services, Networking, and Management*. John Wiley & Sons. doi:10.1002/9781119042655

Francisco, A. (2013). Realizing the Opportunity for Big data in Educatio. *Digital Promise*. Retrieved from http://www.digitalpromise.org

Groves, P., Kayyali, B., Knott, D., & Van Kuiken, S. (2013). The 'big data' revolution in healthcare. *The McKinsey Quarterly*.

Gundotra, V. (2011). Introducing the Google+ project: Real-life sharing, rethought for the web. *The Official Google Blog*.

Halo. (2014). The two-minute guide to understanding and selecting the right analytics. *Halo*. Retrieved from https://halobi.com/2014

Hammond, W. E., Bailey, C., Boucher, P., Spohr, M., & Whitaker, P. (2010). Connecting information to improve health. *Health Affairs*, *29*(2), 284–288. doi:10.1377/hlthaff.2009.0903 PMID:20348075

Harvey, C. (2012). 50 Top Open Source Tools for Big data. *Datamation, ITBusinessEdge*. Retrieved from: http://www.datamation.com/data-cente

Hilbert, M. (2016). Big data for Development: A Review of Promises and Challenges. *Development Policy Review*, *34*(1), 135–174. doi:10.1111/dpr.12142

Insel, T. R., Landis, S. C., & Collins, F. S. (2013). The NIH brain initiative. *Science*, *340*(6133), 687–688. doi:10.1126/science.1239276 PMID:23661744

Jensen, P. B., Jensen, L. J., & Brunak, S. (2012). Mining electronic health records: Towards better research applications and clinical care. *Nature Reviews. Genetics*, *13*(6), 395–405. doi:10.1038/nrg3208 PMID:22549152

Lee, J., Lapira, E., Bagheri, B., & Kao, H. A. (2013). Recent advances and trends in predictive manufacturing systems in big data environment. *Manufacturing Letters*, *1*(1), 38–41. doi:10.1016/j.mfglet.2013.09.005

Loshin, D. (2013). *Big data analytics: from strategic planning to enterprise integration with tools, techniques, NoSQL, and graph*. Elsevier.

Lytle, R. (2013). *Google+ Communities: A beginner's guide*. Mashable.

Miller, J. A., Ramaswamy, L., Kochut, K. J., & Fard, A. (2015, June). Research Directions for Big data Graph Analytics. In *Big data (Big Data Congress), 2015 IEEE International Congress on* (pp. 785-794). IEEE. doi:10.1109/BigDataCongress.2015.132

Nadkarni, A., & Vesset, D. (2014, September). Worldwide Big data Technology and Services 2014–2018 Forecast. *IDC*. Retrieved from http://www.idc.com

Newman, D. (2015). Social media metrics: Using big data and social media to improve retail customer experience. *IBM Big data and Analytics Hub*. Retrieved from: http://www.ibmbigdatahub.com

Nott, C. (2015). A maturity model for big data and analytics. *IBM Big data and Analytics Hub*. Retrieved from http://www.ibmbigdatahub.com

Olanrewaju, T., & Willmott, P. (2013). Finding your digital sweet spot. *Insights and Publications*. Retrieved from http://www.mckinsey.com/insights/business_technology

Palmer, B. (2014). Realizing a return on big data investments—within a year. *IBM Big data and Analytics Hub*. Retrieved from http://www.ibmbigdatahub.com

Patterson, M. (2015). Social Media Demographics to Inform a Better Segmentation Strategy. *Social Media Demographics for Marketers*. Retrieved from http://sproutsocial.com/insights

Rich, R. (2014). Big data: It's all about business value. *Big data Analytics, tmforum*. Retrieved from http://inform.tmforum.org/features-and-analysis/featured/2014

Roski, J., & McClellan, M. (2011). Measuring health care performance now, not tomorrow: Essential steps to support effective health reform. *Health Affairs*, *30*(4), 682–689. doi:10.1377/hlthaff.2011.0137 PMID:21471489

Ruths, D., & Pfeffer, J. (2014). Social media for large studies of behavior. *Science*, *346*(6213), 1063–1064. doi:10.1126/science.346.6213.1063 PMID:25430759

Schefren, R. (2015). Find Your Strategic Sweet Spot– Its What Makes a Business Different: Great Companies Always Know Their Sweet Spot. *BizShifts Trends*. Retrieved from http://bizshifts-trends.com/2015/

Schouten, E. (2012). *Big data As A Service*. Retrieved from: http://edwinschouten.nl/2012/09/19/bigdata-as-a-service/

Schroeck, M., Shockley, R., Smart, J., Morales, D. R., & Tufano, P. (2014). Analytics: The real-world use of big data. IBM Global Business Services & Saïd Business School at the University of Oxford, IBM Institute for Business Value.

Stawski, S. (2015). *Inflection Point: How the Convergence of Cloud, Mobility, Apps, and Data Will Shape the Future of Business*. Financial Times Press.

Thau, B. (2015). Retail product placement: Tapping data to optimize merchandise displays. *IBM Big data and Analytics Hub*. Retrieved from http://www.ibmbigdatahub.com

ADDITIONAL READING

Bendler, J., Wagner, S., Brandt, D. V. T., & Neumann, D. (2014). Taming Uncertainty in Big data. *Business & Information Systems Engineering*, *6*(5), 279–288. doi:10.1007/s12599-014-0342-4

Bitzshift Trends, (2015) Find Your Strategic Sweet Spot– Its What Makes a Business Different: Great Companies Always Know Their Sweet Spot

Chen, H., Chiang, R. H., & Storey, V. C. (2012). Business Intelligence and Analytics: From Big data to Big Impact. *Management Information Systems Quarterly*, *36*(4), 1165–1188.

Gantz, J., & Reinsel, D. (2012). The digital universe in 2020: Big data, bigger digital shadows, and biggest growth in the far east. *IDC iView*. *IDC Analyze the Future*, *2007*, 1–16.

Global Intelligence for the CIO. Fujitsu. Retrieved http://www.i-cio.com/big-thinkers/big-thinkers-of-2014/item/the-big-impact-of-big-data-on-business-and-society

Harmon, R. R., & Demirkan, H. (2015). IT-Enabled Business Innovation[Guest editors' introduction]. *IT Professional*, *17*(2), 14–18. doi:10.1109/MITP.2015.24

IDC Reveals Worldwide Big data and Analytics Predictions for 2015, http://www.idc.com/getdoc.jsp?containerId=prUS25329114]

Lohr, S. (2012). The age of big data. *New York Times, 11*.

McAfee, A., Brynjolfsson, E., Davenport, T. H., Patil, D. J., & Barton, D. (2012). Big data. *The management revolution. Harvard Business Review*, *90*(10), 61–67. PMID:23074865

Sherlin, W. (2015), *Big data – Are You Really Using, or Just Collecting?* Digital Growth Insights, Tufekci, Z. (2014). Big questions for social media big data: Representativeness, validity and other methodological pitfalls. *arXiv preprint arXiv:1403.7400*.

KEY TERMS AND DEFINITIONS

Analytics Maturity Model: Analytics maturity model is a business model which considers the technology to lay out a path to success and business factors like governance, quality of data, leadership, decision making, etc.

Analytics Sweet Spot: The concept comes from sports. It is a point where the combination of factors results in maximum impact achieved relative to a given amount of effort. The analogue in analytics is the most powerful solution that provides the best result, for a given set of inputs or resources. For example in case of banking, FICO score that assesses the capability of a borrower to fulfil his commitment of repayment of loan is an analytic sweet spot.

Big Data Analytics: It is the process of examining large data sets containing a variety of data types using statistical algorithms and machine-learning techniques, to uncover hidden patterns, unknown correlations, market trends, customer preferences and other useful business information to support decision making.

Big Data: Broad term which encompasses a variety of extremely large data sets.

Hadoop: Hadoop is an Apache distributed data processing open source software library that allows distributed processing of big data sets across clusters of computers using simple programming models. Built using Java, it is designed to scale up from single servers to thousands of machines, each offering local computation and storage.

MapReduce: MapReduce is a programming model and software framework for applications that rapidly process vast amounts of data in parallel on large clusters of compute nodes.

NoSQL: NoSQL commonly referred to as "Not Only SQL" represents a framework of databases that allows high-performance and quick processing of information at massive scale. It is a database infrastructure that adapts well to the heavy demands of big data.

Predictive Analytics: Predictive analytics is business intelligence technology which extracts information from existing data sets to determine patterns and predict future outcomes and trends. It helps to unravel unknown events of interest that is to happen in the future.

Social Media: Online communication channels and websites dedicated to community-based input, interaction, content-sharing and collaboration.

Chapter 5
Social Media in Knowledge Management

Srinivasan Vaidyanathan
VIT Business School, Chennai, India

Sudarsanam S. K.
VIT Business School, Chennai, India

ABSTRACT

This chapter discusses in detail about Knowledge Management and how Social Media tools and platforms can be used for Knowledge Management and how they can be integrated into Knowledge Management system. This chapter explains the key aspects of Knowledge Management and Social Media and how Social media can be used to capture both tacit and explicit knowledge and also to share knowledge among the communities of practice both within organizations and also outside the organizations. The chapter provides an overview of using social media to enhance knowledge management and collaboration in a corporate context and gives an insight on how firms get the most value from social media tools like wikis, blogs, microblogging, social tagging and some such similar tools in Knowledge Management. Further research directions based on the review of the literature are proposed.

BACKGROUND

Importance

As novel and evolving technologies, the integration of social tools into knowledge management programs in corporates is gaining utmost importance. Many corporates have been leveraging certain type of social media tools like microblogging and wikis to collect and share knowledge. Social Media has the potential to reinvent the management of knowledge and communication inside and outside the organizational borders. Recent innovations in knowledge management have been associated with emerging concepts such as Web 2.0, enterprise social software, knowledge management 2.0, corporate semantic web, harnessing the collective intelligence, and open innovation. These novel technologies along with the associated emerging concepts are recognized to be critical for creating competitive success in a global

DOI: 10.4018/978-1-5225-0846-5.ch005

business environment. For example, social media can be exploited as a driver for innovation within and outside the company's boundaries. So the importance of the chapter is that how companies may explore these new ways of managing knowledge, communicating and innovating in order to gain or maintain their competitive advantage.

Implication to Organizations

With the current popularity of Internet and Internet based social media, these platforms have become one of the most vibrant and dynamic source of user interaction for large multinational organizations serving millions of customers. These organizations are utilizing their accounts in social media like Facebook and Twitter for interacting with customers, publishing their offers and important announcements and getting user opinions, complaints and feedbacks.

Let us consider the scenario of a large Telecom major. It is serving millions of individual customers who have various types of queries and complaints to be made. The company encourages its customers to post their queries or complaints on its Facebook page or Twitter handle and these are resolved by dedicated executives working online. Such a large company will receive hundreds and thousands of posts in their page daily. If there is a way to effectively store and retrieve relevant knowledge from these posts over a period of history, the executive management can make use of this information to make strategic decisions and plan and implement Business processes.

For example, by exclusively analyzing the geographical trend of the number of network related complaints generated in the past 2-3 months, the management can identify in which telecom circle the network of the company need additional investment. Such specific investment will not only give ROI but also leads to customer satisfaction and improves customer confidence. There are numerous other types of business critical information and knowledge that can be extracted out of the user data.

INTRODUCTION

The 20th anniversary of the landing of an American on the surface of the Moon occasioned many bittersweet reflections. Sweet was the celebration of the historic event itself... Bitter, for those same enthusiasts, was the knowledge that during the twenty intervening years much of the national consensus that launched this country on its first lunar adventure had evaporated... (Fries, S. 1992).

Historian with NASA, USA, here, Fries expressed a deep regret on the fact that if KM had been introduced in the management of the Space's project at NASA, the wealth of knowledge that were accumulated in those who were involved in the expedition (or project) would not have been lost.

Perhaps this sounds a bit ironical. A common and obvious thought should be that NASA, being the headquarter of US's space projects and the origin of many breakthroughs in science and technologies would have the capability to retain the vast amount of knowledge that was generated behind their successful space missions. But, as Fries' study found out, the reality is that most of these knowledge that should have been captured and retained were somehow lost when those who were involved retired, moved on to other opportunities, etc. Having said that, yet another thought should be that, some of that knowledge must have been documented one way or another in notebooks, records that have been used by those who were involved. Even if that would be true, trying to uncover, dig out and pull together these disparate sources of information now will incur magnitudes of efforts that could have been done when a suitable mechanism for systematic Knowledge Management were in place from the start. Seeing from the NASA example and its ramifications, it would not be reasonable to consider "knowledge" as not just something abstract, intangible, but the presence/absence of relevant knowledge can make a difference in an organization's performance capacity.

Knowledge has become the key resource, for a nation's military strength as well as for its economic strength... is fundamentally different from the traditional key resources of the economist – land, labor, and even capital...we need systematic work on the quality of knowledge and the productivity of knowledge ... the performance capacity, if not the survival, of any organization in the knowledge society will come increasingly to depend on those two factors" (Drucker, 1994). As heard from the incredible words of the management Guru, it is evident that knowledge is a key resource and the systematic work on quality and productivity of knowledge is key for the performance capacity of an organization in knowledge society.

It is clear from the above scholarly evidences, Knowledge is trapped in the information silos like emails or on human minds in the form of tacit knowledge. Either knowledge is not captured and made well available with others at the right time or knowledge is evaporated when the project team gets dismantled or the individual members leave the organization. The challenge becomes manifold when the project has a virtual or distributed team organization. Pawlowski & Pirkkalainen (2013), claim that a focus point for research is on distributed teams (local to global, small vs massive), the type of challenges they face, how could social software support in terms of integration with their work, how could they ensure adoption and how could it bridge the gap to other communities or collaborators and setting clear policies that governs and differentiates between internal and external work, customer relations etc. This vindicates that problem will have to be looked at using different theoretical and practical lenses when it comes to Knowledge Management in a distributed team environment.

Knowledge Management Systems should synergize between - the social and structural mechanisms for promoting knowledge discovery, capturing, sharing, application and bleeding-edge IT. The emergence and impact of Social Media makes us rewire knowledge management approaches and poses completely new challenges. Social media has recently emerged as a promising technology for knowledge management. Adopting Social Media has been of paramount importance in corporates as they struggle to manage their exponentially growing volume of vital corporate knowledge thereby getting over core issues with existing knowledge management approaches that are behavioral and technical as called out by Reichental (2013). He goes on to say that many of the benefits we experience in the consumer web space — effective searching, grouping of associated unstructured data sources, and ranking of relevance — will become basic features of enterprise solutions. A heavy reliance on knowledge and IT by corporates to constantly innovate and create business value is a strategic imperative. Several major trends have been identified and analyzed in marrying knowledge management and social media. Increased adoption of social technologies, mobile platforms, business systems on cloud which also helps in the adoption of social media and mobile gadgets are to name a few. These are instrumental in the transformation of knowledge management into social media business.

The purpose of this chapter is:

- To present the past and current status of research on the adoption of social media in Knowledge Management.

- To familiarize the audience with relevant literature and research in this area and to inform what has already been discovered.
- To demonstrate the relationships amongst the prior research after a critical analysis.
- To identify gaps, inconsistencies and discrepancies in the literature.
- To define key concepts and to determine areas that warrant further investigations and research.

KNOWLEDGE MANAGEMENT

Knowledge Management is the process of gathering a firm's collective expertise wherever it resides – in databases, on paper, or in people's heads – and distributing it to where it can help produce the biggest payoff (Justin, 1997). Knowledge Management is the discipline of capturing knowledge-based competencies and then storing and diffusing that knowledge into business, in a systematic and organized manner to improve firm's performance (KPMG, 2000). These core competencies should not become core rigidities in the future. The focus should be on "doing the right thing" rather than "doing things right". Knowledge is not about technology but about mapping processes and exploiting the knowledge database. It is about applying technology to people's minds. This implies that Knowledge Management involves people, technology and organizational processes in overlapping parts (Awad & Ghaziri, 2008).

Wiig (1997) proposed that the objectives of Knowledge Management is "to maximize an enterprise's knowledge-related effectiveness and returns from knowledge assets" through systematic, explicit and deliberate building, renewal and application of knowledge". Rastogi (2000) suggested that Knowledge Management is "a systematic and integrative process of coordinating organization-wide activities of acquiring, creating, storing, sharing, diffusing, developing, and deploying knowledge by individuals and groups in pursuit of major organizational goals".

An integrated KM cycle comprising of three major stages of KM, organizational culture and KM technologies was put together by Dalkir (2005). The three stages of KM include: 1) knowledge capture and/or creation; 2) knowledge sharing and dissemination and 3) knowledge acquisition and application and they interact as given in the Figure 1. The three stages of KM supported by technologies are facilitated by a favorable Organizational Culture that promotes information and knowledge sharing.

Knowledge Management has several integral parts which need to be ensured for the successful implementation and sustenance:

- Using accessible knowledge from outside sources
- Embedding and storing knowledge in business processes, products, and services
- Representing knowledge in databases and documents
- Promoting knowledge growth through the organization's culture and incentives
- Transferring and sharing knowledge throughout the organization, local and global
- Assessing the value of knowledge assets and impact on a regular basis

SOCIAL MEDIA AND KNOWLEDGE MANAGEMENT

Social media refers to the means of interaction among people in which they create, share, and/or exchange information and ideas in virtual communities and networks (Toni, Bäck, Helonen, Heinonen, 2008).

Figure 1. The three stages of Knowledge Management

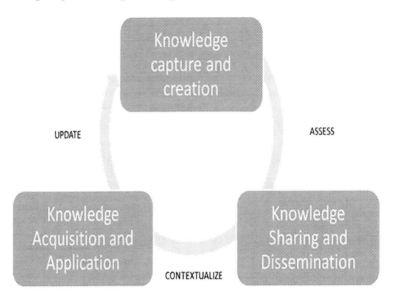

Andreas and Michael (2010) define social media as "a group of Internet-based applications that build on the ideological and technological foundations of Web 2.0 and that allow the creation and exchange of user-generated content." Furthermore, social media depends on mobile and web-based technologies to create highly interactive platforms through which individuals and communities share, co-create, discuss, and modify user-generated content. It introduces substantial and pervasive changes to communication between organizations, communities, and individuals (Jan, Hermkens, 2011). Social Media engagement in corporates is conceived as ingraining knowledge creation and integration through socialization within an extended value network.

A HBR Blog written by Bradley and McDonald (2011) from Gartner, states, Social media & knowledge management seem very similar. Both involve people using technology to access information. Both require individuals to create information intended for sharing. Both profess to support collaboration. But there's a big difference.

Knowledge management is what company management tells the employees that they need to know, based on what they think is important. It reflects a hierarchical view of knowledge to match hierarchical view of the organization.

Social media is how peers show their fellow colleagues what they think is important, based on their experience and in a way that they can judge for themselves. It's chaotic by comparison. There is no predefined index, no prequalified knowledge creators, no knowledge managers and ostensibly little to no structure.

Recognizing the differences and getting the value out of both is a strategic imperative. Business leaders recognize that engagement is the best way to glean value from the knowledge exchanged in social media — and not by seeking to control social media with traditional Knowledge Management techniques. They may need to understand and appreciate the premise that Knowledge should be like water — free-flowing and permeating down and across your organization filling the cracks, floating good ideas to the top and lifting all boats.

Knowledge management (KM) systems today focus on centralized sets of repositories, organized around established business processes. They are expensive to implement and the long-term commitment of the major resources of their deployment, maintenance, and daily operation can be seen as a huge overhead. Subsequently, even customized solutions end up going unused, with the knowledge workers running these custom KM solutions not having the information technology (IT) tools to provide support for their responsibilities. Based on these underutilized KM systems, the continuing evolution of Social Media technologies (Web 2.0) is providing a new KM solution, a collaboration based solution (Levy, 2009). Social networking technologies provide immediate solutions to the large investments for the deployment, maintenance, and daily operations for today's Knowledge Management systems (Burrus, 2010; Diehl, Grabill, Hart-Davidson & Iyer, 2008). It is time for organizations to start looking at tomorrow's knowledge management solution and realize this new solution is a more efficient and effective model for today's enterprise knowledge management systems. Each time a new system is implemented; large investments into systems that have promised automation and seamless integration to share knowledge across the organization rarely become a reality (Fitzgerald & Parise 2009).

Social Media adoption by business firms has been steadily on the rise, with its applications extending to a range of corporate functions, beyond marketing and customer engagement, many of which can be construed as strategic. According to an annual survey conducted by Burson-Marsteller (2012), the number of firms among Fortune 100 companies engaging in Social Media has steadily increased Y-O-Y to a level of 87% in 2011.

Guenard, Katz, Bruno & Lipa (2013) had done a case study of a multinational organization and piloted the creation of a Virtual Technical Network with the following building blocks as shown in Figure 2.

This network enabled a new and better way of working. The network is a combination of social media tools and knowledge management principles with an underlying foundation of inclusive mindset and

Figure 2. Virtual technical network

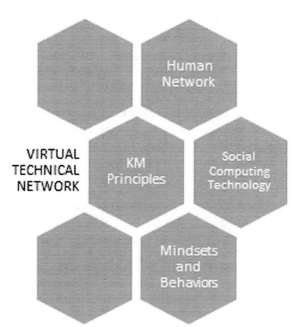

behaviors. It used both the physical technology like social media tools and social technologies like KM principles, network theories, cultural norms, behaviors etc. The firm, by using the VTN to locate and leverage needed knowledge and expertise throughout the organization, has been able to create a global community that not only feels included but also is able to make problems visible and solve them faster, accelerate decision making, and increase innovation. The success stories range from individuals who are better connected in the organization and can make new connections on demand, to improvements in knowledge transfer and application, to quantified business benefits measured by increased efficiencies and cost reductions. In a recent survey, most people in the organization indicated that the VTN is a valuable new way of working and a primary source of knowledge that they would recommend to others.

While the manifestations may differ, the above case study vindicates that there is a lot of potential to tie the knots of Adoption of Social Media in KM incorporating the fundamental building blocks.

CONCEPTUAL FRAMEWORKS FOR KNOWLEDGE MANAGEMENT IN SOCIAL MEDIA

Tacit Knowledge

The Knowledge that resides in the individual's head in forms of experience, know-how, insight, and so on, is the most valuable and significant part of human knowledge existed. It is perceived as an important asset in improving quality of work, decision making, organization learning, productivity, competitiveness, serving customers, producing goods, accuracy of task performance, and major time saving for individuals and organizations. As a result, tacit knowledge sharing is critical for individuals and organizations. (Panahi, Watson & Partridge, 2012). Traditional methods of Knowledge Management are getting irrelevant. The dynamic business environment require different set of KM processes and methodologies.

Social web paradigm can be helpful for tacit knowledge sharing through interactive and collaborative technologies, such as social networking and online discussion forums, where a community of specialized practitioners can share, critique and validate their collective experiential knowledge (Abidi, Cheah & Curran, 2005). Osimo (2005), Steininger, Rückel, Dannerer, & Roithmayr (2010) have also argued that social web platforms are particularly effective tools in facilitating tacit and informal knowledge sharing among individuals.

The framework proposed by Panahi et al., (2012) for Tacit Knowledge Sharing in Social media space involves Social Interactions, Experience Sharing, Informal Relationship & Networking, Observation & Listening and Mutual Swift Trust are key requirements for effect tacit knowledge sharing. Social media tools like Facebook, Pinterest, Tumblr, Google+, LinkedIn and other tools can be used to comply with the key requirements of tacit knowledge sharing. Social media enables synchronous communication in terms of chatting, discussions, story-telling etc. which in turn may facilitate tacit and expertise sharing among experts. Social media also provides opportunities for observation and imitation of best practices, expert locating, informal networking, and a friendly space to talk about ideas and ideals.

Judith (n.d) has proposed a model for optimizing knowledge sharing using social media as given in Figure 3.

The key findings and recommendations of his research are:

Figure 3. A model of optimizing knowledge sharing using social media

- Motivations information and entertainment are major predictors for the use of social mzedia for work purposes it is useful to arrange the social media platforms that are used within organizations so that they fulfill these motivations. Make sure that the platforms are informative, because that is what employees are searching for. But do not forget to create an environment that is entertaining and pleasant to work with.
- Experience has, direct influence on the use of social media for work purposes, so it is important that many employees are experienced in the use of social media. This can be achieved through courses and training, plan room for questions synchronous and a-synchronous, and an ambassador group can be appointed within the organization who are the precursors and who can help others. Reward the positive use of social media
- The attitude towards the use of social media actually appears to influence the use, so a positive attitude is desirable because then the use will increase.
- The organization culture has a positive effect on the level of knowledge sharing within organizations when it supports sharing knowledge. Therefore it is important that within organizations it is expected that everyone actively contributes to the registration and transfer of knowledge and that by doing this contributes to the success of the organization. That employees are encouraged to do so.

Chun Ho Chan, Kai Wah, Wing Yi Lee, Kim To Chan, Kit Leung (2013) have proposed the coding framework of KM processes as given in Table 1.

The following table 2 provides the distribution of coded blogs and Facebook posts in the theme of KM processes. The table 2 figures represent the average number of blog entries / facebook posts that each participant contributed.

The Study of Chun Ho Chan et al., (2013) conclude that the Facebook enhances collaboration and facilitates exchange of ideas better than the blogs. Blogs are more like a diary or a one-way communication. Also, the various options and tools in facebook allows users to view, like, comment, exchange ideas and so this enhances collaboration and interaction. Blogs are restricted to communities of practice and Facebook is able to reach out to peers, subordinates and supervisors far more widely.

Jarche (2013) proposes an effective suite of enterprise social tools which can help organizations share knowledge, collaborate and communicate within Organizations. Also, he has proposed a framework for individual works on how to seek knowledge from social media, filter the information, create new information and then share information with social media if relevant. While the work teams share the complex

Table 1. Coding framework of KM processes

Theme		Definitions
Knowledge Capture:		
	Knowledge Reflection	Reflections on or discoveries of knowledge related to professional practices
	Experience Capture	Personal insights into the meaning and implications of professional experiences
Knowledge Sharing and Dissemination:		
	Knowledge Sharing	Sharing, disseminating or exchanging of ideas and knowledge among the individuals
	Posting questions	Questions that facilitate communication and discussion among users
	Providing feedback	Responses to another post that contribute to knowledge building or sharing
Knowledge Acquisition and Application:		
	Knowledge Construction	Discussion and co-construction on the understanding of a topic or knowledge aera
	Problem solving	Experience of applying knowledge in solving the problems encountered in professional practice

Table 2. Distribution of coded blogs and Facebook posts

	Blogs (n = 53) Mean	Facebook (n=20) Mean
Knowledge Capture	**5.25**	**25.35**
Knowledge Reflection	3.19	10.6
Experience Capture	2.06	14.75
Knowledge Sharing and dissemination	**2.20**	**7.4**
Information Sharing	1.7	1.4
Posting Questions	0.19	1.3
Providing Feedback	0.32	4.7
Knowledge Acquisition and Application:	**3.96**	**2.25**
Knowledge Construction	2.3	0.8
Problem Solving	1.66	1.45

knowledge, the CoPs solve problems and test new ideas, and the Social Networks increase innovation by promoting diversity of ideas thereby forming a connected enterprise as illustrated in Figures 4 and 5.

Individual workers can develop sense-making skills, using frameworks like PKM (Personal Knowledge Mastery), to continuously learn and put their learning to work. For example, they can seek new ideas from their social networks; make sense of these ideas by connecting with communities of practice; try new ideas out alone or with their work teams, and then share these ideas and practices. Essentially

Figure 4. Collaboration and cooperation promoted by enterprise social networks

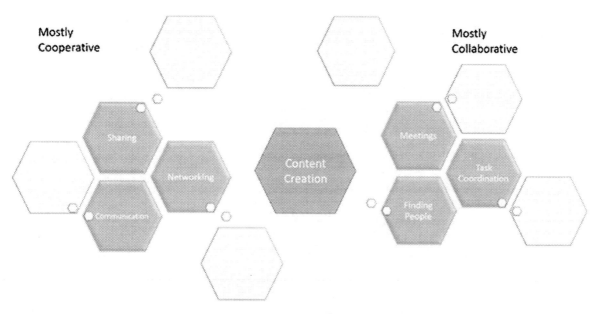

Figure 5. The connected enterprise by social networks

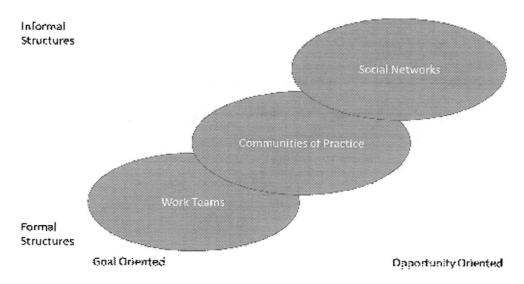

filtering from networks, creating knowledge individually and with teams, and then discerning with whom and when to share as illustrated in the Figure 6.

According to Jarche (2013), Enterprise knowledge sharing will never be as good as individual knowledge networks. Innovation outside of organizations will continue to evolve faster than inside. An organization with hybrid organizational structure that bridges the individual and organizational knowledge sharing will have a major advantage over the other organizations with traditional organization structures.

Figure 6. Personal knowledge mastery

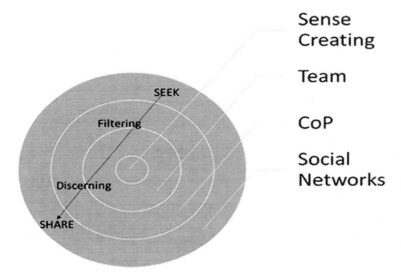

KNOWLEDGE MANAGEMENT USING SOCIAL MEDIA TOOLS

Facebook

Phosaard & Wiriyapinit (2011) work on Knowledge Management via Facebook provides an example of a project plan implemented in Facebook.

The following are the key steps in the implementation of a Project Plan in Facebook:

- The team members to have a Facebook id
- Project Manager to create a group for the team
- Project Manager makes the group private so that only the team members can access it
- Project documents and templates can be kept in google drive and link given to them for the team in Facebook project page
- All project communications can happen through Facebook posts and messengers
- Emails can be sent
- All the KM processes like socialization, externalization, combination and integration will naturally occur through Facebook

Pinterest

Knowledge creation and sharing can happen using Pinterest. The key infographics of the project like Project Plan, Work Breakdown structure, UML diagrams (design documents), Network diagrams (for workflow) etc can be created using Pinterest tools and link can be given to the blog or the Knowledge Management system for more details on the infographics. Also, the infographic can be shared to team members through the share option or by asking them to follow your updates in Pinterest. This way, the project documents can be shared with team members. If the documents are grouped in a unique name, then the team members can search the group name and access the relevant infographics and related KM system updates.

Knowledge Sharing in Social Media

Mvandermeer (2012) has compared the knowledge sharing processes between four most popular social media tools: Twitter, LinkedIn, Facebook and Yammer. His Key Knowledge sharing processes are

- Developing an understanding of 'who knows what',
- Using this understanding to allocate knowledge or information to others (giving knowledge), and
- Using this understanding to retrieve needed knowledge or information from others (receiving knowledge)

Mvandermeer's (2012) conclusions: For the process of developing an understanding of 'who knows what', Twitter scores significantly higher than other services, while Yammer scores significantly lower than most other services. Users of Twitter apparently have the feeling that they get to know a lot about each other through their communication. Because of the limited space for personal information in a Twitter profile, this understanding is likely to be stimulated by the high frequency of messages.

On allocating knowledge, Twitter scores again significantly higher than other services, while LinkedIn scores significantly lower.

For the process of retrieving knowledge, Twitter and Yammer turn out to be most used. The advantage of Twitter in this process is probably the fast communication of the tool. When posing a question, responses often follow quickly. The strong point of Yammer here is the possibility to ask colleagues for help and having the space for an in-depth answer.

This analysis shows that Twitter is a rather strong tool for knowledge sharing, which might support a common claim in the knowledge management literature that communication stimulates knowledge sharing. Twitter is built around communication. Fast and easy communication is the tool's key competence. LinkedIn is more used to build network and keep track of colleagues and friends rather than share knowledge.

Knowledge Sharing using Blogs: Blogs are an excellent social media tool for finding learning resources and for knowledge sharing. In many organizations it is compulsory for staff to use blogs to share knowledge with other staff and customers. *The benefits to organizations (from using blogs) were greater ability to share ideas, and improved access to experts.* In addition to posting information – text, photos, audio, and video blog's readers/followers can add comments, references, links, etc. and participate in a knowledge sharing process. There are many social media tools for creating blogs. Tumblr is a popular social media tool for creating blogs for sharing knowledge.

IMPLEMENTATION APPROACHES

Amongst others, researchers and practitioners have been continuously debating the impact of the adoption process on the success of social software (McAfee, 2009). Whether such applications should be implemented "top-down" (i.e. in the traditional way of implementing corporate software) or "bottom-up" (since corporate social software brings a paradigm shift) (Buhse & Stamer, 2008) is an important point in this debate. There have been arguments that considering force-fitting by management or voluntary adoption and support by employees is a false dichotomy. What should rather be discussed is devising the most adequate ways of management support to bottom-up adoption. Top-down implementation strategies based on management roles such as the Chief Knowledge Officer (CKO) can be found in abundance in the literature, especially in IT-based knowledge management studies. Classical KM approaches often ignore the perspective of knowledge workers (Han & Anantatmula, 2006), as well as the factors motivating knowledge workers to share their knowledge.

An important aspect of a knowledge management implementation strategy is setting knowledge management goals (Richter, Stocker, Muller & Avram, 2012) as given in Table 3.

A firm has to choose between top-down or bottom-up approaches aligning to their KM goals. Case studies by Richter et al., (2012) revealed that the implementation strategy was equally dominant on both. The firm has to strike a balance between exploration as "a continuous investigation of possible use cases for new (open) tools, through a participative approach" and promotion as "the intentional business-aligned and skilled use of the new tools focusing on well-defined usage potential".

An article by BSR STARS (2012), provides guidelines on the selection of the possible knowledge sharing tools that could be used by the communities with the aim to share knowledge with the wider audience. Strengths and Weaknesses that have emerged from their interviews with CoPs are also listed in the Table 4 in order to be able to make a balanced selection for a concrete case.

Table 3. Knowledge management goals

Main Goal	Characteristics of the Goal
Efficient, goal-oriented employee communication and avoidance of information overload	Implementation of open communication channels Support of employees' goal orientation by enhancing communication Improvement of employee-to-employee communication Prevention and control of information overload Decrease of e-mail usage
Efficient knowledge transfer	Preservation and restoration of internal knowledge Break up of knowledge silos Facilitation of intra-organizational knowledge transfer Better access to best practices
The establishment of networks of Experts	Improvement of networking among employees and identification of experts Connecting people with similar contexts, development of expert communities (e.g. yellow pages) Support for wisdom of crowds
Participation of employees and creation of open corporate culture	Sustainable involvement of employees i.e. each employee should be able to contribute actively Prevent employee anonymity within the organization Improve exchange and discussion among the employees to get better insights to support the corporate culture Development of a creative climate Openness of corporate culture allowing employees to participate more
Increased awareness and Transparency	Provide better visibility to common tasks and competences More transparency within decisions and processes Employees and management are aware of each other Cross-cutting issues can be revealed
Support for the innovation potential and secure the future viability of the enterprise	Innovation can be communicated faster and will be better understood Innovation can be initiated from inside and outside New systems guarantee future-orientation and flexibility Sustainability is demonstrated by including the younger generations

Table 4. Knowledge sharing tools and their strengths and weaknesses

Tool/technology	Dimensions	Aim, Example, Strengths and Weaknesses
Facebook	Participation	Community crates the page to the Facebook with the aim to share information/resources to the followers of their community page. Page can be created by focusing only on own community or on wider audience. By focusing on the community's internal communication, the specific information is shared only with the members. By focusing on the wider audience, the page is accessible for all the members and shared information is informative, commercial, focusing on latest news, achievements and so on. In the latter case, the Facebook becomes as part of the community webpage. Facebook's strength - most of the people are using it anyway; they don't have to register to another system. Facebook's weakness - community members may want to separate the personal life and professional life and not to usethe same account as part of the professional community.
Online conference tools (Flashmeeting, GoToMeeting, Skype)	Participation, Synchronous	Online conference tools promote the instant communication and knowledge and information sharing between the community members for increasing the sense of community. One of the members sets up the meeting, shares the link with the others and people join with their own devices to the online meeting. Strength - the possibility to communicate as often as needed and therefor to build the sense of community. The meetings can be in general later re-listened by those members who did not have a chance to participate. The weakness - rather related with the personal barriers than tool – people may be passive participants of the meeting
Google Drive, Dropbox	Reification	GoogleDrive and Dropbox enable to store online the great amounts of the community documents. Documents will be accessed only by selected members or by all the users, depends on the settings. Documents can be managed in different folders.
Twitter	Synchronous, group identity	Twitter is an online social networking site (also microblogging service) that enables users to send and read messages of up to 140 characters (tweets). Communities use Twitter usually with the promotion purposes. Strength – communities can make their websites alive with the Twitter feed in the website. Also it is one of the quickest ways to spread out the news to the larger audience and create awareness. Weakness – Twitter is not for internal communication, more with marketing purposes. Twitter works better for the community if several members continuously tweet. Another weakness is the poor long-term storing capabilities so that Twitter needs to be complemented with a storing tool (such as a weblog or wiki).
Wiki	Asynchronous, group identity	A wiki is a service that enables people to add, modify, or delete content in a collaborative environment. Knowledge sharing via wiki is often focusing more on knowledge creation than just simple information sharing. Usually the content in wiki is being commented, adapted, modified and joint knowledge is being created. Strengths – It is easy to collaboratively edit content. Supports very well a strong group identity and forces members to adapt their views to the group. Weakness – If there are heavy contributions from a large number of people, Wikis tend to get cluttered and it gets increasingly difficult to get an overview. So at some stage a wiki needs editorial roles and regulations.
Weblog	Asynchronous, group identity	A weblog is an informational site published on the web and consists of entries/posts typically displayed in reverse chronological order (the most recent post appears first). Weblogs of the communities are usually focusing on external partners and collaborators with the aim to share information nd knowledge. Usually such weblogs are open to everyone. Strength - weblogs are one of the easiest and quickest ways to reach the wider audience. Entries in the weblogs are usually open to the comments and therefore interesting discussions may occur. Weakness – dynamically updated weblog of the community presumes quite lot of time and therefore persons should be named who are responsible for writing blogposts.
LinkedIn, MeetUp	Group identity	Sites of social networking for people in professional occupations where people are contacting with others generally with the professional aim than personal aim. In general the users create their quite expanded CVs and decide to belong to the different groups. Communities or clusters can create their own pages where they share the information and users may become the members of the community or just follow the community in order to be aware of the latest information. Strengths – Most people are members in these services, so they are very quick to set up Weaknesses – The services are not open and tend to be closed towards outside tools and contents. Therefore the community is dependent on the services offered by the provider, and other services can usually not be integrated easily.

OPPORTUNITIES AND CHALLENGES

Opportunities

In the long run, social media in the enterprise will likely be a boon for global knowledge management. It should mean that many of the benefits we experience in the consumer web space — effective searching, grouping of associated unstructured data sources, and ranking of relevance — will become basic features of enterprise solutions. It's likely we'll see the increasing overlap between public and private data to enhance the value of the private data.

Social media takes knowledge and makes it highly iterative. It creates content as a social object. That is, content is no longer a point in time, but something that is part of a social interaction, such as a discussion. It easily disassembles the pillars of structure as it evolves. As examples: content in a micro-blogging service can shift meaning as a discussion unfolds; conversations in enterprise social networks that link people and customer data can defy categorization; and internal blogs and their comments don't lend themselves to obvious taxonomy.

It's likely that social-media-driven knowledge management will require much less of the "management" component. Historically we've spent far too much time cleaning up the data, validating, and categorizing it. In the future, more of our time will be spent analyzing all the new knowledge that is being created through our social interactions. Smart analysis can result in new insight, and that has powerful value for organizations.

Since businesses and teams operate virtually, social networks can make it easier to manage knowledge with contacts all around the world.

Knowledge management systems integrated with social media help maintain continuous innovations that lead to the creation of new goods and / or services and establish new business processes.

Challenges

According to a survey published by Knowledge Management Review (2011), the two most important challenges in launching KM initiatives are "encouraging cultural adoption of KM" and "encouraging people to share".

The shift to the adoption of enterprise social computing, greatly influenced by consumerization, points to one emergent observation: the future is about managing unstructured content. Let's consider the magnitude of this for a moment. Years of effort, best practices, and technologies for supporting organizational insight in the form of curated, structured insight has to be rethought. It's an enormous challenge, but it may in fact be the best thing that ever happened to knowledge management.

The assumption that an unmediated open group of resources will always come to a better conclusion than a single expert or closed group is dangerous. Companies can collect information from myriad sources and then perform some sort of averaging. In this case, the whole is equal to the sum of its parts, but the key is to maintain the right balance between diversity and expertise. Certain problems are more appropriately addressed by a diversity-based approach than others, but no amount of diversity will help if the group is completely ignorant of the issues. Therefore, firms need to decide which people to involve in group decisions and whether or not each participant should be given an equal voice.

The essence of Web 2.0 is increased interactivity. The more people participate, the more likely that they could divulge proprietary information about themselves or their employers. Regardless of the specific technologies are used, it is how Web 2.0 is implemented and how the associated risks are managed that will be most important. A viewpoint on risks per Nancy Dupre & Frederick (2009) shared the same. Companies must prepare themselves to handle the legal and operational risks abound with Social Networking.

INDUSTRY AND GEOGRAPHICAL DISPERSION

Social Media adoption in global KM cuts across industrial sectors including Financial Services, Insurance, Manufacturing and logistics and Supply Chain, Electrical and Electronics, Education, HR, Software Services, Travel etc. almost all penetrating the entire length and breadth of industrial sectors and lines of businesses. Some of the examples from literature studied reveal this fact. Case and references by Venkataraman & Ranjan Das (2013) is a classic example covering companies across sectors on strategic decisions and social media. Komaromi & Erickson (2011) study on social media use by North American insurance firms vouches for its penetration in Insurance Industry. There have been many evidences on Web 2.0 adoption in education industry.

Geographical coverage is almost all global, though the literature survey hasn't sifted across much of scholarly research from the middle-east geographies. NA and European organizations top the chart. Adoption has been widely studied in these geographies. APAC comes next. Almost all of references and citations used in this review cover the broad spectrum of NA, Europe and APAC regions. There have been some articles and papers touched upon from Australia as well.

CONSISTENCIES AND RELEVANCE

From what has been explored and reviewed in the available literature:

- The dynamic, global and interdisciplinary nature of knowledge and its effective management via implementation of relevant systems is widely researched.
- Knowledge Management practices have been researched intensely in the last ten years and there is a growing body of literature on this area. Importance of state-of-the-art technological implementations for the success of businesses is well emphasized.
- There has been common consensus on the newer school of thoughts on Knowledge Management with the adoption of social media technologies. The paradigm shift facilitated by corporate social software implementations, explaining how technical functionalities support new ways of interaction and thus provides for fundamental changes in Knowledge Management processes has been dealt with universally.
- The role of social networks and collaborative culture in knowledge management processes has been widely accepted. There exists a lot of literature around the adoption of Web 2.0 to collaborate and contribute.
- The virtual evolution and democratization of knowledge has been discussed by many researchers and practitioners. Chosen topic has close association with previous studies and reviewed literature.

INCONSISTENCIES AND GAPS

- Social Media has trained its attention largely on relevance to marketing, customer service, public relations and outreach. Despite possessing characteristics which can potentially position firms as distinct from their competitors and / or create competitive advantages through a variety of mechanisms, all of which may speak to Social Media's strategic potentiality, extant scholarly research has paid very little attention to the relationship between Social Media and a firm's strategic decision making (SDM), per se, in knowledge management dimension or a firm's strategic agenda. A quick perusal of some prominent general management / strategic management focused journals underscores this gap in Social Media related literature (Venkataraman & Ranjan Das, 2013).
- In spite of the massive coverage of Web 2.0 technologies, scholarly research on the topic, particularly in relation to commercial applications, has been limited. Businesses looking to better compete through new means have embraced Web 2.0 but have lacked reliable studies on exactly how and why such applications will help them.
- During the process of surveying the literature, it has been learned that due to the interdisciplinary use of knowledge and the different meanings attributed to knowledge management, there are major differences from study to study. However, some goals are present in almost every study. Such goals are the creation of knowledge repositories, the facilitation of access to knowledge and knowledge sharing and the articulation of knowledge as a vital resource for companies.
- While literature exists on Knowledge Management, Social Media and Virtual teams in their entirety, scholarly research that strings all the three together has been ostensibly sparse.
- Almost all of literature reviewed dealt with exploratory studies and conceptual frameworks. There has been very few empirical research and observational studies come across.

FURTHER RESEARCH DIRECTIONS

As typical of exploratory piece of work, this chapter essentially done to clear the grounds on whether the potentiality exists for Social Media to be seen as a linchpin for sustaining Knowledge Management. While the arguments presented in this paper affirms this notion, we believe that we have scraped only the tip of the ice-berg, specifically since this was developed on top of several limitations particularly that of a paucity of established Social Media related theories in scholarly research and still evolving status of Social Media adoption. However, the key concepts defined and critically analyzed serves to identify the following areas which hold potential for further investigations and research:

- More empirical and case referenced research on social media adoption in Knowledge Management practices
- Scholarly research on Web 2.0 implementation strategies w.r.t. commercial and business applications

CONCLUSION

As set out earlier, this literature review has sought to explore the adoption of social media in Knowledge Management, specifically in terms of the influence this emerging and evolving phenomenon on the various aspects of knowledge management. This review paints a vital area of research with many useful and interesting studies in the recent years. By virtue of its unique and powerful attributes, particularly those which make for speedy, multi-way, transparent communication, Social Media could potentially result in firms being engaged with most current knowledge practices. The characteristics of Knowledge Management, and Social Media were individually reviewed and an attempt made to string both of them together. This study embarked upon demonstrating the relationships amongst the prior researches and to the chosen topic after a critical analysis of the literature. Top five consistencies and relevance and inconsistencies and gaps have been culled out and presented as well. It has been observed that using the lens of Social Media and looking through the related knowledge management practices have not been researched much or addressed sparsely by scholarly literature with only exploratory studies.

REFERENCES

Abidi, S. S. R., Cheah, Y. N., & Curran, J. (2005). A knowledge creation info-structure to acquire and crystallize the tacit knowledge of health-care experts. *IEEE Transactions on Information Technology in Biomedicine, 9*(2), 193–204. doi:10.1109/TITB.2005.847188 PMID:16138536

Andreas K., & Michael H. (2010). Users of the world, unite! The challenges and opportunities of social media. *Business Horizons, 53*(1), 59-68.

Awad, E. M., & Ghaziri, H. (2008). *Knowledge Management.* Pvt. Ltd., Licensees of Pearson Education in South Asia.

Barnes, N. D., & Barnes, F. R. (2009). *Equipping your organization for the social networking game.* Information Management, Arma International.

Bradley, A., & McDonald, M. (2011). *Social Media versus Knowledge Management.* Retrieved from http://blogs.hbr.org/2011/10/social-media-versus-knowledge/

BSR STARS. (2012). *Knowledge Sharing Tools and Practices.* Retrieved from www.bsrstars.se

Buhse, W., & Stamer, S. (2008). *Enterprise 2.0 - Die Kunst, loszulassen.* Berlin: Rhombos.

Burrus, D. (2010). Social networks in the workplace: The risk and opportunity of Business 2.0. *Strategy and Leadership, 38*(4), 50–54. doi:10.1108/10878571011059674

Burson-Marsteller. (2012). *Burson-Marsteller 2011 fortune global 100 social media study.* New York, NY: Burson-Marsteller. Retrieved from http://www.burson-marsteller.com/innovation_and_insights / blogs_and_podcasts/BM_Blog/default.aspx

Chun Ho Chan, R., Kai Wah, S., Wing Yi Lee, C., Kim To Chan, B., & Kit Leung, C. (2013). Knowledge Management using Social Media: A Comparative Study between Blogs and Facebook. *Proceedings of the American Society for Information Science and Technology, 50*(1), 1–9. doi:10.1002/meet.14505001069

Dalkir, K. (2005). *Knowledge Management in Theory and Practice*. Burlington, MA: Elsevier.

Diehl, A., Grabill, J. T., Hart-Davidson, W., & Iyer, V. (2008). Grassroots: Supporting the knowledge work of everyday life. *Technical Communication Quarterly, 17*(4), 413–434. doi:10.1080/10572250802324937

Drucker, P. (1994). *Definition on the "need for Knowledge Management"*. Academic Press.

Fitzgerald, M. (2009). Why social computing aids Knowledge Management. *CIO*, 1-5. Retrieved April 15, 2009, from http://www.cio.com/article/395113/Why_Social_Computing_Aids_Knowledge_Management

Fries, S. (1992). *NASA Engineers and the Age of Apollo*. Retrieved from http://ntrs.nasa.gov/archive/nasa/casi.ntrs.nasa.gov/19920019101.pdf

Guenard, R., Katz, J., Bruno, S., & Lipa, M. (2013). Enabling a New Way of Working through Inclusion and Social Media. *OD Practitioner, 45*(4).

Han, B. M., & Anantatmula, V. (2006). Knowledge management in IT organizations from employee's perspective. In *Proceedings of the 39th Hawaii International Conference on System Sciences*. IEEE Conference Publications

Jarche, H. (2013). *The Knowledge Sharing Paradox*. Retrieved from http://jarche.com/2013/03/the-knowledge-sharing-paradox/?goback=.gde_4453809_member_241895872

Judith, Z. (n.d.). *Social Media adds to knowledge sharing*. Retrieved from http://essay.utwente.nl/63098/1/Zande_van_der_Judith_-s_1254235_scriptie.pdf

Justin, H. (1997). Knowing What We Know. *Information Week*, 46.

Komaromi, K., & Erickson, S. (2011). Using Social Media to Build Community. *Competition Forum, 9*(2).

KPMG Consulting. (2000). *Knowledge Management Research Report 2000*. Retrieved from http://www.providersedge.com/docs/km_articles/KPMG_KM_Research_Report_2000.pdf

Levy, M. (2009). WEB 2.0 implications on knowledge management. *Journal of Knowledge Management, 13*(1), 120–134. doi:10.1108/13673270910931215

McAfee, A. (2009). *Enterprise 2.0: New Collaborative Tools for Your Organization's Toughest Challenges*. Boston, MA: McGraw-Hill Professional.

Mvandermeer. (2012). *Knowledge Sharing Through Social Media Use*. Retrieved from https://www.scanyours.com/knowledge-sharing-through-social-media-use-3/

Osimo, D. (2005). Web 2.0 in government: Why and how. Institute for Prospective Technological Studies (IPTS), Joint Research Center (JRC), European Commission.

Panahi, S., Watson, J., & Partridge, H. (2012). Social Media and Tacit Knowledge Sharing: Developing a Conceptual Model. World Academy of Science, Engineering and Technology.

Parise, S. (2009). Social media networks: What do they mean for knowledge management? *Journal of Information Technology Case and Application Research, 11*(2), 1–11. doi:10.1080/15228053.2009.10856156

Pawlowski, J., & Pirkkalainen, H. (2013). *The use of social software for Knowledge Management in globally distributed settings*. Retrieved, November 2013, from http://www.slideshare.net/jan.pawlowski/research-issues-in-knowledge-management-and-social-media

Phosaard, S., & Wiriyapinit, M. (2011). Knowledge Management via Facebook: Building a Framework for Knowledge Management on a Social Network by Aligning Business, IT and Knowledge Management. *Lecture Notes in Engineering and Computer Science, 2192*(1), 1855–1860.

Rastogi, P. N. (2000). Knowledge management and intellectual capital - The new virtuous reality of competitiveness. *Human Systems Management, 19*(1), 39–48.

Reichental, J. (2013). *Knowledge Management in the age of social media*. Retrieved from, http://radar.oreilly.com/2011/03/knowledge-management-social-media.html

Richter, A., Stocker, A., Muller, S., & Avram, G. (2012). Knowledge management goals revisited: A cross-sectional analysis of social software adoption in corporate environments. The Journal of Information and Knowledge Management Systems, 43(2).

Steininger, K., Rückel, D., Dannerer, E., & Roithmayr, F. (2010). Healthcare knowledge transfer through a web 2.0 portal: An Austrian approach. *International Journal of Healthcare Technology and Management, 11*(1/2), 13–30. doi:10.1504/IJHTM.2010.033272

Toni A., Bäck, A., Halonen, M., & Heinonen, S. (2008, December). Social media road maps exploring the futures triggered by social media. *VTT Research Notes*.

Venkataraman, S., & Das, R. (2013). The Influence of Corporate Social Media on Firm Level Strategic Decision Making. *International Journal of E-Business Research, 9*(1), 1–20. doi:10.4018/jebr.2013010101

Wiig, K. (1997). Knowledge Management: Where Did it Come From and Where Will It Go? *Expert Systems with Applications, 13*(1), 1–14. doi:10.1016/S0957-4174(97)00018-3

KEY TERMS AND DEFINITIONS

CKO: Chief Knowledge Officer who is responsible for formulating and implementing knowledge management strategies in an organization.

Explicit Knowledge: Explicit knowledge is knowledge that can be readily articulated, codified, accessed and verbalized. It can be easily transmitted to others. Most forms of explicit knowledge can be stored in certain media. The information contained in encyclopedias and textbooks are good examples of explicit knowledge.

Knowledge Management and Knowledge Management Systems/Solutions/Services: Knowledge management (KM) is the process of capturing, developing, sharing, and effectively using organizational knowledge. It refers to a multi-disciplinary approach to achieving organizational objectives by making the best use of knowledge. Knowledge management efforts typically focus on organizational objectives such as improved performance, competitive advantage, innovation, the sharing of lessons learned, integration and continuous improvement of the organization. KM efforts overlap with organizational learning and may be distinguished from that by a greater focus on the management of knowledge as a strategic asset and a focus on encouraging the sharing of knowledge. It is an enabler of organizational learning.

Knowledge Sharing: Knowledge sharing is an activity through which knowledge (namely, information, skills, or expertise) is exchanged among people, friends, families, communities (for example, Wikipedia), or organizations.

PKM: Personal Knowledge Mastery to continuously learn and put learning to work through social networks.

Social Media, Social Media Networks and Social Media Tools: Social media are computer-mediated tools that allow people or companies to create, share, or exchange information, career interests, ideas, and pictures/videos in virtual communities and networks. Social media is defined as "a group of Internet-based applications that build on the ideological and technological foundations of Web 2.0, and that allow the creation and exchange of user-generated content."

Social Media Technologies: Social media technologies take on many different forms including blogs, business networks, enterprise social networks, forums, microblogs, photo sharing, products/services review, social bookmarking, social gaming, social networks, video sharing, and virtual worlds.

Social Networking and Social Networking Site (SNS): A social networking service (also social networking site or SNS) is a platform to build social networks or social relations among people who share similar interests, activities, backgrounds or real-life connections. A social network service consists of a representation of each user (often a profile), his or her social links, and a variety of additional services such as career services. Social network sites are web-based services that allow individuals to create a public profile, create a list of users with whom to share connections, and view and cross the connections within the system."

Tacit Knowledge: The Knowledge that resides in the individual's head in forms of experience, know-how, insight, and so on, is the most valuable and significant part of human knowledge existed. It is perceived as an important asset in improving quality of work, decision making, organization learning, productivity, competitiveness, serving customers, producing goods, accuracy of task performance, and major time saving for individuals and organizations.

Web 2.0: Web 2.0 describes World Wide Web sites that emphasize user-generated content, usability, and interoperability. A Web 2.0 site may allow users to interact and collaborate with each other in a social media dialogue as creators of user-generated content in a virtual community, in contrast to Web sites where people are limited to the passive viewing of content.

Section 3
Social Media Metrics

Chapter 6
Social Media Metrics in an Academic Setup

Tasleem Arif
Baba Ghulam Shah Badshah University, India

Rashid Ali
Aligarh Muslim University, India

ABSTRACT

Social media is perhaps responsible for largest share of traffic on the Internet. It is one of the largest online activities with people from all over the globe making its use for some sort of activity. The behaviour of these networks, important actors and groups and the way individual actors influence an idea or activity on these networks, etc. can be measured using social network analysis metrics. These metrics can be as simple as number of likes on Facebook or number of views on YouTube or as complex as clustering co-efficient which determines future collaborations on the basis of present status of the network. This chapter explores and discusses various social network metrics which can be used to analyse and explain important questions related to different types of networks. It also tries to explain the basic mathematics behind the working of these metrics. The use of these metrics for analysis of collaboration networks in an academic setup has been explored and results presented. A new metric called "Average Degree of Collaboration" has been defined to quantify collaborations within institutions.

INTRODUCTION

Man's desire to quantify things is as old as the mankind itself. We derive great pleasure when we are able to represent something in terms of numbers particularly if the measurement at hand is of qualitative nature. Social networks have been around since time immemorial but they attracted attention of the sociologists only in the 1930's (Cooley et al., 1997). Before the advent of computers analysis and understanding of large scale complex networks was almost impossible. The computational power of computers and their ability to store large amounts of data has provided the much needed impetus to the analysis and understanding of large scale complex social networks. These networks have attracted huge attention from the researchers and policy makers because they are being used for a variety of purposes.

DOI: 10.4018/978-1-5225-0846-5.ch006

In the recent past, online social networks have been used for political opinion making, discussing the pros and cons of a product or service, discussing events, etc. It has been observed that these networks have a great deal of impact on the strategy of political figures, political parties, organizations, industries, etc. because they have to adopt to the mood and requirements of the target audience as opinions are formed and revised collectively not individually.

In this contemporary world networks can be found in abundance and everyone talks about them (Katzmair, 2014). A social network is constituted by a number of units (nodes, actors, etc.) that are connected to each other by a defined relationship e.g. "*alice* cites *bob*", "*alice* sends 5 email messages a week to *bob*", "*alice* and *bob* use the same product", "*alice* and *bob* belong to same organization", etc. There are a few wrinkles-the units may be persons, organizations, cities, journal articles, or other types of entities; the relationships may be uni-directional or bi-directional; and the linking relationships may represent categorical relationships or intensity relationships. "*alice* cites *bob*" is a uni-directional relationship; "*alice* cites *bob* very often" is a uni-directional relationship recording intensity; "*alice* and *bob* are friends" is a bi-directional relationship; "*alice* and *bob* are close friends" is a bi-directional relationship recording intensity.

In simple terms a network is an organized collection of nodes or actors and their interconnections or relationships (Jin et al., 2006). Networks can be as simple as blood relations between two individuals or as complex as the World Wide Web. Such networks, where the relationships between actors have some sort of social bearing, are called as social networks. Examples of social networks include e-mail communication networks, economic or business networks, cooperative networks, academic networks. Though the type of link or relationship between actors in any of these networks may be completely different from those in others, they can still be analyzed using a multidisciplinary science called as Social Network Analysis (SNA).

Orgnet.com [1] defines SNA as a tool for analysing relationships and flows between various entities like people, groups, organizations, computers, URLs, etc. In social networks, nodes represents entities like people, groups, organizations, etc. whereas, the edges represents the relationships or flows between the nodes. Using SNA techniques one can have both a visual and a mathematical analysis of relationships in social networks. As a branch of sociology, SNA has emerged as a formal discipline that has borrowed a lot from mathematical notions of graph theory (Mika, 2007). The developments in SNA that we see today are an outcome of contributions from a multitude of disciplines like sociology, social psychology, anthropology, mathematics and computer science (Mika, 2007).

Study of the patterns of interaction and communication in collaborations between various actors has already attracted significant interest from scholars (Wagner & Leydesdorff, 2005a; Wagner & Leydesdorff, 2005b; Wagner & Leydesdorff, 2008; Luo & Hsu, 2009). Advances in data mining and recent developments in social network visualization software have facilitated the study and analysis of intensity and dynamics of these relationships in a visual or graphical manner (Luo & Hsu, 2009). Representation of interactions between entities in terms of nodes and edges i.e. graphs, where nodes represents entities and edges represents interactions, allows one to apply graph theory for the analysis and understanding of underlying collaborations (Luo & Hsu, 2009). Such a study is capable of finding and describing the interactions at micro, macro and universal level.

SNA defines actors and their interactions in quantifiable terms using a set of metrics commonly referred to as social network analysis metrics. Since the use of SNA is not limited to a particular field or type of network the choice of metrics is dependent upon the particular type of network. For example, in an online social network some of metrics are different from those used to model an academic social network. *Engagement* is one such metrics used by Facebook[2] to express reach of an actor in quantifiable terms whereas it may not find any application in an academic social network. SNA can also be used to study dynamic aspects of social networks and for having superior insights into the behaviour of complex systems (Katzmair, 2014).

SNA metrics can be used to understand the behaviour of actors and their relationships. Simple metrics like '*Degree*' provide the number of connections an actor has in the network without taking into consideration the quality of those connections. In SNA the quality of connections can also be expressed in quantities terms as we shall see later in this Chapter. Advance metrics like '*clustering co-efficient*' help predict future connection in the network. For example in a co-authorship based academic social network clustering co-efficient quantifies the possibility of connections between two authors who does not have any direct co-authorship relationship till now but are likely to co-author a publication directly in the future.

The rest of this Chapter is organized in the following way. We first briefly discuss the background and the need for social media metrics. In the next section a discussion on social network analysis and various levels of analysis is provided. This section also explains various social media metrics and the mathematics behind the working of these metrics is also provided. The section next to it explains the role and relevance of these metrics in the analysis and understanding of academic social networks. Then we briefly present the analytical result of a study conducted previously that uses SNA metrics for analysing four different academic collaboration (co-authorship) networks. Towards the end we outline some future research directions followed by conclusions of the Chapter.

BACKGROUND

Social networks have their background in social sciences which primarily use qualitative means of interpreting and analysing things. Because of their social sciences background some of the basic questions about a social network are easy to formulate but difficult to assess. From a network perspective these questions could be related to any of the three: individuals, a group of individuals or the entire network. In social network analysis, one would like to know what groups of individuals are unusually closely interconnected with each other, relative to the average for the population as a whole, among other things. Some of the basic questions that one may have about networks of people include:

- Who is connected to whom and how?
- What is the strength of their connection?
- What is the driving force behind such connections?
- Is there any inclination towards preferential attachment in the network?
- Are there some individuals or group of individuals who are more important for the network than others?
- Does the network have some groups where actors are unusually well connected?
- Are there sub-groupings of individuals who are more closely connected to each other than they are to others in the network?

Though individuals (nodes or actors) have always been at the forefront in social network analysis but the trend is changing. The focus is on the way actors behave in a group rather than individually. A group of actors in a social network is often referred to as "community". Communities are characterised by some intrinsic features which bring some participants in the network closer to each other than others in the network. Finding and analysing communities in social networks is an active research area. Majority of these methods make use mathematical and graph theoretic models for finding communities. The last questions listed above focuses on this aspect and explores if there are communities that can be identified on the basis of mathematical features of their positions within the graph of relationships.

Understanding the social action and behaviour of individuals in communities are of great interest to sociologist, political analysts, business analysts, policy makers, how ideas emerge, proliferate and impact decisions, etc. This is where the mathematics of network graphs comes into play. We need to have procedures to measure the behaviour of individual actors, communities and network as a whole. Using social network or social media metrics one can systematically understand the behaviour of individuals, communities and networks.

There are number of areas in which social network metrics can be used to provide insights into the behaviour of actors of a network. This work provides a brief explanation of major social network metrics with their use in academic social networks. With the help of a collaboration network we try to explain the use of each of these metrics and the insights they provide. We also introduce a new metric "*Average Degree of Collaboration*" for quantifying academic collaborations within institutions.

SOCIAL NETWORK ANALYSIS: LEVELS AND METRICS

There are different levels of social network analysis (Wasserman & Faust, 1994). It may be at actor level, dyadic level, triadic level, subset level, or network level. Whatever be the level of these metrics they provide important information for understanding the structure and dynamics of social networks. At an actor's level SNA uses metrics like centrality, prestige and roles such as isolates, liaisons, bridges, etc. At dyadic level metrics like distance and reachability, structural and other notions of equivalence and tendencies toward reciprocity are explored. At triadic level the metrics of interest include balance and transitivity whereas, cliques, cohesive subgroups, components are important for analysis at the subset level. Metrics like connectedness, diameter, centralization, density, prestige, etc. are used for analysis at network level (Gretzel, 2001).

Social network metrics such as centrality measures (Newman, 2010) (degree centrality, betweenness centrality, closeness centrality and network centrality), average degree, clustering co-efficient, Salton index, density and characteristic path length are often of great interest to the analysis of academic or research collaboration from a network perspective. The study of social networks and their associated metrics is important for social scientists, policy makers, network administrators, etc. as these networks form the underlying structure, which allows for rapid information distribution (Newman, 2006).

Several network analysis measures as proposed in Chelmis and Prasanna (2011) and others can be used to identify prominent actors and discern the structure of communities within social networks. In majority of SNA studies the investigators are interested in capturing the internal connectivity as well as attributes of key nodes in the network (Arif, et al., 2012). In order to identify the leaders in a network, the quantity of interest in many social network studies is "*Betweenness Centrality*" because of its structural significance.

Centrality, as a set of measures, provides information about the relative importance of nodes and edges in a graph (Newman, 2010). Several centrality measures have also been proposed in Chelmis and

Prasanna (2011) to identify the most important actors (leaders) in a social network. These set of metrics play an important role in graph theory and network analysis to measure the importance or prestige of actors (nodes) in a network (Bonacich, 1987; Borgatti, 2005).

Therefore, to answer the above questions in an efficient manner, metrics like betweenness centrality, degree centrality, clustering coefficient, average degree, etc. are used.

- **Degree Centrality:** "*Degree Centrality*" of a node is a straightforward centrality measure as it takes into account the number of links associated with it directly. In a directed graph, e.g. a citation graph, it takes into account the number of edges incident on it. It represents the frequency of activity of individual actors based on the considered relationship. It only considers the number of connections without taking into account the quality of those connections.

Let $A = \left[a_{i,j} \right]$ be the adjacency matrix of a graph G with V vertices and E edges, $A_{v,u}$, an element of the adjacency matrix A is defined by using Equation (1):

$$A_{v,u} = \begin{cases} a_{i,j} = 1, if\ vertex\ 'i'\ is\ adjacent\ to\ vertex\ 'j' \\ a_{i,j} = 0, otherwise \end{cases} \tag{1}$$

For an undirected graph, $G = \left(V, E \right)$ the degree $C_D \left(V \right)$ of a node or vertex $v, \left(v \in V \right)$ can be expressed using Equation (2).

$$C_D \left(v \right) = \sum_{j(j \neq v)} A \left(v, j \right) \tag{2}$$

The degree centrality $C_D \left(G \right)$ of G can be expressed using Equation (3).

$$C_D(G) = \frac{\sum_{i=1}^{|v|} \left[C_D \left(v* \right) - C_D \left(v_i \right) \right]}{H} \tag{3}$$

where $v*$ is the node in G with highest degree centrality and $H = \sum_{j=1}^{|Y|} C_D \left(y* \right) - C_D \left(y_j \right)$. Here $y*$ is the node with the highest degree centrality in a graph X of G with Y nodes. The value of H is maximum when a graph has a star like structure.

- **Eigenvector Centrality:** "*Eigenvector Centrality*" is a more sophisticated version of degree centrality where the number as well as quality of connections is also accounted for. Thus having connections with other high prestige nodes in the network contribute more to the centrality value of the node in question. More the number of connections of a node with other nodes having larger and better connections, the better it's eigenvector centrality. Google's PageRank by Brin and Page (1998) is a variation of eigenvector centrality and Katz Centrality (1953) is closely related to eigenvector centrality.

If A is the adjacency matrix of G (Equation (1)), then, the eigenvector centrality $C_E\left(v\right)$ of a vertex v can be expressed using Equation (4).

$$C_E\left(v\right) = \frac{1}{\lambda} \sum_{u \in N\left(v\right)} x_u = \frac{1}{\lambda} \sum_{u \in G} a_{v,u}\, x_u \qquad (4)$$

where $N(v)$ represents the set of neighbours of the vertex v, λ is a constant, $a_{v,u}$ is the value for edge (v,u) in the adjacency matrix A of the graph and x_u is the eigenvector centrality of the node u.

- **Betweenness Centrality:** "*Betweenness Centrality*" of a vertex v measures how many shortest paths between all pair of vertices in a graph G include the vertex v (Freeman, 1977). In other words, it quantifies the number of times a node acts as a bridge along the shortest path between two other nodes. It is an important measure for identifying nodes which are structurally important for the network. Thus the high betweenness centrality of a node indicates how crucial is the role that node plays in information flow and cohesiveness of the network. These nodes are therefore considered as central and indispensable to the network. Nodes with the high betweenness centrality act as gate keepers.

The betweenness centrality $C_B\left(v\right)$ of vertex v can be expressed using Equation (5).

$$C_B\left(v\right) = \sum_{s \neq v \neq t \in V} \frac{\sigma_{st}\left(v\right)}{\sigma_{st}} \qquad (5)$$

where σ_{st} is the total number of shortest paths from node s to t and $\sigma_{st}\left(v\right)$ is the number of paths that pass through v.

- **Clustering Coefficient:** The "*Clustering Coefficient*" of a node is a measure of the density of edges in the neighbourhood of that node (Watts & Strogatz, 1998). Thus clustering coefficient is a neighbour dependent measure: the better the connectivity in the neighbourhood the better the clustering coefficient. Thus it quantifies the ability of a node's neighbours to form a complete graph, also called a clique. For finding the clustering coefficient of a network the average clustering co-efficient of all the nodes in the network is taken into account. If the clustering coefficient of a network is higher the network is considered to exhibit "*small world*" behaviour (Watts & Strogatz, 1998). To analyse such behaviour Stanley Milgram's (1967) theory of the "*6 Degree of Separation*" utilises the average path length metric. The clustering coefficient of a node v_i in G', where G' is a sub-graph of G induced by the neighbours of v_i can be expressed using Equation (6).

$$C\left(v_i\right) = \frac{number\ of\ edges\ in\ G'}{maximum\ number\ of\ edges\ in\ G'} = \frac{2.m_i}{n_i\left(n_i - 1\right)} \qquad (6)$$

Here, m_i is the number of neighbors of v_i and n_i is the number of connected pairs between all neighbors of v_i. The average clustering coefficient of a graph G with n vertices can be expressed using Equation (7).

$$\bar{C} = \frac{1}{n} \sum_{i=1}^{n} C_i \qquad (7)$$

where $C_i = \dfrac{\lambda_G(v)}{\tau_G(v)}$, $\lambda_G(v)$ is the number of subgraphs of G having 3 edges and 3 vertices including the vertex v, and $\tau_G(v)$ is the number of sub-graphs of G having 2 edges and 3 vertices including v such that both the edges are incident on v.

- **Average Degree:** The "*Average Degree*" of all the nodes in the network is equal to the average number of edges associated directly with all the nodes in the network. It is representative of the frequency of the considered activity of all the actors in the network. For example in co-authorship based academic social networks it is considered a measure of how collaborative the authors are. The average degree of G can be expressed using Equation (8).

$$D_A(G) = \frac{\sum_v d_v}{n} \qquad (8)$$

where d_v is degree of any vertex v and n is the total number of vertices in G.

- **Graph Density:** "*Graph Density*" is a network metric and signifies the number of connections between various actors in the network. It is different from clustering coefficient in the way that it not only considers the connections among neighbours but the entire set of connections in the network. If a graph has more connections and the connections reach towards the upper limit, it is considered dense, otherwise sparse. For an undirected graph G with V vertices and E edges, the density D_G of graph G can be expressed using Equation (9).

$$D_G = \frac{2|E|}{|V|(|V|-1)} \qquad (9)$$

- **Modularity:** "*Modularity*" is one such social network analysis measure that is concerned with the structure of networks or graphs. Since the structure of a network may be divided into small groups which may be connected or disconnected one needs to have an idea of the connectivity in the network. Modularity measures the strength of division of a network into modules (also called groups, clusters or communities). Networks with high modularity have stronger and intense connections between the nodes within modules but sparse connections between nodes in different modules. Modularity is often used in optimization methods for detecting community structure in networks. Suppose a graph G is divided into more than one groups or modules and e_{ii} is 'the percentage of edges in module *i*' and *a_i* is 'the percentage of edges with one end in module *i*', then the modularity *Q* of the graph *G* can be expressed using Equation (10).

$$Q = \sum_{i=1}^{k} \left(e_{ii} - a_i^2 \right) \tag{10}$$

- **Engagement:** The goal of individuals, businesses and organizations using social media is to expand their virtual reach and involve others to follow their activities. In essence the purpose is to engage others not only on specific events, like buying a product, but in as much conversations as possible. Like a good salesman the job of a social media platform is to get the conversation going in the first place. The more the number of actors in a specific event the better the engagement score. The "*Engagement*" metric can have many forms. For example, according to SocialBakers. com[3], on Facebook the value of engagement rate *ER* of an entity on a single day is calculated using Equation (11).

$$ER = \left(\frac{L + C + S}{F} \right) \times 100 \tag{11}$$

where *L*, *C* and *S* stand for number of likes, comments and shares respectively on a single day and *F* stands for number of *fans*. Here, *fans* means the number of entities who liked the page.

METRICS FOR ACADEMIC SOCIAL NETWORKS

Social networks formed amongst academics by way of having some sort of academic relationships are termed as Academic Social Networks. The relationships of interest could be co-authoring a publication, working on a project jointly, co-supervising a thesis, citing publications of other authors, etc. These networks are emerging at a fast pace and gaining a lot of research interests. In such a setup, one may be interested in understanding the structure and dynamics of these networks. The networks formed on the basis of these relationships can be based on a single relationship or multi-relational. SNA metrics can help enumerate various facets of the network including identification of important individuals, connectivity structure and flow of information, etc. These metrics along with some others seeks to answer, *inter alia*, the following questions:

- Who are the bosses in the network?
- Who contributes more to the network in terms of number of connections?
- What is the degree frequency distribution?
- What is the frequency and intensity of the collaboration ties?
- What is the connectivity structure of the network?

    In this section we try to draw parallels between these metrics and their applicability and relevance in analysis of diverse forms of academic social networks. In the end we define a new metric called "*Aver-*

age Degree of Collaboration" which can be used to determine the power of identified institutes to seek external collaborators.

- **Degree Centrality***:* This metrics take into account the strength of relationship studied and is thus directly proportional to the frequency of the activity. In academic social networks higher value of degree centrality of an academic means that he participates in the network frequently. For instance, in a citation network higher degree centrality for an author or paper means that it has been cited frequently but in co-authorship networks it is a measure of how often an author collaborates with other authors in the network. However it does not takes into account the quality of collaborators. It has been observed experimentally by Arif (2015) that higher degree centrality may not be real indicator of the prestige of an actor in the network. Therefore, just having connections with nodes having higher degree centrality may not be an indicator of your importance for the underlying academic social network.

- **Eigenvector Centrality***:* Eigenvector centrality has greater significance in identification of important actors in an academic social network. This is because of the structural importance of such nodes because this node enjoys connections with other quality nodes in the network. Such nodes are synonymous with hubs in the World Wide Web. Owing to this property nodes with higher eigenvector centrality lie at the centre of flow of ideas and information in the network. They have greater proximity with other high profile nodes in the network and thus enjoy the benefit of sensing the flow of information and ideas. In academic social networks like co-authorship networks, where the focus is on joint publications, it provides an idea about the ability of an author to receive new research ideas that spread across the network (Zervas et al., 2014).

- **Betweenness Centrality:** The structural position of nodes with high betweenness centrality allows them to control the flow of information in the network. These nodes occupy strategic positions in the network because of their falling on the shortest paths between other nodes in the network. In academic social networks such nodes possible represent people who are senior or reputed individuals. Because of their having strategic importance in the structure and connectivity in the network removal of such nodes result in breakdown of the information flow and thus the nature of connectivity in the network may change altogether. This may also result in increase in the number of connected components in the network, thus reducing the connectivity. Other academics in the network have some sort of connection with such nodes and those who haven't would like to have connection with such nodes. Analytical results (Newman, 2001) show that in an academic social network such actors play an instrumental role in advancing and proliferation of scientific cooperation. Their removal may result in reducing the connectivity and increasing the modularity of the remnant collaboration graph.

- **Closeness Centrality:** It uses the sum of all the distances to rank how central a node is in the network. It is inversely proportional to the sum of all the distance and is thus a measure of the association of an academic with others in the network. Thus closeness centrality not only takes into account the frequency and prestige of connections but also honours the diversity of connections. Having direct or indirect connections with majority of other nodes in the network will rate a node higher than those have high profile connections on the closeness centrality scale. Our analysis (Arif, 2015) of the closeness centrality shows that nodes having connections with remote nodes have higher value of closeness centrality.

- **Clustering Coefficient:** It is a measure of connectivity in the network which can provide idea about future connections or collaborations in a social network. In case of individual actors the idea is to get an idea about the connectivity around the considered node. This metric has significant importance in academic social networks because it lets you get an idea about the connectivity among the connections of an academic. In addition it also acts as prediction measure as it helps predicting the future evolution of an academic social network. For example in co-authorship academic social networks it provides in percentage terms the chances of future collaborations between any two academics that are indirectly collaborating with each other (Farashbandi et al., 2014).

- **Average Degree:** Degree centrality provides an idea about the contribution of individual nodes to the considered relationship and thus is an individual centric measure but average degree provides a normalized idea about the frequency of connections or collaborations among actors (academic/ scientists in academic social networks). Average degree is a network metric. It factors in the varying potential of contribution of each node in the network. For example, in co-authorship based academic social networks average degree enumerates the collaborative activity of the authors and thus helps in answering how collaborative the authors are in the network. The value of average degree is higher for those academic social networks where team work is at play. If majority of the actors (authors) involve themselves in joint collaboration average degree of the network may be quite higher.

- **Graph Density:** Being a network metric graph density refers to the potential of connectivity in the network. The value of graph density of a network is directly proportional to the diversity of connections in the network, the more the graph density the better the connectivity in the network. In academic social networks it represents the degree of collaboration that takes place in the network (Zervas et al., 2014). If a network is dense majority of actor collaborate with each other and vice versa. For example, in a co-authorship based academic social network higher density means publications with considerably higher number of authors.

- **Modularity:** Modularity is a good measure of collaboration structure within academic social networks. It is a two way sword for academic social networks. In such networks, higher modularity indicates stronger research collaboration within specific groups and lesser collaboration among groups. It may not be good for intra-institutional academic networks to have higher modularity but it may be considered good if modularity is high for inter-institutional academic and research collaboration networks.

- **Average Degree of Collaboration:** In order to quantify the extent of collaboration by the people of an institution, we introduce a new metric '*Average Degree of Collaboration*'. It can be used as a measure to indicate the level of collaboration at the institutional level rather than at the individual level. The need for such a measure was felt as we could not find in the available literature a measure for quantification of the collaborations with outsiders with the people in an institution. The average degree of collaboration $\left(D_{AC} \right)$ may be expressed using Equation (12).

$$D_{AC} = \frac{\left(V_{CG} - V_{LG} \right)}{V_{LG}} \tag{12}$$

where V_{CG} is the number of vertices in the general co-authorship graph and V_{LG} is the number of vertices in the local co-authorship graph of a particular institution.

ANALYTICAL RESULTS

In this section we reproduce the values of various social network metrics obtained in (Arif, 2015) for academic social networks for four IITs. The values for the various social network metrics are listed in Table 1. These values have been obtained from various attributes of co-authorship based academic social networks from joint publications over a ten years period 2005-2014. In Table 1, there are values presented for some more metrics in addition to the metrics we have been discussing in the previous sections. These results explain various important aspects of the collaboration networks studied in (Arif, 2015). Analysis of the values provided in Table 1 shows the level of connectivity, pattern of collaboration and the means to simulate the future behaviour of these networks. We don't go into the detailed analysis of these results as they have been discussed in (Arif, 2015) in a succinct fashion.

Table 1. Values of network metrics

IIT	Delhi	Kanpur	Kharagpur	Madras
Vertices	492	376	414	864
Unique Edges	982	615	818	1436
Edges with Duplicates	1111	389	1290	1546
Total Edges	2093	1004	2108	2982
Average Geodesic Distance	4.495213	4.687331	3.620508	4.892994
Maximum Geodesic Distance	10	12	7	12
Graph Density	0.011169	0.010511	0.0144306	0.005234
Maximum Degree	52	68	58	121
Average Degree	5.484	3.941	5.908	4.516
Maximum Betweenness Centrality	44287.075	21441.269	13577.080	206147.880
Average Betweenness Centrality	610.415	442.803	463.222	1422.853
Maximum Closeness Centrality	0.333	1.000	1.000	0.250
Average Closeness Centrality	0.013	0.044	0.015	0.006
Maximum Eigenvector Centrality	0.048	0.073	0.032	0.045
Average Eigenvector Centrality	0.002	0.003	0.002	0.001
Connected Components	8	14	6	8
Maximum Vertices in a Connected Component	413	299	382	794
Maximum Edges in a Connected Component	1855	848	1993	2773
Average Clustering Coefficient	0.820	0.760	0.799	0.767
Modularity	0.317845	0.365475	0.281603	0.287678

FUTURE DIRECTIONS

Social network analysis is not a new phenomenon but the large scale application of SNA for online and big networks is comparatively new. We are of the view that the methods and metrics are naïve as far their application to online or large social networks is concerned. The sheer size and diversity of these networks present new challenges in application of existing methods and metrics. The present day analysis of large scale social networks use some sort of sampling to understand the structure and behaviour of these social networks. From the exponential growth of these networks it can be understood that whatever the computational power we may have the size and diversity of these networks may still be a challenge. It is therefore required that efforts may be made to design new metrics or the existing metrics may be tuned for analysis of large scale social networks.

It has been observed that in majority of cases social networks exhibit power-law behaviour. In such a scenario average-degree may not be a true representative of degree distribution in the network. It is therefore required that other means may be explored to represent the degree distribution in the network. In addition, the diameter of a graph may get affected by presence of outliers. To have meaningful representation of diameter outliers have to be removed. It is therefore required that some metric like Effective Diameter may be explored that is resilient to outliers.

It has been observed that some online social networks use Engagement as a measure to gauge the virtual reach of an activity. During our investigation we could not find any such metric that has been used in academic social networks. Therefore modifications of Engagement as used in online social networks can be explored in gauging the reach of individual academics/researchers, academic communities or institutions.

CONCLUSION

Social network analysis has been used quite often to discover hidden trends and information from the underlying structure of social networks. Each of such networks is defined by a set of characteristic features which can be described in mathematical terms. Such characteristics features are called social network or social media metrics. These metrics rely heavily on mathematical formulations particularly graph theory. With some modifications these metrics can be applied to a variety of situations but the basics still remain the same.

In this chapter we introduced and discussed the mathematical background of majority of the social media metrics. We purposefully left simple metrics like shares, likes, views, visits, etc. because they are direct measures and do not require any advanced mathematical calculations. We also discussed various levels of network analysis and metrics associated with each level of the analysis. Some of the metrics are individual specific, some others are group or community specific and some others are network specific. Whatever be the level of these metrics each of them plays an important role in overall understanding of the actors and their relationships in the network.

This Chapter also discussed the role and relevance of majority of the social media metrics in analysis of academic social networks. Though metrics like engagement, as defined in this work, may not be directly useful for analysis of academic social networks because there is nothing like shares, likes and comments for academic entities but they can be tuned to fit academic social networks. We can observe some sort of connection between 'Engagement' and 'RG Score' of ResearchGate[4], one of the popular academic networking sites. Casual social networks like Facebook, twitter, etc. are common in use with billions of users but academic social networks like ResearchGate are not that popular. Keeping this thing in mind we thought it worthy to explore the use and relevance of these metrics in evaluation and analysis of academic social networks.

In our earlier studies of academic social networks, we couldn't find a metric to quantify external collaborations of people working with an organization or institution. In this context, we defined a new metric that focuses purely on external collaboration. This can be used to define the prestige of an organization or institution in attracting external collaborators. Institutions with high value for "Average Degree of Collaboration" have high potential for joint research, joint publications with people from other organization and institutions.

REFERENCES

Arif, T. (2015). Understanding Research Collaborations using Social Network Analysis: A Case Study of Indian Institutes of Technology. *International Journal of Advanced Research in Computer Science and Software Engineering, 5*(10), 880–886.

Arif, T., Ali, R., & Asger, M. (2012). Scientific Co-authorship Social Networks: A Case Study of Computer Science Scenario in India. *International Journal of Computer Applications, 52*(12), 38-45.

Bonacich, P. (1987). Power and centrality: A family of measures. *American Journal of Sociology, 92*(5), 1170–1182. doi:10.1086/228631

Borgatti, S. P. (2005). Centrality and network flow. *Social Networks, 27*(1), 55–71. doi:10.1016/j.socnet.2004.11.008

Brin, S. & Page, L. (1998). The anatomy of a large-scale hypertextual Web search engine. *Computer Networks and ISDN Systems, 30*(1), 107-117.

Chelmis, C., & Prasanna, V. K. (2011). Social networking analysis: A state of the art and the effect of semantics. In *Proceedings of 3rd IEEE Conference on Social Computing.* doi:10.1109/PASSAT/SocialCom.2011.23

Cooley, R., Mobasher, B., & Srivastave, J. (1997). Web mining: Information and pattern discovery on the world wide web. In *Proceedings of the 9th IEEE International Conference on Tool with Artificial Intelligence.* doi:10.1109/TAI.1997.632303

Farashbandi, F. Z., Geraei, E., & Siamaki, S. (2014). Study of co-authorship network of papers in the Journal of Research in Medical Sciences using social network analysis. *Journal of Research in Medical Sciences, 19*(1), 41–46. PMID:24672564

Freeman, L. C. (1977). A set of measures of centrality based upon betweenness. *Sociometry, 40*(1), 35–41. doi:10.2307/3033543

Gretzel, U. (2001). *Social network analysis: Introduction and resources.* Retrieved from http://lrs.ed.uiuc.edu/tse-portal/analysis/social-network-analysis/#analysis

Jin, Y., Matsuo, Y., & Ishizuka, M. (2006). Extracting a social network among entities by web mining. In *Proceedings of ISWC'06 Workshop on Web Content Mining with Human Language Technologies.*

Katz, L. (1953). A New Status Index Derived from Sociometric Index. *Psychometrika, 18*(1), 39–43. doi:10.1007/BF02289026

Katzmair, H. (2014). Social Network Analysis: The Science of Measuring, Visualizing and Simulating Social Relationships. *FAS Research,* 207-211.

Luo, Y. L., & Hsu, C. H. (2009). An Empirical Study of Research Collaboration Using Social Network Analysis. In *Proceedings of 2009 IEEE International Conference on Computational Science & Engineering.* doi:10.1109/CSE.2009.253

Mika, P. (2007). *Social networks and the sematic web.* Springer-Verlag.

Milgram, S. (1967). The Small World Problem. *Psychology Today, 2*(1), 60–67.

Newman, M. E. (2001). The structure of scientific collaboration networks. *Proceedings of the National Academy of Sciences of the United States of America, 98*(2), 404–409. doi:10.1073/pnas.98.2.404 PMID:11149952

Newman, M. E. J. (2006). Community centrality. *Physical Review,* 74.

Newman, M. E. J. (2010). *Networks: An Introduction.* Oxford University Press. doi:10.1093/acprof:oso/9780199206650.001.0001

Wagner, C. S., & Leydesdorff, L. (2005a). Mapping the network of global science: Comparing international co-authorships from 1990 to 2000. *International Journal of Technology and Globalisation, 1*(2), 185–208. doi:10.1504/IJTG.2005.007050

Wagner, C. S., & Leydesdorff, L. (2005b). Network structure, self-organization, and the growth of international collaboration in science. *Research Policy, 34*(10), 1608–1618. doi:10.1016/j.respol.2005.08.002

Wagner, C. S., & Leydesdorff, L. (2008). International collaboration in science and the formation of a core group. *Journal of Informetrics, 2*(4), 317–325. doi:10.1016/j.joi.2008.07.003

Wasserman, S., & Faust, K. (1994). *Social network analysis: Methods and applications.* New York: Cambridge University Press. doi:10.1017/CBO9780511815478

Watts, D. J., & Strogatz, S. H. (1998). Collective dynamics of 'small-world' networks. *Nature, 393*(6684), 440–442. doi:10.1038/30918 PMID:9623998

Zervas, P., Tsitmidelli, A., Sampson, D.G., & Chen, N.-S., & Kinshuk. (2014). Studying research collaboration patterns via coauthorship analysis in the field of TeL: The case of Educational Technology & Society journal. *Journal of Educational Technology & Society, 17*(4), 1–16.

KEYWORDS AND DEFINITIONS

Centrality: The relative importance of individuals or actors in a social network can be expressed in terms of its centrality score. It conveys the importance of a node based on particular criteria.

Data Mining: The computational process of finding hidden patterns in the underlying large volumes of data. It has emerged as an interdisciplinary subfield of computer science with backgrounds in database systems, statistics, artificial intelligence and machine learning.

Edges: Edges represent relationship between nodes or vertices in a graph. Edges can be labelled or unlabelled, directed or undirected, weighted or weightless.

Graph: A graph is an object without coordinates and it consists of vertices and edges. Generally a graph is represented as $G= (V,E)$, where V is set of vertices and E is set of edges. A graph can be labelled or unlabelled, directed or undirected, weighted or weightless.

Nodes: Synonymous of vertices in a graph. Nodes represent entities in a graph.

Social Networks: A form of graph where nodes or vertices represent social actors and edges between these nodes represent social relations between the actors of the network.

Social Network Analysis: It is the art and science of analysing actors and their relationships in a social network. SNA rely heavily on mathematical formulations for quantifying social relations and behaviour of individuals, groups, communities, etc.

ENDNOTES

1   Orgnet.com: http://www.orgnet.com/sna.html
2   www.facebook.com
3   http://www.socialbakers.com/
4   https://www.researchgate.net

Chapter 7
Social Media Metrics

S. K. Sudarsanam
VIT Business School, Chennai, VIT University, India

ABSTRACT

Concepts and the theories related to social media are discussed in this chapter. This chapter talks about the various frameworks of social media for the use of organizations in developing social media framework with the business objectives. Definitions and guidelines in respect of social media metrics are mentioned in this chapter. Further it suggests the methods in choosing the right metrics for the key social media objectives in respect of canvassing or product launches. A new Social media metrics framework has been suggested and also the metrics have been identified for each framework group. This Chapter will help Organizations in identifying the key social media metrics for tracking and monitoring the measurement of the performance of one's brands, products, and services in the social media channels. Once the key social media metrics are identified, organizations can choose the right tool to measure the metrics defined. This would help Organizations to improve or enhance their marketing and operational business strategies by leveraging the power and reach of the social media channels. The future directions for research and the references indicated in this chapter would be of great help to researchers in the area of social media metrics.

INTRODUCTION

Buettner (2016) defines Social media as a computer-mediated tool that allow people to create, share or exchange information, career interests, ideas, and pictures/videos in virtual communities and networks . Accordingly to Kaplan and Michael (2010), Social media is "a group of Internet-based applications that build on the ideological and technological foundations of Web 2.0, and that allow the creation and exchange of user-generated content". Furthermore, social media depends on mobile and web-based technologies to create highly interactive platforms through which individuals and communities share, co-create, discuss, and modify user-generated content. They introduce substantial and pervasive changes to communication between businesses, organizations, communities, and individuals (Kietzmann & Hermkens, 2011). These changes are the focus of the emerging field of technoself studies. Social media differ from traditional or industrial media in many ways, including quality, reach, frequency, usability,

DOI: 10.4018/978-1-5225-0846-5.ch007

immediacy and permanence (Agichtein, Castillo, Donato, Gionis, & Mishne, 2008). Social media operates in a dialogic transmission system, many sources to many receivers (Pavlik & MacIntoch, 2015). This is in contrast to traditional media that operates under a monologic transmission model (one source to many receivers). "Social media has been broadly defined to refer to 'the many relatively inexpensive and widely accessible electronic tools that enable anyone to publish and access information, collaborate on a common effort, or build relationships'" (Murthy, 2013). Many Organizations use Social Media to Market their products and services and also use Social Media to communicate with customers or potential customers. Many customers use Social Media to share their experience of using a product or service. So, there is a need for Organizations to track Social Media content on their product and services. Organizations need to analyze Big data and measure certain key metrics. Many Organizations tend to apply the concepts of traditional metrics for measuring the Social Media Metrics. Social Media is defined as a group of organisms which are dynamic, interconnected, egalitarian and interactive and which are beyond the control of any organization (Peters, Chen, Kaplan, Ognibeni, & Pauwels, 2013). The Social media requires a distinct approach to measurement, analysis, and subsequently management. This Chapter discusses in detail the Framework for establishing the key objectives of Organizations, defining the key Social Media Metrics and Benchmarking the metrics with the industry best practices.

THE FRAMEWORK FOR SOCIAL MEDIA

Peters et al. (2013) defined a new theoretical framework for Social Media Metrics. In this framework, the social media constitutes a new kind of organism compared to traditional media. This is explained in Figure 1.

Motives, Content, Social Roles and interactions and Network Structure the four key elements of the SOR (Stimuli-Organism-Response) framework. Actors are the key ingradients of the system and they have dyadic ties with the community. They have motives, create and share content through their social roles and interactions using the network structure they have built in the Social Media over a period of time. So, any organization defining their own Social media metrics, first need to identify the metrics for each of the elements of the SOR framework. The metrics for each of the element of SOR framework are listed in Peters et al. (2013).

Models and frameworks play a key role in going from standard social media definitions and metrics to robust social media measurement. Bagnall and Bartholomew (2013) defines a five-step social media metrics measurement process:

1. Social media measurement starts with measurable objectives that are aligned with desired business outcomes and KPIs.
2. Define the specific metrics necessary to assess performance against the measurable social media objectives. A necessary and important step is setting performance targets for each metric.
3. Populate the Social media model with the metrics defined
4. Gather and analyze the data and evaluate the performance against the objectives and targets.
5. Report the results regularly on dashboards, to stakeholders and interested parties

Figure 1. Social media metrics framework

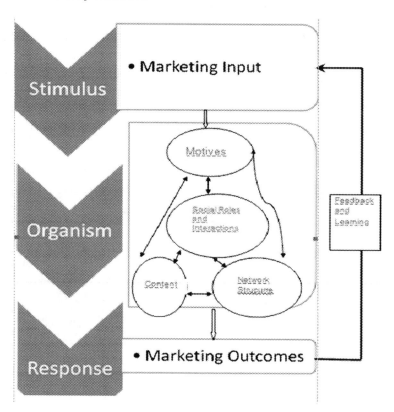

A new type of framework (Bagnall & Bartholomew, 2013) integrates the Marketing Communication Phases with the Marketing Stages. This framework is elaborated in Table 1: AMEC Social Media Framework.

Some of the most positive aspects of the Framework are that it:

- Provides a mechanism to link activities to outputs to outcomes
- Tracks through the familiar sales funnel

Table 1. AMEC social media framework

	Communications / Marketing Stages				
Key Area of Communication	**Awarenss**	**Knowledge/ Understanding**	**Interest/ Consideration**	**Support/ Preference**	**Action**
Public Relations Activity					
Intermediary Effect					
Target Audience Effect					Organization/ Business Results

- The framework is flexible and comprehends several PR use-cases – media relations, reputation, internal communications.
- Helps create a focus on outcomes and business impact.

While using the AMEC Framework in Social Media, two issues were noticed

- The intermediary effect, which in traditional public relations is the impact on the media, seemed at odds with the social world of direct interaction between consumers and brands, and consumers with each other.
- Use of the marketing sales funnel was only relevant in a percentage of social media use-cases and was found to be not the best way to model customer relations and stakeholder relationships

Forrester Research and McKinsey & Company had noted the traditional communications funnel was not necessarily funnel-shaped in social media. They described the discovery process that occurs when investigating companies and brands that often cause the consideration set to expand rather than be reduced, and the fact that a lot of engagement around brands happens post-conversion event.

To overcome these issues a new framework is proposed by AMEC. AMEC team (Bagnall & Bartholomew, 2013) developed the following model They divided Social media metrics into the following groups:

1.   Program metrics. These metrics are directly tied to your campaign objectives or program;
2.   Channel metrics. Metrics that are unique to specific social media channels – Twitter, Facebook, YouTube, Vimeo, LinkedIn, etc.;
3.   Business metrics. Metrics that are designed to measure the impact of the campaign or initiative

Forrester Research has defined the channels as follows:

- Paid are social channels you pay to leverage (e.g. promoted tweets, display ads)
- Owned are channels you own and control (e.g. website, Facebook page)
- Earned is where customers become the channel (e.g. WOM, viral)

Pentin (2010) developed a framework for measuring social media metrics. This is elaborated further in Table 2: IAB Framework.

Table 2. IAB framework

I Intent	A Awareness Appreciation Action Advocacy	b Benchmark
Establish Intentions and Objectives	Define Core KPI metrics by Social Media Platform (Soft Metrics and Hard Financials)	Compare Benchmark with other Social media activity, channels and industry averages

I - Intent: The following are some sample KPIs identified

To build brand awareness, To generate buzz, advocacy or WOM, To generate brand engagement, To shift consumer perceptions, To influence key opinion formers, To generate leads or build prospect base, To stimulate dialogue or relationship with pros, To encourage participation for social event etc

The 4 A's: awareness of social media, appreciation, action and advocacy

The KPIs can be assigned to one or more of the above 4 As. The importance placed on the 4 As depends on the original intent. For example, the activity related to buzz and WOM will focus more on awareness, appreciation and advocacy

B – benchmark

Social media activity benchmarking:

a.   First you need to compare the social media platform with other social media platforms your product or brand uses.
b.   Compare how your objectives perform with other marketing channels which share similar objectives.
c.   Compare how your competitors use social media activity to promote their products or brands.
d.   Compare the social media activity with historical data (trend over a period of time).

Guidelines to define KPIs:
The following three parameters can be used to define KPI (key performance indicators)

•   Social media platform (e.g. blog, microblogging, community forum, social network, fanpage, video forum, social network, fanpage, video sharing site, branded channel widget/application etc).
•   4As
•   Soft metrics AND hard financials

Mavis, Stephanie and Charles (2010) offers following social media metric grouping method. According to them, the social media metrics should be divided into following groups:

1.   Community health group. This group is divided in following four subgroups:
    1.1.   Engagement;
    1.2.   Customer satisfaction;
    1.3.   Social content mobility;
2.   Market perception group. This group is divided in following subgroups:
    2.1.   Thought leadership;
    2.2.   Message resonance;
    2.3.   Market awareness;
    2.4.   Market position;

3. Quantitative group. This group is divided into:
   3.1. Leads/sales/market share;
   3.2. Efficiency of communications

Elliott (2011) offers us to look at social media metrics from following perspective:
The first group is digital, this group is divided in smaller groups such as:

1.1. Social opportunity group. Following social media metrics belong to this group: fans, members, visitors, readers, friends and followers;
1.2. Social health group, this group includes following social media metrics: posts, comments and sentiment;

The second main group is brand group, this group is divided into following subgroups:

2.1. Branding group, following social media metrics are included in this group: awareness, brand attributes, purchase intent;
2.2. Product trial group, following metrics belong to this group: lead generation, coupon redemption and sampling;

Third main group is financial group. Following metrics belong in this group: conversions, revenue and lifetime value (Elliott, 2011).

Pangaro and Wenzek (2015) offers us to divide social media metrics in 5 groups while using CLEAT-framework. The author divides social media metrics into following groups:

1. Context group;
2. Language group;
3. Exchange group;
4. Agreement group;
5. Transaction group.

Next each of these groups are divided into following subgroups: 1. Primary metrics: consumer actions; 2. Secondary metrics: outcome (new & historical); 3. Supporting metrics: group statistics.

Murdough (2009) offers to divide the social media metrics based on the social media campaign aim: First group is named "Deepen relationship with customers".

In this group following metrics are included: numbers of advocates and numbers of comments posted;

The second groups name is "Learn from the community". Following metrics belong to this group: rank of topics discussed; decipher of positive and negative sentiments;

The third groups name is "Drive purchase intent". Following metrics are in this group: leads to ecommerce partners; retail locater results activity and product brochure downloads.

Praude and Skulme (2015) has proposed a social media channel grouping which divides the metrics into the following five groups.

1. Social networks
2. Micromedia

3. Blogs
4. Media Sharing
5. Widgets and social media applications

The Social media metrics are evaluated during each of the consumer purchase decision stages. The purchase decision stages are Need recognition, Information search, Alternative evaluation, Purchase Decision and Post Purchase Behaviour.

Based on the study of all frameworks defined above, a new framework covering groups like Brand Management, Channel Management, Financials and Benchmarks is proposed. The new framework is depicted in Figure 3.

The metrics will be captured and evaluated during the social media campaign initiation, planning, execution and closure phases (for each of the product of the organization).

The Brand Management and Channel management metrics will be tracked continuously throughout the lifecycle of an Organization during the product lifecycle all the release of the new products and service offerings of an Organization.

SOCIAL MEDIA METRICS DEVELOPMENT

Peters et al. (2013) linked theories, framework elements with guidelines for Social media metrics and Dashboards, The pictorial representation of the framework is given in Table 3.

1. Transition from Control to influence: Organizations lose their control over brands or campaigns in social media and they need to use the influence of their engaged customers to promote their social

Figure 3. Proposed Social Media Metrics Framework

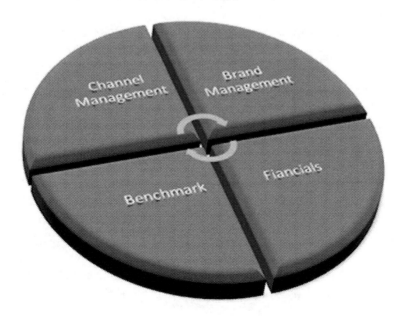

Figure 2. AMEC social media metrics framework

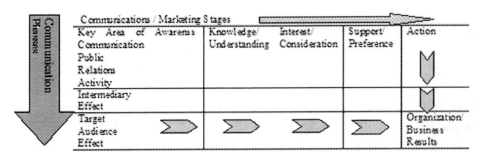

Table 3. Social media metrics theoretical framework and guidelines

Theoretical Framework Theories and Elements			Guidelines for Social Media Metrics and Dashboards
Motives (M)	Social Roles and Interactions (SR & SI)	a)	Transition from Control to Influence
		b)	Shift from States and Means to Processes and Distributions
		c)	Shift from Convergence to Divergence
Content (C)		d)	Shift from Quantity to Quality
		e)	Leverage Transparency and Feedback loops on Metrics
		f)	Balance the Metrics
Network Structure (N)		g)	Cover general to specific
		h)	Shift from Urgency to Importance
		i)	Balance Theory and Pragmatism

media activities. The key metrics that could be measured are influencers, engaged users, listening and responsiveness of brand managers.

2. Shift from states and means to processes and distributions: In Social media, distribution and network is more important than states, so metrics that capture network dynamics is more relevant for social media metric dashboards

3. Shift from convergence to divergence: Brands need to capture adversity and positive sentiment in the network. The dashboards need to include heterogeneity and contingency in case of content relevancy of targeted segments.

4. Shift from Quantity to Quality: Metrics should focus on quality of engaged users rather than the number of users who liked or shared the contents.

5. Leverage Transparency and feedback loops on metrics: Metrics that measure user's influence over a social media or network e.g. Kloutscore (captures the influence of a user, ability to derive an action in social media), edgerank, google rank. The organizations need to be careful while measuring these metrics as they may be skewed over a period of time as they are gamed in social media network.

6. Balance the metrics: Need to develop metrics that balances both quality and quantity to remove the skewed quality metrics. Also, the metrics need to capture the dynamics over a period of time as well.

7. Cover general to specific: Need to have metrics that are general across social media and also metrics that are specific to each of the social media. Also, metrics to take care of level of social media activity (eg likes, shares, comments).

8. Shift from Urgency to importance: Organizations need to develop metrics that capture the essence of discussions, comments, sentiments in social media and need to respond at the right moment to the users to keep them engaged in their brands or products or services. The measurements need to factor the dynamics and heterogeneity of the network.

9. Balance theory and pragmatism: Metrics to be built with theoretical rigor and also of practical relevance. Metrics to be built in dashboards that both meet organizational objectives and also relevance for the organization.

The above nine guidelines need to be kept in mind while developing the social media metrics.

SOCIAL MEDIA METRICS

The following are the best social media metrics used by most of the organizations (Kaushik, 2012)

1. Conversion Rate
2. Amplification
3. Applause
4. Economic Value

Let us know discuss about the each of the above metrics in detail.

Conversion Rate

It is measured as no. of comments per post. This can be measured for any social media network. Many organizations promote their brand in social media. To achieve a higher conversion rate, organizations need to understand the target audience, brand attributes, strength of brands and value additions to followers and ecosystem. Organizations would be required to use a tool which will measure conversion rates across all social media networks and this would require buying or developing such tools.

The six principles of persuasion mentioned by Cialdini are reciprocity, consistency, social proof, authority, scarcity and liking. They serve to boost conversions in social media marketing if correctly used.

1. **Reciprocity:** Conversion rate improves quite significantly if quality content is offered to the customer and customer turns influencers for the brand. In Inbound Marketing there are many companies offering at the beginning free quality content and then informing their clients that if they want more detailed reports they can collaborate. Organizations also reach out to influencers in network or communities to increase their conversion rates.

2. **Consistency:** This principle is encountered in social media marketing as offering for a free license of a product for a month or so to a potential customer and then if the customer is happy with the product he will buy the product. The e-mail address of a potential customer is the most valuable

for the company, so it is willing to offer trial versions of the product to obtain the contact details of interested customers.

3. **Social Proof:** The social proof principle in online social media can be proved by the number of fans/ followers in networks like Facebook or Twitter, by the number of visualization of YouTube videos or simply, by the number of likes and shares of posts. Another way in which this principle is used is by informing potential customers about best sold products, which might convince the customers to make a decision based on the number of other customers that made the same decision in the past.

4. **Authority:** Cialdini explains that people follow the advice of those with authority and expertise in a particular domain or business. They can be roped in as brand ambassadors to increase the conversion rate of the brand among his or her followers.

5. **Liking:** Some people tend to have similar interests as certain set of people who may represent a brand or a customer of a certain product. This enables them to be engaged more with the brand and in turn increase the conversion rate.

6. **Scarcity:** This principle is meant to show customers that product offerings are for a limited amount of time and for a limited quantity. Amazon and Flipkart offer products with discounts for a limited period of time and quantity.

Amplification Rate

It is measured as the rate at which the user's followers consume content and share it across their networks. For example, in twitter its measured as no. of retweets per tweet. Once the user's 1st network friends or followers find the shared content valuable, they will share it across to their network and the contents start to reach bigger group of customers

On Facebook, Google Plus: Amplification = # of Shares per Post

On a blog, YouTube: Amplification = # of Share Clicks per Post (or Video)

Applause Rate

Is measured as no. of likes per post (in facebook) or no. of favourite clicks per post (in twitter). The applause rate helps organizations to find out what the social media users like and what they like to view etc. Facebooks insights will measure the applause rate.

Economic Value

can be derived from micro and macro conversions (eg order of a catalogue, review of the product, an enquiry phone call). It is the sum of long term and short term revenue and cost savings. Organizations would require tools to measure macro and micro conversions across B2C, B2B and other channels. Google analytics will help capture the economic value metrics from all the participating social media channels. There are other tools also which help capture the economic value metrics.

Social Media Framework (With Metrics)

The Channel Management Metrics, Brand Management Metrics, Financial Metrics and Benchmark are proposed for the new framework. These metrics are elaborated in detail in Figure 5.

Figure 4. Social Media Metrics Framework with guidelines

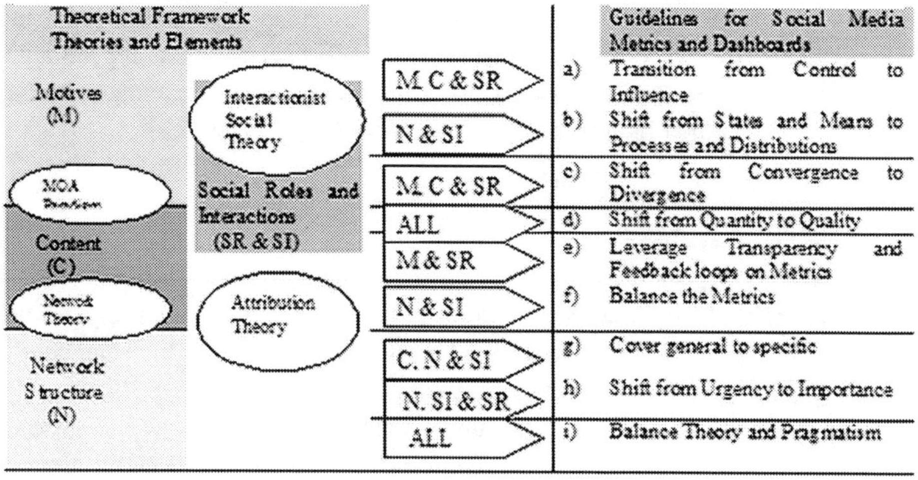

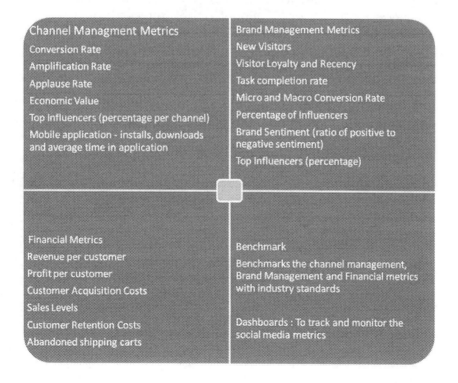

Figure 5. Proposed Framework with Social Media Metrics

FUTURE RESEARCH DIRECTIONS

There is a need to improve the existing social media frameworks which could be used by Organizations to map their business objectives into metrics that could measure the success of the campaigns or product launch or customer feedback on the product and services offered by an organization. The future research need to focus on metrics focused on a particular social media for a particular objective. For example if you need to measure customer satisfaction twitter and facebook are the right social media to focus on. The tools used to measure and report metrics are focused mostly on a particular social media. There is a need to have an integrated tool which would measure all the metrics across all the social media channels. This would greatly reduce the cost of social media performance measuring and reporting for organizations. Organizations also could direct the user traffic from their websites to social media networks to gather customer feedback on their brands, products and services.

CONCLUSION

In this chapter the social media frameworks, guidelines to develop metrics, metric definitions and key social media metrics have been discussed in detail. The key social metrics which can be used for measuring the marketing campaigns and product launches are Conversion rate, amplification rate, applause rate, economic value, social value, engagement rate, percentage of influencers, Kloutscore, Edgerank, Google rank. Organizations need to measure the dynamism and heterogeneity of metrics over a period of time and also they need to respond at the right time with the right response and not very early in the discussion threads. Also, the focus should be on quality of metrics than the quantity. Organizations would need to research on social media frameworks, theories, develop guidelines for defining and measuring metrics, develop ability and tools to trace business objectives with metrics and measure the success of their objectives in the social media networks. Such an integrated approach would help CMOs to justify the investment made in Social media networks and also help businesses reach and service wider range of customers faster. In Business speed is the key and leveraging the power of social media would help businesses to grow faster and outsmart the competition in this dynamic and ever changing landscape.

REFERENCES

Agichtein, E., Castillo, C., Donato, D., Gionis, A., & Mishne, G. (2008). Finding high-quality content in social media. In *Proceedings of the 2008 International Conference on Web Search and Data Mining*. New York, NY: ACM Digital Library.

Baer, J. (2012). *A field guide to the 4 types of content marketing metrics* [PowerPoint slides]. Retrieved from http://www.slideshare.net/jaybaer/a-field-guide-to-the-4-types-of-content-marketing-metrics

Bagnall, R., & Bartholomew, D. (2013). *AMEC Social Media Measurement Framework* [PDF document]. Retrieved from Lecture Notes Online Web site: http://www.social-media-measurement-framework.org/wp-content/uploads/2014/06/Social-Media-Measurement-Framework.pdf

Buettner, R. (2016). *Getting a Job via Career-oriented Social Networking Sites: The Weakness of Ties.* Paper presented at the 49th Annual Hawaii International Conference on System Sciences, Kauai, HI. doi:10.1109/HICSS.2016.272

Cialdini, R. B. (1993). *Influence: The psychology of persuasion.* New York, NY: Harper Business.

Cialdini, R. B., & Goldstein, N. J. (2004). Social influence: Compliance and conformity. *Annual Review of Psychology, 55*(1), 591–621. doi:10.1146/annurev.psych.55.090902.142015

Cialdini, R. B., Wosinska, W., Barrett, D. W., Butner, J., & Gornik-Durose, M. (1999). Compliance with a request in two cultures: The differential influence of social proof and commitment/consistency on collectivists and individualists. *Personality and Social Psychology Bulletin, 25*(10), 1242–1253. doi:10.1177/0146167299258006

Elliott, N. (2011), *Which Social Media Marketing Metrics Really Matter? (And To Whom?).* Retrieved from http://blogs.forrester.com/nate_elliott/11-02-23-which_social_media_marketing_metrics_really_matter_and_to_whom

Ioanid, A., Militaru, G., & Mihai, P. (2015). Social Media Strategies for Organizations using influencer's power. *European Scientific Journal.* Retrieved from http://eujournal.org/index.php/esj/article/view/6144

Kaplan, A. M., & Michael, H. (2010). Users of the world, unite! The challenges and opportunities of social media. *Business Horizons, 53*(1), 59–68. doi:10.1016/j.bushor.2009.09.003

Kaushik, A. (2012). Best Social Media Metrics: Conversation, Amplification, Applause, Economic Value. *Vikalpa, 37*(4), 92–97. Retrieved from http://www.vikalpa.com/pdf/articles/2012/Pages-from-Vikalpa374-69-111.pdf

Kietzmann, J. H., Hermkens, K., McCarthy, I. P., & Silvestre, B. S. (2011). Social media? Get serious! Understanding the functional building blocks of social media. *Business Horizons, 54*(3), 241–251. doi:10.1016/j.bushor.2011.01.005

Lee, K. (2014). *Know What's Working on Social Media: 19 Free Social Media Analytics Tools.* Retrieved May 22, 2016 from https://blog.bufferapp.com/social-media-analytics-tools

Marx, S. (2010). *Measuring Social Media and Its Impact on Your Brand.* Cisco.

Murdough, C. (2009). Social Media Measurement: It's Not Impossible. *Journal of Interactive Advertising, 10*(1), 94–99. doi:10.1080/15252019.2009.10722165

Murthy, D. (2013). *Twitter: Social Communication in the Twitter Age.* Cambridge, MA: Polity.

Pangaro, P., & Wenzek, H. (2015). Engaging consumers through conversations: A management framework to get it right across converged channels. *Procedia: Social and Behavioral Sciences, 213*, 628–634.

Pavlik, J. V., & MacIntoch, S. (2015). *Converging Media* (4th ed.). New York, NY: Oxford University Press.

Pentin, R. (2010). *A new framework for measuring social media activity* [PowerPoint slides]. Retrieved from http://www.slideshare.net/Ifonlyblog/iab-measurement-framework-for-social-media-final4-3

Peters, K., Chen, Y., Kaplan, A. M., Ognibeni, B., & Pauwels, K. (2013). Social Media Metrics —A Framework and Guidelines for Managing Social Media. *Journal of Interactive Marketing*, *27*(4), 281–298. doi:10.1016/j.intmar.2013.09.007

Praude, V., & Skulme, R. (2015). Social Media Campaign Metrics in Lativia. *Procedia: Social and Behavioral Sciences*, *213*, 628–634. doi:10.1016/j.sbspro.2015.11.462

ADDITIONAL READING

Alba, J. W. A., Lynch, J., Weitz, B., Janiszewski, C., Lutz, R., Sawyer, A., & Wood, S. (1997). Interactive Home Shopping: Consumer, Retailer, and Manufacturer Incentives to Participate in Electronic Marketplaces. *Journal of Marketing*, *61*(3), 38–53. doi:10.2307/1251788

Ambler, T. (2003). *Marketing and the Bottom Line*. London: FT Press.

Ansari, A., Koenigsberg, O., & Stahl, F. (2011). Modeling Multiple Relationships in Social Networks. *JMR, Journal of Marketing Research*, *48*(4), 713–728. doi:10.1509/jmkr.48.4.713

Arora, R. (1982). Validation of an S–O–R Model for Situation. Enduring, and Response Componentsof Involvement. *JMR, Journal of Marketing Research*, *19*(6), 505–516.

Bandura, A. (1971). *Social Learning Theory*. New York: General Learning Press.

Batra, R., & Ray, M. (1985). How Advertising Works at Contact. In L. F. Alwitt & A. A. Mitchell (Eds.), *Psychological Processes and Advertising Effects* (pp. 13–44). Hillsdale, NJ: Lawrence Erlbaum Associates.

Belk, R. W. (1975). Situational Variables and Consumer Behavior. *The Journal of Consumer Research*, *2*(3), 157–164. doi:10.1086/208627

Berger, J., & Milkman, K. L. (2012). What Makes Online Content Viral? *JMR, Journal of Marketing Research*, *49*(2), 192–205. doi:10.1509/jmr.10.0353

Berger, J., Sorensen, A. T., & Rasmussen, S. J. (2010). Positive Effects of Negative Publicity:When Negative Reviews Increase Sales. *Marketing Science*, *29*(5), 815–827. doi:10.1287/mksc.1090.0557

Blau, P. M. (1974). Presidential Address: Parameters of Social Structure. *American Sociological Review*, *39*(5), 615–635. doi:10.2307/2094309

Burt, R. S. (1980). Models of Network Structure. *Annual Review of Sociology*, *6*(1), 79–141. doi:10.1146/annurev.so.06.080180.000455

Burt, R. S. (2011). An Experimental Study of Homophily in the Adoption of Health Behavior. *Science*, *334*(6060), 1269–1272. doi:10.1126/science.1207055

Chen, Y., Fay, S., & Wang, Q. (2011). The Role of Marketing in Social Media: How Online Consumer Reviews Evolve. *Journal of Interactive Marketing*, *25*(2), 85–94. doi:10.1016/j.intmar.2011.01.003

Chintagunta, P. K., Gopinath, S., & Venkataraman, S. (2010). The Effects of Online User Reviews on Movie Box Office Performance: Accounting for Sequential Rollout and Aggregation Across Local Markets. *Marketing Science, 29*(5), 944–957. doi:10.1287/mksc.1100.0572

Coralio, B., Calvó-Armengol, A., & Zenou, Y. (2006). Who's Who in Networks Wanted: The Key Player. *Econometrica, 74*(5), 1403–1417. doi:10.1111/j.1468-0262.2006.00709.x

Damon (2010). The Spread of Behavior in an Online Social Network Experiment. *Science, 329*(5996), 1194–1197. doi:.10.1126/science.1185231

Edvardsson, B., Tronvoll, B., & Gruber, T. (2011). Expanding Understanding of Service Exchange and Value Co-creation: A Social Construction Approach. *Journal of the Academy of Marketing Science, 39*(2), 327–339. doi:10.1007/s11747-010-0200-y

Eisenbeiss, M., Blechschmidt, B., Backhaus, K., & Freund, P. A. (2012). The (Real) World Is Not Enough: Motivational Drivers and User Behavior in Virtual Worlds. *Journal of Interactive Marketing, 26*(1), 4–20. doi:10.1016/j.intmar.2011.06.002

Fader, P. S., & Winer, R. S. (2012). Introduction to the Special Issue on the Emergence and Impact of User-generated Content. *Marketing Science, 31*(3), 369–371. doi:10.1287/mksc.1120.0715

Farris, P.W., Bendle, N.T., Pfeifer, P.E., & Reibstein, D.J. (2006). *Marketing Metrics:*

Folkes, V.S. (1988). Recent attribution research in consumer behavior: A review and new directions. *The Journal of Consumer Research, 14*(1), 548–565.

Freeman, L. (2006). *The Development of Social Network Analysis.* Vancouver: Empirical Press.

Galeotti, A., & Goyal, S. (2010). The Law of the Few. *The American Economic Review, 100*(4), 1468–1492. doi:10.1257/aer.100.4.1468

Gensler, S., Völckner, F., Liu-Thompkins, Y., & Wiertz, C. (2013). Managing Brands in the Social Media Environment. *Journal of Interactive Marketing, 27*(4), 242–256. doi:10.1016/j.intmar.2013.09.004

Godes, D., Mayzlin, D., Chen, Y., Das, S., Dellarocas, C., Pfeiffer, B., & Verlegh, P. et al. (2005). The Firm's Management of Social Interactions. *Marketing Letters, 16*(3), 415–428.

Granovetter, M. (1973). The Strength of Weak Ties. *American Journal of Sociology, 78*(1), 1360–1380. doi:10.1086/225469

Hanneman, R.A., & Riddle, M. (2011). *Concepts and Measures for Basic Network Analysis.*

Hartmann, W. R. (2010). Demand Estimation with Social Interactions and the Implications for Targeted Marketing. *Marketing Science, 29*(4), 585–601. doi:10.1287/mksc.1100.0559

Hennig-Thurau, T., Malthouse, E. C., Friege, C., Gensler, S., Lobschat, L., Rangaswamy, A., & Skiera, B. (2010). The Impact of New Media on Customer Relationships. *Journal of Service Research, 13*(3), 311–330. doi:10.1177/1094670510375460

Hoffman, D. L., & Fodor, M. (2010). Can You Measure the ROI of Social Media Marketing? *MIT Sloan Management Review, 52*(1), 41–49.

Joseph, W. A., & Hutchinson, J. W. (1987). Dimensions of Consumer Expertise. *The Journal of Consumer Research*, *13*(2), 411–454.

Kadushin, C. (2012). *Understanding Social Networks: Theories, Concepts, and Findings*. Oxford University Press.

Katona, Z., Zubcsek, P. P., & Sarvary, M. (2011). Network Effects and Personal Influences: The Diffusion of an Online Social Network. *JMR, Journal of Marketing Research*, *48*(3), 425–443. doi:10.1509/jmkr.48.3.425

Kelley, H. H. (1967), Attribution Theory in Social Psychology. In David Levine (Ed.). *Nebraska Symposium on Motivation* (pp: 192-238). Lincoln, NE: University of Nebraska Press.

Kozinets, R. V., Valck, K., Wojnicki, A. C., & Wilner, S. J. S. (2010). Networked Narratives: Understanding Word-of-mouth Marketing in Online Communities. *Journal of Marketing*, *74*(2), 71–89. doi:10.1509/jmkg.74.2.71

Kusum, L. A., Donald, R. L., & Scott, A. N. (2003). Revenue Premium as an Outcome Measure of Brand Equity. *Journal of Marketing*, *67*(5), 1–17.

Labrecque, L., Esche, J., Mathwick, C., Novak, T. P., & Hofacker, C. F. (2013). Consumer Power: Evolution in the Digital Age. *Journal of Interactive Marketing*, *27*(4), 257–269. doi:10.1016/j.intmar.2013.09.002

Liu-Thompkins, Y., & Rogerson, M. (2012). Rising to Stardom: An Empirical Investigation of the Diffusion of User-generated Content. *Journal of Interactive Marketing*, *26*(2), 71–82. doi:10.1016/j.intmar.2011.11.003

MacInnis, D. J., Moorman, C., & Jaworski, B. J. (1991). Enhancing and Measuring Consumers' Motivation, Opportunity, and Ability to Process Brand Information from Ads. *Journal of Marketing*, *55*(4), 32–53. doi:10.2307/1251955

Mallapragada, G., Grewal, R., & Lilien, G. (2012). User-generated Open Source Products: Founder's Social Capital and Time to Product Release. *Marketing Science*, *31*(3), 474–492. doi:10.1287/mksc.1110.0690

Malthouse, E. C., Haenlein, M., Skiera, B., Wege, E., & Zhang, M. (2013). Managing Customer Relationships in the Social Media Era: Introducing the Social CRM House. *Journal of Interactive Marketing*, *27*(4), 270–280. doi:10.1016/j.intmar.2013.09.008

Mavis, T. A., Stephanie, M. N., & Charles, H. N. (2010). The Influence of C2C Communications in Online Brand Communities on Third, our literature review reveals many disjoint studies on Customer Purchase Behavior. *Journal of the Academy of Marketing*, *38*(5), 634–653. doi:10.1007/s11747-009-0178-5

Mead, G. (1934). *Mind, Self and Society*. Chicago, IL: University of Chicago Press.

50 Metrics Every Executive Should Master. Upper Saddle River, NJ: Prentice Hall.

Mizerski, R. W., Golden, L. L., & Kernan, J. B. (1979). The Attribution Process in Consumer Decision Making. *The Journal of Consumer Research*, *6*(3), 123–140. doi:10.1086/208756

Moe, W. W., & Trusov, M. (2011). The Value of Social Dynamics in Online Product Ratings Forums. *JMR, Journal of Marketing Research*, *48*(3), 444–456. doi:10.1509/jmkr.48.3.444

Netzer, O., Feldman, R., Goldenberg, J., & Fresko, M. (2012). Mine Your Own Business: Market-structure Surveillance Through Text Mining. *Marketing Science, 31*(3), 521–543. doi:10.1287/mksc.1120.0713

Noort, V., Guda, H., Voorveld, A. M., & Reijmersdal, E. A. V. (2012). Interactivity in Brand Web Sites: Cognitive, Affective, and Behavioral Responses Explained by Consumers' Online Flow Experience. *Journal of Interactive Marketing, 26*(4), 223–234. doi:10.1016/j.intmar.2011.11.002

Park, C. W., & Mittal, B. (1985). A Theory of Involvement in Consumer Behavior: Problems and Issues. In J. N. Sheth (Ed.), *Research in Consumer Behavior* (pp. 201–231). Greenwich, CT: JAI Press Inc.

Paulo, A., Pavlidis, P., Chatow, U., Chen, K., & Jamal, Z. (2012). Evaluating Promotional Activities in an Online Two-sided Market of User-generated Content. *Marketing Science, 31*(3), 406–432. doi:10.1287/mksc.1110.0685

Pauwels, K., Ambler, T., Clark, B., La Pointe, P., Reibstein, D., Skiera, B., . . . Wiesel, T. (2008). Dashboards and Marketing: Why, What, How and What Research Is Needed? MSI Working Paper, Marketing Science Institute, Report 08-203.

Ransbotham, S., Kane, G. C., & Lurie, N. H. (2012). Network Characteristics and the Value of Collaborative User-generated Content. *Marketing Science, 31*(3), 387–405. doi:10.1287/mksc.1110.0684

Reibstein, D., & Srivastava, R. (2005). Metrics for Linking Marketing to Financial Performance. *Marketing Science Institute Special Report* 85–109.

Seraj, M. (2012). We Create, We Connect, We Respect, Therefore We Are: Intellectual, Social, and Cultural Value in Online Communications. *Journal of Interactive Marketing, 26*(4), 209–222. doi:10.1016/j.intmar.2012.03.002

Sinan, A., & Walker, D. (2011). Creating Social Contagion Through Viral Product Design: A Randomized Trial of Peer Influence in Networks. *Management Science, 57*(9), 1623–1639. doi:10.1287/mnsc.1110.1421

Sonnier, G. P., McAlister, L., & Rutz, O. J. (2011). A Dynamic Model of the Effect of Online Communications on Firm Sales. *Marketing Science, 30*(4), 702–716. doi:10.1287/mksc.1110.0642

Sridhar, S., & Srinivasan, R. (2012). Social Influence Effects in Online Product Ratings. *Journal of Marketing, 76*(5), 70–88. doi:10.1509/jm.10.0377

Stephen, A. T., & Toubia, O. (2010). Deriving Value from Social Commerce Networks. *JMR, Journal of Marketing Research, 47*(2), 215–228. doi:10.1509/jmkr.47.2.215

Stewart, D. W., & Pavlou, P. A. (2002). From Consumer Response to Active Consumer: Measuring the Effectiveness of Interactive Media. *Journal of the Academy of Marketing Science, 30*(4), 376–396. doi:10.1177/009207002236912

Sun, M. (2012). How Does the Variance of Product Ratings Matter? *Management Science, 58*(4), 696–707. doi:10.1287/mnsc.1110.1458

The SAGE Handbook of Social Network Analysis. John Scott, Peter J. Carrington, editors. SAGE Ltd., 364–367.

Tirunillai, S., & Tellis, G. J. (2012). Does Chatter Really Matter? Dynamics of User-generated Content and Stock Performance. *Marketing Science, 31*(2), 198–215. doi:10.1287/mksc.1110.0682

Trusov, M., Bodapati, A. V., & Bucklin, R. E. (2010). Determining Influential Users in Internet Social Networks. *JMR, Journal of Marketing Research, 47*(4), 643–658. doi:10.1509/jmkr.47.4.643

Vries, De., Lisette, S.G., & Leeflang, P.S.H. (2012). Popularity of Brand Posts on Brand Fan Pages: An Investigation of the Effects of Social Media Marketing. *Journal of Interactive Marketing, 26*(2), 83–91.

Wang, X., Yu, C., & Wei, Y. (2012). Social Media Peer Communication and Impacts on Purchase Intentions: A Consumer Socialization Framework. *Journal of Interactive Marketing, 26*(4), 198–208. doi:10.1016/j.intmar.2011.11.004

Weinberg, B. D., Ruyter, K., Dellarocas, C., Buck, M., & Keeling, D. I. (2013). Destination Social Business: Exploring an Organization's Journey with Social Media, Collaborative Community and Expressive Individuality. *Journal of Interactive Marketing, 27*(4), 299–310. doi:10.1016/j.intmar.2013.09.006

Wiesel, T., Pauwels, K., & Arts, J. (2011). Marketing's Profit Impact: Quantifying Online and Offline Funnel Progression. *Marketing Science, 30*(4), 604–611. doi:10.1287/mksc.1100.0612

Yadav, M., Valck, K., Henning-Thurau, T., Hoffman, D. L., & Spann, M. (2013). Social Commerce: A Contingency Framework for Assessing Marketing Potential. *Journal of Interactive Marketing, 27*(4), 311–323. doi:10.1016/j.intmar.2013.09.001

Zhang, K., Evgeniou, T., Padmanabhan, V., & Richard, E. (2012). Content Contributor Management and Network Effects in a UGC Environment. *Marketing Science, 31*(3), 433–447. doi:10.1287/mksc.1110.0639

Zhang, X., & Zhu, F. (2011). Group Size and Incentives to Contribute: A Natural Experiment at Chinese Wikipedia. *The American Economic Review, 101*(4), 1601–1615. doi:10.1257/aer.101.4.1601

Zhang, Z., Li, X., & Chen, Y. (2012). Deciphering Word-of-Mouth in Social Media: Text-based Metrics of Consumer Reviews. *ACM Transactions on Management. Information Systems, 3*(1), 1–22.

KEYWORDS AND DEFINITIONS

AMEC: International Association for Measurement and Evaluation of Communication.

Audience Growth Rate: A comparison of your audience today to your audience yesterday, last week, last month, etc.

Average Engagement Rate: Individual post engagement compared to overall followers.

Bounce Rate: The percentage of people who land on your page and immediately leave, without viewing any other pages rate at which people leave your site after viewing only one page.

Conversions: The number of people who achieved a desired result. This could be paying for a product, signing up for a trial, completing a form, or any other goal you've set up for your campaign.

CPC: Cost per click.

Dashboard: It is a user interface that resembles an automobile's dashboard, organizes and presents information in a way that is easy to read.

Engagement: The total number of likes, shares, and comments on a post.

Exit Rate: The percentage of people who leave your site from a given page. It's possible these people have browsed other pages of your site before exiting.

Funnels: The paths that visitors take toward converting.

Impressions: A look at how many people saw your post.

Inbound Links: The number of sites linking back to your website or page.

Leads: Potential conversions. These include anyone with the need or interest to pursue your product or service.

Metrics: Standards of measurement by which efficiency, performance, progress, or quality of a plan, process or product can be assessed.

Metrics Framework: A set of definitions of metrics.

Metric Theory: A metric theory is a combination of a metric framework, a set of definitions of attributes (qualitative or quantitative) and a mapping from the framework to the set of attributes, representing the hypothesis that each metric is a good predictor of the associated attribute.

M-O-A: Motivation, Opportunity and Ability.

Reach: A measurement of the size of audience you are communicating with.

Response Rates: These can be measured in two ways, either as the speed with which you respond to comments and replies on social media, or how quickly your marketing or sales department follows up with leads from social.

Social Marketing Analytics: The discipline that helps companies measure, assess and explain the performance of Social Media initiatives in the context of specific Business objectives.

Social Media: Websites and applications that enable users to create and share content or to participate in social networking.

Social Media Metrics: The use of data to gauge the impact of social media activity on a company's revenue.

Time on Site: A measure in minutes and seconds of how long a visitor stays on your site before exiting.

Valid Metrics Framework: A Framework that provides a mechanism to link activities to outputs to outcomes, tracks through the familiar sales funnel and helps create a focus on outcomes.

Visits vs. Unique Visits: Visits count each time a person visits your site or page, regardless of whether or not they have visited before. Uniques count each person only once.

WOM: Word of Mouth.

Section 4
Conceptual Business Models in Social Media Environment

Chapter 8
Social Media:
An Enabler for Governance

N. Raghavendra Rao
FINAIT Consultancy Services, India

ABSTRACT

Social Media is becoming increasingly important in society and culture; making people to join together on common interests and share opinions through internet. Most of the business organizations have been using social media as a communication tool for public relations and marketing. It is high time government departments should engage citizens of their country for interaction through social media. There are many schemes and programs initiated by the government need the attention of their citizens in a country. Government departments are required to form strategies to involve their citizens for making use of their schemes and programs. This chapter stresses the need for making use of social media by a government creating awareness of the schemes and programs to their citizens. Further it explains the importance of the interaction with their citizens through social media for good governance.

INTRODUCTION

Social media are nothing more than a special class of websites. They can be considered as second generation websites. First generation websites are those that are created by an organization or authority to upload information to be read by the users of their site. This model can be said as one-to many. Social media websites by contrast are platforms that provide users the ability and tools to create and upload their own mini websites or web pages. The content on these sites is created by the participants. This can be said as many-to-many model. Participants in this model are active in creating, commenting, rating and recommending content. Social media sites have three distinct characteristics. They are 1) majority of the content is generated by users, 2) high degree of participation and interaction between users, and 3) easily integrated with other sites. Social media are different from industrial or traditional media such as newspapers, television channels, and films.

Social media are relatively inexpensive and accessible to enable any one to publish or access information compared to industrial media, which generally require significant resources to publish information.

DOI: 10.4018/978-1-5225-0846-5.ch008

One common feature in social media and industrial media is capability to reach small or large audiences. For an example either a blog post or a television show may reach none or millions of people. The features that help to know the differences between social media and industrial media depend on one's understanding. Some of the features are described below:

1. Reach: Both industrial and social media technologies provide scale and enable any one to reach a global audience.
2. Accessibility: The means of production for industrial media are typically owned privately or by government. Social media tools are generally available to everyone at little or no cost.
3. Usability: Industrial media production typically requires specialized skills and training. Most of social media does not need specialized skills. In fact anyone can create and manage a social media site.
4. Time Period: he time taken between communications produced by industrial media can be long compared to social media. In the case of social media, communication will be virtually instantaneous responses.
5. Feasibility: Once a magazine article is printed and distributed, changes cannot be made to the same article. In the case of social media it can be altered almost instantaneously by comments or editing.

SOCIAL MEDIA TOOLS AND APPLICATIONS

Social media is the collective of online communications channels dedicated to community based input, interaction, content sharing and collaboration. Social media sites applications are dedicated to forums, micro blogging, social networks, social book marking, and social curation.

- **Forums:** Forums are like social mixers where every one is at equal level discussing with others. This can be considered as many to many communication tools. This tool allows anyone to start a topic and anyone to respond to one member or at equal levels. Content is usually a particular topic of interest to most of them.
- **Micro Blogging:** Micro Blogging is a web service that allows the subscriber to broadcast short messages to other subscribers of the service. Micro posts can be made public on website and/ or distributed to a private group of subscribers. Subscribers can read micro blog posts online or request that updates be delivered in real time to their email id as an instant message or sent to a mobile device as SMS text message.
- **Social Networking:** Online social networking brings people with common interests, ideas, goals, and experiences together. Some of the most popular social networks are face book, linked in and twitter.
- **Facebook:** Face Book is a popular free social networking websites that allows registered users to create, profiles, upload photos and video, to send messages and keep in touch with friends, families and colleagues.
- **Linkedin:** Linkedin is a social networking site designed specifically for the professionals. The goal of the site is to allow registered members to document and establish network among people they know and trust professionally.

- **Twitter:** Twitter is online social networking service that enables users to send and read short 140 character messages called "Tweets". Registered users can read and post tweets, but unregistered users can only read.
- **Social Curation:** Social Curation is collaborating sharing of web content organized around one or more particular themes or topics.
- **Blog:** It is a regularly updated website or web page. This is managed by an individual or a small group. This is written in an informal or conversational style.
- **Social Book Marking:** Social book marking is a user defined Taxonomy System for book marks. Taxonomy is sometimes called folksonomy and the book marks are referred as tags. Unlike storing book mark in a folder on one's computer tagged pages are stored on the web.
- **Wiki:** A wiki is online tool that enables users to add, amend, connect and post information for other users to see.
- **My Space:** This is a social networking site.

NEED FOR GOVERNMENT BE CONNECTED VIA SOCIAL MEDIA

Social media are a new initiative for government reaching their citizens at a phenomenally low cost. Further they enable citizens to interact with their government. The following points give an idea of the importance of social media in governance.

1. Schemes and programs: It is easy for government to highlight the important points in their schemes and programs to their citizens.
2. Online Reputation Management: Once citizens become aware of the schemes and programs of their government, they will express their views and make comments. Government can keep track of their citizen's views and comments. Further they can analyze and respond to them. They can also correct any wrong perception floating around.
3. Relationships: Government should personalize their services with innumerable choices in the hands of citizens. It has become imperative to add personal touch in their approach.
4. Role of Citizens: It would be better to create situations where citizens get a chance to discuss among themselves on any social media platform. Citizens can jointly talk to the government for modification and improvements of the schemes and programs.

Government and Governance

Growth of internet has provided scope of multiple applications. Governments everywhere in both developed and developing nations have started making use of internet in their functioning. The idea behind these governments moving from manual work to IT enabled system through internet is to improve governance. One needs to be clear about the distinction between government and governance. A quotation going back to 1656 is relevant in understanding the distinction: "Wise Prince ought not to be admired for their Government, But Governance". Government refers to actions carried out within a formal legal setting. Governance involves all activities of government along with informal activities. Further that can be outside a formal government setting that is meant to achieve goals.

Coordination for E-Governance

UNESCO defines E-Governance as Governance refers to the exercise of political, economic and administrative authority in the management of country's affairs including citizen's articulation of their interests and exercise of their legal rights and obligations. E-Governance may be understood as the performance of this governance through disseminating information to the public, and other agencies, and for performing government administrative activities.

UNESCO's definition indicates the importance of coordination among the government departments to provide and improve the government services, transactions with citizens, business community, and other departments of government.

Existing E-Governance Practice

E-Governance adopted by many government departments is in isolation and scattered pattern. This procedure lacks an integrated approach toward E-Governance. Information available with one department is not easily accessible by other departments. This is due to lack of standardization and uniformity in platform, data, and software. Instead of sharing the data, departments go for creations of their own data.

Case Illustration

Managing natural resources and economic development in a country are considered mutually antagonistic because promoting one would result in damaging the other (Tiwari 2010). Generally economic development is given more importance to remain competitive in the globalization scenario. It is important that a government in a country should realize the necessity for integrating natural resources concerns into economic development activity. Careful assessment is required to assess the stress on the earth's surface. A good natural resources management agenda is needed especially in the developing countries. The agenda should concentrate to reduce the stress on natural resources and to manage environmental issues in urban areas.

The type of data and information for the purpose of analysis and framing policies for natural resources management varies from country to country (Chapin, Kofnas & Floke 2009). It also depends on the availability of natural resources and its uses in the respective areas in a country. A well structured database and information systems are required by the authorities who are involved in planning and framing the policies for managing the natural resources under their control. Developing countries need a model that helps them to manage their country's resources judiciously. It is a general practice in many countries that the government assigns the responsibility to one department or more than one department for managing the components of natural resources. In most of the cases there will not be co-ordination among the departments for handling the issues related to natural resources management.

It is needless to say that nature belongs to all of us. It is important that the authorities who are involved in managing the natural resources are expected to be aware of structural composition and functions of natural resources (Quazi 2009). Natural resources management is inter-disciplinary where co-ordination is required among the various government departments. It is advisable to form a core team consisting of the representatives of various departments along with environment and bio-technology experts. Citizens who live close to the natural resources should be a part of the core team.

GEOGRAPHICAL DATA FOR A COUNTRY

The details of natural resources, population, and location of industries, educational institutions, towns and cities are available with a government in their information systems. The above data is classified as under.

- **Forests:** Data related to different types of forests such as moist tropical forests, dry tropical forests, mountain sub tropical forests, mountain temporal forests, sub alpine forests and alpine scrubs. Classification of forests varies form country to country.
- **Water Resources:** Data related to fresh water, lakes, rivers, ground water and oceans falls under this category.
- **Minerals:** Data related to metallic and non metallic falls under this category.
- **Agricultural Land:** Data related to cultivable and non cultivable land will be stored under this category.
- **Industrial Areas:** This will contain data pertaining to various industries such as automobiles, textiles, pharmaceuticals, consumer durables, and consumer related products.
- **Urban Areas:** Data related to residential, road, transport infrastructure and utility falls under this category.
- **Rural Areas:** Data related to the areas which do not fall under the category of urban areas can be considered under this category.
- **Service Units:** Data related to educational institutions, health care units, and other related units fall under this category.
- **Business Units:** Data related to trading organizations, financial institutions, hospitality units and other similar units fall under this category.

The above classified data will be useful for framing policies to manage resources in a country. While framing policies related to the management of natural resources, government can discuss and get the views of their citizens in the social media sites exclusively created for this purpose.

Natural Resources and Environmental Management

Industrialization and urbanization has become a world wide phenomenon. Industrialization and urbanization raise many environmental issues. It is because of the requirements of people living in urban and industrial areas are increasing. Managing their requirements need to be assessed properly.

The relationship between the availability of natural resources and its consumption can be established from the quantitative and textual data in any particular area (Chiras & Reganold 2010). Further it helps to address the environmental issues. This also helps the policy makers to understand in minimizing environmental hazards and avoiding the depletion of resources (Conroy & Paterson 2013) . The details pertaining to water usage, solid waste products, disposition of packing materials and other related information are available with the government departments. This will be more useful for environmental management. The type if data required for analyzing environmental issues are:

1. Under ground composition of urban areas
2. Water Usage

3. Disposition of wastage and
4. Air Pollutants

Composition of Urban Areas

Earth is being dug up in developing countries very frequently for the purpose of laying lines for communication, electricity, water pipes, sanitary and sewage lines. Generally it is not well planned activity especially in the developing countries. The details of the information pertaining to every area in cities and sub-urban areas are required for analysis. This data is required for town planners for action.

Water Usage

The data related to water consumption by residents and industrial services and business sectors are available with the different departments in any government.

Disposition of Wastage

The advancement in the package industry has created a good scope for marketing of the products manufactured across the globe. Demand for packed products is on the rise in the developing countries. Disposal of every kind of packaging materials at the end are to be carried out by the civic authorities. Statistics of discarded packing materials is required for allocation of places in cities and sub-urban areas.

Air Pollution

Oxygen and nitrogen are the major constituents of the atmosphere. Coal, fuel oil, and gasoline used by citizens emit carbon mono oxide. This human activity is contributing to changes in the atmosphere. The largest single source of the emission from automobile pollution in air is from the above factors. The health of human beings is affected by this pollution. The policy makers need to think of workable solutions for air pollutants.

Remote Sensing Application in Urban Areas

Planned development does not seem to take place in the developing countries in respect to urbanization. Information in respect to cities and suburban areas infrastructure is needed constantly (Hoornweg D, 2011). Remote sensing systems are more useful for getting data related to buildings, transport and utility infrastructure and environment assessment. This data will be useful for framing policies by the department in the government. Data for Environmental Management Analysis is given in the Table 1

Scenario in the Developing Countries

Governments in developing countries have the data pertaining to natural resources as described in the previous paragraphs of this chapter. E-Governance adopted by many government departments is in

Table 1. Data for environmental management analysis

Modules	Contents
Water Usage	• Residents • Industrial Sector • Service Sector • Business Sector
Disposal of Waste	**Packing Materials** • Textiles Jute, Sacks, Bags • Milk and Juice Cartons • Glass Bottles • Aluminum Cans • Steel Strapping • Corrugated Cartons and Boxes • Wood Pallets, Boxes and Craters **Solid Waste** • Industrial Waste • Municipal Waste
Air Pollutants	• Particles • Sulphur Di Oxide • Nitrogen Oxide • Hydrocarbons • Carbon Mono Oxide
Under Ground Composition of Urban Areas	• Communication Lines • Electricity Lines • Water Main Lines • Sanitary Sewage Lines • Story Water Lines

isolation and scattered pattern. This procedure lacks an integrated approach by the government. Information available with one department is not easily assessable by the other department. This is due to lack of standardization and uniformity in platform, data and software. Instead of sharing the data, the departments take efforts for creation of their own data. Lack of integration of data in respect of natural resources, many important points escape the attention of the government while preparing a comprehensive master plan for managing the natural resources in a country. Further their approach is mostly due to economics and opportunity rather to avoid misuse of natural resources. Mostly governments do not have the professional expertise in advising to manage the natural resources. Policies also keep changing depending on which elected political party is in the power.

Importance of Social Media for Governance

Prior to internet became popular, print media used to highlight the views of citizens in their papers. Advent of social media channel, many citizens in a country can take part in the discussions and expressing their views on the issues pertaining to them. Now it would be better that the government announces its tentative plans and policies in the social networking sites to get the views of the citizens (Gillin 2009). Citizens who have experience, knowledge and expertise can express their views on the government's tentative plans and policies. Many of them will be willing to express their views because of their interest in the management of natural resources.

Need for Social Media Channels for Citizens in India

It would be better if the government indicates their tentative plans and policies relating to deforestation in hilly area, preserving wild life animals, use of pesticides, mining, waste land reclamation, and disposal of waste materials. Once the government uploads their tentative approach on the above matters on the social media channels, citizens can express their views and narrate the incidents taken place in the various locations in India.

Following are some of the issues related to natural resources management in India have been discussed by a group of research scholars among themselves for their academic interest in their social media sites. It would be better the government creates a social media site exclusively for the citizens to discuss and express their views on the issues related to their country. The government can know the issues related natural resources, environment, noise pollution and other related issues from the citizens' perspective (Crowe 2012).

- Deforestation in a Hilly Area: Hilly region near Chotta Nagpur used to be a good forest area toward the turn of the century and used to receive fairly frequent afternoon showers favoring tea plantations. Following the destruction of forests rain fall declined in Chotta Nagpur area to such an extent that tea gardens also disappeared from the region.
- Waning Rain fall in Ooty: The ubnormal rain fall at Ooty in Nilgiris Mountains has been found to be closely associated with declining forest cover in these regions. Earlier the Nilgiris had luxuriant forest cover and annual rain fall used to be much higher.
- Deforestation in the Himalayas: Deforestation in Himalayas, involving clearance of natural forests and plantation of mono cultures like pinus rox burghi, eucalyptus camadulenis and other related plantations of monocultures have upset the ecosystem by changing various soil and biological properties. Nutrient cycling has become poor, original rich germ plasma is lost and the area is covered by exotic weeds. These areas are not able to recover and are losing their fertility.
- Wayanand Wildlife Sanctuary: The Wayanad wildlife sanctuary was affected by the displacement of tribal families living in that area. They were promised to allocate land in some other area for their dwelling. In the process of allocation of land, some tribal families got and many others did not get the land as promised to them. As a result of this the tribal felt cheated and they encroached into the forest in large numbers, cutting down the trees and started constructing huts and digging wells causing a violent encounter with the forest officials, ultimately causing injuries and deaths to the people.
- Valimik Tiger Reserve: The tribal living in the valmiki tiger reserve area in Bihar state felt that they have been deprived of their legitimate ancestral rights to collect firewood and fodder from the forest. Their employment was also lost due to the "Project Tiger". The jobless villagers felt cheated and started indulging in the destruction of forest and started engaging themselves in unsocial activities.
- Waste Land Reclamation: Economically unproductive land is generally used for dumping waste materials. This type of usage of land creates health problems to people who are living near by.
- Plastic Materials: Plastic has become a part of modern living. Right from packaging to making toys and various other items are made out of plastic. Normally they are petroleum products where alkaline oxides are polymerized to form plastics such as polythene. They are non-bio degradable being novel to the environment and hazardous to the earth.

- Noise Pollution during Diwali: Diwali is the festival of lights in India. There has been concern over the noise levels generated during Diwali. It is required that the manufacturers of fireworks should mention the noise levels on the labels of crackers.
- Environmental Awareness: Making environmental education as a part of a subject at the school stage will inculcate a feeling respecting the mother earth among the students.

Discussion on Natural Disasters on Social Media Platforms

Chennai is a city in India. This city has experienced heavy rains in the last week of November and first week of December 2015. This year's monsoon particularly has created havoc in Chennai. A group of architects, urban planners and environmental specialists discussed about the disaster created by the heavy rains in Chennai on their social media group channel. The following is the gist of the professionals' views regarding the reasons for the damage suffered by the city due to natural disaster. One of the participants has expressed that the citizens of Chennai are paying the price for unscrupulously developing real estate on the city's natural reserves, lakes and marsh lands. The fact remains that the increasing population has forced the city to reclaim land and expand its boundaries. The challenge lies in executing infrastructure development for this expanded city in a smart and sustainable manner.

Other participants indicated that permanent solutions are ignored and looking instead only at quick, and patchwork alternatives. They felt that the government authority can use the guidance of the institute of town planners of India and Indian Institute of Architects for plans constructing buildings. Increasing density within the city and expanding its boundaries with better connectivity in a scientific manner is the way forward. The reason behind the current water logging is because most water bodies have filled up and have lost their internal links. Rivers and lakes are to flourish their flow. Their needs are to be respected. The problem is house construction sites are becoming smaller and buildings are getting closer. Any construction activity during the monsoon is a threat to neighboring buildings as the soil is likely to slide.

In Chennai it can be seen imbalanced, sporadic growth areas driven by economics and opportunity rather than by cohesive master plan. A cohesive master plan is required that takes into account a holistic approach by placing nature, environment and urban expansion on equal pedestals. Developing residential and commercial projects in low lying areas need to be avoided. If developments are to take place storm water and sewage provisions should be designed to withstand double the normal capacity.

Nature always provides for a natural path for water to run off to the nearest lake or water body. When this is ignored and the path is blocked, there will not be alternative options. This will lead us for a perfect mess. This is exactly what has happened in Chennai. Local bodies have classified some areas as ecologically sensitive. These areas are required to be avoided for construction of building projects. Environment impact assessment reports are to be prepared objectively for issuing no objective certificates by the concerned authorities. It is unfortunate that with modern education systems being inspired solely by the west. In this process localized design principles in architecture and engineering lost its importance.

Cyclones, typhoons and hurricanes occur across the world. Sensible design, proper engineering and most importantly regular maintenance is required to ensure that buildings cope with these conditions. Hongkong is hit by a typhoon almost every year with wind velocities crossing 100 Km per hour. Still the buildings can withstand it.

A participant who happens to be an environment expert is of the strong opinion that reclaiming harsh lands and water bodies is definitely not the ethical thing to do. Further the expert fuels that we need to understand our city's ecology and topography. As all neighborhoods seem flat surface, most of the time citizens are clueless about the water flow in their regions. Only during the monsoon people will realize that they have converted watershed areas into commercial zones. A deeper understanding of the terrain is required. Many massive infrastructure projects have encroached on water bodies. It is felt before taking any large scale infrastructure project is under taken, the project in charge group should study the impact of such construction on the city's sub structures. Worldwide water bodies are respected and looked at as the natural long spaces of a city (Olteanu, Castilo, Diakopoulos & Aberer 2015). We borrow so many western concepts that are out of sync with culture, but why not adapt the good ideas.

Discussion on Ecological Cycles by a Group of Research Scholars on Social Media Channel

Right from ancient civilizations rivers have been the life of our cities and towns. Mohenjadaro, Harappa, Egypt and China thrived alongside fertile river banks. River water was used for irrigation, drinking, commerce and transport. As early as 18th century, communities from Chennai (Earlier known as Madras) had travelled by boat to a place called Mahabalipuram. The distance would be around 50 Kms. The entire water system was an intricate inter linked ecosystem. River, rivulets, canals, lakes and temple tanks led to the Adyar creek that finally joined the sea.

The newly developed Mahindra world city near Chennai has successfully integrated water systems linking storm water drains to the adjoining lake. Future cities need to respect these ecological cycles along with water management.

Trash Dump Site at Chitalapakkam Lake

Chitalapakkam Lake is near Chennai. This lake continued to be a garbage dumping site. It is a plain health hazard to the people in the locality. Garbage is also being burnt here. It has severe long term effects. Dumping sites should not be anywhere near a residential or school area. The metric tons of waste from houses, offices, commercial complexes and the streets get dumped at a site adjoining the lake. A NGO (Non Government Organization) has been involved in segregating bio-waste from the land fill manually and processing them for several years. They could cover only six tones of house hold garbage. The remaining garbage invariably ends up contaminating the water body, which is becoming more polluted. A primary health centre and a school are located next to the site, posing sanitation hazards.

A citizen, who comes to fish at the cleaner end of the lake, recalled that the lake used to be much cleaner when he grew up in this locality. A petition filed by a lawyer requested the court for restraint of dumping at the site, which is barely an acre. Garbage is piled here every day of the year, while the local authorities are removing the garbage on a weekly basis. The trash levels have increased in addition to the locality's households, commuters to the nearby place taking the road also add to the trash.

During the rains, the garbage levels increased and have reportedly just returned to the original status. But the stench hovers in the air and one can smell it even from several kilometers away. The local government agency is waiting for an approved dumping site from the government to be allocated for this purpose. The local government agency feels by norms a place of five acres of land space is required for dumping garbage. The chitlapakkam Lake has also over the years shrunk from 90 acres to its present 40 odd acres.

The above it the gist of discussion took place among by a group of citizens on their social media sites.

Recycle Demolition Debris

The global average contribution of construction and demolition waste is set to be around 50% of total solid waste generated in major cities. The numbers in Indian metros are not tracked, but safe estimate will be fairly close to this general worldwide statistics.

Construction and demolition of waste can be broadly categorized based on the sources of generation such as extracted soil, road and infrastructure waste, demolition waste and other complex wastes generated from project sites. The problem is further intensified with the general landfills. There is a pressing need for our building industry to recognize the global best practices in the area of construction and demolition of waste recycling.

It is usually the most land scarce areas that are first to innovate successfully. Hongkong and Singapore are considered pioneers in this area and manage to divert between 60-90% of their construction and demolition wastes from landfills. These high numbers are largely due to legal processes that are put in place along with the required incentives to ensure success in implementation. Their laws often describe step-wise processes for demolition, codes on the use of recycled aggregates and building standards that mandate inclusion of recycled construction and demolition materials.

While waste management is one part of the concern, there is a larger worry about the availability of resources. There is indiscriminate sand mining in the river beds and beaches that causes extensive damage to the environment. Strategies to recycle construction and demolition of wastes would lower the demand on river sand. The reduced demand will in turn preserve our natural ecology.

The above ecologic issue in respect of construction and demolition of waste require the attention of the government. An architect feels that the Indian standards for construction, project construction management have some indications on the inclusion of recycle material in constructed projects. These standards are required to be standardized and passed as bench marks for using recycled construction and demolition materials in the construction projects. This will improve the ecology in the construction sector.

Role of Social Media in Natural Calamities This is another a gist of discussion on social media channel pertaining to recycle of demolition debris.

When Chennai was to face with rains and floods in November & December 2015, social media came to the rescue of the residents. As phone networks remained jammed, most people used whatsapp. Twitter and Face Book have been made use of to share information, pictures, and extending help. The role of social media has been a life saver, as several people were given help, while others came forward to do it.

People of Chennai turned crusaders in many places. Citizens took to twitter to offer their homes to strangers seeking shelter from the rain and floods. Images and videos of helpful Samaritans were soon uploaded in social media sites. Live updates of the situation in the social media sites saved many people from getting caught unguarded. When there was no access to news, these social media were information providers (Imran Muhammad, Castillo Carlos, Diaz Fernando, & Vieweg Sarah, 2015). Several help groups used the online media, as it was the only virtual communication room to get in contact with emergency numbers of ambulance. The constant stream of whatsapp forwards and other social media channels also helped to distribute a substantial amount of food items and other requirements of the people who are stuck in the flood affected areas. Another group of citizens played a crucial role in providing weather forecasting and updates in the various social media groups.

DISCUSSION

It is interesting to note many aspects related to natural resources, handling of solid waste, natural disaster, recycle of demolition debris and environmental issues are being discussed by the various groups on their social media channels. It will be highly useful if an exclusively social media channel is created by a government for knowing the views, opinions, suggestions and professional approach from their citizens (Simon, Goldberg, & Adini 2015). Further the government can announce its proposed policies and plans pertaining to natural resources management and other related issues on its social media sites. There are many forms of social networking channels available for interaction with the citizens in a country (Hestres 2013). Each type of site has its strengths and advantages. The following few sites give an overview of the usefulness of the social media forms (Vijayendra & Pillai 2011).

- **Linkedin**
  - Research and connect with professionals in environment consultancy
  - Creation of groups where different individuals, professionals and expert collaborate on ideas to achieve a particular objective in the area of natural resources management
  - Link with similar type of projects in the other parts of a country
- **Twitter**
  - Tweet photos of environmental practices
  - Involve citizens in number of conversations on relevant green issues
  - Experts championing green causes
  - Retweet interesting posts about environmental issues including news articles and published articles
- **Face Book**
  - Share interesting environmental stories from the news on one's face book page
  - Upload photos of environmental activities in the country
  - Share other people's posts on relevant issues

FUTURE RESEARCH DIRECTIONS

Social media is an open box of potential. This is particularly true with natural resources management and environmental issues (Wending, Radisch, & Jacobzone 2013) . The opportunities that social networking and social media sites provide are yet to be fully utilized by the government. These sites can be used to promote good environmental practices, share ideas of best practices, awareness of government policies and plans (Kawasaki & Fitzpatrick 2015). Business houses are already utilizing social media channels for promoting their business activities. Similarly the government should involve the citizens of the country to express ideas and suggestions on the issues related to their country. The government should engage the experts in social media for developing a business model for them (Golden, 2012). Research scholars can also develop a prototype model for the government for interaction with their citizens on social media channels.

CONCLUSION

This chapter explains that the government is having the data of the country's natural resources and its utilization with them. Even the government has the required data; many issues related to the resources are escaping the attention of the government. It may be noted that a group of citizens and professionals are already discussing and expressing their views on the resources, disasters and environmental issues on their social media channels. It is high time that the government makes use of social media sites for better governance involving their citizens.

REFERENCES

Adam, C. (2012). *Disasters 2.0: The Application of Social Media Systems for Modern Emergency Management*. Taylor & Francis Inc.

Alexandra, O., Carlos, C., Nicholas, D., & Karl, A. (2015). Comparing Events Coverage in Online News and Social Media: The Case of Climate Change. *International Conference Web and Social Media*.

Chapin, F.S., Kofnas, G.P., & Floke, C. (2009). *Principles of Ecosystem Stewardship: Resilience- Based Natural Resource Management in a Changing World*. London: Springer.

Chiras Daniel, D., & Reganold John, P. (2010). *Natural Resource Conversation Management: Management for a Sustainable Future*. Prentice Hall.

Conroy, M. J., & Paterson, J. T. (2013). *Decision Making in Natural Resource Management: A Structured Adaptive Approach*. Willey-Blackwell.

Gillin, P. (2009). *The New Influencers- Marketers Guide to New Social Media*. Quill Driver Books

Golden, M. (2012). *Social Media: Strategies for Professionals and their firms*. Wiley and Sons. doi:10.1002/9781119200352

Hestres, L. E. (2013). *Preaching to the Choir: Internet-Mediated Advocacy, Issue Public Mobilization and Climate Change: New Media and Society*. Sage Journals.

Hoornweg, D. (2011). *Cities and Climate Change: Responding to an Urgent Agenda*. World Bank Publication.

Kawasaki, G.,, & Fitzpatrick, P. (2015). *The Art of Social Media for Power Tips for Power users*. Penguin.

Muhammad, I., Carlos, C., & Diaz, F. V. S. (2015, July). Processing Social Media Messages in Mass Emergency A Survey. *ACM Computing Surveys*, *47*(5), 67.

Quazi, S. A. (2009). *Principles of Physical Geography*. APH Publishing Corporation.

Tiwari, A. K. (2010). *Infrastructure for Sustainable Rural Development*. New Delhi: Regal Publications.

Tomer, S., Avishay, G., & Brunia, A. (2015, October). Socializing in Emergencies- A review of the Use of Social Media in Emergency Situations. *International Journal of Information Management*, *35*(5), 609–619. doi:10.1016/j.ijinfomgt.2015.07.001

Vijayendra, H., & Pillai, A. (2011). *Social Media Simplified- Twitter, Face Book- Beyond Casual Networking*. New Delhi: Ocean Paper Backs.

Wending, C., Radisch, J., & Jacobzone, S. (2013). *The use of Social Media in Risk and Crisis Communication*. OECD Working Papers on Public Governance no 25. OECD Publishing.

KEY TERMS AND DEFINITIONS

Eco System: A Biological community and its physical environmental exchanging matter and energy.

Ecology: Study of interactions of living organisms with their biotic and abiotic environment.

Governance: Exercise of political, economic, and administrative authority in the management of country's affairs including citizen's articulation of their interests.

Land Fill: Solid wastes are dumped into the low lying areas.

Natural Disasters: Hazards that destroy or damage wild life habitats, damages property and human settlements.

Social Media: It uses web based technology to quickly disseminate knowledge and information to a large number of users.

Social Networks: This allows people to build personal web pages and then connect with friends to share content and communicate.

Urbanization: Increasing concentrations of people in cities.

Chapter 9
Social Media:
An Enabler in Developing Business Models for Enterprises

N. Raghavendra Rao
FINAIT Consultancy Services, India

ABSTRACT

Rapid changes are taking place in global business scenario. It has become a necessity for enterprises to adapt to these changes. Social media facilitates business enterprises to make use of the opportunities in the global market. Social media has become an important source of information for the stakeholders of business enterprises. Structured, semi-structured, and unstructured data from social media provide a good scope for developing business models for enterprises. This chapter mainly talks about developing the conceptual business models in the sectors such as automobiles, textiles and software developing companies. Further, this chapter explains making use of the concepts such as virtual reality, multimedia and cloud computing with the data from social media in developing conceptual business models.

INTRODUCTION

The existing ways of doing business are constantly changing and opportunities in the present global markets have to be exploited at a rapid pace (Evans 2010). Business enterprises need to realize that managing technical knowledge as well as innovative process in conducting business in the way that is required to remain competitive in the global market is necessary. Every business enterprise has unique challenges to face in its sector. It is high time they take advantage of making use of social media for their business (Choudhary 2012). Even the most stable industries and the strongest brands can be blown to bits by the emerging concepts in information and communication technologies. Technology is forcing business enterprises to rethink their business models and organizational designs. Further the technology facilitates to rebalance their share in the market place. Smaller organizations that are fast and flexible can now outmaneuver the traditional large enterprises by employing new technology. The new technology enables them to deliver goods and services to their customers at a faster pace and lower cost. This

DOI: 10.4018/978-1-5225-0846-5.ch009

chapter talks about the three conceptual business models developed by making use of the concepts such as multimedia, virtual reality and cloud computing along with the data from social media. The essence in these models is the importance of the data and information from social media.

Need for a Business Model

The problem arises when the organizations are spending too much time tinkering with the existing business models of their organizations instead of relaying their teams around the potential to do something extraordinary in the market place (Alpert 2012). Tinkering is like painting a car when the engine is weak. The challenge today is to develop sustainable business that is compatible with the current economic reality. Now it has become imperative for every business enterprise to make use of data from social media that will help them in developing conceptual business models for their products and services (van Belleghem 2012). Developing a conceptual business model is nothing but identifying the relevant concepts in information and communication technology and making use of them with data from a social media in developing a business model suitable to a business enterprise (Brogan 2010).

Trends in Management Concepts

One can find from the analysis of trends in management in every decade a new concept has been emerging. The moment it emerges, it is considered as "Next Big Thing" or "Next Important Concept". In 1950's "Brain Storming" concept has become popular. It was considered to be very important factor in involving the employees in business enterprises to generate new ideas. In 1960's and 1970's sensitivity groups have played an important role in business enterprises. Group leaders of this group were considered to be 'Gurus'. They were expected to lead group managers. Then it was a practice 'Gurus' would make brief opening remarks and they would wait for response from the group managers. Then the 'Gurus' would facilitate them to express and try to clarify. It was a hope that 'Inner Manager' would emerge. More research would follow on their deliberations. The era 80's was considered as the age of quality management. During this period quality control, quality circles, six sigma and other related approaches were followed for enhancing workers performance. Later the focus has been shifted to production and operation costs. The idea has been to reduce production and operation costs through total quality management, just in time, inventory, flexible manufacturing systems and efficient supply chain management. However reduction in cost alone is no longer enough being an effective strategy. Later retaining and developing customers has become critical. Then the focus has been shifted customer relationship management.

Data in the Present Marketing Scenario

Traditionally the major source of data has been from expanding customer relationship management application. In the present business scenario, the complexity of data sources is on increase. The data sources which contribute to complexity are 1) Primary Data 2) Secondary Data 3) Internet Data 4) Device Data and 5) Supply Chain Data.

Primary data provides data related to surveys, experiments, and observations. Secondary data is based on business data, reports from industries, market place and competitors' data. The source of internet data is from social media, and social networking. The data from the device are such as mobile phones, sensors and RF Data. Vendor data and pricing form supply chain data are considered as another important source.

Consumers Approach in the Digital Age

To days consumers thinking have changed. Many of them do not read news papers. They fast forward through television commercials, and they consider unsolicited e-mails as junk (Davidow 2011). This is because they have new options that better fit their digital life style. They can choose from the marketing messages received by them. They would prefer marketers who talk with them, not at them. Today's consumers want relevant interactive communication across the digital power channels such as web sites and social media (Bilton 2013).

Social Media in Marketing Perspective

Social Media provide marketers with a new platform to reach out their customers at a phenomenally low cost. Most importantly they are real time and allow a marketer to capture markets alive. It is now the marketer's responsibility to ensure that the content generated through social media is constantly updated as to keep the business alive. Social media allow customers to listen different brands of products. Proper strategy can lead to customers turning into marketers for certain brands (Brito Michael, 2014). At the same time one negative opinion can multiply and cause a serious blow to the brand's image. If effectively utilized, Social media can empower companies as well as customers to have a two way communication (Haryal & Pillai 2011). Further it facilitates an openness which can go a long way in building the trust of the customers. Once this trust is established and the enterprise starts reasoning with the customer's needs. Then it can be said that social media have achieved their objectives.

Social media can be said very important to the extension of an enterprises business (Bradley & Mark 2011). It is because social media allow sharing of knowledge and insights in developing business processes. Further it enables executives in business enterprises to work together closely for achieving predefined tasks.

Concept of Virtual Reality

Before any major change has to be effected in a business enterprise in the area of product development or adding new features in the existing product or changing a business process, the enterprise would like to visualize before it is implemented (Chorafas & Steinmann 1995). Visualization of the above activities is possible through stimulation. This kind of simulation can be termed as virtual reality. The concept of virtual reality facilitates in visualizing the new ideas for business purposes. The elements constituting virtual reality are audio, voice, graphics, images, sound and motion sensing. These elements along with numerical and textual data facilitate the creation of real time simulation. Business enterprises have choices to evaluate their new ideas by making use of the concept of virtual reality. Simulated outputs resulted from virtual reality application programs help to visualize and visiblize the proposed ideas of business enterprises. They also help to visualize hypothetical cases in business and interact with the applications developed with the virtual reality concept. It may be noted that the concept of multimedia is required in virtual reality applications. The concept of virtual reality is the seed of innovation for developing a business model. Visualization, visibilization, and visitraction are the terms associated in virtual reality.

- **Visualization**: Information and communication technology has made visualization process as important component in the development of advanced business applications. Presentation of output through simulated data facilitates to analyze and take decisions.
- **Visibilization**: Visibilization makes mapping of physical reality with virtual reality for end users to understand the output generated through simulated data.
- **Visitraction**: Visitraction is the process of visualization of concepts, characteristics or phenomena lacking a direct physical interpretation. This results in establishing a link between the concepts and ideas.

COMPONENTS OF MULTIMEDIA

The components of multimedia are graphics, images, animation, video, audio, and tactile. Virtual reality imitates the way the real object or scene looks and changes. The components of multimedia support the virtual reality concept while creating or designing a prototype model of a product to be produced by an organization.

Cloud Computing

Cloud computing provides mechanism for sharing and coordinating the use of resources. This mechanism enables the creation of geographically and organizationally distributed components of virtual computing systems.

Cloud computing supports the concept of virtualization in respect of applications, devices, networking, storage, and servers. Further it can be said that cloud computing facilitates the economies across the globe closely inter connected and integrated.

Case Illustration 1

An Indian based ROA Motor Bikes Ltd has been manufacturing motor bikes for Indian and global markets. They have been in the market over a period of two decades. Their products are well received in both the markets. Till recently their market share has been encouraging. Due to the globalization policy followed by many countries, the global market is now open to many players across the globe. ROA Motor bikes ltd has started losing hold on the market due to globalization. ROA Motor Bikes Ltd has decided innovating new methods and business processes in production and marketing of their motor bikes.

They have decided to hire the services of the domain experts who have rich experience in the motor bikes sector. They have identified the domain experts living in France and Korea. It has been agreed among themselves that the domain experts and their team members will operate from their respective countries. Further it has been agreed to use the concepts of virtual reality, cloud computing and social media in developing business models for ROA Motor Bikes Limited.

Social Media and Conceptual Design Approach

The domain experts felt that it would be better to interact with young automobile engineers in their respective countries who have passion to do something different. So the domain experts have created a social media site exclusively for young automobile engineers. The young automobile engineers have been invited to express their views and suggestions on the existing motor bikes models manufactured by ROA Motor Bikes Limited in the social media site created for them. The views and suggestions discussed by the young automobile engineers among themselves have posted them in the social media site. The domain experts downloaded the data and information from the above site and stored in the datawarehouse created in the cloud computing environment by ROA Motor Bike Limited. The domain experts have analyzed and considered the feasible features from the above data. They have designed a motor bike from their professional experience along with the feasible features suggested by the young automobile engineers. Their design has taken care of the real world requirements. Simulated version of a motor bike has been tested and experiments have been carried out on the computer systems. The domain expert team members have immersed themselves in every aspect of design and testing. Working in front of a large screen of a computer system has given a sense of being actually testing a bike in a real world perception. The concept of virtual reality has helped them to look from the real world situation.

Later the domain experts have posted an invitation in the social media site inviting the young automobile engineers to test the bike created under virtual reality concept at their office. Some of the young engineers have tested the bike at the expert's office. This testing has given a sense of being actually riding a motor bike in a real world.

This experience induced them to interact with their friends. Further they persuaded them to visit the domain expert's office to experience by them. Many more young engineers tested the simulated bike. They have given their feedback to the domain experts. Some fine tuning has taken place on the basis of their feedback. After this the final design of a motor bike to ROA Motor Bikes Limited, similar type of testing by engineers has taken place in India before the design was frozen.

It may be noted that the domain experts have made use of the resources of ROA Motor Bikes Limited from their respective countries. The software such as CAD/CAM, Multimedia, Data mining, Text mining, and Virtual Reality are required for the design of a motor bike. They are made available to them by ROA Motor Bikes Limited. Cloud computing environment facilitated the use of the above mentioned software by the domain experts from their respective countries . The data and information provided by the young automobile engineers in the exclusive social media site created for this purpose helped the domain experts to think in an innovative way.

Case Illustration 2

OAR Limited is a management and information technology consultants based in India. Their team consists of professionals who have rich experience in the areas of management and information and communication technology. OAR Limited has been in consultancy business over a period of three decades. Their consultancy in management and information technology based business solutions has helped many business enterprises to improve their business. OAR Limited has offices in western and eastern countries including India. The consultants of OAR Limited are based in different parts of the globe. In recent times their valuable clients have started feeling the impact of competition due to globalization policy followed by many countries. One of the clients of OAR Limited has felt that managing technical knowledge as well as innovative process in conducting business is the way to remain competitive in the global market. The client has requested them to design a knowledge repository system for the purpose of innovative approach for their business needs. In response to their request OAR Limited has decided to develop a business model for knowledge repository system. They have applied the concepts of knowledge management and information technology disciplines for developing a knowledge repository system.

Case Illustration 3

3G textile mill is one of the leading textile mills in India. This textile mill has been in the business over five decades. Uniqueness of this mill is managed by a management team consisting of a president, senior vice president and vice president who belong to three different generations. Their approach and decisions are based on their experience, business insight and education. Their mill products are for ladies and men. They also manufacture readymade garments for men and ladies. 3G textile mill has been making profits even though the three management team members follow their own methods. Every team member has his own information system for his product related activities such as purchase of materials, production design and marketing.

Vice President of the mill felt that the concept of social media is to be made use of for their business. As a maiden venture he attempted in getting feedback from their customers for designing a cloth material. He has selected a cloth material for ladies. A sample cloth material has been designed with his experience, knowledge and also with the inputs from the domain experts in their organization. The concepts of virtual reality and multimedia are applied in creating a material with the different combination of colors. While designing the cloth material, the types of dyes available in the market are also kept in mind.

The marketing department of the mills has created an exclusive social media channel for the prospective customers to express their opinions of the proposed design of a cloth material. The proposed design of the material is uploaded in the site. Vendors of dyes have been informed to visit the social media site to get an idea the types of dyes are to be supplied once the proposed design is finalized.

Interactions with the prospective customers on the social media site have facilitated them to understand their needs and tastes. This has helped the mills to design a cloth material from the data and information from the social media site created exclusively by the marketing department.

METHODOLOGY

OAR Limited has created a core team consisting of selected experts in their organization who are based in different countries. The task of the core team is to identify the important factors related to the business in the globalization scenario. These factors should be the base for designing a business model in knowledge repository system. Further the company has created a social media site exclusively for the core team. This site will enable the core team to exchange ideas and interact among themselves for designing a business model for "Knowledge Repository System".

The important element in this model is the resource for knowledge. How broad or narrow its knowledge base depends upon the requirements of a business enterprise. A business enterprise has to know the industrial scenario for their products. This will help the enterprise to know its competitive advantages and disadvantages in the market. Further it will help them to identify the gaps in their system. Innovative processes can be thought of in bridging the existing gaps by making use of knowledge repository system.

Social Media and the Core Team

The members of the core team who work at the different locations in the globe shared their experience and knowledge in the social media site created exclusively for them (Chaney 2009). The constant interaction among the team members could successfully integrate their ideas under different business environment towards the completion of developing a business model.

The word "Capital" or "Asset" as suffix to "Intellectual" is not used in strict accounting terminology. It is only a term referred for "Intangible Assets". It may be noted that the meaning of both the terms is the same. The core team has classified the components of intangible assets under four heads.

1. Market assets represent business enterprise's brand image, distribution network and collaboration.
2. Intellectual property assets are patents, copyrights, design rights, trademarks, and trade secrets.
3. Human centered assets indicate knowledge and entrepreneurial ability of employees in business enterprises.
4. Infrastructure assets consist of business processes, methods and information systems.

The core team came to the conclusion that the above components need to be assessed properly. These assessments will enable business enterprises to conduct their business smoothly. Knowledge sharing network by the core team in the social media site has resulted in developing a workable business model. Resource for knowledge base created by the core team helps to develop a business model for knowledge repository system.

Summary of the Above Illustrations

A business enterprise can take advantage of unique knowledge and resources where ever they are located. It may be technology expert or domain expert. Till recently the standard model of development of a product or service has been a linear process from research through to design, development and manufacturing. Now many of these processes are carried out concurrently and collaborating through social media sites created exclusively for this purpose. Case Illustration-1 demonstrates how wide range of technologies can stimulate innovative approach. Case illustration – 2 explains that the need for a business enterprise's requirements to evaluate the core competence in relation with their products and services. The elements in external competency are patents, brands, monopoly and trade secrets. The element in internal competency consists of process technology, distribution channels, and advantages in costing and size of plants. The core competency in an organization is the collective learning especially in coordinating diverse skills and integrating multiple streams of technologies. Knowledge networking is needed in the present business scenario. It is a process of management and information technology disciplines where people share information, knowledge and experiences to develop new knowledge for handling new situations. It may be noted that Knowledge repository system stimulates innovative thinking through knowledge transfer. Services of professionals and domain experts through the exclusively created social media sites present the potential scope in the world of business in developing business models. Case Illustration-3 gives an overview of the approach followed by the textile mill to design a cloth material for ladies making use of the concepts such as virtual reality and multimedia. The feedback from the prospective customers on the social media channel facilitated them to finalize the design of the cloth for production. Further vendors who supply dyes and raw cotton are able to get the required information for supplying the materials as per the requirements of a new design. Customers' tastes are becoming more homogeneous around the globe. The feedback on social media channel facilitates to innovative approach (Gallo 2012).

FUTURE RESEARCH DIRECTIONS

Many business enterprises are under the impression that social media is meant only for marketing and brand awareness (Brown 2011). Most of them are not aware that social media can be used for improving business processes and developing new business models (Gillin 2009). The three case illustrations discussed in this chapter give an idea in making use of the various concepts in information technology and management in developing business models under social media environment. There is a good scope for developing business models with an innovative approach from the data in the social media site exclusively created for this purpose.

CONCLUSION

Social media is no longer confined to interaction among friends and relatives only. It may be noted that social media channel can create an efficient frame work to leverage in business environment (Gillin 2009). Technology does not drive change. It enables change.

REFERENCES

Alpert, J. (2012). *The Mobile Marketing Revolution*. New Delhi: Tata McGraw Hill Education Private Limited.

Bilton, N. (2013). *Hatching Twitter UK*. Sceptre.

Bradley Anthony, J., & Mark, P. (2011). *The Social Organization Boston*. Harvard Business Review Press.

Brito, M. (2014). Your Brand, the Next Media Company. In *How a Social Business Strategy Enables Better Content, Smarter Marketing, Deeper Customer Relationships*. Indiana Polis.

Chorafas Dimitris, N., & Steinmann. (1995). *Virtual Reality Practical Applications in Business and Industry*. Prentice Hall.

Choudhary, P. (2012). *The Unlimited Business Opportunities on the Internet*. Xcess Info store Private Limited

Chris, B. (2010). *Social Media 101 Tactics and Tips to develop your Business online*. John Wiley and Sons Inc.

Davidow William, H. (2011). *Over connected- The Promise and Threat of the Internet.* London: Headline Publishing Group.

Eileen, B. (2011). *Working the Crowd Social Media Marketing for Business.* British Informatics Society Limited.

Evans, D. (2010). *Social Media Marketing- An Hour a Day.* New Delhi: Wiley India Private Limited.

Gallo, C. (2012). *The Power of Four Square- 7 Innovative Ways to get your customers wherever they are.* New Delhi: Tata McGraw Hill Education Private Limited.

Gillin, P. (2009a). *Secrets of Social Media Marketing.* Quill Driver Books.

Gillin, P. (2009b). *The New Influencers- A Marketers to Social Media.* Quill Driver Books.

Haryal, V., & Pillai, A. (2011). *Social Media Simplified Twitter; Face Book-Beyond Casual Networking.* New Delhi: Ocean Paper Backs.

Paul, C. (2009). *The Digital Hand Shake- Seven Proven Strategies to grow your Business using Social Media.* John Wiley and Sons Inc.

van Belleghem, S. (2012). The Conversation Company boost Your Business through Culture. In *People and Culture.* London: Koga Page.

KEY TERMS AND DEFINITIONS

Conceptual Business Model: A Business model is designed on the basis of ideas from the various sources.

Core Team: A team consisting of domain experts who perform multi disciplinary activities.

Data Warehouse: A large data store containing organizations historical data which is used primarily for data analysis and data mining.

Data Mining: The process of analyzing large data sets in a data ware house to find number of obvious patterns.

Knowledge Repository System: An information system contains information pertaining to skill gained through experience and education.

Text Mining: The process of analyzing the textual content in a data ware house.

Virtual Reality: A system in which images that look like real and three dimensional objects are created by a computer system.

Section 5
Software Tools for Analysis and Research in Social Media Sites

Chapter 10
Employing the Sentiment Analysis Tool in NVivo 11 Plus on Social Media Data:
Eight Initial Case Types

Shalin Hai-Jew
Kansas State University, USA

ABSTRACT

Sentiment analysis has been used to assess people's feelings, attitudes, and beliefs, ranging from positive to negative, on a variety of phenomena. Several new autocoding features in NVivo 11 Plus enable the capturing of sentiment analysis and extraction of themes from text datasets. This chapter describes eight scenarios in which these tools may be applied to social media data, to (1) profile egos and entities, (2) analyze groups, (3) explore metadata for latent public conceptualizations, (4) examine trending public issues, (5) delve into public concepts, (6) observe public events, (7) analyze brand reputation, and (8) inspect text corpora for emergent insights.

INTRODUCTION

For those conducting research in the social sciences and other fields that overlap with human behavior, it is important to integrate insights from social media—given its wide adoption and popularity. Any social issue, by definition, has a public facing side. People go online to self-express and vent, to rally others to their cause, to raise public consciousness, and to engage in political activities. In an era of openness, as people go online to post status updates, selfies, tips, and resources—as messages, audio, video, and multimedia—the social media platforms that host such contents enable access to the direct shared digital contents as well as metadata and trace data. This all makes for torrents of public information made available by social media platforms through their application programming interfaces (APIs) and other means. The available social media data include contents (textual and multimedia, such as messaging, profile data, Tweetstreams, crowd-sourced encyclopedia articles, and others), metadata (tags), trace data

DOI: 10.4018/978-1-5225-0846-5.ch010

(like interaction information), and others. For all the mystique and subjectivity of human connectivity, such social information may be collected within and across social media platforms, through the Web and Internet, for machine-processing and extracted insights. In some cases, social media insights (from user-generated data) are central to the research, and in others, it is complementary and peripheral.

Individual and mass sentiments are seen as possible indicators of a precursor event, an early signal, if you will. If people's communications on social media platforms are read as part of a sentient human sensor network, it may be possible to use such messaging as an early warning of anything with mass or destructive potential. Social media has been accused of enabling people to fall into massthink and to speed the sharing of misinformation, outrage, and judgment, and pushing the speed of events, to enable "tempests in a teacup." In environments where speed is key, people may suspend their critical filters and sense of disbelief, and go with unvetted information. For many, whatever is top-of-mind is simply shared as part of a quick status update, and information that is sent by a known individual or "friend" is merely retweeted and propagated throughout social media platforms without too much oversight, if any. As T. Haile, CEO of Chartbeat observed, people share information socially without reading the original shared article (Jeffries, 2014). Such records become then part of the public record and are eminently capturable, viewable, and analyzable. Mass sentiment may also be read as indicators of public attitudes about particular public figures, products, services, policies, and other in-world phenomena. Researchers have made headway in using computational linguistic analysis to explore the underlying causes behind sentiments and emotions, including multi-clause (and more complex) causes (Chen, Lee, Li, & Huang, 2010, p. 179). Other studies have probed how verbs—whether positive or negative or "bipolar-preference" (balanced in terms of both positive and negative polarity) in polarity preference—affect their direct objects (the nouns that receive the verb's action): "Given clear-cut polarity preferences of a verb, nouns, whose polarity is yet unknown, can now be classified. We reached a lower bound of 81% precision in our experiments, whereas the upper bound goes up to 92%" (Klenner & Petrakis, 2012, p. 35).

The intuition is that the observed expressed sentiments and emotions, whether explicit or implicit, are somehow reactive to something, whether from within or without, whether from a single cause or multiple causes. In one case, the research team used combinations of prepositions, conjunctions (subordinate and coordinate), "light verbs," "reported verbs," epistemic markers, and others (Chen, Lee, Li, & Huang, 2010, p. 183). There has also been work on respective cultures and proclivities to particular ideas based on cultural preconditioning. Likewise, there have been studies of individuals who tend to be suggestible and vulnerable to responding to others' ideas and instigations, even through remote messaging such as through social media.

Sentiment analysis is a subfield of natural (ordinary) language processing (NLP), which involves the formal computational study of evolved human languages. NLP draws on techniques from computer science, artificial intelligence (AI), computational linguistics, and text analytics (Luo, Chen, Xu, & Zhou, 2013, p. 53). Work in text summarization as a general category and computational sentiment analysis as a specific approach has been ongoing for the past decade. Recent advancements in research-enhancing software tools have enabled researchers without command-line and developer skills to access data that would not be available otherwise. Researchers are able to process textual data with increased affordances, such as fast machine "remote" reading or non-reading (as compared to human "close-reading" of text) and the extraction of identified themes or concepts and sentiment analysis.

QSR International's rollout of NVivo 11 Plus (on September 29, 2015) has much heralded because of some novel capabilities; this upgrade features a new sentiment analysis tool, which involves comparing a text or text corpus against a sentiment lexicon set (or dictionary) which quantifies words based on where each falls in a positive-negative sentiment continuum. Sentiment analysis, as practiced, is fairly coarse-grained with only the polarities of "positive" and "negative". There is a value in the parsimonious approach of focusing on two dimensions—the binary of either positive or negative; this polar approach is even more valuable given that a majority of stances tend towards the broad middle or the neutral. It may also be assumed that some percentage of a population may be indifferent to the particular issue. This schema is simple, but it actually has wide application. Sentiment labels may be applied to various objects: a person with certain dispositional tendencies in a personality; public opinion about a topic; a text or text corpus in a particular domain (think of the label of economics as a "dismal" science), and others. Beyond the "positive" or "negative" dimensions, there are more fine-grained emotion-based analyses that may be done based on some core emotion models (including anger, sadness, surprise, fear, disgust, joy, and contempt), and there are even personality models applied. [Combined with the theme extraction component, which captures a kind of topic modeling (the identification of topical or concept-based patterns from text), the sentiment analysis feature offers additional analytical awareness.]

Another related branch of research involves the automated identification of whether a text or a text corpus is subjectively or objectively composed. In a sense, sentiment analysis serves as a bridge to more complex analyses. While the polarities are superficially simple, sentiment analysis may be analyzed in a granular way—with close-in readings of sentiments labeled as positive or negative and studies of those communicating the respective sentiments and the related ideas. Depending on the respective dataset, sentiment manifests in different ways and through different words and sentence structures. Sentiment analysis may be integrated with research-based hypothesizing, predictive analytics, and decision-making. Sentiment may be studied as deeply held "biases" (an assumed natural part of egos based on unique worldviews and local experiences) that tend to be more stable over time, or shallowly held (ephemeral, transient, and changing over time) opinion commitments. Intuitively, people's emotions and thinking are different between a cold- and rest-state vs. an emotionally hot-state, in the context of fast-changing events. Over longitudinal time, people's attitudes and emotions may change, based on new learning or other social influences or other factors.

Sentiments are studied as parts of general trajectories: an issue may capture the public imagination, begin with a certain common sentiment (or not), change directions in terms of polarities, coalesce around a particular state of equilibrium, possibly change directions, harden into a particular stance, and then dissipate from public interest and memory. A current trending issue may get overtaken by a different issue. In other settings, there may be no convergence of public sentiment to one pole or another, whether negative or positive, but remain generally neutral. On mainstream media, typified by soundbytes, surveys are taken to interpret favorability ratings for public figures, with popularity seen as a vote for the individual's message or policy platform. Public figures embody messages by their apparent lived lives and their groomed appearances. Or there have been reports of the "Internet" having spoken, which is shorthand for public opinion. Theoretically and practically, some cultures may be more amenable to accepting certain ideas and practices than others, and this may be seen at a macro level based on broad sentiments. It is said that leaders cannot move ahead of their populace or risk being removed from power and office.

If "perception is reality," as the old saw goes, then it is a powerful force, which can activate people to certain behaviors, like voting, purchasing a particular product or service, or participating in a certain social event. Based on classic perception research, people are social organisms interacting with their physical environment and each other in a social environment, with interaction effects and mutual influences among these factors: perception is culturally mediated and shaped by experiences, history, and language (Michaels & Carrello, 1981). When engaging in an environment and perceiving reality, people are not purely rational agents, even as they strive to calculate their own interests and the optimal ways to achieve those objectives. Some limiting factors are cognitive (given limited human capabilities and a complex world) and informational. How people arrive at trusting an unknown other is one case-in-point, with emotional or non-rational factors affecting some of the decision-making. People who are perceived as good-looking may also evoke non-epistemic or unvalidated trust in others (Bascandziev & Harris, 2014); people often conflate appealing appearances with trustworthiness, at least initially, based on a "beauty premium" but may bring a "beauty penalty" into play if heightened expectations are not met (Wilson & Eckel, 2006), and likewise with likeability and implicit trust (Rotter, 1980, as cited in Doney & Cannon, 1997). Further, people's emotional and dispositional states affect their perceptions, and perceptions help form people's stable worldviews and senses of reality. [In general, it is broadly thought that those who are optimistic and positive tend to wear the proverbial rose-colored glasses, and those who tend to be cynical and pessimistic tend to wear "black lens" ("Dispositional affect," Feb. 17, 2014); of the two groups, those who are more pessimistic tend to be more accurate in their assessments.]

Sentiments themselves are not an inert force. How people feel about an issue can be highly motivating of their ensuing actions. Researchers have explored whether empathy or sympathy lead to altruistic or prosocial behavior. Empathy and sympathy are not the same thing:

Empathy is defined as an affective state that stems from the apprehension of another's emotional state or condition, and that is congruent with it. Thus, empathy can include emotional matching and the vicarious experiencing of a range of emotions consistent with those of others. In contrast, sympathy refers to an emotional response stemming from another's emotional state or condition that is not identical to the other's emotion, but consists of feelings of sorrow or concern for another's welfare (Eisenberg & Miller, 1987, pp. 91 – 92).

In a review of the literature, Eisenberg and Miller (1987) found some association between some measures of empathy and some measures of prosocial behavior but nothing definitive. Another research team found that people tend to sympathize with identifiable victims and their unique situations (vs. statistical victims), even though their contributions could help many more people if channeled to statistical victims; when made aware of the discrepancy in valuing some lives over others, though, individuals will reduce their giving to identifiable victims but not shift their support to statistical ones (Small, Loewenstein, & Slovic, 2007). Researchers have found that sympathy for others was a pre-requisite for human happiness and life satisfaction in various cultures (Kitayama & Markus, 2000).

When inspired, people may take action in various ways. They may express their ideas to others face-to-face and through social media. They may organize others to take action. As social and empathic beings, people can share their emotional states with each other, with sentiments and attitudes transmitting between people and groups. They may donate money to a cause. They may take part in a social event or a larger social movement. Generally, sentiments are not directly correlated 1-1 to action; rather, there has long been an observed gap between professed sentiments and taken actions. This is known classically as the difference between "cheap talk" and "costly signaling". The "cheap talk" comes about because people create public personas which are often social constructions or contrivances for the building of status (and for other reasons). The "costly signaling" is considered much more of an important signal because there is an actual investment or cost to taking most actions. It is easier to not take actions because of both costs and risks. In terms of members of a group who might take certain actions, this often depends on a number of factors, such as the social organization of the group (particularly the power structure), the aspirational motivations of its members, the leadership, and other factors. For some, the public expression of the sentiment is already personally perceived as action taken (such as retweeting a microblogged message), and additional steps may seem excessive. In the same way that sparking people to action requires some major impetus, oftentimes, achieving the sufficient momentum to create virality is difficult because messages have to popularize beyond particular silos and broadcast across different social networks, such as those which are not traditionally inter-connected. Observed sentiments may be strongly held and committed, or they may be transitory.

Social media platforms are considered important testbeds for how people interact, share information, and spark each other to emotions. Of particular interest has been the phenomenon of online social virality, the fast (even exponential) sharing of information via social media platforms, potentially resulting in fast-onset mass events. Contents evoking positive or negative sentiments have differing effects on those consuming the informational contents. One research team writes:

Content that evokes either positive (awe) or negative (anger or anxiety) emotions characterized by activation (i.e., high arousal) is more viral. Content that evokes deactivating emotion (sadness) is less viral. These results hold controlling for how surprising, interesting, or practically useful content is (all of which are positively linked to virality), as well as external drivers of attention (e.g., how prominently content was featured) (Berger & Milkman, 2010, p. 2).

People experiencing increased general arousal (whether through consumption of emotional information or physical exertion) are more receptive to the transmission of emotion (Berger, 2011).

Core Research Questions and Sub-Questions

This chapter addresses four core research questions. First, how does the new sentiment analysis tool (and the theme extraction one) in NVivo 11 Plus work, and what are their capabilities? Second, in the context of some social media, what is knowable based on the sentiment analysis tool? Third, what are some effective methodologies to enhance sentiment extraction in this context? And fourth, are there ways to validate or invalidate the sentiment analysis assessment (using other software tools applied to the same dataset, and other methods)? There are related sub-research questions below:

1. **Functions of the Sentiment Analysis Tool (and the Theme Extraction Tool) in NVivo 11:** What are the functions and capabilities of the sentiment analysis tool in NVivo 11? The theme and subtheme extraction tool?
   ◦ How does the algorithmic classifier apparently work?
2. **Data Knowability:** Based on various text datasets from various social media platforms (extractable using widely available software tools), what is knowable and assertable from the sentiment analysis tool in NVivo 11? What level of confidence may be attained with the findings? What is not apparently knowable?
   ◦ How do the respective datasets from the various social media platforms differ? Why do they differ?

- ◦ Is there a degree of data amount and density that has to be achieved for meaningful sentiment analysis? Or does sentiment analysis work effectively with sparse data? If so, at what thresholds?
- ◦ Are there certain types of social media data that seem more amenable to sentiment analysis? Why? How so?
- ◦ Are there certain types of social media data that seem more resistant to sentiment analysis? Why? How so?

3. **Effective Methodologies:** What methods enhance the ability to apply sentiment analysis techniques to particular types of social media data? Are there ways to increase the effectiveness of sentiment analysis?

4. **External Validity:** What are some ways to test the external validity of the extracted sentiment information?

To these ends, various types of social media platforms were used, including a microblogging social media platform, a crowd-sourced open-source encyclopedia, an image- and video-sharing site, and others. The idea is that this approach will not require hard-core state-of-the-art "big data" sentiment analysis capabilities, which have been around for years, but which require high-end command-line developer skills, access to cloud computing, and complex data visualization capabilities. Rather, this approach involves using some basic chaining of available software tools to capture text sets from various social media platforms (namely Network Overview, Discovery, and Exploration for Excel or "NodeXL Basic," Maltego Chlorine 3.6.1, and web browser-based data scrapers, in addition to NCapture of NVivo 11 Plus), the application of the sentiment analysis, and human analyses of the results.

The Research Approach

Eight basic approaches were conceptualized, as an initial typology of applications of sentiment analysis to social media data, using NVivo 11: (1) the profiling of an ego or agent account, (2) the description of a group with interacting members, (3) the study of metadata based on a seeding term, (4) the analysis of sentiment around an issue based on a particular stimulus term or phrase, (5) the sentiment around a concept, (6) the sentiment around an event or phenomena, (7) the sentiment around a brand (generically conceptualized) and related ephemera, and (8) the sentimental gist around particular formalized individual texts and text corpora. To explore what these real-world datasets might look like, a general theme with sufficient breadth was selected from which to draw focal seeding or source terms. The data extractions would all generally be discrete-time ones for cross-sectional data, not continuous streaming data or periodic-time extractions; also, the research will be applied to data at-rest. While social media data may be studied historically (backwards in time, in historical time periods) and may be applied to potential future events (based on projections), this study is focused on contemporaneous data and current sentiment. This work is novel because it draws on the capabilities of a new tool which is applied to datasets from social media that are originally captured and representative of a particular time and context.

Delimitations

It is beyond the purview of this work to even partially qualify the general assertions that may be made from the extracted data. Even so, it seems valuable to make some initial observations.

- **Incomplete Information:** What is captured in social media is partial information. What is articulated on social media may well mask what is not articulated, and many extant opinions and concepts may go unexpressed and hidden to researchers. There are (silent) topics which do not appear at all in social media, and other times, only a fairly skewed angle of a topic is addressed on social media. Another aspect of incomplete information is the lack of documentation about what is happening "under the hood" in various software tools that enable data extraction from social media platforms and then sentiment analysis tools. Without sufficient information, researchers will not have full information about how data is being extracted and processed.
- **Limited Voices:** The respective social media platforms do not represent the ideas of a complete cross-section of respective societies; rather, they are select parts of a tech-savvy and fairly electronically social part of a population; these are specific demographic portions of a society.
- **Data Fidelity Concerns:** The fidelity of the extracted information and the ensuing analyses may be challenging. How the data is sampled will result in various limitations. Multimedia files are not usually included in sentiment analyses that are generally only applied to textual data. Those who would make assertions of sentiment should do so with the proper qualifying information to contextualize the assertions. Researchers should be able to describe the strengths and limitations of the data.
- **Data Ethics Challenges:** There are also concerns about data ethics. The broad public has access to unprecedented ways to share user-generated contents (UGC) to share broadly without the oversight of formal curators and editors, and these affordances are seen as a *de facto* public good. However, there have also been other voices critiquing such sharing because of the sense that there are those who employ the information for commercial and / or privacy-infringing ends. Some have argued that there are local cultural imperatives to enable "not seeing" and masking certain aspects of culture, and broad open-access and open-sourcing may hinder respectful digital curation. It helps to note that the data here have been shared broadly and are available through the social media sites themselves (through their APIs).

The main point of the delimitation section is to suggest that assertions should be tempered given the facts of the data limitations. In this chapter, users are also advised to use other extra-tool methods at data validation.

REVIEW OF THE LITERATURE

In the early history of computer-enabled semantic analysis of texts, the focus was on the semantics in a language, or the meaning-bearing words. Terms and phrases were identified as having varying degrees of positive or negative associations and were weighted as such. Sentiment analysis, or "opinion mining," also focused on the intensity of the polar stances of texts and text corpuses—with positive and negative at the polar ends of the continuum. This topic was studied under other names as well, such as "subjectivity" and "point of view" (Katz, Ofek, & Shapira, 2015, p. 162). Early in the field, automatic text categorizations were tested against human or manual sentiment tagging on canonical data sets (to acquire baseline measures against which the computer program results would be compared). Early work also was applied to varying genres of texts—such as formally structured writing like reports, novels, poetry, and other literary works—to test their robustness across contexts. In the digital humanities, texts have been studied using some machine processing to understand the nature of languages, various genres of writing, character interactions, and a wide range of other insights. With the advent of analyses of social media, opinion-laden texts like online reviews, Tweetstreams, comment streams, user-generated encyclopedia entries, and other texts have been studied.

In intervening years and up through the present, the technique has been applied to a variety of text corpora with applications to larger and larger datasets, including streaming data (data created on-the-fly through social media, for instance); further, the application is not only to datasets at rest but streaming datasets. The intuition is that people's actions are often explained and justified using language, and language itself may be potent and instigational or activating. Language may be the outside indicators that help analysts understand others' private, internal states. The ability to measure language direction (positive or negative) and strength or intensity may enable people to anticipate event onset and direction. For example, the observed timings of messages may be combined with sentiment analysis to identify potential emergent social events (Tsolmon, Kwon, & Lee, 2012, p. 266).

Early work in sentiment analysis. One early sentiment analysis tool was found to have a 74% accuracy rate when applied to a set of 410 reviews in four different topical domains but to show varying levels of accuracy (from 66% to 84%) within-sets (Turney, 2002, p. 417). An early sentiment analysis tool involved the following steps:

The algorithm has three steps: (1) extract phrases containing adjectives or adverbs, (2) estimate the semantic orientation of each phrase, and (3) classify the review based on the average semantic orientation of the phrases. The core of the algorithm is the second step, which uses PMI-IR (Pointwise Mutual Information and Information Retrieval) to calculate semantic orientation (Turney, 2001, as cited in Turney, 2002, p. 424).

Sentiment analysis tools applied to pre-selected contents tend to be more accurate than general sentiment tools applied to a variety of types of textual data because dedicated sentiment tools somewhat "overfit" to particular text sets and are more sensitive to the vagaries of those particular sets. The semantic orientation was characterized by a numerical rating for words and phrases to capture overall sentiment. Another research team achieving early work in this area noted that "thwarted expectations" narratives may be misinterpreted by a machine as laudatory when in fact it expresses disappointment (Pang, Lee, & Vaithyanathan, 2002, p. 85). This latter works suggests that there are ways to "game" sentiment analysis systems, which may cause accuracy rates to plummet, such as in cases of active deception.

Another intuition from this early work was that there may be different patterns seen in various genres of texts. Some genres of texts may trend positive or negative or neutral, in general; knowing how genres trend may provide a reference point against which texts from that genre set may be compared. It is said that a majority of people's comments tend towards neutral (in terms of average polarity) for social media data sets, and the outliers that express ideas that are positive or negative and with high intensity tend to be rarer.

The various terms extracted from a text indicating positive and negative polarities may provide further insights about potential dynamics. While early research focused on particular semantic words (unigrams) or n-grams of sequential text (bigrams or two-grams, three-grams, and so on), later works integrated a more complex mix of informative lingual elements, such as various parts of speech, syntactic features, and others. Sentiment analysis generally works with unstructured (unlabeled) text. Broadly speaking, the text is processed into separate pieces, analyzed for sentiment, and then, the subject matter linked to the sentiment is extracted:

Opinion mining typically occurs in two or three stages, although more may be needed for some tasks (e.g., Balahur et al., 2010). First, the input text is split into sections, such as sentences, and each section tested to see if it contains any sentiment: if it is subjective or objective (Pang & Lee, 2004). Second, the subjective sentences are analysed to detect their sentiment polarity. Finally, the object about which the opinion is expressed may be extracted (e.g., Gamon, Aue, Corston-Oliver, & Ringger, 2005). (Thelwall, Buckley, Paltoglou, & Cai, 2010, p. 2546)

So where do the sentiments come from to determine the positive-negative polarity? There are some main approaches. One method is to compare the test text set against sentiment-labeled dictionaries or word sets. The words then are pre-labeled, based on either the native language or, more distantly, translated into another language and compared against a sentiment dataset in that foreign language. Researchers have worked through many of the issues of understanding positivity and negation, including sentiment direction switches (reversions of polarity) and sentiment direction shifts (mitigations to the intensity of a particular sentiment direction) based on contextual phrasing, proximity between terms, and the study of sentiment polarity within lexical units (Machová & Marhefka, 2013, pp. 155 – 156). Another approach is to use a sentiment dictionary or word set that has been manually annotated with particular terms from dedicated (or general language-based) lexicons. This is especially relevant for smaller data test sets, and may be particularly relevant in specific contexts or domains (maybe in circumstances of focused research questions). The use of sentiment-based lexicon dictionaries is a form of *a priori* definition of sentiments. How affect is conceptualized and understood differs in different research cases, and the affective relevance also varies. It makes sense to extract both topics and sentiments simultaneously from social media (Fu, Yang, Huang, & Cui, 2015) because topics and sentiments may be understood as somewhat complementary to understanding the meanings in a text or text set.

Another approach is the use of machine learning (formerly datamining), in which various machine-learning algorithms or analytical processes are directly applied to the text to identify and extract patterns from the text set; these are done without pre-made advance lists of labeled terms. Machine learning algorithms use a floating (or sliding) window approach to look at individual word occurrences, word pairs, word triples (three-grams), and other combinations to extract sentiment. Compound messages are disaggregated and analyzed in their component parts and for separate orientation counts. (A human parallel involves the parsing out of simultaneously mixed sentiments.) In the more sophisticated programs, sarcasm, irony, humor, and other nuances in human communications are considered in the determination of sentiment orientation. "Active learning" is defined as using "unlabeled examples for manual annotation on the basis of their informativeness for the classification task" (Koncz & Paralič, 2013, p. 347). The statistical modeling method of "conditional random fields" has also been used with active learning in order to capture the context of textual and speech expressions to identify sentiment analysis (Zhang, Xie, Yang, Sun, Liu, & Choudhary, 2014, p. 60). Active learning is also applied to extract domain-specific sentiment lexicon (Park, Lee, & Moon, 2015). There have been traditions for tapping data from particular contexts for contextualized sentiment analysis methods (Katz, Ofek, & Shapira, 2015).

General practice involves using a percentage of the data as a training set (70% or so) and the rest of the data as the test set (30% or so) to see which extracted data models are the most accurate in data modeling. Some common machine learning classifiers include popular ones such as Naïve Bayes (NB),

Maximum Entropy (ME), Support Vector Machines (SVMs), and Logistic Regression Models (LR) (Luo, Chen, Xu, & Zhou, 2013, p. 58), as well as Decision Tree and K Nearest Neighbor. Still others use multiple classifiers to assess sentiment, while applying complex computational means to extract which combination of approaches is most effective. [Ensemble machine learning efforts have also been applied to sentiment analysis (Rong, Nie, Ouyang, Peng, & Xiong, 2014). These ensemble machine learning methods involve techniques known as "bagging" ("bootstrap aggregation") and "boosting" and "random subspace" and were found to "substantially improve the performance of individual base learners for sentiment classification" (Wang, Sun, Ma, Xu, & Gu, 2014, p. 77). Another approach used a Bayesian ensemble learning method to "reduce the noise sensitivity related to language ambiguity and therefore to provide a more accurate prediction of polarity" (Fersini, Messina, & Pozzi, 2014, p. 26). Another team describes a "blending technique" that "performs inference over multiple sources of data simultaneously," such as two sentiment-based lexicon sets to use the overlapping emotion-based data (Poria, Cambria, Howard, Huang, & Hussain, 2015). These innovative methods look to be very promising and may well define the state of the field eventually but are well beyond the purview of this work.

Besides the actual text processing work, there are various ways to pre-process the data to enhance the sentiment analysis (Haddi, Liu, & Shi, 2013). And clearly, there may be additional data post-processing after initial data analyses, based on the particular domain. In one work, this post-processing was referred to as "pruning the feature set" or otherwise modifying the textual data pulled out as one sentiment or another. The learning from testing various models on a variety of data enable integrating the new learning into the respective classifiers for improved performance (usually defined as accuracy and efficiency).

There has also been work done on subjectivity–objectivity identification, which aims to label whether a text tends to be based more on subjective (ego-based and opinionated) or objective (factual) writing, whether the tendencies are explicit or implicit. In some cases, particular syntactic words (vs. semantic ones) are extracted for analysis; adjectives, adverbs, and verbs (as parts of speech) are particularly informative of opinion and sentiment (Luo, Chen, Xu, & Zhou, 2013, p. 55). For another research group, in the Chinese context, they found "particular symbols, key words, and emotional sentences" as important indicators of emotional tendencies in terms of short-text sentiment analysis in microblogs, instant messages, and short reviews (Huang, Zhao, Liu, & Wang, 2015, p. 169). Multi-classifiers use a range of semantically informative terms (including abbreviations and emoticons), parts of speech, syntactic dependencies, and negation to classify or categorize text based on apparent sentiment. In some multi-classifiers, unique aspects of the text corpus may be extracted for meaning, such as repeated letters or extended form spelling ("waaaay cool") or punctuation (!!!!) for emphasis (Liu & Chen, 2015).

Machines capture the high dimensionality of the concepts in a text and are able to capture virtually all concepts in a text corpus whereas human labeling of sentiment and key words is necessarily more brief and limited. (A term describing this phenomenon is "curse of dimensionality.") With machine processing, the dimensions themselves may be reduced further through various types of text summarizations. Generally, various sentiment analysis research processes require human interventions and machine ones, in differing trade-offs.

With the popularization of the World Wide Web (WWW) and Internet, and the move to social media platforms of much of the world's populations, researchers have moved to studying the sentiments expressed on various social media platforms. More sophisticated AI systems are able to comprehend "the visual, auditory, and written information" that humans can use but also "more exotic forms of data that stream through computers and networks. Imagine how smart you would be if you could see through thousands of eyes, hear distant sounds, and read every word as it is published. Then slow the world down to a pace where you can sample and ponder all of this at your leisure, and you'll get an idea of how these systems experience their environment" (Kaplan, 2015, p. 4).

Conceptualizing Sentiment

At the most basic, sentiment may be conceptualized also as a binary, either positive or negative, with no neutrality category; some conceptualizations have a three-category concept: positive, negative, or neutral (in which case the information is often not counted). A more nuanced approach may conceptualize sentiment as a polarity, with positive and negative at the polar ends, and then various shades or gradations of sentiment in-between. There is also the capturing of an intensity indicator of opinion strength (Luo, Chen, Xu, & Zhou, 2013, p. 54), or how strongly a person has a particular sentiment on a particular topic. (In some cases, the intensity of an emotion may be understood by the inclusion of so-called "booster words." Metaphors, punctuation, word choices, word sequences, and other factors may also reveal sentiment intensity.) The concept of sentiment analysis is applied at a high level as something culturally agnostic (independent of a specific culture), in a sense, and applicable across cultures, even as language itself and how it is wielded, is highly culturally sensitive and culture-specific.

Sentiment may be conceptualized as something that is temporally dependent, such as when emotions are high and issues are trending. Some sentiments are difficult to maintain over long periods of time but may spark based on the presence of particular stimuli and social context. Sentiments are also thought to be influenced by social peers or those closest to us, based on social psychology. Finally, sentiment may also be conceptualized as something that is dispositionally-based and somewhat more permanent or time-invariant. That would be positive or negative personalities, or an upbeat vs. a negative personality or affect. Positive affect is related to high-energy while negative affect is linked to the opposite. One project studied social networks "connecting individual agents...endowed with distinct sentiment states or 'views of the world'" at particular periods: "sentiment neutrality, exuberant optimism, non-exuberant optimism, exuberant pessimism and nonexuberant pessimism" (Gomes, 2015, p. 224). In this work, the researcher modeled collective and evolving states of optimism and pessimism and convergence to constant levels of each for particular periods, from local micro interactions among members with the various five-sentiment states. Gomes (2015) writes:

The analysis has revealed that, in continuous-time, a sentiment model built upon a complex network delivers a stable steady-state outcome in which constant positive shares of sentiment states coexist in the long-run. This result continues to hold in a discrete-time version of the model for a homogeneous network of connectivity degree 1. However, when assuming higher degrees of connectivity and, thus, a more realistic network, endogenous fluctuations emerge for admissible and reasonable parameter values. Therefore, by conceiving a relatively simple local interaction structure, where individuals holding distinct beliefs or distinct 'views of the world' establish contact and influence each other, one was able to justify the formation of waves of optimism and pessimism. These waves emerge as the direct result of the mechanics of the model, without the need for assuming any external shock (Gomes, 2015, p. 238).

The research may be applied to understand positive and negative waves of human sentiment at macro levels within larger populations (albeit emerging from micro- or individual- decisions and interactions). One application of this insight is to understanding the "animal spirits" of business cycles based on systemic "persistent aggregate volatility" based on the interaction effects of people's different sentiments on each other (Gomes, 2015, p. 238). In a sense, the prior research is a way to tell when the mood reaches a particular threshold and changes in a crowd and leads to potential localized or broad-scale mass action.

While some projects involve studying micro (individual or ego-level) actions that may manifest as macro-level patterns of behavior, there are also studies at micro levels. One approach involves the study of individual messaging to identify latent or otherwise-hidden personality traits. One research team identified nine basic categories of statistically different sentiment-based user profiles on Twitter (based on a dataset of more than 36,000 users) (Gutierrez & Poblete, 2015, p. 24). In this work, the authors used the following sequence:

1. Building a dataset, containing public tweets retrieved from user timelines.
2. Processing for each user his / her tweets and extracting the sentiment polarity (positive and negative) for each one.
3. Clustering users according to common properties in their sentiment polarity distributions, following both positive and negative dimensions.
4. Identifying independent profiles according to the values of sentiment strength along each polarity axis: positive and negative (Gutierrez & Poblete, 2015, p. 25).

Social Media Data

Different social media platforms employ technological features and enablements that allow people to interact in and relate to each other in different ways. Based on the platform features and end-user policies, certain types of connections may be "privileged" over others. There are dedicated sites with defined types of interactions: marketplaces, dating sites, social funding, co-writing and co-editing of shared wiki encyclopedias, open-source code-sharing and version control, news-based chatter, profession-based slideshow sharing, room-renting sites, and others. There are microblogging sites that enable on-the-fly short-text status updates. There are image- and video-sharing sites that enable multi-medial collaborations.

The data from social media are unstructured, which means that they are not pre-labeled in certain types as compared to data in traditional databases represented in data tables and worksheets. Social media data are multimodal and multimedial (consisting of audio, video) and dynamic (real-time and interactive). They are considered empirical data because they are data-in-the-wild created mostly by real people in a real-world context. These datasets tend to be noisy, with a high noise-to-signal ratio. The noise comes from the informality of the interactions and the many attempts at "astroturfing" or creating manipulated or artificial impressions of "grassroots" events; often people will include the uses of robot and cyborg social media accounts to magnify apparent opinion and to try to spark viral popularity and behavior. The technologies of social media encourage the development of parasocial relationships or "one-way relationships with a media character or avatar representation, without a true human connection" (Hai-Jew, 2009) that exist in the imagination and encourage mass fandom and acolytes. Such parasocial loyalties are encouraged by media and commercial entities that stand to gain from the commercialization of personalities.

Social media do not exist in isolation from the effects of traditional mainstream media. There has been plenty of research on the agenda-setting role of conventional mainstream media and also their bi-directional interactive effect on social media (Roberts, Wanta, & Dzwo, 2002; Wallsten, 2007; Meraz, 2009), and it is not a stretch to assume that mainstream media may affect sentiment responses in the broader population and in segments of particular interest groups. Broadly speaking, mainstream media may be considered sending out a "call," and social media offering a "response"—based on classic power dynamics and basic communications.

With the advent and popularization of computational sentiment analysis techniques simultaneous with the rise of social media-based sharing, researchers have started looking for ways to apply the first to the latter. Social media provides rich target datasets of "opinionated data" from "forum discussions, reviews, blogs, micro blogs, social networks and Twitter" (Fattah, 2015, p. 434). Based on the social media sites' end user license agreements (EULAs) and policies, the shared data is often released for public use, and this data is then captured and used for a variety of potential research applications. The popularization of social media has meant the sharing of a broad range of contents that would not be available otherwise.

Online mediated relationships tend to be comprised of weak, superficial, and transitory ties. The broad use of social media and the changing cultures of informational sharing have meant that even intimate data may be broadly self-disclosed and electronically shared. One example is from the microblogging site, Twitter:

In social psychology, it is generally accepted that one discloses more of his/her personal information to someone in a strong relationship. We present a computational framework for automatically analyzing such self-disclosure behavior in Twitter conversations. Our framework uses text mining techniques to discover topics, emotions, sentiments, lexical patterns, as well as personally identifiable information (PII) and personally embarrassing information (PEI). Our preliminary results illustrate that in relationships with high relationship strength, Twitter users show significantly more frequent behaviors of self-disclosure (Bak, Kim, & Oh, 2012, p. 60).

One early challenge about how to exploit social media data was in how to handle very different and noisy data. On various sites, the messages are brief: short messaging service (SMS), microblogs, short "social reviews," brief chatroom interactions, commenting on shared online resources, tagging, and so on. The observed communications were so different from "natural language" that some termed the observed communications as "unnatural language," which would require a more granular approach for sentiment analysis than n-gram counts (Blamey, Crick, & Oatley, 2012, p. 207). Using a dataset of user-generated commentary from MySpace, a research team created a new algorithm (named SentiStrength) to identify sentiment and emotions (treated as integrated elements) from short and informal texts and "exploit the de facto grammars and spelling styles of cyberspace" and was able to detect positive emotion with 60.6% accuracy and negative emotion with 72.8% accuracy (Thelwall, Buckley, Paltoglou, & Cai, 2010, p. 2544).

Twitter has 316 million active users (which has been compared unfavorably to "Facebook's 1.5 billion, and even Instagram's 400 million") and a market valuation at below $20 billion (from a high of $40 billion at its IPO) (Bilton, Oct. 5, 2015). Even so, this microblogging site is a major social force and widely cited across mainstream media. As such, it is often the subject of much research. Different sentiment analyzers have been created to capture value from Twitter messaging directly. One team, which created SentiCircles, used a lexicon-based approach for sentiment analysis on Twitter.

Different from typical lexicon-based approaches, which offer a fixed and static prior sentiment polarities of words regardless of their context, SentiCircles takes into account the co-occurrence patterns of words in different contexts in tweets to capture their semantics and update their preassigned strength and polarity in sentiment lexicons accordingly. Our approach allows for the detection of sentiment at both entity-level and tweet-level. We evaluate our proposed approach on three Twitter datasets using three different sentiment lexicons to derive word prior sentiments. Results show that our approach significantly outperforms the baselines in accuracy and F-measure for entity-level subjectivity (neutral vs. polar) and polarity (positive vs. negative) detections (Saif, He, Fernandez, & Alani, 2015, p. 1).

Another strategy involves using multiple classifiers and various strategies for weighting new terms (Fattah, 2015). One classifier designed from Twitter microblogging messages (tweets) uses "classifier ensembles formed by Multinomial Naive Bayes, SVM, Random Forest, and Logistic Regression" to improve accuracy in positive or negative classification (da Silva, Hruschka, & Hruschka, Jr., 2014, p. 170). Another group developed a method to use brand-based n-grams (sequences of contiguously placed words) and statistical analysis to augment a Twitter-specific lexicon for sentiment analysis for a more parsimonious, efficient, and accurate classifier (Ghiassi, Skinner, & Zimbra, 2013, p. 6266).

Various social media platforms have evolved their own grammars, such as the uses of #hashtags to identify topics but also to self-label emotions (Mohammad, 2012) and the @ symbol to indicate social media accounts. There are non-standard lexical variants of words, with letters dropped and contractions used because of length limits to certain types of messaging. Another factor was that many datasets tended to contain a number of languages, requiring adaptations for multilingual sentiment expression (Severyn, Moschitti, Uryupina, Plank, & Filippova, 2015). New terminology and hashtags may appear without any prior warning to enable people to share ideas around a particular (often breaking) event. In one case, researchers described their strategy to integrate two languages (in this case, Chinese and English) and bilingual language sets to analyze sentiments for more accuracy (Yan, He, Shen, & Tang, 2014). In another case, researchers applied of "hybrid features and multilingual, machine-translated data (even from other languages)" to identify relevant language features for sentiment classification within and between languages to enhance sentiment analysis (in this case, testing English and Spanish datasets) (Balahur & Perea-Ortega, 2015, p. 547); this research team used a combination of supervised learning along with "features sentiment dictionaries, emoticon lists, slang lists and other social media-specific features" (p. 549). A research team used an ontology-based approach to extract lexico-syntactic patterns in text to study microblogging messages and tested their classifier to messages about mail service in UK and Canada (Thakor & Sasi, 2015).

Sentiment analysis processes developed to understand formal and structured texts were limited in their application to idioms, requiring the additional extraction of idiom features for idiom recognition (Williams, Bannister, Arribas-Ayllon, Preece, & Spasić, 2015, p. 7375); idioms are multi-word expressions whose meanings are not particularly clear from the words used in the expressions, and they are often used to "imply an affective stance toward something rather than a neutral one" (Williams, Bannister, Arribas-Ayllon, Preece, & Spasić, 2015, p. 7376).

The language used in Web 2.0 applications such as blogging platforms, realtime chats, social networks or collaborative encyclopaedias shows remarkable differences in comparison with traditional texts. The presence of informal features such as emoticons, spelling errors or Internet-specific slang can lower the performance of Natural Language Processing applications. In order to overcome this problem, text normalization approaches can provide a clean word or sentence by transforming all non-standard lexical or syntactic variations into their canonical forms (Mosquera & Moreda, 2012, p. 241).

Microblogging platforms have become very popular ways of sharing opinions on everyday life topics. To accommodate these types of messaging, another research team applied an ontological structure on the labeled information:

Towards this direction, text-based sentiment classifiers often prove inefficient, since tweets typically do not consist of representative and syntactically consistent words, due to the imposed character limit. This paper proposes the deployment of original ontology-based techniques towards a more efficient sentiment analysis of Twitter posts. The novelty of the proposed approach is that posts are not simply characterized by a sentiment score, as is the case with machine learning-based classifiers, but instead receive a sentiment grade for each distinct notion in the post. Overall, our proposed architecture results in a more detailed analysis of post opinions regarding a specific topic (Kontopoulos, Berberidis, Dergiades, & Bassiliades, 2013, p. 4065).

The data on social media are not only textual data but include multimedia forms. Some methods for data analysis involve turning multimedia into textual data, through transcriptions, annotations, and coding. In other approaches, there are moves to directly process sentiment from the multimedia files without the intermediate step of rendering embedded data into textual data. There are various methods for extracting sentiment from audio conversations (Bhaskar & Nedungadi, 2015). There has been some early work in combining text and imagery for combined multimedia sentiment analysis (Cao, Ji, Lin, & Li, 2014). Researchers have developed methods for extracting sentiment from "audio, visual and textual modalities as sources of information"; in one study, researchers were able to achieve 80% accuracy purported against a YouTube dataset (Poria, Cambria, Howard, Huang, & Hussain, 2015). Another study focused on opinion-mining information in two languages (English and Italian) from YouTube, and this methodology relied on the use of "tree kernels to automatically extract and learn features" (Severyn, Moschitti, Uryupina, Plank, & Filippova, 2015, p. 1).

The analysis of social media data is challenging in another regard, and that is the inclusion of virtually all known languages on the Internet (as expressed by UTF-8 character set). Multiple languages may be used in one microblog post, and there are all sorts of datasets that include multiple language entries. The study of emotions on microblogs written in Chinese pose different challenges, given single-character emotional words in colloquial Chinese; single terms may be understood very differently in a stand-alone context vs. in combined sequences, and a single-character emotional word is polysemous (Huang, Zhao, Liu, & Wang, 2015, pp. 169 - 170). While various languages are patterned, each has unique features which affect how sentiment may be interpreted and extracted. Most annotated sentiment corpora are off a base language, and many pre-defined sentiment language sets are based on the most popular global languages (English, Chinese, and others). The annotated sentiment sets from one language do not apply effectively—without adjustments—to other languages because of differences in word meanings, word usage, cultures, writing styles, and communications contexts. The work of automatic translation from one language to another also is limited because languages, by their nature, are polysemic or multi-meaninged, and a wooden one-to-one translation of terms does not necessarily capture meaning. To improve cross-lingual sentiment classification, researchers have worked on improving machine methods: one team has proposed "the combination of uncertainty-based active learning and semi-supervised self-training approaches to incorporate unlabelled (sic) sentiment documents from the target language in order to improve the performance of cross-lingual methods. Further, in this model, the density measures of unlabelled (sic) examples are considered in active learning part in order to avoid outlier selection

The empirical evaluation on book review datasets in three different languages shows that the proposed model can significantly improve the performance of cross-lingual sentiment classification in comparison with other existing and baseline methods" (Hajmohammadi, Ibrahim, Selamat, & Fujita, 2015, p. 67).

Time and Sentiment

There have been findings at the macro levels of communities. For example, one finding has been that there may be diurnal rhythms in expressed sentiment, such as times of day when people are more prone to collectively have a particular positive or negative sentiment. One researcher studied the diurnal stability of investors' collective valuation of financial assets based on data from a large-scale social network:

Employing user-assigned valuation indicators attached to time-stamped messages, I show that investors' sentiment towards assets, which is fairly constant during most of the day, dips markedly and regularly in the morning. When looking at messages posted by different subsamples of users, I find that both level and variability of investor sentiment decrease with trading experience. Not only are more experienced investors as a group less optimistic than novice investors, their valuations are also substantially less variable over the course of the day. The findings provide empirical support for assumptions and results that feature prominently in theoretical and empirical descriptions of investor behavior (Drerup, 2015, p. 1).

It has been approximately 14 years in since some of the initial sentiment analysis work was done. Since then, it has been applied to marketing ("brand sentiment"), policy-making, emergency response situational awareness, and other areas. Sentiment analysis may be applied to automated systems involving using sentiment to support "social tag recommender systems" (Luo, Chen, Xu, & Zhou, 2013, p. 58) to connect people on social media, to recommend resources or products and services to purchase, and other automated services. Sentiment analysis is applied also to e-learning and collaborative learning environments (Ortigosa, Martin, & Carro, 2014; Colace, Casaburi, De Santo, & Greco, 2015), often to increase the adaptivity of automated learning supports (such as AI-based tutor support). Awareness of human users' affect and sentiment may strengthen intelligent user interfaces in a number of contexts from games to tutoring systems to information systems (Schuller, 2015). The awareness of learners' changing mood states may enable personalized support for learners based on their emotional states (Ortigosa, Martín, & Carro, 2014). Temporal sentiment analysis on social media is studied for event prediction (Preethi, Uma, & Kumar, 2015). In the research literature, people's user-generated content is thought to enable the tapping of human sensor networks for intelligence.

The relationship between humans and machines in various analytical sequences varies. Sometimes, people just design the algorithms and the computer programs are run automatically over text, and people use the results of the sentiment analyses outputs. In other situations, people select and process the data over which such analyses are run. This chapter shows a machine-assisted sentiment analysis in which the human researchers play critical roles. In this approach, people benefit from computerized affordances for "distant reading" or "not-reading" (per terms by Franco Moretti), text classification (into sentiment categories), and combined with topic extraction capabilities. The efficiencies of using a computational approach extends what human researchers are able to achieve. Further, sentiment analysis is conceptualized here as human researcher centered, with the need for "close reading" for additional discourse and multi-medial content analysis for fuller understandings.

Technology Dependency

In terms of conducting sentiment analysis on data from social media platforms, it is important to observe that this research is very technology dependent. The user-generated content (UGC) is shared through technological means, maintained in cloud-based data centers, made available through application programming interfaces (or other public-facing interfaces), extracted using technologies, and analyzed technologically. This is not to say that technologies may be skipped at some junctures in the process, but on the whole, this process is deeply reliant on technological knowledge and capabilities.

Among the various technological approaches for sentiment extraction for analysis, there is not a clear consensus in the literature about the optimal approach—based on accuracy and efficiency. Each new work that appears baselines against a particular model and its accuracy and efficiency. While machine learning generally outperforms machine learning (as compared to human-produced analysis), unique cases vary.

What may work optimally may depend on the particulars of the context. Also, researchers are often limited to packaged software packages with graphical user interfaces (GUIs), or built-in software packages with command-line interfaces (as in R and Python). Researchers may have to experiment with the various software and their affordances in order to choose an optimal approach.

EXTRAPOLATING SENTIMENT FROM THE REAL WORLD: EIGHT EXEMPLAR CASES

In the introduction, four main objectives were described: (1) to better understand the functions of the sentiment analysis tool (and the theme extraction one) in NVivo 11 Plus, (2) explore the data knowability from various social media platform data using this tool, (3) identify some effective methodologies to increase sentiment analysis, and (4) explore some initial ways to test the external validity of the sentiment analysis findings. To begin to address these questions, a sufficiently broad and overarching topic was selected from which to create seeding (or source) terms for eight different types of data extractions: (1) ego- or entity-based personality profiles, (2) group profiles, (3) folk tagging metadata, (4) trending public issues, (5) public conceptualizations through shared data, (6) public events, (7) "brand" reputation (generically conceptualized), and (8) particular text corpora. These are not particularly aligned data types, but they are somewhat easily available given the popular social media platforms and the technology tools on the market.

NVivo 11 Plus

NVivo is one of the state-of-the-art qualitative and mixed methods data analysis tools on the market today. In late September 2015, QSR International released NVivo 11 Plus, with two new auto-coding features: sentiment analysis and theme extraction. In combination, these two new features enable machine-speed analysis of text data in a way that complements human analytics capabilities.

Automated Sentiment Analysis

The sentiment analysis tool is applied based on the base language for the particular NVivo project. Most users of NVivo go with the underlying base language (generally selected by region with the purchase of the software) and do not change it. NVivo enables a number of base languages (listed in alphabetical order): Chinese (PRC) or simplified pinyin, English (US), English (UK), French (France), German (Germany), Japanese (Japan), Portuguese (Brazil), and Spanish (Mexico). [To access the base language in the NVivo suite, go to File -> Info -> Project Properties -> General -> Text content language (in the dropdown menu)]. While a wide number of UTF-8 character set enabled languages may be used in any one NVivo project, there is only one base language against which spell checks, stopwords lists, and sentiment analyses are conducted. For those who want sentiment analysis conducted against a number of languages, they may pre-process all the various languages first…before running the NVivo sentiment analysis tool. The NVivo 11 Plus Auto Code Wizard will enable some updates with a built-in language pack to detect sentiment in the sources. All the sentiment analyses in this chapter were based on "English (US)".

The continuum of sentiment using the NVivo sentiment analysis tool are the following: very negative, moderately negative, moderately positive, and very positive. The results are expressed in an explorable and interactive intensity matrix consisting of four main columns. The intensity matrix cells will show darker the more applicable the particular sentiment is for the particular term. In NVivo 11 Plus, users may double-click on the cells of the resultant intensity matrix to retrieve a list of the text coded to each category, and they can further access back-links to the original source documents that were analyzed using the sentiment analysis feature. One visual way to conceptualize this tool is in Table 1, "Analyzing the Identified Sentiment Text Sets, which conceptualizes the various categories of sentiments as sets of textual data, represented as words, phrases, sentences, and paragraphs.

In Figure 1, this shows the "Four Basic Categories of Coded Sentiment in NVivo 11 Plus," as visualized in the Select Project Items pop-up window.

Prior to the broad public release of the sentiment analysis tool in the NVivo 11 Plus rollout in late September 2015, one of the QSR International staff members described the tool to the author in an email (when asked about the underlying lexicon dictionary or set):

The key thing to understanding the sentiment analysis is that content can be coded to more than one category (both positive and negative). One helpful way of looking that results may be to pull up content that has been coded at both positive and negative, and/or to leave this content out of exploration of the content coded as exclusively positive or negative. This coding is based on a dictionary of terms, by which content is 'scored,' hence the possibility of coding in multiple categories (Jacobs, personal email, Sept. 14, 2015).

This is not to say that the tool enables customizing the underlying sentiment dictionary. Rather, it is possible to analyze text coded to particular categories of sentiment (positive or negative), and then it is possible to remove words and phrases from the coded selection so that they are not included in the particular sentiment analysis categorization. Beyond uncoding selected text, it is also possible to re-code the

Table 1. Analyzing the identified sentiment text sets

Very Negative	Moderately Negative	Moderately Positive	Very Positive
{ }	{ }	{ }	{ }

Figure 1. Four basic categories of coded sentiment in NVivo 11 Plus

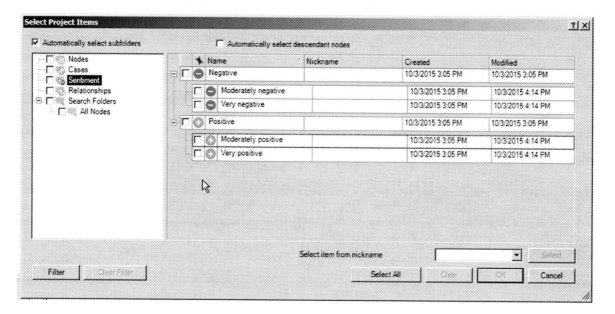

highlighted text to any of the four sentiment categories. (The sentiment dictionary itself is not changed. What may be changed is only the removal of the coded text from a certain category of sentiment for that particular sentiment analysis context.)

Automated Theme Extraction

The new theme extraction capability enables users to automatically extract themes and sub-themes from the text or text corpus for further exploration. This theme extraction is a type of topic modeling, with automatic extraction of important (frequently occurring) concepts and sub-concepts. This provides a high-level text summarization of some of the main concepts from the text. In addition, the more traditional text queries—text search, word frequency count, and such—may also be applied to the sentiment-analyzed data.

The ability to examine the extracted words enables deeper exploration. What words belong in each sentiment category in a particular text corpus? What do the topic words suggest about the conversations being held or the views being shared? In terms of word frequency counts, what do these indicate about the focuses of the positive sentiment and the negative sentiment? In closer inferential readings of the messaging, what are the apparent underlying rationales and values underlying the expression of positive sentiment (and likewise, negative sentiment)?

The Data

For both the sentiment analysis and the theme extraction features, there has to be a certain threshold of data amount and density for there to be successful sentiment and theme extractions. If there is insufficient text with sentiment words, a sentiment count is not possible, and the tool will return a message of "The Auto Code Wizard could not find any sentiment coding references to create." Likewise, if there is insufficient thematic or conceptual words in a text set, the software will return a message: "No themes were identified in the selected source(s)." Lists of words do not work as well as text with sentences and paragraphs. So, at the low end, there has to be a sufficient threshold of text to capture sentiment and theme data; likewise, there are upper limits for data processing. If there is too much data to process, the software will return a failure message. There are adjustments that may be made, such as coding in a coarser way by paragraph level instead of sentence level, which may ease the computational expense of the data processing. As for the actual lower and upper bounds of text required, this is not information that is published, and the author has only run several dozen applications of the sentiment analysis tool and the theme extraction tool—but has observed tool behavior at both lower and upper bounds.

This suggests that data pre-processing would benefit the process to ensure that the data collected is as valid as possible and of sufficient size for analytical insight (and to benefit from machine processing). Since social media often involve image, audio, video, and other types of data, it is important to render such content into text form, so they may be included in both the sentiment analysis and the theme extraction. Video transcription may be transcoded into a consumable form in NVivo, for example. Likewise, data post-processing will likely require human analytics (and potentially branch to other data extraction, data processing, and analytical work).

SOME TYPES OF POTENTIAL ASKABLE QUESTIONS

The sentiment analysis tool enables asking questions about various types of social media data. The conceptualized enablements are as follows: (1) profiling the personalities of egos and entities through related social media account data, (2) describing the personalities of groups with interacting members (in ego neighborhoods, *ad hoc* networks, editing groups, and others) through network analysis and then sentiment analysis, (3) exploring metadata (folksonomic related tag networks and article networks) to surface latent public conceptualizations, (4) examining trending public issues through socially shared data and discourse sets, (5) delving into public concepts through socially shared data and discourse sets, (6) observing public events through socially shared data and discourse sets, (7) analyzing broad-scale brand reputation through socially shared data and discourse sets, and (8) inspecting various individual texts and text corpuses for emergent insights.

In Table 2, "Types of Targeted Social Media Platform Data, Sentiment Analysis, and Askable Questions," the first column lists the initial case types, and the correlating cell to the right includes potential types of research questions that may be asked from the resulting sentiment analysis data. Here, the types of askable questions do not slip into the realm of interventions to change the direction of individual or mass sentiments. The questions in this table were created with the assumption that a researcher is taking a discovery approach, with possibly implied hypotheses and questions, but without fully identified *a priori* hypotheses. Another assumption is that the researcher has methods to externally validate the findings, such as through other methods of running sentiment analyses on the text set and other methods of analyzing the imagery, audio, websites, videos, and multimedia linked to the particular social media platform text set. The validity of particular interdictive or corrective actions in the context of a context and a strategy go well beyond the purview of the table. Likewise, other forms of active decision-making in light of the discovered sentiments are also beyond the scope of this table. The table is set up to be general and not specific to a particular context.

In *Figure 2,* "One Approach to the Sentiment Analysis Process with NVivo 11 Plus," this visual begins with either an *a priori* pre-defined research question (an implied process) or a general exploratory one. The researcher goes to extract information from a web-facing social media platform or wiki site (or some other data source). The reference to NCapture is not actually a requirement since there are a

Table 2. Types of targeted social media platform data, sentiment analysis, and askable questions

Types of Targeted Social Media Platform Data Extractions for the Text Sets	Potential Types of Askable Questions
Case 1. Ego and entity profiling	• What is the general sentiment of messaging from this social media account? *What are the general issues discussed?* *Are there "signatures" or "tells" to the social media account?* *What perspective(s) is/are shared through the social media account?* • What is apparently the desired public image? *Are there latent topics and sentiments? What data leakage (unintended data sharing) is observed (and with how much confidence)?* *What messages are purposively not included? What communications are explicitly "shut down"?* • What does the sentiment of the particular social media account suggest about the individual (and his / her disposition)? (if available) • What are some potential anticipated near-term, mid-term, and long-term future behaviors and actions of this individual based on available information? (if available)
Case 2. Interactive group (entity) profiling	• What is the general sentiment of the shared messages among the members of the particular interacting group? • What is the formal messaging? The informal? The explicit and the implicit? • What does the sentiment reveal about the level of agreement in the group? *Is there factional splitting over issues, and if so, which ones?* *What are the issues which bring out positive sentiment?* *What are the issues which bring out negative sentiment?* • How does group sentiment change over time? What is the rate of such changes? • What do the sentiment measurements suggest about the dynamics within the group? • What does the sentiment suggest about where this group might be headed in terms of near-term actions, mid-term actions, and long-term actions? (if available)
Case 3. Metadata: related tags network(s) (based on a folksonomy); article networks	• What are the public sensibilities revealed in the related tags networks in terms of connected co-occurring tags? • What is the sentiment from the related tags network? (if any) • How much may be learned from the sparsity or density of extracted folk-applied tags? • What are the topical interrelationships revealed in article networks on a crowd-sourced and open-access online encyclopedia? • What do the findings suggest about public understandings about the seeding topic? Public attitudes? Public rationales (writ large)? Public opinions? *What are the mental models individuals have vs. the conceptual models held by experts?*
Case 4. Trending issue(s)	• How is the issue trending—with positive or negative sentiment (or what mix of sentiment)? • Who are those who see the issue in a positive light? Is it possible to categorize them? Who are those who see the issue in a negative light? Is it possible to categorize them? *What are the rationales for the various stances based on their own self-reported express reasons?* • What do the extracted sentiments and intensity of sentiments suggest about actions that people may take? • What do the sentiments suggest about the direction of this issue? In the near-term? Mid-term? Long-term? • Who are those individuals and groups who have the highest influences on this issue? Why? (including social network analysis data)

continued on following page

Table 2. Continued

Types of Targeted Social Media Platform Data Extractions for the Text Sets	Potential Types of Askable Questions
Case 5. Public concept(s)	• Based on the text set, what is the dominant sentiment(s) related to the concept? Less dominant sentiment(s) related to the concept? • Which sub-groups maintain which attitudes? *What are the apparent underlying causes for the particular sentiment?* *What is the reasoning for why various groups take different stances on the concept?* • What are the mental models individuals have vs. the conceptual models held by experts? • What are the differences between different cultures' senses of this term? What might account for this difference?
Case 6. Event(s) or temporal phenomenon/phenomena	• What are the predominant sentiment(s) about the particular event(s) or phenomenon (phenomena)? What are the less predominant sentiment(s)? • Who are the groups who comprise those with positive sentiment toward the issue? Negative sentiment? • What are the expressed rationales for holding particular opinions? • How does the sentiment related to an issue trend over time? What are messages or awarenesses which affect public opinion?
Case 7. Brand(s) (generically conceptualized)	• What is the predominant sentiment(s) about a particular brand? The less predominant sentiment(s) about a particular brand? • What ideas, personalities, and phenomena are related to a brand? What types of relatedness are observed? • Who are the groups who hold the particular sentiment? *What are their expressed rationales for holding certain opinions?* • How do competing brands compare based on people's respective sentiments about each? • What are some potential strategies for changing people's brand perceptions? *What are some aspects of counter-messaging?*
Case 8. Text and text corpora (formal and informal texts, structured by particular expectations of a field or domain)	• What is the predominant sentiment for a particular text or text corpora? Less popular sentiments? *Based on an analysis of the manuscript, what are the core reasons why the text seems to a particular positive or negative sentiment?* • What are the main extracted themes and sub-themes in the text (or text corpus)? *Why do these themes seem to have salience?* • What are some apparent underlying reasons for the sentiment?

number of ways to download, scrape, or otherwise access publicly-available and non-private data from various sites; these alternative paths are shown with the dashed lines. The contents are ingested into an NVivo 11 project. The data may be left uncoded, or the user may choose to code the data. The text is run through the sentiment analysis tool. The researcher may choose to make some changes to the sentiment analysis tool parameters or to the analyzed data, or both, and to re-run another sentiment analysis assessment to acquire more refined insights. Then, he or she may draw conclusions and be done—for this phase of the research. Or, it is possible to run the data through other software tools for comparison data about sentiment to decide how much confidence to put into the findings. The data may be continually refined with other analytical capabilities. For example, in social media data, there are often images, audio files, video files, and multimedia contents. Without text versions, these cannot be analyzed computationally with the broadly available tools in the market today. Manual analyses of these objects may be done to enable complementary analyses. A hands-on human-based analysis enables researchers to get more granular and fine-grained understandings. For example, researchers may identify sets of unusual

Figure 2. One approach to the sentiment analysis process with NVivo 11 Plus

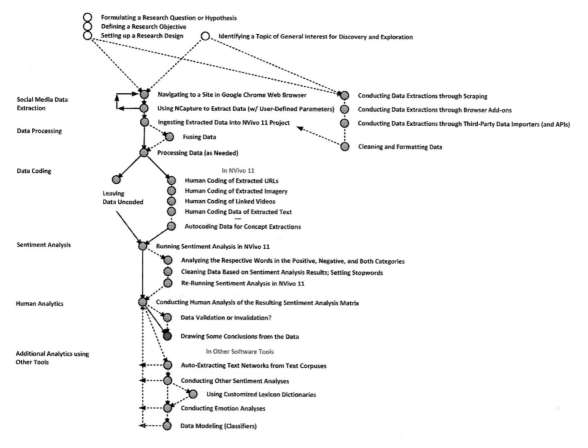

One Approach to the Sentiment Analysis Process with NVivo 11

words and distinct concepts labeled positive and negative vs. more common words labeled positive and negative respectively. There may be value in analyzing terms labeled both positive and negative. There may be unique and new identified symbology and phraseology encoded in the communications. In these described research contexts, there is always a "human in the loop," but to what degree and in what position in the sequence differs.

Within NVivo, there are other queries that may be applied to the research data, to attain other insights (such as text frequency counts, word search trees, locational mapping if lat-long data is available, and others). There are also various types of data exploration that may be achieved with other software tools—to extract word networks from a text corpus, for example. One of the nodes at the bottom of the diagram (Figure 2) suggests that there may be efforts at data validation or invalidation through other methods of research and knowing. Results (in)validation may well have to occur outside the NVivo tool and likely would involve other software tools and techniques. That validation approach will be critical for high-value high-cost assertions but also for general research standards. Also, it is highly likely that any assertions will have to be qualified and restrained because these approaches will not support broad assertions. These techniques do not result in N=all datasets, and the methods will collect noise and ingest distortion. The lack of validation of sentiment analysis of user-generated texts is a major concern. Some authors have suggested some potential mitigation methods:

For the external validity of these sentiment reports, i.e., the applicability of the results to target audiences, it is important to well analyze data of the context of user-generated content and their sample of authors. The literature lacks an analysis of external validity of sentiment mining reports and the sentiment mining field lacks an operationalization of external validity dimensions toward practically useful techniques.

From a kernel theory, we identify multiple threats to sentiment mining external validity and study three of them empirically 1) a mismatch in demographics of the reviewers sample, 2) bias due to reviewers' incidental experiences, and 3) manipulation of reviews. The value of external validity threat identifying techniques is next examined in cases from Goodread.com. We conclude that demographic biases can be well detected by current techniques, although we have doubts regarding stylometric techniques for this purpose. We demonstrate the usefulness of event and manipulation bias detection techniques in our cases, but this result needs further replications in more complex and more competitive contexts. Finally, for increasing the decisional usefulness of sentiment mining reports, they should be accompanied by external validity reports and software and service providers in this field should incorporate these in their offerings. (Wijnhoven & Bloemen, 2014, p. 262)

Depending on the various datasets, sometimes, machine-enabled analyses result in more accurate sentiment analyses, and in other cases, human sentiment coding is more effective. There are numerous complexities to the varying respective sentiment analysis contexts; one takeaway point is that there are tradeoffs between efficiencies and accuracy in every context. Arriving at what would work optimally in a situation will require some actual research and testing, and even then, there are likely qualifying observations to the data.

The above sequence requires a fair amount of work, particularly in a research context where in-depth insights are required. One run-through of this sequence, for each of the examples below, takes about half a day, including the image renderings and write-up. More complex data extractions would require more human concentration and effort. There can be many more complex stepwise approaches for more complex sentiment analyses, such as those involving data pre-processing and data post-processing. The cost to this work here assumes that the researcher has foundational understandings of the target social media platforms and of the particular domain in which the research findings are applied.

For this research, eight initial case types were conceptualized to test using the sentiment analysis tool (and the theme extraction tool) in NVivo 11 Plus. These include the following:

1. Profiling the personalities of egos and entities through related social media account data,
2. Describing the personalities of groups with interacting members (in ego neighborhoods, *ad hoc* networks, editing groups, and others) through network analysis and then sentiment analysis,
3. Exploring metadata (folksonomic related tags networks and article networks) to surface latent public conceptualizations,
4. Examining trending public issues through socially shared data and discourse sets,
5. Delving into public concepts through socially shared data and discourse sets,
6. Observing public events through socially shared data and discourse sets,

7. Analyzing broad-scale brand (generically conceptualized) reputation through socially shared data and discourse sets, and

8. Inspecting various individual texts and text corpora for emergent insights.

Topic Selection

To simplify topic selection, one over-arching real-world concept was identified as sufficiently broad and contemporaneous to use for selecting the seeding terms for the eight cases: the European Union (EU). This topic enables data extractions of various types from a range of social media platforms. On the multiple days when social media data extractions are occurring, there will likely be some trending topic or other—based on serendipity alone. There are no actual solid assertions made about the topic. Of course, such analyses would benefit from having a researcher with a solid background in the topic and intimacy with the data. The European Union, as a political entity, is comprised of 28 member states located mostly in Europe. The member states interact with each other and the world based on policies set by various supranational institutions that set policy and practices around political decision-making, a single market, shared defense, and a monetary union. At the time of the writing of this chapter, the EU was under political duress with the influx of Syrian refugees escaping violence in their homeland, the aftermath of the political wrangling to support the Greek economy (or countenance "grexit" or the Greek exit from the Eurozone), the incursions of Russia into Ukraine on the EU's eastern flank, and other issues.

Case 1: Profiling the Personalities of Egos and Entities through Social Media Account Data

An Askable Question: What is the personality disposition of the social media account holder(s) based on expressed sentiment in messaging and interactions?

An "ego" or "entity" on social media often refers to an individual or group, respectively, that may be understood through a personality frame. Generally, there are two types of ego or entity data available on social media: static data like self-created profiles representing the individual or group, and then the shared dynamic data like short text messages, images, audio, video, and other contents used for inter-communications, interactions, and broad sharing. How individuals communicate and what they express have been studied to create models of the users, in order to adapt online services to their interests (Abel, Gao, Houben, & Tao, 2011). The dynamism in the latter data involves the engagement with others on social media. On social media, there is plenty of information both "by" vs. "about" particular egos and entities. The first may offer ways to capture an original voice, a limited line-of-sight worldview, a personality, and those types of data. The latter may capture more of a public sense of a public persona.

Based on the EU theme, then, multiple verified user accounts were identified on Twitter for the data extractions. Several of the initial ones were public but did not enable data extractions, so those were not pursued. For highly public and official organizational accounts, it is often likely that a team is working on the messaging. This is true also with highly busy and public figures. While it may be unclear whether an account represents the messaging by proxies or others, it is at least clear that most accounts follow certain rules of messaging, so there is consistency in the message. The "by" approach tends to offer more of a sense of direct voice of the ego or entity behind the user account.

NCapture (a plug-in to Internet Explorer and Google Chrome) was used to capture the two respective Tweetstreams in this section. The extractions from Twitter result in files with the extension .nvcx, which are then opened into an NVivo project. This plug-in enables the download of upwards of 3,500 Tweets of a given public user account on Twitter, in interaction with the Twitter API.

The @Europarl_EN (https://twitter.com/Europarl_EN/), representing the European Parliament, account had 13,000 Tweets, 9,886 following, 175,000 followers, 81 favorites and 11 lists on the Twitter site at the time of the data extraction. The captured Tweetstream from this account consisted of 3,225 of the most recent Tweets. The sentiment analysis resulted in the following: Very negative: 211; Moderately negative: 185; Moderately positive: 193; and Very positive: 116. These results may be seen in Figure 3

The EU External Action Service (EEAS) holds a Twitter account @eu_eeas (available at https://twitter.com/eu_eeas/) with 13,600 Tweets, 1,822 following, 113,000 followers, 71 favorites, and 27 lists, at the time of the data extraction. The account was started in October 2009. The sentiment analysis of its Tweetstream, with 3,227 captured Tweets, were skewing a little negative. The sentiment metrics were as follows: Very negative: 301; Moderately negative: 226; Moderately positive: 199; and Very positive: 60. This may be viewed in Figure 4.

A further autocoded theme extraction of the Tweetstream showed top-level themes related to its organizational interests. This may be seen in Figure 5.

Another two data extractions were done to focus on crowd-sourced data about targeted egos and entities. Two sentiment analyses were run on crowd-sourced articles about two public figures on Wikipedia. The "Angela Merkel" page on Wikipedia (https://en.wikipedia.org/wiki/Angela_Merkel) describes this powerful Chancellor of Germany. Her profile on Wikipedia showed a wide range of sentiment: Very negative: 23; Moderately negative: 27; Moderately positive: 32; and Very positive: 19. These results may be a reflection of her stature and her polarizing stances on various high-profile issues. Figure 6 shows these results in a bar graph.

Figure 3. @Europarl_EN Tweetstream on Twitter represented in a sentiment bar chart

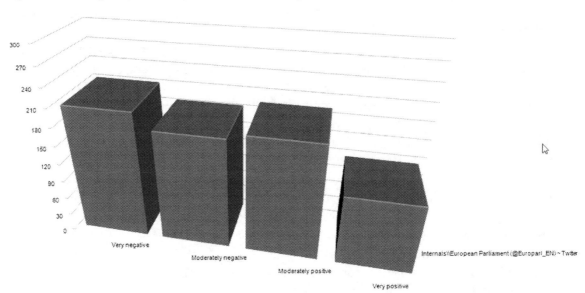

Figure 4. @eu_eeas Tweetstream on Twitter represented in a sentiment bar chart

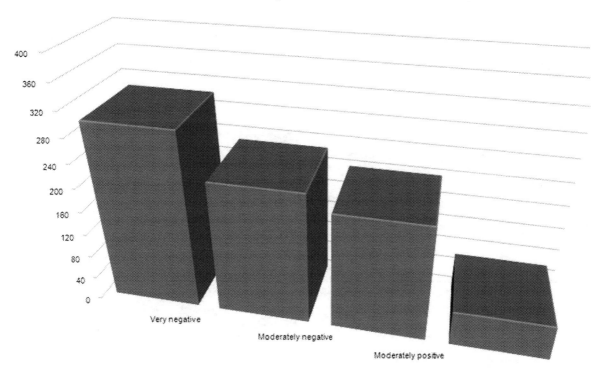

Figure 5. @eu_eeas Tweetstream on Twitter Represented in an auto-extracted theme coding structure

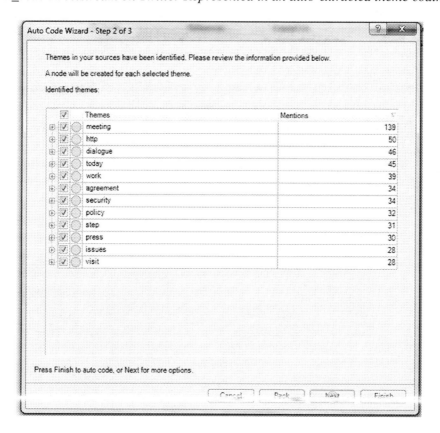

Figure 6. "Angela_Merkel" article on Wikipedia represented in a sentiment bar chart

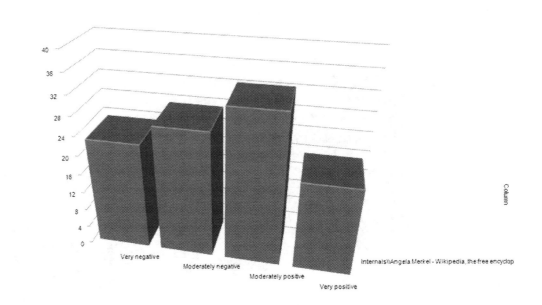

Auto Code Sentiment Results 10-7-2015 10.51 AM

A similar data extraction was done with a "Mario_Draghi" article on Wikipedia. His profile on Wikipedia showed less polarized sentiment: Very negative: 8; Moderately negative: 17; Moderately positive: 11; and Very positive: 1. Figure 7 shows these results in a bar graph.

Also, an entity may represent a group of people working in coordination. In this case, it is possible, for example, to capture the sentiment "about" the European Central Bank based on its crowd-sourced page on Wikipedia. The resulting sentiment analysis metrics were as follows: Very negative: 43; Moderately negative: 42; Moderately positive: 40, and Very positive: 5. The sentiment outcomes may be seen in Figure 8.

The resulting theme-based extraction is depicted as a bar chart in Figure 9. Such summaries, a this high level, give a quick gist of the topics addressed.

Another Europe-based entity is the North Atlantic Treaty Organization (NATO). A sentence-level sentiment analysis of the "NATO" article on Wikipedia had the following results: Very negative: 15; Moderately negative: 20; Moderately positive: 14; and Very positive: 2 (Figure 10).

An autocoded theme extraction was also applied to the article, with some of the results viewable in Figure 11.

Figure 7. "Mario_Draghi" article on Wikipedia represented in a sentiment bar chart

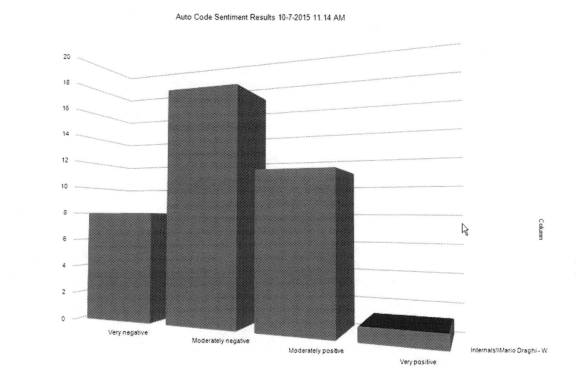

Figure 8. "European_Central_Bank" article on Wikipedia represented in a sentiment bar chart

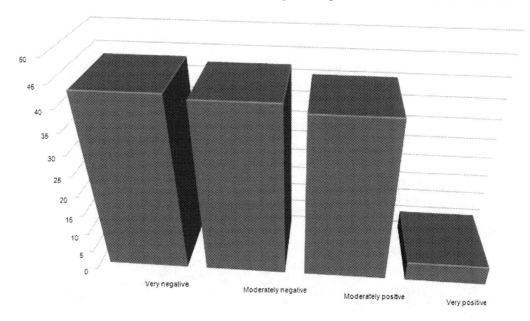

Figure 9. "European_Central_Bank" article on Wikipedia represented in a theme extraction bar chart

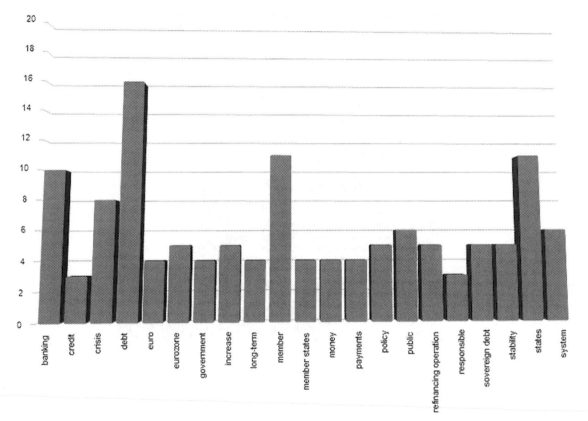

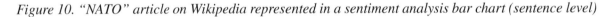

Figure 10. "NATO" article on Wikipedia represented in a sentiment analysis bar chart (sentence level)

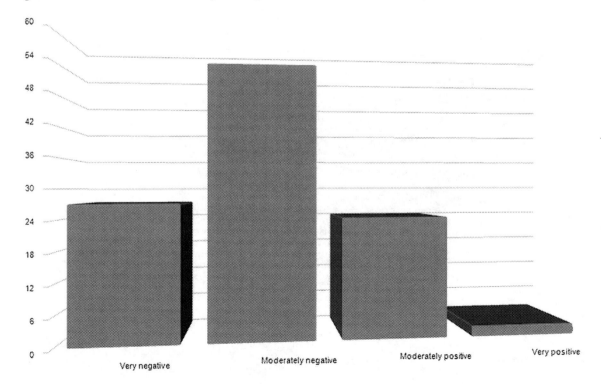

Figure 11. "NATO" article on Wikipedia represented in a theme extraction coding node structure

Name	Sources	References	Created By	Created On	Modified By	Modified On
command	1	8	NV	10/11/2015 10:46 AM	NV	10/11/2015 10:46 AM
military command outp	1	1	NV	10/11/2015 10:46 AM	NV	10/11/2015 10:46 AM
military command struct	1	2	NV	10/11/2015 10:46 AM	NV	10/11/2015 10:46 AM
military structure	1	3	NV	10/11/2015 10:46 AM	NV	10/11/2015 10:46 AM
strategic commanders	1	1	NV	10/11/2015 10:46 AM	NV	10/11/2015 10:46 AM
supreme commanders	1	1	NV	10/11/2015 10:46 AM	NV	10/11/2015 10:46 AM
countries	1	5	NV	10/11/2015 10:46 AM	NV	10/11/2015 10:46 AM
allied countries	1	1	NV	10/11/2015 10:46 AM	NV	10/11/2015 10:46 AM
candidate countries	1	1	NV	10/11/2015 10:46 AM	NV	10/11/2015 10:46 AM
contact countries	1	1	NV	10/11/2015 10:46 AM	NV	10/11/2015 10:46 AM
participating countries	1	1	NV	10/11/2015 10:46 AM	NV	10/11/2015 10:46 AM
third countries	1	1	NV	10/11/2015 10:46 AM	NV	10/11/2015 10:46 AM
forces	1	6	NV	10/11/2015 10:46 AM	NV	10/11/2015 10:46 AM
allied land forces	1	1	NV	10/11/2015 10:46 AM	NV	10/11/2015 10:46 AM
armed force	1	1	NV	10/11/2015 10:46 AM	NV	10/11/2015 10:46 AM
conventional forces	1	2	NV	10/11/2015 10:46 AM	NV	10/11/2015 10:46 AM
direct forces	1	1	NV	10/11/2015 10:46 AM	NV	10/11/2015 10:46 AM
peacekeeping force	1	1	NV	10/11/2015 10:46 AM	NV	10/11/2015 10:46 AM
member	1	6	NV	10/11/2015 10:46 AM	NV	10/11/2015 10:46 AM
16 member nations	1	1	NV	10/11/2015 10:46 AM	NV	10/11/2015 10:46 AM
28 member states	1	1	NV	10/11/2015 10:46 AM	NV	10/11/2015 10:46 AM
european states	1	1	NV	10/11/2015 10:46 AM	NV	10/11/2015 10:46 AM
member state subject	1	1	NV	10/11/2015 10:46 AM	NV	10/11/2015 10:46 AM
permanent member	1	1	NV	10/11/2015 10:46 AM	NV	10/11/2015 10:46 AM
requiring member state	1	1	NV	10/11/2015 10:46 AM	NV	10/11/2015 10:46 AM
military	1	21	NV	10/11/2015 10:46 AM	NV	10/11/2015 10:46 AM
active military	1	1	NV	10/11/2015 10:46 AM	NV	10/11/2015 10:46 AM
combined military spen	1	1	NV	10/11/2015 10:46 AM	NV	10/11/2015 10:46 AM
military affairs	1	1	NV	10/11/2015 10:46 AM	NV	10/11/2015 10:46 AM
military command outp	1	1	NV	10/11/2015 10:46 AM	NV	10/11/2015 10:46 AM

A sentiment analysis at cell level is the most granular form (assuming the traditional cellular structure of information vs. the key-value pairs in big data datasets). The next size higher would be sentence-level and then paragraph level. A paragraph-level sentiment analysis of the "NATO" article on Wikipedia was also run, with the following results: Very negative: 27; Moderately negative: 54; Moderately positive: 24, and Very positive: 2. While the numbers are different for each category, the general relative dynamics seem the same, per Figure 12.

Case 2: Describing the Personalities of Groups with Interacting Members

An Askable Question: What is the personality disposition of the coalesced group based on expressed sentiment in messaging and interactions?

Case 2 may seem similar to an "entity" or a group. This is conceptualized somewhat differently, however. The idea here is that a group of interacting individuals on a social media platform are captured based on some aspect of interaction. For example, a group of individuals may be identified interacting via an email system or a microblogging platform or an image-sharing site. This network may be a formal one—in a declared group based on invited membership, for example—or it may be an informal one, based on having a shared interest in a particular discussion (such as one labeled by a #hashtag). Once such groups are identified, then each of the members' Tweetstreams or other related textual information may be collected to capture the dynamic personality of the group as sentiments. This data may be treated

Figure 12. "NATO" article on Wikipedia represented in a sentiment analysis bar chart (paragraph level)

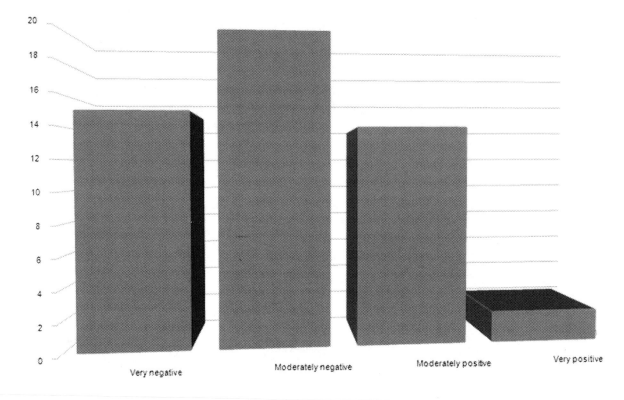

in a summary way, or the respective individual text streams may be analyzed individually for sentiment and then cross-compared.

The above method then requires potential use of network analysis to identify the respective groups formed via social media platforms. While those who create relationships on social media tend to be linked only by fleeting and weak ties, new media culture has enabled people to share even intimate details with a broad audience. In Granovetter's classic work (1973), in what he termed "a fragment of a theory" (p. 1378), even loosely linked nodes may be highly important to the network because of their potential bridging functions—connecting network that would not otherwise be linked and enabling rich cross-fertilization of ideas and extending communities' reach.

A walk-through of how this could work was seeded with the #euro hashtag on the Twitter microblogging site, based on the Network Overview, Discovery and Exploration for Excel (NodeXL) tool (with a built-in hard limit of 18,000 extractions). This data extraction resulted in a sociogram of 5,213 vertices (individual social network accounts) and 4,882 unique edges (relationships, such as replies-to and re-tweets) in the week leading up to the day of the data extraction. The graph diameter (maximum geodesic distance) was 19, and the average geodesic distance was 6.6. There were 2,172 groups or clusters.

First, a sentiment analysis was run on the range of self-created profiles of those who were part of this *ad hoc* network of communicators who recently labeled one of their messages with #euro. The profile descriptors were found to be as follows: Very negative: 130; Moderately negative: 208; Moderately positive: 317; and Very positive: 148. These results may be seen in Figure 13.

From extracted word pair lists, no sentiments were obtainable, probably due to data sparsity in English and also the mixed languages included in the set. Analyses were conducted of the extracted Tweets as a

Figure 13. Self-created profiles of #euro hashtag network on Twitter (basic and friends)

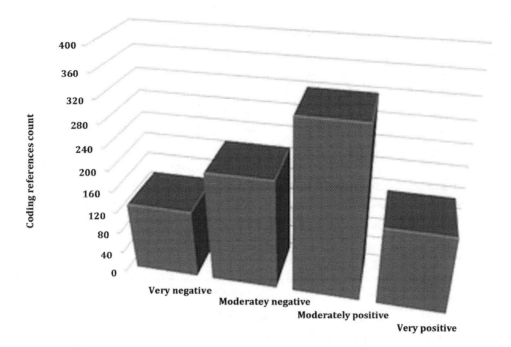

composite group. There were 17,909 messages in the dataset. Even though the contents were ingested into the NVivo 11 Plus project in multiple ways—as a dataset, as a .txt file, as a .docx file—no sentiments were extractable, and also no themes were extractable. To capture individual Tweetstreams from each of the respective communicators in the *ad hoc* #euro hashtag network would require a high investment of time and effort, so that was not directly done.

Case 3: Exploring Metadata (Folksonomic Related Tags Networks and Article Networks) for Latent Public Conceptualizations

An Askable Question: What can metadata (such as related tags networks and article networks) reveal about hidden public conceptualizations and mental models?

On social media, a wide range of metadata is captured. One category of metadata is tags or the labels users apply to their shared contents. Another type may be interrelationships between linked files on an open-access and crowd-sourced online encyclopedia. These two sources of texts are explored in Case 3 as possible ways to capture latent or hidden insights of a public mindset. The concept of a "mental model" is that it is a conceptualization of a topic by a non-expert as compared to a "conceptual model" as understood by experts in a field.

Related Tags Networks on Flickr

Some common metadata on social media platforms are tags, textual descriptors that users upload with their multimedia contents, including imagery, video, audio, slideshows, and other elements. These tags are considered informal types of data because the labeling is not done by professional librarians but by amateurs or non-professionals. To this end, such user-generated forms of classification are known as folksonomies (based on "folk" understandings and wisdom as compared to "taxonomies"). Some direct latent insights from related tags networks may be from the direct and indirect connections people make between tags based on co-occurrences.

A related tags network is seeded by a focal word that serves as a tag. At one degree, a related tags network shows the focal tag and all co-occurring tags that are linked to the focal tag at a certain threshold (most commonly co-occurring to least-commonly co-occurring). At 1.5 degrees, a related tags network captures the transitivity in the ego neighborhood of the focal node (it shows the likelihood that the "alters" in the 1-degree ego neighborhood co-occur among themselves along with the focal node). At two (2) degrees, the related tags network captures the ego neighborhood of the focal (source or seed) node, the transitivity between the "alters" of the initial ego neighborhood, and also the ego neighborhoods of the "alters". The data extractions for this section were done with two-degree data extractions in order to capture as much textual data as possible from this type of network graph to optimally meet a minimum threshold for sentiment analysis and for theme extraction respectively. However, it is important to note that higher order connectivity past 1.5 or 2 degrees may well end up with the data becoming almost pure noise (with little signal).

To capture a related tags network from Flickr, the open-source and free Network Overview, Discovery and Exploration for Excel (NodeXL Basic) tool was used to extract the data and to conduct early data processing. "Eurail" was used as a seeding term to extract a two-degree related tags network from Flickr, and the clustering algorithm used was the Clauset-Newman-Moore clustering algorithm (which resulted in the identification of nine groups). The extracted related tags network graph consisted of 412 vertices, with 1,388 unique edges. The graph may be viewed in Figure 14.

Figure 14. "Eurail" related tags network on Flickr (2 deg.) (NodeXL)

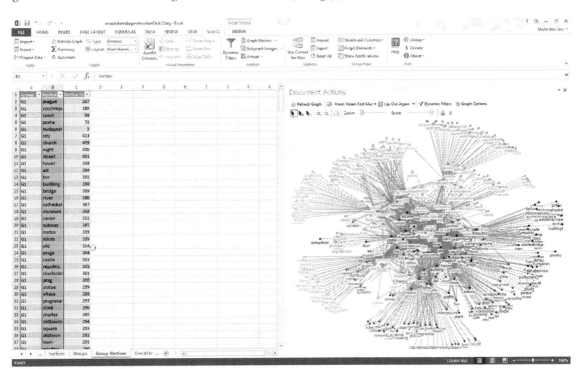

Another visualization of the "Eurail" related tags network extracted graph, with the groups in partitions and related thumbnail images for the vertices, may be seen in Figure 15.

A sentiment of the two-degree "Eurail" related tags network showed only one very negative reference and one moderately positive one (in Figure 16).

Another two-degree related tags network was extracted from Flickr using "Brussels" as the seeding term. A network graph with 748 vertices and 3,591 unique edges was extracted, and eight (8) groups were identified within this graph. This graph may be viewed in Figure 17.

The two-degree "Brussels" related tags network text was analyzed for sentiment in NVivo 11 Plus, but no sentiments were extractable. Specifically, the message returned was: "The Auto Code Wizard could not find any sentiment coding references to create." When a theme autocoding (automated coding by computer algorithm and other computational resources) was attempted, no themes could be extracted either. This was not surprising because a related tags network tends to be fairly sparse, and these extractions were abstractions of abstractions, several steps out from the original sources. To conceptualize

Figure 15. "Eurail" related tags network on flickr (2 deg.) (NodeXL)

Figure 16. Sentiment analysis matrix of the "Eurail" related tags network on Flickr (2 deg.)

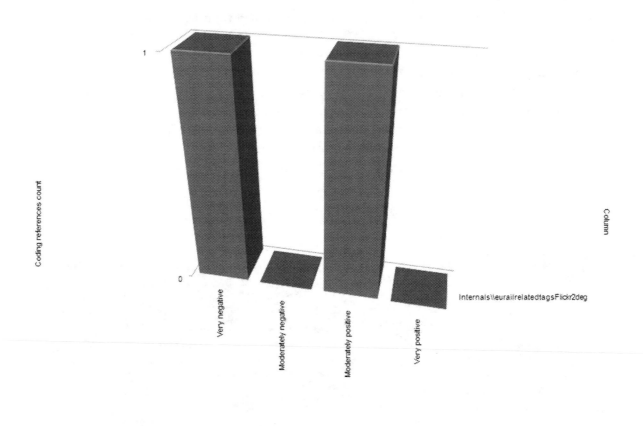

this, imagine concentric circles, with image content at the center circle, tagging as the next circle out, sentiment analysis as the third circle out (or auto-extracted themes as the third circle out).

Article Networks on Wikipedia

An article network captures the interrelationships between linked articles on a system. These are considered declared relationships based on directional public linkage (out-links, in-links). Article networks on Wikipedia show the outlinks from a particular page (each page as an article), and the resulting graphs have vertices labeled by the title of the article. Holistically, these offer a sense of related contents and topics. Ideally, the systems should have sufficient mass of data to provide a rich overview of a topic. Article networks are extracted based on the linkage metadata of open sites (in this case, one built on the MediaWiki understructure).

Figure 17. "Brussels" Related Tags Network from Flickr in Partitioned Groups (2 deg.) (NodeXL)

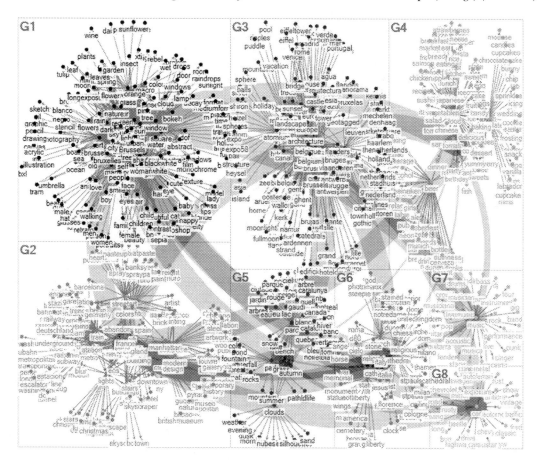

A one-degree "Eurozone" article network on Wikipedia resulted in a network consisting of 157 vertices and 156 unique edges (outlinks). The graph diameter (maximum geodesic distance) was two. At a one-degree network, a sentiment analysis of this network did not result in any extracted sentiments or themes. The network graph itself may be viewed in Figure 18.

A 1.5 degree "Eurozone" article network resulted in a graph with 25,734 vertices and 38,152 unique edges, and a maximum geodesic distance of 4 (graph diameter). Some 31 groups or clusters of related articles were identified. A sentiment analysis of this article network resulted in the following: Very negative: 11; Moderately negative: 7; Moderately positive: 10, and Very positive: 3. The actual extracted intensity matrix may be seen in Figure 19.

In a bar chart, the sentiment analysis results of the "Eurozone" article network on Wikipedia at 1.5 degrees may be seen in Figure 20.

A two-degree article network extraction was attempted multiple times, but they resulted in software crashes usually after some 60,000 nodes had been identified by NodeXL. The sentiment analysis of an article network is again an abstraction of an abstraction. At the core of a concentric circle display would be the Wikipedia articles co-evolved by contributors over time; then in the next concentric circle out would be the article network, and in the ring furthest from the center would be the sentiment analysis.

Figure 18. A One-degree article network graph of "Eurozone" on Wikipedia (NodeXL)

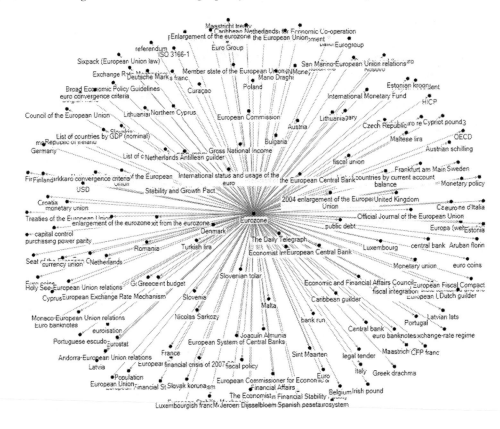

Figure 19. Sentiment analysis of "Eurozone" article network on Wikipedia (1.5 deg.)

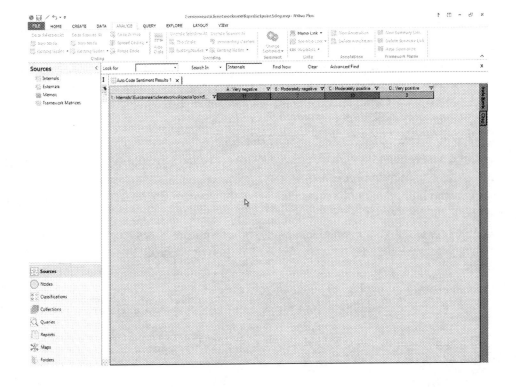

Figure 20. Sentiment analysis of "Eurozone" article network on Wikipedia (1.5 deg.)

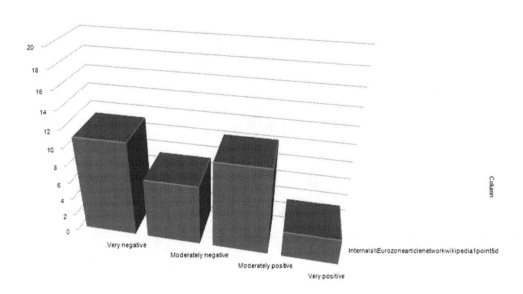

By Contrast

As a point of contrast, it may help to get a sense of what the "Eurozone" article on Wikipedia looks like. This capture involves the text, imagery, and hyperlinks, from the landing page: https://en.wikipedia.org/wiki/Eurozone (which is captured as a .pdf page using NCapture of NVivo). The captured sentiments were as follows: Very negative: 6; Moderately negative: 29; Moderately positive: 12, and Very positive: 3 (Figure 21).

Three sentences were coded to the Very positive group (Figure 22).

When looking at metadata for sentiment analysis, it may also help to capture some of the underlying content data to see how those compare and to support hypothesizing about what is occurring.

Case 4: Examining Trending Public Issues through Socially Shared Data and Discourse Sets

An Askable Question: What is the sentiment-based tone, positive or negative, of a trending public issue based on social media data, and what are some of the underlying issues informing the sentiment?

Figure 21. A bar chart of extracted sentiment of the "Eurozone" article page on Wikipedia

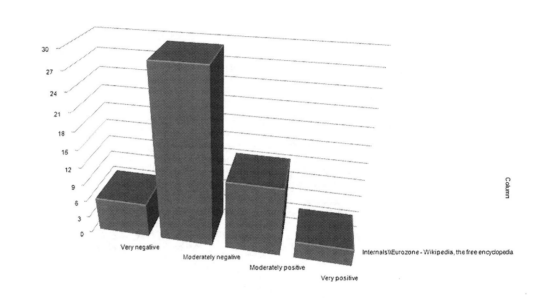

Auto Code Sentiment Results 10-3-2015 3.08 PM

One of the main rationales for capturing social media data linked to real-world trending issues is to create situational awareness, so the proper responses may be made. Trends invariably spark, spread, popularize, and then sunset. The time spans may be short-term, mid-term, or long-term. Trends may shift directions based on various opinions, public personas, in-world events, and funding. Some trends may re-spark in the future. In general, trends may be sparked and maintained by mainstream media, which affect public opinion and also spill over into social media. A public issue often involves a number of objective facets, stakeholder groups, and points-of-view.

A sentiment analysis was run on the crowd-sourced "European_migrant_crisis" article (Wikipedia 2016) available on Wikipedia. The sentiment analysis showed negative trending: Very negative: 144; Moderately negative: 96; Moderately positive: 65, and

Very positive: 6. This may be seen in Figure 23.

It is possible to double-click on each category in order to read the underlying text coded to that category. This is shown in Figure 24.

Another approach to understand how a public issue is trending may be to capture messaging from a microblogging site. One may use a hashtag label about a particular location, in an effort to capture the respective issues trending in that locale. #Europe of course would be referring to a large geographic and socio-cultural space, with any possible number of potential issues. A recent hashtag search seeded with

Figure 22. Identifying the verbatim sentences coded to the "very positive" category of sentiment

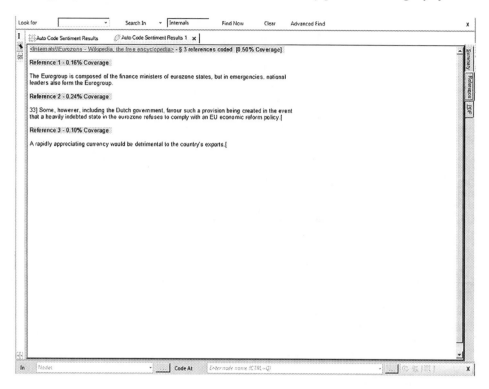

Figure 23. "European_migrant_crisis" article on Wikipedia represented in a sentiment bar chart

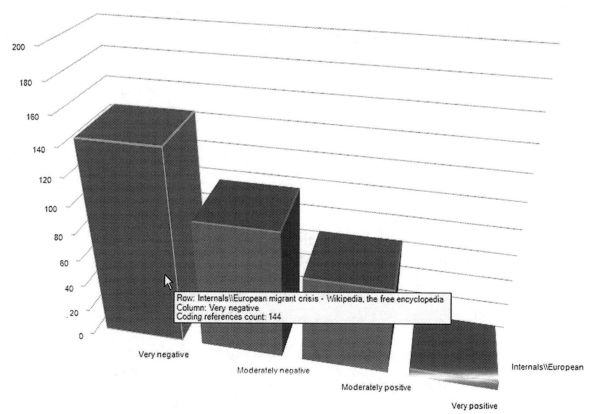

Figure 24. European_migrant_crisis article on Wikipedia (an exploration of the underlying coded text)

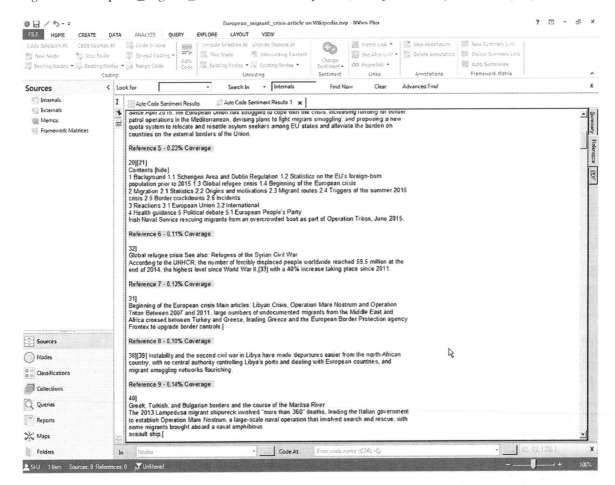

#Europe resulted in a network graph with 3,345 vertices and 3,550 unique edges, and a graph diameter of 14 (maximum geodesic distance). From these, there were 1,405 clusters or groups. A sentiment analysis of the shared messages around #europe found the following results: Very negative: 234; Moderately negative: 186; Moderately positive: 594, and Very positive: 161. This is visualized in Figure 25.

On social media, there are various ways to capture trending issues. There may be images and video available on content-sharing sites. There may be mainstream media articles as well as academic articles. There may be blog posts.

Case 5: Delving into Public Concepts through Socially Shared Data and Discourse Sets

An Askable Question: What is the sentiment-based tone, positive or negative, of a public concept based on social media data, and what are some of the underlying issues informing the sentiment?

A "concept" refers to an idea or notion. Understanding how the broader public understands certain phenomena may better inform those working on particular policies or issues or goals. A one-degree

Figure 25. #Europe hashtag search on Twitter represented in a sentiment bar chart

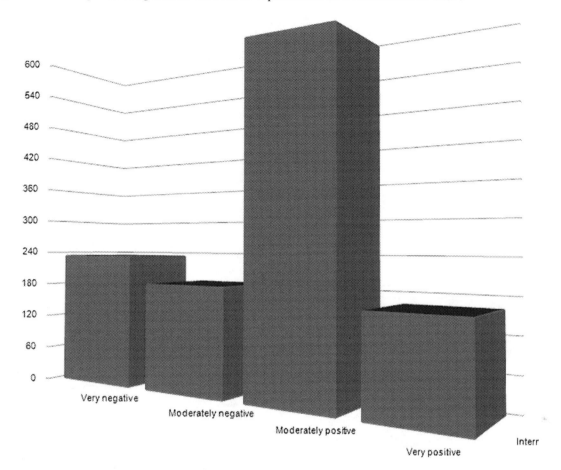

article network of "Trade_mark_law_of_the_European_Union" (available at https://en.wikipedia.org/wiki/Trade_mark_law_of_the_European_Union) on Wikipedia captured a 20-node (vertex) network; a graph visualization using the Harel-Koren Fast Multiscale Layout Algorithm may be seen in Figure 26.

A sentiment analysis of the results of this one-degree network resulted in the following: Very negative: 2; Moderately negative: 0; Moderately positive: 1, and Very positive: 0. This may be viewed as Figure 27.

Another concept is the so-called "right to be forgotten." The "Right_to_be_forgotten" article on Wikipedia (available at https://en.wikipedia.org/wiki/Right_to_be_forgotten) revealed a range of sentiments in the collected text: Very negative: 21; Moderately negative: 48; Moderately positive: 24, and Very positive: 7 (Figure 28).

A top-level theme extraction was conducted on the "Right_to_be_forgotten" article on Wikipedia (Figure 29).

The top-level theme extraction may be seen in Figure 30.

It is possible to customize autocoded data to some degree…such as by removing texts that do not fit a particular sentiment category (or a theme category for that matter) and re-coding that text to another category (if desired). NVivo enables "uncoding" of certain texts, too, as a human "check" on the autocoding.

Figure 26. "Trade_mark_law_of_the_European_Union" article network on Wikipedia (1 deg.)

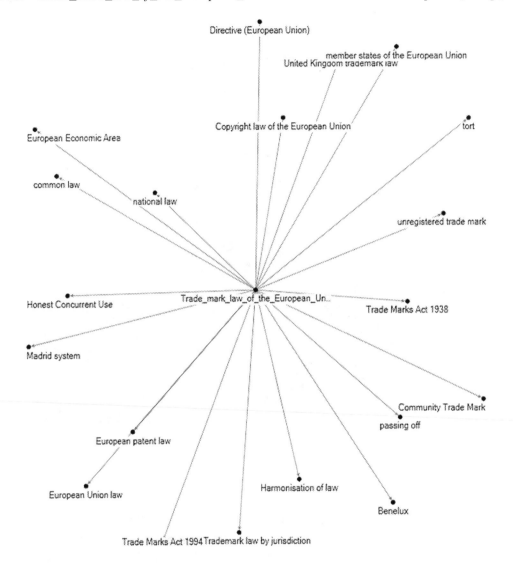

Case 6: Observing Public Events through Socially Shared Data and Discourse Sets

An askable question: What is the sentiment-based tone, positive or negative, of a social (or non-social) event based on social media data, and what are some of the underlying issues informing the sentiment?

An "event" is used to refer to an occurrence in time, with some way to demarcate a start and an end point, or in some research T1 (Time 1) and T2 (Time 2). Social events are those in which a number of people participate with some degree of cooperation and interactivity. Events may be studied prior to their occurrence (in an anticipatory way), during their unfolding, and post-event (such as in historical analyses). Events are generally thought to have recognizable trajectories, with various types of starts, middles, and ends. Social media platforms are thought to inform on human events—by leaders signal-

Figure 27. "Trade_mark_law_of_the_European_Union" article on Wikipedia sentiment analysis bar chart

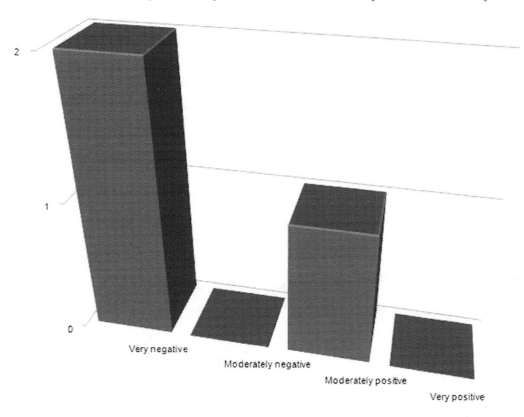

Figure 28. "Right_to_be_forgotten" article on Wikipedia represented in a sentiment analysis bar chart

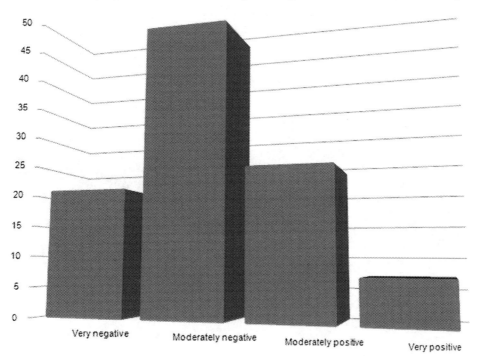

Figure 29. "Right_to_be_forgotten" article on Wikipedia represented in a top-level theme extraction view

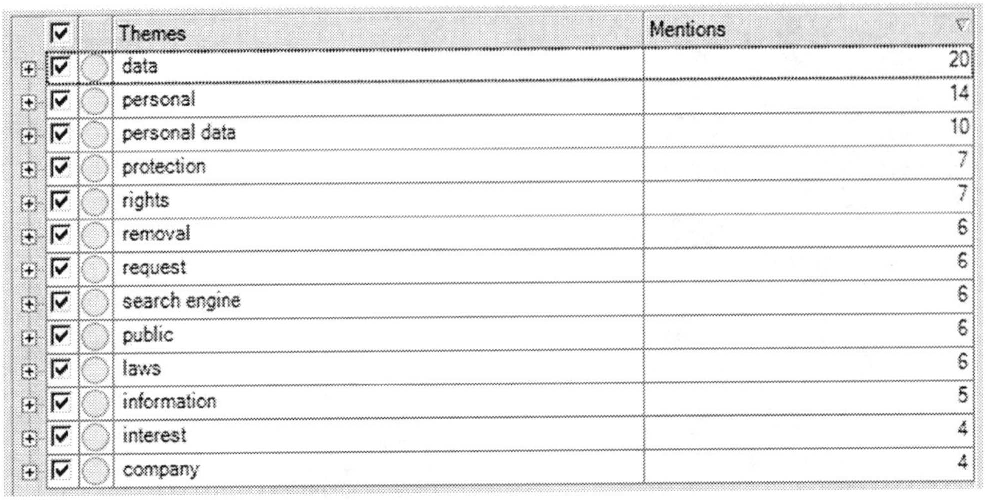

			Themes	Mentions	▽
⊞	☑	○	data		20
⊞	☑	○	personal		14
⊞	☑	○	personal data		10
⊞	☑	○	protection		7
⊞	☑	○	rights		7
⊞	☑	○	removal		6
⊞	☑	○	request		6
⊞	☑	○	search engine		6
⊞	☑	○	public		6
⊞	☑	○	laws		6
⊞	☑	○	information		5
⊞	☑	○	interest		4
⊞	☑	○	company		4

Figure 30. "Right_to_be_forgotten" article on Wikipedia represented in a theme extraction bar chart

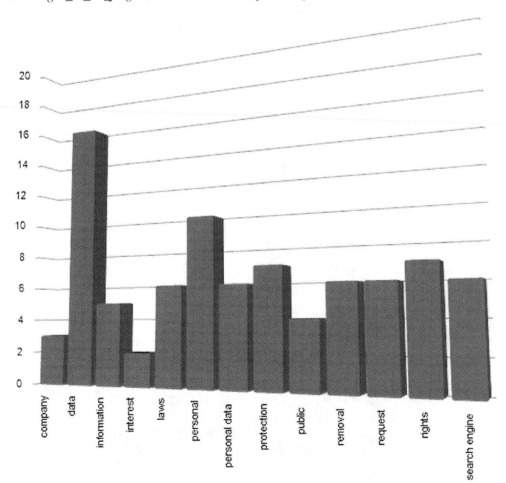

ing calls for actions, by incendiary messaging proliferating through networks around the world (or in particular regions), by collective emotions surging and waning, by geographical hotspots heating up and cooling off, and other indicators.

At the time of this chapter's writing, multiple terrorist bombings occurred in Turkey. The @byegmeng account is the official one for the Turkish Prime Minister's Press and Information interests (available at https://twitter.com/byegmeng). At the time of the data extraction, it had 2,349 Tweets, 226 following, 4,138 followers, and 13 favorites. The @byegmeng Tweetstream was extracted, with 3,099 microblogging messages. A sentiment analysis of this Tweetstream showed the following: Very negative: 106; Moderately negative: 134; Moderately positive: 201, and Very positive: 40 (Figure 31).

To capture more of a sense of public perceptions (instead of an official word), a #turkey hashtag extraction was captured in the same time frame. This resulted in an *ad hoc* network with 13,031 vertices (representing user accounts of those engaged in labeling their messages with #turkey) and 16,748 unique edges. The maximum geodesic distance or graph diameter of this network was 14. One thousand nine hundred and ninety groups (1,990) were identified. The resulting sentiment analysis was as follows: Very negative: 6449; Moderately negative: 2406; Moderately positive: 2101, and Very positive: 516 (Figure 32). This does show that the shading of the intensity matrix is relative to the amounts in each of the categories.

A theme extraction from the Tweets in the extracted #turkey ad hoc network resulted in the following theme extractions (Figure 33). The top-level themes indicate a focus on the attention-getting bombings.

Another analysis was done from the extracted #turkey hashtag search. A summary profile was extracted from all the texts used in the descriptions of the related user accounts on Twitter, and this text was

Figure 31. @byegmeng user account on Twitter Tweetstream expressed as a sentiment bar chart

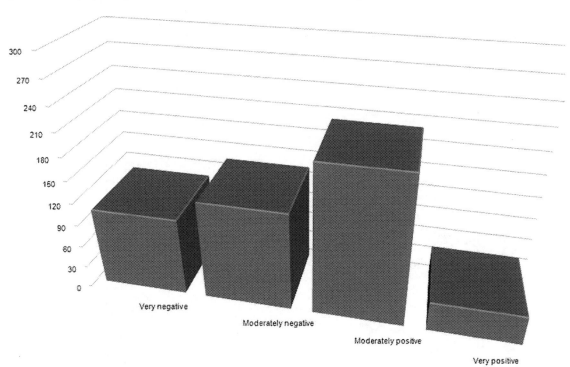

Figure 32. #turkey hashtag search on Twitter represented in a sentiment analysis bar chart

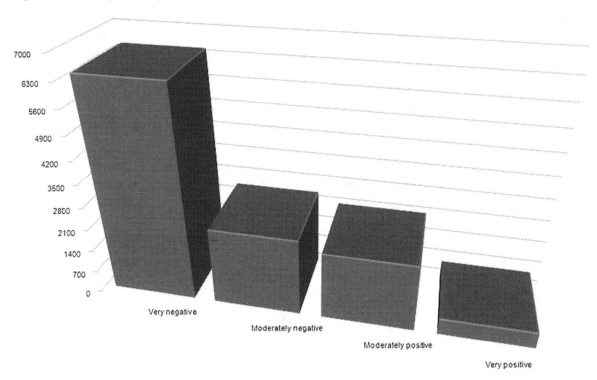

Figure 33. #turkey hashtag search on Twitter represented in top-level theme extractions

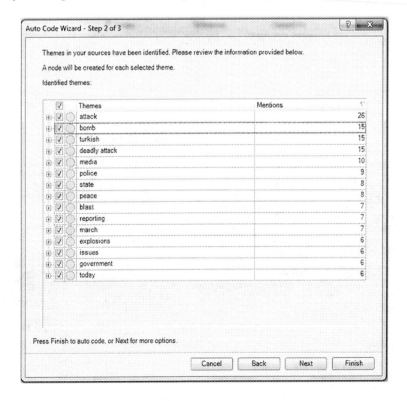

analyzed for sentiment. The sentiment results were as follows: Very negative: 496; Moderately negative: 705; Moderately positive: 941, and Very positive: 345 (Figure 34).

A naïve approach might suggest that the profiles might be generally positive since they are created by the users, but a more real-world understanding may be that people's profiles represent interests in the world, and the world is a complex place. To probe more deeply, a theme extraction was conducted on the user accounts' profiles from the #turkey hashtag search on Twitter.

Finally, the Tweetstream for another user account @POLITICOEurope (verified to a media organization and http://www.politico.eu/) was captured, resulting in 2,117 Tweets. At the time of the data extraction, this account (available at https://twitter.com/POLITICOEurope) had 3,562 Tweets, 259 following, 39,200 followers, 261 favorites, and 9 lists. Analyzed at the cell level, these microblogging messages were coded as having the following sentiments: Very negative: 338; Moderately negative: 336; Moderately positive: 209, and Very positive: 67 (Figure 36).

In terms of the extracted sentiments, the issues of the day and the recent few prior days may be seen (Figure 37).

NVivo 11 Plus enables the extraction of a sociogram from Twitter data (Figure 38).

It also enables the physical identification of those communicating in the Tweetstream @POLITICOEurope (Figure 39).

Figure 34. Profile descriptions for #Turkey hashtag search on Twitter represented in a sentiment analysis bar chart

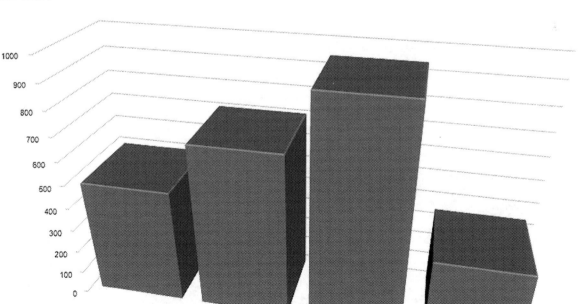

Figure 35. Profile descriptions for #Turkey hashtag search on Twitter theme extractions in coded nodes

Name	Sources	References	Created By	Created On	Modified By	Modified On
Autocoded Themes						
attack	1	15	NV	10/11/2015 1:36 PM	NV	10/11/2015 1:36 PM
blast	1	7	NV	10/11/2015 1:36 PM	NV	10/11/2015 1:36 PM
bomb	1	14	NV	10/11/2015 1:36 PM	NV	10/11/2015 1:36 PM
bomb attack police	1	4	NV	10/11/2015 1:36 PM	NV	10/11/2015 1:36 PM
bombing aftermath	1	2	NV	10/11/2015 1:36 PM	NV	10/11/2015 1:36 PM
bombing civilians	1	1	NV	10/11/2015 1:36 PM	NV	10/11/2015 1:36 PM
sucide bomb blast	1	3	NV	10/11/2015 1:36 PM	NV	10/11/2015 1:36 PM
suicide bombings	1	2	NV	10/11/2015 1:36 PM	NV	10/11/2015 1:36 PM
terrorist bombing	1	2	NV	10/11/2015 1:36 PM	NV	10/11/2015 1:36 PM
deadly attack	1	5	NV	10/11/2015 1:36 PM	NV	10/11/2015 1:36 PM
explosions	1	6	NV	10/11/2015 1:36 PM	NV	10/11/2015 1:36 PM
government	1	5	NV	10/11/2015 1:36 PM	NV	10/11/2015 1:36 PM
issues	1	6	NV	10/11/2015 1:36 PM	NV	10/11/2015 1:36 PM
march	1	5	NV	10/11/2015 1:36 PM	NV	10/11/2015 1:36 PM
media	1	10	NV	10/11/2015 1:36 PM	NV	10/11/2015 1:36 PM
peace	1	7	NV	10/11/2015 1:36 PM	NV	10/11/2015 1:36 PM
police	1	9	NV	10/11/2015 1:36 PM	NV	10/11/2015 1:36 PM
reporting	1	7	NV	10/11/2015 1:36 PM	NV	10/11/2015 1:36 PM
state	1	8	NV	10/11/2015 1:36 PM	NV	10/11/2015 1:36 PM
today	1	5	NV	10/11/2015 1:36 PM	NV	10/11/2015 1:36 PM
turkish	1	13	NV	10/11/2015 1:36 PM	NV	10/11/2015 1:36 PM
turkey game	1	1	NV	10/11/2015 1:36 PM	NV	10/11/2015 1:36 PM
turkish army	1	2	NV	10/11/2015 1:36 PM	NV	10/11/2015 1:36 PM
turkish authority	1	2	NV	10/11/2015 1:36 PM	NV	10/11/2015 1:36 PM
turkish capital	1	1	NV	10/11/2015 1:36 PM	NV	10/11/2015 1:36 PM
turkish doctors	1	2	NV	10/11/2015 1:36 PM	NV	10/11/2015 1:36 PM
turkish security services	1	1	NV	10/11/2015 1:36 PM	NV	10/11/2015 1:36 PM
turkish soldier friends	1	1	NV	10/11/2015 1:36 PM	NV	10/11/2015 1:36 PM
turkish staple crop	1	1	NV	10/11/2015 1:36 PM	NV	10/11/2015 1:36 PM
turkish streets	1	1	NV	10/11/2015 1:36 PM	NV	10/11/2015 1:36 PM
turkish streetsrt	1	1	NV	10/11/2015 1:36 PM	NV	10/11/2015 1:36 PM

Figure 36. Tweetstream of @POLITICOEurope user account on twitter represented as a sentiment analysis bar chart

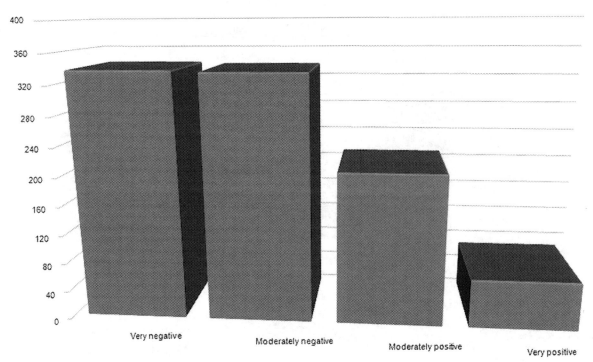

Figure 37. @POLITICOEurope user account on Twitter represented in a theme extraction bar chart

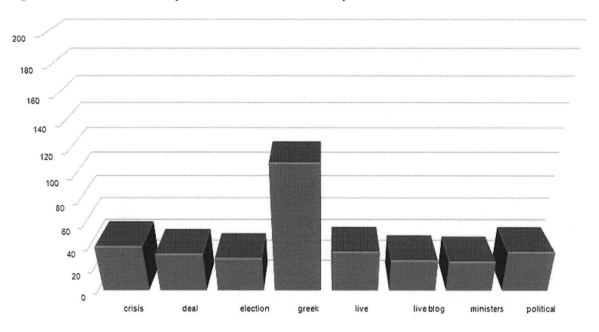

Figure 38. @POLITICOEurope user account on Twitter in a network sociogram

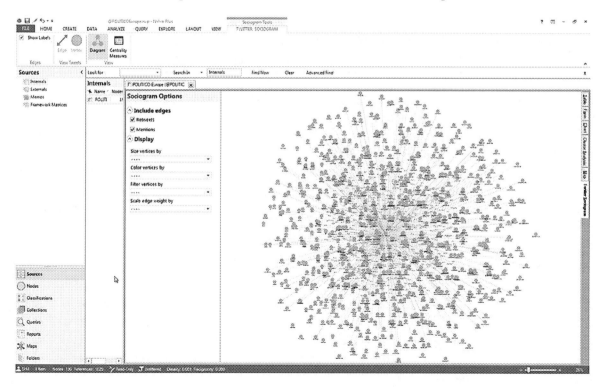

Figure 39. @POLITICOEurope user account on Twitter on a geographical map

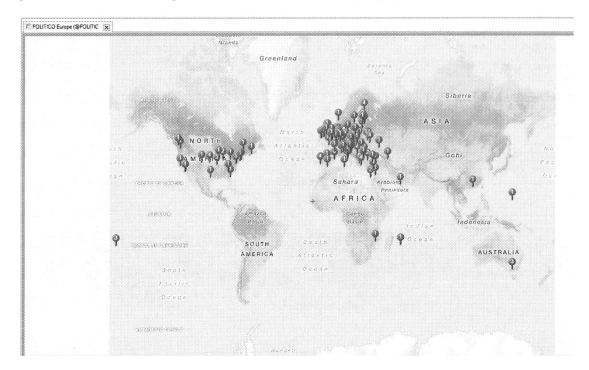

Case 7: Analyzing Broad-scale Brand Reputation (Generically Conceptualized) through Socially Shared Data and Discourse Sets

An Askable Question: What is the nature of a particular brand (generically conceptualized) based on extracted expressed sentiments?

To capture how sentiment analysis might apply to generic brand reputations, two data extractions were run. One was for the crowd-sourced "Vatican" article in Wikipedia (https://en.wikipedia.org/wiki/Holy_See). A sentiment analysis of the contents found that the bulk of the related words were either moderately positive or moderately negative, followed by very positive and then very negative. A bar chart showing these results is available in Figure 40.

An automated theme extraction from the same article showed a range of high-level topics (shown in alphabetical order in a bar chart), in Figure 41.

Another well-known European "brand" involves the airplane maker, Airbus. The sentiment analysis applied to the crowd-sourced "Airbus" article on Wikipedia (https://en.wikipedia.org/wiki/Airbus) reveals one of the more symmetrically balanced sentiment analyses, with low counts of "Very negative" (10) and "Very positive" (4) sentiment, but most coding to the "Moderately negative" (46) and "Moderately positive" (40) classifications (almost in a bell curve). The 3D bar chart visualization may be seen in Figure 42.

A number of themes were extracted from the "Airbus" article. The node set may be seen in Figure 43.

Figure 40. Holy_See article on Wikipedia sentiment analysis bar chart

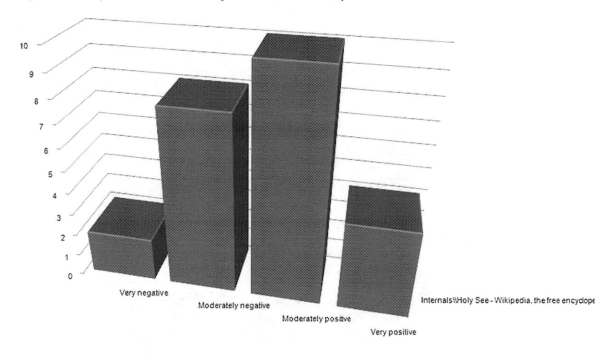

Figure 41. Holy_See article on Wikipedia theme extraction bar chart

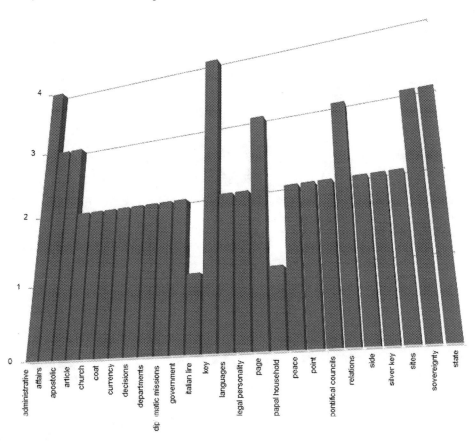

Figure 42. "Airbus" article on Wikipedia sentiment analysis bar chart

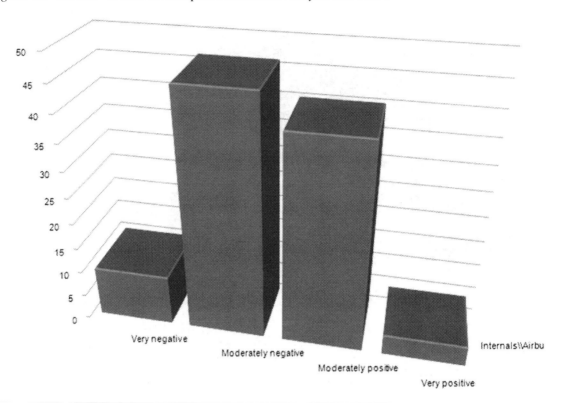

Figure 43. "Airbus" article on Wikipedia theme extraction in a coded node set

Autocoded Themes						
Name	Sources	Referen	Created	Created	Modified	Modifie
aid	1	4	10/7/20	NV	10/7/201	NV
federal aid	1	1	10/7/20	NV	10/7/201	NV
government aid	1	1	10/7/20	NV	10/7/201	NV
launch aid	1	2	10/7/20	NV	10/7/201	NV
aircraft	1	16	10/7/20	NV	10/7/201	NV
airliner	1	7	10/7/20	NV	10/7/201	NV
company	1	13	10/7/20	NV	10/7/201	NV
design	1	11	10/7/20	NV	10/7/201	NV
development	1	5	10/7/20	NV	10/7/201	NV
engineering	1	5	10/7/20	NV	10/7/201	NV
flight	1	4	10/7/20	NV	10/7/201	NV
fuel	1	5	10/7/20	NV	10/7/201	NV
government	1	9	10/7/20	NV	10/7/201	NV
jet	1	4	10/7/20	NV	10/7/201	NV
launch	1	4	10/7/20	NV	10/7/201	NV
manufacturers	1	5	10/7/20	NV	10/7/201	NV
market	1	7	10/7/20	NV	10/7/201	NV
orders	1	5	10/7/20	NV	10/7/201	NV
page	1	4	10/7/20	NV	10/7/201	NV
partner	1	3	10/7/20	NV	10/7/201	NV
passenger	1	4	10/7/20	NV	10/7/201	NV
production	1	12	10/7/20	NV	10/7/201	NV
section	1	3	10/7/20	NV	10/7/201	NV
shareholders	1	4	10/7/20	NV	10/7/201	NV
subsidies	1	4	10/7/20	NV	10/7/201	NV
support	1	4	10/7/20	NV	10/7/201	NV
technology	1	4	10/7/20	NV	10/7/201	NV
work	1	4	10/7/20	NV	10/7/201	NV

Case 8: Inspecting Various Individual Texts and Text Corpora for Emergent Insights

An Askable Question: In assessing a collection of related or pseudo-related texts, what is the predominant sentiment, and what are the underlying themes behind that sentiment? What are lesser sentiments, and what are the underlying themes behind those?

The prior cases involved user-account-related microblogging messaging, datasets of microblogging messages based around particular hashtags (hashtagged seeding or source terms), related tags networks, and article networks from a crowd-sourced encyclopedia, and others. In this section, by contrast, this uses a collection of texts in a related corpus to fast-read the texts for sentiment and thematic insights. In this example, the articles selected related to the Greek economy and its contested role in the Eurozone. The 100 articles were downloaded from two proprietary databases and a Google Scholar search.

Initially, there were several tries at sentiment extraction from these articles. After multiple failures, the list was limited to 50 full-length academic articles, and the resulting intensity matrix was extracted (Figure 44). Down the left column are the articles with their original file names left intact. Quite a few of

Figure 44. An intensity matrix of sentiment of related articles based on a related article set

	A : Very negative	B : Moderately negative	C : Moderately positive	D : Very positive
1 : Internals\\1061670	38	47	35	17
2 : Internals\\1288484	62	47	57	15
3 : Internals\\13608746%2E2013%2E779784	22	26	21	7
4 : Internals\\1404369	42	33	56	13
5 : Internals\\1452-595X1004391K	37	13	15	12
6 : Internals\\1601643	33	25	27	19
7 : Internals\\1848946	18	12	19	11
8 : Internals\\1-s2.0-S0164070413001286-main	25	39	22	4
9 : Internals\\20202974	65	63	100	43
10 : Internals\\20453138	24	23	34	10
11 : Internals\\20752845	43	115	63	15
12 : Internals\\23071701	9	18	8	5
13 : Internals\\23265969	25	32	35	17
14 : Internals\\23289410	10	15	18	5
15 : Internals\\25096899	11	11	8	3
16 : Internals\\25481928	173	149	64	21
17 : Internals\\27515971	36	78	40	13
18 : Internals\\3330768	15	35	32	21
19 : Internals\\40263651	23	10	12	8
20 : Internals\\40278457	25	17	38	19
21 : Internals\\40470466	70	70	80	33
22 : Internals\\40657771	52	47	60	23
23 : Internals\\40728488	22	19	48	21
24 : Internals\\4122458	25	26	27	15
25 : Internals\\41288358	27	33	41	6
26 : Internals\\41377887	24	38	48	23
27 : Internals\\41478275	27	37	36	10
28 : Internals\\41581131	59	44	30	19
29 : Internals\\41962514	23	16	16	9
30 : Internals\\422387	22	32	21	12
31 : Internals\\4380428	27	27	23	6
32 : Internals\\4380468	20	21	21	10
33 : Internals\\4543315	36	46	27	11
34 : Internals\\5092570	10	9	14	1
35 : Internals\\643195	28	36	47	29
36 : Internals\\669855	118	73	72	32
37 : Internals\\8th_June_2015	12	22	10	6
38 : Internals\\9 Suhail Abboushi	16	11	9	3

the articles seem to be fairly neutral across the sentiment categories: Very negative, Moderately negative, Moderately positive, and Very positive. There are some which show sentiment emphases.

Next, the full corpus of texts was analyzed for theme extractions. In Figure 45, the uploaded articles may be seen in the background as .pdf files, and the window with the Auto Code Wizard – Step 2 of 3 shows the processing.

The autocoded themes may be seen in an alphabetical node listing in Figure 46.

The automated theme extraction may also show the results in an intensity matrix (Figure 47). Down the left column are the unique articles…and across the column headers are the various topics. The numbers in the cells of this intensity matrix show the numbers of occurrences of that term in the particular source. (This method is sometimes used by researchers to mass-read a large number of articles and then to select out those that contain the contents of interest for the particular project.)

Comparing Sentiment Analysis Outcomes

As mentioned earlier, the resulting sentiment analysis may be vetted by human oversight of the coded text, and changes may be made. There are also other machine-ways to offer some comparisons—although

Figure 45. The identification of themes from a set of extracted articles based on Greek finances and the Eurozone topic

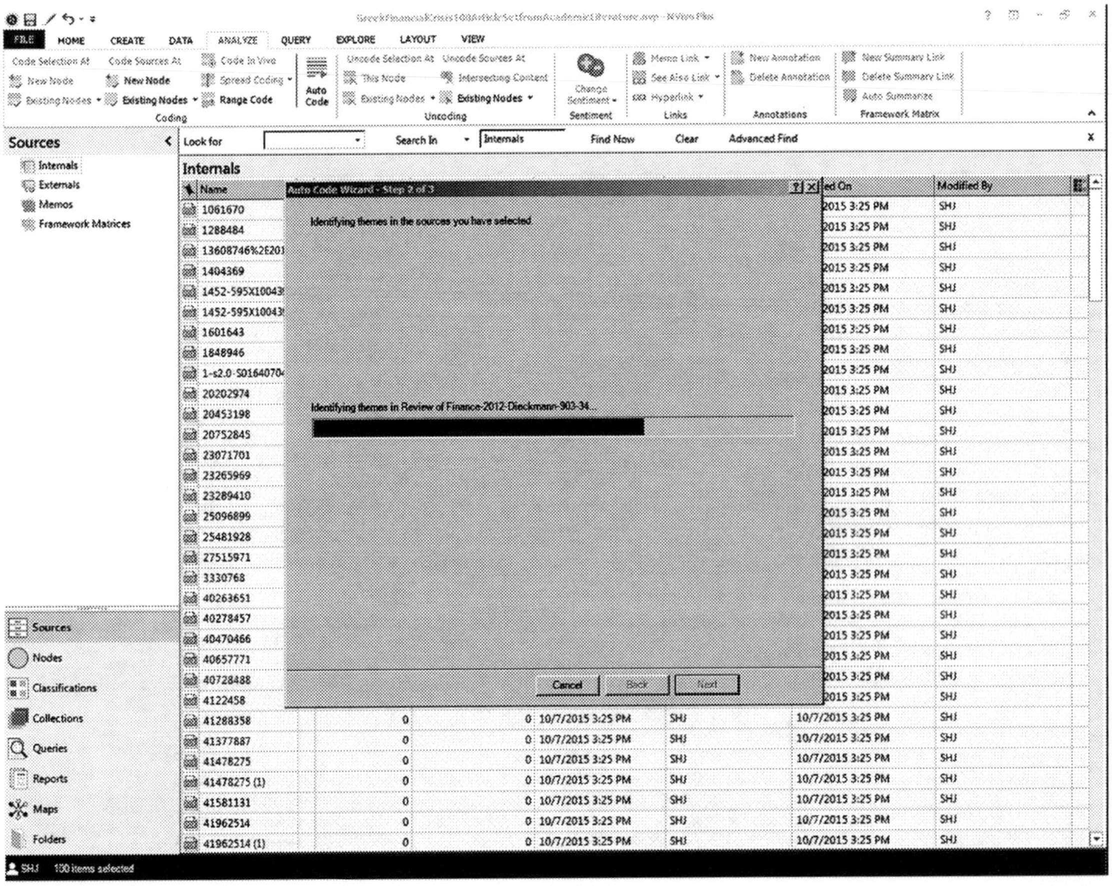

Figure 46. 100 academic and popular article set about Greek financial crisis: theme extraction

Autocoded Themes							
Name	Sources	Referen	Created	Created	Modified	Modifie
bank	60	441	10/7/20	NV	10/7/20	NV
bond	38	172	10/7/20	NV	10/7/20	NV
capital	46	177	10/7/20	NV	10/7/20	NV
change	61	181	10/7/20	NV	10/7/20	NV
countries	63	257	10/7/20	NV	10/7/20	NV
credit	44	139	10/7/20	NV	10/7/20	NV
crisis	84	374	10/7/20	NV	10/7/20	NV
current	69	248	10/7/20	NV	10/7/20	NV
debt	60	353	10/7/20	NV	10/7/20	NV
economic	85	552	10/7/20	NV	10/7/20	NV
economy	64	203	10/7/20	NV	10/7/20	NV
effects	59	170	10/7/20	NV	10/7/20	NV
european	68	272	10/7/20	NV	10/7/20	NV
government	84	401	10/7/20	NV	10/7/20	NV
greek	77	678	10/7/20	NV	10/7/20	NV
increase	57	179	10/7/20	NV	10/7/20	NV
interest	57	137	10/7/20	NV	10/7/20	NV
international	56	146	10/7/20	NV	10/7/20	NV
level	59	157	10/7/20	NV	10/7/20	NV
market	68	406	10/7/20	NV	10/7/20	NV
measures	49	144	10/7/20	NV	10/7/20	NV
national	52	212	10/7/20	NV	10/7/20	NV
period	56	140	10/7/20	NV	10/7/20	NV
policy	72	435	10/7/20	NV	10/7/20	NV
political	68	465	10/7/20	NV	10/7/20	NV
prices	50	166	10/7/20	NV	10/7/20	NV
public	73	358	10/7/20	NV	10/7/20	NV
rate	59	363	10/7/20	NV	10/7/20	NV
risk	46	184	10/7/20	NV	10/7/20	NV
sector	53	163	10/7/20	NV	10/7/20	NV
social	58	285	10/7/20	NV	10/7/20	NV
sovereign	33	166	10/7/20	NV	10/7/20	NV

the results are not directly comparable. The data extractions available by the various software tools on the market vary, and the sentiment analysis tools in the respective tools differ (although most do not sufficiently describe what is going on "under the hood"). It is possible to run data extractions at the same time and with different software tools on different machines, but given the complexity of the data and the rate-limiting of various social media APIs, the extracted sets are often very different.

Some might then suggest that the sentiment analyses should be done using the same dataset. The challenge is that the data are not interchangeable across the tools. NVivo 11 Plus can use data from NodeXL, but Maltego Chlorine 3.6.1 data is not as easily exported and used in other tools. NodeXL cannot take data from NVivo 11 Plus or Maltego Chlorine. Maltego Chlorine cannot take data directly from NVivo 11 Plus or NodeXL. Also, the respective tools only capture data from certain social media platforms. The software tools do not work equally adeptly across social media platforms. What this means is that validating or invalidating findings by using a mix of methods may be much easier asserted than done.

A Test Run of #Europe Hashtag Search on Twitter

To see how this might work, a parallel query around the #europe hashtag search on Twitter was conducted. To review, the sentiment analysis of the #europe hashtag search (based off a dataset created with

Figure 47. 100 academic and popular article set about Greek financial crisis: theme extraction

	A : bank	B : bond	C : capital	D : change	E : countries
1 : Internals\\1061670	3	0	6	3	2
2 : Internals\\1288484	0	0	0	1	1
3 : Internals\\13608746%2E2013%2E779784	0	1	0	0	1
4 : Internals\\1404369	0	0	0	2	1
5 : Internals\\1452-595X1004391K	4	5	2	2	9
6 : Internals\\1452-595X1004391K (1)	4	5	2	2	9
7 : Internals\\1601643	0	0	2	1	3
8 : Internals\\1848946	0	0	0	2	0
9 : Internals\\1-s2.0-S0164070413001286-main	1	7	0	0	3
10 : Internals\\20202974	0	0	1	0	1
11 : Internals\\20453198	0	0	0	1	0
12 : Internals\\20752845	0	0	0	3	3
13 : Internals\\23071701	4	0	3	2	1
14 : Internals\\23265969	0	0	0	3	0
15 : Internals\\23289410	0	0	0	2	1
16 : Internals\\25096899	0	0	0	0	1
17 : Internals\\25481928	0	0	0	2	0
18 : Internals\\27515971	0	0	0	0	3
19 : Internals\\3330768	1	0	0	2	1
20 : Internals\\40263651	0	0	0	3	0
21 : Internals\\40278457	2	0	2	1	0
22 : Internals\\40470466	0	0	2	4	5
23 : Internals\\40657771	2	1	2	2	4
24 : Internals\\40728488	2	0	11	5	8
25 : Internals\\4122458	0	0	0	1	0
26 : Internals\\41288358	0	0	0	2	0
27 : Internals\\41377887	5	0	0	4	1
28 : Internals\\41478275	0	0	3	0	0
29 : Internals\\41478275 (1)	0	0	3	0	0
30 : Internals\\41581131	15	2	6	0	15
31 : Internals\\41962514	3	0	4	0	2
32 : Internals\\41962514 (1)	3	0	4	0	2
33 : Internals\\422387	0	0	0	6	3
34 : Internals\\4380428	0	0	1	4	2
35 : Internals\\4380468	1	0	2	0	13
36 : Internals\\4543315	0	0	0	1	0
37 : Internals\\5092570	13	9	1	2	4

NodeXL) resulted in the following: Very negative: 234; Moderately negative: 186; Moderately positive: 594, and Very positive: 161. This was visualized earlier in Figure 25.

Maltego Chlorine 3.6.1 is a penetration testing tool that enables the capturing of messaging from Twitter. Its basic sequence for the "Tweet Analyser" machine goes as follows:

Finding Tweets
run(tweets)
run(pullURLs)
run(pullHashTags)
run(TweetSentiment)
Extracting data
run(TweetToWords)
Extracting data

The tool works iteratively, with required pauses between each machine-enabled extraction based on the limits in Twitter's application programming interface. Figure 48 shows the bubble view at the

Figure 48. Exploding "Bubble View" of the #Europe "Tweet Analyser" machine using Maltego Chlorine 3.6.1

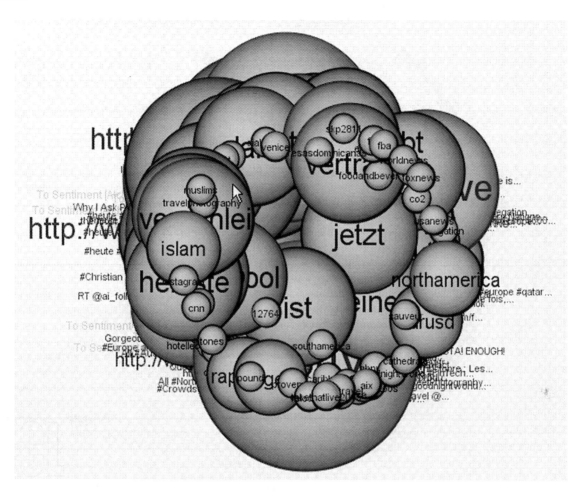

beginning of the second iteration. Those using Maltego may keep this "machine" running for a length of time, and its limits on vertices can top out upwards of 10,000 or more nodes. The more that is captured, often, the more complexity may be seen until a certain limit at which point the complexity likely plateaus or drops off. By the third iterations, there were about 600 "entities" (nodes, vertices)—to use the nomenclature within Maltego.

In Figure 49, the view shows the extraction of #europe hashtagged messaging. Three nodes around that central node show the trend of positive, negative, and neutral. Zooming into the messages shows the "Twit" (the user account identifier on Twitter) and the specific Tweeted message (or a portion of the message).

In Figure 50, the same data may be viewed through the "Entity List" view with some more specifics. Exporting this list, though, is not as simple as a simple copy-paste or save-as.

Figure 51 shows that it is possible to highlight and export the sentiment nodes with their linked messages for easier categorical analysis.

Figure 49. #Europe "Tweet Analys er" machine with built-in sentiment analysis (Maltego Chlorine 3.6.1)

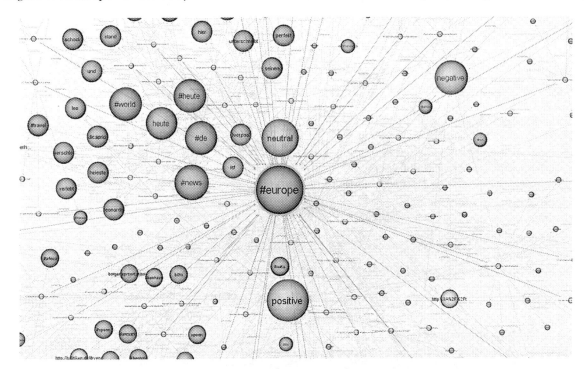

Figure 50. Entity view of #Europe "Tweet Analyser" machine using Maltego Chlorine 3.6.1 (with embedded sentiment analysis)

∆ Nodes	Type	Value	Weight	Incoming	Outgoing	Bookmark
#1101	Hashtag	#1101	100	1	0	
#Enfermita ☐☐ pero apoyandi	Twit	#Enfermita ludischudc/8/ud33ludn8a pero apova...	100	1	17	
#Europe	Phrase	#Europe	0	0	65	
#Europe http://t.co/7Cuy5SDt	Twit	#Europe http://t.co/?Cuy5SSDWA	100	1	2	
#Europe is dancing Selena Gom	Twit	#Europe is dancing Selena Gomez @kelenagomez...	100	1	5	
#absence	Hashtag	#absence	100	1	0	
#africa	Hashtag	#africa	100	2	0	
#airline	Hashtag	#airline	100	1	0	
#allies	Hashtag	#allies	100	2	0	
#anthropology	Hashtag	#anthropology	100	1	0	
#asia	Hashtag	#asia	100	1	0	
#aurora	Hashtag	#aurora	100	1	0	
#bahrain	Hashtag	#bahrain	100	1	0	
#bible	Hashtag	#bible	100	1	0	
#bitcoin	Hashtag	#bitcoin	100	1	0	
#boyfriend	Hashtag	#boyfriend	100	1	0	
#business	Hashtag	#business	100	2	0	
#business #europe 3 strategie:	Twit	#business #europe 3 strategies to learn from rich...	100	1	5	
#business #europe The Last 10	Twit	#business #europe The Last 10 Things This....	100	1	5	
#buzz	Hashtag	#buzz	100	1	0	
#canada	Hashtag	#canada	100	1	0	
#capsulecloset	Hashtag	#capsulecloset	100	1	0	
#castle	Hashtag	#castle	100	1	0	
#cdanclair	Hashtag	#cdanclair	100	1	0	
#china	Hashtag	#china	100	1	0	
#cia/#mossad	Hashtag	#cia/#mossad	100	1	0	
#ck	Hashtag	#ck	100	1	0	
#climate	Hashtag	#climate	100	1	0	
#colombia	Hashtag	#colombia	100	1	0	
#crypto	Hashtag	#crypto	100	1	0	
#cryptocurrency	Hashtag	#cryptocurrency	100	1	0	
#daech	Hashtag	#daech	100	3	0	
#denmark	Hashtag	#denmark	100	1	0	

Figure 51. Shift-clicking to capture the positive, negative, and neutral sentiments node in Maltego Chlorine 3.6.1

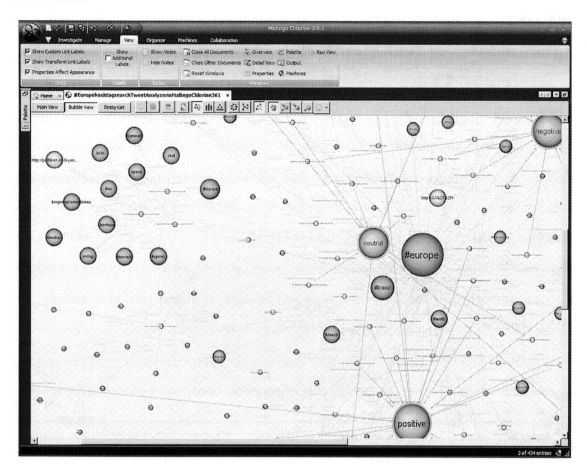

So back to the question of verification, this extraction shows some agreement as to the slightly greater positive trending and some negative messaging. However, at this high level, that is not saying much.

As for using NodeXL's new sentiment analysis feature, the labeling is on words and word pairs and are created from lists of separate positive words and negative words. This tool also has a customization feature to enable people to use their own words for categorizing. (However, if the changes are only to a few words, the overall effect on the sentiment labeling outcomes is likely to be marginal. There will not likely be an overall shift in polarity, for example.) The author tried multiple times to set up the beta sentiment analysis feature. (She has used the NodeXL software for over 3 years.) The output was not sufficiently clear or defined to be useful in this case to validate or invalidate prior findings. This may be viewed in Figure 52.

Discussion

To recap, the sentiment analysis tool of NVivo 11 Plus enables asking questions about various types of data, including social media data. The novel conceptualized enablements were as follows: (1) profiling the personalities of egos and entities through related social media account data. (2) describing the per-

Figure 52. A screenshot of the sentiment analysis setup in NodeXL

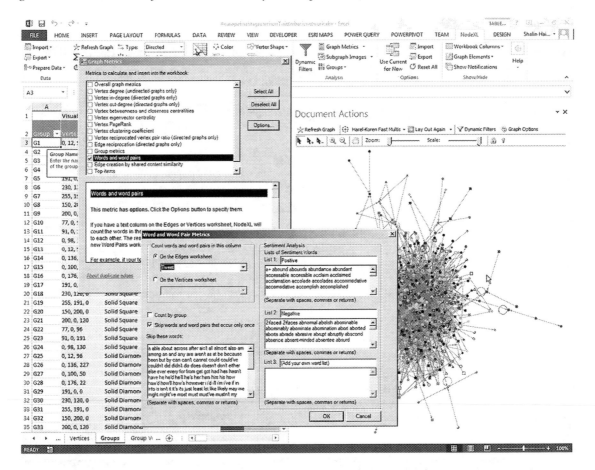

sonalities of groups with interacting members (in ego neighborhoods, *ad hoc* networks, editing groups, and others) through network analysis and then sentiment analysis, (3) exploring metadata (folksonomic related tag networks and article networks) to surface latent public conceptualizations, (4) examining trending public issues through socially shared data and discourse sets, (5) delving into public concepts through socially shared data and discourse sets, (6) observing public events through socially shared data and discourse sets, (7) analyzing broad-scale brand reputation through socially shared data and discourse sets, and (8) inspecting various individual texts and text corpuses for emergent insights. This chapter provided an example or two of each of the prior.

The four basic questions for this chapter involved probing the following: (1) the new sentiment analysis and theme extraction autocoding tools in NVivo 11 Plus; (2) some features of data knowability from social media using these tools; (3) effective methodologies to enhance sentiment extraction from social media data, and (4) ways to (in)validate the sentiment analysis.

In the body of the chapter, much attention has been paid already to how the sentiment analysis and theme extraction autocoding functions work. One other point should be made here—which is that it is critical to ensure that web pages are fully loaded before attempting data extractions, in order to fully achieve the data extractions using NCapture of NVivo.

Per the second area of study, the application of these two autocoding features to eight different types of data from social media have been described. Some basic observations may be shared. Data amount and density is a critical factor in enabling sentiment analysis and theme extraction. This means that sparse related tags networks will be less effective for the NVivo 11 Plus sentiment analysis tool than collections of research articles or Wikipedia pages. Also, data with sentiment-laden terms tend to work better for sentiment analysis than those with more objective terms.

Third, some methods to enhance sentiment extraction from social media data include the following.

- **Data Extraction:** In terms of data extraction to map different phenomena—egos and entities, events, concepts, and so on—it is important not to fall into deterministic assumptions. There are a variety of ways to use social media to "get at" particular targets, and even though social media platforms may be designed for particular uses, there are often many other ways they may be used to extract information.

- **Inclusion of Textual Data from Multimedia Sources:** For multimedia contents, they should be turned into textual data (such as transcripting audio files and videos).

- **Data Pre-Processing:** It would help to focus on data pre-processing. Text corpus datasets of articles (and other merged datasets) should be de-duplicated, so that repeated information will not skew the autocoding results.

- **Need for Human Analysis:** The broad-scale summary sentiment analysis classifications should not be used independent of an analysis of the underlying text and its themes. Human close reading of textual data will be important to the analysis.

- **Awareness of the Data Context:** Researcher understanding of the data context will clearly be important in terms of surfacing insights from the sentiment analysis.

- **Importance of Researcher Hypothesizing:** Researcher hypothesizing may add value to the extracted sentiments. What would their expectations be for sentiment, and why? How do the hypotheses compare to what was actually found?

- **Employment of Network Analysis Techniques:** Also, network analysis may be helpful in extracting data to identify *ad hoc* networks discussing issues based around #hashtags and keywords on microblogging sites…and on extracting related tags networks from content-sharing sites.

To the fourth point, based on the need for research rigor, users will need to interrogate the sentiment coding and the theme extraction. In this initial work, it would seem difficult to directly confirm or disconfirm the sentiment analysis findings from NVivo 11 Plus. There are a number of dependencies for the extraction of social media data (from various social media platforms). Multiple computers run using the same software to extract social media platform data from their respective APIs often result in very different datasets on platforms like Twitter because of how dynamic the data is and also because of how the API works. If the same data set is used to compare sentiment analysis on different analytical tools, there are still differences because of differing sentiment dictionaries and different data processing methods. (This is assuming that the data can be sufficiently transcoded to be readable in the various software tools. In this case, each of the test software extracted its own set based on the same seeding terms…but there was not a transferable core dataset usable for sentiment analysis across the three software tools used.) This is not to say that the effort should not be made to (in)validate the findings based on common practices of testing findings. A few examples of aligned sentiment analyses (using Maltego Chlorine, with the AlchemyAPI sentiment analysis tool, and NodeXL) were shared prior.

There can also be validating or invalidating the sentiment analysis based on comparing the results to the world, to see how observed sentiment may manifest in people's real-world choices and actions. How to systematize this may be quite a challenge but a worthwhile one.

FUTURE RESEARCH DIRECTIONS

In Table 2, "Types of Targeted Social Media Platform Data, Sentiment Analysis, and Askable Questions," some generic types of questions were suggested based on the various types of information extractions available from respective social media platforms. The questions suggested discrete extractions from particular social media platforms, but that is clearly an artificial limitation. After all, textual datasets of all sorts may be queried and mixed-and-matched. Data may be extracted from a number of social media platforms and analyzed together or analyzed and compared.

The ability to apply machine autocoding of sentiment and of themes from text sets have a variety of other applications. For example, based on a particular topic with global implications, what are the various expressed ideas by those from different geographical regions, those in different age categories, those in different language groups, those in different cultural groups? How do these respective groups respond to an issue when an issue is related to a breaking or emergent event? Often, the first step in any number of new discoveries begins with asking bold and audacious questions. (In the research literature, there are a number of applications of sentiment analysis to enhance e-governance, service provision, online teaching and learning, marketing, law enforcement, national security, communications studies, and other areas.)

For many researchers who use qualitative, mixed methods, and/or multi-methods research approaches, sentiment may be one variable that has not directly been considered. The new sentiment analysis feature in NVivo 11 makes it possible to efficiently explore sentiment in various text datasets to add analytical richness. This chapter provided an overview of some applications of the new sentiment analysis tool applied to a number of different types of extracted social media datasets (using NodeXL Basic, Maltego Chlorine 3.6.1, and web browser-based data scrapers, in addition to NCapture of NVivo). The data extractions in this work were drawn from Twitter (microblogging site), Flickr (image- and video-sharing site), and Wikipedia (open crowd-sourced encyclopedia). In terms of future directions for research, one easy approach would be to tap other online spaces where people gather and interconnect online. These may be large-scale spaces like email systems, social networking sites, video sharing sites (with downloaded transcripts), image-sharing sites (with image annotations), digital bulletin boards, immersive games, immersive virtual worlds, and other virtual communities.

There is a need for new insights on effective ways to pre-process the textual data for insightful analysis. Likewise, it would help to have further insights on data post-processing for various research. As mentioned earlier, it will be important to find ways to test the sentiment outcomes and the theme extractions—with other datasets, methods, and tools, in order to validate or invalidate results, or at least to temper assertions from the findings. This sentiment analysis feature (combined with the theme extraction one) may be much more powerful when chained with other software tools that extend its analytical capabilities. Even within NVivo, there are other tools that benefit the insights from the sentiment analysis tool—such as human coding, automated concept extraction, text frequency counts, text searches, matrix queries, and data visualizations. The geospatial mapping of microblogging messages may be used to add another dimension to the data. Certainly, users may conduct more related research after initial autocoding.

CONCLUSION

Researchers may apply NVivo 11 Plus well beyond the realm of social media—to anything text-based (and enabled around one of the base languages that NVivo 11 Plus enables). This may be applied to research notes, manuscripts, metadata sets, transcripts, and other data types. Sentiment analysis has been applied to journalistic article sets, historical documents, letters, journal entries, and other texts. The applications of broadly available sentiment analysis are broad and deeply promising. They may be used to explore topics, individuals, practices, locations, cultures, languages, and others.

ACKNOWLEDGMENT

I am grateful to Jason Flett (of QSR International, the maker of NVivo 11 Plus) for discussing the sentiment analysis tool with me via web conference and emails. Thanks to Kansas State University for their support of my research work. Without access to these impressive technologies and the time to explore them, I would not be able to achieve this work—no matter how many nights and weekends I spend on the research.

REFERENCES

Abel, F., Gao, Q., Houben, G.-J., & Tao, K. (2011). Analyzing temporal dynamics in Twitter profiles for personalized recommendations in the Social Web. In *Proceedings of WebSci '11*. doi:10.1145/2527031.2527040

Bak, J. Y., Kim, S., & Oh, A. (2012). Self-disclosure and relationship strength in Twitter conversations. In *Proceedings of the 50th Annual Meeting of the Association for Computational Linguistics*.

Balahur, A., & Perea-Ortega, J. M. (2015). Sentiment analysis system adaptation for multilingual processing: The case of tweets. *Information Processing & Management, 51*(4), 547–556. doi:10.1016/j.ipm.2014.10.004

Bascandziev, I., & Harris, P. L. (2015). In beauty we trust: Children prefer information from more attractive informants. *The British Journal of Developmental Psychology, 32*(1), 94–99. doi:10.1111/bjdp.12022 PMID:24164592

Berger, J. (2011). Arousal increases social transmission of information. *Psychological Science, 22*(7), 891–893. doi:10.1177/0956797611413294 PMID:21690315

Berger, J., & Milkman, K. L. (2010). *Social transmission, emotion, and the virality of online content.* Wharton Research Paper. Retrieved October 3, 2015, from http://robingandhi.com/wp-content/uploads/2011/11/Social-Transmission-Emotion-and-the-Virality-of-Online-Content-Wharton.pdf. 1 – 53.

Bhaskar, J. K. S., & Nedungadi, P. (2015). Hybrid approach for emotion classification of audio conversation based on text and speech mining. *Procedia Computer Science, 46*, 635 – 643.

Bilton, N. (2015, Oct. 5). Jack Dorsey returns to a frayed Twitter. *The New York Times.*

Blamey, B., Crick, T., & Oatley, G. (2012). R U:-) or:-(? Character- vs. word-gram feature selection for sentiment classification of OSN corpora. In *Research and Development in Intelligent Systems: XXIX*. Academic Press.

Cao, D., Ji, R., Lin, D., & Li, S. (2014). A cross-media public sentiment analysis system for microblog. In *Multimedia Systems* (pp. 1–8). Springer; doi:10.1007/978-1-4471-4739-8_16

Chen, Y., Lee, S. Y. M., Li, S., & Huang, C.-R. (2010). Emotion cause detection with linguistic constructions. In *Proceedings of the 23rd International Conference on Computational Linguistics* (Coling 2010).

Colace, F., Casaburi, L., De Santo, M., & Greco, L. (2015). Sentiment detection in social networks and in collaborative learning environments. *Computers in Human Behavior*, *51*, 1061–1067. doi:10.1016/j.chb.2014.11.090

da Silva, N. F. F., Hruschka, E. R., & Hruschka, E. R. Jr. (2014). Tweet sentiment analysis with classifier ensembles. *Decision Support Systems*, *66*, 170–179. doi:10.1016/j.dss.2014.07.003

Dispositional Affect. (2014, Feb. 17). In *Wikipedia*. Retrieved Sept. 28, 2015, from https://en.wikipedia.org/wiki/Dispositional_affect

Doney, P. M., & Cannon, J. P. (1997, April). An examination of the nature of trust in buyer-seller relationships. *Journal of Marketing*, *61*(2), 35–51. doi:10.2307/1251829

Drerup, T. (2015). Diurnal rhythms in investor sentiment. *Journal of Behavioral and Experimental Finance*. .10.1016/j.jbef.2015.07.002

Eisenberg, N., & Miller, P. A. (1987). The relation of empathy to prosocial and related behaviors. *Psychological Bulletin*, *101*(1), 91–119. doi:10.1037/0033-2909.101.1.91 PMID:3562705

Fattah, M. A. (2015). New term weighting schemes with combination of multiple classifiers for sentiment analysis. *Neurocomputing*, *167*, 434–442. doi:10.1016/j.neucom.2015.04.051

Fersini, E., Messina, E., & Pozzi, F. A. (2014). Sentiment analysis: Bayesian ensemble learning. *Decision Support Systems*, *68*, 26–38. doi:10.1016/j.dss.2014.10.004

Fu, X., Yang, K., Huang, J. Z., & Cui, L. (2015). Dynamic non-parametric joint sentiment topic mixture model. *Knowledge-Based Systems*, *82*, 102–114. doi:10.1016/j.knosys.2015.02.021

Ghiassi, M., Skinner, J., & Zimbra, D. (2013). Twitter brand sentiment analysis: A hybrid system using n-gram analysis and dynamic artificial neural network. *Expert Systems with Applications*, *40*(16), 6266–6282. doi:10.1016/j.eswa.2013.05.057

Gomes, O. (2015). Sentiment cycles in discrete-time homogeneous networks. *Physica A*, *428*, 224–238. doi:10.1016/j.physa.2015.01.084

Granovetter, M. S. (1973). The strength of weak ties. *American Journal of Sociology*, *78*(6), 1360–1380. doi:10.1086/225469

Gutierrez, F. J., & Poblete, B. (2015). Sentiment-based user profiles in microblogging platforms. In *Proceedings of HT '15*. doi:10.1145/2700171.2791027

Haddi, E., Liu, X., & Shi, Y. (2013). The role of text pre-processing in sentiment analysis. In *Proceedings of 2013 Information Technology and Quantitative Management* (ITQM 2013).

Hai-Jew, S. (2009, Sept.) Exploring the immersive parasocial: Is it you or the thought of you? *MERLOT Journal of Online Learning and Teaching,* 5(3). Retrieved Oct. 9, 2015, from http://jolt.merlot.org/vol5no3/hai-jew_0909.htm

Hajmohammadi, M. S., Ibrahim, R., Selamat, A., & Fujita, H. (2015). Combination of active learning and self-training for cross-lingual sentiment classification with density analysis of unlabeled samples. *Information Sciences, 317,* 67–77. doi:10.1016/j.ins.2015.04.003

Huang, Z., Zhao, Z., Liu, Q., & Wang, Z. (2015). An unsupervised method for short-text sentiment analysis based on analysis of massive data. Intelligent Computation in Big Data Era. doi:10.1007/978-3-662-46248-5_21

Jeffries, A. (2014, Feb. 14). You're not going to read this but you'll probably share it anyway. The Verge. Retrieved Aug. 26, 2016, from http://www.theverge.com/2014/2/14/5411934/youre-not-going-to-read-this

Kaplan, J. (2015). *Humans Need Not Apply: A Guide to Wealth and Work in the Age of Artificial Intelligence.* New Haven, CT: Yale University Press.

Katz, G., Ofek, N., & Shapira, B. (2015). ConSent: Context-based sentiment analysis. *Knowledge-Based Systems, 84,* 162–178. doi:10.1016/j.knosys.2015.04.009

Kitayama, S., & Markus, H. R. (2000). The pursuit of happiness and the realization of sympathy: Cultural patterns of self, social relations, and well-being. In *Culture and Subjective Well-Being.* The MIT Press.

Klenner, M., & Petrakis, S. (2012). Polarity preference of verbs: What could verbs reveal about the polarity of their objects? In G. Bouma, A. Ittoo, E. Métais, & H. Wortmann (Eds.), *Natural Language Processing and Information Systems.*

Koncz, P., & Paralič, J. (2013). Active learning enhanced document annotation for sentiment analysis. In A. Cuzzocrea, C. Kittl, D.E. Simos, E. Weippl, & L. Xu (Eds.), *Availability, Reliability, and Security in Information Systems and HCI.* Springer. doi:10.1007/978-3-642-40511-2_24

Kontopoulos, E., Berberidis, C., Dergiades, T., & Bassiliades, N. (2013). Ontology-based sentiment analysis of twitter posts. *Expert Systems with Applications, 40*(10), 4063–4074. doi:10.1016/j.eswa.2013.01.001

Liu, S. M., & Chen, J.-H. (2015). A multi-label classification based approach for sentiment classification. *Expert Systems with Applications, 42*(3), 1083–1093. doi:10.1016/j.eswa.2014.08.036

Luo, T., Chen, S., Xu, G., & Zhou, J. (2013). Sentiment Analysis. In T. Lu, S. Chen, G. Xu, & J. Zhou (Eds.), Trust-based Collective View Prediction. Springer. doi:10.1007/978-1-4614-7202-5_4

Machová, K., & Marhefka, L. (2013). Opinion mining in conversational content within web discussions and commentaries. In A. Cuzzocrea, C. Kittl, D.E. Simos, E. Weippl, & L. Xu (Eds.), *Availability, Reliability, and Security in Information Systems and HCI.* Springer. doi:10.1007/978-3-642-40511-2_11

Meraz, S. (2009). Is there an elite hold? Traditional media to social media agenda setting influence in blog networks. *Journal of Computer-Mediated Communication, 14*(3), 682–707. doi:10.1111/j.1083-6101.2009.01458.x

Michaels, C. F., & Carello, C. (1981). *Direct Perception*. Englewood Cliffs, NJ: Prentice-Hall, Inc.

Mohammad, S. M. (2012). *#Emotional Tweets*. In the First Joint Conference on Lexical and Computational Semantics (*SE$M), Montréal, Canada.

Mosquera, A., & Moreda, P. (2012). The study of informality as a framework for evaluating the normalization of Web 2.0 texts. In G. Bouma, A. Ittoo, E. Métais, & Hans Wortmann (Eds.), *Natural Language Processing and Information Systems*.

Ortigosa, A., Martín, J. M., & Carro, R. M. (2014). Sentiment analysis in Facebook and its application to e-learning. *Computers in Human Behavior, 31*, 527–541. doi:10.1016/j.chb.2013.05.024

Pang, B., Lee, L., & Vaithyanathan, S. (2002). Thumbs up? Sentiment Classification using Machine Learning Techniques. *Proceedings of the Conference on Empirical Methods in Natural Language Processing (EMNLP)*. doi:10.3115/1118693.1118704

Park, S., Lee, W., & Moon, I.-C. (2015). Efficient extraction of domain specific sentiment lexicon with active learning. *Pattern Recognition Letters, 56*, 38–44. doi:10.1016/j.patrec.2015.01.004

Poria, S., Cambria, E., Howard, N., Huang, G.-B., & Hussain, A. (2015). Fusing audio, visual and textual clues for sentiment analysis from multimodal context. *Neurocomputing*. doi:10.1016/j.neucom.2015.01.095

Preethi, P. G., Uma, V., & Kumar, A. (2015). Temporal sentiment analysis and causal rules extraction from Tweets for event prediction. *Procedia Computer Science, 48*, 84 – 89. doi:10.1016/j.procs.2015.04.154

Roberts, M., Wanta, W., & Dzwo, T.-H. (2002). Agenda setting and issue salience online. *Communication Research, 29*(4), 452–465. doi:10.1177/00936502002029004004

Rong, W., Nie, Y., Ouyang, Y., Peng, B., & Xiong, Z. (2014). Auto-encoder based bagging architecture for sentiment analysis. *Journal of Visual Languages and Computing, 25*(6), 840–849. doi:10.1016/j.jvlc.2014.09.005

Saif, H., He, Y., Fernandez, M., & Alani, H. (2015). Contextual semantics for sentiment analysis of Twitter. *Information Processing & Management*, 1–15.

Schuller, B. W. (2015). Modelling user affect and sentiment in intelligent user interfaces. In *Proceedings of the IUI 2015*. doi:10.1145/2678025.2716265

Severyn, A., Moschitti, A., Uryupina, O., Plank, B., & Filippova, K. (2015). Multi-lingual opinion mining on YouTube. *Information Processing & Management*, 1–15.

Small, D. A., Loewenstein, G., & Slovic, P. (2007). Sympathy and callousness: The impact of deliberative thought on donations to identifiable and statistical victims. *Organizational Behavior and Human Decision Processes, 102*(2), 143–153. doi:10.1016/j.obhdp.2006.01.005

Thakor, P., & Sasi, S. (2015). Ontology-based sentiment analysis process for social media content. *Procedia Computer Science, 53*, 199 – 207. doi:10.1016/j.procs.2015.07.295

Thelwall, M., Buckley, K., Paltoglou, G., Cai, D., & Kappas, A. (2010). Sentiment strength detection in short informal text. *Journal of the American Society for Information Science and Technology*, *61*(12), 2544–2558. doi:10.1002/asi.21416

Tsolmon, B., Kwon, A.-R., & Lee, K.-S. (2012). Extracting social events based on timeline and sentiment analysis in Twitter corpus. In G. Bouma, A. Ittoo, E. Métais, & H. Wortmann (Eds.), *Natural Language Processing and Information Systems*. doi:10.1007/978-3-642-31178-9_32

Turney, P. (2002). Thumbs Up or Thumbs Down? Semantic Orientation Applied to Unsupervised Classification of Reviews. *Proceedings of the Association for Computational Linguistics*. arXiv:cs.LG/0212032

Wallsten, K. (2007). Agenda setting and the blogosphere: An analysis of the relationship between mainstream media and political blogs. *Review of Policy Research*, *24*(6), 567–587. doi:10.1111/j.1541-1338.2007.00300.x

Wang, G., Sun, J., Ma, J., Xu, K., & Gu, J. (2014). Sentiment classification: The contribution of ensemble learning. *Decision Support Systems*, *57*, 77–93. doi:10.1016/j.dss.2013.08.002

Wijnhoven, F., & Bloemen, O. (2014). External validity of sentiment mining reports: Can current methods identify demographic biases, event biases, and manipulation of reviews? *Decision Support Systems*, *59*, 262–273. doi:10.1016/j.dss.2013.12.005

Williams, L., Bannister, C., Arribas-Ayllon, M., Preece, A., & Spasić, I. (2015). The role of idioms in sentiment analysis. *Expert Systems with Applications*, *42*(21), 7375–7385. doi:10.1016/j.eswa.2015.05.039

Wilson, R. K., & Eckel, C. C. (2006). Judging a book by its cover: Beauty and expectations in the trust game. *Political Research Quarterly*, *59*(2), 189–202. doi:10.1177/106591290605900202

Yan, G., He, W., Shen, J., & Tang, C. (2014). A bilingual approach for conducting Chinese and English social media sentiment analysis. *Computer Networks*, *75*, 491–503. doi:10.1016/j.comnet.2014.08.021

Zhang, K., Xie, Y., Yang, Y., Sun, A., Liu, H., & Choudhary, A. (2014). Incorporating conditional random fields and active learning to improve sentiment identification. *Neural Networks*, *58*, 60–67. doi:10.1016/j.neunet.2014.04.005 PMID:24856246

ADDITIONAL READING

Hai-Jew, S. (2014, Sept.). *Using NVivo: An Unofficial and Unauthorized Primer*. Retrieved Aug. 26, 2016, from http://scalar.usc.edu/works/using-nvivo-an-unofficial-and-unauthorized-primer/index

KEY TERMS AND DEFINITIONS

Application Programming Interface (API): A computer application that developers to create tools for certain limited functionalities (such as accessing metadata or data from a social media platform).

Autocoding: Using computer algorithms and other resources to automatically code data.

Brand: An identifying mark or name, often linked to a certain reputation.

Classifier: A software tool which categorizes words or concepts.

Diurnal: During the day.

Emotion: An affect, a state-of-mind.

Exploratory Data Analysis: The examination of data to "see what is there" without necessarily a research hypothesis.

External Validity: The generalizability of research from a limited context to a more general one.

Idiom: A colloquial expression, a sequence of words with meanings that are not directly deducible from the particular used terms.

Lexicon: The vocabulary of a branch of knowledge or knowledge domain.

Lexicon Dictionary: A standard listing of words from a particular field or domain.

Machine Learning: Algorithmic applications that enable computers to identify patterns in data, without explicit programming to find and extract a specific phenomena.

N-gram: A contiguous sequence of n-number items (such as words) in a sequence in a text or text corpus.

Opinion: A subjective judgment or point-of-view about a particular topic.

Positive: Good or affirmative.

Profile: A brief description of a person or organization (an ego or an entity).

Negative: Bad or undesirable.

Semantic: Containing meaning.

Sentiment: An attitude, emotion, or opinion about a particular topic.

Social Media: Online applications that enable people to interact, share contents, and collaborate around shared interests.

Stopwords List: An editable list of words which are excluded from natural language processing.

Strength: Intensity of an emotion, sentiment, or belief.

Syntactic: Related to word and phrase arrangement to create correctly structured sentences.

Tag: A brief textual descriptor of multimedia contents.

Topic Modeling: The automated extraction of theme clusters from a text or text corpus (collection of texts).

User-Generated Content (UGC): Any of a range of digital contents created by the broad public and distributed via social media platforms.

Valence (in Psychology): A sense of intrinsic attractiveness or aversiveness of a thing, person, or event.

Validation: Confirmation.

Web Browser: A software application to enable the accessing of information from the World Wide Web based on uniform resource locators (URLs).

Web Browser Plug-In (Add-On): A software extension which adds functionality to a web browser, such as to enhance the speedy extraction of desired data or to block certain websites or to protect privacy.

Chapter 11

Capturing the Gist(s) of Image Sets Associated with Chinese Cities through Related Tags Networks on Flickr®

Shalin Hai-Jew
Kansas State University, USA

ABSTRACT

To introduce how related tags networks may be extracted from Flickr® and used for "gist" and other analysis, this chapter describes the related tag networks associated with some of the cities of the People's Republic of China (used as seeding terms). The software used for the data extractions (from the Flickr® API) and the creation of various graph visualizations is the free and open-source Network Overview, Discovery and Exploration for Excel (NodeXL Basic), available on Microsoft's CodePlex platform.

INTRODUCTION

Web 2.0 brought with it the broad-scale open-access sharing of digital contents on social media platforms. People shared digital imagery, videos, "pins," slideshows, six-word memoirs, novels, digital learning objects, and other informational contents; they shared pithy thoughts in microblogging messages. People also shared messages with others, friended and unfriended them, interacted over the digital artifacts, tagged their digital contents as well as those of others, liked and favorited digital artifacts, and engaged socially. The phenomena of "consumer-generated media" (CGM) is thought to create new dynamics (Yanai, Kawakubo, & Barnard, 2012, p. 63). Their actions on the various platforms resulted not only in publicly accessible repositories of contents, but they also enabled access to floods of metadata and metainformation, raw data about data, and more processed information about information. Some researchers summarize this phenomenon:

DOI: 10.4018/978-1-5225-0846-5.ch011

Social media sites share four characteristics: (1) Users create or contribute content in a variety of media types; (2) Users annotate content with tags; (3) Users evaluate content, either actively by voting or passively by using content; and (4) Users create social networks by designating other users with similar interests as contacts or friends. In the process of using these sites, users are adding rich metadata in the form of social networks, annotations and ratings. Availability of large quantities of this metadata will lead to the development of new algorithms to solve a variety of information processing problems, from new recommendation to improved information discovery algorithms.(Lerman, Plangprasopchok, & Wong, 2007, p. 65)

A number of social media platforms have created application programming interfaces (APIs) to allow broad public access to both some of those informational contents and labeling metadata. These APIs may be accessed by automated programs used to scrape information, and they may be accessed by applications that are less complex to use than command-line based programs. Researchers, particularly in the fields of data mining, have worked to turn some of that metadata into information. One type of metadata of interest are folk-created tags, freeform, unstructured keywords used to describe or label images and videos. Collective tagging—by individuals working individually and in groups—lead to a common informal and non-hierarchical classification system, dubbed a "folksonomy." This portmanteau term of "folk" and "taxonomy" was created by Thomas Vander Wal in 2004 (Vander Wal, "Folksonomy," Feb. 2, 2007). Others refer to informal tagging as "lightweight annotation" or "lightweight semantic scaffolding." If formal tags come in "sets" that are non-redundant, then informal tags come in "bags" that have duplicates and redundancies. Indeed, there are some patterned differences between informal tagging and formal indexing (Rorissa, 2010). Some structured data may be extracted from freeform tags for analysis (Rattenbury, Good, & Naaman, 2007). Informal tagging is of nominal expense to the service providers as compared to formal tagging, but the captured tags have limits and enable only some kinds of information capture.

Folksonomies are understood to be amateur created, and as such, the applied terms of not formally defined or hierarchically structured; they are non-exclusive. Such tags may be explored in the context of the particular described digital artifact, but they may also be collected into networks related to certain seeding tag terms, which may enable insights into collective perceptions of particular phenomena. One writer went so far as to describe the tagging feature on Flickr® as "feral" (as in in-the-wild and non-domesticated):

The most interesting—and the most feral—aspect of Flickr is the tagging. Instead of providing a set list of possible keywords, Flickr allows users to type in any tag they like. Each photo can have as many tags as desired. If Jane clicks on one of the tags on a photo her friend Nina took, Jane is shown all Nina's photos that have that particular tag. From that page, she can continue by clicking the link titled "see all public photos tagged with [the tag]". This gives some very interesting results. Since there are no predefined rules for how to tag your photos, nobody has complete control of the ways in which photos are presented, yet vast pools of photographs of specific places or events are gathered and made accessible. Different tags produce very different kinds of description, narrative or argument.(Walker, 2005, p. 4).

Related tags networks are concept-based abstractions that exist several steps out from the original taggers (individuals who provided the keyword labels) and the digital contents (the target images, slideshows, articles, videos, or tagged objects). Related tags networks are depicted visually in node-link diagrams, in which the nodes or vertices are entities (the tags), and the links or edges are relationships (co-occurrence ties between tags that are often used together to describe digital artifacts). Tag clusters may be extracted from the network based on tag usage analysis.

Initially, tagging systems were created so that users could self-organize their uploaded contents and simultaneously enable others to search for and find relevant images based on keyword and hashtagged labels that described the uploaded contents. Tags originally were conceptualized as knowledge management tools. However, many observed that such tags were highly noisy and not particularly representative of the uploaded contents. Some words used as tags have more informational value than others.

A visually representative tag (such as sunset, sky, tiger) easily suggests the scene or object an image may describe even before the image is presented to a user. On the other hand, tags like 2009, Asia, and Canon often fail to suggest anything meaningful related to the visual content of the annotated image. In other words, images annotated by a visually representative tag are visually coherent by containing similar visual content (Sun & Bhowmick, 2010, p. 472).

For tags to enhance query performance, they have to be visually representative of the linked contents. To that end, some researchers strived to automatically rank tags based on their informational value in relation to the linked imagery (Liu, Hua, Yang, Wang, & Zhang, 2009). There have been efforts to use a follow-on retagging system in order to add informational value to tags (Liu, Hua, Wang, & Zhang, 2010) to make them more representational of the image contents.

Another common motivation for tagging is to enhance the profile of an account and its image-stream and video contents. On social media platforms, profile building may be conceptualized as "any information on the social network that is connected to the user's profile" (Thomas-Jones, 2010, p. 58). These digital content annotations could be used to attract others with similar interests for possible online (and offline) interchanges and intercommunications. In an "attention economy," tags may help capture attention and popularity (whether bursty and ephemeral or continuing and longer-term). Historically, on Flickr, tags were thought to be used to calculate image "interestingness" for showcasing on the site. From another perspective, tags related to user accounts may be analyzed to infer users' topics of interest and to profile accounts (Chen & Shin, 2010).

Various strategies have been suggested to enhance the semantical descriptions of photos by building on folksonomy tagging. One approach involves capitalizing on the collective knowledge of community on Flickr® by extending tagging metadata based on the adding of similar tags to those applied by the user and enabling a more open tagging system (Sigurbjörnsson & van Zwol, 2008, p. 327). The "narrow" folksonomy of individuals tagging their submitted contents may be enhanced by the "broad" folksonomy enabled by larger groups. People tag for a number of motivations, such as for self-reminding of the shared contents and for socializing. In some cases, people tag in order to share information in real time during shared activities (Ames & Naaman, 2007, p. 977). One work described the uses of metadata, including tagging, to capture toponyms (place names) and other details, in order to collect location information to identify the most probable physical locations of a given image. Many Flickr® images are location-agnostic (given that many photographers do not enable the location-awareness of their devices or choose not to share locational data in the "exchangeable image file format" or "EXIF" information) (Serdyukov, Murdock, & van Zwol, 2009). Tagging may be used with vision algorithms to refine image retrieval (Kennedy, Naaman, Ahern, Nair, & Rattenbury, 2007). In a different study, some 42% of 52 million photos in the dataset included geotagging (Clements, Serdyukov, de Vries, & Reinders, 2010).

and such locational images were used to predict users' favorite locations and to predict likely favorite locations in other cities with similar features.

Some researchers suggest that the types of tags assigned to a photo "may be radically divergent depending on whether the tagging is performed by the photographers, their friends, or strangers looking at their photos" (Marlow, Naaman, boyd, & Davis, 2006, p. 34). The point-of-view and the experience with the imagery affect the informal descriptors applied to the digital contents. Author-based tagging may result in self-expression and interpretation of the imagery, capturing biographical information and the "mood" of the images and their contents (Rafferty & Hidderley, 2007, p. 407). The personalization of the imagery tagging may not itself be negative in the tagging because images may be consumed interpersonally and socially. The tie of photos to another individual's life and self-expression (as a framing tool) may enhance others' appreciation for the images, and these digital artifacts and digital albums may be read as personality and individual social performance. Along similar lines, people go to Flickr® to browse socially (exploring the images shared by those who are their contacts) (Lerman & Jones, 2006, pp. 7 - 8). On social media platforms, the sense of others' social presence affects people's motivations for content sharing and tagging; on Flickr, a user's contacts represent "social presence" and increased awareness of these others may increase tagging (Nov & Ye, 2010, pp. 129 - 130).

The expressed interests of people's Flickr® accounts may be used to understand the purpose of the social media account; these insights may be used by the service provider to filter and personalize the images called up by those individual's text-based searches for others' imagery (for a more sensitive tag-based search) (Lerman, Plangprasopchok, & Wong, 2007). Flickr® falls into the category of "creative outlet" to provide opportunities to broadcast contents to a broad audience in a four-quadrant social media matrix (with Relationship, Self-Media, and Collaboration as the other categories in addition to Creative Outlet) (Zhu & Chen, 2015, p. 337). Groups on Flickr® may be conceptualized as special interest groups (SIGs) and the tagging of group members may also be seen as expressions of users' interests (Lerman, Plangprasopchok, & Wong, 2007, p. 65). Other researchers have compiled a non-comprehensive list of Flickr® group types: geographical / event groups (those based on particular physical areas and events), content groups (groups based on particular interests), visual style groups (groups that focus on particular photographic techniques), "quality indicator groups" [groups set up for "the identification and regroupment of (perceived) high quality photography"], and "catch-all groups" defined as groups without content-oriented rules (Negoescu & Gatica-Perez, 2008, p. 418). An analysis of hundreds of Flickr® groups suggested that there was what the authors termed low group loyalty, with users "sharing about 9.6 photos in the same group (with median of 5.1)" and low photo repurposing among groups (Negoescu & Gatica-Perez, 2008, pp. 425 – 426).

Among individuals in a community (or a virtual group), there is often interpretation, egocentric meaning, and intentionality behind image sharing, and there may be shared mental models of imagery and image sets for the select audiences. For example, images based on a shared conference may be (hash) tagged with a unique identifier for the event, and the participants share common understandings, cultural values, and concepts. On Flickr, individuals have formed groups for collective image sharing and may share some tagging conventions, based on social emulation. Whether a user generated the contents or only came across it may affect how works are described. People may label images quite differently from machine-vision-based auto-tagging programs. In Figure 1, the inner-most circle of the concentric circles shows the ego; the next circle out shows the social groups around that ego; the largest circle shows the larger publics that interact with and view the user-created contents. At each level out, there are differing

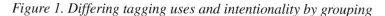

Figure 1. Differing tagging uses and intentionality by grouping

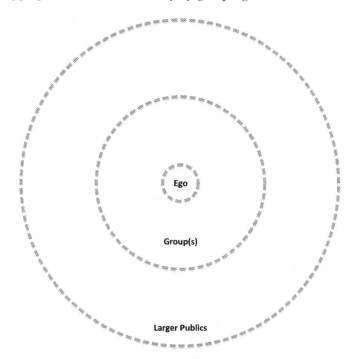

dynamics and relationships to the digital imagery contents around which people interact. An image or video artifact evokes personal experiences, memories, thoughts, and contexts to the image-taker that would be absent from outsiders just looking at the image or video. An intimate group which shared an experience may have a more powerful experience from shared images and videos in a narrowcast way (sharing among a targeted group of friends and acquaintances) than the broader public, which is more distant from the actual context in which the images and videos were captured. For example, a vacation pic may show a natural phenomenon of interest beyond the local interest. No matter what the original context of the tagging, whether for individuals organizing their own collections or groups sharing images of interest or research-based objectives, the tags themselves may be used for informational value independent of the original purpose of their creation. Web 2.0 "works with the principle of weak co-operation, where a huge amount of individual contributions build solid and structured sources of data" and apparently self-focused self-production actions become social (Prieur, Cardon, Beuscart, Pissard, & Pons, 2008, p. 1). Even without initial intentionality to be social, the initial publicizing of user-created contents may lead to interactivity:

They discover cooperative opportunities simply by making their individual productions public. Public space is seen as an opportunity for one's visibility, leading to relation making and eventually actual cooperation with different levels of involvement. And this cooperation can work in a very large scale precisely because it is non-demanding (Prieur, Cardon, Beuscart, Pissard, & Pons, 2008, p. 1).

While the social connections may be backgrounded for many users, there are clear social network effects on Flickr. For example, social networks on Flickr® have been found to affect particular uses of camera models.

First, a pair of friends on Flickr has a significantly higher probability of being congruent, i.e., using the same brand, compared to two random users (27% vs. 19%). Second, the degree of congruence goes up for pairs of friends (i) in the same country (29%), (ii) who both only have very few friends (30%), and (iii) with a very high cliqueness1 (38%). Third, given that a user changes her camera model between March-May 2007 and March-May 2008, high cliqueness friends are more likely than random users to do the same (54% vs. 48%). Fourth, users using high-end cameras are far more loyal to their brand than users using point-and-shoot cameras, with a probability of staying with the same brand of 60% vs 33%, given that a new camera is bought. Fifth, these "expert" users' brand congruence reaches 66% (!) for high cliqueness friends (Singla & Weber, 2009, p. 252).

Various Dependencies for Related Tags Network Captures

To convey a sense of the dependencies for related tags networks, Figure 2, " Some Different Interface Factors that May Affect the Contents of Related Tags Networks" illustrates how socio-technical spaces are co-evolved by their users interacting with the technical system (with its affordances and enablements). Users do have a large voice in terms of the services provided because they will move on if their needs are not met. On the other hand, providers of social media platform services also have power by how they harness the technology, define the end user license agreements (EULAs), and enforce policies. They also define the terms of tagging. Different tagging systems enable different tagging rights. Some restrict the ability to tag only to the individuals or groups who uploaded the particular resources (self-tagging). Open systems for tagging enable collective "free for all" sorts of tagging, for any who would care to participate. Many enable a mix of user-based and user-identified-friends access to tagging. For example, in an image sharing site, users may capture images using smart phones and mobile devices, and their apps may enable them to upload directly to the social media platform. That use case scenario may mean that tags are applied on-the-fly and may capture terms which are top-of-mind (but without sufficient reflection or mindfulness). If images are bulk-tagged, that will affect the level of detail per each digital artifact. If there are groups using a content-sharing social media platform, that may affect tagging behaviors. Whether the original photographer returns to add more tags may depend on the individual's motivations for sharing the imagery, his or her motivations, his or her authorizing environment, and so on. If the social media platform also enables machine-vision-based auto-tagging, that will affect which tags are included in a related tags network. How the application programming interface (API) works in terms of enabling related tags extractions will affect what researchers may observe. The software tool used to extract information may result in the capturing of some data and not others, and then how that data is processed and visualized and analyzed also will be affected by the software. Finally, the training and background of the researchers will affect how the information is used and exploited. The various dependencies would be challenging to measure and codify. The abstract conceptualization in Figure2 is not inclusive of all dependencies.

This chapter explores related tag networks extracted from Flickr®, one of the most popular platforms for digital image and video sharing in a service provided by Yahoo! Inc. A variety of data and metadata related to each image (and video) are captured on this platform: the image itself, the photographer,

Figure 2. Some different interface factors that may affect the contents of related tags networks

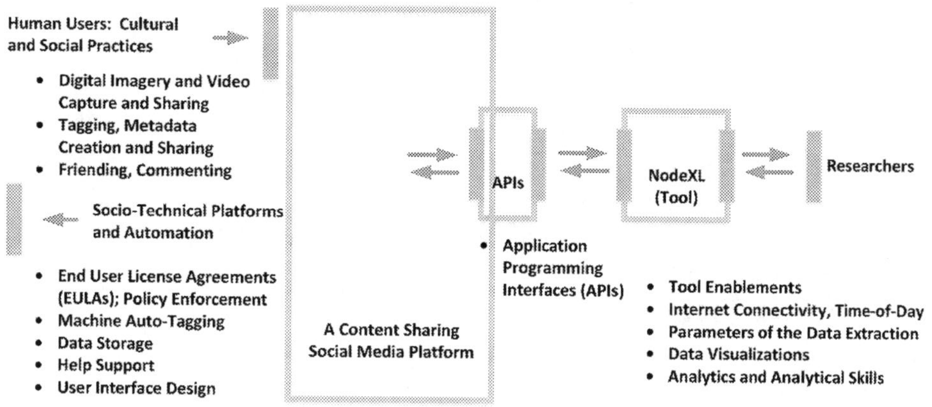

profile, information about the camera and settings, the gelocational data, the groups, tags, and feedback on the photo page. In terms of abstracted network information, there are also user networks—based on how user member accounts are grouped, how individuals interact (such as through friending, commenting, co-tagging), and geographical, regional, linguistic, and cultural features. There are also related tags networks, which capture dyadic co-occurrence of tags based on a particular probability threshold. (Related tags networks capture common-occurring tags more than novel, unique, or distinct ones.) There are insights to be gained that would be non-obvious otherwise and that would not be seeable at the local user level based just on the Flickr® platform and its regular use. Known as the site that captures the "social nature of photography," Flickr offers a range of features that enable people to build image collections, annotate their images, and interact with others. A recent technological feature uses machine vision to "view" and automatically suggest tags for images, which has led to expressions of angst by some long-time Flickr® users who would prefer to maintain direct human control over their tagging and who have suggested that the automated tagging has been inaccurate in some cases (one suggested that the auto-tagger listed "birds" in multiple images that did not contain any birds, for example). During the time of this chapter's creation, news was released that an image of two individuals were labeled as "gorillas" by Google's auto-tagging of its images; Google reached out shortly thereafter to apply a fix to the artificial intelligence applied to their image recognition capabilities but not before the scandal had spread on social media and mainline media (Schupak, July 1, 2015). Machine-based object recognition is a fairly new capability in the public sphere. This means that tagging now is not purely unmediated. Tag recommender systems also mediate the tagging). The interactions between Flickr's tens of millions of users around the world (who've uploaded tens of billions of photos) and the platform's technological affordances affect the types of tags created and ultimately the related tags networks that appear.

The types of terms that people use represent various parts of speech: nouns (people, places, things), proper nouns (names), verbs, adverbs, adjectives, acronyms, gerunds, and others. There are also abbreviations and acronyms. Slang terms are also common. There are references to technologies which enable certain types of image captures ("iphonography" and "gopro"). Often, photographer names and other personal touches are included in the tags. For example, one tagged object contained many of the typical descriptors but also simultaneously "cliché Saturday" and "out of your comfort zone" and "troiled&proud." (which in an urban dictionary is described as an experience of "poopy debauchery") ("troil," Urban

Dictionary, March 21, 2010). So, too, there are names of the respective cameras or technologies used in the image capture. In one sample, it read "10mm fisheye" to describe the lens and also "fullframe". There are also geotags, which indicate the physical locations of the image (or video) capture. Some tags are event-based. Some tags are conceptual (ideas-based) and / or emotional.

One term used by some researchers to describe populist and amateur tagging is "democratic indexing," which suggests access by the masses to such labeling. The uses of "non-imposed semantic structures" for folk tag labeling by authors (those who create and upload the images) means that the extracted structures (author-indexed databases) are not predetermined but emerge organically based on common speech (Rafferty & Hidderley, 2007, pp. 402 and 407). Researchers have described where subjective and amateur tagging falls short: depending on the context, the respective tags may be overly broad, overly specific, incorrectly used, written in private code (or undefined notations), concatenations of multiple words, ambiguous, or synonymous (such as using singular and plural forms of the same word) (Rafferty & Hidderley, 2007, p. 403). Author-created tags are poor ways to find visual contents since plenty of information from the visual image is not able to be understood from the tags alone. This is a special challenge in contexts when broad access to particular contents is desirable.

One research team advocates human sorting and simple machine vision analysis to complement the tagging for searchability of Flickr's images, particularly its Creative Commons attribution images, for broader usage (Hietanen, Athukorala, & Salovaara, 2011). This group observed: "The fact that our 147,306 searches to over 25 million CC-By images returned only under 3 million images suggests that most of the images cannot be easily found through common searches. It means that only 12 percent of the CC-By licensed images are easily findable" (Hietanen, Athukorala, & Salovaara, 2011, p. 267).

As a matter of fact, a research team found plenty of noise in tagging data: "When the image is tagged with a visual concept by a Flickr® user, there is a roughly 50/50 chance that the concept actually appears in the image" (Kennedy, Chang, & Kozintsev, 2006, p. 252). Even if tags were more appropriately placed, by nature, words (tag terms) are polysemous and require some work to disambiguate. Yet, to engage with a complex world, people also need to have comfort with ambiguity and indefinition (Deemter, 2010). There is power to words that allow "borderline cases" (Deemter, 2010, p. 8). While unstructured bottom-up tagging lacks the cleanness of more professional tagging, these approaches enable people to share other types of knowledge: For example, Flickr® tags are shared as a way for people to contribute "local" and "personal" knowledge (Kipp, Buchel, & Neal, 2012, p. 1).

Related tags networks are depictions of interrelationships between tags which are linked by co-occurrence. For example, related tags networks from Flickr® are tag networks that are often used together to describe images and videos uploaded to that content-sharing social media platform. Users of Flickr® may post up to 75 tags per digital content (image or video), and tags may be single words, symbols, or phrases. Images and videos may be tagged by others who are given access to an individual's Flickr® friends list. As such, co-occurrence indicates something about context and association. When a particular tag appears, users are also talking about other elements or details.

Flickr® also has an auto-tagging feature which uses image recognition technology and computer algorithms to describe apparently neutral aspects of an image, such as whether an image was taken in the daytime or the nighttime, indoor or outdoor, the core nature of the image (skyline, architecture, water, waterfront, building, text, sign), and other aspects. On the site, the robot-contributed tags are marked differently than those selected by the person who uploaded the image. Such tags may be removed by the person or group who uploaded the image, but some have complained on the Flickr® site that they have collections of thousands, and it would be infeasible to manually delete all robot-created tags (there is not apparently a global account-level option of disallowing automatically created tags). On the Flickr® site at the time of the chapter's creation in mid-2015, a pop-up window about "Tags BETA" (auto-tagging) read: "Tags are keywords that make photos easier to find in Flickr® search. The ones you add will show up in dark gray. Flickr's friendly robots will try to help out by adding some for you; these will appear with justr a gray outline." Said another way, the Flickr-ness of the online social media platform and the nature of the data extraction tool both affect the information that is ultimately extracted. What is extracted shows the data captured, but the dependencies underlying the capture may not be fully clear.

A related tags network from Flickr, as extracted using NodeXL, tends to be sparse, with a limited number of included tags. Related tags networks, by nature, are also extremely sparse, especially in comparison to the referred-to contents; they are a type of meta-metadata about metadata, and essentially a skim off of big data. The succinctness is not necessarily a negative, especially if this extracted information may be revelatory or insightful. Datamining is often about extracting outsized insights from information. In the 1.5 and 2 degree tag networks, there are not that many clusters—approximately three to ten or so. While there is cognitive manageability in sparsity and power also in visual summary, it is not clear where the limits are set for such networks (is it a feature of the Flickr® API or a built-in limitation of NodeXL)? Better understanding what influences the extracted related tags networks will help researchers not over-assert from their results.

What to Do with Related Tags Network Data?

So how should related tags networks be used? What do they mean exactly? In one sense, these are the words that come to mind in relation to digital imagery and videos when people upload these digital artifacts. Collectively, these may show mental conceptualizations at a macro level that might be non-obvious at the individual or local level. Once graphed, these networks may be explored visually to see which tags have direct relationships to a source tag (whether this is a word, hashtag, or phrase). Then, too, it may help to see which transitive relationships exist in 1.5-degree related tag networks. High transitivity in a related tags network might show intensive ties between tags; low transitivity in a related tags network might show sparse relational ties among tags. Then 2-degree related tags networks may be examined for more diffuse tag relationships. Related tags networks may be used to identify latent topics and tag relationships that would be non-obvious otherwise. In all these network types, it may help to identify anomalies or surprises for further exploration. There may be leads for additional tags to explore (and to possibly use as seeding tags for related tags network extractions). Subgraphs may be extracted for tags beyond the two-degree network.

Adjusting the Aperture

The level of granularity of focus may affect what may be observed and asserted. In terms of units of analysis, a related tags network may be analyzed at the various levels: the individual tag, dyadic tag relationships, tag clusters, tag motifs, the related tags network graph level, and then inter-related related tags networks. The related tags networks may be captured at various degrees: 1, 1.5, and 2 (at least with these tools), and they may be captured at even higher degrees (although meanings become much more complex and potentially diffuse with the addition of degrees). The folksonomy tags themselves may be compared against more structured and formal taxonomic systems (with controlled vocabularies).

To introduce how related tags networks on Flickr® may be extracted and used for "gist" analysis, this chapter describes the extraction of tag networks related to some of the well-known cities of the People's Republic of China (used as seeding terms). They include, in alphabetical order, the following: Beijing, Chengdu, Chongqing, Dalian, Guangzhou, Hangzhou, Harbin, Hong Kong, Jinan, Macau, Nanjing, Ningbo, Qingdao, Shanghai, Shenyang, Shenzhen, Tianjin, Urumqi, Wuhan, Xiamen, and Xian The selected cities were used as seeding terms to extract related tags networks in both 2014 and 2015 in order to get a sense of related tags networks from Flickr. The nature of the seeding tags will affect the resulting extracted tags and the related tags networks; in this case, the city names will pull tags relating to places, landmarks, geographical features, tourist activities, regular human activities, people, nature, and typical Flickr® data such as camera types and professional and amateur image description tags. In other words, there are invariants in terms of image and video tagging which will appear given the nature of the seeding term, the social media platform, and the uploaded contents.

The software used for the data extractions (from the Flickr® API) and the creation of various graph visualizations is the free (no-cost) and open-source Network Overview, Discovery and Exploration for Excel (NodeXL), available on Microsoft's CodePlex platform. The version of NodeXL used was 1.0.1.336.

AN EXPLANATION OF DEGREES IN A NETWORK

Generally, a one-degree network includes the target (source or seeding) tag and other tags with which it co-occurs at a certain threshold level. In other words, not all tags that co-occur with the seeding one will be listed, but only those that appear at a certain probability. At 1.5 degrees, the network consists of the seeding term, all the "alters" in that network (the tags that have a direct relationship with the seeding tag at a certain threshold), and this includes any ties between those alters with each other (which is an indicator of transitivity). The clusters will have varying degrees of internal coherence and describability, and many of these are not apparently mutually exclusive in terms of type. In other words, multiple clusters may contain place names, for example. Finally, a 2 deg. network consists of the target tag, its ego neighborhood of direct ties ("alters"), and the ego neighborhoods of those alters (the direct ties for those "alters" in addition to the target tag). At two degrees, the resulting network includes tags that are relationally more distant from the original seeding tag. This means that there is increased potential to discover surprise tag connections and informational meaning through weak ties. Such multi-degree related tags networks may have a more free-associational feel and have more of an overall sense of an indirect and diffuse pseudo-narrative. Still, the visual graph has to be legible and human-readable for use. The extracted data may be visualized in different ways, based on a variety of layout algorithms, for a wide range of looks-and-feel of the underlying data.

There are other graph metrics. The number of nodes or vertices provides a sense of the size of the network. The number of edges or links shows the amount of interconnectivity in the network. (The types of nodes and links vary depending on the type of network graph depicted.) Reciprocation between vertex pairs and edges show the directionality in the graph. The maximum geodesic distance or graph diameter shows the breadth of the network through the maximum number of hops required to move from the two furthest nodes from each other (from one end of the graph to the furthest other side). The average geodesic distance indicates the average number of hops needed to move from any one node to any other node, across the graph. To see how this works, broadly speaking, please see the example below.

Seeding City Name: "Beijing"

A one-degree related tags network extraction of "Beijing" results in a graph with 106 vertices and 105 unique edges. This related tags network data is depicted in a horizontal sine wave graph in Figure 3.

To provide an example of what follows, a data extraction was done for "Beijing" and also for "#Beijing." The first is a keyword extraction, and the latter is a hashtag extraction. Both related tags networks extracted were fully similar: both had 106 vertices with 105 unique edges. In other words, the related tags API in Flickr® treats both keywords and hashtags similarly (at least at the time of the data extraction). This may be seen in Figure 4. The seeding terms are at 3 o'clock in the ring lattice graphs, and they are circled in red. This visualization shows the similar extracted one-degree related tags network graphs.

A 1.5-degree related tags network of "Beijing" results in 106 vertices, 2,745 unique edges, and two groups. This extraction shows some transliteration of words from non-English languages using the al-

Figure 3. "Beijing" Related Tags Network on Flickr® (1 deg.)

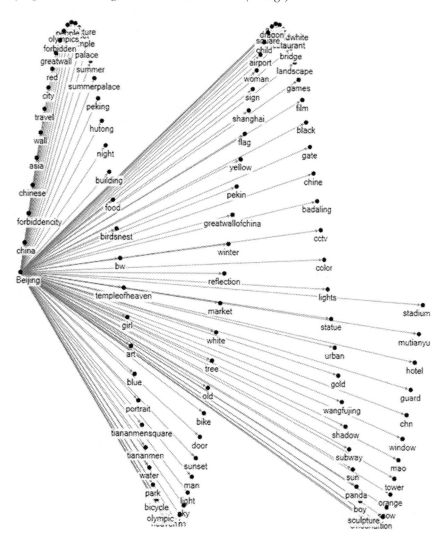

Figure 4. "Beijing" and "#Beijing" related tags network on Flickr® (1 deg.)

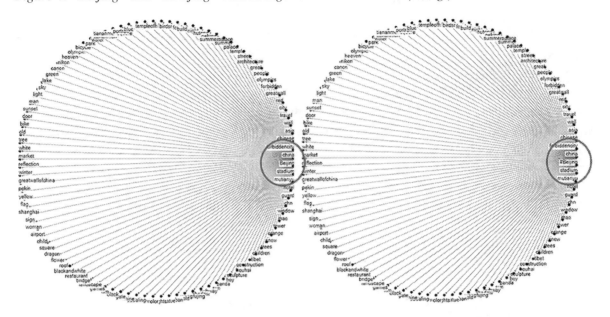

phabet. Typos and misspellings are also part of the tag graph. There are mentions of other locales. There are mentions of architecturally and culturally interesting landmarks. This graph may be seen in Figure 5.

A two-degree related tags network extracted from "Beijing" as the seeding city resulted in 1,243 vertices, 5,891 unique edges, and 11 clusters. This network has a reciprocated vertex pair ratio of 0.0833 and a reciprocated edge ratio of 0.15379. The maximum geodesic distance (graph diameter) is 4, and the average geodesic distance is 3.314. The graph density is 0.0038. These metrics were the same for both 2014 and 2015.

In one sampled image, its tags included all the following: Beijing, Peking, 北京, arndalarm, China, 中国, Platz des himmlischen Friedens, Tiananmen Square, 天安门广场, 天安門廣場的地方, Tian An Men, 天安門, 天安门, IMG_3609_7.0K+10_e+0.5… and an auto-tagged label "outdoor." There were terms in simplified Chinese as well as complex Chinese. Some terms are synonymous. It is helpful to note that Flickr® is "a naturally multilingual database" however, people tend not to be as willing to function crosslingually or to translate image searches into unknown other languages (Artiles, Gonzalo, López-Ostenero, & Peinado, 2007, pp. 196 and 203).

REVIEW OF THE LITERATURE

Humans have a range of complex needs, personal and professional, individual and social, cognitive and across a 10-motivation framework "for sharing information and social support in social media" (Oh & Syn, 2015, p. 4). These researchers extracted the 10 motivation variables based on a meta-analysis of published research and studied how these manifested differently among users on different social media platforms. The motivations were enjoyment, self-efficacy, learning, personal gain, altruism, empathy, community interest, social engagement, reputation, and reciprocity (Oh & Syn, 2015, p. 5). These mo-

Figure 5. "Beijing" related tags network on Flickr® (1.5 deg.)

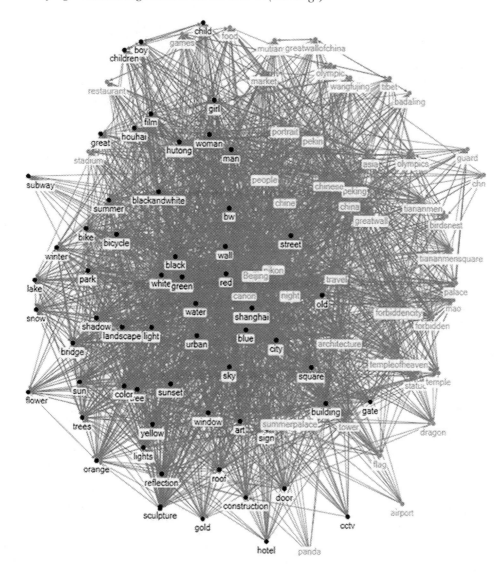

tivational elements were measured across multiple social media platforms to see their varying degrees of influence on people's behaviors on that platform. Based on surveys, the authors found the following measures of Cronbach's alpha of survey statements for each motivation factor for Flickr: enjoyment (.747), self-efficacy (.731), learning (.784), personal gain (.871), altruism (.776), empathy (.731), community interest (.697), social engagement (.747), reputation (.782), and reciprocity (.779) (Oh & Syn, 2015, p. 7); these measures suggest that the survey test is a reliable measure for these variables on Flickr® (and they were similarly high for the other social media platforms studied: Facebook, Twitter, Delicious, and YouTube. The authors discovered the following about general motivations for those engaged on social media:

Figure 6. " Beijing" related tags network on Flickr® (2 deg.) (2014 and 2015)

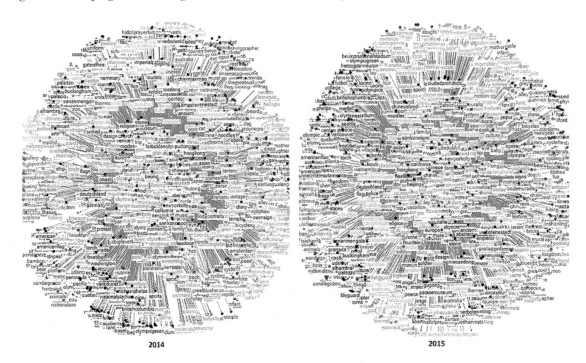

2014   2015

Learning is the most highly influential motivation and social engagement is the second. These are followed by reciprocity, reputation, altruism, enjoyment, self-efficacy, and community interests, although their mean ratings are almost tied with one another. Personal gain is the least influential and empathy second from last (Oh & Syn, 2015, p. 7).

The 10 motivations are positively correlated with each other and the correlations are statistically significant at the 99% level. The authors write, "Learning, the most influential motivation, is statistically significant in strong correlation ($r > .50$) with enjoyment, self-efficacy, altruism, empathy, community interest, social engagement, and reciprocity. Those who are motivated by learning would likely be motivated by the other motivations, except personal gain or reputation" (Oh & Syn, 2015, p. 7). These researchers found correlations between altruism and reciprocity and altruism and empathy. Enjoyment and self-efficacy are "strongly correlated with one another" (Oh & Syn, 2015, p. 8). Those who are motivated by reputation building also tend to engage in reciprocity behavior. Personal gain is "strongly correlated with community interest only" (Oh & Syn, 2015, p. 9). The authors summarize some of their insights across social media platforms:

Overall, both learning and social engagement are ranked as the top two across all types of social media except Delicious, in which learning and altruism are the top two, while social engagement is ranked fourth. Reciprocity and reputation are ranked together in the middle in most of the social media. Both empathy and personal gain are the two least influential motivations across all of the social media.

The rank orders of motivations across social media differ slightly. In Facebook, social engagement is the most highly influential motivation, while learning is the most highly influential motivation in other social media. In both Facebook and Delicious, altruism is ranked relatively high (second in Delicious and third in Facebook). In Twitter, self-efficacy is ranked third. In Flickr, enjoyment is ranked highly at third, compared to other media. In YouTube, reciprocity, reputation, self-efficacy, and enjoyment are ranked slightly higher than those in other social media (Oh & Syn, 2015, p. 11).

There are partially formal approaches to tagging as well, such as projects related to the tagging of photographs in the Library of Congress photostream in Flickr®. Two researchers analyzed the Flickr® member discussions surrounding the photos and analyzed the photostream tags in relation to "two knowledge organization systems: the Thesaurus for Graphic Materials (TGM) and the Library of Congress Subject Headings (LCSH)". The authors found the following:

Thirty seven percent of the original tag set and 15.3% of the preprocessed set (after the removal of tags with fewer than three characters and URLs) were invalid or misspelled terms. Nouns, named entity terms, and complex terms constituted approximately 77% of the preprocessed set. More than a half of the photostream tags were not found in the TGM and LCSH, and more than a quarter of those terms were regular nouns and noun phrases. This suggests that these terms could be complimentary (sic) to more traditional methods of indexing using controlled vocabularies (Stvilia & Jörgensen, 2010, p. 2477).

Comparing informal tagging with formal tagging shed light on alignments and non-alignments across the tag corpus. There are benefits to bringing together the bottom-up tagging of folk taggers with the top-down tagging of those professionals using a controlled and *a priori* vocabulary.

Flickr, a digital image sharing service and social media platform, was created in 2004 by Ludicorp and sold to Yahoo in 2005. Currently, it is one of the most popular social media platforms on the Web. In August 2011, its users numbered more than 51 million, and its members had posted more than six billion images (De Meo, Ferrara, Abel, Aroyo, & Houben, 2013, p. 14:6). For years, it has been known as a site that captures "the social nature of photography" because it enables broad image sharing, commenting and intercommunications, friending, and coordinated group activities and interests. It has been called a "photographic club" whose members engage in "photography as serious leisure" (Cox, Clough, & Marlow, 2008, p. 1). As a service, it offers 1,000 GB of data storage for users for free. It also has service-enhanced pay channels and services. Users may also choose to keep their photo and video collections private (with membership by invitation only and no public-access) or sharable only among their selected friends. At the time of this chapter's writing, there was a Recent Photos feature, a World Map with location-identified imagery, various galleries and collections, a Commons area (a place serving as "the world's public photography archives"). There is also a Creative Commons collection which enables access to images under generous licensure.

According to Flickr's The App Garden, the flickr.tags.getRelated "returns a list of tags 'related' to the given tag, based on clustered usage analysis." The seeding tag (or "tags source") for the data extraction is "the tag to fetch related tags for." To use the Flickr® API, a user must request a key and secret from the App Garden and input that into their version of NodeXL to conduct the extraction. The Flickr® API allows third-party websites and applications to communicate with Flickr® and access information as part of integrated services and mash-ups. Flickr® is seen as being transparent:

Flickr is transparent: every username, every group name, every descriptive tag is a hyperlink that can be used to navigate the site, and unless it has been 1http://www.flickr.com designated private, all content is publicly viewable and in some cases, modifiable. (Lerman & Jones, 2006, p. 1)

Flickr® tags may be understood as keywords, and they relate to each other based on a certain threshold of correlation, such as on a keyword correlation matrix. Flickr® enables the capturing of "Flickr clusters, which, provided a popular tag, give related tags grouped into clusters" (Begelman, Keller, & Smadja, 2006, p. 3). One limit noted back in 2006 was that Flickr® did not keep records of who viewed an image (Lerman & Jones, 2006). That observation is apparently still true today.

Flickerati have commented on why they enjoy Flickr® An author collected some of the reasons for user appreciation of Flickr®, including the idea that the user community can self-organize, that users are respected and that their preferences are responded to by Yahoo, that photographers can showcase their talents on the site, that the site can provide "collective memory," that the forums involve quality discussions, and that the site is easy-to-use (Tik, 2005). Some of the observations were about tagging. #17 read: "Tagging is intuitive and remarkably successful even though no standards exist." #30 read: "The tagging system works because of the redundancy. Even though not all photos are tagged correctly, enough results show up to make this method very effective." #s 46 and #47 also dealt with tagging, reading respectively: "No hierarchy here. Flickr is self-categorizing. Tagging images helps you organize your collection and makes it easier for others to find. Members and friends can add to your tags which add value to your work," and "Tags also bring people together and channel their creativity" (Tik, 2005). Another summarized the social order on Flickr:

The social order of Flickr, though less obvious and restrictive than the photo club identified by Schwartz (1987), is quite specific, embodying values which are summarized by Tik (2005) from users' comments as stressing open entry (Tik's point 42), high activity (44), lack of hierarchy (46), learning (51), diversity (52, 73), creativity (60, 74), and positivity (61) (Cox, Clough, & Marlow, 2008, p. 11).

In a study of five million Flickr® users and an image set of 150 million photos, researchers have found that there are a large number of registered users are inactive on the platform, with 39% who had never uploaded any public photos or used any public-facing functionalities; 23% of users who hadn't uploaded any public photos but who had used communications functionalities, and then 19% who had uploaded public photos but not used communications functionalities, and another 19% who had both uploaded public photos and used communications functions (described as "contacts, comments or group participation") (Prieur, Cardon, Beuscart, Pissard, & Pons, 2008, pp. 3-4). Of those 38% who were actually active on the site, the average number of posted photos was 915 (with a max number at 75,737) (p. 3). The researchers found a small minority of users producing a large amount of contents and organizing these contents through "creating or animating group, tagging pictures, organizing contests, defining reputation of others, etc." (Prieur, Cardon, Beuscart, Pissard, & Pons, 2008, p. 4). "Star" photographers on Flickr® were seen to cultivate that stardom by posting comments, favoriting others' work, and participating in groups. The authors observe: "Social activity is a necessary condition to reputation: one of the prominent Flickr® stars is also the top commentator on the site (51,400 comments posted in 18 month of activity) (Prieur, Cardon, Beuscart, Pissard, & Pons, 2008, p. 5). At the time of the research, 8% of Flickr® users were in groups (vs. 49% of pro users), which the researchers interpreted as a case of an "active minority" affecting "the structuring of the whole community" (Prieur, Cardon, Beuscart,

Pissard, & Pons, 2008, p. 5). Flickr® is also a site that involves more formalized endeavors such as the creation and sharing of historical image collections by university libraries, university archives, and public libraries (Jett, Senseney, & Palmer, 2012).

Tagging on Flickr

Not all images uploaded into Flickr® have tagging. Those who use Flickr® may upload imagery and choose not to tag at all (Marlow, Naaman, boyd, & Davis, 2006, p. 36). The quality of the tags may vary. For example, individuals who are taking photos using mobile devices may be uploading on-the-fly and tag based on whatever concepts are top-of-mind; they may not return to review what tagging they had applied or to add more. They may bulk-tag a mass-uploaded set of images and tags, with varying levels of applicability of the tagging. The various friend networks may also tag their friends' images, and that may change what shows up in the tagging system. In one study, there was an initial classification for different types of tags based on the relationship between the tag and the image content, in part, and also in how the tag was used by the particular individual or group, among other factors (Angus, Thelwall, & Stuart, 2007).

Researchers have looked into why people using Flickr® tag images, and they have found a mix of intrinsic and extrinsic motivations. In one research project, intrinsic motivations include "enjoyment" and "commitment to the community," and extrinsic motivations include "self-development" and "reputation building"; in addition to those variables, "tenure in the community" was also studied to explore participation in the Flickr® community in terms of artifact sharing, meta-information sharing, one-to-one connections, and one-to-many connections (Nov, Naaman, & Ye, 2009, p. 559). The length of tenure in Flickr® was found to positively affect metainformation sharing but result in diminished levels of information-artifact sharing. The research team elaborated:

The causality of the relationship between tenure and the measured factors is unclear. One way to explain the increase in joining social structures may be the effect of greater embeddedness in the community: As people form relationships with others (both one-one and one-to-many), they become more comfortable with activity and exposure on Flickr, they get to know new people, and through them, even more people.

Thus, the social aspect of the community has a positive effect on continued participation. The construct of feedback (Burke et al., 2009) could help explain this relationship: People stick around because they are involved with more contacts and groups, which is likely to lead to more feedback. However, positive effects of feedback would also suggest a correlation between number of photos to contacts and groups, which was not found in our study (Nov, Naaman, & Ye, 2009, p. 563).

In discussions on the Flickr® API group on the Flickr® site, various individuals have posted their research findings on the average numbers of tags per digital object on the site. An early research studied cited an average of 3.74 (Rattenbury, Good, & Naaman, 2007, p. 108) to 8.94 tags (Huiskes & Lew, 2008, p. 40). More recent postings suggest between 8 – 10 (MariannaBolognesi, Oct. 3, 2012, FlickrAPI Group). Another suggested that a majority or 70% of sampled images had 10 tags or fewer, and a minority had from the maximum of 75 and other counts down to the 10 *stevefaeembra, 3 years ago, FlickrAPI Group). Neither of the latter two sources provided more in-depth information.

In the academic research literature, a number of works highlight the use of tags for various purposes. Even from the early years of the platform, researchers strove to induce ontologies from tags on Flickr® (Schmitz, 2006). Researchers have worked to use tags for meaning-making. One involves the "landmark finding problem" and the use of human-created tagging and Flickr® groups to identify landmark images on Flickr® (Abbasi, Chernov, Nejdl, Paiu, & Staab, 2009). Another research project involves the use of vernacular geography tagging (from volunteered geographic information) to explore the concept of city cores among Flickr® users (Hollenstein & Purves, 2010). The authors describe some of their findings:

Between 0.5–2% of tags associated with georeferenced images analyzed describe city core areas generically, while 70% of all georeferenced images analyzed include specific place name tags, with place names at the granularity of city names being by far the most common. Using Flickr metadata, it is possible not only to describe the use of the term Downtown across the USA, but also to explore the borders of city center neighborhoods at the level of individual cities, whilst accounting for bias by the use of tag profiles (Hollenstein & Purves, 2010, p. 21).

The mining of tags involves the pursuit of "data leakage" or the unintended revelation of information. One example of this may be the revelation of a user account's physical location based on clues in the tags. Another may be unintended information leakage based on what may be unintentionally revealed in terms of word choices. (In the same way, the images may be considered unintentionally informative if there are images in the background that the photographer may not have intentionally captured and shared.) There may be unintentional self-disclosures of identity and context (Popescu & Grefenstette, 2010).

Another example of tag mining involves the use of Flickr® tags as an indicator of collective happiness in various cities. In this study, Flick tag corpuses were compared against a happiness index dictionary to compare varying happiness measures of different cities (You, DesArmo, & Joo, 2013).

One research team created a method for extracting "Flickr distance" (a form of semantic correlation) among visual concept pairs identified in Flickr. The researchers calculated Flickr distance for any two concepts on the Flickr® tagging database by calculating "the square root of Jensen-Shannon (JS) divergence between the visual language models corresponding to the concepts. If two concepts are more likely to appear in the same photo, the square root of JS divergence of their visual language models tends to be small; otherwise large" (Wu, Hua, Yu, Ma, & Li, 2008, p. 32). Other researchers found that how people tend to tag fairly uniformly and typically independent of the social sharing platforms that they're using; however, on Flickr, users were found to occasionally deviate and use non-homogeneous or outlier tags (De Meo, Ferrara, Abel, Aroyo, & Houben, 2013). On Flickr, the researchers found "strong correlation" between "the intensity of tagging and the intensity of friending activities" (De Meo, Ferrara, Abel, Aroyo, & Houben, 2013, p. 14:3).

If the "views" of an image on Flickr® were treated analogically as disease reproduction (a common analogy for propagation), then popular photos' reproduction numbers would be between 1 and 190, much higher than even highly infectious diseases—so social networks can be efficient transmission mediums (Cha, Mislove, Adams, & Gummadi, 2008, p. 18). While many strive to position their imagery for viral spreading, multiple research teams have found that a very small subset of images actually go viral (or propagate exponentially). It turns out that digital contents are not so easy to spread widely through social media platforms. One team found that many photos do show a rise in popularity "during the first few days after they are uploaded"; further, after the first 10 – 20 days, most pictures "enter a period of steady linear growth" over extended periods of time, without slowing even after 1 – 2 years (Cha, Mislove, & Gummadi, 2009, p. 721). Users of Flickr® tend to discover interesting photos slowly. The authors also discovered the following:

... (a) even popular photos do not spread widely throughout the network, (b) even popular photos spread slowly through the network, and (c) information exchanged between friends is likely to account for over 50% of all favorite markings, but with a significant delay at each hop (Cha, Mislove, & Gummadi, 2009, p. 721).

Image information shared across social links tend to propagate in a matter of days, and "most fans of a given picture are within a few hops of the picture uploader" for high content locality (Cha, Mislove, & Gummadi, 2009, p. 728). In other words, social cascades matter in the dissemination of content, but the speed of dissemination is slower than many may think. The tendency to back-link and reciprocate on Flickr® was a major factor in social networking on Flickr, with users creating and receiving links "in proportion to their outdegree and indegree" (Mislove, Koppula, Gummadi, Druschel, & Bhattacharjee, 2008, pp. 29 – 30). A comparison of tagging behaviors across social media platforms suggests that Flickr® users "show a greater tendency towards tag avoidance than users of other systems" (Heckner, Neubauer, & Wolff, 2008, p. 8). Another study found that abstract images tended to receive more tagging than representational ones; images that were more visually complex tend to receive more tagging; also, tags with "identifiable people, dates, or locations" tend to appear earlier in the list of tags" (Golbeck, Koepfler, & Emmerling, 2011).

To explore how related tags networks may be captured and visualized for analytical purposes, a basic research methodology was followed. This is described in the next section.

"CHINESE CITIES" AS SEEDING KEYWORDS: A COLLECTION OF ASSOCIATED RELATED TAGS NETWORKS FROM FLICKR®

To explore some aspects of related tags networks on Flickr, the author conducted data extractions using the NodeXL tool to access Flickr® data through its related tags API. The cities selected were the following (with most written in pinyin): Beijing, Chengdu, Chongqing, Dalian, Guangzhou, Hangzhou, Harbin, Hong Kong, Jinan, Macau, Nanjing, Ningbo, Qingdao, Shanghai, Shenyang, Shenzhen, Tianjin, Urumqi, Wuhan, Xiamen, and Xian. The 1-degree and 1.5-degrees networks were extracted in June 2015; the two-degree networks were extracted in September 2014 and June 2015, nine months apart, in order to try to capture changes over time (but resulted in the surprising finding of no changes at two degrees and with the same data extraction parameters in that time period). Some of the city names were crawled using the actual simplified Chinese characters but did not result in any data extractions. This may reflect how Flickr handles UTF-8 tags.

Network Overview, Discovery and Exploration for Excel (NodeXL) is a no-cost open-source tool that enables the visualization of network graphs. It has additional functionality of extracting data from social media platforms (Facebook, Twitter, MediaWiki-based platforms, YouTube, and Flickr, among others). In Figure 7, this screenshot shows the data worksheets to the left and the graph (visualization) pane to the right. There is an interactive component: when data records to the left are highlighted, their counterparts are highlighted in the graph pane to the graph; likewise, when a node or link or branch or

Figure 7. The "Import from Flickr® Related Tags Network Window" and general work interface for NodeXL

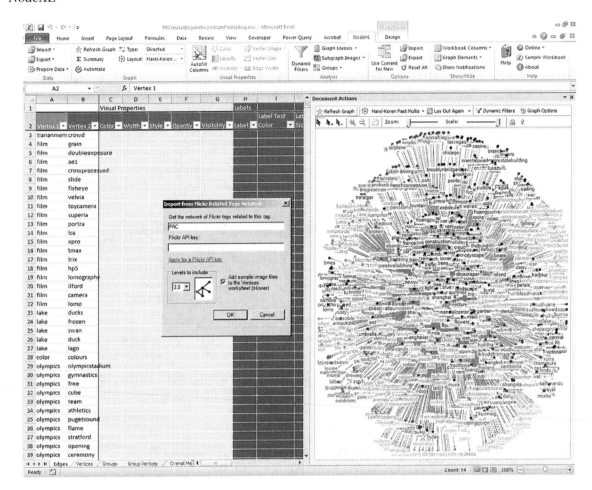

cluster to the right is highlighted, the linked information to the left is highlighted. A basic sequence of the data extraction from Flickr® is shown in Figure 8, "Capturing a Related Tags Network from Flickr® (General Steps)."

Seeding City Name: "Chengdu"

A one-degree related tags network of "Chengdu" results in 77 vertices and 76 unique edges. The resulting graph, laid out with the Fruchterman-Reingold force-based layout algorithm, may be seen in Figure 9. The tags are represented all in lower case, without capitalization, without camel case. There are expressions of enthusiasm ("abigfave"), colloquial phrasing ("chinglish"), camera specifications, a historical leader (mao), animal mentions ("giantpanda"), and place mentions ("leshan").

A 1.5-degree related tags network of "Chengdu" results in 77 vertices, 1,450 unique edges, and three groups. The graph visualization here may be seen in Figure 10, laid out with the Harel-Koren Fast Multiscale layout algorithm. (The groups are more easily seen with the color-based graph depiction in

Figure 8. Capturing a related tags network from Flickr® (General Steps)

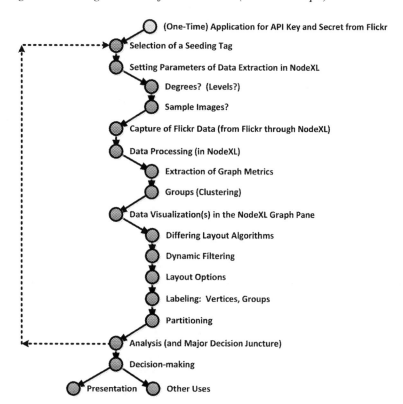

the electronic version of the chapter.) There are some clusters that more clearly tell a pseudo-story, of photography-related elements or travel in China or wildlife in China.

For both 2014 and 2015, the related tags network for "Chengdu" at the two-degree data extraction resulted in 1,130 vertices and 4,358 unique edges and 9 groups. The reciprocated vertex pair ratio is 0.058, and the reciprocated edge ratio is 0.109. The maximum geodesic distance (graph diameter) is 4, and the average geodesic distance is 3.32. The graph density is .00034. The two side-by-side graphs may be viewed at Figure 11.

Seeding City Name: "Chongqing"

A one-degree related tags network of "Chongqing" results in 80 vertices and 79 edges. In the graph visualization, Figure 12, the thumbnail images created a visceral sense of some of the terms in the network.

At 1.5 degrees, the "Chongqing" related tags network consists of 80 vertices, 1,583 unique edges, and three clusters. The resulting graph is shown in Figure 13 and is displayed using the Harel-Koren Fast Multiscale layout algorithm, with the groups in partitions.

A two-degree related tags network with the seeding term "Chongqing" resulted in 989 vertices, 4,414 unique edges, and 8 groups for both 2014 and 2015. The reciprocated vertex pair ratio is .07, and the reciprocated edge ratio is .13. The maximum geodesic distance or diameter is 4, and the average geodesic distance is 3.28. The graph density was 0.0045. The graphs from this extraction may be seen in Figure

Figure 9. "Chengdu" related tags network on Flickr® (1 deg.)

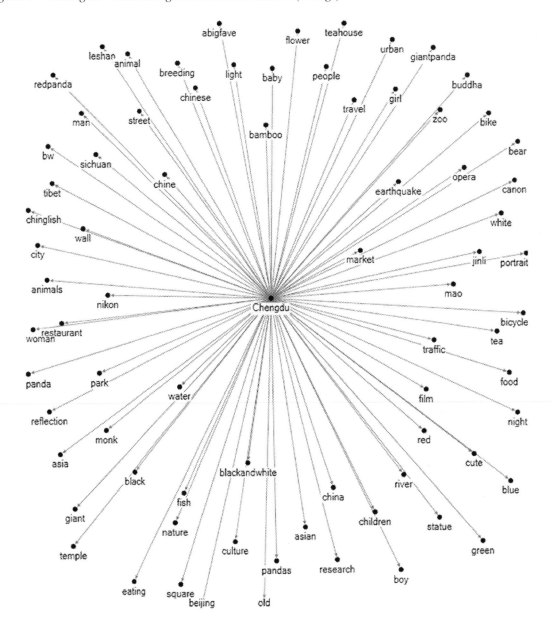

14. Both the 2014 and the 2015 graphs were laid out using the Fruchterman-Reingold force-based layout algorithm, but the left one was iterated several times, resulting in smoother outer edges.

Seeding City Name: "Dalian"

For "Dalian," its one-degree related tags network results in 98 vertices and 97 unique edges. These direct tag ties are illustrated with the Fruchterman-Reingold layout algorithm in Figure 15. This visualization shows one large connected component of one degree. This directional graph only shows outlinks to other tags from the "Dalian" seeding tag in the center.

A 1.5-degree related tags network for "Dalian" on Flickr® shows 98 vertices, 2,436 unique edges, and four clusters (Figure 16).

Figure 10. "Chengdu" related tags network on Flickr® (1.5 deg.)

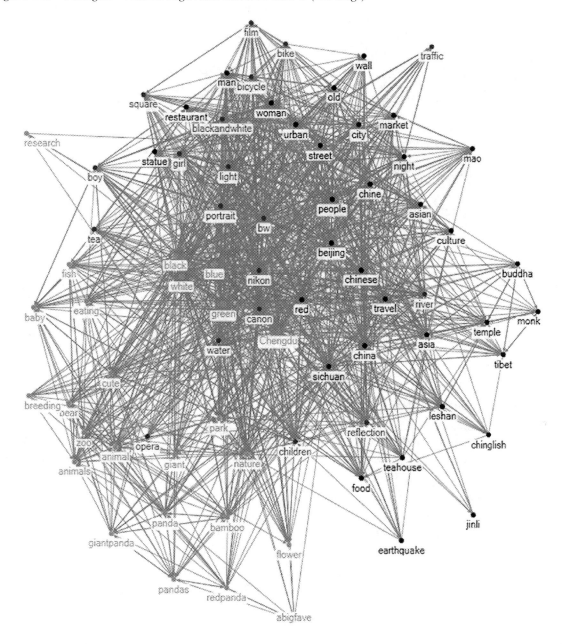

The two-degree related tags networks seeded with "Dalian" were the same in 2014 and 2015. The network consists of 1076 vertices, 5,214 unique edges, and 10 groups. These graphs have a reciprocated vertex pair ratios of 0.0903, and the reciprocated edge ratio is 0.1657. The maximum geodesic distance or graph diameter is 4, and the average geodesic distance is 3.3138. In Figure 17, the graph data are depicted using the Harel-Koren Fast Multiscale layout algorithm.

Figure 11. " Chengdu" related tags network on Flickr® (2 deg.) (2014 and 2015)

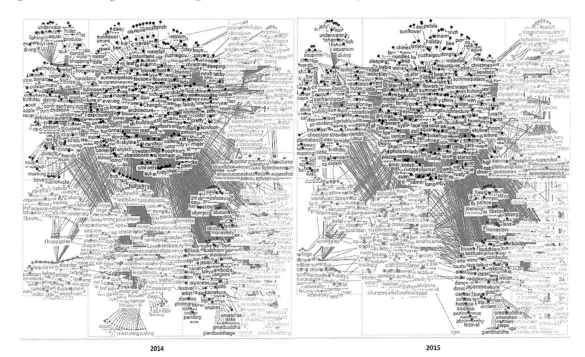

2014   2015

Seeding City Name: "Guangzhou"

A one-degree related tags network of "Guangzhou" results in a data extraction of 92 vertices and 91 unique edges. This graph is visualized using the Harel-Koren Fast Multiscale layout algorithm in Figure 18. This graph shows the uses of multiple languages in reference to "Chinese." It also shows reference to "Canton," a more archaic reference to Guangzhou.

A 1.5-degree related tags network for "Guangzhou" results in 92 vertices, 2,277 unique edges, and seven groups. In Figure 19, this is shown in a partitioned graph with the clusters placed using the Harel-Koren Fast Multiscale layout algorithm.

The graph metrics for a two-degree related tags network for "Guangzhou" resulted in 1,024 vertices, 5,057 unique edges, and 13 groups, for data extractions in both 2014 and 2015. The reciprocated vertex pair ratio is 0.089, and the reciprocated edge ratio is 0.164. The maximum geodesic distance (graph diameter) is 4, and the average geodesic distance is 3.24. The graph density is 0.0048. The two networks are shown in Figure 20 side-by-side. On the left, the Harel-Koren Fast Multiscale layout algorithm was used, and on the right, the same layout algorithm was used but the clusters were partitioned. A two-degree network gives a sense of the interconnectedness of various tags and also the potential for exponential growth of a related tags network. In this "use case," the related tags give a sense of how people form very human ties with place and each other. City names also seem to evoke other city names, which expands the sense of relatedness of place.

Figure 12. " Chongqing" related tags network on Flickr® (1 deg.)

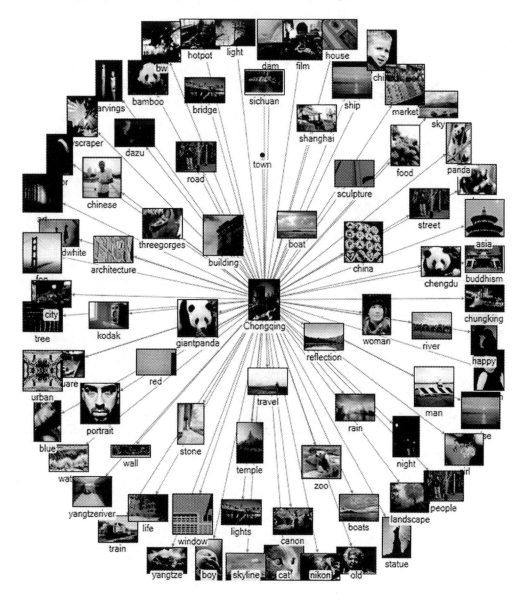

Seeding City Name: "Hangzhou"

A one-degree related tags network for "Hangzhou" resulted in a graph with 68 vertices and 67 unique edges. This graph is visualized in a vertical sine wave in Figure 21.

At 1.5 degrees, the "Hangzhou" related tags network resulted in 68 vertices and 1,460 unique edges, in 2 groups or clusters. The resulting graph may be seen in Figure 22, with the groups in their own partitions, and the vertices (tags) laid out using the Fruchterman-Reingold force-based layout algorithm.

For "Hangzhou," two-degree related tags networks extracted in 2014 and 2015 were extracted with the same metrics: 746 vertices, 3,449 unique edges, and 6 groups. The reciprocated vertex pair ratio is

Figure 13. " Chongqing" related tags network on Flickr® (1.5 deg.)

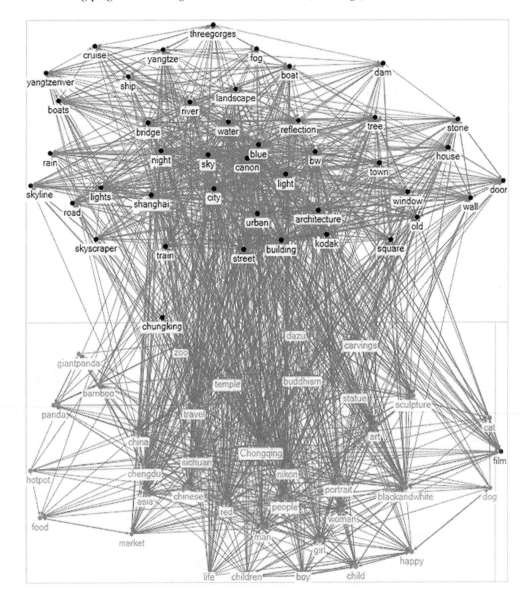

0.0908, and the reciprocated edge ratio is 0.1664. The maximum geodesic distance (graph diameter) is 4, and the average geodesic distance is 3.078 (which shows a concentrated network and fairly close ties between the extracted tags). The graph density is 0.0062. These graphs may be seen in Figure 23.

Seeding City Name: "Harbin"

The one-degree "Harbin"-seeded related tags network contains 54 vertices and 53 unique edges. This network graph is drawn using a horizontal sine wave layout algorithm in Figure 24. This related tags network mentions Harbin's famous ice sculptures and its ice festival, among other features.

Figure 14. " Chongqing" related tags network on Flickr® (2 deg.) (2014 and 2015)

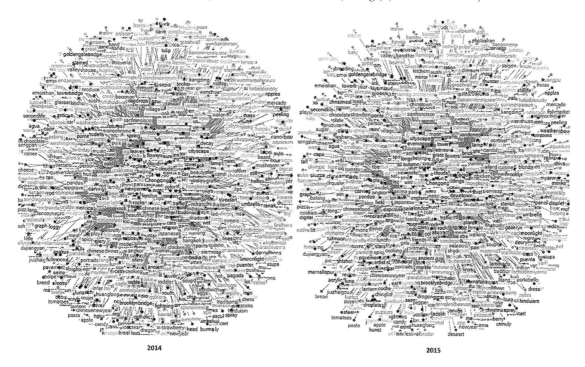

At 1.5 degrees, the "Harbin" related tags network on Flickr® results in 54 vertices, 716 unique edges, and two groups. In Figure 25, this related tags network is shown on a grid layout.

A two-degree related tags network based on "Harbin," resulted in two similar graphs with 955 vertices, 3,067 unique edges, and 8 clusters. The graphs have a reciprocated vertex pair ratio of 0.03825 and reciprocated edge ratio of 0.07369. The graphs have a maximum geodesic distance (graph diameter) of 4, and the average geodesic distance is 3.333. The graph density is 0.00337. This figure may be seen in Figure 26.

Seeding City Name: "Hong Kong"

A one-degree related tags network of "Hong Kong" ("Fragrant Harbor") results in a network of 49 vertices and 48 unique edges. Figure 27 shows this graph.

A 1.5-degree related tags network for "Hong Kong" consists of 49 vertices, 945 unique edges, and two clusters. This graph is depicted in Figure 28, using a random layout and partitioned groups.

A two-degree related tags network seeded with "Hong Kong" was found to be similar between 2014 and 2015. The graphs have 625 related tags as vertices, 2,707 unique edges, and 9 groups or clusters. The reciprocated vertex pair ratio is 0.07038, and the reciprocated edge ratio is 0.13151. The maximum geodesic distance (graph diameter) is 4, and the average geodesic distance is 3.00637. The graph density is 0.00694. The resulting data visualization may be seen in Figure 29.

Figure 15. " Dalian" related tags network on Flickr® (1 deg.)

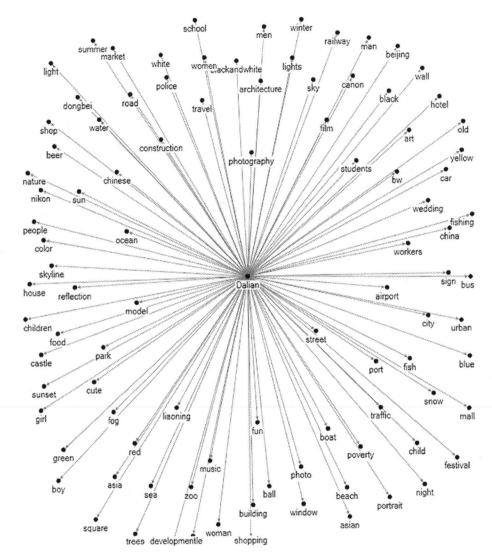

Seeding City Name: "Jinan"

A one-degree related tags network for "Jinan" reveals 35 vertices and 34 unique edges. This graph may be seen in Figure 30.

The 1.5- degree related tags network for "Jinan" consists of 35 vertices, 423 unique edges, and two groups. The resulting graph visualization may be seen in Figure 31; this was created using the Harel-Koren Fast Multiscale layout algorithm and partitions.

A two-degree related tags network extraction for Jinan in both 2014 and 2015 resulted in the same metrics: 594 vertices, 1,930 unique edges, and eight groups. For these networks, the reciprocated vertex pair ratio is 0.046638, and the reciprocated edge ratio is 0.089119. The maximum geodesic distance (graph diameter) is 4, and the average geodesic distance is 3.11327. The graphs may be seen in Figure 32.

Figure 16. " Dalian" related tags network on Flickr® (1.5 deg.)

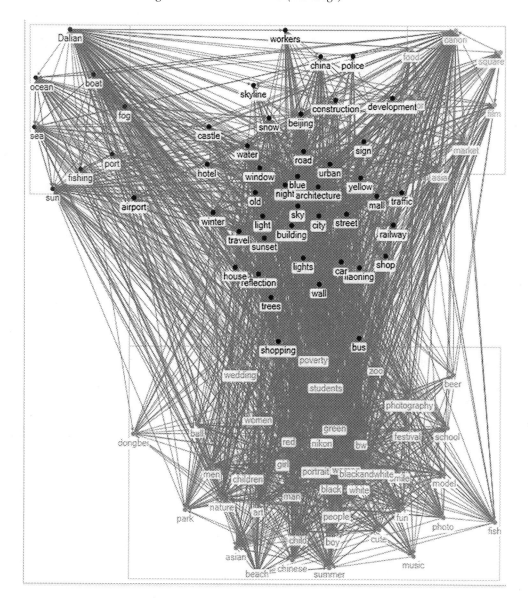

Seeding City Name: "Macau"

The one-degree "Macau" related tags network resulted in a graph with 57 vertices and 56 unique edges. Some unique aspects of the city may be observed, with mentions of local landmarks but also famous activities like "gambling". Also, one of the tags is SAR for the "special administrative region," which describes a political relationship. The direct one-degree related tags network linked to "Macau" has 57 vertices. This graph may be seen in Figure 33.

The 1.5-degree "Macau" related tags network contains 57 vertices, 1,025 unique edges, and three groups. This is depicted using a circle (ring lattice graph) layout in a partitioned graph in Figure 34.

Figure 17. " Dalian" related tags network on Flickr® (2 deg.) (2014 and 2015)

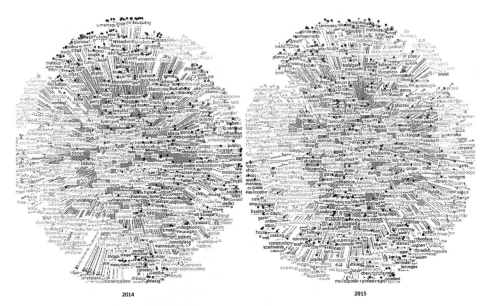

2014   2015

Figure 18. " Guangzhou" related tags network on Flickr® (1 deg.)

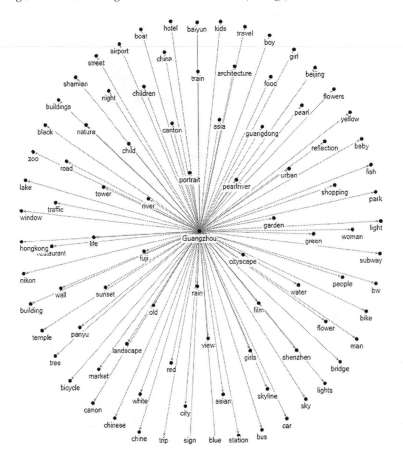

Figure 19. " Guangzhou" related tags network on Flickr® (1.5 deg.)

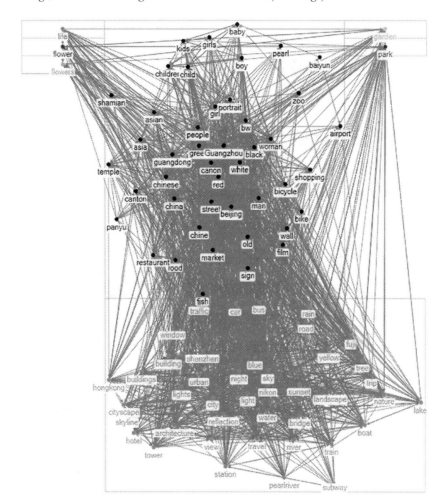

The two-degree version of the related tags network for "Macau" has 845 vertices, 3,417 unique edges, and 9 groups—for both 2014 and 2015. The reciprocated vertex pair ratio is 0.049447, and the reciprocated edge ratio is 0.00.09447, and the reciprocated edge ratio is 0.094235. The maximum geodesic distance is 4, and the average geodesic distance is 3.175. Intriguingly, the metrics are the same for both 2014 and 2015, even though the 2015 extraction resulted only in a "partial network captured only" notice (which may have also happened in 2014 (even though the author did not note that per se).

Seeding City Name: "Nanjing"

A one-degree related tags network for "Nanjing" results in 79 vertices and 78 unique edges. The resulting graph is depicted in Figure 36 and is built on a random layout.

At 1.5 degrees, the "Nanjing" related tags network contains 79 vertices, 1,858 unique edges, and three groups. This network is laid out with a grid algorithm in Figure 37.

A two-degree network of the "Nanjing" related tags network on Flickr® resulted in graphs with 935 vertices, 4,344 unique edges, and nine clusters. The reciprocated vertex pair ratio is 0.08302, and the

Figure 20. " Guangzhou" related tags network on Flickr® (2 deg.) (2014 and 2015)

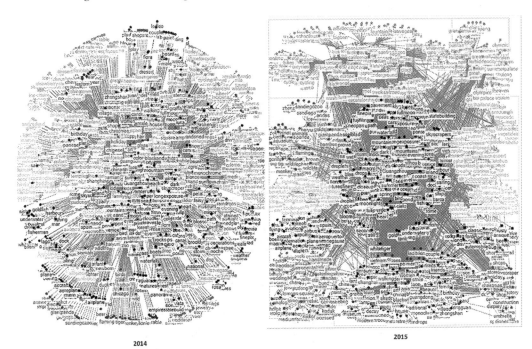

2014

2015

Figure 21. " Hangzhou" related tags network on Flickr® (1 deg.)

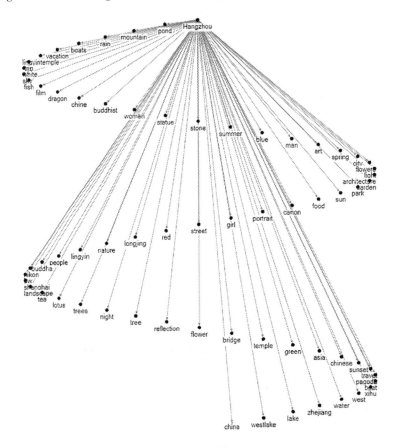

Figure 22. " Hangzhou" related tags network on Flickr® (1.5 deg.)

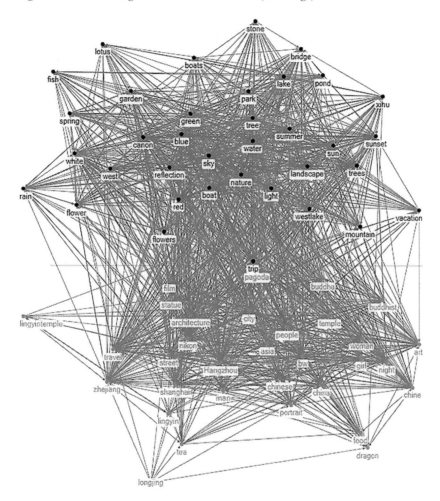

reciprocated edge ratio is 0.153315. The maximum geodesic distance (graph diameter) is 4, and the average geodesic distance is 3.197. These side-by-side graphs may be seen in Figure 38.

Seeding City Name: "Ningbo"

A one-degree related tags network for "Ningbo" contains 54 vertices and 53 unique edges. In Figure 39, this is shown in a grid layout format.

At 1.5 degrees, the "Ningbo" related tags network has 54 vertices, 998 unique edges, and three groups. The resulting graph is depicted in Figure 40, with the Harel-Koren Fast Multiscale layout algorithm.

The two-degree related tags networks of "Ningbo" were the same in 2014 and 2015. The networks contain 677 vertices each, 2,889 unique edges, and 9 groups. The reciprocated vertex pair ratio is 0.073978, and the reciprocated edge ratio is 0.13776. The maximum geodesic distance (graph diameter) is 4, and the average geodesic distance is 3.09. These side-by-side graphs may be seen in Figure 41.

Figure 23. " Hangzhou" related tags network on Flickr® (2 deg.) (2014 and 2015)

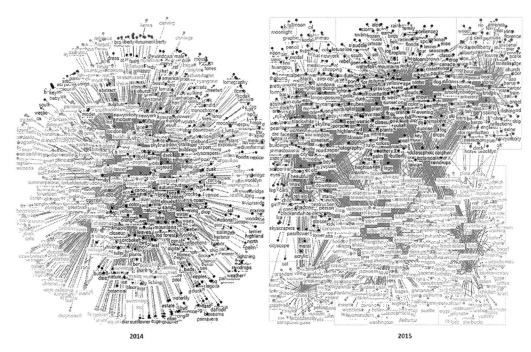

2014   2015

Figure 24. " Harbin" related tags network on Flickr® (1 deg.)

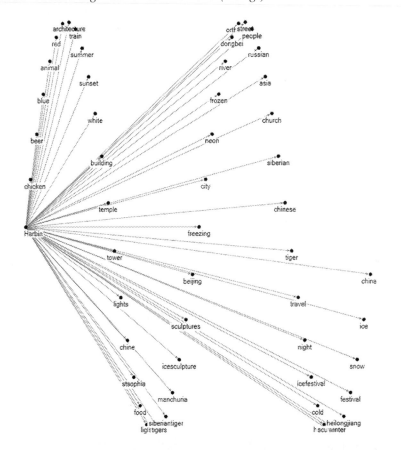

Figure 25. " Harbin" related tags network on Flickr® (1.5 deg.)

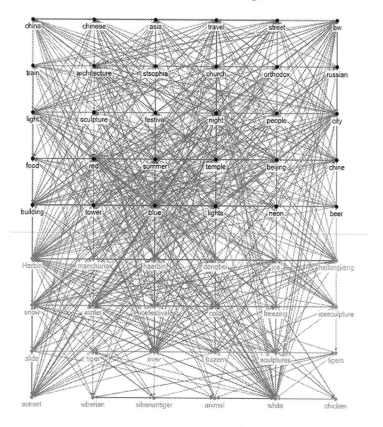

Figure 26. " Harbin" related tags network on Flickr® (2 deg.) (2014 and 2015)

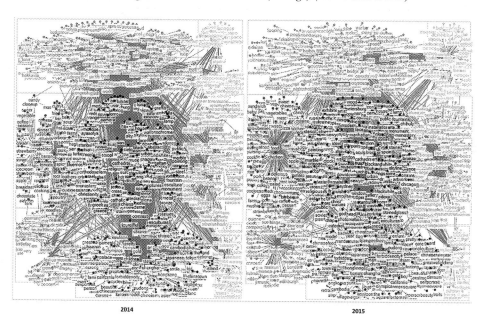

Figure 27. " Hong Kong" related tags network on Flickr® (1 deg.)

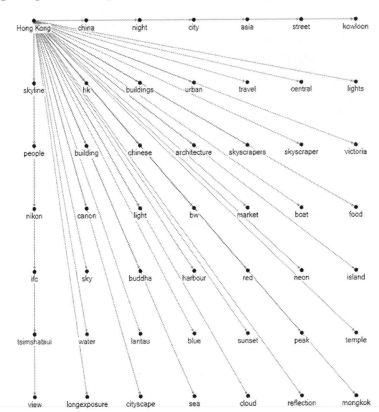

Seeding City Name: "Qingdao"

A one-degree related tags network around "Qingdao" contains 77 vertices and 76 unique edges. This graph may be seen in Figure 42.

At 1.5 degrees, the "Qingdao" related tags network contains 77 vertices, 1,582 unique edges, and three groups. In Figure 43, this related tags network is depicted using the Fruchterman-Reingold force-based algorithm.

So what to make of this graph? There is a variant of the spelling of the city's name, Qingdao vs. Tsingtao. There are clear differences between general to specific terms. Singular and plural versions of a term are treated as separate tags. The handling of capitalization is not clear, with some tags capitalized on the Flickr® site, but the extracted tags are written in lower case. Capitalization, lower case, camel case, and other variants all seem to be nulled, and the lower case is the given form in the graph visualizations.

A two-degree related tags network of Qingdao, in both 2014 and 2015, resulted in a graph of 1,004 vertices, 4,183 unique edges, and 10 groups. The reciprocated vertex pair ratio of this related tags network is 0.0681818, and the reciprocated edge ratio is 0.1276596. In this graph, the maximum geodesic distance is 4, and the average geodesic distance (average number of hops between any two nodes) is 3.249. These graphs may be seen in Figure 44.

Figure 28. " Hong Kong" related tags network on Flickr® (1.5 deg.)

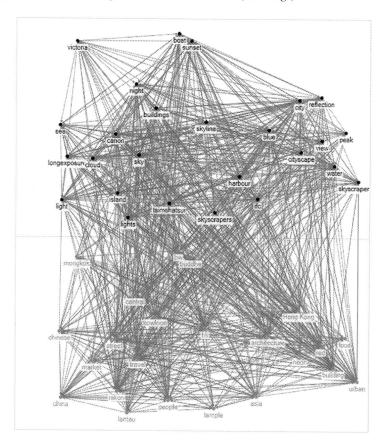

Figure 29. " Hong Kong" related tags network on Flickr® (2 deg.) (2014 and 2015)

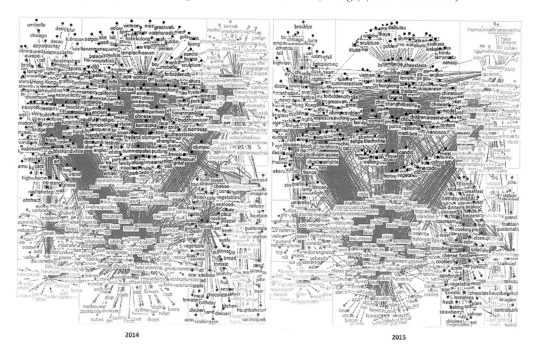

2014

2015

Figure 30. " Jinan" related tags network on Flickr® (1 deg.)

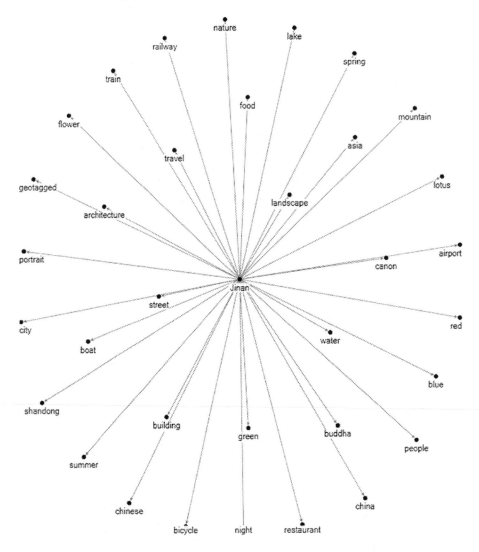

Seeding City Name: Shanghai

A one-degree related tags network around the term "Shanghai" resulted in a graph with 88 vertices and 87 unique edges. The related tags included landmarks in the city and also media organizations (like the Shanghaiist). The resulting graph may be seen in Figure 45.

At 1.5 degrees, the "Shanghai" related tags network has 88 vertices, 2269 unique edges, and two groups. Figure 46 shows two main clusters that are grouped and boxed. The layout algorithm is the Harel-Koren Fast Multiscale one.

At two degrees, the "Shanghai" related tags network for both 2014 and 2015 has 934 vertices, 4,786 unique edges, and 9 groups. The reciprocated vertex pair ratio is 0.09494, and the reciprocated e3dge ratio is 0.173422. The maximum geodesic distance (graph diameter) is 4, and the average geodesic distance is 3.1931. The graph density is 0.00549217. The side-by-side graphs may be seen in Figure 47.

Figure 31. "Jinan" related tags network on Flickr® (1.5 deg.)

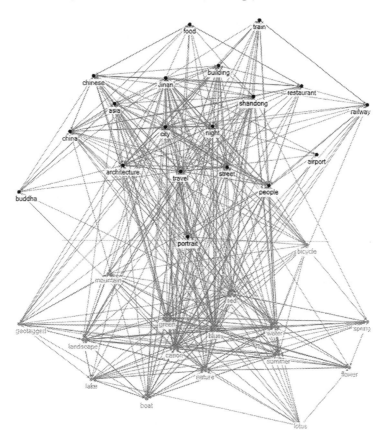

Figure 32. " Jinan" related tags network on Flickr® (2 deg.) (2014 and 2015)

2014

2015

Figure 33. " Macau" related tags network on Flickr® (1 deg.)

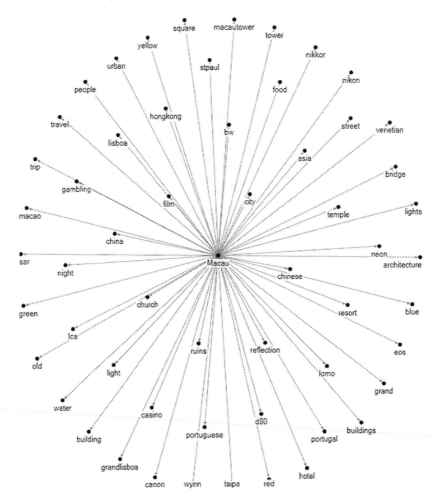

Seeding City Name: Shenyang

A one-degree related tags network based on the source tag "Shenyang" results in a graph with 67 vertices (tags) and 66 unique edges. This graph is depicted in Figure 48. This graph has some thumbnail images included, but some vertices lack images.

A 1.5-degree related tags network for "Shenyang" may be seen in Figure 49. This graph consists of 67 vertices, 1,323 unique edges, and two groups. The graph is laid out using the Fruchterman-Reingold force-based layout algorithm and is partitioned to increase its readability.

The two-degree related tags network for "Shenyang" for both 2014 and 2015 had 894 vertices, 3,804 unique edges, and 7 groups or clusters. The reciprocated vertex pair ratio was 0.060, and the reciprocated edge ratio was 0.1136. The maximum geodesic distance (graph diameter) was 4, and the average geodesic distance was 3.18. Finally, the graph density was 0.0047.

Figure 34. " Macau" related tags network on Flickr® (1.5 deg.)

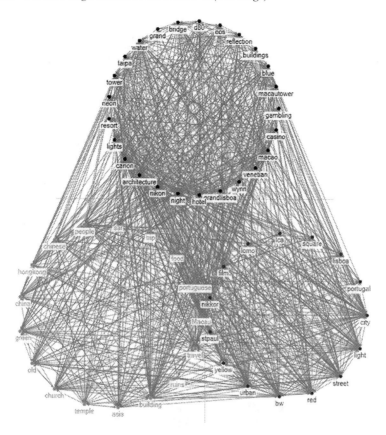

Figure 35. " Macau" related tags network on Flickr® (2 deg.) (2014 and 2015)

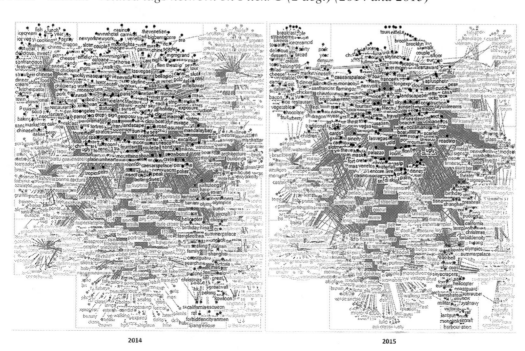

2014   2015

Figure 36. " Nanjing" related tags network on Flickr® (1 deg.)

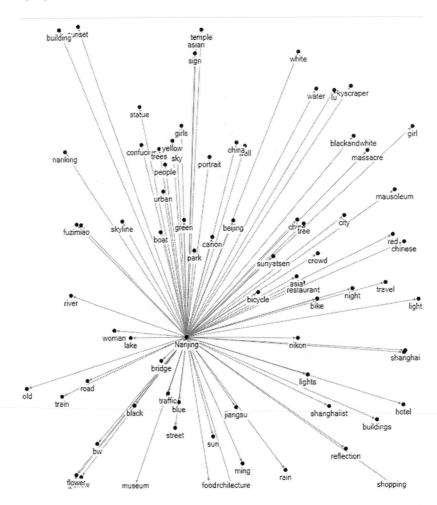

Seeding City Name: Shenzhen

A one-degree related tags network of "Shenzhen" on Flickr® results in 100 vertices and 99 unique edges. This depiction may be seen in Figure 51.

A 1.5-degree related tags network from "Shenzhen" results in 100 vertices, 2,637 unique edges, and three groups. Tags for other cities, travel destinations, activities, and such are included. Broadly speaking, the main groupings include location-based tourist-based features (as the largest cluster), separate sensory features (as the second-largest cluster), and a smaller mixed set of tags with generic image features like "blackandwhite" and "child." The graph is depicted in Figure 52.

The two data extractions for related tags networks for "Shenzhen" (at two degrees) were similar for both 2014 and 2015. This network involved 989 vertices, 5,387 edges, and 8 groups. The reciprocated vertex pair ratio was .099, and the reciprocat4ed edge ratio was 0.18. The maximum geodesic distance or graph diameter was 4, and the average geodesic distance was 3.197. This graph may be seen in Figure 53.

Figure 37. " Nanjing" related tags network on Flickr® (1.5 deg.)

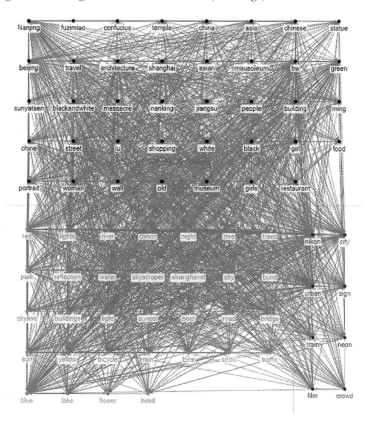

Figure 38. " Nanjing" related tags network on Flickr® (2 deg.) (2014 and 2015)

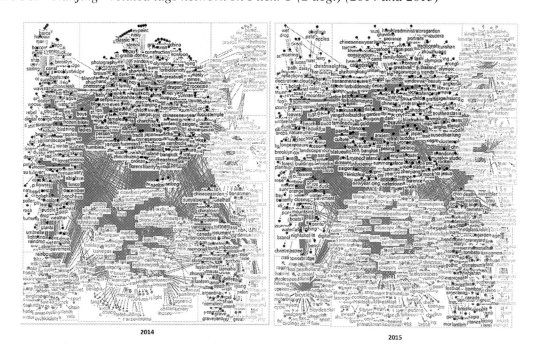

Figure 39. " Ningbo" related tags network on Flickr® (1 deg.)

Seeding City Name: Tianjin

A one-degree related tags network seeded with "Tianjin" results in a network with 78 vertices and 77 unique edges. This may be seen in Figure 54.

At 1.5 degrees, the "Tianjin" related tags network on Flickr® contains 78 vertices, 1848 unique edges, and three groups. This network is laid out in Figure 55 using the random layout algorithm.

The two-degree related tags network for "Tianjin" involves 935 vertices, 4,317 unique edges, and 10 groups or clusters. The reciprocated vertex pair ratio is 0.086, and the reciprocated edge ratio is 0.15844. The maximum geodesic distance (graph diameter) is 4, and the average geodesic distance is 3.2239. The graph density is 0.00494338.

Figure 40. " Ningbo" related tags network on Flickr® (1.5 deg.)

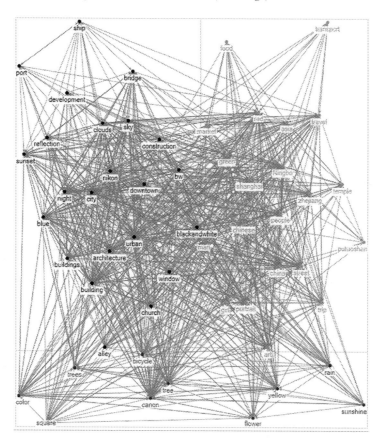

Figure 41. " Ningbo" related tags network on Flickr® (2 deg.) (2014 and 2015)

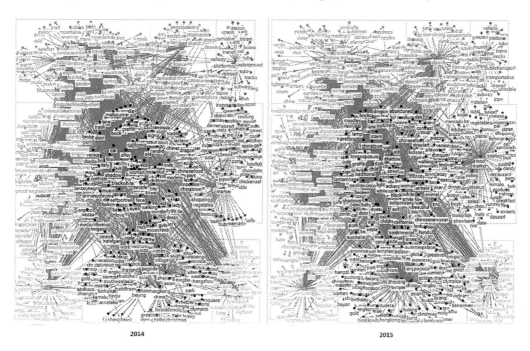

2014   2015

Figure 42. " Qingdao" related tags network on Flickr® (1 deg.)

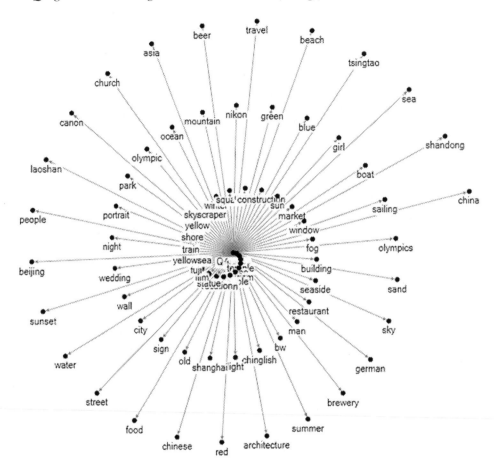

Seeding City Name: Urumqi

The one-degree related tags network based on "Urumqi" has 57 vertices and 56 unique edges. Some of the tags indicate religion and culture related to the city. The resulting graph in Figure 57 shows a random layout with related pictures included as thumbnails.

At 1.5 degrees, the "Urumqi" graph has 57 vertices, 859 unique edges, and two groups. This graph may be seen in Figure 58, which is laid out in a partitioned graph using Harel-Koren Fast Multiscale layout algorithm.

The two-degree related tags network for the "Urumqi" tag resulted in the same metrics for both 2014 and 2015. Both networks contain 810 vertices, 3,090 unique edges, and 6 groups. As with all the other two-degree graphs, there are no self-loops (given the type of network captured). The reciprocated vertex pair ratio is 0.05, and the reciprocated edge ratio is 0.0964. The maximum geodesic distance (graph diameter) is 4. The average geodesic distance is 3.1759. The graph density is 0.0047.

The two-degree "Urumqi" related tags networks are shown as a side-by-side with the 2014 graph on the left depicted using the Harel-Koren Fast Multiscale layout algorithm; on the right, the 2015 graph is

Figure 43. " Qingdao" related tags network on Flickr® (1.5 deg.)

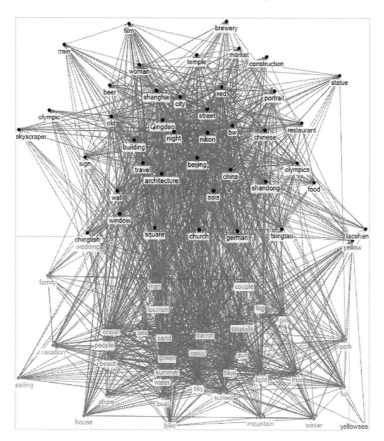

Figure 44. " Qingdao" related tags network on Flickr® (2 deg.) (2014 and 2015)

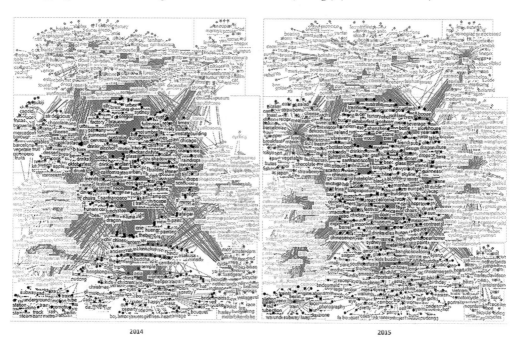

Figure 45. " Shanghai" related tags network on Flickr® (1 deg.)

created using the Fruchterman-Reingold force-based layout algorithm and partitions for the respective groups (in Figure 59). While the underlying data is the same for both years, the different layout methods were used to showcase these to evoke something of how layout parameters can change the look-and-feel of the data.

Seeding City Name: Wuhan

The one-degree related tags network for Wuhan is 78 vertices with 76 unique edges. This graph may be seen in Figure 60 with the random layout algorithm.

A 1.5 degree related tags network of "Wuhan" on Flickr® consists of 78 vertices, 1,693 unique edges, and three groups. This data is laid out as a graph in Figure 61, based on a grid layout.

The two-degree graphs for "Wuhan" from 2014 and 2015 were similar, with 981 vertices, 4,234 unique edges, and 12 groups. The reciprocated vertex pair ratio is 0.079, and the reciprocated edge ratio is 0.147. The maximum geodesic distance or graph diameter was 4, and the average geodesic distance was 3.26. The graph density was 0.0044. This is depicted in Figure 62.

Figure 46. " Shanghai" related tags network on Flickr® (1.5 deg.)

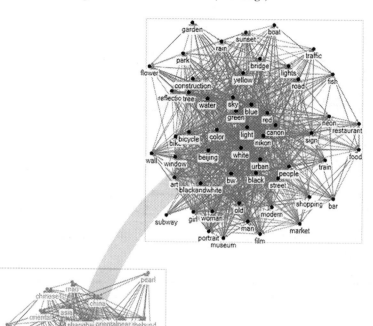

Figure 47. " Shanghai" related tags network on Flickr® (2 deg.) (2014 and 2015)

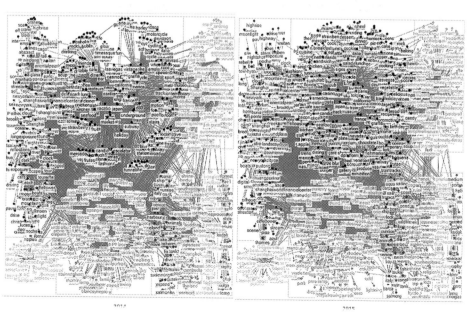

Figure 48. " Shenyang" related tags network on Flickr® (1 deg.)

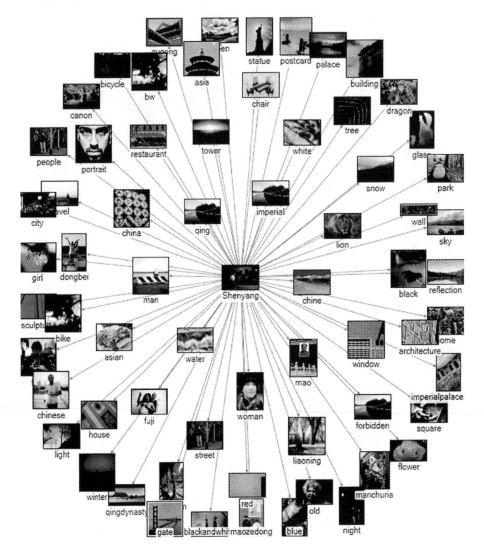

Seeding City Name: Xiamen

A one-degree related tags network seeded with "Xiamen" was extracted from Flickr® using NodeXL. This resulted in 57 vertices and 56 unique edges. The resulting graph may be seen in Figure 63.

A "Xiamen" related tags network at 1.5 degrees results in 57 vertices, 1,092 unique edges, and two groups. Figure 64 shows a depiction of this network in a partitioned graph with the vertices laid out using the Harel-Koren Fast Multiscale layout algorithm.

The two-degree related tags network graphs for both 2014 and 2015 were similar: 675 vertices, 2,973 unique edges, and 6 groups. Both graph metrics included reciprocated vertex pair ratios at 0.080 and reciprocated edge ratios at 0.1486. The graph density is 0.0065. The graph diameter is 4, and the average geodesic distance is 3.097. These graphs may be viewed in Figure 65.

Figure 49. " Shenyang" related tags network on Flickr® (1.5 deg.)

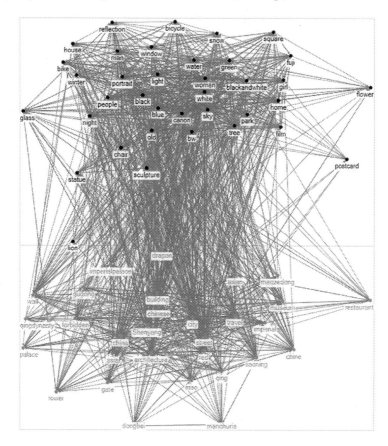

Figure 50. " Shenyang" related tags network on Flickr® (2 deg.) (2014 and 2015)

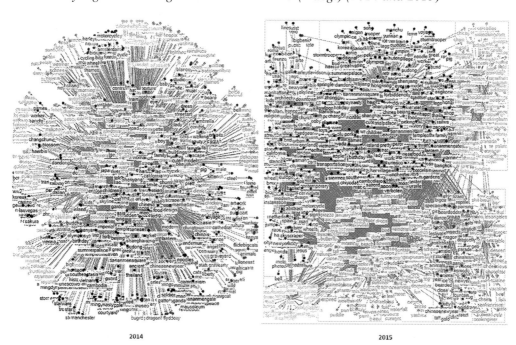

2014   2015

295

Figure 51. " Shenzhen" related tags network on Flickr® (1 deg.)

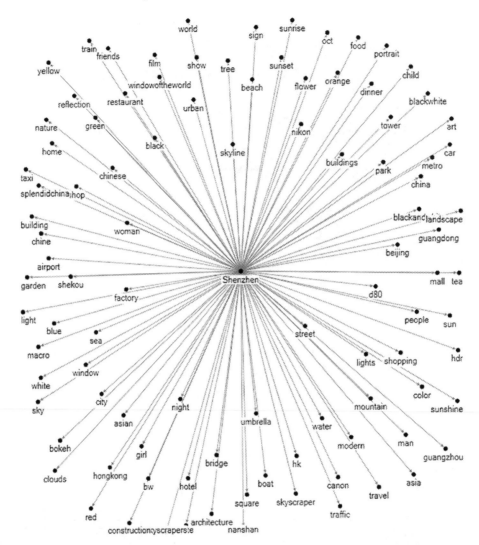

Seeding City Name: Xian

A one-degree related tags network for "Xian" was found to have 90 vertices and 89 unique edges. The resulting graph is depicted in Figure 66.

A 1.5-degree related tags network for "Xian" resulted in 90 vertices and 1,780 unique edges in 3 groups. This is depicted in Figure 67 using the Fruchterman-Reingold force-based algorithm.

As with the other related tags networks, the "Xian" extracted data for both 2014 and 2015 resulted in 1,257 vertices and 5,185 unique edges, in 10 groups. The maximum geodesic distance (graph diameter) is 4, and the average geodesic distance is 3.3. The graph density is .003. Its reciprocated vertex pair ratio is .044, and the reciprocated edge ratio is .084. The side-by-side graph is shown at Figure 68.

Figure 52. " Shenzhen" related tags network on Flickr® (1.5 deg.)

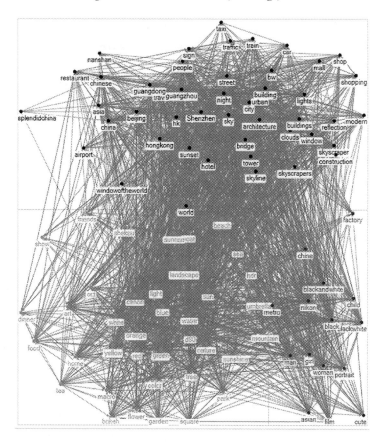

Figure 53. " Shenzhen" related tags network on Flickr® (2 deg.) (2014 and 2015)

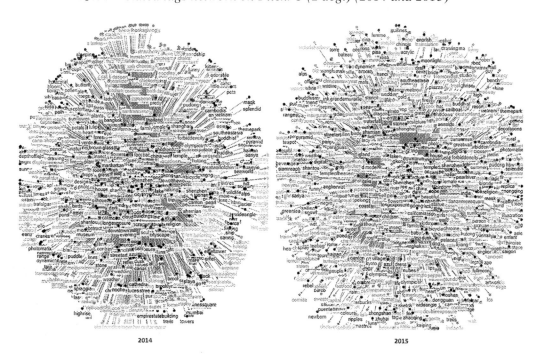

Figure 54. " Tianjin" related tags network on Flickr® (1 deg.)

DISCUSSION

This chapter used a number of Chinese cities as seeding tags to extract related tags networks from Flickr® at 1 degree, 1.5 degrees, and 2 degrees, in order to explore what related tags networks look like and how they may be used for user awareness and research. Related tags networks showcase tags that co-occur in usage in the description of imagery (and videos) uploaded on Flickr. This research demonstrates a limited use case in that the seeding terms are all of a type. Referring to the locations by geotagging would result in yet a different set of insights. The limitation is an artificial one because there are a wide range of seeding (or source) tags that may be used to extract related tags networks to capture different

Figure 55. " Tianjin" related tags network on Flickr® (1.5 deg.)

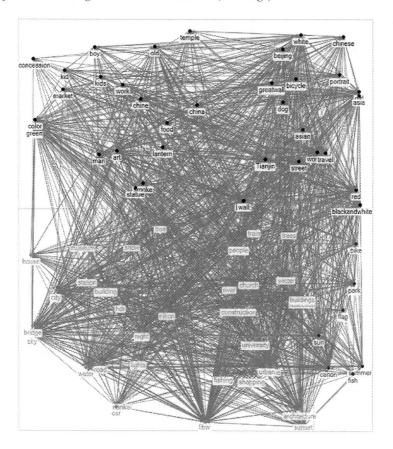

Figure 56. " Tianjin" related tags network on Flickr® (2 deg.) (2014 and 2015)

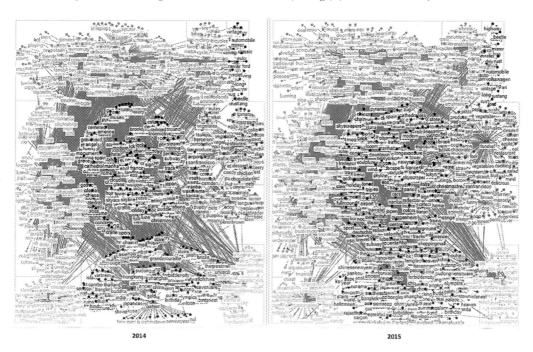

2014   2015

Figure 57. " Urumqi" Related Tags Network on Flickr® (1 deg.)

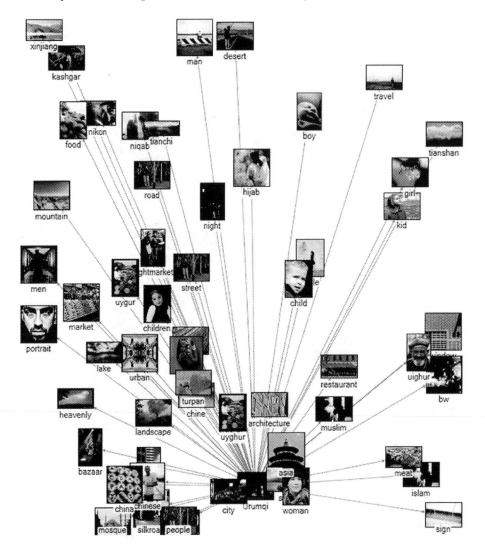

information. In this case, the related tags networks resulted in tags addressing aspects of daily life activities (and tourism activities) in the respective cities, important landmarks, geolocational information, travel destinations, related cities (culturally, geographically), political structures, wildlife and nature, and technical aspects of photography.

In exploring these particular results, it may help to explore some other questions:

1. What are some recurring related tags that may be seen across cities?
2. What are some recurring tag clusters across cities? (such as b/w, types of cameras, landmarks, activities, cultural aspects like religions, language insights, and historical events)?
3. What is the relative popularity of the respective cities based on cross-city related tags networks comparisons and contrasts?

Figure 58. " Urumqi" related tags network on Flickr® (1.5 deg.)

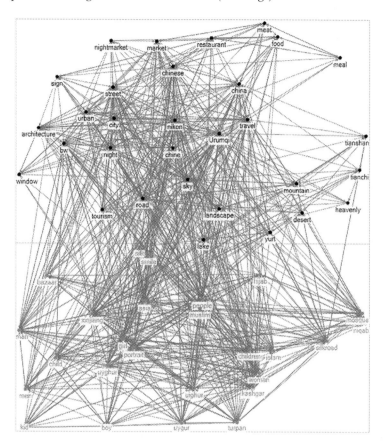

Figure 59. " Urumqi" related tags network on Flickr® (2 deg.) (2014 and 2015)

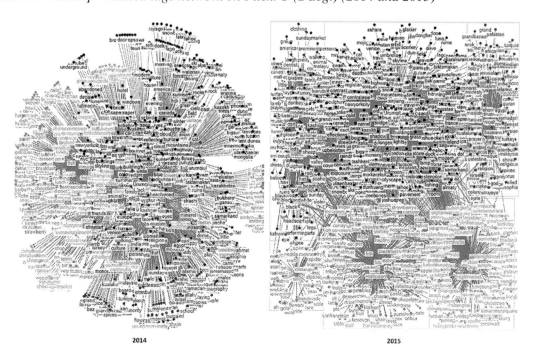

Figure 60. " Wuhan" related tags network on Flickr® (1 deg.)

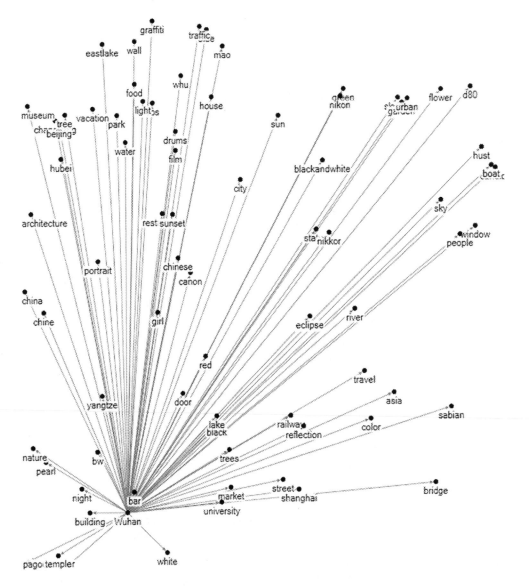

4. What are some cultural insights about the respective cities based on the related tags networks on Flickr?

5. What are potential causes of (geo)locational patterns in related tags networks?

6. How well do related tags networks "represent" or evoke particular cities (or locations) at 1 deg., 1.5 deg., and at 2 deg.? What city information is not addressed in the tags?

7. How do related tags networks seeded with the names of particular cities evolve over time? What do these changes show about the collection of imagery and videos? What do the changes suggest about the city and its environs and its peoples? What do changes in related tags networks suggest about the tagging savvy of the users? (How do such related tags networks compare across social media platforms, and what may be learned by comparing such related tags networks based on different underlying social media platforms)?

Figure 61. " Wuhan" related tags network on Flickr® (1.5 deg.)

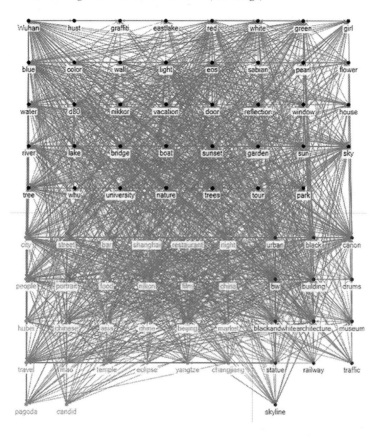

Figure 62. " Wuhan" related tags network on Flickr® (2 deg.) (2014 and 2015)

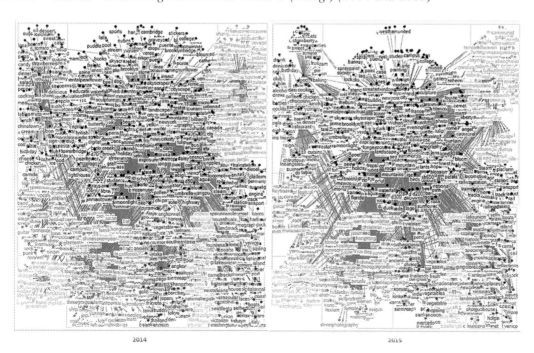

Figure 63. " Xiamen" related tags network on Flickr® (1 deg.)

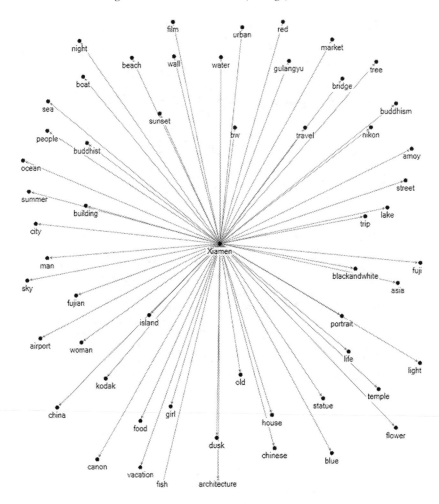

8. What sorts of sentiment analysis may be applied to various cities or locales through the related tags? How may these be accurately understood?
9. How do the related tags networks surrounding cities compare with direct tag analysis of tags linked to particular images or particular videos?
10. As compared to the personal tagging on various images from the related Flickr® dataset, what sorts of information does not show up in the related tags networks? What unique tags (even while popular) are used to identify particular cities, and are they fairly evocative? Does the "threshold" or "filter: for such tags (only including the most popular ones) mean that certain idiosyncratic tags never make it into the related tags network?

Querying Related Tags Networks

To generalize from this approach, a wide variety of other questions may be asked but would be specific to the research questions and the respective domains. Broad and generic questions that may be asked from the analysis of related tags networks from Flickr could include the following:

Figure 64. " Xiamen" related tags network on Flickr® (1.5 deg.)

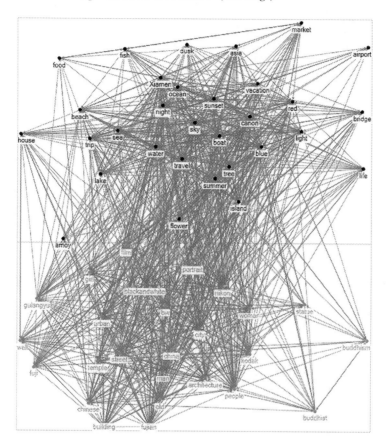

Figure 65. " XIamen" related tags network on Flickr® (2 deg.) (2014 and 2015)

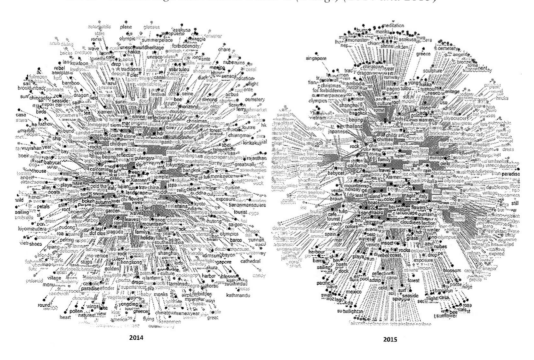

2014   2015

Figure 66. " Xian" related tags network on Flickr® (1 deg.)

Basics

- What related tags are evoked in relation to a particular seeding or source tag?
- What are the relationships between the tags? What are some possible explanations for the respective tags' co-occurrence?

Fresh Seeding Terms

- Any sort of word (well beyond city names) may be used as a seeding term, even if it seems that initially there may not be any tagging using that particular term. For example, emotions and sentiments, brands, people's names, symbols, numbers, technologies, and other content sets may be used to draw out relatedness.

Figure 67. " Xian" related tags network on Flickr® (1.5 deg.)

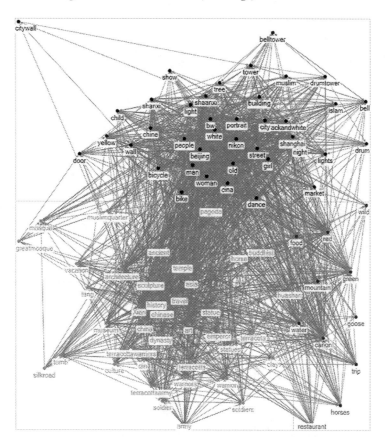

Figure 68. " Xian" related tags network on Flickr® (2 deg.) (2014 and 2015)

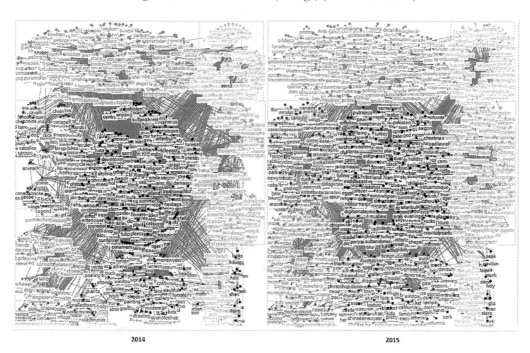

2014   2015

Interventions

- What are some ways to change the outcomes of tagging behaviors, to either create new ties or to reduce or disappear current ones? (For example, if a brand is linked with a negative phenomenon, is there a way to lessen that sense of a tie?)

FUTURE RESEARCH DIRECTIONS

Related tags networks enable the exploration of metadata built on big data. The extracted networks may be used for discovery and providing leads for further research. They may offer a sense of word-based and light visual thumbnail-based gist of the topic. While tags are machine-extracted based on co-occurrence relationship, there is clearly an important role for human analysis. Some simple questions about related tags networks may be:

- What are the relationships between the extracted tags in a particular cluster? Is there a way to summarize the tags in a cluster such as the defining of extracted variables in a data-reducing principal component analysis?
- What is the relevance of dense transitivity connections in a 1.5 degree related tags network vs. sparse transitivity connections? Do dense connections suggest a large underlying dataset of images and video with many shared understandings of tags? Do sparse connections suggest that the collective human taggers do not share common understandings of the image and video contents that they are uploading? Does it mean that the content set in Flickr® is sparse? Does a sparse 1.5-degree network suggest that the image and video contents are in the early stages of collection?
- Which "alters" tags tend to have more connections, and why? What might explain their connectivity or co-occurrence with other related tags?
- What does tag co-occurrence suggest about the context of the tags' usage and their meaning (as extrapolated from the context)?
- What may be asserted about related tags networks with fewer clusters (2-3) vs. those with more (8 – 12)? Does the prior have less diversity and the latter have more diversity of concepts? Of image and video contents (in the underlying data)?
- What information does not show up then in related tags networks? Related image analysis? Related video analysis? (If the underlying dataset of images is fully available, what may be seen by comparing the related tags network and its underlying content dataset?)

More generally, this approach does show how related tags networks offer a "skim" of the underlying data, albeit with a full sense of how the resulting networks were extracted (such as the threshold that must be met for a tag to be included in a particular related tags network). At this point, it is still not clear how extracted related tags networks may be cross-checked and cross-referenced and verified, except by direct data scraping access to the Flickr® API and the mapping of those results using another network graphing tool and conducting direct comparisons. It may be that there will be additional information available about each of the steps in Figure 2 where the resulting related tags network may be influenced.

Light Assertions

The unique aspects of the related tags networks aside, there are some light assertions that may be made from the respective related tags networks: the direct ties of related tags at 1 degree, the transitivity at 1.5 degrees, and the dispersion of meaning and the explosions of complexity at 2 degrees. At a very high level, tags that are collectively associated by co-occurrence may reveal something about people's perceived and lived experiences as they interact around imagery and videos on the Flickr® social media platform. The inclusion of related thumbnail imagery may convey hints of visuals. Delving into the multi-lingual nature of tags may shed light on geographical regionalisms, languages, and cultures.

Some of the questions that may be asked and partially answered using such related tags networks include the following:

1. Is it possible to use extracted tags as a summary of the underlying image and video contents? What sorts of image- and video- contents (in the Flickr® collection) may be inferred from the pithy related tags? Are there gaps in imagery that may be identified?
2. What do the related tags networks suggest about the state of tagging (particularly around the seeded topic)?
3. What sorts of parts-of-speech are represented in related tags networks? What languages?
4. What are some ways you would describe each of the clusters in the related tags groupings?
5. What cultural information may be ascertained from related tags networks from social media platforms?
6. What are ways to use synonyms and transforms to access different related tags networks around the same topic?
7. What do the related tags networks suggest about the people and groups who are doing the tagging? (How much confidence may be placed in the research impressions?)
8. Why are related tags networks so apparently static and little-changing? (Is this a factor of how Flickr® creates these or of the fact that the results only cull a few groups from a large dataset or a mix of tags?)
9. Is there a benefit to extracted related tags networks of outlier tags, and what would those possibly show instead of the most probable or likely tag associations?
10. What are systematic ways to identify related tags that are most promising to pursue for further research?
11. What are some non-intuitive sorts of seeding terms that may be used to evoke elusive meanings—such as the uses of particular symbols, emotions, phrases, equations, or other terms?
12. Is it possible to identify geography and cultural influences of various taggers by their word choices?
13. Is it possible to see how related tags networks look with auto-tagging vs. without auto-tagging?

There are various ways to explore the dimensionality of tags. For example, the digital contents—the imagery, the videos—may be extracted and analyzed as the contents related to the tags. [Thumbnail images related to a particular tag may be part of the data extraction, but such samples are only very fleetingly and superficially representational. Of the literally tens of millions of potential candidate images for a particular tag, why was a particular one chosen? Was the selection done by machine or by human? What were the criteria for the image selection, or was the selection purely random? It is unclear how Flickr® has linked such thumbnails to particular tags, but specific recurring thumbnails are used to represent the tags. In some related tags networks, there are no available thumbnails for illustration.

The geolocational data may be analyzed. The physical regions around which particular tags were used may surface other insights. One team used explorative pattern mining to create profiles of locations using Flickr (Lemmerich & Atzmueller, 2011). The time aspect of the tagging may be observed, in order to see when individuals who've participated in using particular tags may have engaged with the platform. Social networks around particular tags may be extracted and analyzed.

If the seeding terms are of various kinds, the resulting related tags networks may be explored based on unique features of those.

- For example, if the seeding terms are based on an event or shared human activity, what may be seen about those types of related tags networks? What language do participants use to describe their activity?
- If there is an original social phenomenon or new technology, what are the related tags networks around that?
- If a popular personality or real-life individual is used to seed a related tags network, what may be seen in those related tags networks?
- If a latitude-longitude or other physical place marker is used to seed a related tags network, what may be seen in that type of related tags network?

Using the Flickr® social media platform and NodeXL, the two resources used for the capture of related tags networks, it is possible to also capture user networks, with formal declared friending and also ad hoc relationships created by commenting on Flicrk imagery and videos. These data extractions may complement related tags networks, particularly if there are certain user accounts which are high contributors to particular tags and data sets. There are also ways to capture information about Flickr® groups and networks related to their members and image and video artifacts.

CONCLUSION

This chapter introduced related tags networks focused on a select list of cities in modern China as seeding terms; these networks were extracted from Flickr® at 1, 1.5, and 2 degrees, using NodeXL. As such, this work explores a case of the use of metadata for informational value, based on a limited use case.

This chapter provided a sense of some of the questions that may be asked. This approach assumes that the technologies remain static and unchanging. That is clearly not a realistic assumption. There are constant changes with technologies. Any of a number of changes will affect the dependencies referred to in Figure 2. For example, if the related tags networks go out another half-degree or a whole degree, what other insights may be possible (balanced against what introduced noise and what network graph unwieldiness)? What if the thumbnail images were canonical and representative of the particular tag set, what could be learned from that? What if the depicted images were partially morphs of the set, what could be discovered from that? (For example, would visual patterns from the collected imagery possibly emerge and provide new human insights?)

The research value of exploring related tags networks is only just beginning to be explored by researchers. This explains the dearth of research citations of prior work. This work contributes a light approach to such data extractions and analysis. Certainly, there are a number of ways to build on this research approach and this light work.

ACKNOWLEDGMENT

I am grateful to the team supporting NodeXL Basic for making this tool available. The topic for this chapter was selected in part based on my four years living and working in the People's Republic of China, at Jiangxi Normal University (Nanchang, Jiangxi Province) and Northeast Agriculture University (Harbin, Heilongjiang Province). Also, thanks to those who critiqued this chapter for their helpful insights.

REFERENCES

Abbasi, R., Chernov, S., Nejdl, W., Paiu, R., & Staab, S. (2009). Exploiting Flickr tags and groups for finding landmark photos. In Proceedings of the CIR 2009, (LNCS), (vol. 5478, pp. 654-661). Springer-Verlag.

Ames, M., & Naaman, M. (2007). Why we tag: Motivations for annotation I mobile and online media. In *Proceedings of CHI 2007 Tags, Tagging & Notetaking*.

Angus, E., Thelwall, M., & Stuart, D. (2008). General patterns of tag usage among university groups in Flickr. *Online Information Review, 32*(1), 89 – 101. DOI .10.1108/14684520810866001

Artiles, J., Gonzalo, J., López-Ostenero, F., & Peinado, V. (2007). Are users willing to search cross-language? An experiment with the Flickr image sharing repository. Evaluation of Multilingual and Multi-modal Information Retrieval. *Lecture Notes in Computer Science, 4730*, 195–204.

Begelman, G., Keller, P., & Smadja, F. (2006). Automated tag clustering: Improving search and exploration in the tag space. In *Proceedings of WWW 2006*.

Bolognesi. (2012, Oct. 3). *Average number of tags associated to each photo?* FlickrAPI Group. Retrieved June 23, 2015, from https://www.flickr.com/groups/api/discuss/72157631682781762/

Cha, M., Mislove, A., Adams, B., & Gummadi, K. P. (2008). Characterizing social cascades in Flickr. In Proceedings of WOSN '08. doi:10.1145/1397735.1397739

Cha, M., Mislove, A., & Gummadi, K. P. (2009). A measurement-driven analysis of information propagation in the Flickr social network. In *Proceedings of the WWW 2009*. doi:10.1145/1526709.1526806

Chen, X., & Shin, H. (2010). Extracting representative tags for Flickr users. In *Proceedings of the 2010 IEEE International Conference on Data Mining Workshops*. doi:10.1109/ICDMW.2010.117

Clements, M., Serdyukov, P., de Vries, A. P., & Reinders, M. J. T. (2010). Using Flickr geotags to predict user travel behaviour. In *Proceedings of SIGIR '10*. doi:10.1145/1835449.1835648

Cox, A. M., Clough, P. D., & Marlow, J. (2008). Flickr: A first look at user behaviour in the context of photography as serious leisure. *Information Research, 13*(1), 1–19.

De Meo, P., Ferrara, E., Abel, F., Aroyo, L., & Houben, G-J. (2013). Analyzing user behavior across social sharing environments. *ACM Transactions on Intelligent Systems and Technologies, 5*(1), Article 14. DOI:10.1145/2535526

Deemter, K. V. (2010). Not Exactly. In *Praise of Vagueness*. Oxford, UK: Oxford University Press.

Golbeck, J., Koepfler, J., & Emmerling, B. (2011). An experimental study of social tagging behavior and image content. *Journal of the American Society for Information Science and Technology, 62*(9), 1750–1760. doi:10.1002/asi.21522

Heckner, M., Neubauer, T., & Wolff, C. (2008). Tree, funny, to_read, google: What are tags supposed to achieve? In Proceedings of SSM '08.

Hietanen, H., Athukorala, K., & Salovaara, A. (2011). What's with the free images? A study of Flickr's Creative Commons attribution images. In *Proceedings of MindTrek '11*.

Hollsenstein, L., & Purves, R. S. (2010). Exploring place through user-generated content: Using Flickr tags to describe city cores. *Journal of Spatial Information Science, 1*, 21–48. doi:10.5311/JOSIS.2010.1.3

Huiskes, M. J., & Lew, M. S. (2008). The MIR Flickr retrieval evaluation. In *Proceedings of MIR '08*. doi:10.1145/1460096.1460104

Jett, J., Senseney, M., & Palmer, C. L. (2012). Enhancing cultural heritage collections by supporting and analyzing participation in Flickr. In *Proceedings of ASIST 2012*. doi:10.1002/meet.14504901287

Kennedy, L., Naaman, M., Ahern, S., Nair, R., & Rattenbury, T. (2007). How Flickr helps us make sense of the world: context and content in community-contributed media collections. In *Proceedings of MM '07*. doi:10.1145/1291233.1291384

Kennedy, L. S., Chang, S. F., & Kozintsev, V. (2006). To search or to label? Predicting the performance of search-based automatic image classifiers. In *Proceedings of the 8th ACM International Workshop on Multimedia Information Retrieval*.

Kipp, M. E. I., Buchel, O., & Neal, D. R. (2012). Exploring digital information using tags and local knowledge. In *Proceedings of ASIST 2012*. doi:10.1002/meet.14504901318

Lemmerich, F., & Atzmueller, M. (2011). Modeling location-based profiles of social image media using explorative pattern mining. In *Proceedings of the 2011 IEEE International Conference on Privacy, Security, Risk, and Trust, and IEEE International Conference on Social Computing*. doi:10.1109/PASSAT/SocialCom.2011.186

Lerman, K., & Jones, L. A. (2006). *Social browsing on Flickr*. arXiv:cs/0612047v1

Lerman, K., Plangprasopchok, A., & Wong, C. (2007). Personalizing image search results on Flickr. Association for the Advancement of Artificial Intelligence.

Liu, D., Hua, X.-S., Wang, M., & Zhang, H.-J. (2010). Retagging social images based on visual and semantic consistency. In *Proceedings of WWW 2010*. doi:10.1145/1772690.1772848

Liu, D., Hua, X.-S., Yang, L., Wang, M., & Zhang, H.-J. (2009). Tag ranking. In *Proceedings of 18*th *International Conference on World Wide Web 2009*. doi:10.1145/1526709.1526757

Marlow, C., Naaman, M., boyd, d., & Davis, M. (2006). HT06, tagging paper, taxonomy, Flickr, academic article, to read. In *Proceedings of HT'06*.

Mislove, A., Koppula, H. S., Gummadi, K. P., Druschel, P., & Bhattacharjee, B. (2008). Growth of the Flickr social network. In Proceedings of the WO SN '08. doi:10.1145/1397735.1397742

Negoescu, R.-A., & Gatica-Perez, D. (2008). Analyzing Flickr groups. In *Proceedings of CIVR '08*. doi:10.1145/1386352.1386406

Nov, O., Naaman, M., & Ye, C. (2009). Analysis of participation in an online photo-sharing community: A multidimensional perspective. *Journal of the American Society for Information Science and Technology, 61*(3), 555–566.

Nov, O., & Ye, C. (2010). Why do people tag? Motivations for photo tagging. *Communications of the ACM, 53*(7), 128–131. doi:10.1145/1785414.1785450

Oh, S. & Syn, S.Y. (2015). Motivations for sharing information and social support in social media: A comparative analysis of Facebook, Twitter, Delicious, YouTube, and Flickr. *Journal of the Association for Information Science and Technology*, 1 - 16.

Pennebaker, J. W. (2011). *The Secret Life of Pronouns: What our Words Say about Us*. New York Bloomsbury Press.

Popescu, A., & Grefenstette, G. (2010). Mining user home location and gender from Flickr tags. In *Proceedings of the 4*th *International AAAI Conference on Weblogs and Social Media*.

Prieur, C., Cardon, D., Beuscart, J. S., Pissard, N., & Pons, P. (2008). *The strength of weak cooperation*. Retrieved May 30, 2015, from http://arxiv.org/ftp/arxiv/papers/0802/0802.2317.pdf

Rafferty, P., & Hidderley, R. (2007). Flickr and Democratic indexing¨ Dialogic approaches to indexing. *New Information Perspectives, 59*(4/5), 397–410.

Rattenbury, T., Good, N., & Naaman, M. (2007). Towards automatic extraction of event and place semantics from Flickr tags. In *Proceedings of SIGIR 2007*. doi:10.1145/1277741.1277762

Rorissa, A. (2010). A comparative study of Flickr tags and index terms in a general image collection. *Journal of the American Society for Information Science and Technology, 61*(11), 2230–2242. doi:10.1002/asi.21401

Schmitz, P. (2006). Inducing ontology from Flickr tags. In *Proceedings of the WWW 2006*.

Schupak, A. (2015, July 1). Google apologizes for mis-tagging photos of African Americans. *CBS News*. Retrieved July 2, 2015, from http://www.cbsnews.com/news/google-photos-labeled-pics-of-african-americans-as-gorillas/

Serdyukov, P., Murdock, V., & Van Zwol, R. (2009). Placing Flickr photos on a map. In *Proceedings of SIGR '09*. doi:10.1145/1571941.1572025

Sigurbjörnsson, B., & van Zwol, R. (2008). Flickr tag recommendation based on collective knowledge. In *Proceedings of the WWW 2008*. doi:10.1145/1367497.1367542

Singla, A., & Weber, I. (2009). Camera brand congruence in the Flickr social graph. In *Proceedings of WISDM '09*. Retrieved June 23, 2015, from https://www.flickr.com/groups/api/discuss/72157631682781762/

Stvilia, B., & Jörgensen, C. (2007/2008). End-user collection building behavior in Flickr. In *Proceedings of the American Society for Information Science and Technology*.

Stvilia, B., & Jörgensen, C. (2010). Member activities and quality of tags in a collection of historical photographs in Flickr. *Journal of the American Society for Information Science and Technology*, *61*(12), 2477–2489. doi:10.1002/asi.21432

Sun, A., & Bhowmick, S. S. (2010). Quantifying tag representativeness of visual content of social images. In *Proceedings of MM '10*. doi:10.1145/1873951.1874029

Thomas-Jones, A. (2010). *Putting the social in social networks. In The Host in the Machine: Examining the Digital in the Social* (pp. 57–75). Oxford, UK: Chandos.

Tik, J. (2005). Why is Flickr so successful? *Flickr Central*. Retrieved May 30, 2015, from https://www.flickr.com/groups/central/discuss/36512/

Troil. (2010, Mar. 21). In *Urban Dictionary*. Retrieved June 20, 2015, from http://www.urbandictionary.com/define.php?term=troil

Vander Wal, T. (2007, Feb. 2). *Folksonomy*. Retrieved June 22, 2015, from http://www.vanderwal.net/folksonomy.html

Walker, J. (2005). Feral hypertext: When hypertext literature escapes control. In Proceedings of HT '05.

Wu, L., Hua, X.-S., Yu, N., Ma, W.-Y., & Li, S. (2008). Flickr distance. In *Proceedings of MM'08*. doi:10.1145/1459359.1459364

Yanai, K., Kawakubo, H., & Barnard, K. (2012). Entropy-based analysis of visual and geolocation concepts in images. In Multimedia Information Extraction: Advances In Video, Audio, And Imagery Analysis For Search, Data Mining, Surveillance, And Authoring. John Wiley & Sons, Inc.

You, S., DesArmo, J., & Joo, S. (2013). Measuring happiness of U.S. cities by mining user-generated text in Flickr.com: A pilot analysis. In *Proceedings of ASIST 2013*.

Zhu, Y.-Q., & Chen, H.-G. (2015). Social media and human need satisfaction: Implications for social media marketing. *Business Horizons*, *58*(3), 335–345. doi:10.1016/j.bushor.2015.01.006

ADDITIONAL READING

Hansen, D. L., Schneiderman, B., & Smith, M. A. (2011). *Analyzing Social Media Networks with NodeXL: Insights from a Connected World*. Amsterdam: Elsevier.

KEY TERMS AND DEFINITIONS

Algorithm: A set of instructions or process for a computer to achieve a particular function or problem-solving.

Bag: A set of words with some recurring terms.

Co-occurrence: Concurrence or coincidence (relationship) in the same text "set" or "bag" or "corpus".

End user license agreement (EULA): A legally binding agreement between users of a service and the providers of the service.

Exchangeable image file format (EXIF): A standard defining formats for digital imagery.

Folksonomy (also known as an "ethnoclassification"): A collaboratively created folk+taxonomy or metadata structure of labels for objects, with the "folk" describing the non-expert aspects of bottom-up popular tagging and the "taxonomy" referring to a classification structure.

Geolocation: Identifying the physical location of a thing (such as from online information).

Geotag: Metadata about a digital resource that indicates precise physical location of that object (or the location of its capture).

Gist: The central essence of a thing.

Graph: A diagram depicting entities and the relationships between the entities.

Invariant: A "constant" variable or factor that is unchanging.

Lat-long: Latitude and longitude coordinates to indicate a specific location on Earth.

Metadata: Data about data (including tags that describe digital contents).

Morph: A combined image comprised of a number of other images (in this case referred to in a static vs. dynamic form).

Open tagging: A freeform approach to folk tagging of objects.

Repository: A collection of objects, often curated.

Robot: An automated agent.

Semantics: Meaning-bearing words.

Set: A set of words without any redundancy.

Tag: A freeform or unstructured keyword used to label images and videos on Flickr.

Tag recommender: A system that identifies similar or related terms to a human tagger (usually for a more complete set of labels for a digital object).

User: An individual or group which accesses particular online services, such as those of a content-sharing social media platform.

Chapter 12

Real–Time Sentiment Analysis of Microblog Messages with the Maltego "Tweet Analyzer" Machine

Shalin Hai-Jew
Kansas State University, USA

ABSTRACT

For social media to work as a "human sensor network" or a relevant source for "eventgraphing" for some fast-moving events, it is important to be capture real-time and locational information. It may help to not only capture information from a particular social media platform but from across the Web. In such a context, Maltego Carbon 3.5.3/Chlorine 3.6.0's Tweet Analyser "machine" (with AlchemyAPI built-in) and used in combination with other "transforms," may serve the purpose—at least for initial and iterated sampling of the related messaging. This tool may be used to capture information from social media accounts.. social media accounts, linked URLs, geolocational information, and other information of research value. Maltego is an open-access tool with a community version and a proprietary commercial version available by subscription. Maltego Chlorine's Tweet Analyzer has a built-in sentiment analysis feature.

INTRODUCTION

Whether explicit or implicit, part of the social media "bargain" that some social media companies have made with the general public is to not only ingest people's data, but to share the public-facing information. Such sharing involves corporate citizenship and good public relations. It enables datamining research that is value-added to the collected data. These companies enable open-access to some of their data through application programming interfaces (API) instead of merely leveraging the data for advertising and in-company research purposes. Content that is publicly released by their respective creators (the social media users) is available to the masses, and the privately held information is available based on

DOI: 10.4018/978-1-5225-0846-5.ch012

authenticated access (usually those of the original content creator). For most social media platforms, access is enabled by registering with the target social media platform service (usually with email-verified accounts) and the use of access keys. Those using software applications to access social media platform databases often use proper OAUTH (an open standard used to enable resource owners to authorize third parties to access server resources, without revealing who is making the query). A majority of social media holdings are open-access, with very low costs of entry. (Command-line access through high-level programming languages is enabled through the Web and Internet; third-party software tools—many of them open-source and free—enable easier data access and data visualizations.)

Twitter, one of the world's foremost microblogging sites, has long been a favorite with datamining researchers and the broad public. Twitter has enabled access via its application programming interfaces (APIs), enabling two broad types of data capture: the extraction of captured recent historical data (static) and also real-time (or near real-time) and continuous streaming data (dynamic). The static API enables the download of public streams (multi-user streams and topic streams), user streams (single users), and site streams (multiple stream extractions simultaneously, used for servers) ("The Streaming APIs," 2015). The streaming and iterated API enables the near-real-time capture of emergent communications. This feature may be used as a perpetual or continuously-running dashboard.

While developers have tapped into Twitter's APIs and scraped data (in Javascript Object Notation / JSON; comma separated values / .csv formats; hypertext markup language / HTML, and extensible markup language / XML), the general public itself has often had limited access—often through software tools, web interfaces, or limited applications. This lack of access is especially the case for continuous or dynamic data extractions. Also, most research require close human readings of the captured messaging and trained coding for sensemaking. Most researchers do not have the access to sentiment analysis tools or content network creation tools based on the extracted contents.

A new "machine" in Maltego Carbon 3.5.3 / Chlorine 3.6.0, though, enables near real-time topic-based microblogging extractions from Twitter and near real-time sentiment analysis (with the built-in AlchemyAPI for English language text, not the Unicode characters). In addition, the other affordances of this software tool—extracting data from the Surface Web—means that researchers that are interested in using this to capture a sense of the fast-changing collective mindset (as expressed on both Twitter and on the Surface Web) may be able to achieve a fairly broad and accurate sampling of unfolding events and / or socio-cultural phenomena. Researchers can reach out beyond a (somewhat porously) bounded system and into the larger Web and Internet ecosystems. The affordances of this "machine" (a designed macro) are tailor-made for using Twitter data for a "human sensor network" (the usage of on-ground data shared from social media accounts) and for "eventgraphing" (mapping out unfolding events). Knowing real-world sentiments enable individuals to both react and pro-act, such as to correct misperceptions, particularly when there is a level of broad-scale predictivity about the direction of public opinion based on a particular topic or issue (Nguyen, Wu, Chan, Peng, & Zhang, 2012, p. 1).

In the literature, both approaches are important use cases for human awareness of in-world events. This chapter introduces the Tweet Analyser™ "machine" with a few real-world examples. The data extractions and data visualizations for this chapter were conducted using the proprietary versions of Maltego Carbon 3.5.3 and Chlorine 3.6.0; there is also a community and open-source version of this tool but with a cap on the amount of nodes extracted (the community version tops out at a dozen vertices; the proprietary version enables extractions of over 10,000+). Even with 10,000 nodes, that may not actually be at-scale of what is available.

Delimitations

Maltego Chlorine 3.6.0 was created as a penetration "pen" testing tool to probe weaknesses and vulnerabilities for online networks. Since the tool's creation eight years ago, Paterva, a S. African-based software company, has evolved the tool through various iterations, and it is currently one of the foremost Web security tools available. IBM is the company behind AlchemyAPI. While it has a predominant position in network security and intrusion detection, it also has application in academic and other research (Hai-Jew, 2014). This chapter highlights a particular "machine" or scripted function for data collection on the Surface Web. Within Maltego Chlorine, there are dozens of "machines" and numerous "transforms," and each may be used in a stand-alone way, or in combination with others. The "transform" method of disambiguating what an entity is is by "entity linking" or seeing what other relationships it has with other nodes. The Tweet Analyzer functions should not be conflated with an overview of Maltego Chlorine, which has numerous other functions. Also, this approach describes one general "use case" of in-world event awareness (and engagement), but the Tweet Analyser itself may be applied in a wide range of other applications as well. A "transform" in Maltego refers to the ability to link various types of information to other correlated information on the Surface Web; for example, an "alias" may be transformed into personally identifiable information (PII), a phone number, an email, a social media account, and so on. [Note: All other references to the Tweet Analyzer machine will use the American English spelling.]

Review of the Literature

To simplify, a "human sensor network" is supposed to enable awareness of real-world on-ground events based on their folk-reportage from the frontlines of whatever events are occurring. "Eventgraphing" refers to the mapping out of a particular event, particularly the individuals who are participating in and communicating about that event on social media. The idea is that somewhere in this cyber-physical confluence, there are insights to be had: trending opinions, popular concepts, influential individuals, influential clusters, geographical phenomena, and other potential drivers (vs. barriers)-to-action.

Twitter for Real-World Awareness

In some ways, the inherent design and culture of Twitter make it a powerful tool for situational awareness and datamining. The 140-character limitation per message forces a succinctness and focus, often resulting in the stripping out of structural aspects of language. Known as the "SMS (short message service) of the Internet," Twitter is about brevity; it is about being in the moment and sharing status updates about what is top-of-mind. The ease of text, photo, and video updates—calling up the Twitter site or a related app and hitting "Tweet"—is nominal. The installed base of users includes 288 million monthly active users, and 500 million Tweets sent per day; some 77% of the accounts are not within the U.S. ("About," 2015) The social media platform supports 33 languages. It has 40 million Vine (video service) users. The speed of information sharing does not encourage the oversight of the executive mind or the "internal censor" that might control what people share. Shared video and imagery may be done without full vetting of what has actually been captured and is knowable from the data. If there is data leakage at the individual level, this is multiply-so for a range of accounts. In addition to the information that may be ascertained en masse, there are also other types of information capturable such as geolocational information [from account tagging, message tagging, and exchangeable image file format (EXIF) data in digital photos and digital video]. Ideally, real-time data for awareness would include both the time and the physical space of particular messaging, and there would be a fast machine-read of the data for issues that merit fast attention.

On Sentiment Analysis

One mass-scale study of messaging in both Facebook and Twitter found that a majority of the messaging tended to be neutral (77.26% on Facebook and 67.27% on Twitter), and then, of those broadly identified as containing sentiment…to be mostly positive (14.74% on Facebook, and 25.88% on Twitter) and a minority as negative (8% on Facebook, 6.85% on Twitter). (Lucia, Akcora, & Ferrari, 2013, p. 372). The researchers note that Facebook friends tend to be real-life acquaintances, with messages directed to a more private audience, whereas Twitter followers may often be non-real-life acquaintances and messages directed to a more public audience (p. 371). These findings may be helpful to offer a rough baseline of understandings of sentiment in social media messaging. In this case, it helps to understand that sentiment is not broadly distributed across all messaging and that expressed sentiments tend towards the positive. In the cited study, the studied dataset consisted of ten of the most recent messages of 11 million Twitter user accounts, with the messaging posted between 2008 and 2013; the actual crawl or data extraction occurred between December 2012 – 2013 (Lucia, Akcora, & Ferrari, 2013, p. 370).

In terms of the integrated AlchemyAPI, the makers of this tool describe how their machine learning algorithm has been trained on a training set of 200+ billion words—through the use of text from the Web. (To stay up-to-date, the algorithm is re-trained monthly to stay atop the current uses of online English.) The AlchemyAPI approach to textual analysis involves both a combined linguistic and statistical analysis technique to account for the lack of traditional linguistic structure and amount of noise in Tweeted data. Gangemi (2013) summarized: "AlchemyAPI uses machine learning and natural language parsing technology for analyzing web or text-based content for named entity extraction, sense tagging, as well as for relationships and topics" (p. 357). In a whitepaper released by the makers of this tool, the approach taken to accommodate data from social media is explained:

Linguistic analysis takes a basic grammatical approach to understand how words combine into phrases, and how those phrases combine into sentences. While this approach works well with editorialized text (e.g., news articles and press releases), it does not perform as well when it comes to user-generated content, often filled with slang, misspellings and idioms. Statistical analysis, however, understands language from a mathematical standpoint and works well on "noisy" content (e.g., tweets, blog posts, and Facebook status updates). The combination of these two approaches allows for increased accuracy on a variety of content. ("Sentiment analysis with AlchemyAPI: A hybrid approach," 2013).

The brevity of microblogging messages is a challenge for those using computers to disambiguate the meanings and the communicator intentions.

Sentiment analysis of tweets data is considered as a much harder problem than that of conventional text such as review documents. This is partly due to the short length of tweets, the frequent use of informal and irregular words, and the rapid evolution of language in Twitter (Saif, He, & Alani, 2012, p. 510)

In another sense, the succinctness of Tweets forces some degree of fast-editing for those sharing messages (as does the character count-down in Twitter). While AlchemyAPI is capable of deeply nuanced analysis based on semantics and on adjectival and adverbial descriptors [negation words (which change the polarity or direction of the assertion), amplifiers (words that strengthen the emphasis or intensity of the assertion), diminishers (words that weaken the emphasis or intensity)], what may be seen in Maltego Carbon / Chlorine's Tweet Analyzer is an indicator of basic polarities: positive, negative, and neutral. The machine collection and (sentiment) analysis of such messaging may be done at Web scale with sufficient computational processing and storage capabilities. Web 2.0, the Social Web, offers plenty of possibilities for opinion mining (Petz, Karpowicz, Fürschuβ, Auinger, Stríteský, & Holzinger, 2014).

Maltego Carbon 3.5.3 and Chlorine 3.6.0's Tweet Analyzer

Finally, it may help to have a sense of how the Tweet Analyzer works. Essentially, this tool is seeded with some text that indicates a conversation of interest; the request runs through Paterva servers, and the data is captured and communicated in network graph format (along with an "entity list" data table). As with most other cases of network analysis, the levels of analysis may be micro, meso, and macro; the data may be analyzed in as granular an entity as a node (or link), a motif, a cluster, or the entire network (for which general metrics are available). The data may also be extracted (albeit a little awkwardly) for data visualizations and analysis in other tools.

In a live-and-real-time context, with large amounts of trending data, it is fully possible to hit data limits on one machine, and it may make more sense for some to having the iterations running on multiple machines and data collection happening in a staggered sequence—unless an improved collection environment is possible (or unless the pruning machine is used to delete irrelevant information). Clearly, for multiple analyses to co-occur, it may help to have a server version of Maltego installed, and the server version of this tool does enable real-time collaborative communications.

In this work, Maltego's Tweet Analyzer enables the capturing of a gist and a glimpse of an unfolding issue. Even at the maximum of 10,000-nodes, given Twitter's capabilities, that amount may be a small amount of the messaging available on the target text (which itself may only capture a portion of the communications on the particular trending event or topic). For an actual N = all, and real-time captures for high-value real-time decision-making, going with the commercial company that has direct access to the Twitter "firehose" and to at-scale sentiment analysis is advisable. Also, given the fast decay of such information and the dynamics of fast-moving events, a more organized approach to such tracking would be necessary to create actual real-time awareness.

ENGAGING PUBLIC OPINION OF EVENTS AND SOCIO-CULTURAL PHENOMENA THROUGH DYNAMIC TWEET EXTRACTIONS AND SENTIMENT ANALYSIS

To illustrate how the Tweet Analyzer works, several trending terms were selected based on some basic criteria.

- The terms have to reflect an issue with potential global implications. The issues have to be of sufficient interest and high publicity to result in microblogging messages from multiple global locations and to capture multi-lingual messaging. The social networks forming around the conversation should be geographically disparate and varied.

- There should be a macro sense of a large-scale conversation, not just localized ones about large-scale issues.
- There has to be a sense of the issue being highly popular or "trending," in order to capture a sense of the "event" and simultaneity.
- The topic should also have related websites and other presences on the Web and Internet in order to showcase Maltego's capabilities beyond the Tweet Analyzer (although those capabilities will only be minimally and peripherally introduced).

Often, such issues have a lot of play on mass media, demonstrating in part their agenda-setting influence. For each of the Tweet Analyzer data extractions, there were at least two iterations. The number of nodes was set to 10,000, so as not to artificially limit the tool. However, the rate-limiting aspects of Twitter meant that the initial extraction only runs for a minute or two before pausing for 240 seconds (four minutes) before the next run. Time variations may occur based on a number of factors, such as the popularity of the search term, the parameters of the data extraction (whether 12, 50, 255, or 10,000+ vertices are desired), how many others may be accessing the Twitter APIs at the particular time, Web traffic, the busy-ness of the Maltego servers, and other reasons. The data extractions showcased here were captured over several consecutive work days. The rollout of Maltego Chlorine also occurred during the same time period, which is why some of the screenshots are of the Tweet Analyzer in Maltego Carbon 3.5.3 and others in Maltego Chlorine 3.6.0. Figure 1 shows a general sequence of how real-time Tweets are extracted from Twitter and analyzed.

Figure 1. Sequence of a real-time Tweet Analyzer

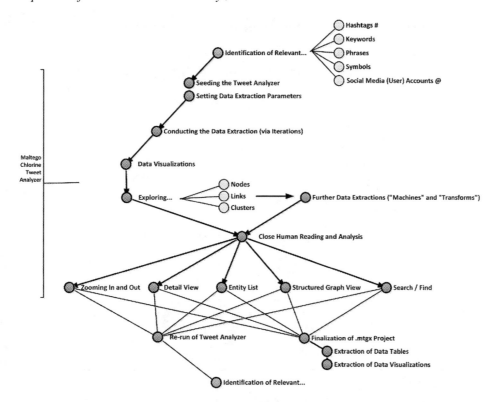

Essentially, the first step involves the planning for how to seed the Tweet Analyzer "machine." This step is depicted as a simple approach based on identifying hashtags, keywords, phrases, symbols, or @ social media accounts, but in reality, there is often some deep thought that must go into research questions and research designs. If the search is purely exploratory, then the investment in strategy and tactics may be somewhat less. The next steps all occur within Maltego: seeding the Tweet Analyzer, setting the data extraction parameters, conducting the data extraction, visualizing the data, exploring the data for informational value, conducting further data extractions, interacting with the data visualizations for human close reading and analysis, and then deciding further data extractions from the Surface Web (as needed). This paragraph describes the process as somewhat linear, but this process may also be quite recursive—as needed. Data may be extracted from Maltego for further analysis in other tools.

Three terms were selected to showcase the Tweet Analyzer: "H7N9," "ISIS," and "Iran." For one reason or another, all three were in the headlines of some of the popular online news sources. This work does not take a stance on any of the topics.

Example 1 Target: "H7N9"

A Tweet Analyzer run on the keyword "H7N9" captured other related terms: "one health," "pandemic," "flu," "emergency," "scientists," "mutating," "bird flu," "#china," and others. The anxieties related to this term may be seen in the size of the "negative" bubble in Figure 2. Interestingly, the messages of warning

Figure 2. Bubble view of "H7N9" keyword search on Twitter using the Tweet Analyzer

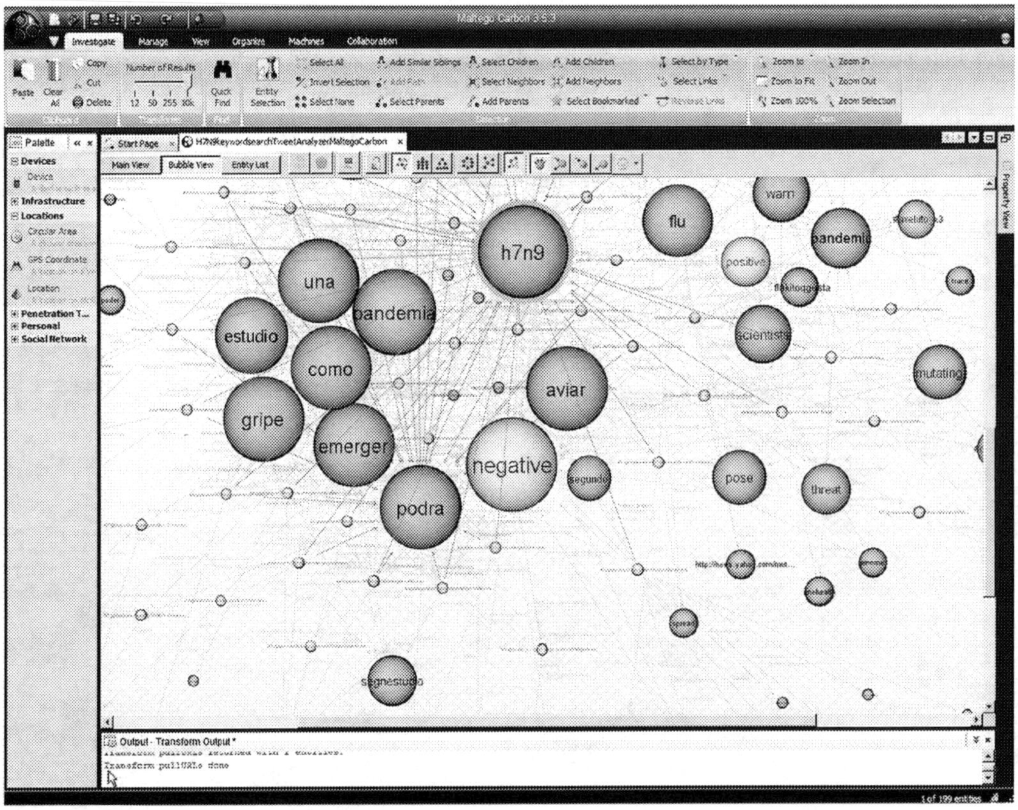

of a potential pandemic tracked closer to the "positive" sentiment. In terms of languages represented in the Tweets, English, Chinese, Japanese, French, and Spanish were readily represented.

Figure 3 shows an entity list resulting from the two iterations of the "N7N9" Tweet Analyzer extraction.

In Figure 4, there is a structured graph view of the H7N9 network. This shows clustering of some of the social media accounts in Twitter but also links to other resources on the Surface Web.

In Figure 5, there is a broadened search of other related contents to the issue based on Maltego Carbon 3.5.3 "transforms".

Example 2 Target: "isis"

In terms of a Tweet Analyzer extraction based around the keyword "ISIS," the trending phrases were terms like "spy, "ransacking," "assyrians," "ancient," "antiquities," "shariah," and "coalition." There were threads of conversations trending negative, positive, and neutral (as indicated by the AlchemyAPI tool). The trending words may be used to indicate a type of text summarization of the ongoing Tweets. A researcher who is interested in the actual communicator of a particular message may zoom in to see the @ account name. It is also possible to extract clusters of social groups engaging in particular conversations.

Figure 3. Entity list for "H7N9" keyword search on Twitter using the Tweet Analyzer

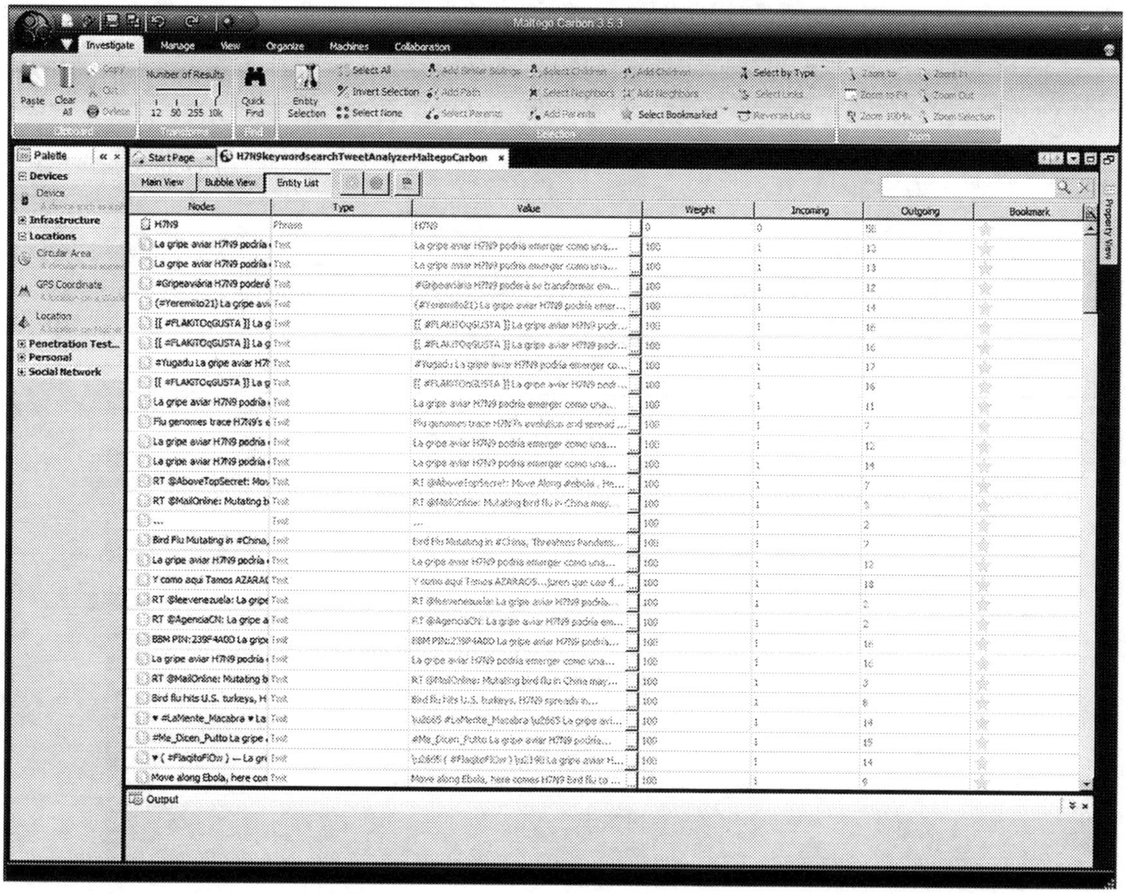

Figure 4. Structured view for "H7N9" keyword search on Twitter using the Tweet Analyzer

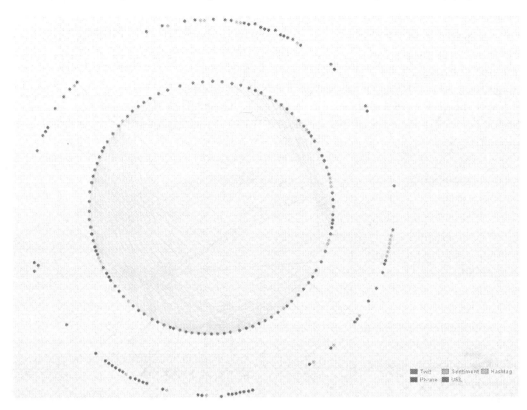

Figure 5. A broadened search for "H7N9" keyword search on Twitter using transforms (bubble view)

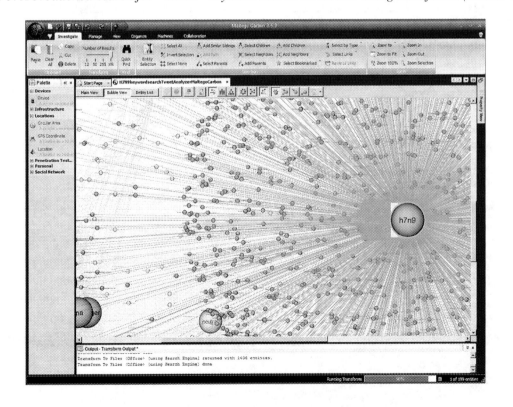

Particular nodes may be highlighted in order to view direct ties to other nodes; further, parent, child, or other levels of relations may be indicated and selected…and copied…for more in-depth analysis, as may be seen in Figure 6.

In Figure 7, the entity list for the "ISIS" data extraction shows a list of Tweets. Each row contains a record that may be further analyzed in the Detail View.

In Figure 8, there are clusters of interrelated discussants and resources that may be seen in the structured ring lattice view. This is drawn with the same data from the ISIS extraction in the initial Tweet Analyzer. At the bottom right of the image is the legend that describes what the various objects represent. A zoomed-in view brings out the specifics. This view shows the macro level of the networked graph.

Another structured view of the same network is shown in Figure 9. This view is a more classic parent-child structure from top-down. The various data views enable ways to interact with the data. In any of the views, it is possible to highlight particular clusters or branches and to analyze those in more depth. At any time, it is possible to highlight a node or a branch or a cluster and to conduct additional "machines" or "transforms" for more information. Maltego also enables the writing of memos or notations

Figure 6. Bubble view for "isis" keyword search on Twitter using the Tweet Analyzer

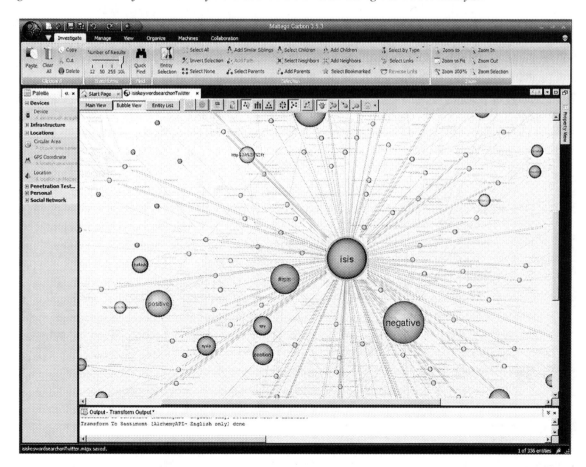

to attach to various nodes for record-keeping (assuming a long-term observation of particular trending / non-trending phenomena). Parts of a large graph may also be broken off and pasted into new graphs to be saved as new projects in order to enable more in-depth probes and analyses.

Finally, in Figure 10, "transforms" were performed on the focal node, with an explosion of new related resources identified by Maltego Carbon 3.5.3.

Example 3 Target: "Iran"

Finally, "Iran" was chosen for the third example. At the time of the data extraction, mass media outlets had broad news coverage of the world's leading nations negotiating with Iran over its nuclear program. The Tweet Analyzer extraction for this showed a mix of local and national and international interests. There were terms like "idiocy" used in relation to the "GOP." More generally, there were discussions of "#human rights," "Geneva," "#us," and other terms. There were some topics that could be understood as conspiracy theories. Some of the initial ideas may be seen in Figure 11. The negative trending view for many of the related discussions on Twitter was found to hold for days.

Figure 7. Entity list view for "isis" keyword search on Twitter using the Tweet Analyzer

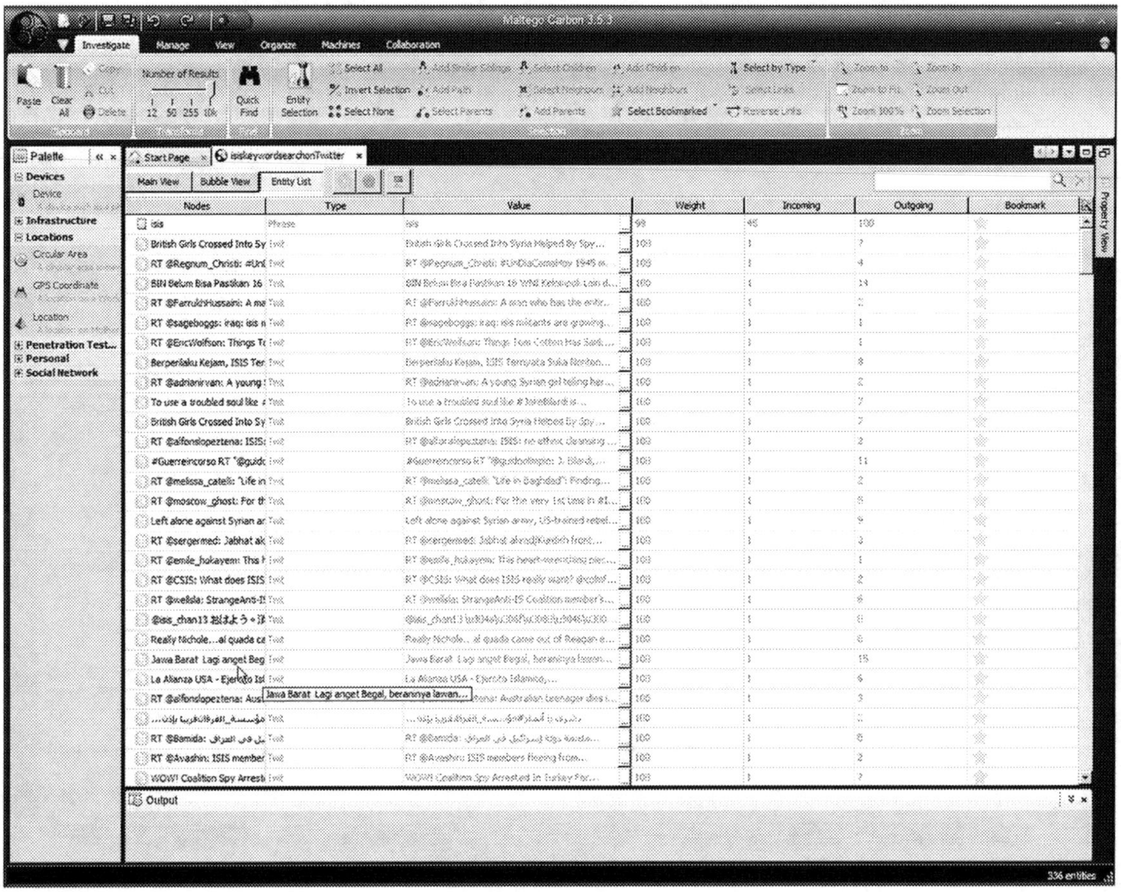

Figure 8. Zoomed-out structure view for "isis" keyword search on Twitter using the Tweet Analyzer

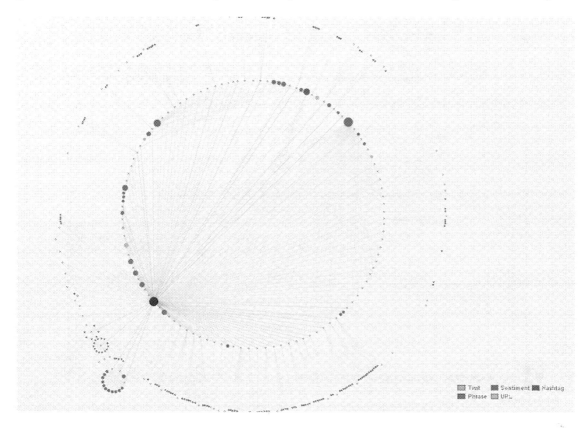

Figure 9. Zoomed-out structure view for "isis" keyword search on Twitter using the Tweet Analyzer

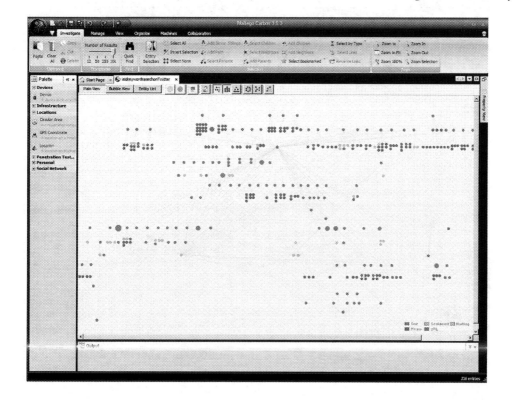

Figure 10. A broadened search for "isis" keyword search on Twitter using transforms (bubble view)

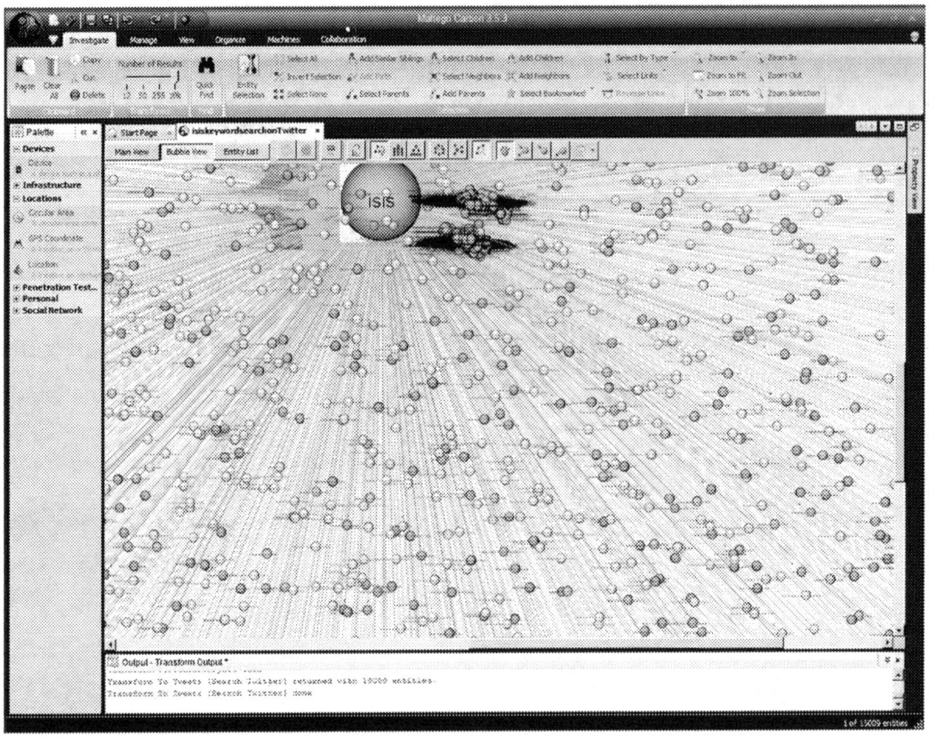

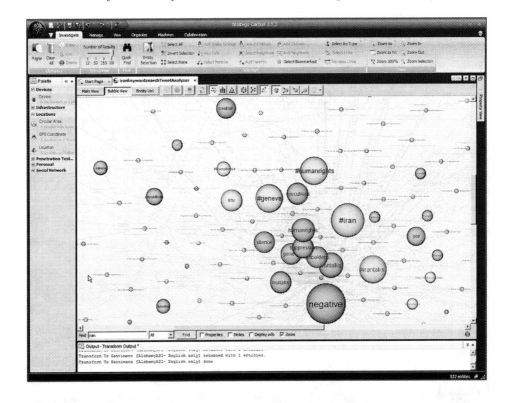

Figure 11. Bubble view of "Iran" keyword search on Twitter using the Tweet Analyzer

In Figure 12, the entity list from the "Iran" Tweet Analyzer data extraction may be viewed. The right scrollbar enables close-in views of all the records captured for the data extraction.

In Figure 13, a ring lattice view of the structured graph from the "Iran" Tweet Analyzer extraction may be viewed. Small clusters of users interacting around the communications may be seen here.

In terms of related "transforms" to the focal seeding term, that endeavor resulted in an explosion of related contents, as may be seen in Figure 14.

Another new feature in Maltego Carbon 3.5.3 involves the ability to extract geo-tagged Tweets based on latitude-longitude information. The city linked to the negotiations around Iran's nuclear program is Lausanne, Switzerland. Google Maps shows the latitude and longitude used for this location on Earth, and the screenshot of this tool may be seen in Figure 15.

The "46.5198,6.6335,1600m" seed is placed in the Circular Area "transform" with a circular area defined. All the logged Tweets from that targeted location were captured, and a few were found to include "Iran" in the Tweeted message, as may be seen in Figure 16. (An actual serious search would focus on the known locale of where the diplomats are meeting, and the target circle would be broadened. For basic proof-of-concept for an example, this simpler approach was used.)

Figure 12. Entity view of "Iran" keyword search on Twitter using the Tweet Analyzer

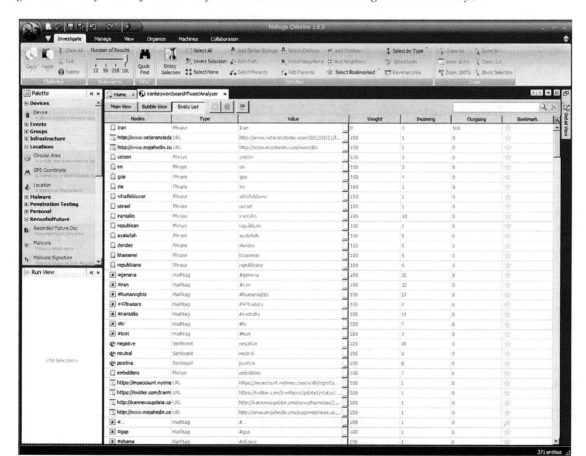

Figure 13. Structured view of "Iran" keyword search on Twitter using the Tweet Analyzer

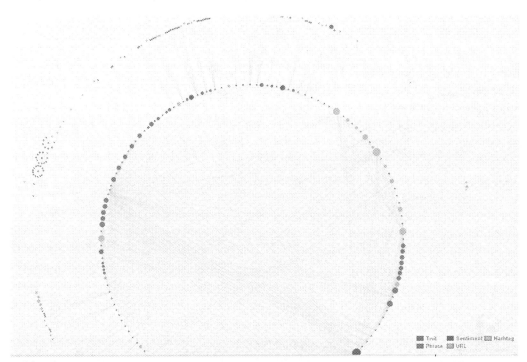

Figure 14. A broadened search for "Iran" keyword search on Twitter using transforms (bubble view)

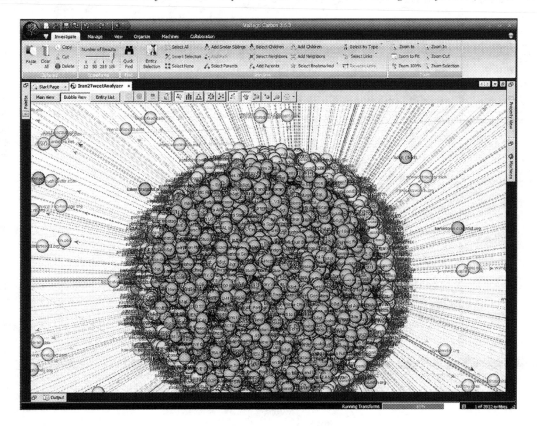

Figure 15. A screenshot of the Google Maps "Earth" view of Lausanne, Switzerland, at the defined latitude and longitude

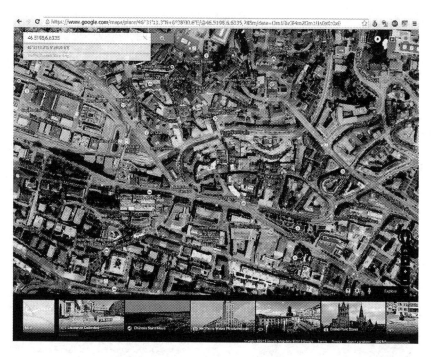

Figure 16. Lausanne, Switzerland, circular area search for tweets

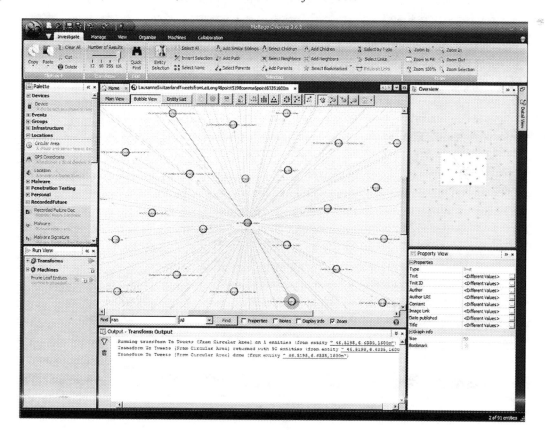

Other Analyses

Besides the types of analyses above, there are some other approaches.

For those who may want to understand which messages were deemed "positive," "negative," or "neutral" by the AlchemyAPI, researchers may highlight the sentiment node and select all parent nodes and extract those for further perusal and analysis. (This may be done already in the graph visualization, but others may prefer to have this in a data table format.) Figure 17 shows what this visualization may look like.

Researchers go to the Investigate tab -> Selection area -> Select Parents. Figure 18 shows the "Select Parents" function. Right-click and copy as list

Another option is to copy everything into a new graph for further data extractions and analysis in Maltego. This may be visualized in Figure 19.

Another approach involves individual profiling and group profiling through network analysis. There is a large literature about the nature of social networks and "partisan sharing" (people tending to share information with other like-minded individuals, indicative of selective exposure) and homophilous ties (people tending to "friend" others who are similar to themselves). There is plenty of research on how

Figure 17. "Parent Nodes" identified as trending negative based on "Politics" tweet analyzer in Maltego Chlorine's Tweet Analyzer

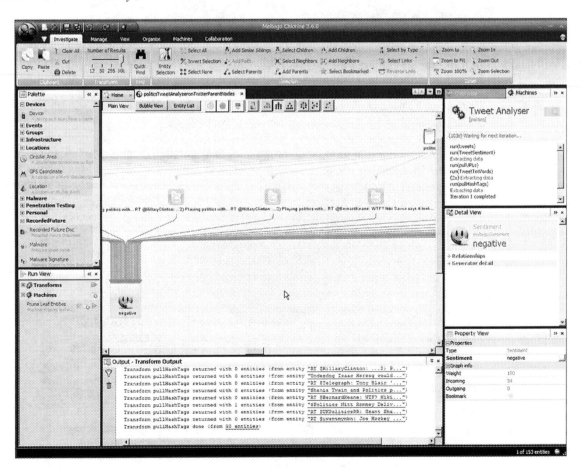

Figure 18. "Parent Nodes" identified as trending negative based on "Politics" tweet analyzer in Maltego Chlorine's Tweet Analyzer

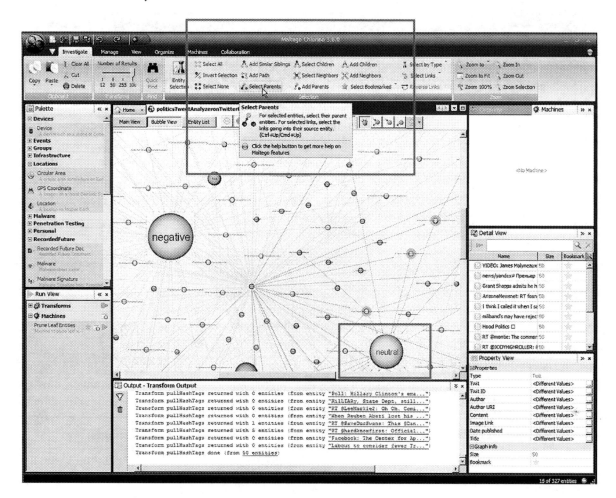

information moves through networks and how individuals and groups are brought around to certain beliefs and practices by social influence. There is well established theory in these areas, which may be further pursued.

Another approach involves extracting available geolocational data from the Tweets in order to understand the centers-of-geographical-mass in terms of locational participation. Currently, multiple sources suggest that only 1 – 2% of Tweets include locational data that is actually geographically mappable.

The Tweets do not only contain textual messages. Uniform Resource Locators (URLs) may be extracted from the messaging for further analysis. Photos, videos, and other elements may also be traced back for content analysis.

Another approach is to use a social media account and engage others in a topic of interest to see if it is possible to add fresh insights or to enliven a particular conversation. People are sparked by animating ideas and animating others, and for many issues, it is important to engage with others on social media for additional learning and information collection.

Figure 19. Copying parent nodes of the "negative" bubble to a new graph for semantic clusters

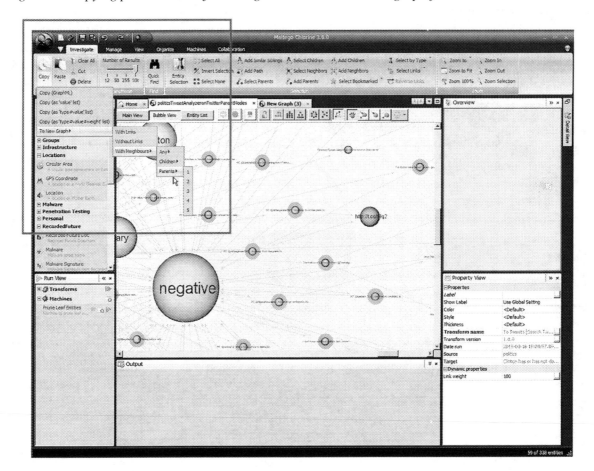

DISCUSSION

In the near-term, sentiments generally will vary and be fairly volatile, particularly over contested issues. In some cases, only the "negative" or only the "positive" sentiments are dominant. Over the mid- to longer-term horizons, the topics of interest can be expected to change, based on the issues of the then-moment.

These three examples using the Maltego Tweet Analyzer machine affords some insights. Based on the sequences of the extractions, how the machine is seeded is an important aspect of the type of data that is returned. Within Maltego, there are many ways to add to the dataset, well beyond Twitter and onto the Surface Web and Internet. The "cyborg" approach magnifies human capabilities of near-real-time awareness of select trending issues. While the tool itself is sufficiently easy to wield, there is assumed expertise in knowing which messages to pursue and which user accounts to explore.

There are many right ways to learn about the cyber-physical confluence, and the expertise necessary to draw solid conclusions likely requires deep expertise. Even just understanding how communities use social media to interact and to create changes requires rich expertise.

FUTURE RESEARCH DIRECTIONS

There are multiple research directions that may be taken to build on this initial work, which is the first academic publication of its kind about Maltego's Tweet Analyzer ("Analyser" in the British spelling). It would be helpful to have a model that defines which nodes, links, and clusters to pursue for additional analytical depth, particularly for a live, evolving, and emergent event. It may help to know if there are strategic times at which to collect the most informative Tweets for particular objectives; such insights would enhance research in "eventgraphing" from social media. Researchers may share insights about how other "machines" and "transforms" within Maltego Chlorine 3.6.0 (or whichever is the extant version at the time) may be used effectively to enhance the reach of the Tweet Analyzer "machine." Researchers may share insights about other tools and techniques that would complement the approach described here. There is room in the research for the sharing of unique cases of how this tool was used for awareness, human sensor networks, and eventgraphs.

CONCLUSION

Certainly, there is value to going beyond using one tool and a few strategies for exploration but to engage a variety of tools and tactics. As others have noted before, there is a wide range of techniques and tools for social media analytics (Batrinca & Treleaven, 2015). For those interested in pursuing "human sensor networks" and "eventgraphing" of emergent events, however, Maltego Chlorine's Tweet Analyser offers some pretty critical capabilities.

ACKNOWLEDGMENT

Thanks to iTAC at Kansas State University for funding several years of subscriptions for the use of Paterva's Maltego software. Some of the information about the AlchemyAPI came from webinars offered by IBM Watson.

REFERENCES

About. (2015). *Twitter*. Retrieved March 16, 2015, from https://about.twitter.com/company

Batrinca, B., & Treleaven, P. C. (2015). Social media analytics: A survey of techniques, tools, and platforms. *AI & Society*, *30*(1), 89–116. doi:10.1007/s00146-014-0549-4

Gangemi, A. (2013). A comparison of knowledge extraction tools for the Semantic Web. In P. Cimiano et al. (Eds.), *ESWC 2013. 361 – 366*. Berlin: Springer-Verlag. doi:10.1007/978-3-642-38288-8_24

Hai-Jew, S. (2014). *Conducting Surface Web-Based Research with Maltego Carbon*. Scalar Platform. Retrieved March 15, 2015, from http://scalar.usc.edu/works/conducting-surface-web-based-research-with-maltego-carbon/index

Lucia, W., Akcora, C. G., & Ferrari, E. (2013). Multi-dimensional conversation analysis across online social networks. In *Proceedings of the 2013 IEEE Third International Conference on Cloud and Green Computing*. doi:10.1109/CGC.2013.65

Nguyen, L. T., Wu, P., Chan, W., Peng, W., & Zhang, Y. (2012). Predicting collective sentiment dynamics from time-series social media. In Proceedings of WISDOM '12.

Petz, G., Karpowicz, M., Fürschuß, H., Auinger, A., Stříteský, V., & Holzinger, A. (2014). Computational approaches for mining user's opinions on the Web 2.0. *Information Processing & Management, 50*(6), 899–908. doi:10.1016/j.ipm.2014.07.005

Saif, H., He, Y., & Alani, H. (2012). *Semantic sentiment analysis of Twitter. In Proceedings of ISWC 2012*. Springer-Verlag Berlin Heidelberg.

Streaming APIs. (2015). *Twitter*. Retrieved March 16, 2015, from https://dev.twitter.com/streaming/overview

ADDITIONAL READING

Hai-Jew, S. (2014). *Conducting Surface Web-Based Research with Maltego Carbon*. Scalar Platform. Retrieved March 15, 2015, from http://scalar.usc.edu/works/conducting-surface-web-based-research-with-maltego-carbon/index

KEY TERMS AND DEFINITIONS

Disambiguation: Clarifying the meaning of a word or phrase, also known as "entity linking".

Eventgraphing: The mapping of an event by capturing various types of information about people communicating about the event and the contents of their messages; the use of social graphs to describe an event.

"Firehose": A term which colloquially refers to a large output of data as if water through a firehose.

Human Sensor Network: The collecting of people's social media messaging in order to understand a particular event or phenomena.

Internet: Interconnected computer networks.

"Machine": A function in Maltego Chlorine; a macro Maltego: A multi-use software tool that enables penetration testing by mapping.

Surface: Web structures and other information.

Named Entity: A proper noun or name.

Network Graph: A 2D or 3D visualization of entities and their relationships (often in various forms of node-link diagrams).

Penetration Testing: The testing of computer networks for vulnerabilities; intrusion detection.

Scraping: Extracting unstructured textual or multimedia or other data from websites through automated means.

Sentiment Analysis: The capturing of human attitudes and emotions (as specific descriptive terms or as simpler polarities like "positive," "negative," or "neutral").

Surface Web: The Web browser-accessible part of the World Wide Web (not including the Deep Web).

"Transform": A function in Maltego Chlorine that enables the transforming of one type of related data to other types (such as a phone number to an email address to a name).

Tweet Analyzer: A Maltego Chlorine machine that enables the real-time extraction of microblogging messaging from Twitter and the analysis of those messages using the AlchemyAPI.

World Wide Web: Interlinked hypertext (http) documents and pages.

Chapter 13

Exploring Public Perceptions of Native–Born American Emigration Abroad and Renunciation of American Citizenship through Social Media

Shalin Hai-Jew
Kansas State University, USA

ABSTRACT

There has been little work done on American emigration abroad and even less done on the formal renunciation of American citizenship. This chapter provides an overview of both phenomena in the research literature and then provides some methods for using the extraction of social media data and their visualization as a way of tapping into the public mindsets about these social phenomena. The software tools used include the following: Network Overview, Discovery and Exploration for Excel (NodeXL Basic), NVivo, and Maltego Carbon; the social media platforms used include the following: Wikipedia, YouTube, Twitter, and Flickr.

INTRODUCTION

Renunciation is the most unequivocal way in which a person can manifest an intention to relinquish U.S. citizenship. -- U.S. Department of State

The vast majority of people in the world are a member of a country; for many, their national identity is an integral part of their sense of self and their lifestyles. Being an American is an important part of life for the 320 million citizens of the U.S. However, there are still annual cases of native-born U.S. citizens

DOI: 10.4018/978-1-5225-0846-5.ch013

who choose to irrevocably renounce their citizenship for a variety of reasons. This chapter explores the relatively uncommon phenomena of American expatriations and the rare extreme cases of citizenship renunciations; based on the idea of nationality as in-part based on the human imagination, this work will include research into social media to capture a sense of the public discourse around this topic. (The social media approaches will include sampling from an open- and crowd-sourced encyclopedia; a massive collection of videos on a video content sharing site; a microblogging site, and a digital image and video sharing site. The types of data extractions will include the following: article networks on Wikipedia; video networks on YouTube; #hashtagged conversations on Twitter; keyword searches on Twitter; user networks on Twitter, and related tags networks on Flickr.)

To gain a sense of the size of this issue, it may help to acquire a sense of the numbers. The world population (at the time of this writing) is 7.3 billion people. There are currently 320 million Americans. Of this population, 35% of hold an American passport. At any one time in the world, there are 7.6 million Americans living abroad; this expatriate community "would constitute the 13th largest U.S. state by population size" (Stcherbatcheff, June 28, 2014). (Another source suggests that at any one time there are 3-6 million Americans abroad in 160 different countries (excluding the military, which is apparently counted differently) ("American diaspora," Jan. 17, 2015). (Note: An "expatriate" or "expat" is a person who lives outside his or her native country.)

The "expat" community are comprised of those who are exploring the world, serving their country, living abroad with foreign spouses; those working at various organizations abroad; those stretching retirement dollars by living in countries with lower costs of living; and others. Many are military personnel (who are not often counted as expats even if they live abroad). These are, in the migration literature, the mobile ones as compared to the broadly immobile others. In 2014, there were about 3,500 Americans who renounced their citizenship to the Internal Revenue Service (IRS). [According to Section 6039G of the Health Insurance Portability and Accountability Act, IRC section, the IRS of the U.S. Treasury has to release a quarterly publication of the individuals who've chosen to expatriate. One example may be viewed here, for the quarter ending March 31, 2014, for example: Quarterly Publication of Individuals Who Have Chosen to Expatriate (https://s3.amazonaws.com/public-inspection.federalregister.gov/2014-10139.pdf) .

The citizens of the U.S. and those long-term residents with green cards who choose to renounce their citizenship and permanently emigrate from the U.S. are a small minority. In 2014, according to records from the Internal Revenue Service (IRS) of the U.S. Treasury, there were 3,415 former Americans who went through this irreversible process ("Quarterly Publication of Individuals, Who Have Chosen to Expatriate, as Required by Section 6039G," IRS; A record 3,415 Americans…, Feb. 12, 2015). The prior quarterly public dataset is created when exit tax forms are filed with the IRS; these numbers do not include "consular expatriations," and it is unclear if that data is available through the U.S. State Department. With those caveats about the undercounting, that is 3,415 out of 320,090,857 Americans on Jan. 1, 2015, according to the U.S. Census ("Census Bureau projects U.S. and World Populations on New Year's Day," Dec. 29, 2014). The named number of American emigrants is 1/100,000th (.000010658%) of the population. While these numbers are quite small, a visual of the statistics collected by the deVere Group, a financial advisory firm serving many American expatriates, suggests that there may be an upward trend (Picchi, Feb. 12, 2015), at least in the near-term. The 3,415 is a small subset even of the total 7.6 million Americans who live outside the U.S. (Picchi, Feb. 12, 2015); that would be 4/10,000 (.000449342%). Those Americans who renounce their citizenship self-select into a very rare group. Just as a factor of chance given these numbers of individuals and the dynamism of politics and people's vary-

Figure 1. American renouncement of citizenship by the numbers

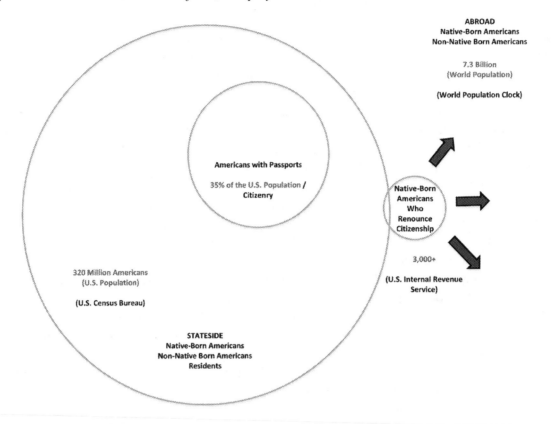

ing opinions, there will always be some who choose to emigrate and renounce citizenship. A political science understanding of migration assumes that some degree of migration is inherent in the "anarchical" global political system (Ahmed, 1997, p. 178).

Indeed, Americans who may be even minimally adventuresome will find a number of paths that they can take abroad. Tourism and travel are an important part of the American lifestyle. Various religious, civic groups, student clubs, and professional groups go abroad to engage in development and aid projects. There are government-to-government exchanges. There are study abroad programs. Various entrepreneurial and career endeavors may bring people abroad. Even if Americans are mono-lingual, much of the world has populations with high levels of English fluency. The U.S. has a number of institutions—military, international businesses, diplomatic corps, and religious institutions—with global reach and global interests. This broad reach means a broad exposure to the world, which means that there are many factors that may create paths abroad. There are entities that encourage American travel.

The Association of Americans Resident Overseas (AARO) describes how the U.S. government set up programs to encourage young Americans to venture abroad during the Cold War. In 1946, the Fulbright Program was established; in1961, the Peace Corps was created. Both encouraged intercultural exchanges. A recent call to go abroad came from websites that highlighted the challenges to the U.S. economy and encouraged overseas work to make especially younger Americans more hirable (McGath, 2013). This phenomenon may be an indicator of the cyclical nature of immigration to the U.S. based in large part on the economic health of the country (Flowers, Dec. 10, 2015). One case in point involves

Figure 2. Recent American renunciation of citizenship (derived from "A record 3,415 Americans...," Feb. 12, 2015, CNN Money)

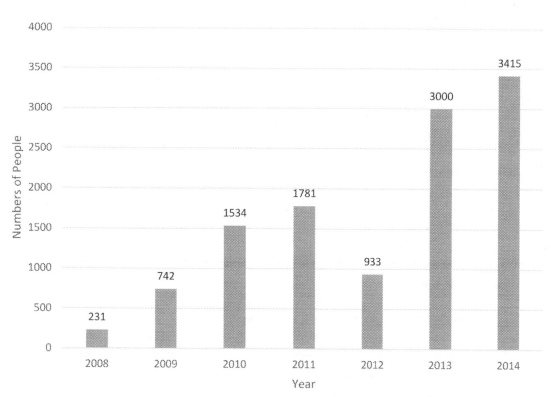

the dynamics around the U.S.-Mexico border. From 2005-2010, Mexicans left in droves: 170,000 from 1995 – 2000, 356,000 from 2005 – 2010. Not only was the traffic headed *el norte* severely lowered, but many retirees left as well with the severe drop in value of their homes and stocks. A Pew report suggested that Mexican migration to the U.S. fell to less than zero or may have even reversed (Passel, Cohn, & Gonzalez-Barrera, 2012).

Protecting Against Strategic "Brain Drain"

As a liberal-democratic nation, the U.S. has a system based on the respect of human rights, including the freedom to emigrate Post-WWII, the U.S. created programs like the Fulbright Program (1946), U.S. Peace Corps (1961), and others to encourage Americans to travel abroad to engage the world to increase mutual understandings. Strategically, the U.S. was a sending country in one aspect, but it also had a concurrent interest in protecting its most highly educated against relocation abroad. It has interests in maintaining a creative population of individuals who may contribute to industry and learning. In that sense, it has interests in knowing where some of its top talent may be headed (and knowing if there is a failure in placing the highly educated in gainful employment stateside). "Brain drain" is a colloquial term which refers to the loss of intellectual and innovation capacity to another country. [A more nuanced view suggests that those who are educated in the open West and return to their home countries are the "new Argonauts" who benefit not only the countries in which they were university-educated and may have worked for some years but also their sending countries in terms of new industries (Saxenian, 2006); this is a book which advocates open networks and a non-zero-sum sense of the world.] Some sending countries' governments encourage their citizens to go abroad to work (international labor migration) because that often means remittances to family members remaining in the sending countries in foreign currencies as well as some tax collection in the sending countries. However, these are usually for service and labor positions, not those involving higher education and high-demand skills. The so-called migration-development nexus is a complex dynamic (Faist, 2008).

There are more formal counts of U.S. born individuals with science and engineering doctorates. A 2004 study involved surveying those just about to graduate with such desirable degrees and found that less than 3% of the survey respondents (289 of the 24,558) had plans to work or study abroad at the time of their receiving their doctorates. This finding was part of a long-term trend: "Except for two brief up-turns, the number of U.S.-born S&E doctorate recipients with definite plans to work or study abroad has been about 300 – 400 each year since the mid-1960s" (Burrell, 2004, n.p.). In general, the destinations of choice were friendly countries, namely, "Canada, the UK, Germany, France, Japan, Switzerland, and Australia" for those with definite plans (Burrell, 2004, n.p.).

In terms of the expression of intent to go abroad in a survey, using the IBOPE-Zogby firm, since 2005, "Nearly 40% of young Americans 18 to 24 are thinking about leaving the U.S. to seek opportunity abroad" (Adams, 2011). For all the concerns about American out-migration in some quarters, the nation's Potential Net Migration Index (PNMI), a measured based on a 2009 Gallup Poll, is not particularly high, which does not portend large demographic shifts. The PNMI subtracts the number of adults who would move out of a country from those who would move to that same country and represents that percentage as a portion of the total adult population. The higher the PNMI, the greater the desirability of the country as an end destination for migrants. In a sense, this is a measure of potential population churn, assuming migration were frictionless and a matter of will alone (in this theoretical construct): "The U.S. has a PNMI of 60%, less than a quarter of top-ranked Singapore's 260%. Other countries that rank higher than the U.S. include New Zealand (175%), Canada, (170%), Australia (145%), France (70%) and the U.K. (65%)" (Rice, 2010). In terms of aggregated Gallup surveys in 154 countries from 2010 - 2012, the PNMI scores for major regions still put the Americas at the top (13), then Europe (10), then the Middle East and North Africa (4); in terms of the potential net migration index, Asia (-6) and Sub-Saharan Africa (-24) would experience net population losses (Esipova, Pugliese, & Ray, 2014).

Locations of the U.S. Expatriates

So where exactly are these expatriates? Several research sources, published from the 1990s to the present, address this issue. These works show changing preferred destinations. Host country characteristics are an important factor in their selection by American émigrés. One study from 1996 found that U.S. citizens were "more likely to reside in rich and close countries than in distant and poor countries and that the foreign country's ties to the U.S. immigrant population and the use of the English language are important determinants of where Americans settle abroad. Political conditions and U.S. military presence also influence the choice of foreign residence" (Bratsberg & Terrell, 1996, p. 788).

The largest fraction (40.3%) resides in North America, followed by those in Europe (33.0%), Asia (16.9%), South America (3.9%), Oceania (3.7%), and Africa (2.1%). For individual countries, the largest groupings of Americans are found in Mexico, Canada, the United Kingdom, Germany, and the Philippines. Relative to the population of the foreign country, the largest U.S. influence is in Israel, where Americans make up 3.1 percent of the population. Compared to the immigrant population in the United States, Israel again has the largest number of U.S. citizens; there are 2.3 times as many Americans in Israel as there are immigrants from Israel in the United States. At the other end of the scale is Cuba; there are 436 times as many Cubans in the United States as there are Americans in Cuba. (Bratsberg & Terrell, 1996, p. 790)

A more recent source suggests regional shifts and changing preferences.

Nearly one-third (32.2%) live in countries in Latin America and the Caribbean. In fact, the U.S. ranks ninth in the percentage of its emigrants that reside in that part of the world. The next most popular destination for American emigrants is Europe, at 28.3%. Around 12.6% of U.S. emigrants reside in other parts of Northern America, and there are small numbers of American emigrants living in Oceania (4.2%) and Africa (2.7%). (Rice, 2010)

An unofficial 2011 U.S. Department of State source lists the following (with general regions in alphabetical order):

- Africa: 171,000
- East Asia and Pacific: 864,000
- Europe: 1,612,000
- Near East: 870,000
- South Central Asia: 212,000
- Western Hemisphere: 2,591,000

By descending order, the most popular regions would be the following: Western Hemisphere, Europe, Near East, East Asia and Pacific, South Central Asia, and Africa. The summary Wikipedia entry has a composite table with numbers of Americans in various countries (more specifically) based on a number of sources. This source suggests that there are 6,320,000 Americans abroad currently Table 1).

Table 1 should be treated as handling very rough numbers because it is not clear how the data was collected, the veracity of the various sources used, the methods used for counting, the rounding, and so on. Still, there are benefits in using some general way of visualizing a rough sense of where Americans may be located.

RENUNCIATION OF AMERICAN CITIZENSHIP

In one sense, U.S. citizenship involves a basket of social goods to citizens, and in this exchange, citizens maintain a list of citizenship and civic-based responsibilities. A back-of-the-napkin description of this exchange would involve a government providing security, basic welfare, national defense, infrastructure, public health, public education, national prestige, foreign diplomacy, monetary management, and so on, and citizens provide loyalty to the state, compliance with laws, and owed tax revenues. How people perceive this exchange is probably fairly variant. The exit-voice-loyalty argument suggests that people leave a particular nation-state in situations when they are sufficiently discomfited, unable to make their voices heard in the polity, and so they move on to another nation in order to have their needs met. Ultimately,

Table 1. Destination countries for the American diaspora

Country (and Region)	American Populations
Mexico	738,100
Philippines	300,000
Israel	200,000
Liberia	160,000
Canada	137,000
Costa Rica	130,000
South Korea	120,000
United Kingdom	115,000
Germany	107,755
France	100,000
Australia	99,349
China	71,439
Brazil	70,000
Colombia	60,000
Hong Kong	60,000
India	60,000
Japan	51,321
Italy	50,000
Malaysia	40,000
Ireland	38,000
Argentina	37,000
Norway	33,509
Bahamas	30,000
Lebanon	25,000
Panama	25,000
New Zealand	21,462
Qatar	15,000
Honduras	15,000
Chile	12,000
Taiwan	10,645
Bermuda	8,000
Kuwait	8,000

("American Diaspora," 2015)

a nation-state needs to govern well (provide services, listen to citizens, respect human rights), provide a proper ideology, control borders, and minimize corruption in order to maintain itself (Ahmed, 1997, pp. 180 - 185). On these counts, the U.S. is generally seen as a solid bet.

Figure 3. *"American Diaspora" in 2015 table mapped from Wikipedia (in Tableau Public)*

What does the actual renunciation of American citizenship entail? According to the U.S. Department of State, Section 349(a)(5) (§ U.S.C. 148(1)(5) of the Immigration and Nationality Act (INA) describes the rights of a U.S. citizen to renounce his or her citizenship. By making a formal and signed oath re-nunciation of nationality in front of a diplomatic or consular officer of the U.S. in a foreign state, the individual can make this status official. Apparently, the signing is preceded by an interview, and followed by a period of reflection, and then an actual renunciation ceremony, in some U.S. consulates. Anything less—such as such declarations by mail or through an agent or "while in the United States"—essentially has no legal effect. The renunciation of citizenship is a personal decision, and as such, this may not be done by one individual for another. A minor who has renounced his or her citizenship before age 18 may have his or her citizenship reinstated within six months of turning 18. Guardians cannot renounce citizenship for an "incompetent." Expatriations are not fully official tax-wise until notification and tax satisfaction certificates are filed with the IRS and Department of State (with the filing of Form 8854 or "Initial and Annual Expatriation Information Statement").

The renunciation of citizenship involves "all the rights and privileges associated with citizenship," including that of physically remaining stateside (Renunciation of American Citizenship"). The State Department clarifies on its site that an individual could end up being stateless after renouncing their American citizenship "unless they already possess a foreign nationality." This section continues:

Even if not stateless, former U.S. citizens would still be required to obtain a visa to travel to the United States, or show that they are eligible for admission pursuant to the terms of the Visa Waiver Pilot Program (VWPP). Renunciation of U.S. citizenship may not prevent a foreign country from deporting that individual to the United States in some non-citizen status. ("Renunciation of U.S. Nationality")

Being born in the U.S. is synonymous with U.S. citizenship (from the perspective of the U.S. government). The U.S. apparently does not recognize dual citizenship.

While the U.S. does not formally recognize dual citizenship, it does not take a stand against it. In the United States, for example, a child born in a foreign country to U.S. citizen parent(s) may be both a U.S. citizen and a citizen of the country of birth. Also, a U.S. citizen may acquire foreign citizenship by marriage, or a naturalized U.S. citizen may not lose the citizenship of their country of birth. U.S. law does not mention dual nationality or require a person to choose one citizenship over another. (Schachter, 2006, p. 3)

The renunciation of citizenship does not mean that the individual is no longer liable for legitimate tax, legal, and / or military obligations. The State Department page elaborates: "Persons who wish to renounce U.S. citizenship should be aware of the fact that renunciation of U.S. citizenship may have no effect whatsoever on his or her U.S. tax or military service obligations (contact the Internal Revenue Service or U.S. Selective Service for more information). In addition, the act of renouncing U.S. citizenship does not allow persons to avoid possible prosecution for crimes which they may have committed in the United States, or escape the repayment of financial obligations previously incurred in the United States or incurred as United States citizens abroad." ("Renunciation of U.S. Nationality")

Even if the renunciation of citizenship goes through, the former American citizens may re-apply to enter the U.S. and to theoretically go through the process of applying for U.S. citizenship again. However, that is a long process to apply for permanent residency.

BROADSCALE REASONS FOR AMERICAN EMIGRATION

The recent rise in American citizens renouncing their citizenship has been attributed to the passing of some federal laws to tighten up American tax regimes, most specifically, the Foreign Account Tax Compliance Act (FATCA).

Tax Compliance

The most recent spate of applications to renounce American citizenship has been attributed, in part, to the passing of the Foreign Account Tax Compliance Act (FATCA), which passed as part of the 2010

Hiring Incentives to Restore Employment (HIRE) Act. U.S. tax laws have long required all Americans who earn money anywhere to pay taxes on their earning (above a certain amount). One author writes:

The U.S. is the only country that taxes its citizens on worldwide income, instead of where they earn the money. That means that an American who lives in Australia, for instance, has to file taxes in both countries, although they are exempt from paying U.S. taxes on their first $97,600 of earnings. (Picchi, Feb. 12, 2015)

By contrast, the IRS view is simple: "If you are a U.S. citizen or resident alien, the rules for filing income, estate, and gift tax returns and paying estimated tax are generally the same whether you are in the United States or abroad" ("U.S. Citizens and Resident Aliens Abroad," 2015). Several journalists suggest that the numbers of those relinquishing their U.S. citizenship may be expected to grow. One author observes: "A survey from deVere last year found that almost four out of five of its clients, who are primarily American expatriates, said they would consider handing in their passports because of the law, which is called the Foreign Account Tax Compliance Act, or FACTA" (Picchi, Feb. 12, 2015). Another suggests that the new thicket of American laws over the taxation of Americans working abroad may create sufficient cost and frustration to Americans abroad to encourage changes of citizenship. Companies themselves face a new range of compliance issues in hiring Americans (Stcherbatcheff, June 28, 2014). Some suggest that Americans' interests while abroad are not sufficiently represented by the U.S. government (Stcherbatcheff, June 28, 2014).

FATCA has resulted in the requirement for those Americans living abroad to complete complicated tax paperwork in order to report their foreign assets, often requiring the hiring of specialized accountants and paying $1,000 for these services for each tax filing. At the same time, FATCA has required foreign banks to reveal foreign accounts held by Americans (at risk of facing a 30% withholding tax on various types of payments from the U.S. In this context, there are "expats who no longer want to deal with complicated tax paperwork, a burden that has only gotten worse in recent years" (A record 3,415 Americans…, Feb. 12, 2015). For some, relinquishing U.S. citizenship is about simplifying their lives and preserving wealth (A record 3,415 Americans…, Feb. 12, 2015). To relinquish citizenship, American citizens must show that they have been compliant with U.S. tax laws for at least the five years preceding the date of relinquishment of citizenship. If their net worth is greater than $2 million, or their average net income tax for the five previous years is $155,000 or more, there is an "expatriation tax," effective June 16, 2008 ("Expatriation Tax," June 28, 2014). A certain amount of wealth is exempted ($668,000); one journalist has likened this exit tax as a kind of "capital gain tax as if you sold your property when you left" and is the last chance for the U.S. of taxing the individual (Wood, May 3, 2014). Citizenship may not only be relinquished, it may also be denied by the state.

Forced Loss of Citizenship

While it may be difficult (and rare) to actually lose American citizenship, it is not impossible. There are potentially expatriating acts, which are assessed by the U.S. Department of State. By definition, a citizen "owes permanent allegiance to the United States" ("Advice about Possible Loss of U.S. Nationality and Dual Nationality," 2015). The U.S. Department of State's Bureau of Consular Affairs writes:

Section 349 of the INA (8 U.S.C. 1481), as amended, states that U.S. nationals are subject to loss of nationality if they perform certain *specified* acts *voluntarily* and *with the intention to relinquish* U.S. nationality. Briefly stated, these acts include:

1. Obtaining naturalization in a foreign state upon one's own application after the age of 18 (Sec. 349 (a) (1) INA);
2. Taking an oath, affirmation or other formal declaration of allegiance to a foreign state or its political subdivisions after the age of 18 (Sec. 349 (a) (2) INA);
3. Entering or serving in the armed forces of a foreign state engaged in hostilities against the United States or serving as a commissioned or non-commissioned officer in the armed forces of a foreign state (Sec. 349 (a) (3) INA);
4. Accepting employment with a foreign government after the age of 18 if (a) one has the nationality of that foreign state or (b) an oath or declaration of allegiance is required in accepting the position (Sec. 349 (a) (4) INA);
5. Formally renouncing U.S. nationality before a U.S. diplomatic or consular officer outside the United States (sec. 349 (a) (5) INA);
6. Formally renouncing U.S. nationality within the United States (The Department of Homeland Security is responsible for implementing this section of the law) (Sec. 349 (a) (6) INA);
7. Conviction for an act of treason against the Government of the United States or for attempting to force to overthrow the Government of the United States (Sec. 349 (a) (7) INA). ("Advice about Possible Loss..." 2015)

One lawyer writes on this issue: "Aside from declaring your allegiance or citizenship to a foreign country, the only other ways you can lose US citizenship is if you: served in a 'policy level position' in a foreign government; committed treason, such as by fighting in a war against the US voluntarily; formally renounce US citizenship at a US Embassy or to the US Attorney General; (and) acted in a manner considered totally inconsistent with any possible intent to keep a US citizenship" (LaMance, Mar. 27, 2014).

A Review of the (Scant) Literature

One of the earliest works about American expatriates is J. Bainbridge's *Another Way of Living: A Gallery of Americans Who Choose to Live in Europe* (1968). In this book, the author used a convenience sample of expatriates he encountered while traveling through Europe. He portrayed his subjects as those who had somehow failed in their lives stateside and had to go abroad to find fulfillment. In the introduction, Bainbridge wrote: "The subjects of this book are a happier breed. They are Americans who have been blessed with a second chance, and have chosen to use it to make a new life in Europe" (p. 1). In this book, the author decried the sense of U.S. chauvinism and the treatment of those Americans living abroad as somehow suspect. Generally, Americans were described as a migratory people who tended to move "every seventh year" (Bainbridge, 1968, p. 3). [This observation somewhat updates and echoes Alexis De Toqueville's observations of the restless American personality in *Democracy in America* (Vol. II, 1840).]

Who were these Americans he met who were abroad? The author, in 1968, pointed to citizens going abroad to fulfill military commitments (with the U.S. stepping into Britain's shoes as the new imperial power, as he described it), commercial and financial interests, religious and cultural outreach, and, for a small group simply because they "want to" (Bainbridge, 1968, pp. 3 – 4). Of these expatriates, the author notes, very few actually renounce citizenship (Bainbridge, 1968, p. 5). Then as now, Bainbridge found artists and writers who utterly rejected what they saw the U.S. as standing for (Bainbridge, 1968, p. 9), so some left for ideological and political reasons. However, most tended to maintain their American citizenship even as they lived abroad, even for extended periods.

In a book published in 1992, the authors focused on individual and social-psychological level reasons for why Americans would live abroad, with a focus on two countries—Australia and Israel. These included marriage, employment, a desire for adventure, ideology, and personal fulfillment. In general, they go abroad to pursue opportunities, and they are not moving in large groups or for reasons generally of extraordinary events ("economic dislocation, political repression, and religious persecution") but more mundane reasons (Dashefsky, DeAmicis, Lazerwitz, & Tabory, 1992, p. 7). In their research, the authors strove to answer three basic questions: "(1) What accounts for the motivation of migrants to move? (2) What are the sources of the adjustment problems the migrants experience? 93) What explains whether the migrants remain or return to the United States?" (p. v).

In general, the authors summarized that those who are in "loosely integrated stages of life cycle are more prone to migrate" (p. vi). Even then, the authors pointed to a paucity of data of American expats. Migration, here, is simplified as a measure of fertility, mortality, and (out)migration, or births, deaths, and "the measure of population movement in space" (p. 2). Human migrants tend to gravitate towards destinations that are somewhat similar to their areas of origin (Goldscheider, 1971, p. 66, as cited by Dashefsky, DeAmicis, Lazerwitz, & Tabory, 1992, p. 3). Those who emigrate do not generally include "the most dispossessed or politically oppressed" but tend to be "well-educated, white, young adults who have enormous economic opportunities at home"; many move as individuals or young couples or family units with children (Dashefsky, DeAmicis, Lazerwitz, & Tabory, 1992, pp. 4-5).

In justifying their research, the authorship team provided a sense of the scope of emigration from 1900 – 1979:

Despite the flow of immigrants coming to American shores, there has generally been an ebb of migrants leaving. In the twentieth century hundreds of thousands of Americans have left to settle elsewhere. According to Warren and Kraly (1985, p. 5), 789,000 U.S. citizens have emigrated in the period 1900 – 1979. Indeed, it is a subject not frequently studied systematically, perhaps because of the ideological bias favoring the view of America as the great 'melting pot' which sociologists recently have suggested is less factual than fanciful a notion (Newman, 1973; Dashefsky, 1976; Alba and Chamlin, 1983). In fact, Warren and Kraly (1985, p. 5) have reported that the number of emigrants leaving the United States between 1900 and 1979 represented approximately one third the number of all immigrants. (Dashefsky, DeAmicis, Lazerwitz, & Tabory, 1992, pp. 5 - 6)

The authors constructed their research in part based on the accessibility of national statistics from Australia and Israel. They also conducted surveys and interviews. The researchers identified two main categories for American migration: expressive ones and instrumental ones.

Expatriate Americans tend to stay abroad for the following reasons: marriage, particularly to a native person; family ties in the new country; satisfaction with the job and standard of living, "religioethnic experiences," and feeling "more at home in the new country" (Dashefsky, DeAmicis, Lazerwitz, & Tabory, 1992, p. 147). A variable linked to Americans leaving their overseas destinations were an initial migration due to the "adventure motive." In general, Americans generally lived abroad for only a few

Table 2. Motivations for American migration

Goals of Migration		
(Locus of concern)	**Expressive**	**Instrumental**
Self	**Group A** Adventure / travel Alienation Religioethnic identity and self-fulfillment	**Group B** Entrepreneurship Job opportunities Attending School
Others	**Group C** Family unity Spouse's desire to return to homeland Alienated family head	**Group D** Medical service personnel Educational service personnel

(Dashefsky, DeAmicis, Lazerwitz, & Tabory, 1992, p. 40)

years as sojourners. Not even those holding permanent resident visas were found to intend to stay. The researchers identified special vulnerabilities for Americans in transitory stages of life—described as those dealing with marriage, job status, or military transitions (Dashefsky, DeAmicis, Lazerwitz, & Tabory, 1992, p. 60). While the authors conceptualize that it is in the interests of developed nations to "deter efforts to force migrants to change citizenship or otherwise make a permanent, formal commitment to one society or another. Few will surrender their citizenship, and they see no reason why they cannot live abroad for 20 years or longer while still retaining their status, particularly if they are American citizens" (Dashefsky, DeAmicis, Lazerwitz, & Tabory, 1992, p. 155). They suggest that (dis)satisfaction with living in a particular society is based on "friendship, family, and occupational relationships," government has limited power in changing up the individual decision-making (Dashefsky, DeAmicis, Lazerwitz, & Tabory, 1992, pp. 154 – 155).

The Problems of Accurate Counting

For some years, the U.S. Immigration and Naturalization Service (INS) counted or estimated U.S. emigration flows. Between 1918 – 1950, they estimated that there were 789,000 U.S. citizens who emigrated (abroad), and between 1908 to 1957, they estimated 4.8 million alien emigrants (to the U.S.). When the INS discontinued collecting data on U.S. emigration in 1957, a range of academics and other researchers used a variety of means to try to extrapolate that data because of its importance for policy. Various researchers tapped a variety of data sources, including administrative data, decennial censuses, UN data, foreign countries' data, and others, and the conclusions were often highly variant (Bratsberg & Terrell, 1996, pp. 788 - 789).

The U.S. Census Bureau does not collect data on those who emigrate from the U.S. In 1995, a researcher with the U.S. Census Bureau conducted research and wrote a white paper on how to extrapolate U.S.-born citizen expatriate numbers. His approach involved cobbling a number of foreign and domestic data sources and applying statistical methods. As the author noted, many nations do not collect foreign resident information in their censuses or surveys. Those that do collect such data may not include age, sex, race, or other information that may be of interest. For his work, Fernandez used materials from four main sources: the Census Bureau's main library, the Bureau's Center for Information Research (CIR) library, the United Nations Statistical library in NY, and the library of the Population Research Center

(PRC) at the University of Texas at Austin. In his exploration, he found gaps in the data; he also had to restructure the data into queryable datasets to run his statistical analyses. He used foreign census and selective administrative data. He wrote:

...the methodologies currently used by the Census Bureau to estimate and project the U.S. population still lack a believable estimate of that elusive process: emigration. For a long time we have not had a current, empirically-based, measure of the annual emigration rate of the U.S. population by age, sex, and race. Although compared to the annual volume of foreign immigration to the U.S. annual emigration from the U.S. is probably small, lack of a reliable figure for the net annual outflow of persons from the U.S. inhibits us: (1) in making more accurate estimates and projections of the U.S. population, and (2) in determining more precisely the population coverage error in our decennial censuses. (Fernandez, 1995, n.p.)

The min-max estimation ranges were pretty wide. In the prior two censuses, the U.S. government had relied on foreign countries' counts of enumerated U.S. citizens in their territories but did not separate out those that were citizens by birth vs. those by naturalization. To address this gap, he wrote a whitepaper with the layering on of the intercensal (between censuses every 10 years) "cohort survival method of analytical demography" to the State Department's U.S. citizen registration data to estimate the annual rate of U.S.-born emigration. In the first phase of his research, he used the data on U.S. persons living abroad based on foreign country censuses. He used reverse survival to bring forward the age-sex cohorts of U.S.-born persons in the most recent two censuses of the foreign country. He created averages from both the forward and reverse survival processes "to generate a single estimate of annual net emigration of U.S. born persons to the particular country." He did this for a number of countries (listed in alphabetical order): Australia, Brazil, Canada, France, Great Britain, Ireland, Mexico, New Zealand, Sweden, Switzerland, and Venezuela (Fernandez, 1995, n.p.). He also applied some Bayesian probabilities based on State Department statistician estimates that only about 60% of U.S. citizens abroad register at U.S. posts, and 50% of those are actually U.S. native born persons. He wrote about how he used such data:

Hence, for a selected group of countries with no census data on foreign residents but whom I judged nontrivial recipients of U.S. born emigrants, I used the annual State Department registration counts and their suggested proportions to broadly estimate the total number of U.S. born residents in these countries for the years 1970 and 1980. Subsequently, for these countries I chose the same age sex patterns of U.S. residents as in countries with reported census data and similar cultural background (e.g. Canada Australia; Mexico Venezuela; etc.) and then applied the cohort survival method accordingly to estimate U.S. emigration. These latter estimates, obviously, are mainly dependent on the assumptions proffered by the State Department on U.S. emigrants registration levels. (Fernandez, 1995, n.p.)

Using these methods, Fernandez (1995) projected that there were some 48,000 U.S. native-born emigrants annually. [As a point of comparison, a 1996 work said that the U.S. Bureau of the Census assumed an annual emigration of 160,000 persons when constructing population estimates, although these may include more than U.S.-born emigrants; the U.S. Department of State was said to have estimated 2.6 million U.S. citizens in a foreign country in 1993, not counting U.S. government employees and dependents of the U.S. military or its civilian employees (per the U.S. Immigration and Naturalization Service, 1994) (Bratsberg & Terrell, 1996, p. 788)].

Another researcher has worked to try to understand the rate of U.S.-born emigration using survival analysis and time-series data. The researcher explained: "A time one (T1) population of either U.S. born or U.S. citizens is survived to a future time (T2) for which we have a comparable observed population total (e.g. from a Census). The difference between the survived and observed population is used to measure net migration" (Schachter, 2006, p. 2). To get a sense of how such census data may be muddy, one researcher explains:

While true from a legal standpoint, given that Census data is self-reported, people born in the U.S. often do not report having U.S. citizenship in international data sources. For example, in the 2001 Spanish Census, of 21,000 people born in the United States, 9,000 were Spanish citizens, while 12,000 were counted as foreigners. That those who hold both U.S. and Spanish citizenship are only counted as Spanish further complicates the matter. In addition, the use of U.S. born as your defining universe potentially misses a number of U.S. citizens who were born outside the United States, either to American parent(s), or those who have since become naturalized U.S. citizens. (Schachter, 2006, p. 2)

He went on to advocate the use of U.S.-born data because that is not reliant on how countries define citizenship, even if this set "misses naturalized citizens and those born abroad of American parents, (because) it is a consistent measure, comparable across countries" (Schachter, 2006, p. 3). Some datasets include U.S. military personnel, but others do not. Schachter (2006) said that before the military presence in Iraq and Afghanistan, it was said that there were 253,000 U.S. military personnel abroad and an equal number of dependents and Department of Defense civilian personnel (p. 5). Another challenge with data is whether the numbers from two censuses are comparable given different definitional standards and methods (Schachter, 2006, p. 14).

In 2009, another researcher used a fresh tact, by drawing on administrative earnings records to understand the emigration of foreign workers from the U.S., a phenomenon which may have effects on government planning. J.A. Schwabish inferred emigration status by examining the longitudinal earnings patterns of foreign-born workers stateside by using three datasets from the IRS: the Detailed Earnings Records, the Numerical Identification System (Numident), and the Master Beneficiary Record (Schwabish, 2009, p. 1). He was looking for those with a stream of positive earnings followed by zero earning; that pattern suggested that the individual had left the country (Schwabish, 2009, p. 2). (It is not clear if he omitted those who had passed on.) For this study, he focused on those ages 16 to 62 in order to avoid capturing information about those who had retired. He separated out those who emigrated from the U.S. and those who left both the U.S. and the Social Security system. He found 1 – 1.5 percent of the foreign-born working population emigrates from the U.S. annually. He wrote:

These estimates suggest that the number of foreign-born workers who emigrate each year doubled between the late 1970s and late 1990s, rising from about 200,000 to 400,000. A smaller portion—between about 0.8 and 1.2 percent of foreign-born workers—emigrates from the United States and exits the Social Security system annually. This suggests that the number of foreign-born workers who emigrated each year from Social Security grew from about 150,000 to 330,000 over the same period. (Schwabish, 2009, p. 2)

Using a logit-regression analysis based on demographic features of the study population, Schwabish found that those with lower earnings were more likely to emigrate; further, he found that emigrating decreased with age at an increasing rate. In an environment with data constraints, he examined the probability of foreign-born immigrants in the U.S. workforce emigrating from the U.S. in the 26-year period covered by the data (Schwabish, 2009, p. 25). As he pointed out, there was little in the way of data that followed people from one country to another.

[Note: The U.S. has international social security agreements, known as "totalization agreements," to strive to ensure that foreign workers in the U.S. do not pay for social security in both the sending and host countries ("U.S. International Social Security Agreements," 2015).] In the past, a "residual method" of counting was used, which was a simple estimation: project the foreign-born population by adding estimates of new immigrants and subtracting estimated deaths for an estimated population (Warren and Peck, 1980, as cited by Schwabish, 2009, p. 4).

A Residual Calculation Method

$$E = P_{1960} - D + I - P_{1970}$$

$$E = P_{1960}' - P_{1960}' \times (1 - s) + I - P_{1970}$$

$$E = P_{1960}' \times s + I - P_{1970}$$

The residual calculation went as follows, with E = net number of foreign-born emigrants in the U.S. during a decade time-period; P_{1960} as the foreign-born population of the select age cohort in 1960; P_{1970} as the foreign-born population of the select age cohort in 1970; D as the number of foreign-born immigrant deaths stateside (overall); s as the survival probability of the foreign-born; I as the total number of immigrants in the U.S. between 1960 and 1970.

What is going on below is this, with the equation to solve for E.

$$E = P_{1960} - D + I - P_{1970}$$

Figure 4. An illustration of the residual method for calculating American emigration

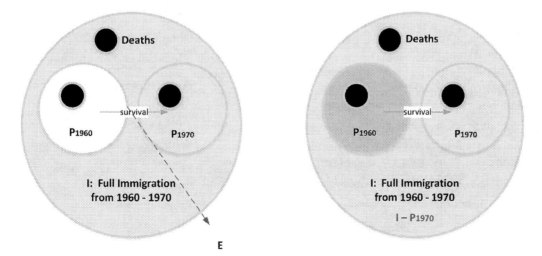

Line 1: The number of foreign-born emigrants in the age cohort from the U.S. in the 10-year-period studied (E) equals the population of foreign-born immigrant population of the select age cohort in 1960 minus known deaths plus the full set of immigrants from 1960 through 1970 inclusive minus the population of the foreign-born population of the select age cohort in 1970. What is left over should be those who did not die but also who do not show up in the 1970 population. (So 1960 and 1970 may be understood as discrete times 1 and 2 or "T1" and "T2" in a survival analysis.) P_{1960} and P_{1970} may be understood as discrete constants (starting and ending #s of the foreign-born emigrant population) and "D" and "I" are dynamic rates (and apply to the larger full-set of the immigrant population), with D as the numbers of deaths and the I as the numbers of immigrants (out-going and in-coming to the set)

$$E = P_{1960}' - P_{1960}' \times (1 - s) + I - P_{1970}$$

Line 2: In the above, the equation starts with the known population of the age cohort of foreign-born immigrants. Subtracted from that are the set of those expected to be lost based on the survival rate. From this is subtracted those who survived to 1970. What is left is another interpretation of E (the foreign-born immigrants to the U.S. who re-emigrated elsewhere and left the system). The P_{1960}' is used to indicate that those who are assumed to have died may be left out of the new calculation, so the only "survival" has to do with whether they survive to 1970 (vs. dying along the way). Likewise the ' prime symbol in the third line.

$$E = P_{1960}' \times s + I - P_{1970}$$

Line 3: In the third equation, which is very similar to the second one, the beginning age cohort of the foreign-born immigrant population in the U.S. is multiplied by the survival rate, and those who made it to 1970 are discounted through subtraction. What is left is then those who have left the system through re-emigration.

Ultimately, these measured those who disappeared from the system without other explanations. There was the assumption of a binary categorical outcome: whether the individual is present or absent.

This residual method of counting populations is still used as a baseline measure (against which other measures are compared). The residual refers to the error rate or gap between the actual numbers vs. the projected ones (based on a particular regression formula or model). Such regression models may be reweighted in order to make them more accurate.

Nowadays, even more sophisticated "survival analyses" statistical methods exist that enable even closer modeling of populations and changes to their makeup and with much smaller time increments ("spells") than decades. They include "censoring" representations to account for members who have either not entered the population set at the beginning of the study or those who have not left the population set at the end of the study. These new models enable the integration of population data to test the model's accuracy and to refine the model for more accurate projections.

Counting American Emigration Today

Often, the act of emigration is carried out with full intentions of returning. In 2001, the U.S. Congress considered the issue of how to count Americans abroad. As part of the public record, the legislators recounted the challenges that the U.S. Census Bureau asserted that they would face in trying to achieve this count (when asked in 1999 if they could include this in the 2000 census). The record reads:

The reasons behind the desire to count overseas Americans are clear, reasonable and justified. Many Americans abroad continue to pay taxes and vote here in the United States. Many are only overseas temporarily and will soon return. When they return of course they begin to use the resources in the States and communities where they will reside. Many overseas Americans recognize the civic importance of participating in the census and want to do their part. ("Americans Abroad, How Can We Count Them?" 2001, p. 1)

Some of the challenges mentioned include how the Census Bureau is supposed to determine actual citizenship vs. non-citizenship and fraud. Administrative records may not be sufficiently accurate from other organizations. Should such a count be voluntary or not? How may privacy be protected? How can this be done in a way that is not burdensome to either the citizens or the government? What if there are challenges to assigning a "home state" given long residence abroad? (p. 22) If there are mistakes, how may these be rectified? The report describes other challenges.

Unclaimed Citizenship

Many American citizens also do not official claim their citizenship status:

There are hundreds of thousands of persons in Canada and Mexico alone who are U.S. citizens but may lack documentation such as a U.S. passport to establish that fact, especially since U.S. citizens are not required to have a U.S. passport in order to travel to those countries. Moreover, there are thousands of persons around the globe who are in fact U.S. citizens, but have never chosen to make that fact of record by applying for documentation as a U.S. citizen. Yet a person's status as a U.S. citizen is determined by the laws enacted by Congress regardless of whether a person has come forward to confirm that status. ("Americans Abroad, How Can We Count Them?" 2001, p. 15)

Transient Citizenship without Documentation

There are also many who may have transiently been American who no longer have documentation of that.

*Additionally, there is a universe of persons--of unknown size---who, while clearly **U.S.** citizens at birth or some other point in their lives, lack current evidence that they remain **U.S.** citizens. In some instances, this involves complex adjudications, retrieval of records pertaining to past generations, and other pro-tracted procedures to determine if a person acquired, has retained, or may have lost U.S. citizenship even before one gets to the question of how to count such persons. ("Americans Abroad, How Can We Count Them?" 2001, p. 21)*

Fast Decay of Consular Information

Besides those challenges, the State Department only renews passports every decade (unless there are special circumstances). U.S. embassies and consulates keep purely voluntary self-reporting records by citizens abroad, and those who actually volunteer information are considered a small minority. The information that is provided suffers high decay, or it is not relevant for long. Congressional members also note that the State Department does not have the expertise to conduct or validate a census. In other words, the challenge is global in scope and non-trivial.

Besides the interest of government to start counting American citizens living abroad, there are some statistics of interest (relevant to 2000).

The Departments of Commerce and Transportation travel and .... tourism statistics reflect that Americans make more than 60 million trips abroad each year. According to the Department of Education, the number of U.S. students studying abroad each year has grown to 114,000. The Department of State issued over 7 million U.S. passports in FY-2000. The population of Americans abroad is very complex. Americans abroad include, for example, the more than 44,000 children born abroad to U.S. citizen parents each year for whom we issue Consular Reports of Birth Abroad. We also issue more than 6,000 Reports of Death of U.S. Citizens Abroad each year. More than 2,500 U.S. citizens are arrested abroad each year and serve sentences in foreign prisons. There are also some 400,000 recipients of U.S. Federal benefits such as Social Security and Veterans benefits abroad, which includes both citizens and non-citizens ("Americans Abroad, How Can We Count Them?" 2001, p. 18).

To fulfill government responsibilities, the U.S. needs to have an accurate count and sense of the geographical distribution of American citizens abroad for emergency evacuations and assistance in time of natural disasters or political restiveness ("Americans Abroad, How Can We Count Them?" 2001, p. 52).

With the prior information introducing the topic generally, what follows are some initial probes of the topic on social media. This is not a particular topic that may be top-of-mind for many, but there may be some insights in a broad skim of some social media platforms.

A View from Social Media

A political community is largely "imagined because the members of even the smallest nation will never know most of their fellow-members, meet them, or even hear of them, yet in the minds of each lives the image of their communion," wrote B. Anderson (2006, 1983, p. 6), in his *Imagined Communities*. If citizenship is, in part, the product of imagination—an imagined community in the view of B. Anderson (2006, 1983), then social media may be a way of understanding those who perceive themselves as members (even aspirational ones) and also those who may actually be members and their direct (also imagined) perceptions. Researchers have found empirical evidence from Twitter to suggest that social media sites are used to reproduce "social behavior we have evolved over thousands of years" (Quercia, Capra, & Crowcroft, 2012, p. 305). The larger questions which researchers have started to tease out were what aspects of people's lives may be reflected in social media and how much actual overlap there is (such as in the concept of the cyber-physical confluence).

Citizenship is a personal issue, not only as defined by U.S. law (as in related to the individual person as in "person-specific")), but it is also highly personal as in private and closely held. While expatriates are not particularly hard to find, the small subset of those who have relinquished U.S. nationality can be especially hard to find. Instead of striving to elicit information directly, this chapter involves using datafied social media information to capture some of the ideas in the public mind (writ large) about issues related to citizenship, U.S. emigration, and the renouncement of citizenship. (A secondary motive is to showcase some of the ways to extract social media data to complement more traditional research.) Historically, based on prior research, Americans have approached American emigration with puzzlement and suspicion. How sophisticated are the public sensibilities in relation to this issue? Are there gaps in understandings? Are there points of high emotion?

Many of the words related to citizenship are potent and emotional ones: birthright, loyalty, and patriotism. A "citizen" is an insider; a "citizen" belongs. Likewise, there are terms linked to the renouncement of citizenship, with other potent labels on the other polarity, like traitor, fugitive, spy, draft dodger, tax dodger, outsider, and other terms. These terms are freighted with public and private meaning and emotion. Citizenship is a critical element of identity for most. The stories about American citizenship while abroad are those of unsuspecting Americans who are "big blue walking passports" for those overseas who may want to become Americans—so the stories go. Often, the popular stories are of those who arrive at the U.S. with various ambitions and sometimes nefarious intentions. There are those taking part in "birth tourism" in order to have children who have American citizenship. The idea of native-born Americans renouncing citizenship seems somewhat heretical. In many ways, this population of individuals is fairly hidden except for those close to them. This is except for when individuals are fairly high profile; in the popular media, there are stories of pop stars who renounce their citizenship to protect their wealth (such as Tina Turner in 2013) (Kamen, Nov. 12, 2013). While mainstream media offer occasional articles about citizenship renouncement, the new public square exists on social media platforms, where individuals self-express, engage in online conversations, collect and share information, and otherwise engage. On the Surface Web, there are some sites which clearly encourage American renunciations of citizenship. To capture the tone of some of the sites, one site has as its tagline, "Because, U.S. citizenship is a problem to be solved" ("Relinquishment and renunciation guide—RenunciationGuide.com," 2015).

With the collection of so much digital information on social media platforms, the companies behind many of them commissioned application programming interfaces (APIs) to enable some limited access to their data for many: app developers, researchers, direct users of the social media platforms, and the general public. This next part involves the use of multiple software tools to collect data from some widely known platforms to showcase how public opinion regarding American emigration and American renunciation of citizenship may be explored. The main tool used is Network Overview, Discovery and Exploration for Excel (NodeXL); also used are NVivo (with its NCapture plug-in to Chrome and Internet Explorer) and Maltego Carbon. In general, the information collected are of two types: structural and content. Structural information refers to relational data represented as inter-relational networks (content networks, user networks, and others); content information refers to the messaging and multimedia (the exchanged or shared contents). In most cases, the extracted data are a sample of what is available, very rarely an N of all. Extractions from proprietary and commercial databases of contents are highly protected and rate-limited. (Wikipedia article networks are usually comprehensive. This may be because the data extraction actually is accessing open and publicly available data hosted through the MediaWiki technological substructure.)

Machine- and Human-Based Analyses

So how is extracted social media information used for ascertaining public opinions? Structurally, user networks may be analyzed to understand the social entities interacting with each other on particular platforms and across platforms and over the Web and Internet. Structurally, informational contents may be analyzed in order to understand which concepts co-occur in proximity. Metadata labeling various types of multimedia is also often used as tagging networks to further understand connected concepts, even as those doing the tagging may not themselves be aware of the connections. In terms of content analysis, this may be done with both machine-readings and human-readings. Machine-based types of readings involve frequency counts and text-based concordances to show the contexts in which various terms or phrases are used. Where machines may process large amounts of information in negligible amounts of time, human close readings often require the appropriate context and time (with human reading rates at 400 – 800 words per minute depending on whether the person is reading academically, or skimming / scanning). Various observations may be made from social media data—which may be understood as empirically obtained information. What is on social media platforms is what the world of people will create given the constraints of modern life.

What follows are light samples of information available on social media that may be exploited to provide glimpses and insights on public opinion on a social topic that is not often directly in the public mind. A more in-depth analysis of the topic in social media would require a much longer work, the application of machine-based linguistic analysis, human coding of the "take" of digital contents, and other approaches. Any assertions would likely do well to be qualified based on the fact that most are samples (without any current clear indicators of what percentage of the available set has been collected); the fact that some social media accounts are human, some cyborg, and some robots (and that many of the accounts are "fronts"); that certain platforms attract certain demographics (and ultimately certain subsets of a population), and so on.

Article Networks on Wikipedia

A basic approach may begin with Wikipedia, which is a crowd-sourced encyclopedia edited by people (and robots). With 4.7 million articles in its English-language version ("Size of Wikipedia," Feb. 19, 2015), this can offer a broad scale sense of a topic. An "article network" then shows the out-links from that article to other pages on Wikipedia. The articles in Wikipedia are considered summary ones based on edited publications; this online encyclopedia's popular articles are considered fairly well vetted, but those that are part of the long tail are much less so and often considered then less trustworthy.

The one-degree article network for "List_of_former_United_States_citizens_who_relinquished_their_nationality" article network on Wikipedia provides an overview of some of these individuals, their basis for citizenship (*jus soli* or "right of the soil" or *jus sanguinis* or "right of blood" or naturalized). There are a variety of professional roles described. Those listed are a fairly selective list, often for individuals with historical significance.

The article network for "Emigration_from_the_United_States" on Wikipedia shows some mentions of FATCA, political ideologies, bureaucratic offices, various locales with American communities and expatriates, and other related issues.

The article network for "American_diaspora" on Wikipedia addresses some of the bridging reasons that may bring people abroad. There are also links to pages for various locations.

Figure 5. List_of_former_United_States_citizens_who_relinquished_their_nationality article network on Wikipedia (1 deg.)

The article network for "Foreign_Account_Tax_Compliance_Act" reveals ties to various locations, to businesses that deal with tax issues, capital flight, and also individuals with some tie to the issue.

Video Networks on YouTube

Google's YouTube is a video-content sharing site with over a billion users and local presences in 75 countries ("Statistics," 2015). A "video network" based on YouTube holdings is a listing of related videos based on titles, meta-tags, and textual labels applied to the videos.

Figure 6. "Emigration_from_the_United_States" article network on Wikipedia (1 deg.)

A "United States" video network on YouTube shows the link of the U.S. to issues of military, governance, immigration, policies, politics, and technologies. Some of the videos express challenges to U.S. policies.

An "expat" video network on YouTube shows expat communities from various regions of the world, with both a sharing of experiences and information. There days in the lives of expats as well. The various clusters, indicated by color, show similarity ties based on regions for some and language clusters for others.

#hashtagged Conversations on Twitter

One of the main ways that trending events may be observed in near-real-time is to use the streaming API on Twitter. Another API involves the capturing of #hashtagged conversations that have occurred within the past week on Twitter. Depending on how disambiguated the #hashtagged label is for a particular conversation, information may be collected around #hashtagged events, thrown-discussions, and

Figure 7. "American_diaspora" article network on Wikipedia (1 deg.)

topic-based engagements. (Even if a hashtag is not fully disambiguated, it can have value because the resulting messages may be sorted into various categories for analysis.)

The #expat hashtagged conversation surfaces a range of issues, with some of the messages displayed along the edge (link) in the vertical sine wave data visualization.

In terms of the concept of #abroad, a range of discussants may be seen labeling their discussions in Figure 12. The contents of the Tweets are accessible in the data extraction but are not shown in this particular data visualization.

In terms of the concept of #stateless, this data extraction seems to have resulted in the capturing of a main discussion as contrasted to also smaller discussions among smaller groups. This conversation network is represented as a ring lattice graph with the nodes (vertexes) labeled with the names of the social media accounts' users and the links (edges) labeled with the Tweet. Topics and events are highly time sensitive on social media, and there can often be bursty events depending on in-world events, powerful media organizations and individuals on social media, and other factors.

Figure 8. "Foreign_Account_Tax_Compliance_Act" article network on Wikipedia (1 deg)

Keyword Searches on Twitter

A "keyword search" on Twitter often captures a more disparate range of discussions by capturing messages with the particular focal word mentioned. In a sense, this is much more disparate since there is not a purposive labeling of conversations with a selected label. Sometimes, what is collected may be much more difficult to make coherent or to even identify any extant relationships. Sometimes, the conversations held are narrowcast microchats among a few. Sometimes, self-looped conversations are captured, with people essentially Tweeting to themselves without an outsider reply or interaction (at least on that particular topic).

The "American" keyword search on Twitter brings out a network of many discussants with a wide variety of disparate conversations.

A search for "mycountry" results in a fairly sparse graph with both user account names and messaging shared.

Figure 9. A "United States" video network on YouTube

An "emigrant" keyword search highlights a range of microchats around the topic. The messaging is in the dataset but was not visually reflected in Figure 16.

User Networks on Twitter

There are ways to map the social networks of particular user accounts on a number of social media platforms. One organization that may be used to seed a network extraction is the Association of Americans Resident Overseas. This organization was founded in 1973 as a not-for-profit and non-partisan organization to represent U.S. citizens living abroad.

Figure 10. An "Expat" video network on YouTube

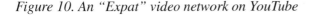

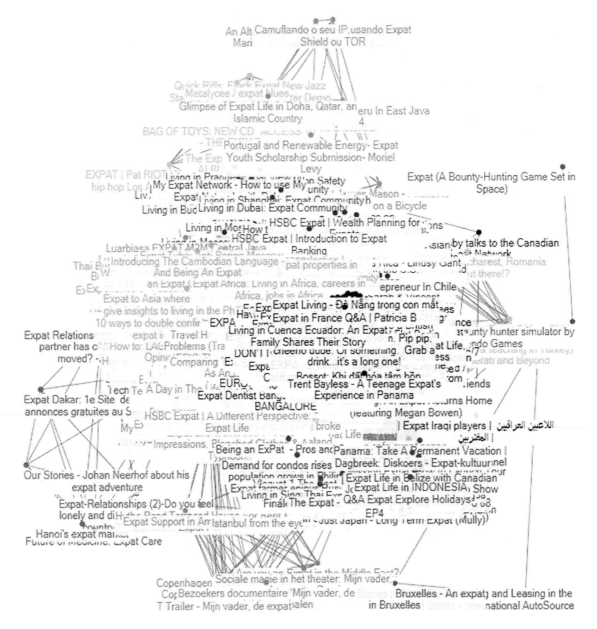

In Figure 17, @aaro clearly has broad reach and the interests of some government consulates and some mainline media organizations. There are some names of accounts that are eliciting expat stories (via @ExpatBlog, for example). Figure 17 is represented by Table 3, which contains the metrics of the extracted data. Such metrics may be analyzed for certain structural features of the network, which may suggest particular insights about the power dynamics and information sharing in the network. The vertices refer to the numbers of nodes or entities in the network; the edges refer to the links or ties. The actual nature of the links or ties depend on the social media platform that is the source of the data extraction. Self-loops include forms of self-referential relating on the social media platform. The maximum edges

Figure 11. "#expat" hashtag conversation network on Twitter (basic network)

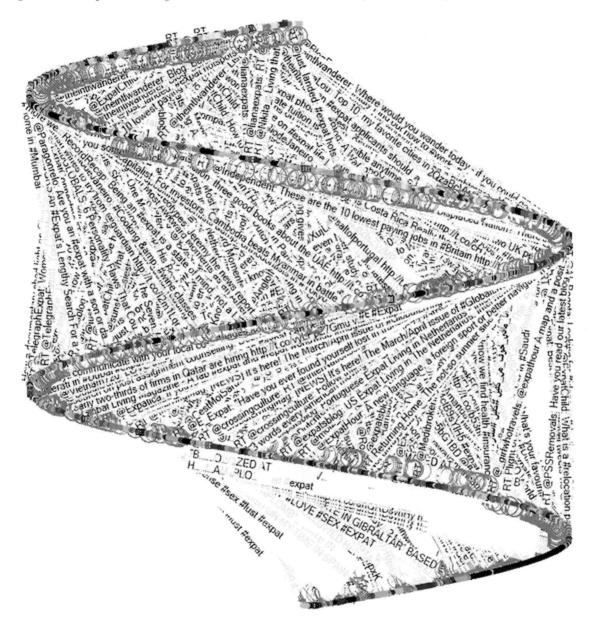

in a connected component show the size of the largest cluster. The maximum geodesic distance indicates the diameter of the graph or the farthest points between two nodes in the network. The average geodesic distance shows the average hops between any two nodes in the network. The graph density gives an indication of the amount of connectivity found in the network as a fraction of the possible connectivity if every node was connected to every other node.

There are also ways to capture Tweetstreams from an account for textual and other forms of analysis. A Tweetstream is a collection of microblogged messages.

Figure 12. "#abroad" hashtag conversation network on Twitter (basic network)

A cluster analysis of the Tweetstream shows not only some active accounts linked to @aaro but also some issues, such as FATCA and Social Security interests.

Also, a word cloud may be made of the captured Tweets in order to summarize the messaging and to provide a gist of the concepts. From the 1,121 recent Tweets, there are other accounts of active users (@uscitizenabroad and @repubabroad). There are plenty of keywords. There are not any #hashtagged conversations.

Figure 13. "#stateless" hashtag conversation network on Twitter (basic network)

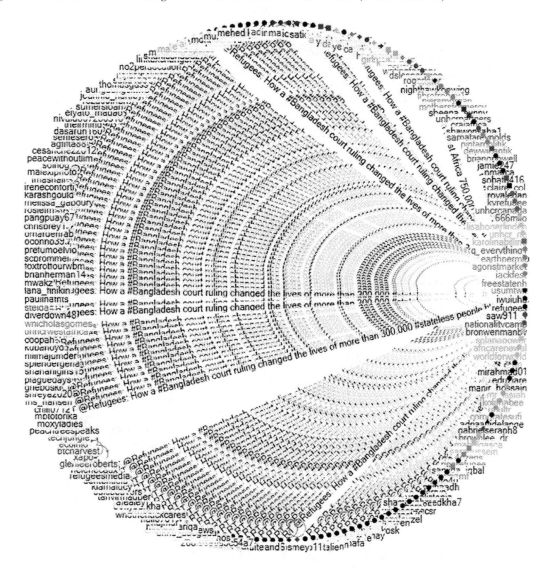

The URL of the organization may be used to analyze its http network or those other sites that it is connected to or which connect to it. Using Maltego Carbon, transforms may be run on the data in order to extract related email accounts, telephone numbers, documents, and other types of data.

The entity list underlying the data visualization in Figure # of the http networks of www.aaro.org provides insights on the geographical reach of the site. An actual footprinting of the site would result in the revelation of the locations of its servers.

A Level 2 footprinting provides more of a socio-technological sense of the network, the human-based accounts and underlying technological infrastructure of www.aaro.org. In Figure 23, this shows the ability to zoom in on any of the nodes or links for further exploration. (This screenshot was captured based on Maltego Carbon 3.5.3. The research overlapped with the changeover of the Maltego tool from Carbon 3.5.3 to Chlorine 3.6.0.)

Figure 14. "American" keyword search on Twitter (basic network)

Related Tags Networks on Flickr®

Flickr®, owned by Yahoo, is a content sharing site that enables the sharing of both digital images and videos. A related tags network extracted from Flickr® is built on the tags used to label particular digital resources. The seeding tag is analyzed for its relationship to other tags that co-occur with it, to form a kind of folksonomy or amateur tag classification.

The terms related to "citizen" in part show the nature of the multimedia collection, with some mentions of particular cameras and other words. Many of the terms here are inherently neutral while others are positive in evocation, like, "grandmother."

Figure 15. "mycountry" keyword search on Twitter (basic network)

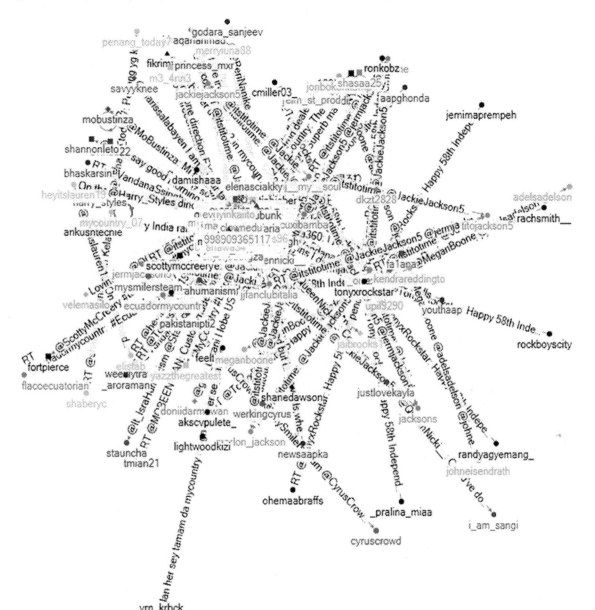

A run of "non-citizen" for a related tags network on Flickr® was run but came up empty. Instead, "foreigner" was used. Here various locations were evoked. Also, "racist" (a word which trends negative) was one of the tags.

A data extraction of "Americana" shows a Flickr tag network evoking California, Los Angeles, New Mexico, Arizona, and other locales. There is "bluegrass," "diner," "road trip," and "route66". There are also terms like "abandoned" and "decay."

Figure 16. "emigrant" keyword search on Twitter (basic network)

Finally, "expatriate" was used to seed a related tags network from Flickr®. Various locations were evoked. The male gender was evoked. "Worker" was another direct link. A thumbnail image was captured during the data extraction, and the imagery was integrated in the graph.

DISCUSSION

The issues of American emigration and the renunciation of U.S. citizenship are issues that are simultaneously micro-, meso, and macro-: they affect individuals, their close families and friends and colleagues, and the larger national polity. On the policy side, this is an issue of interest because of the possible implications for the nation of out-migration and the loss of skills, other contributions, and potential, of each out-migrating citizen. This chapter showcased the application of some basic network analysis applied to extracted social media data for glimmers of public awareness of and attitudes towards the particular topic. In mining data, there are direct and indirect methods to capture public consciousness

Figure 17. @aaro user network on Wikipedia (1 deg.)

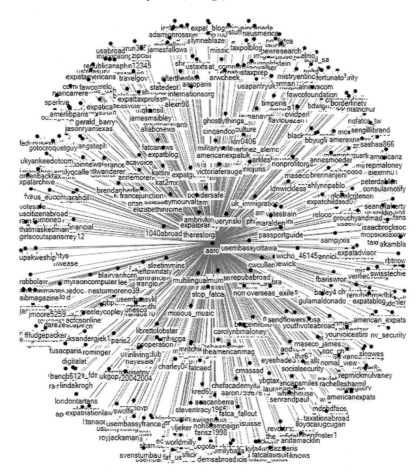

Figure 18. @ aaro Twitterstream Map of the locations of the microblogging messages (tweets)

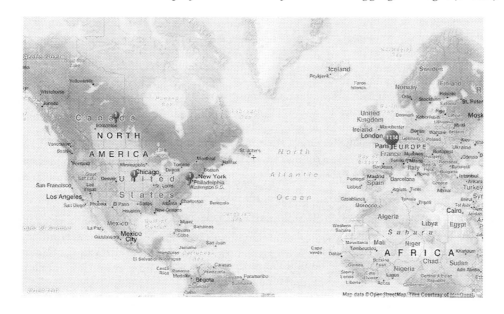

Table 3. Graph metrics table for the @aaro user network Twitter

Graph Metric	Value
Graph Type	Directed
Vertices	439
Unique Edges	469
Edges With Duplicates	201
Total Edges	670
Self-Loops	197
Reciprocated Vertex Pair Ratio	0.075342466
Reciprocated Edge Ratio	0.140127389
Connected Components	1
Single-Vertex Connected Components	0
Maximum Vertices in a Connected Component	439
Maximum Edges in a Connected Component	670
Maximum Geodesic Distance (Diameter)	2
Average Geodesic Distance	1.990899
Graph Density	0.002449527
Modularity	Not Applicable
NodeXL Version	1.0.1.335

Figure 19. @aaro Tweetstream cluster as a word branch

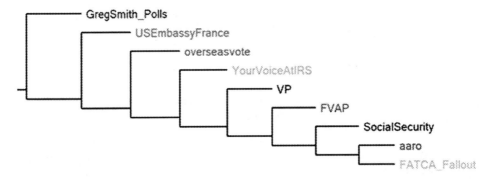

and points-of-view. The use of social media platforms and social media data must include sensitivity to the nuances of each platform, the types of information that is available, the subgroups of populations that are represented in each platform, and the potential quirks of the extracted data from each platform (and by each method). Such data can also be highly dynamic and evolving, particularly data in microblogging sites (as compared to article networks on Wikipedia or video networks on YouTube). What is in the public consciousness varies, with some issues forefronted, others backgrounded, and much ultimately forgotten. Some ideas may be viewable only through closer analysis of the digital products of human creation at the macro levels, at the group levels of consciousness.

Figure 20. A word cloud of the tweetstream of @aaro account on Twitter

Figure 21. Http networks of www.aaro.org on the web and internet

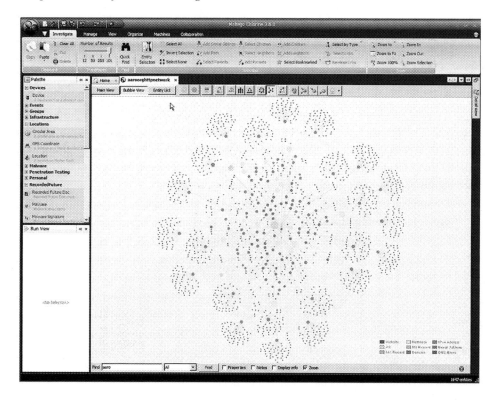

Figure 22. The entity list for the aaro.org http network and a sense of geographical reach

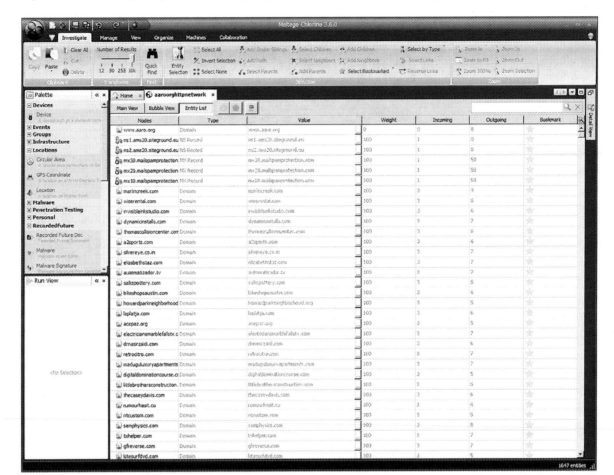

Some issues never emerge into broad public consciousness but are in the collective subconscious, and there are issues that exist in the collective unconscious, latent, quiet, hidden, but tappable. Some of these indirect methods of tapping online conversations and metadata may help illuminate some of these more latent issues in the public conscious, subconscious, and unconscious—for further exploration.

FUTURE RESEARCH

To update this work, it is important to note that the United States' current presidential election cycle has stirred up interest in migrations to Canada. A somewhat tongue-in-cheek but also pragmatic pre-election article summarizes some of the requirements that have to be met in order to emigrate: a clean FBI background check, sufficient settlement funds (ranging from $12,164 to $32,191 in Canadian dollars depending on the family size), and other considerations. Canada itself ranks higher than the U.S. in terms of living costs (ranking 3rd compared to the U.S.'s 19th in the world ranking, according to a Deutsche Bank survey of prices). This article also describes requisite adjustments and lifestyle changes that Americans may encounter as they seek to resettle abroad (Morgan, Aug. 21, 2016). It seems that

Figure 23. L2 footprinting of the aaro.org site for social-structural information

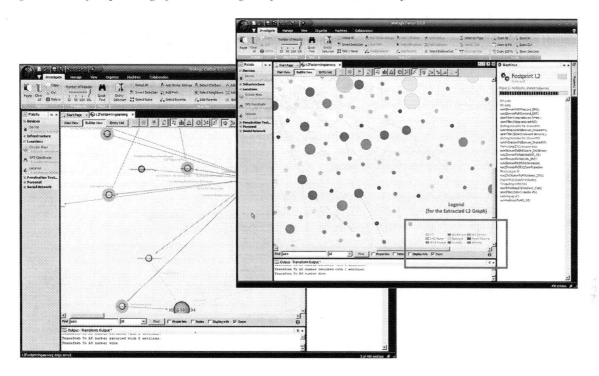

Figure 24. "citizen" related tags network on Flickr (1 deg.)

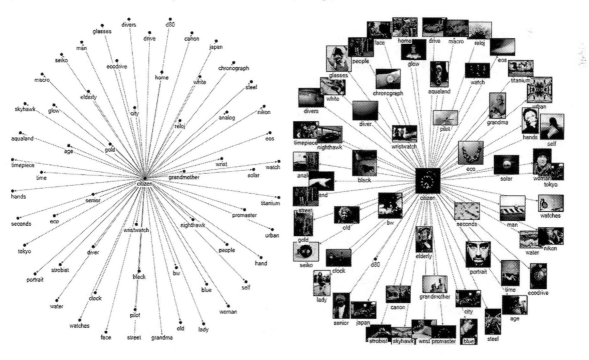

Figure 25. "foreigner" related tags network on Flickr® (1 deg.)

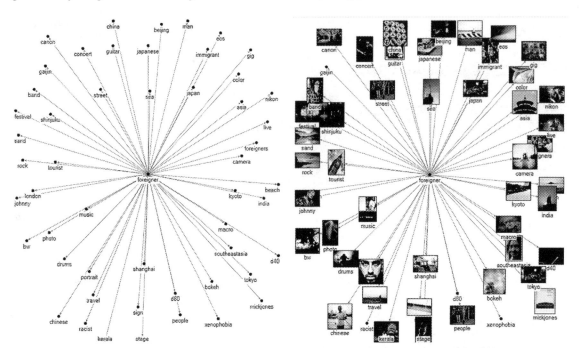

Figure 26. "Americana" related tags network on Flickr® (1 deg)

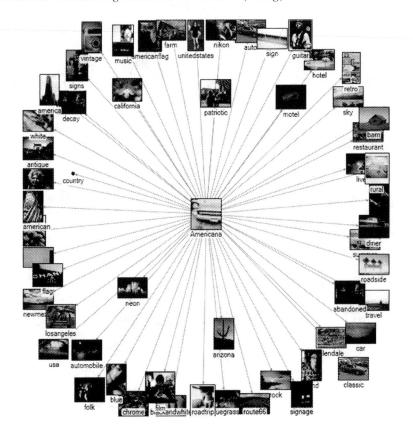

Figure 27: "expatriate" Related Tags Network on Flickr® (1 deg.)

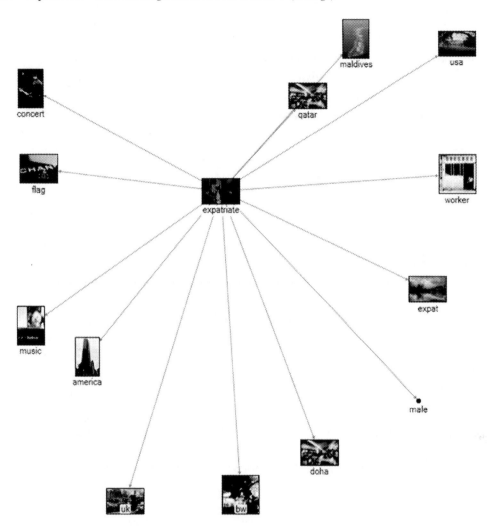

this issue of national out-migrations (as contrasted to the current mass migrations of Syrians from civil war and state failure) manifests in new ways all the time, and political concerns are also a constant part of the equation.

In terms of potential future research, there is much more that can be learned about why people may choose to exit from their U.S. citizenship and their lives afterwards in a receiving country. There may be work done to understand who may self-select for such a choice. It would be interesting to examine the commercial industries and government entities that surround such choices. It may help to understand who is doing the recruiting for such individuals (nation states, businesses, individuals, and others) and why.

On the social media platform side, there are other approaches that may shed fresh light on the topic. One obvious approach would be to use geolocational information to identify location themes, attitudes, and concerns. Regions with high concentrations of American expats may be focused on to gain a sense of the public conversations on the topic of citizenship, for example. Or, there may be the exploitation of spatiotemporal data, particularly around trending events in physical space. There are also text scraping and text analysis approaches using various high-level programming tools and linguistic analysis packages, multimedia scraping using web-browser-based plug-ins, text summarization software programs, and other approaches. Also, there are a range of other seeding words that may be used for the data extractions. Different social media platforms may be tapped for other insights. Different sequences of applying these queries may also help surface fresh insights: for example, to find seeding words, a researcher could begin with a natural language analysis of a core document and use extracted words as leads from that process. Or a researcher could start with an article network on Wikipedia for some lead terms. A hashtag conversation may lead to @accounts for further exploration and network graphing. There is a universe of question types that may be addressed using social media surrounding a particular topic.

CONCLUSION

Ultimately, this chapter was about the application of a range of techniques that could be applied to social media data to explore something of the public mind (the broad conscious, subconscious, and unconscious mind) on a topic based on collective electronic social spaces. While the approaches are quite rudimentary, the potential is enormous. In the special case in which these techniques were applied, there were some light observations about American emigration and the relatively rare cases of renunciation of U.S. citizenship for ex-Americans.

ACKNOWLEDGMENT

This was originally conceptualized and realized as a project in a graduate course on International Migration (Sociology 738) at Kansas State University. I want to thank Dr. Alisa Garni for her wonderful class, high demands for intellectual rigor, and general support for all of her students.

REFERENCES

A record 3,415 Americans ditch their passports. (2015, Feb. 12). *CNN Money*. Retrieved Feb. 22, 2015, from http://money.cnn.com/2015/02/12/pf/americans-expat-citizenship-passports/

Adams, B. (2011). *The Great Escape*. Retrieved Jan. 31, 2015, from http://online.barrons.com/articles/SB50001424052748703827804577056023254214872#printMode

Advice about possible loss of U.S. nationality and dual nationality. (2015). U.S. Department of State, Bureau of Consular Affairs. Retrieved Feb. 22, 2015, from http://travel.state.gov/content/travel/english/legal-considerations/us-citizenship-laws-policies/citizenship-and-dual-nationality.html

Ahmed, I. (1997). *Exit, voice and citizenship. International Migration, Immobility and Development: Multidisciplinary Perspectives*. Oxford, UK: Beg Publishers.

American Diaspora. (2015, Jan. 17). In *Wikipedia*. Retrieved Jan. 31, 2015, from http://en.wikipedia.org/wiki/American_diaspora

Americans Abroad, How Can We Count Them ? (2001, July 26). Hearing before the Subcommittee of the Census of the Committee on Government Reform. House of Representatives. 107th Congress. Serial 107-13.

Anderson, B. (2006). *Imagined Communities: Reflections on the Origin and Spread of Nationalism.* New York: Verso.

Bainbridge, J. (1968). *Another Way of Living: A Gallery of Americans Who Choose to Live in Europe.* New York: Holt, Rinehart and Winston.

Bratsberg, B., & Terrell, D. (1996). Where do Americans Live Abroad? *International Migration Review, 30*(3), 788 – 802. Retrieved Jan. 31, 2015, from http://www.jstor.org/stable/2547637

Burrell, J.S. (2004, June). *Emigration of U.S.-born S&E Doctorate Recipients.* InfoBrief. SRS Home. NSF 04-327.

Census Bureau projects U.S. and world populations on New Year's Day. (2014, Dec. 29). U.S. Census Bureau. CB14-TPS.90. Retrieved Feb. 22, 2015, at http://www.census.gov/newsroom/press-releases/2014/cb14-tps90.html

Dashefsky, A., DeAmicis, J., Lazerwitz, B., & Tabory, E. (1992). Americans Abroad: A Comparative Study of Emigrants from the United States. New York: Springer Science + Business Media, LLC. doi:10.1007/978-1-4757-2169-0

Emigration from the United States. (2015, Jan. 27). In Wikipedia. Retrieved Jan. 31, 2015, from http://en.wikipedia.org/wiki/Emigration_from_the_United_States

Esipova, N., Pugliese, A., & Ray, J. (2014, Jan. 17). Potential Net Migration Index declines in many countries: Southern Europe's economic troubles make it less attractive. Gallup. Retrieved April 29, 2015, from http://www.gallup.com/poll/166796/potential-net-migration-index-declines-countries.aspx

Expatriation Tax. (2014, June 28). Internal Revenue Services. Retrieved Feb. 22, 2015, at http://www.irs.gov/Individuals/International-Taxpayers/Expatriation-Tax

Faist, T. (2008). Migrants as transnational development agents: An inquiry into the newest round of the migration-development nexus. *Population Space and Place, 14*(1), 21–42. doi:10.1002/psp.471

Fernandez, E. W. (1995, Jan). *Estimation of the Annual Emigration of U.S. Born Persons by Using Foreign Censuses and Selected Administrative Data: Circa 1980.* U.S. Bureau of the Census, Population Division. Working Paper No. 10.

Flowers, A. (2015, Dec. 10). Immigration projections rebound with the economy. *DataLab.* Retrieved Jan. 31, 2015, from http://fivethirtyeight.com/datalab/immigration-projections-rebound-along-with-the-economy/

Foreign Account Tax Compliance Act. (2015, Feb. 14). In *Wikipedia.* Retrieved Feb. 22, 2015, from http://en.wikipedia.org/wiki/Foreign_Account_Tax_Compliance_Act

Kamen, A. (2013, Nov. 12). In the loop: Tina Turner formally 'relinquishes' U.S. citizenship. *The Washington Post.*

LaMance, K. (2014, Mar. 27). Reinstatement of U.S. citizenship lawyers. *Legal Match*. Retrieved Feb. 22, 2015, from http://www.legalmatch.com/law-library/article/reinstatement-of-us-citizenship-lawyers.html

List of former United States citizens who relinquished their nationality. (2015, Feb. 18). In *Wikipedia*. Retrieved Feb. 22, 2015, from http://en.wikipedia.org/wiki/List_of_former_United_States_citizens_who_relinquished_their_nationality

McGath, T. (2013, Sept. 17). Get out While You Can: Why Young Americans Should Emigrate. *Alternet*.

Morgan, D. (2016, Aug. 21). So you want to move to Canada? CBS News. Retrieved Aug. 21, 2016, from http://www.cbsnews.com/news/so-you-want-to-move-to-canada/

Passel, J. S., Cohn, D., & Gonzalez-Barrera, A. (2012). *Net migration from Mexico falls to zero—and perhaps less*. Pew Research Center. Retrieved Mar. 5, 2015, from http://www.pewhispanic.org/2012/04/23/net-migration-from-mexico-falls-to-zero-and-perhaps-less/

Peck, D. (2013, June 19). Why so many Americans are Leaving the U.S. --in 1 Big Chart. Chartist. *The Atlantic*.

Picchi, A. (2015, Feb. 12). Record number renouncing American citizenship. *CBS News. Moneywatch*.

Quercia, D., Capra, L., & Crowcroft, J. (2012). The social world of Twitter: Topics, geography, and emotions. In *Proceedings of the Sixth International AAAI Conference on Weblogs and Social Media*. Association for the Advancement of Artificial Intelligence.

Relinquishment and renunciation guide—RenunciationGuide.com. (2015). Retrieved Mar. 8, 2015, at http://renunciationguide.com/

Renunciation of U.S. Nationality. (n.d.). U.S. Department of State, Bureau of Consular Affairs. Retrieved Feb. 22, 2015, from http://travel.state.gov/content/travel/english/legal-considerations/us-citizenship-laws-policies/renunciation-of-citizenship.html

Rice, M. (2010, June 4). Not Everyone Wants to Live in America. *Forbes Magazine*.

Saxenian, A. (2006). *The New Argonauts: Regional Advantage in a Global Economy*. Cambridge, MA: Harvard University Press.

Schachter, J. P. (2006). *Estimation of Emigration from the United States using International Data Sources. United Nations Expert Group Meeting on Measuring International Migration: concepts and Methods*. New York: United Nations Secretariat, Dept. of Economic and Social Affairs, Statistics Division.

Schwabish, J. A. (2009). *Identifying Rates of Emigration in the United States Using Administrative Earnings Records*. Congressional Budget Office, Working Paper Series.

Size of Wikipedia. (2015, Feb. 19). In *Wikipedia*. Retrieved Mar. 5, 2015, from http://en.wikipedia.org/wiki/Wikipedia:Size_of_Wikipedia

Statistics. (2015). In *YouTube*. Retrieved Mar. 8, 2015, at http://www.youtube.com/yt/press/statistics.html

Stcherbatcheff, B. (2014, June 28). Why Americans abroad are giving up their citizenship. *Newsweek*. Retrieved Mar. 3, 2015, from http://www.newsweek.com/why-americans-abroad-are-giving-their-citizenship-256447

U.S. Citizens and Resident Aliens Abroad. (2015). Internal Revenue Service. Retrieved Mar. 5, 2015, from http://www.irs.gov/Individuals/International-Taxpayers/U.S.-Citizens-and-Resident-Aliens-Abroad

U.S. International Social Security Agreements. (2015). Social Security Administration. Retrieved Mar. 5, 2015, from http://www.ssa.gov/international/agreements_overview.html

Wood, R. W. (2014, May 3). Record numbers renounce U.S. citizenship—and many aren't counted. *Forbes Magazine*. Retrieved Feb. 22, 2015, from http://www.forbes.com/sites/robertwood/2014/05/03/americans-are-renouncing-citizenship-at-record-pace-and-many-arent-even-counted/

ADDITIONAL READING

Hai-Jew, S. (2014). *Querying Social Media with NodeXL*. Scalar Platform. Retrieved March 12, 2015, at http://scalar.usc.edu/works/querying-social-media-with-nodexl/index

Hansen, D. L., Schneiderman, B., & Smith, M. A. (2011). *Analyzing Social Media Networks with NodeXL: insights from a Connected World*. Elsevier.

KEY TERMS AND DEFINITIONS

Article Network: A network graph displaying the relationships between article pages on a wiki site (or some other platform).

Census: An official count of the population.

Citizenship: The formal membership to a state.

Content Network: A relational graph depicting interrelationships between concepts (expressed as words).

Emigration: The out-migration of people from one state to another, sometimes volitionally and sometimes by force (of circumstance like a natural disaster or government edict, by threat, or other factors).

Hashtag: # (a symbol used to indicate a related conversation to a topic).

http Network: A network graph displaying interlinked web pages on the WWW.

***Jus Sanguinis*:** Right of blood (to citizenship).

***Jus Soli*:** Right of the soil (to citizenship).

Microblog: A social media platform which enables the real-time sharing of short text messages, URLs, images, and video contents.

Naturalization: A formal process which enables a foreign-born individual to become a citizen of the country.

Passport: A formal government document used by citizens to travel.

Related Tags Network: A network graph built with co-occurring tags.

Renunciation: The formal rejection of something.

Social Media: A range of technologies which enable people to create identities, interact with others, share information, and engage in mediated digital ways.

Surface Web: The Web which is accessible by current-generation Web browsers (often not including the dynamic data in the Deep Web).

Tweetstream: A collection of microblogging messages (such as those related to one user account or an event or a particular topic of conversation).

Chapter 14

Finding Automated (Bot, Sensor) or Semi–Automated (Cyborg) Social Media Accounts Using Network Analysis and NodeXL Basic

Shalin Hai-Jew
Kansas State University, USA

ABSTRACT

Various research findings suggest that humans often mistake social robot ('bot) accounts for human in a microblogging context. The core research question here asks whether the use of social network analysis may help identify whether a social media account is fully automated, semi-automated, or fully human (embodied personhood)—in the contexts of Twitter and Wikipedia. Three hypotheses are considered: that automated social media account networks will have less diversity and less heterophily; that automated social media accounts will tend to have a botnet social structure, and that cyborg accounts will have select features of human- and robot- social media accounts. The findings suggest limited ability to differentiate the levels of automation in a social media account based solely on social network analysis alone in the face of a determined and semi-sophisticated adversary given the ease of network account sock-puppetry but does suggest some effective detection approaches in combination with other information streams.

INTRODUCTION

With the popularization of social media, masses of people have gone online to interact, collaborate, and share; in their midst, non-human social media accounts have likewise proliferated. These automated and semi-automated accounts include social bots, sensor-based accounts, and human-assisting robots as well as cyborg accounts (human-assisted machine accounts; machine-assisted human accounts). When people interact on social media platforms, whether they are microblogging, gaming, sharing photos, or

DOI: 10.4018/978-1-5225-0846-5.ch014

making connections with others, many generally assume that they are interacting with other people. On a number of social media platforms today, there are accounts that are masks for algorithmic actors—robots and sensors, as well as cyborgs (accounts representing human-assisted robots or robot-assisted humans).

The online social ecology benefits from many of the efficiencies and tasks of automated agents, whether their presence is noticed and identified or not. On microblogging sites, robots ('bots) are used to send out critical messaging alerts about traffic, weather, environmental hazards, and missing children. On Wikipedia, vetted robots contribute to the coherence and functioning of the site by "injecting public domain data, monitoring and curating content, augmenting the MediaWiki software, and protecting the encyclopedia from malicious activity" (Halfaker & Riedl, 2012, p. 80). The Wikimedia Foundation Inc. also runs their own scripts to control against page vandalism and vulgarity; it has human staff to control against public relations manipulations and personal attacks (Safer, Apr. 5, 2015). Rambot, the encyclopedia's first officially sanctioned robot, inserted census data into articles about countries and cities. Robots traverse virtually all social media platforms in order to collect information and provide services.

There are high hopes expressed in the research literature for the services that robots may provide to humans. One research team identified a range of early and functional chatterbot roles: digital assistant, information provider, and general chat (Tatai, Csordás, Kiss, Szaló, & Laufer, 2003, p. 9). Socialbots may be deployed in swarms across social media to mend hard feelings and promote social comity:

Swarms of 'bots could be used to heal broken connections between infighting social groups and bridge existing social gaps. Socialbots could be deployed to leverage peer effects to promote more civic engagement and participation in elections (Hwang, Pearce, & Nanis, 2012, p. 40).

Social robots may be disarming; they may sooth communal feelings; they may mediate. Sensor networks, many with data flowing on social media platforms, are seen as potentially providing cost-savings and other efficiencies for government services (Ylagan, 2014). For examples, sensors may inform people of traffic congestion on the public roads; they may inform about hazardous chemicals or bioagents in the environment; they may enhance security awareness at critical sites..and broadcast select and relevant information broadly.

On the other hand, there have also been disruptive automated agents that have been deployed on social media platforms to dupe human users into revealing sensitive information to compromise their finances, protected information, and personal security. They autogenerate and distribute spam broadly to sell a variety of goods and services, to promote misinformation, and to manage (false) impressions. Some are used to "socially engineer" people into revealing sensitive information with risk implications for companies and even to national security. In one study, researchers created algorithmic agents to present as friends of friends on Facebook in order to access targeted individual's private information in order to launch attacks against corporate employers of those targeted individuals (Elyashar, Fire, Kagan, & Elovici, 2013); their conclusion was that they were able to access 50 – 70% of the queried employees' private data in the targeted organizations even though these individuals. These researchers show that such "homing agents" enable organization intrusion and mining (Elyashar, Fire, Kagan, & Elovici, 2013; Elishar, Fire, Kagan, & Elovici, 2012). The automation of such compromises means that this may be done at negligible cost and at mass scale (Boshmaf, Muslukhov, Beznosov, & Ripeanu, 2012). Hired (or manipulated) "sybils" or "paid participants" often come at much higher cost than automation, even when developing markets are exploited for such applications of human labor. Robot accounts (including sensor-based ones) are used for both benign and malign purposes.

People would benefit from being able to discern the presence of automated agents in their social media environments since so many human activities are conducted in those spaces. While some social media accounts are clearly flagged as robots or sensors, there are many cyborg ("cybernetic organism") accounts which do not self-identify as such (as humans and machines messaging). Even more concerning are socialbots that often literally pass as humans on virtually all popular social media platforms. The growing sophistication of the design of socialbots, particularly informed by research in linguistics, psychology (particularly personality and emotion research), communications, and computer science, means that traditional methods of ferreting out 'bot accounts are not as effective. For the general public, which generally does not have access to either the back-end data or the computing expertise to discern robots, it may help to have some additional ways of perusing an account to understand its underlying "nature," if you will.

In this social and interrelational context, socialbots embed in social networks of people, cyborgs, and other robots. Is it possible to ascertain the essential nature of an account (defined here as whether it is controlled and driven by a robot or sensor, cyborg, or fully human entity) by applying network analysis to the target account, its messaging, and direct "alters" in its network? More specifically, what are some of the capabilities of Network Overview, Discovery, and Exploration for Excel (NodeXL) in this practical application?

REVIEW OF THE LITERATURE

The main concern expressed in the research literature is that people who engage on online social networks may be unduly influenced by malicious automated agents ("malbots") that create an illusion of "personhood." These malicious scripted agents may spread mis-information, redirect human traffic to compromised websites, create a false sense of viral enthusiasm through astroturfing, or swipe private information under the guise of online friendship or professional relationship. "Sociable technology" promises friendship but delivers only the "illusion of intimacy" and "performance" of identity (Turkle, 2011, p. 1, 12). There have been widely documented cases of stock market manipulations and political election manipulations based on automated agents. There have been accidental shocks to high frequency stock trading with hacked news accounts that mis-reported information. Socialbot attacks on online social networks pose a risk to "discourse and democratic processes" and that such bots have demonstrated capabilities to "shape and influence" the social graph (Mitter, Wagner, & Strohmaier, 2013). The points of compromise may be many, with people's computers and accounts compromised to create false "follower markets," to raise the popularity of 'bot- or cyborg-driven accounts, botnets (robot networks), and hashtagged conversations. In massively multiplayer online role-playing games (MMORPGs), automated agents are a corrupting influence and ruin a sense of fair play (Woo, Kang, & Kim, 2012).

While the scope of this issue is not clear, the research literature does suggest a wide proliferation of adversarial socialbot networks headed by botherder (command and control) software and human coders (or hackers) with malicious intentions to automate social engineering (Huber, Kowalski, Nohlberg, & Tjoa, 2009; Boshmaf, Muslukhov, Beznosov, & Ripeanu, 2011). People fall for social engineering schemes when they unthinkingly adhere to social cues (Singer & Friedman, 2014, p. 40). A colloquial term for this exploit is "hacking the wetware," or attacking a system by compromising the human staff or membership because they are often the weakest link in a socio-technical system. Coordinated 'bot networks may be identified and studied to understand their particular aims (Perez, Birregah, Layton,

Lemercier, & Watters, 2013). Researchers point to the usage of social network sites as command-and-control infrastructures to run botnets (Kartaltepe, Morales, Xu, & Sandhu, 2010).

Pursuing Revelatory "Tells" or Unintended Reveals of Actual Identity

In the common parlance, a "tell" is an unconscious action that may betray a ruse or deception, particularly in games of strategy and chance, such as poker. In popular culture, reading tells is often a subtle endeavor, involving astute observations of near-invisible facial or physical micro-expressions or communications clues (like Freudian slips, word choices, silences, or changes in conversation topics). This sense of "tell" assumes an unconscious slippage based on human psychology and / or physiology. In this context, a "tell" is a kind of design slippage that reveals a 'bot or automated agent (or a cyborg social media account) that is attempting to pass as a human. This does not suggest anything near sentience (or consciousness or unconsciousness) of the automated agent; rather, the idea is that the "tell" is a limitation of the bots' human designer, who put out a flawed creation. Information technology (IT) security analysts have studied the spatio-temporal patterns of social spammers in order to identify distinguishing characteristics. Using social honeypots, one research team identified a strategy in timing, with peaks in spamming activity around holidays, namely, around Columbus Day, Halloween, and Thanksgiving, with the researchers suggesting that legitimate users might be spending more time online then (Webb, Caverlee, & Pu, 2008, p. 5). Geographically, the "spam profiles almost never overlap with the locations of their targets" (Webb, Caverlee, & Pu, 2008, p. 2). The various profiles also used "thousands of URLs and various redirection techniques to funnel users to a handful of destination web pages" (Webb, Caverlee, & Pu, 2008, p. 2), which shows the centralized work. Some have applied textual stylometry (a form of quantitative content analysis) to discern chatter robots (as a class of identifiable authors) and to infer the intelligence of the communicator (whether artificial intelligence or human) (Ali, 2014). The trajectory of large-scale spam campaigns has also been studied (Stringhini, Kruegel, & Vigna, 2010, p. 8). In terms of spam messaging, there are certain types of promotions:

An analysis of 200 million tweets revealed that 50% of spam tweets were used to promote free music, games, books, jewelry, electronics and vehicles. Also, gambling and financial products, such as loans, are promoted via spam on Twitter (Zangerle & Specht, 2014, p. 587).

Researchers suggest that "automated social engineering" is a serious risk given the human tendency to anthropomorphize machines (see them as human), cognitively create narrative structures with only a few data points, and generally fail to recognize that they're dealing with a computer program and not a person. The more people interacted with particular 'bots, the less "neurotic" the robots might seem and the more human-like over time (Holtgraves, Ross, Weywadt, & Han, 2007, p. 2163). A 'bot's use of a person's first name was a factor in the perception of the robot as having a personality. The researchers also observed that communications variables affected perceptions of the bot:

Specifically, a relatively high degree of familiarity on the part of the bot – and hence a positively polite style – resulted in perceptions of a more skilled conversationalist. And a bot who responded relatively quickly was perceived as more conscientious and extraverted than a bot who responded more slowly.

Finally, similar to human interactants, participants preferred not to chat (as evidenced by shorter chat times) with a bot they perceived as being high in neuroticism. (Holtgraves, Ross, Weywadt, & Han, 2007, p. 2172)

Twitter, like other social media platforms, has undergone "botification" (Hwang, Pearce, & Nanis, 2012, as cited in Edwards, Edwards, Spence, & Shelton, 2014, p. 372), with some 5% of its users identified as bots (D'Onfro, 2013). When Instagram purged its rolls of inactive accounts and spam accounts, they deleted some 15% of extant accounts (Griffin, Dec. 19, 2014). The estimated ranges of 'bots on Twitter range from 14 million to about 23 million based on various mainstream news accounts. In one research study, human users of Twitter found Twitterbots "credible, attractive, competent in communication, and interactional. Additionally, there were no differences in the perception of source credibility, communication competence, or interactional intentions between the bot and human Twitter agents" (Edwards, Edwards, Spence, & Shelton, 2014, p. 372).

Link click rates of uniform resource locators (URLs) offered by 'bots in social media contexts range up to 76.1%, and they may lead to "shady webshops, phishing websites, or malware" (Lauinger, Pankakoski, Balzarotti, & Kirda, 2010, p. 1). Available since 2002, shortened URLs have been used in text messages to mask questionable destinations:

Based on our investigations of a URL shortener service, we find that around 80% of shortened URLs contained spam-related content. The extent of spam might be larger due to the lack of spam blocking features (Klein & Strohmaier, 2012, p. 87).

Social media users who are susceptible to interacting with social media robots tend to use Twitter for a conversational purpose; tend to be more open and social since they communicate with many different users; use more social words, and show more affection than non-susceptible users; the friending of 'bots ranged from an average acceptance rate of 59.1% to some 80% (Wagner, Mitter, Körner, & Strohmaier, 2012, p. 41). More recent research has been conducted to identify those who are most susceptible to interacting with socialbots on Twitter, with the two main risk factors having a high "kloutscore" (a metric of social influence) and also those having the highest number of friends in the system as the "strongest predictors of whether or not an individual will interact with a social bot…" of the 13 variables studies (Wald, Khoshgoftaar, Napolitano, & Sumner, 2013, p. 10). A later study used regression trees to identify variables correlated with users' susceptibility to socialbots. This team found that "users who use more negation words (e.g. not, never, no) tend to interact more often with bots, which means they have a higher susceptibility level. Further, users who tweet more regularly (i.e. have a high temporal balance) and users who use more words related with the topic death (e.g. bury, coffin, kill) tend to interact more often with bots than other susceptible users" (Wagner, Mitter, Körner, & Strohmaier, 2012, p. 47). Claudia Wagner, et al. observed that more socially active individuals online "would develop some kind of social skills or capabilities to distinguish human users from social bots. This is obviously not the case and suggests that attacks of social bots can be effective even in cases where users have experience with social media and are highly active" (Wagner, Mitter, Körner, & Strohmaier, 2012, p. 47). It is not a stretch to imagine the ease of creating a robot that would fit right in with the "selfie" and social performance cultures of some online social sites.

Socialbots: "Hello, World!"

Essentially, socialbots are merely automated computer programs designed to function on online social networks as intelligent and emotional agents. They must be designed to hold their own autonomously on social media platforms.

A socialbot is an automation software that controls an account on a particular OSN, and has the ability to perform basic activities such as posting a message and sending a connection request. What makes a socialbot different from self-declared bots (e.g., Twitter bots that post up-to –date weather forecasts) and spambots is that it is designed to be stealthy, that is, it is able to pass itself off as a human being. This allows the socialbot to compromise the social graph of a targeted OSN by infiltrating (i.e., connecting to) its users so as to reach an influential position. This position can be then exploited to spread misinformation and propaganda in order to bias the public opinion (Boshmaf, Muslukhov, Beznosov, & Ripeanu, 2011, p. 93).

Spambots use a variety of methods to achieve their ends. One researcher team described four types across a range of social media platforms: "displayer" bots that display some spam contents on profile pages; "bragger" bots that post messages (usually status updates) on their own feeds, so the messages show on direct recipient feeds but not on recipient profiles; "poster" bots that send direct messages to each victim, and "whisperer" bots which send private messages to recipients (Stringhini, Kruegel, & Vigna, 2010, p. 5).

Precursors to today's socialbots were the humble chatbot. These artificial intelligence (AI)-humanoid-based robots would "chat" with individuals who visited the site. One or two sentences in an interchange with a human, they would be at the ends of their repertoires and would be repeating the same factoid again and again. Chatbots ("conversational agents," "embodied conversational agents," or "natural language agents") have been around since the mid-1960s, with the first chatbot systems originated at the Massachusetts Institute of Technology (Weizenbaum 1966, 1967, as cited in Shawar & Atwell, 2005). In semantic spaces, the dominance of language enabled the empowerment of "the superficial but often-credible natterings of chatterbots" (Kennedy & Eberhart, 2001, p. 187). Versions of them proliferated with spoofed email accounts.

Some online 'bots became virtually "embodied" as avatars in the Second Life virtual world. Some were designed to wander around and collect data and engage in simple interactions and generally blend in the environment; further, they were used to conduct social experiments within this virtual environment (Friedman, Steed, & Slater, 2007, pp. 252 - 253). Automated avatars in Second Life apparently show an uncanny similarity to human behaviors:

They meet, spend time together and make friends. This behavior suggests that avatars construct an online social network, an Internet-based network that represents the social relationships existing among human beings (Varvello & Voelker, 2010, p. 9).

Their social networks resemble "natural networks more than other online social networks," and their presence has a "fundamental impact on the SL social network" because of their high sociality, but the relationships themselves are "fragile" and fleeting (Varvello & Voelker, 2010, p. 9), typified by weak links. The removal of 'bot avatars from a social network on Second Life was found to change the network from "a small-world network" (Varvello & Voelker, 2010, p. 9). Finally, the bot-avatars themselves were humanlike in terms of gathering in popular places in Second Life to socialize; they maneuvered into virtual proximity ("interaction range") to other avatars to communicate (Varvello & Voelker, 2010, p. 10). What distinguishes socialbots from the chatbots of the past is that they actually strive to create "substantive relationships among human users" and strive to shape "the aggregate social behavior and patterns of relationships between groups of users online" (Hwang, Pearce, & Nanis, 2012, p. 40).

Multiple studies have found that people often cannot discern the difference between machines and humans in these contexts. The low detection rates for the automata are in part due to the sophistication of socialbots (social network robots), which have now been designed to observe their environments, learn how others interact, emulate human activities, improvise based on the conversation, and manage "multiparty interactive situations" at a time (instead of just maintaining dyadic (one-to-one) conversations (Kumar & Rosé, 2014, p. 24:3). Socialbots are being sensitized to how to interact with humans, with the requisite social niceties through a "sense-think-act" approach:

Social robots have a lot to learn from their older siblings: physical robots. Socialbots learn the shape of the social graph and observe what people are talking about, perform analyses to decide whom to interact with and what to say, and execute their plan by following and posting (Marra, 2012, p. 44).

Various design features of socialbots were created to simulate social presence by human "mirroring". The observation that humans tend to be closer on a social network graph when they share ideas and terminology and opinions provides a pathway for a socialbot to cozy up to a human by having shared interests. Such tactics enable both a simulated humanity and a simulated relating. In 2011, the Web Ecology Project sponsored a competition in which bots purposefully ingratiated themselves (using anthropocentric language) into particular social networks and built social capital and credibility through the observed language of the online social networks and by offering "cute cat photos" (@tinypirate & @ AeroFade, 2012, p. 41) Human accounts are "cloned" in order to pass as human, along with the natural language capabilities and on-the-fly scanning of the Web for information to share on public discussions of public interest (Ferrara, Varol, Davis, Menczer, & Flammini, 2014). Human stratagems have been embedded in the design of socialbots. The understanding of "human factors" in perception, cognition, and memory have been brought to bear as well. To wit, a basic dictum in the research literature on human deception is that those who are deceived, at some level, choose to be. To avoid cognitive dissonance, people tend to select certain information to believe and ignore conflicting information because of the psychological discomfort that may cause. In context, people may be unwilling to entertain the idea that their close friend or follower online is a computer program running based on sophisticated scripts. Humans may take disparate pieces of information and weave mental narratives and fill in gaps as part of a Gestalt psychological function. Socialbots are designed to communicate as people by showing solidarity, showing tension release, and agreeing, based on human patterns of intercommunications per Bales' Interaction Process Analysis (Kumar & Rosé, 2014, p. 24:4).

Socialbots communicate through a kind of "virtual telecopresence" in "electronic proximity" with people—through the mediation of social media platforms. This synthetic sociality is applied in a range of contexts:

Social bots differ from other types of computer programs in that they are specifically designed to communicate with humans in place of humans. In the case of instrumental social bots, computer programs replace direct human assistance with automated response systems that make information sharing more efficient. And, in the case of communicative social bots, computer programs mimic human interaction in providing people with entertainment, interpersonal training, or psychological comfort (Zhao, 2003, p. 448).

Modern-day 'bots that are designed to pass as humans are created to control for their own "tells"—such as speed of message response, content depth and informational novelty, digital life backstopping, and other factors. Some socialbots emulate circadian patterns to pretend sleep to emulate people (Ferrara, Varol, Davis, Menczer, & Flammini, 2014, p. 4). Ronson (2015) described the harrowing experience of having an "infomorph" socialbot using his name Tweeting out fake information but collecting actual followers he knew; the academics that created the 'bot would not take down the account until they were roundly publicly called out and shamed. The traps used to identify 'bots—such as the uses of nonsense messaging to see which 'bots would still friend the account (without much in the way of discrimination)—used to be sufficient to identify the 'bots. Today, similar deployed honeypot traps (usually setups that humans would not find appealing) fail to catch the majority of 'bots on a mainstream microblogging site. There is much more blurring between human and 'bot behaviors.

Intuitively, any human electronic presence may be machine-imitated. The more sophisticated socialbots were built by individuals informed by linguistics, psychology, sociology, human inter-communications, and computer science—to inform the bots' psycho-social behavior. Present-day socialbots have simulated personalities and emotions. Malicious socialbots join social networks and lurk; they elicit and collect sensitive information and send it back to their human handlers for exploitation. They create false impressions.

When a social robot has to interact through a thin channel—think 140 characters of text, online imagery, or short video link, for example—the illusion of the full person behind the account is much easier to maintain, even over time. A thicker multi-dimensional channel, online, is not that much harder to spoof given the ease of account creation and the still-low-levels of verifiability of accounts online. If an individual is trying to check out the humanity of an account holder, he or she will likely require not only a range of software tools, a skeptical mind, and access to a database of verified people—but a determined spoofer can still create individuals out of online bits and bytes that can be very hard (if not impossible) to distinguish from the real and to disprove. As a small historical point, the objective for creating artificial intelligence (AI) to be non-discernible from an actual person—as defined in the Turing Test (1950)—has been achieved for some years now, without fanfare.

The presence of cyborg accounts—in which a human participates as well as the computer—adds further potential confusion. The interactions between human and machine in cyborg accounts on Twitter may be as follows:

Cyborgs have become common on Twitter. After a human registers an account, he may set automated programs (i.e., RSS feed/blog widgets) to post tweets during his absence. From time to time, he participates to tweet and interact with friends. Cyborgs interweave characteristics of both humans and bots (Chu, Gianvecchio, Wang, & Jajodia, 2010, p. 21).

The presence of human and automated communications elements provides more fuzziness about the nature of the account. Is the individual just highly prolific and efficient, or are there automated elements at play? (Social media accounts may also shift over time, from human to robot and back and forth. There are a number of ways that accounts may be deployed and maintained.)

Is It or Isn't It?

In a naïve sense, a number of easily observable and superficial indicators may reveal something of the underlying nature of a social media account. One researcher found that "spammy" names often led to both "bad human actors" and bots with names generated by poor algorithms (Freeman, 2013). The respective profiles of some malicious automated accounts on social media platforms may have some suspicious features such as information captured from a grab-bag of online sites.

Other indicators may be temporal, such as the time patterning of when a particular account shares information, or how (inhumanly) quickly it responds to messages. An elicitation may cause the revealing of the automation—by probing the account with some interactions to see essentially how well coded the 'bot is in terms of interactions. Another surface indicator may be the type of accessible messaging: does the account just stay on messaging and emphasize one point-of-view, or is there a sense of real-world diversity and whimsy?

The intuition here is that 'bots are often created to create a magnifier effect—to achieve much with low expenditures of effort or blowback. Since online credibility is often understood as a feature of a number of "friends," there are robots that enable "mass friend adding" to artificially raise numbers. Likewise, if people are interested in a particular topic or issue, they may artificially raise mass comments using robot-based services or their own 'bots in this form of "astroturfing". In this sense, for example, most spambots cut to the chase. They collect as much information as possible in as short a time as possible and often will exploit the collected data as quickly as possible. This single-minded focus on mass-collection efficiency may mean that the spambot or botnets will not work as stealthily as possible: "Greedy bots that send spam with each message are easier to detect by the social network administrators. On the other hand, a low-traffic spam campaign is not easy to detect" (Stringhini, Kruegel, & Vigna, 2010, p. 8). Some botnets on Twitter are used to squelch citizen dissent against their government and to disrupt actual human Twitter protests (including "smearing protesters"); many such 'bots do not create networks but engage at a high rate around particular issues (Gallagher, 2015). Another common "tell" with some spambots involves the uses of different account names on the same messaging (duplicate Tweets) to mask their connectivity to one actor (Wang, 2010, p. 338). The @ function in Twitter is often mis-used not to maintain clear lines of communication but to draw others' networks into the bot's messaging in order to attract more people to click on malicious links and to hijack trending (bursty) topics (Wang, 2010, p. 335). Various on-platform mechanisms are often misused by malicious agents:

The reply and mention functions are designed to help users to discover each other on Twitter. However, the spam account utilize the service to draw other user's attention by sending unsolicited replies and mentions. Twitter also considers this as a factor to determine spamming. The number replies and mentions in one account is measured by the number of tweets containing the reply sign "@" in the user's 20 most recent tweets. (Wang, 2010, p. 339)

Some 15% of account profiles of spamming accounts on social media were found to be copied from other profiles, which is on par with email spam profile copying (Webb, Caverlee, & Pu, 2008, p. 7). The demographic details of these "fakester" accounts also shared similar demographic details, with the following observation: "all of the profiles are female and between the ages of 17 and 34 (85.9% of the profiles state an age between 21 and 27). Additionally, 1,476 (99.3%) of the profiles report that they are single. None of these characteristics are particularly surprising because they all reinforce the deceptive nature of these profiles. Specifically, these demographic features make each profile appear as though it was created by a young, "available" woman" (Webb, Caverlee, & Pu, 2008, p. 8). Spam accounts tend to create more messaging than legitimate users "and are more likely to follow other spammers than legitimate users" (Chu, Gianvecchio, Wang, & Jajodia, 2010, p. 22). On YouTube, researchers found that fraudulent accounts there tended to be registered as males (vs. females), and tended to be registered more recently but were "more active than legitimate profiles" in terms of viewing and interacting with other videos albeit without uploading their own (Bulakh, Dunn, & Gupta, 2014, pp. 1111 and 1114); their main role was to promote particular videos to fraudulently drive human traffic for video views. There have been observed blackhat (attacker) efforts to create botnets to stealthily exfiltrate information without triggering those monitoring for anomalies in network traffic (Nagaraja, Houmansadr, Piyawongwisal, Singh, Agarwal, & Borisov, 2011).

Those who administer such social networks are in an "arms race" with spammers who would exploit their systems for illicit gain. Simply put, they have to generally put into place policies, technologies, practices, training, and systems (such as those enabling human reportage of suspicious account activities), to enable accurate detection of malicious automated or semi-automated agents. If their system is too coarse, too many 'bots exist and victimize the human users. If their system is too fine, there may be false positives, and legitimate accounts may be accidentally suspended—annoying human users (who tend to have long memories and a tendency to share their displeasure across a lot of networks). On the other hand, users of a social media platform may also be irritated when their accounts are compromised by spammers who steal their credentials and co-opt their account and friend networks to send spam. Recent research suggests that many such human victims will dump an old account and go to a new one after a compromise occurs, resulting in account churn (Zangerle & Specht, 2014).

While 'bots "wildly populate social media ecosystems," their design and synthetic emulation of (implied) people still reveal "signatures of engineered social tampering" (Ferrara, Varol, Davis, Menczer, & Flammini, 2014, p. 1). The "Bot or Not!" model which was created based on analysis of socialbot activity on Twitter focused on six classes of features: the number of retweets (many more by social bots than people); account age (much shorter account ages for 'bots); number of Tweets (less for socialbots); number of replies (less for socialbots); number of mentions (much more for people); number of times retweeted (much more for people), and username length (much longer for the socialbots) (Ferrara, Varol, Davis, Menczer, & Flammini, 2014, p. 6). This online tool enables identified users to be able to test social media accounts for their respective levels of botness, with a classification ranking on a percent scale of likelihood of being a 'bot, with 80% - 100% suggestive of a danger zone for being a robot. The tool enables access to additional information about the respective accounts as well.

Another approach involves the creation of a supervised machine learning algorithm for a predictive model to identify "non-personal" Twitter accounts from mass-scale Twitter data. ("Machine learning," formerly known as data mining, is used to identify patterns in data.) The idea is that the model may be able to identify "non-personal" Twitter users, which are understood as machine accounts, organization accounts, "individual accounts that only post career information, and "spam users that post commercial or malicious content" (Guo & Chen, 2014, p. 18:3). In this work, the researchers used geographical patterning from the microblogging messages. The underlying assumption for this latter work seems to be that Twitter was made to be a social networking platform for individuals, sort of each with their own voices, and non-personal Twitter users are trying to change up their respective power and influence through various system manipulations. The resulting classifier was not particularly accurate, but the study lays the groundwork for future tools that may be much more accurate.

This push for cost-benefit efficiencies means that if one strategy is shown to work, that effort will beget many other similar ones to try to maximize gains before system administrators and individuals become aware and a counter-measure is put into place. It may also mean that the account lifespan is shorter than for other accounts. The behavior of a robot of any kind may be analyzed to understand its core and peripheral functions, given that these are scripted "puppets" for human puppet masters, and both overt and latent objectives may be logically ferreted out. For example, simpler bots, whether licit or illicit, are deployed on social media platforms to edit and distribute data; collect information; monitor the online context; manage impressions; support pranking and trolling; steal information, and other purposes. Beyond its observable behavior, a bot's code may also be analyzed to get an extended sense of its purpose(s). Merely observing behavior on the one hand still leaves a wide range of latent or infrequent or stealth behaviors unobserved.] Is the information which is shared original or not? (Some 'bots scrape data from the Web in order to share potentially related contents to an online conversation.) Is the identity backstopped with actual ways to connect in the real world and real human records findable on the Deep (or Hidden) Web and government databases (at least in Western democracies)? If there are cross-platform presences apparently linked to the same account (such as based on http networks), do these other presences add or detract from the potential validity of the identity?

There are also robots which are designed to enhance the work of human editors and writers to a crowd-sourced online encyclopedia built on a wiki platform. These are robots which have been vetted by a volunteer board and which must abide by certain site-based policies before they may be deployed.

Sensor Data on Tweetstream

In terms of sensor networks on social media sites, there seem to be two general types. One type involves the collection of information from persistent sensors and computer systems and delivered through social media accounts. Many of these types are related to weather and air quality. The other type is from wearable computers (like watches, cameras, glasses, and others) and mobile devices, which involve the sharing of human biometric information and locations on various social media accounts. The capturing, recording, and sharing of biosensor information about an individual is part of the "quantified self" movement, in which individuals purposefully choose to record aspects of their lives and to share that with others. (Microsoft researcher Gordon Bell was one of the very earliest such quantified selves.) Researchers have been advancing the integration for a Web of Things type of network in connecting everyday life objects with the Web and Internet (Gao, Zhang, & Sun, 2011), and these types of information streams are being shared through some social media accounts. Researchers have identified drivers for integrating sensor and social networks: meeting the needs of human actors who want to share their data and see others' data, and understanding aggregate behavior (such as vehicle traffic conditions) to enhance awareness and decision-making (Aggarwal & Abdelzaher, 2011, p. 381). Differing sensor platforms release multimodal types of data, which may be challenging to share coherently on some social media platforms; in this sense, data integration may be challenging. Another long-standing concern related to the privacy of people's information from their wearable and mobile devices. [Note: To clarify, this is not about the "human sensor network" or "citizen sensor network," which uses public human-shared information to understand an on-ground situation (particularly emergency situations). In this "use case," machines and people peruse public messaging on social media to try to understand human experiences and senses of a situation.].

For years now, there has been work by researchers to use computers to identify 'bot and cyborg accounts on social media platforms through classification algorithms. These methods involve analyzing a shortlist of information about the respective accounts, their behaviors, and other features (Chu, Gianvecchio, Wang, & Jajodia, 2010).

USING NETWORK ANALYSIS TO FIND AUTOMATED AND SEMI-AUTOMATED ACCOUNTS ON SOCIAL MEDIA

In the spirit of the Social Web 2.0, robots have gone social alongside humans. They are active throughout the Internet and proliferate broadly on social network sites, which are some of the most visited websites on earth. Six of the top-20 most-visited sites on the World Wide Web (WWW) are social network ones. Electronic social network analysis may be brought to bear on the question of the underlying nature of an account—whether 'bot, cyborg, human, or sensor. This approach may add another layer of knowledge to the question and may leave an impression (a sense of whether an account is a 'bot or cyborg or sensor or human) but may require additional research and information to know for sure.

This network analysis approach to discern the nature of an account does have some precedence in the research literature. Human social networks have been observed to be tiered and affected by various "personal facts" of geography, family, education, and employment; at individual levels, cognitive limits affect the social network tier sizes and structures; human social networks "are known to have very different network properties as compared to other non-human networks…" (Hirschman, St. Charles, & Carley, 2011, p. 321). Such human idiosyncrasies suggest that those may be differentiators from the social networks created by non-human or partially human agents. Graph based features—the number of friends and followers, the contents in recent tweets—have been used to identify spambots in Twitter (Wang, 2010, p. 335). There is also precedence for the extracting of conversations around being hacked and gleaning information about that experience and what people did to try to deal with that issue (Zangerle & Specht, 2014, p. 587).

Going Beyond Surface Observables to Underlying Networks

What are the types of information that may be ascertained of a target social media account using Network Overview, Discovery, and Exploration for Excel (NodeXL)?

- **Membership Patterns:** Who is in the "ego neighborhood" of the target social media account on the particular social media platform at one-degree? What is its network at 1.5 degrees? Two degrees? What is the social media account membership like at these various degrees? Are the relationships simply extant and undirected or two-arrowed and reciprocated? If homophily (in-group preference; the preference to bond with others who are similar) is accurate, what would the network findings look like? If so-called tiered homophily is applicable in human social networks, with a few very strong ties, some general friend ties, and then a more diffuse network of weak ties of acquaintances, would robot networks show similar patterns? Cyborg networks? Sensor networks? Or would they display quite different networks of connectivity? If heterophily (the preference to bond with others who are dissimilar to the self) is accurate, what would the findings suggest?

- ◦ Which social media accounts are part of the two-degree network? Which groups or clusters may be found in this network? What do these clusters suggest about network interests and sub-graph memberships? What do these links suggest about the focal social media account?
- **Relationship Patterns:** When there is a 'bot / sensor / cyborg / human network, who follows? Why? What relational patterns may be seen? When there is a 'bot / sensor / cyborg / human network, who is usually followed by these accounts? What can these follower – following links say about the respective focal social media account?
- **Interactional Patterns:** How are the various entities in the network interacting with each other?
- **Messaging and Contents:** What are some of the messages shared from the account for a certain select time period? What were the emphases? The mood? The advocacy? The sentiments? The links? The hashtagged campaigns or movements or trends? What do these messages possibly say about the focal social media account? What types of websites were linked to? What sorts of images, audio, video, and other multimedia?
  - ◦ **Exchanged Messages:** What are exchanged messages between various accounts? Do these messages indicate coordination? (Particularly, what is being exchanged between private channels—assuming the researcher is privy to these as an insider.)
  - ◦ **Types of Information Streams:** What information stream is being offered? Where does the data come from? What form is it in? Is it easy to read and interpret?
  - ◦ **Advocacy?** If there are hashtagged campaigns, which are the other accounts taking part? Are there similarities in names and behaviors between such linked accounts? If so, could that indicate possible coordination or collusion? Is there a botnet or sensornet or cyborg-net or human-net of colluders that may be identified?
  - ◦ **Coordination:** Are there any indicators of coordinated activities (beyond communication) between the entities in the respective networks? Are there references to in-world events or activities?
- **Geographical Patterns:** In terms of geolocation coordinates of the accounts on the social network, are there indications of physical co-location? Are there observable geolocational patterns? Are there spatial patterns in the subgraphs? Are there spatial patterns in various hashtagged campaigns? Other advocacy actions? What could these suggest about the underlying nature of the focal social media account?
- **Time Patterns:** Are there any time zone patterns? Are there times when the network members are more active, and if so, would this suggest co-locational factors?
- **Cross-Type Comparisons:** What are some observable differences between the social and / or content (or multi-modal) networks of the various types of accounts (bot, sensor, cyborg, and human) on the respective social media platforms?

In this chapter, the research question is: What is the observable relationship between the type of automated or semi-automated social media account (robot, sensor, cyborg, or human) and its network structure as identified by NodeXL, and are there observable indicators of such identities?

To initially and provisionally explore the research question, verified 'bot, sensor, cyborg, and human accounts were identified on Twitter and Wikipedia. Both social media sites have developed policies around automation ("Automation rules and best practices," July 10, 2013; "Wikipedia:Bot policy," Nov. 19, 2014). Both social media sites are highly popular and receive a lot of human traffic, making both target-rich environments for potential social engineering and fraud (which are main impetuses for malicious socialbot attacks). Verified accounts were used to seed the research because so many accounts on online social networks are built on lightweight identity credentials, and it would be unfortunate to misidentify an account as a certain type. The networks were extracted at the 1.0, 1.5, and 2.0-degree ranges. These were then initially analyzed to see if there may be leads from such analyses. This approach is not definitive nor prescriptive by any means. This exploratory work was created as an early probe to see how this form of structure mining and content analysis may be applied to the question of analyzing a social media account of unknown origins to discern its likely humanness or its machine-ness. [Some may argue, with some grounds, that a robot is a tool that is human-coded/scripted for particularly human aims, and that is so, but machine and human capabilities do diverge, and it is important to understand the nature of the "other."] Also, this work was set up to understand how NodeXL might enhance analytical capabilities for this "use case" in a very complex environment.

Some simple hypotheses:

- **Hypothesis 1:** Purely automated social media account networks will have a lot less diversity and heterophily in their networks than non-automated (human) networks. Robots and sensor accounts on social networks will tend to connect with other entities potentially created by the same 'bot master or sensor network lead. These automated accounts will be much more hierarchical and less of a distributed and diffuse network (not like wearable sensor types of networks).
- **Hypothesis 2:** The degree of the nodes in automated social media account's networks will likely have one dominant account and a lot of other follower accounts (if these emulate a botnet structure). (The real-world social networks would likely have multiple groups and social centers of gravity.)
- **Hypothesis 3:** Cyborgs on social media platforms are popularly referred to as 'bot-assisted humans or human-assisted 'bots. Mixed cyborg social media account networks would likely involve some aspects of humans and some aspects of machines. As such, their social network structures would likely have a mix of features from automated and non-automated sorts of networks. These may show a lack of smooth handoffs between the human and the machine and maybe a bifurcation of messaging and message types.

About NodeXL Basic

Network Overview, Discovery, and Exploration for Excel (NodeXL Basic) is a free and open-source add-on to a more recent version of Excel (on Windows). Essentially, it enables the graphing of relational data using a variety of layout algorithms. It also enables the extraction of a range of publicly available social media platform data (through their respective application programming interfaces or "APIs") and the mapping of that data in various types of network graphs. There are a variety of tools for network analysis including the extraction of core graph metrics, motif census, vertex-edge labeling, dynamic filtering, and other features. The use of this tool in this chapter is a focused use case and does not actually represent anywhere near the full functionality of the tool. This visual (network) analytics software tool itself is distributed off of Microsoft's CodePlex site. A special "software library," the NodeXL MediaWiki Importer, enabled extraction of the Wikipedia network data (Keegan, Ceni, & Smith, 2013).

AN OVERVIEW OF THE BASIC NETWORK EXTRACTION AND ANALYSIS PROCESS

Before NodeXL is applied to the work of understanding the core nature of social media accounts, it may help to understand the basics of the data extraction, mapping, and analytics process.

Mapping Social Media Accounts and Networks as Graphs in NodeXL Basic

The extraction of a network for a particular account is built on a layer of dependencies. the results of a data extraction depend on the following: (1) the data extraction parameters the person uses for the data extraction, (2) the time period when a data extraction is conducted, (3) the speed of connectivity of the computer used, (3) the application programming interface features for the particular social media platform (including restrictive features like rate-limiting, white-listing, and others), (4) the nature of the underlying data (some types of data are more stable and less dynamic than others), (5) the way relationships (expressed as links and edges) are defined within both the social media platform and NodeXL, (6) the way the captured data is processed (both within NodeXL and outside of this tool), (7) the way the data is graphed visually, and, finally, (8) the way the cumulative information is human-analyzed. There may well be other intervening factors as well. At this point, it is not clear how much each listed factor affects actual outcomes.

These factors mean that the extracted information for this context is likely a partial set, not a full one. In that sense, there cannot really be claims of an N=all in the "big data" sense. Assertions that are made need to be qualified and nuanced for accurate impressions. At this stage, network analysis looks like it may enable some deeper awareness of various accounts, but it may not fully provide a definitive label of robot-hood, cyborg-hood, sensor-hood, or person-hood. The resulting network graphs are highly readable and may feel accessible to a common user. This accessibility has pros and cons. The downside is that people may assume that they understand what a graph means and over-generalize or over-assert. Also, while NodeXL is fairly easy to use, network analysis itself often involves a learning curve, particularly about the underlying statistics, variant terminology, and theorizing. It makes sense to invest the effort and time for fuller understanding before venturing to use the tool and method for public claims. Also, it's a good idea to read the context-sensitive annotations about each type of network extraction in the "More about this option" section, which includes details about how relationships are defined in the particular social media platform and within NodeXL. (Such details should generally accompany the network graphs, if those are used for research purposes.)

Using Network Analysis to "Guess" at the Nature of a Social Media Account

Figure 1 is an early conceptualization of how this process of using network analysis to identify an underlying identity feature of a social media platform account could work. While the process may seem one-directional in the visual, practically speaking, this would be a semi-recursive process, as needed. Also, while there is a path to stopping the analysis, the reality is that there may be no exact definitive "tell" without a robust empirically-derived information set.

For the purposes of this work, there will be an informal or "folk" categorization of these various account types. Figure 2 separates out automation in three general categories: wholly machine-run accounts, semi-automated cyborg accounts, and non-automated or fully human accounts.

Figure 1. Robot, sensor, cyborg, or human?: Exploring a target account on social media

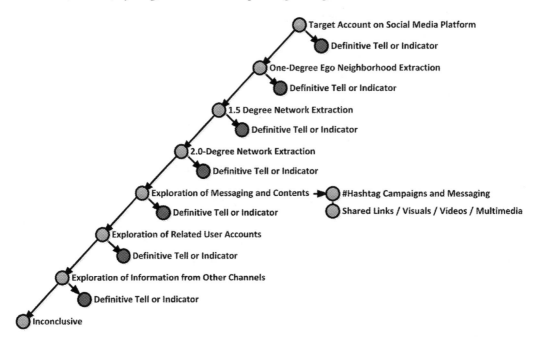

Figure 2. Types of automated, semi-automated, and non-automated accounts on social media

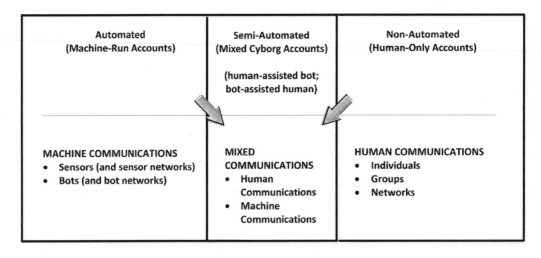

TRIAL RUNS OF NETWORK ANALYSES ON SELECT ACCOUNTS (ON TWITTER AND WIKIPEDIA)

Two social media platforms were used for this initial exploration: Twitter and Wikipedia. The first is a popular microblogging site, and the latter is a crowd-sourced encyclopedia built on the MediaWiki software tool. Both social media platforms are widely used and widely known. Both enable broad public access to their data. Twitter was chosen because of known 'bots and sensor networks; Wikipedia was chosen because of flagged 'bots. To simplify the work, identified robot, sensor, cyborg, and human accounts were used for a thin exploration.

Microblogging 'Bots, Sensors, Cyborgs, and Humans on Twitter

Robot Social Media Account: @DearAssistant

The @DearAssistant 'bot is a social media account linked to the Wolfram Alpha site, and it manages to connect those who would have a quant-based query to access the services and computational capabilities of the site (Figure 3).

This @DearAssistant 'bot account included 2,092 vertices, with 2,107 unique edges.

Maybe more about the integration of the 'bot in human use. This would suggest that a highly popular 'bot would likely show a network with a diversity of people who appreciate the service (Figure 4).

By scaling down the graph pane image in NVivo and then zooming in and using the panning function, users may be able better see positionality and interrelationships up close. The popularity of this

Figure 3. @DearAssistant Bot Account (Linked to Wolfram Alpha) on Twitter (1 deg.)

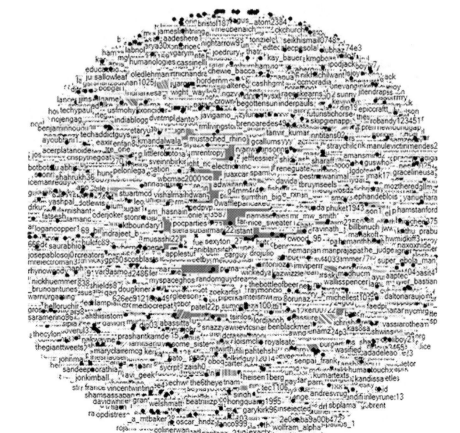

Figure 4. Scaled Down and Zoomed in View of the @DearAssistant Bot Account (Linked to Wolfram Alpha) on Twitter (1 deg.)

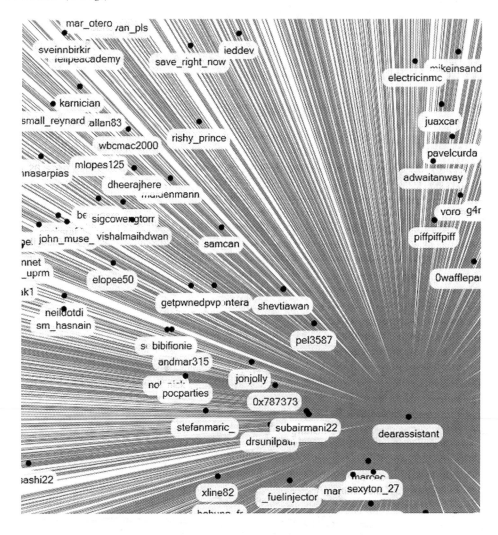

'bot site and its high-end functionality may make this an outlier case and therefore not directly useful in this quest for "tells" of bot-ness by examination at the node and close-in network levels.

Sensor Social Media Account: @BeijingAir

@BeijingAir is one of the better-known sensor-based accounts on Twitter. A U.S. Embassy website linked to the @BeijingAir account on Twitter describes this monitor as "a resource for the health of the American community" ("U.S. Embassy Beijing Air Quality Monitor," 2014), but the broad sharing of this information gives the sense of this sensor network as leveraging the power of public awareness and pressure to improve air quality. Indeed, this @BeijingAir site has been labeled "a diplomatic sore point" between countries (Wong, 2013). The air quality sensors measure particulates less than 2.5 micrometers in diameter, which may cause lung and health problems. The $PM_{2.5}$ information on this account is

Tweeted as the amount of particulate matter in the air at the location of the sensor ranging as follows: good (0-50), moderate (51- 100), unhealthy for sensitive groups (101 – 150), unhealthy (151 – 200), very unhealthy (201 – 300), and hazardous (301-500). Alongside the ratings is information about which members of the broad public should be concerned and the steps they should take to deal with the air quality issues. The types of messaging include the day, the time, the levels of particulate matter in the air, and the air quality level; sometimes, there is data on a 24-hour average. Most if not all of the data seems machine generated. The profile itself describes the specific machines used for monitoring. The express goal is to monitor air quality in Beijing, Chengdu, Guangzhou, Shanghai, and Shenyang. The scale used by the U.S. Embassy enables a broader range of air quality index measures than those used in-country which top-out at 500 but real-world measures at 755 at one reading well "beyond index" level of toxicity (Wong, 2013).

A one-degree network extraction of the @BeijingAir ego neighborhood on Twitter identified 2,005 vertices and 2,004 unique edges (Figure 5).

Figure 5. @BeijingAir ego neighborhood on Twitter (1 deg.)

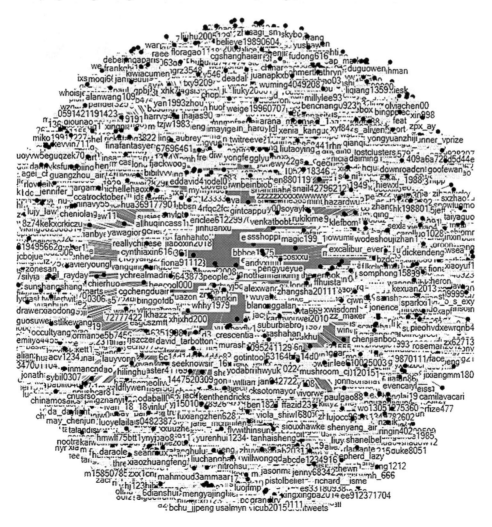

This original account was started in July 2008. At the time of the data extraction, there were 53,500 Tweets, 4 following, and 39.500 followers. It was noticed that this account followed four others, and those others could be similar accounts related to the potential objectives of the focal sensor site on the social media platform (Figure 6).

A log-in into Twitter revealed that @BeijingAir was following @Shenyang_Air, @CGShanghaiAir, @CGChengduAir and @Guangzhou_Air. There were some placeholder accounts also for @ShandongAir and @ShanghaiAir, which might indicate placeholding (or even possibly cybersquatting). A check of the other accounts showed that they each followed each other, suggesting collusion. A network extraction of the five related accounts resulted in a network with 6,524 vertices and 7,607 edges. In this network,

Figure 6. The @BeijingAir following accounts (a sensor network)

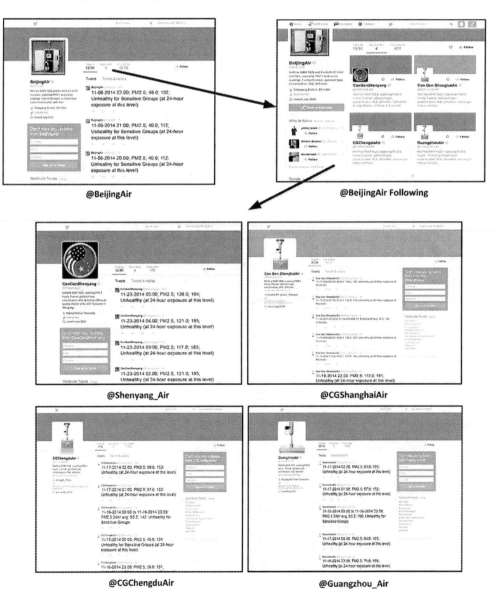

five groups (clusters) were identified. The accounts seem to be a mix of people and accounts indicated by numbers alone (Figure 7).

To see if there is any sense of differentiation between the sizes of the five related "air" accounts, the same data underlying Figure 8 was re-visualized to see if the lead account could be identified through several metrics. Using the Dynamic Filters, it is possible to identify the nodes which connect the network based on their betweenness centrality measures. The main nodes are the original ones that belong in the network, with the slider set at 1.9.

If the In-Degree slider is set fairly high, it is possible to identify the nodes with the highest in-degree, which may be an indicator of popularity. Interestingly, @cgshanghaiair had the highest in-degree even though others in this network joined Twitter earlier: April 2012 for @CGShanghaiAir, July 2008 for @BeijingAir, May 2011 for @Guangzhou_Air, May 2012 for @CGChengduAir, and June 2012 @ Shenyang_Air.

The Time Zone UTC Offset (in constant seconds) shows a spike in the general geographical locations of the related air quality sensors (Figure 9).

Figure 7. The @BeijingAir following user network on Twitter with all five related accounts represented

Figure 8. Betweenness centrality filtering in the @BeijingAir following user network on Twitter with all five related accounts represented

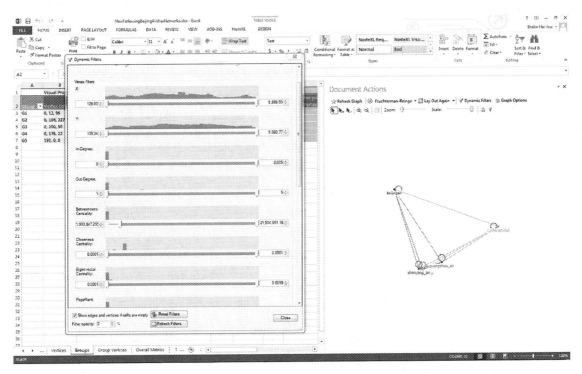

Figure 9. Locating to geographical location with the time zone UTC offset

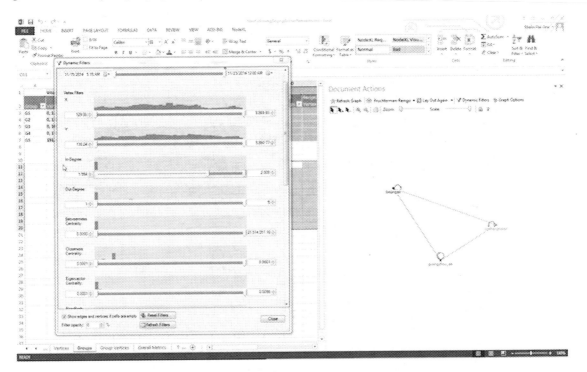

To get a sense of the entities speaking about this sensor account on Twitter, a keyword search for <@ BeijingAir> was conducted. The inclusion of the <@> was to capture messages that were purposefully sent to the site owner to their attention (Figure 10).

A perusal of this "keyword" search in NodeXL shows that this community consists of individuals, interest groups (such as environmental ones), events, and those with apparent area interests (based on the account names). This search shows those conversation and sending Tweets with the @BeijingAir addressee. The @BeijingAir account does not broadcast these messages on its feed, but this attribution by those communicating about it and sharing its data are following Tweeting conventions. This network consists of 95 vertices with 88 unique edges.

A simple keyword search for "BeijingAir" resulted in the following graph. The intuition behind a keyword search is that it will bring up unlabeled mentions of the term. This network consists of 133 vertices and 141 unique edges. Eighteen groups (clusters) were identified in this network. The communicators using this term I the week prior to the data extraction consist of celebrities, humans, sensor

Figure 10. @BeijingAir search network on Twitter

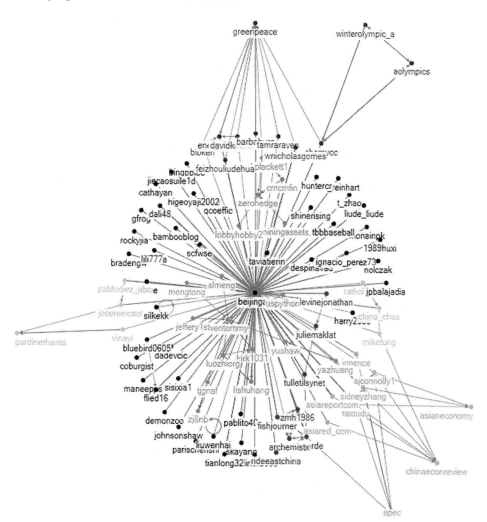

networks, news organizations, and others. This is a less dense network because in part this is about a snapshot of conversations in which a particular term was mentioned. Here, the vertices are labeled by the account name, and the edges are labeled with the Tweet (Figure 11).

A hashtag conversation around #BeijingAir was also captured. These capture the social media accounts and the messaging with the #BeijingAir hashtag label. This particular data extraction resulted in 10 vertices, with 8 unique edges. This network does not seem to have many members, and of the members, just a few are communicating with each other. It may be that the communicators are more satisfied Tweeting messages to the @BeijingAir account than maintaining a hashtagged conversation (Figure 12).

Cyborg Social Media Account: @MarsCuriosity

The @MarsCuriosity is a well-known "cyborg" account with several NASA employees working to create the voice of the Mars rover and then the sharing of machine-created messaging from the rover itself

Figure 11. BeijingAir keyword search network on Twitter

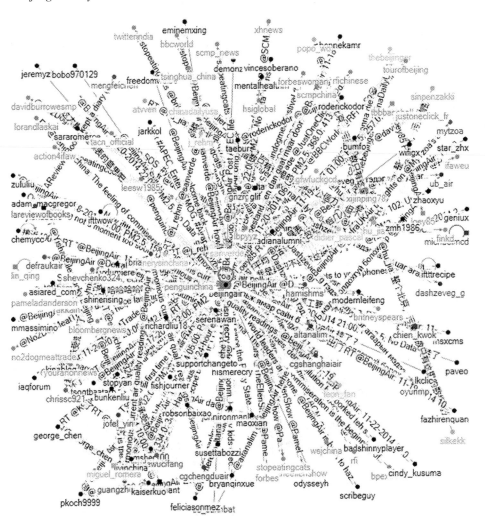

Figure 12. #BeijingAir search network on Twitter

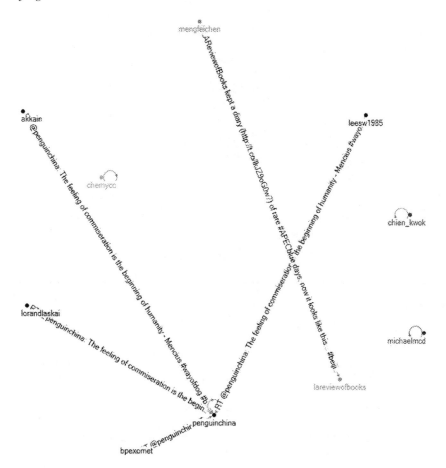

(such as history-making images from Mars, which is an average of 225 million kilometers / 139 million miles) (Figure 13).

On the day of the data extraction, the "ego neighborhood" for @MarsCuriosity on Twitter showed 2,282 vertices and 2,260 unique edges. The graph itself shows a broad range of apparently human accounts as well as 'bots (some linked to news organizations that follow various accounts in order to have early leads on possible news stories). At the time of the data extraction, based on its formal Twitter landing page (https://twitter.com/marscuriosity), the account itself had 2,788 Tweets, 161 following, 1.74 million followers, 316 favorites, and six lists, all to emphasize the smallness of the actual captured sample of recent connections.

Bots, Cyborgs, and Humans on Wikipedia

The second social media platform used for this chapter is Wikipedia, a crowd-sourced online encyclopedia which is often one of the most popular and most-visited site on the Web. As a platform, it enables the broad uses of benign and community-minded 'bots. A group of volunteers are assigned to a Bot Approvals Group to decide whether a particular bot account may be approved for use on Wikipedia. There

Figure 13. @MarsCuriosity user network on Twitter (1 deg.)

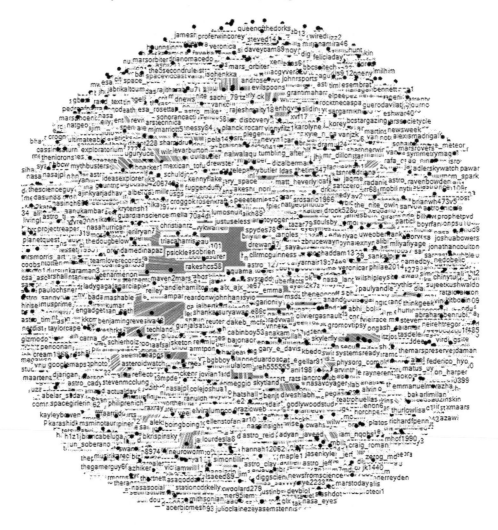

is also responsiveness to human complaints about 'bots and their functions. One that has been featured in an academic article is Xqbot:

In October 2008, the editor applied for a bot flag for her xqbot in order to request speedy deletions of orphan pages or remains of moved pages. In November 2008, the bot flag was assigned and the bot started working. Soon after this, the bot activities included over ten different tasks such as correcting double redirects, fixing links on disambiguation pages, adding missing references tags in articles, and the setting of interwiki-links. All these tasks were mainly focused on quality improvements to encyclopedic articles (Müller-Birn, Dobusch, & Herbsleb, 2013, p. 85).

Interestingly, there are Wikipedia bots that analyze new editors' activities and identify vandals so as to block them against creating future damage (Halfaker & Riedl, 2012, p. 80).

Robot Social Media Account: User:Xqbot

To get a sense of what the User:Xqbot article network looks like, a 1-degree extraction was conducted. Figure # shows the results. Here, the User:Xqbot page is in the center and links to one other user and multiple pages that link to online tools and a category label (Figure 14).

The network is sparse and seems to mostly connect to other pages related to computing machines and machine tools. A 1.5 degree data visualization shows the actual sparse network of User:Xqbot displaced by a new center page, "Programming_language." Here, User:Xqbot is a small and peripheral part of the "Programming_language" network. It seems fairly clear that when a 'bot is created for a type of editorial function, it is not out there trying to link to other pages on Wikipedia. Only two groups were identified in this network, so there is not a lot of diversity of groups per se. [The network here is a multimodal one because the various Wikipedia pages may represent various types of data: users (editors), topics, categories, or others.] (Figure 15).

A two-degree extraction of the User:Xqbot article network on Wikipedia results in a graph with 17,990 vertices and 29,856 unique edges. A way to understand this is that at two degrees out, the "tell" on the bot network almost disappears because the high connectivity simply links the bot to a wide variety of

Figure 14. User:Xqbot user article network on Wikipedia (1 deg.)

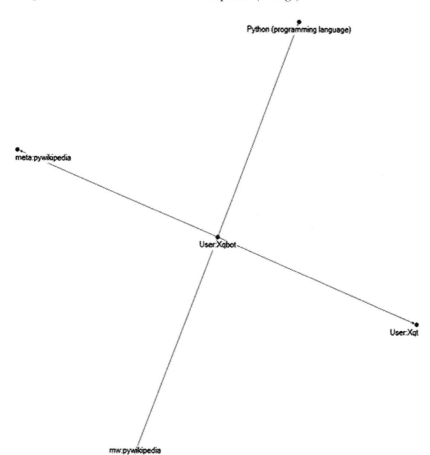

Figure 15. User:Xqbot user article network on Wikipedia (1.5 deg.)

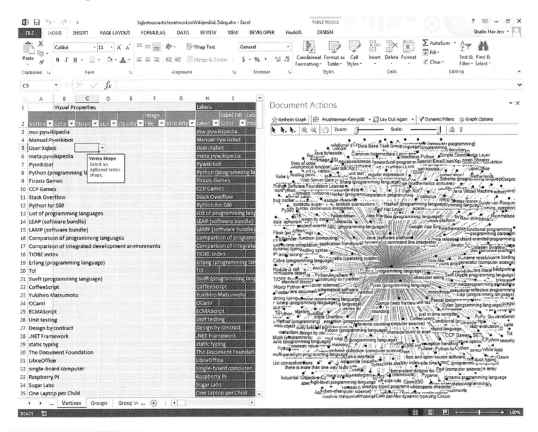

other pages. (This graph looks different from the others in part because the names of the various pages were not used as labels for the vertices. The size of the network itself is already prohibitive in terms of using additional labeling. The colors of the different clusters do suggest a diversity of interconnected groups within this two-degree article-article network.)(Figure 16).

The same dynamic of a sparse 1-degree network crawl vs. a 1.5 degree network crawl of a verified User:GiftBot article network on Wikipedia may be seen, with the same displacement of the original network once the degree size is changed (a phenomenon which will occur with any originally sparse network)(Figure 17).

Human Social Media Account: User:Dsimic

"User:Dsimic" was selected as a convenience case against which to compare the initial 'bot on Wikipedia in part because of recent postings on a technology-based issue. By comparison, a human-based user in Wikipedia tends to be at the center of a network of interests and of other possible users. Such a data extraction provides a gist about the individual's areas of expertise and interests because of the links based on editing behavior within the platform (Figure 18).

At a 1.5 degree extraction, the richness of connectivity and ideas is further emphasized (Figure 19).

Figure 16. User:Xqbot user article network on Wikipedia (2 deg.)

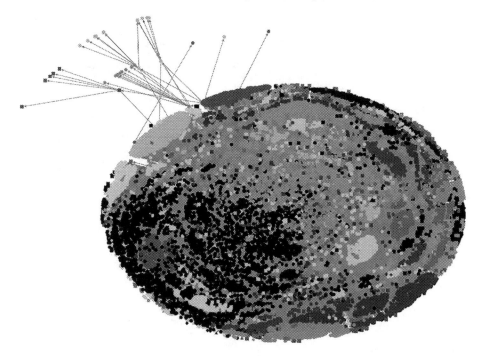

Figure 17. User:GiftBot user article network on Wikipedia (1 deg. on the left; 1.5 deg. on the right)

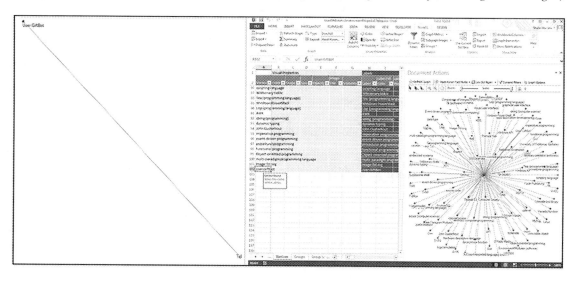

This 1.5 degree article network for "User:Dsimic" involves 8,200 vertices, with 9,788 unique edges, with 30 groups. A 2-degree network would likely devolve into incoherence (although it could be extracted and then information filtered to make the information much more accessible).

Figure 18. User:Dsimic article network on Wikipedia (1 deg.)

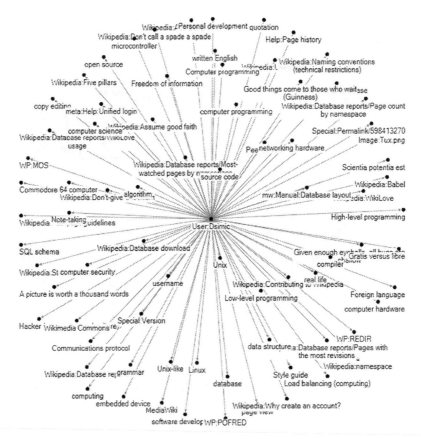

Figure 19. User:Dsimic article network on Wikipedia (1.5 deg.)

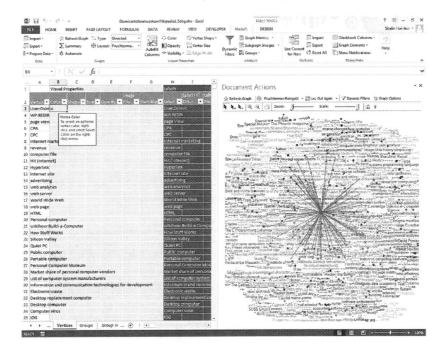

Robot Social Media Account: User:Bluebot

A more integrated 'bot though may link to a wide range of contents. One example would be User:Bluebot on Wikipedia (Figure 20).

In other words, it may be that a sparse initial network and then diversity of connections that displace a 'bot is not a "tell" of robothood. This is a network which shows a degree of diversity.

Human Social Media Account: User:Tawker

Human accounts in Wikipedia are often related to those who create contents as authors. Macro-scale network analysis has been applied to subject areas in order to study the impact of author expertise on whether they contributed to "pivotal artifacts" in a knowledge domain or whether they served a bridging function with generalist boundary-crossing knowledge between two subject matter domains (Halatchliyski, Moskaliuk, Kimmerle, & Cress, 2013).

The next example involves a network extraction of User:Tawker on Wikipedia. This network has some apparent 'bots in the article network, but the actual original account links to a person. This ego neighborhood would belie the concept of "homophily" or selective attachment between social media accounts of a type (bot-to-bots, humans-to-humans). In this case, the human ("Tawker") has linked 'bot attachments ("User:AntiVandalBot/FAQ," Oct. 25, 2006) (Figure 21).

Cyborg Social Media Account: User:Huggle

Finally, a data extraction was conducted on an identified cyborg account, User:Huggle. This shows the sparseness of an initial 1 deg. extraction but then much more complexity with higher-degree extractions (Figure 22).

Figure 20. User:Bluebot article network on Wikipedia (1 deg., 1.5 deg., 1.5 deg.)

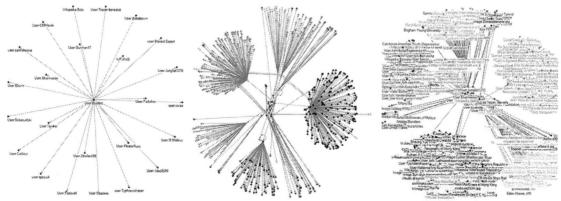

Figure 21. User:Tawker article network on Wikipedia (1 deg.)

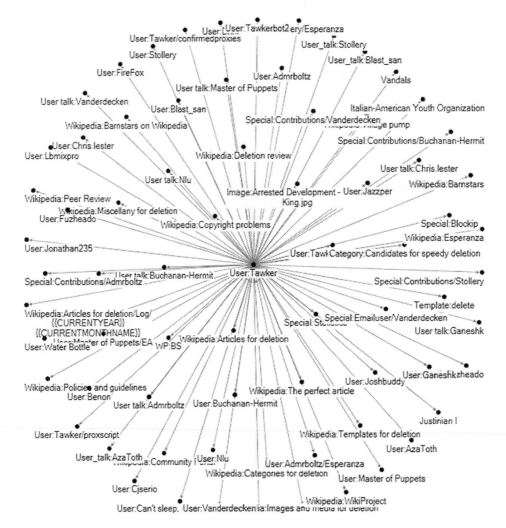

Figure 22. User:Huggle cyborg article network on Wikipedia (1 deg., 1.5 deg., and 2 deg.)

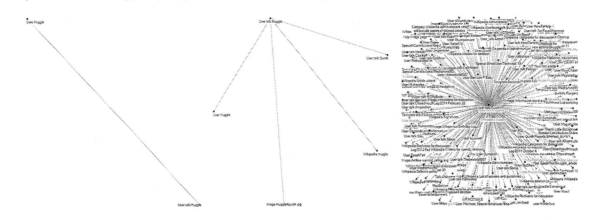

DISCUSSION

To review, the core question is whether there is an (observable) relationship between the underlying type of automated or semi-automated social media and its network structure, and further, whether there are indicators of certain identity type (robot, sensor, cyborg, or human) for the social media account. With NodeXL, it is possible to learn more about the network connections between a focal social media account and the membership of its direct ties "ego neighborhood" and also further out an extra half-degree to a degree. [The accuracy of the approach depends in part on the completeness of the captured network since various degree and betweenness centrality measures are not considered robust in a context of incomplete data (such as when a social media platform API only enables access to a small percentage of the available data).The general argument though is that having some data is valuable even if incomplete if the assertions made from that data are qualified and delimited/bounded.] The tool enables the analysis of relationship patterning, interactions, geographical patterns, and time patterns. This work suggests that a human analyst may compare across types of known accounts on various platforms to identify indicators which may suggest whether an underlying social media account is automated, semi-automated, or fully human (or robot, sensor, cyborg, or human).

Another implied question involves whether such indicators of account types could possibly apply across various social media platforms. For example, if robots tend to follow other robots on Twitter, is this pattern also common on a non-microblogging social media site such as a content-sharing one? Or if sensor-based social media accounts tend to have a lot of robot-based followers on Twitter, would this same pattern be seen on Facebook or Wikipedia? The types of accounts studied were deeply limited here because the purpose was only to explore an initial proof-of-concept. (There are likely many other types of automated agents that were not included in this initial work.) A more systematic and in-depth research approach would enhance the quality of potential assertions. This approach was limited because the research was seeded with already identified and verified account types. What would be more effective would be to explore unknown accounts and see what information may be extrapolated and accurately understood.

Were the hypotheses borne out based on the initial research? The first hypothesis about automated networks having less diversity and heterophily was not necessarily borne out in robotic accounts on social media (particularly once the network extraction went to two degrees). This hypothesis was especially contradicted by 'bot accounts that offered desirable services, which resulted in linkage to plenty of human-driven accounts as well as other robot-based accounts. In a sense, this hypothesis was partially borne out in terms of automated sensor networks that sample the environment and Tweet almost pure data, such as those sensors that sample air quality and send data through the social media account. Hypothesis 2 suggested the capability of identifying lead 'bots in botnets, and that is theoretically possible to see based on degree, betweenness and closeness centrality measures, and eigenvector centrality. Some of those metrics were analyzed for the @BeijingAir sensor network on Twitter, with some attendant insights. This alone, though, may not lead to the identification of a lead 'bot per se because a number of factors may affect those variables. Hypothesis 3, which suggested that cyborg-social media account networks would have aspects of both automated and non-automated networks was only partially borne out. It would seem like cyborg networks more closely represent human networks and do not necessarily reflect as much in the way of purely automated social media accounts. In other words, there is much more connectivity with a wide range of apparently human-based social media accounts and less of those that are obviously 'bots by naming convention and number identifiers.

Time and Other Factors

Cross-sectional or slice-in-time data collection has obvious limits because these only offer snapshots of available data. The examples here only showed slice-in-time sampled data. It may be that network analysis (applied to understand various types of social media accounts) may be more effective as an iterated exploratory process, with systematic sampling and observations enabled over some period of time. After all, online networks can be highly dynamic, with generally weak ties evolving over time.

Dynamic Filtering

There are ways to enhance the network analysis process itself by applying dynamic filters to the information, re-visualizing the data (based on select network metrics), and posing exploratory questions. For example, NodeXL enables dynamic (interactive) filtering of visualized graph information based on a range of dimensions depending on the extracted data. On Twitter, #hashtagged conversations among agents may be filtered based on a mix of edge and vertex dimensions. Edge dimensions include inception of relationship date and Tweet date. Vertex filters include Polar R, Polar Angle, in-degree, out-degree, betweenness centrality, closeness centrality, eigenvector centrality, PageRank, clustering coefficient, reciprocated vertex pair ratio, followed, followers, Tweets, favorites, time zone UTC offset (a proxy of physical location), and joined Twitter date. User networks on Twitter may be filtered based on edge descriptors: relationship dates and Tweet dates. If an account's messaging is highly regularized based on time, could that indicate a sensor? Or if an account's messaging is idiosyncratic time-wise, could that indicate a human actor? If a cluster of accounts that interacts were all created in a particular short time span (and maybe in a proxemics location), could that indicate their creation for use as a socialbot-net for manipulations? This electronic social network analysis research approach may be used in conjunction with other processes, such as content analysis. For example, what messaging is being shared? Is there an obvious advocacy agenda in the messaging? What URLs are being shared? What images? What videos? What contents? Who is being targeted with the messaging?

Human communications have been studied for years for various "tells" of their hidden states: their personalities, psychological states, moods, intellect, knowledge, class, gender, and other aspects. Such reads have been achieved face-to-face but also remotely using all forms of communications from the individual or group. Of promise are a range of linguistic "lie detectors" used to assess people and their levels of deception based on linguistic indicators in speech and written expressions. Linguistic analysis is applied predictively as well to project how individuals (and groups) will make decisions and progress on various dimensions (such as creativity or leadership) in time. There are qualitative differences between actual experiences being described and fabricated ones; however, oftentimes, computational linguistics programs applied to such detection can only give probabilities of likelihood on a continuum of deception to honesty, and the only absolute indicator of deception as a logical discrepancy. James W. Pennebaker (2011), a social psychologist with decades of work in computational linguistic analysis of people's communications, suggests that every Tweet is "like a fingerprint" that can reveal people's "motivations, fears, emotions, and the ways they connect with others and themselves" (p. 2). Statistical analysis of counts of semantic or meaning-bearing content terms may indicate various aspects of the true state of the world (even if hidden), and so, too, can the counts of syntactic or "style" or "function" words, including pronouns, articles, prepositions, auxiliary verbs, negations, conjunctions, quantifiers, and adverbs (Pennebaker, 2011, p. 22). What is known about human communications—describable by computers—may be compared against the created communications of robots for revelatory tells (except in cases where programs are used to emulate particular human communicators, with their idiosyncrasies). For example, because people communicate with certain patterns of language for certain contexts (Pennebaker, 2011, p. 246) their communications may differ from those of robots without that socially-ingrained and culturally-based contextual awareness. Whereas human communicators may have "immediacy clusters" based on local geographies and cultures (Pennebaker, 2011, pp. 249- 251), robots created without any geographical grounding will not register with such linguistic tendencies.

There has been a "survival analysis" applied to human Wikipedia editor accounts in order to understand the time-based departure dynamics. Overall departure rates decrease over time, so those who choose to leave generally do so early in their interactions on Wikipedia (Zhang, Prior, Levene, Mao, & van Liere, 2012). Low-frequency editors tended to have a shorter lifetime than medium-frequency editors, who were then also less likely to have "a long lifetime than high-frequency editors" (Zhang, Prior, Levene, Mao, & van Liere, 2012, p. 4). High engagement early on may be indicative of a longer-term commitment; however, as the authors point out, theirs is a correlational observation, and the actual underlying causative variables still need to be explored. This idea of "survival analysis" may be applied to a wide range of account types in order to study how robotic accounts fare given that robots, too, will ultimately sunset and be replaced by newer models with different capabilities. The understanding of the life cycles of various social media accounts may be a promising approach alongside the study of the survival analysis of particular (robot-, sensor-, cyborg-, and human-social media account-centered) networks themselves.

Caveats to the Approach

In the research literature, robot identification is often designed into systems that are automated, fast, scalable, and machine-accurate (with error rates not often spilling into the double-digits percentage-wise and many with error rates at a percent of a percent only). The approach here is manual. It is slow. The extracted and processed information is noisy. The conclusions that may be drawn seem conditional and quite error-prone. The work presented here is highly exploratory and early. That is not to say that more sophisticated methods based on network analysis of ego neighborhoods of social media accounts on social media platforms may not be insightful, or that this approach may not be effective in more expert hands. However, as of this moment, it would seem that there are more effective approaches based on machine-observed signatures, network traffic analysis, and other approaches.

FUTURE RESEARCH DIRECTIONS

Network analysis applied to the exploration of social media accounts to understand their types clearly has value to surface some types of information. For accuracy, though, the techniques have to broaden, and the research aperture has to be widened to collect more data. At this point, it still does not seem that an account may be definitively identified one way or another if there is a concerted effort to camouflage the actual account identity. Per the game tree in the figure "Robot, Sensor, Cyborg, or Human?: Exploring a Target Account on Social," this endeavor may well end with "Inconclusive" because of the noisy social spaces and the affordances of clever scripting, coding, and impression management. Network analysis offers a number of data points, but those are not sufficient to necessarily absolutely rule on the identity of a social media account one way or another particularly if there is active effort at creating confusion about identity.

Another challenge involves the lack of clarity of a way forward to scale the approach if certain "tells" of automated agentry are found that may be broadened to social media platform scale. This challenge would involve fine-tuning any such approach for accuracy of detection with as few mistakes (false negatives, false positives) as possible.

Online social media platforms are deeply mixed spaces. Humans are watching for the machines, and computing machines are deployed to watch people and to extract meaningful data such spaces by using human-created data in human or citizen sensor networks to monitor events and public sentiment.

What gives humans this distinct advantage is their ability to deal with semantics and leverage extensive background knowledge, experience, common sense, and complex reasoning, even with fuzzy data or inconsistent information. Although traditional sensors merely report encoded observations, humans process observations via their intellect and available contextual knowledge (Sheth, 2009, pp. 81 – 82).

In such an environment, the agents (human and computer) that dominate are those that are situationally aware and accurately informed. In game theory, a "dominated strategy" is one that is in a given losing position, no matter which branch of the game tree is actualized. On social media platforms, it is a dominated (losing) strategy to trust first and verify later; rather, cybersecurity professionals would suggest that it is important to verify first and then trust sparingly and conditionally. In this light, NodeXL may be used as a tool for people to explore their online friends and followers and targets-of-interest to get a clearer sense of just exactly who or what they're dealing with actually. The steps do not stop here.

What may initially seem like "costly signaling" and relational investment may actually be the "cheap talk" of malicious automated agents phishing for compromising information or photos. What data is shared may lack integrity, and the purveyors of that information may be part of robotic networks spewing messages to artificially control for impression management. With this awareness, human users may retract the "swift trust" and promiscuous friending that is part of social media culture and take a more real-world approach ("verify first and trust sparingly") may be applied. Social media users may work harder to (dis)confirm online identities by (de)linking to real-world persons through "identity binding" (Boshmaf, Muslukhov, Beznosov, & Ripeanu, 2012).

Certain "calls to action" via social media accounts may be manipulations by those botmasters behind the robotic social media accounts. With such knowledge, human users may maintain a cooler head and not engage in unthinking, emotionally-driven, and mass actions.

Online spacing are hunting grounds for those human predators who would use others' gullibility and naivete for their own gain. The deployment of non-human robotic and cyborg accounts may sometimes be harnessed to such predatory ends. Human users may block levels of access to their own private social networks and sensitive information. They may notify those who run the respective social media platforms to disable malicious social media accounts. They may prevent the release of their physical locations along with their shared messaging and digital contents.

CONCLUSION

Human behaviors are eminently observable, machine-learnable, and often machine-emulable. In human interactions, people pattern based on common practice, observation, emulation, and these harden into cultural practices. In terms of the Turing test (1950), a little-mentioned but fundamental aspect of it defines a relationship between machines and humans: that of machine mimicry of people and machine deception of people in order to "pass." J. Markoff (2015) proposes that those who design automated systems build with a sense of human interest in mind in order to find "common ground" between humanity and machine, not because machines have inherent interests but because machines may be designed with outsized and disruptive capabilities that may change up people's lifestyles and livelihoods. Computational capabiliites may stand to augment human capabilities, but if designed and instantiated in unthinking ways, they may lead to harm.

Of course, "influence agents" on social networks may be fully human and still malicious or in the control of others in the way of "gold farmers" in immersive games. Robots (and cyborgs) may be totally benign, beneficent, capable, and human-helpful. What may have started out as benign may suddenly turn malicious, per the "black swan" scenario. Actual situational awareness in social media will require the understanding of positions and roles in the environment and knowledge of whose interests are being advocated and to what intermediate and ultimate ends. In other words, savvy users of social media must be able to discern what the messaging is, what the calls to action are, and what the real-world implications of following certain paths will be. They have to be able to differentiate the fake from the real, simulacra from the actual.

ACKNOWLEDGMENT

Thanks to Dr. Marc A. Smith for encouraging the creation and evolution of this work.

This work would not exist without the affordances of NodeXL (Network Overview, Discovery, and Exploration for Excel). I am grateful to the team that creates NodeXL.

The pre-identified robot accounts used in this chapter were selected so that the author would not accidentally mis-name or call out a human social media account as a robot one; however, in the real world and a non-publishing context, such assertions may be made with some accuracy and caution—and without any potential public harm.

I am grateful to the two anonymous respondents for their double-blind critiques, which resulted in some additional revisions.

REFERENCES

Aggarwal, C.C. & Abdelzaher, T. (2011). Integrating sensors and social networks. In *Social Network Data Analytics*. Springer-Science + Busines Media.

Ali, N. (2014, May). *Text stylometry for chat bot identification and intelligence estimation*. (Dissertation). University of Louisville, Dept. of Computer Engineering and Computer Science. Retrieved July 16, 2015, from http://ir.library.louisville.edu/cgi/viewcontent.cgi?article=1030&context=etd

Automation rules and best practices . (2013, July 10). Retrieved Nov. 22, 2014, from https://support.twitter.com/articles/76915-automation-rules-and-best-practices#

Boshmaf, Y., Muslukhov, I., Beznosov, K., & Ripeanu, M. (2011). The socialbot network: When bots socialize for fame and money. In *Proceedings of ACSAC 11*.

Boshmaf, Y., Muslukhov, I., Beznosov, K., & Ripeanu, M. (2012). Key challenges in defending against malicious socialbots. *5th Usenix Workshop on Large-scale Exploits and Emergent Threats: Botnets, Spyware, Worms, New Emerging Threats and More*. Retrieved May 11, 2015, from https://www.usenix.org/conference/leet12/workshop-program/presentation/boshmaf

Bot Policy. (2014, Nov. 19). In *Wikipedia*. Retrieved Nov. 22, 2014, from http://en.wikipedia.org/wiki/Wikipedia:Bot_policy

Bulakh, V., Dunn, C. W., & Gupta, M. (2014). Identifying fraudulently promoted online videos. In *Proceedings of WWW '14 Companion*. doi:10.1145/2567948.2578996

Chu, Z., Gianvecchio, S., Wang, H., & Jajodia, S. (2010). Who is tweeting on Twitter: Human, bot, or cyborg? In *Proceedings of ACSAC '10*.

D'Onfro, J. (2013, Oct. 4). Twitter admits 5% of its 'users' are fake. *Business Insider*. Retrieved from http://www.businessinsider.in/Twitter-Admits-5-Of-Its-Users-Are-Fake/articleshow/23479699.cms

Edwards, C., Edwards, A., Spence, P. R., & Shelton, A. K. (2014). Is that a bot running the social media feed? Testing the differences in perceptions of communication quality for a human agent and a bot agent on Twitter. *Computers in Human Behavior*, *33*, 372–376. doi:10.1016/j.chb.2013.08.013

Elishar, A., Fire, M., Kagan, D., & Elovici, Y. (2012). Organizational intrusion: Organization mining using socialbots. In *Proceedings of the 2012 International Conference on Social Informatics*.

Elyashar, A., Fire, M., Kagan, D., & Elovici, Y. (2013). Homing socialbots: Intrusion on a specific organization's employee using socialbots. In *Proceedings of 2013 IEEE/ACM International Conference on Advances in Social Networks Analysis and Mining*.

Ferrara, E., Varol, O., Davis, C., Menczer, F., & Flammini, A. (2014). *The rise of social bots*. Retrieved Nov. 17, 2014, from http://arxiv.org/pdf/1407.5225.pdf

Freeman, D. M. (2013). Using Naïve Bayes to detect spammy names in social networks. In Proceedings of the AISec'13.

Friedman, D., Steed, A., & Slater, M. (2007). Spatial social behavior in Second Life. In the proceedings of IVA 2007. *LNAI*, *4722*, 252–263.

Gallagher, E. (2015, Mar. 18). Tracking the Mexican botnet: Connecting the Twitterbots. *Revolution News*. Retrieved March 25, 2015, from http://revolution-news.com/tracking-the-mexican-botnet-connecting-the-twitterbots/

Gao, L., Zhang, C., & Sun, L. (2011). RESTful Web of Things API in sharing sensor data. *IEEE Xplore*. Retrieved Nov. 15, 2014, from http://ieeexplore.ieee.org/stamp/stamp.jsp?arnumber=6006157

Griffin, A. (2014, Dec. 19). Instagram's spam account purge leaves accounts shedding millions of followers. *The Independent.* Retrieved Dec. 19, 2014, from http://www.engadget.com/2014/12/19/instagram-purges-spam/

Guo, D., & Chen, C. (2014). Detecting non-personal and spam users on geo-tagged Twitter network. *Transactions in GIS, 18*(3), 370–384. doi:10.1111/tgis.12101

Halatchliyski, I., Moskaliuk, J., Kimmerle, J., & Cress, U. (2013). *Explaining authors' contribution to pivotal artifacts during mass collaboration in the Wikipedia's knowledge base.* New York: Springer Link.

Halfaker, A., & Riedl, J. (2012). Bots and cyborgs: Wikipedia's immune system. IEEE, 79 – 82.

Hirschman, B. R., St. Charles, J., & Carley, K. M. (2011). Leaving us in tiers: Can homophily be used to generate tiering effects? *Computational & Mathematical Organization Theory, 17,* 318–343. doi:10.1007/s10588-011-9088-4

Holtgraves, T. M., Ross, S. J., Weywadt, C. R., & Han, T. L. (2007). Perceiving artificial social agents. *Computers in Human Behavior, 23*(5), 2163–2174. doi:10.1016/j.chb.2006.02.017

Huber, M., Kowalski, S., Nohlberg, M., & Tjoa, S. (2009). Towards automating social engineering using social networking sites. In *Proceedings of the 2009 International Conference on Computational Science and Engineering.* IEEE. DOI doi:10.1109/CSE.2009.205

Hwang, T., Pearce, I., & Nanis, M. (2012). Socialbots: Voices on the fronts. *Interaction, 19*(2), 38–45. doi:10.1145/2090150.2090161

Kartaltepe, E. J., Morales, J. A., Xu, S., & Sandhu, R. (2010). Social network-based botnet command-and-control: Emerging threats and countermeasures. In Proceedings of ACNS 2010, (LNCS), (vol. 6123, pp. 511 – 528). Berlin: Springer-Verlag.

Keegan, B. C., Ceni, A., & Smith, M. A. (2013). Analyzing multi-dimensional networks within MediaWikis. In *WikiSym '13.* doi:10.1145/2491055.2491056

Kennedy, J., & Eberhart, R. C. (2001). *Swarm Intelligence.* San Francisco: Morgan Kaufmann Publishers, Academic Press.

Klien, F., & Strohmaier, M. (2012). Short links under attack: Geographical analysis of spam in a URL shortener network. In *Proceedings of HT '12.*

Kumar, R. & Rosé, C.P. (2014). Triggering effective social support for online groups. *ACM Trans. Interact. Intell. Syst., 3*(4), Article 24. DOI:.10.1145/2499672

Lauinger, T., Pankakoski, V., Balzarotti, D., & Kirda, E. (2010). Honeybot, your man in the middle for automated social engineering. In *LEET' 10, 3ʳᵈ USENIX Conference on Large-Scale Exploits and Emergent Threats.* Retrieved Nov. 19, 2014, from https://www.sba-research.org/wp-content/uploads/publications/autosoc-leet2010.pdf

Markoff, J. (2015). *Machines of Loving Grace: The Quest for Common Ground between Humans and Robots.* New York: HarperCollins.

Marra, G. (2012). Socialbots are robots, too. In Socialbots: Voices on the fronts. Academic Press.

Mitter, S., Wagner, C., & Strohmaier, M. (2013). Understanding the impact of socialbot attacks in online social networks. In *WebSci '13*.

Müller-Birn, C., Dobusch, L., & Herbsleb, J. D. (2013). Work-to-rule: The emergence of algorithmic governance in Wikipedia. In *Proceedings of C&T '13*.

Nagaraja, S., Houmansadr, A., Piyawongwisal, P., Singh, V., Agarwal, P., & Borisov, N. (2011). Stegobot: A covert social network botnet. In Proceedings of IH 2011, (LNCS), (vol. 6958, pp. 299 – 313). Berlin: Springer-Verlag.

Pennebaker, J. W. (2011). *The Secret Life of Pronouns: What our Words Say about Us*. New York Bloomsbury Press.

Perez, C., Birregah, B., Layton, R., Lemercier, M., & Watters, P. (2013). REPLOT: Retrieving Profile Links On Twitter for suspicious networks detection. In *Proceedings of the 2013 IEEE / ACM International Conference on Advances in Social Networks Analysis and Mining*.

Registered Bots. (n.d.). In *Wikipedia*. Retrieved from http://en.wikipedia.org/wiki/Wikipedia:Bots/Status

Ronson, J. (2015). *So You've Been Publicly Shamed*. New York: Riverhead Books.

Safer, M. (2015, Apr. 5). Wikimania. 60 Minutes. *CBS News*. Retrieved April 6, 2015, from http://www.cbsnews.com/news/wikipedia-jimmy-wales-morley-safer-60-minutes/

Shawar, B. A., & Atwell, E. (2005). Using corpora in machine-learning chatbot systems. *International Journal of Corpus Linguistics*, *10*(4), 489–516. doi:10.1075/ijcl.10.4.06sha

Sheth, A. (2009). Citizen sensing, social signals, and enriching human experience. Semantics & Services. *IEEE Internet Computing*, 80–85.

Singer, P. W., & Friedman, A. (2014). *Cybersecurity and Cyberwar: What Everyone Needs to Know*. Oxford, UK: Oxford University Press.

Stringhini, G., Kruegel, C., & Vigna, G. (2010). Detecting spammers on social networks. In Proceedings of ACSAC '10. doi:10.1145/1920261.1920263

Tatai, G., Csordás, A., Kiss, A., Szaló, A., & Laufer, L. (2003). Happy chatbot, happy user. *LNAI, 2792*, 5–12.

@tinypirate & @AeroFade. (2012). A socialbots competition. In *Socialbots: Voices on the fronts*.

Turkle, S. (2011). *Alone Together: Why We Expect More from Technology and Less from Each Other*. New York: Basic Books.

U.S. Embassy Beijing. (n.d.). *Air Quality Monitor*. Embassy of the United States. Retrieved from http://beijing.usembassy-china.org.cn/aqirecent3.html

User:AntiVandalBot/FAQ. (2006, Oct. 25). Retrieved Nov. 23, 2014, from http://en.wikipedia.org/wiki/User:AntiVandalBot/FAQ

Varvello, M., & Voelker, G. M. (2010). Second Life: A social network of humans and bots. In *Proceedings of NOSSDAV'10*. doi:10.1145/1806565.1806570

Wagner, C., Mitter, S., Körner, C., & Strohmaier, M. (2012). When social bots attack: Modeling susceptibility of users in online social networks. In Proceedings of #MSM2012 workshop.

Wald, R., Ghoshgoftaar, T. M., Napolitano, A., & Sumner, C. (2013). Predicting susceptibility to social bots on Twitter. *IEEE IRI 2013*. doi:10.1109/IRI.2013.6642447

Wang, A. H. (2010). Detecting spam bots in online social networking sites: A machine learning approach. In Data and Applications Security XXIV, (LNCS), (vol. 6166, pp. 335 – 342). International Federation for Information Processing. doi:10.1007/978-3-642-13739-6_25

Webb, S., Caverlee, J., & Pu, C. (2008). Social honeypots: Making friends with a spammer near you. In *5th Conference on Email and Anti-Spam (CEAS)*. Retrieved Nov. 15, 2014, from http://www.ceas.cc/2008/papers/ceas2008-paper-50.pdf

Wong, E. (2013, Jan. 12). On scale of 0 to 500, Beijing's air quality tops 'crazy bad' at 755. *NY Times Online*. Retrieved Nov. 15, 2014, from http://www.nytimes.com/2013/01/13/science/earth/beijing-air-pollution-off-the-charts.html?_r=1&

Woo, J., Kang, A. R., & Kim, H. K. (2012). Modeling of bot usage diffusion across social networks in MMORPGs. In *Proceedings of WAS A 2012*. doi:10.1145/2425296.2425299

Ylagan, A. (2014, July 15). Governments can bridge costs and services gap with sensor networks. *O'Reilly Radar*.

Zangerle, E. & Specht, G. (2014). *'Sorry, I was hacked": A classification of compromised Twitter accounts*. Academic Press.

Zhang, D., Prior, K., Levene, M., Mao, R., & van Liere, D. (2012). Leave or stay: The departure dynamics of Wikipedia editors. In Proceedings of ADMA, (LNAI), (vol. 7713, pp. 1 – 14). Berlin: Springer-Verlag.

Zhao, S. (2003). Toward a taxonomy of copresence. *Presence (Cambridge, Mass.)*, 12(5), 445–455. doi:10.1162/105474603322761261

ADDITIONAL READING

Hansen, D. L., Schneiderman, B., & Smith, M. A. (2011). *Analyzing Social Media Networks with NodeXL: Insights from a Connected World*. Amsterdam: Elsevier.

KEY TERMS AND DEFINITIONS

Algorithmic Agent: A robot.
Automated Agent: A robot.
Botmaster: A human agent who is running a botnet (and benefitting from the data collected by the robots).

Cheap Talk: Communications between players that do not affect the payoffs of a game (in game theory) (as compared to costly signaling), also communications which do not cost the communicator much if anyting.

Costly Signaling: Actions and communications taken by a player that are expensive to him / her and which indicate the seriousness with which the player is signaling.

Cyborg ("Cybernetic Organism"): A social media account that is run by both a human and automated agents.

Machine Learning: Data mining; the use of various algorithms to identify associational patterns in data.

Malbot: A malicious robot.

Network Analysis: The study of interrelationships between agents and other entities in order to understand the agents, the relationships, communications dynamics, the ecosystem, and other factors.

Compilation of References

@tinypirate & @AeroFade. (2012). A socialbots competition. In *Socialbots: Voices on the fronts.*

A record 3,415 Americans ditch their passports. (2015, Feb. 12). *CNN Money.* Retrieved Feb. 22, 2015, from http://money.cnn.com/2015/02/12/pf/americans-expat-citizenship-passports/

Abbasi, R., Chernov, S., Nejdl, W., Paiu, R., & Staab, S. (2009). Exploiting Flickr tags and groups for finding landmark photos. In Proceedings of the CIR 2009, (LNCS), (vol. 5478, pp. 654-661). Springer-Verlag.

Abel, F., Gao, Q., Houben, G.-J., & Tao, K. (2011). Analyzing temporal dynamics in Twitter profiles for personalized recommendations in the Social Web. In *Proceedings of WebSci '11.* doi:10.1145/2527031.2527040

Abidi, S. S. R., Cheah, Y. N., & Curran, J. (2005). A knowledge creation info-structure to acquire and crystallize the tacit knowledge of health-care experts. *IEEE Transactions on Information Technology in Biomedicine, 9*(2), 193–204. doi:10.1109/TITB.2005.847188 PMID:16138536

About. (2015). *Twitter.* Retrieved March 16, 2015, from https://about.twitter.com/company

Abroms, L. C., & Lefebvre, R. C. (2009). Obama's wired campaign: Lessons for public health communication. *Journal of Health Communication, 14*(5), 415–423. doi:10.1080/10810730903033000

Adam, C. (2012). *Disasters 2.0: The Application of Social Media Systems for Modern Emergency Management.* Taylor & Francis Inc.

Adams, B. (2011). *The Great Escape.* Retrieved Jan. 31, 2015, from http://online.barrons.com/articles/SB5000142405 2748703827804577056023254214872#printMode

Advice about possible loss of U.S. nationality and dual nationality. (2015). U.S. Department of State, Bureau of Consular Affairs. Retrieved Feb. 22, 2015, from http://travel.state.gov/content/travel/english/legal-considerations/us-citizenship-laws-policies/citizenship-and-dual-nationality.html

Aggarwal, C.C. & Abdelzaher, T. (2011). Integrating sensors and social networks. In *Social Network Data Analytics.* Springer-Science + Busines Media.

Agichtein, E., Castillo, C., Donato, D., Gionis, A., & Mishne, G. (2008). Finding high-quality content in social media. In *Proceedings of the 2008 International Conference on Web Search and Data Mining.* New York, NY: ACM Digital Library.

Ahmed, I. (1997). *Exit, voice and citizenship. International Migration, Immobility and Development: Multidisciplinary Perspectives.* Oxford, UK: Beg Publishers.

Aladwani, A. M. (2014). The 6As model of social content management. *International Journal of Information Management, 34*(2), 133–138. doi:10.1016/j.ijinfomgt.2013.12.004

Alexandra, O., Carlos, C., Nicholas, D., & Karl, A. (2015). Comparing Events Coverage in Online News and Social Media: The Case of Climate Change. *International Conference Web and Social Media.*

Ali, N. (2014, May). *Text stylometry for chat bot identification and intelligence estimation.* (Dissertation). University of Louisville, Dept. of Computer Engineering and Computer Science. Retrieved July 16, 2015, from http://ir.library.louisville.edu/cgi/viewcontent.cgi?article=1030&context=etd

Ali-Hassan, H., Nevo, D., & Wade, M. (2015). Linking dimensions of social media use to job performance: The role of social capital. *The Journal of Strategic Information Systems, 24*(2), 65–89. doi:10.1016/j.jsis.2015.03.001

Alpert, J. (2012). *The Mobile Marketing Revolution.* New Delhi: Tata McGraw Hill Education Private Limited.

American Diaspora. (2015, Jan. 17). In *Wikipedia.* Retrieved Jan. 31, 2015, from http://en.wikipedia.org/wiki/American_diaspora

Americans Abroad, How Can We Count Them ? (2001, July 26). Hearing before the Subcommittee of the Census of the Committee on Government Reform. House of Representatives. 107th Congress. Serial 107-13.

Ames, M., & Naaman, M. (2007). Why we tag: Motivations for annotation I mobile and online media. In *Proceedings of CHI 2007 Tags, Tagging & Notetaking.*

Anderson, B. (2006). *Imagined Communities: Reflections on the Origin and Spread of Nationalism.* New York: Verso.

Andreas K., & Michael H. (2010). Users of the world, unite! The challenges and opportunities of social media. *Business Horizons, 53*(1), 59-68.

Angus, E., Thelwall, M., & Stuart, D. (2008). General patterns of tag usage among university groups in Flickr. *Online Information Review, 32*(1), 89 – 101. DOI .10.1108/14684520810866001

Anstead, N., & Chadwick, A. (2012). *Parties, election campaigning, and the Internet: Toward a comparative institutional approach.* London, UK: Routledge.

Aral, S., Dellarocas, C., & Godes, D. (2013). Social media and business transformation: A framework for research. *Information Systems Research, 24*(1), 3–13. doi:10.1287/isre.1120.0470

Aral, S., & Weill, P. (2007). IT assets, organizational capabilities, and firm performance: How resource allocations and organizational differences explain performance variation. *Organization Science, 18*(5), 763–780. doi:10.1287/orsc.1070.0306

Arif, T., Ali, R., & Asger, M. (2012). Scientific Co-authorship Social Networks: A Case Study of Computer Science Scenario in India. *International Journal of Computer Applications, 52*(12), 38-45.

Arif, T. (2015). Understanding Research Collaborations using Social Network Analysis: A Case Study of Indian Institutes of Technology. *International Journal of Advanced Research in Computer Science and Software Engineering, 5*(10), 880–886.

Artiles, J., Gonzalo, J., López-Ostenero, F., & Peinado, V. (2007). Are users willing to search cross-language? An experiment with the Flickr image sharing repository. Evaluation of Multilingual and Multi-modal Information Retrieval. *Lecture Notes in Computer Science, 4730,* 195–204.

Ashley, C., & Tuten, T. (2015). Creative Strategies in Social Media Marketing: An Exploratory Study of Branded Social Content and Consumer Engagement. *Psychology and Marketing, 32*(1), 15–27. doi:10.1002/mar.20761

Athey, S., & Ellison, G. (2009). *Position auctions with consumer search (No. w15253).* National Bureau of Economic Research. doi:10.3386/w15253

Automation rules and best practices . (2013, July 10). Retrieved Nov. 22, 2014, from https://support.twitter.com/articles/76915-automation-rules-and-best-practices#

Awad, E. M., & Ghaziri, H. (2008). *Knowledge Management.* Pvt. Ltd., Licensees of Pearson Education in South Asia.

Baer, J. (2012). *A field guide to the 4 types of content marketing metrics* [PowerPoint slides]. Retrieved from http://www.slideshare.net/jaybaer/a-field-guide-to-the-4-types-of-content-marketing-metrics

Bagnall, R., & Bartholomew, D. (2013). *AMEC Social Media Measurement Framework* [PDF document]. Retrieved from Lecture Notes Online Web site: http://www.social-media-measurement-framework.org/wp-content/uploads/2014/06/Social-Media-Measurement-Framework.pdf

Bainbridge, J. (1968). *Another Way of Living: A Gallery of Americans Who Choose to Live in Europe.* New York: Holt, Rinehart and Winston.

Bak, J. Y., Kim, S., & Oh, A. (2012). Self-disclosure and relationship strength in Twitter conversations. In *Proceedings of the 50th Annual Meeting of the Association for Computational Linguistics.*

Baker, D., Buoni, N., Fee, M., & Vitale, C. (2015). *Social Networking and its effects on companies and their employees.* Retrieved November 29, 2015, from https://www.neumann.edu/academics/divisions/business/journal/Review2011/SocialNetworking.pdf

Bakshi, K. (2004). *Tools for end-user creation and customization of interfaces for information management tasks.* (Doctoral dissertation). Massachusetts Institute of Technology.

Balahur, A., & Perea-Ortega, J. M. (2015). Sentiment analysis system adaptation for multilingual processing: The case of tweets. *Information Processing & Management, 51*(4), 547–556. doi:10.1016/j.ipm.2014.10.004

Banning, S. A., & Sweetser, K. D. (2007). How much do they think it affects them and whom do they believe?: Comparing the third-person effect and credibility of blogs and traditional media. *Communication Quarterly, 55*(4), 451–466. doi:10.1080/01463370701665114

Baptista, J. (2009). Institutionalisation as a process of interplay between technology and its organisational context of use. *Journal of Information Technology, 24*(4), 305–319. doi:10.1057/jit.2009.15

Baptista, J., Newell, S., & Currie, W. (2010). Paradoxical effects of institutionalization on the strategic awareness of technology in organizations. *The Journal of Strategic Information Systems, 19*(3), 171–183. doi:10.1016/j.jsis.2010.07.001

Bardhan, I., Krishnan, V., & Lin, S. (2013). Business value of information technology: Testing the interaction effect of IT and R&D on Tobin's Q. *Information Systems Research, 24*(4), 1147–1161. doi:10.1287/isre.2013.0481

Barnes, N. G., Lescault, A. M., & Holmes, G. (2015). *The 2015 Fortune 500 and Social Media: Instagram Gains, Blogs Lose.* UMass Dartmouth. Retrieved December 08, 2015, from http://www.umassd.edu/cmr/socialmediaresearch/2015fortune500andsocialmedia/

Barnes, N. D., & Barnes, F. R. (2009). *Equipping your organization for the social networking game.* Information Management, Arma International.

Bascandziev, I., & Harris, P. L. (2015). In beauty we trust: Children prefer information from more attractive informants. *The British Journal of Developmental Psychology, 32*(1), 94–99. doi:10.1111/bjdp.12022 PMID:24164592

Batrinca, B., & Treleaven, P. C. (2015). Social media analytics: A survey of techniques, tools, and platforms. *AI & Society, 30*(1), 89–116. doi:10.1007/s00146-014-0549-4

Bayus, B. L. (2013). Crowdsourcing new product ideas over time: An analysis of the Dell IdeaStorm community. *Management Science*, *59*(1), 226–244. doi:10.1287/mnsc.1120.1599

Beer, D. D. (2008). Social network(ing) sites... revisiting the story so far: A response to Danah Boyd & Nicole Ellison. *Journal of Computer-Mediated Communication*, *13*(2), 516–529. doi:10.1111/j.1083-6101.2008.00408.x

Begel, A., DeLine, R., & Zimmermann, T. (2010). *Social media for software engineering*. Paper presented at the 2010 FSE/SDP Workshop on the Future of Software Engineering Research (FoSER), Santa Fe, NM.

Begelman, G., Keller, P., & Smadja, F. (2006). Automated tag clustering: Improving search and exploration in the tag space. In *Proceedings of WWW 2006*.

Behringer, N., & Sassenberg, K. (2015). Introducing social media for knowledge management: Determinants of employees' intentions to adopt new tools. *Computers in Human Behavior*, *48*, 290–296. doi:10.1016/j.chb.2015.01.069

Bell, J., & Loane, S. (2010). "New Wave" Global Firms: Web 2.0 and SME Internationalisation. *Journal of Marketing Management*, *26*(3-4), 213–229. doi:10.1080/02672571003594648

Bennett, S. (2013). How does HR use Social Media. *Adweek*. Retrieved November 23, 2015, from http://www.adweek.com/socialtimes/hr-social-media/492469

Bennett, S., Maton, K., & Kervin, L. (2008). The 'digital natives' debate: A critical review of the evidence. *British Journal of Educational Technology*, *39*(5), 775–786. doi:10.1111/j.1467-8535.2007.00793.x

Berger, J., & Milkman, K. L. (2010). *Social transmission, emotion, and the virality of online content*. Wharton Research Paper. Retrieved October 3, 2015, from http://robingandhi.com/wp-content/uploads/2011/11/Social-Transmission-Emotion-and-the-Virality-of-Online-Content-Wharton.pdf. 1 – 53.

Berger, J. (2011). Arousal increases social transmission of information. *Psychological Science*, *22*(7), 891–893. doi:10.1177/0956797611413294 PMID:21690315

Bernal, J. (2010). *Web 2.0 and social net working for the enterprise - Guidelines and examples for implementation and management within your organization*. New Delhi: Pearson.

Bertolucci, J. (2013). Big data Analytics: Descriptive Vs. Predictive Vs. Prescriptive. *Big data Analytics, Information Week*. Retrieved from: http://www.informationweek.com

Bhargava, R. (2006). *5 Rules of Social Media Optimization (SMO)*. Retrieved from http://www.rohitbhargava.com/2006/08/5_rules_of_soci.html

Bhaskar, J. K. S., & Nedungadi, P. (2015). Hybrid approach for emotion classification of audio conversation based on text and speech mining. *Procedia Computer Science*, *46*, 635 – 643.

Bhattacharya, R. (2015). *Social Commerce*. Retrieved November 06, 2015, from http://www.happiestminds.com/white-papers/social_commerce.pdf

Bianco, J. S.Jamie Skye Bianco. (2009). Social networking and cloud computing: Precarious affordances for the "prosumer." *WSQ:Women's Studies Quarterly*, *37*(1/2), 303–312. doi:10.1353/wsq.0.0146

Bilton, N. (2013). *Hatching Twitter UK*. Sceptre.

Bilton, N. (2015, Oct. 5). Jack Dorsey returns to a frayed Twitter. *The New York Times*.

Blamey, B., Crick, T., & Oatley, G. (2012). R U:-) or:-(? Character- vs. word-gram feature selection for sentiment classification of OSN corpora. In *Research and Development in Intelligent Systems: XXIX*. Academic Press.

Blanchard, O. (2012). *Social media ROI*. New Delhi: Pearson.

Bolognesi. (2012, Oct. 3). *Average number of tags associated to each photo?* FlickrAPI Group. Retrieved June 23, 2015, from https://www.flickr.com/groups/api/discuss/72157631682781762/

Bonacich, P. (1987). Power and centrality: A family of measures. *American Journal of Sociology, 92*(5), 1170–1182. doi:10.1086/228631

Borgatti, S. P. (2005). Centrality and network flow. *Social Networks, 27*(1), 55–71. doi:10.1016/j.socnet.2004.11.008

Boshmaf, Y., Muslukhov, I., Beznosov, K., & Ripeanu, M. (2011). The socialbot network: When bots socialize for fame and money. In *Proceedings of ACSAC 11*.

Boshmaf, Y., Muslukhov, I., Beznosov, K., & Ripeanu, M. (2012). Key challenges in defending against malicious socialbots. *5ʰ Usenix Workshop on Large-scale Exploits and Emergent Threats: Botnets, Spyware, Worms, New Emerging Threats and More*. Retrieved May 11, 2015, from https://www.usenix.org/conference/leet12/workshop-program/presentation/boshmaf

Bot Policy. (2014, Nov. 19). In *Wikipedia*. Retrieved Nov. 22, 2014, from http://en.wikipedia.org/wiki/Wikipedia:Bot_policy

Boudreau, K. J., & Lakhani, K. R. (2013). Using the crowd as an innovation partner. *Harvard Business Review, 91*(4), 60–69.

Bowden, J. (2015). Reasons to Explore Big data with Social Media Analytics. *Social Media Today*. Retrieved from: http://www.socialmediatoday.com

Boyd, D., & Crawford, K. (2012). Critical questions for big data: Provocations for a cultural, technological, and scholarly phenomenon. *Information Communication and Society, 15*(5), 662–679. doi:10.1080/1369118X.2012.678878

Bradley Anthony, J., & Mark, P. (2011). *The Social Organization Boston*. Harvard Business Review Press.

Bradley, A., & McDonald, M. (2011). *Social Media versus Knowledge Management*. Retrieved from http://blogs.hbr.org/2011/10/social-media-versus-knowledge/

Braojos-Gomez, J., Benitez-Amado, J., & Llorens-Montes, F. J. (2015). How do small firms learn to develop a social media competence? *International Journal of Information Management, 35*(4), 443–458. doi:10.1016/j.ijinfomgt.2015.04.003

Bratsberg, B., & Terrell, D. (1996). Where do Americans Live Abroad? *International Migration Review, 30*(3), 788 – 802. Retrieved Jan. 31, 2015, from http://www.jstor.org/stable/2547637

Breschi, S., & Lissoni, F. (2001). Knowledge spillovers and local innovation systems: A critical survey. *Industrial and Corporate Change, 10*(4), 975–1005. doi:10.1093/icc/10.4.975

Brin, S. & Page, L. (1998). The anatomy of a large-scale hypertextual Web search engine. *Computer Networks and ISDN Systems, 30*(1), 107-117.

Brito, M. (2014). Your Brand, the Next Media Company. In *How a Social Business Strategy Enables Better Content, Smarter Marketing, Deeper Customer Relationships*. Indiana Polis.

Brooks, S. (2015). Does personal social media usage affect efficiency and well-being? *Computers in Human Behavior, 46*, 26–37. doi:10.1016/j.chb.2014.12.053

Brown, B., Chui, M., & Manyika, J. (2011). Are you ready for the era of 'big data'. *The McKinsey Quarterly, 4*, 24–35.

Brynjolfsson, E., Hitt, L. M., & Kim, H. H. (2011). *Strength in numbers: How does data-driven decisionmaking affect firm performance?*. Available at SSRN 1819486

BSR STARS. (2012). *Knowledge Sharing Tools and Practices.* Retrieved from www.bsrstars.se

Buettner, R. (2016). *Getting a Job via Career-oriented Social Networking Sites: The Weakness of Ties.* Paper presented at the 49th Annual Hawaii International Conference on System Sciences, Kauai, HI. doi:10.1109/HICSS.2016.272

Bughin, J., & Chui, M. (2010). *The rise of the networked enterprise: Web 2.0 finds its payday.* Retrieved from http://www.mckinsey.com/insights/high_tech_telecoms_internet/the_rise_of_the_networked_enterprise_web_20_finds_its_payday

Buhse, W., & Stamer, S. (2008). *Enterprise 2.0 - Die Kunst, loszulassen.* Berlin: Rhombos.

Bulakh, V., Dunn, C. W., & Gupta, M. (2014). Identifying fraudulently promoted online videos. In *Proceedings of WWW '14 Companion.* doi:10.1145/2567948.2578996

Burrell, J.S. (2004, June). *Emigration of U.S.-born S&E Doctorate Recipients.* InfoBrief. SRS Home. NSF 04-327.

Burrus, D. (2010). Social networks in the workplace: The risk and opportunity of Business 2.0. *Strategy and Leadership, 38*(4), 50–54. doi:10.1108/10878571011059674

Burson-Marsteller. (2012). *Burson-Marsteller 2011 fortune global 100 social media study.* New York, NY: Burson-Marsteller. Retrieved from http://www.burson-marsteller.com/innovation_and_insights/blogs_and_podcasts/BM_Blog/default.aspx

Cachia, R., Compano, R., & Da Costa, O. (2007). Grasping the potential of online social networks for foresight. *Technological Forecasting and Social Change, 74*(8), 1179–1203. doi:10.1016/j.techfore.2007.05.006

Cai, J., Liu, X., Xiao, Z., & Liu, J. (2009). Improving supply chain performance management: A systematic approach to analyzing iterative KPI accomplishment. *Decision Support Systems, 46*(2), 512–521. doi:10.1016/j.dss.2008.09.004

Camison, C., & Villar-Lopez, A. (2012). On how firms located in and industrial district profit from knowledge spillovers: Adoption of an organic structure and innovation capabilities. *British Journal of Management, 23*(3), 361–382. doi: 10.1111/j.1467-8551.2011.00745.x

Cao, D., Ji, R., Lin, D., & Li, S. (2014). A cross-media public sentiment analysis system for microblog. In *Multimedia Systems* (pp. 1–8). Springer; doi:10.1007/978-1-4471-4739-8_16

Carpenter, C. (2012). Copyright infringement and the second generation of social media websites: Why Pinterest users should be protected from copyright infringement by the fair use defense. *Journal of Internet Law, 16*(7), 9–21. doi: 10.2139/ssrn.2131483

Casalo, L. V., Flavian, C., & Guinaliu, M. (2010). Relationship quality, community promotion and brand loyalty in virtual communities: Evidence from free software communities. *International Journal of Information Management, 30*(4), 357–367. doi:10.1016/j.ijinfomgt.2010.01.004

Census Bureau projects U.S. and world populations on New Year's Day. (2014, Dec. 29). U.S. Census Bureau. CB14-TPS.90. Retrieved Feb. 22, 2015, at http://www.census.gov/newsroom/press-releases/2014/cb14-tps90.html

Cha, M., Mislove, A., & Gummadi, K. P. (2009). A measurement-driven analysis of information propagation in the Flickr social network. In *Proceedings of the WWW 2009.* doi:10.1145/1526709.1526806

Cha, M., Mislove, A., Adams, B., & Gummadi, K. P. (2008). Characterizing social cascades in Flickr. In Proceedings of WOSN '08. doi:10.1145/1397735.1397739

Chai, S., & Kim, M. (2010). What makes bloggers share knowledge? An investigation on the role of trust. *International Journal of Information Management, 30*(5), 408–415. doi:10.1016/j.ijinfomgt.2010.02.005

Champoux, V., Durgee, J., & McGlynn, L. (2012). Corporate Facebook pages: When "fans" attack. *The Journal of Business Strategy, 33*(2), 22–30. doi:10.1108/02756661211206717

Chang, H. L., & Chou, C. Y. (2012). *Shaping proactivity for firm performance: Evaluating the role of IT-enabled collaboration in small and medium enterprises.* Paper presented at the 16th Pacific Asia Conference on Information Systems (PACIS 2012), Ho Chi Minh City, Vietnam.

Chan, N. L., & Guillet, B. D. (2011). Investigation of social media marketing: How does the hotel industry in Hong Kong perform in marketing on social media websites? *Journal of Travel & Tourism Marketing, 28*(4), 345–368. doi:10.1080/10548408.2011.571571

Chantanarungpak, K. (2015). Using e-portfolio on social media. *Procedia: Social and Behavioral Sciences, 186*, 1275–1281. doi:10.1016/j.sbspro.2015.04.063

Chapin, F.S., Kofnas, G.P., & Floke, C. (2009). *Principles of Ecosystem Stewardship: Resilience- Based Natural Resource Management in a Changing World.* London: Springer.

Chelmis, C., & Prasanna, V. K. (2011). Social networking analysis: A state of the art and the effect of semantics. In *Proceedings of 3rd IEEE Conference on Social Computing.* doi:10.1109/PASSAT/SocialCom.2011.23

Chen, X., & Shin, H. (2010). Extracting representative tags for Flickr users. In *Proceedings of the 2010 IEEE International Conference on Data Mining Workshops.* doi:10.1109/ICDMW.2010.117

Chen, X., Wang, C., & Zhang, X. (2013). *All online friends are not created equal: Discovering influence structure in online social networks.* Paper presented at the Pacific Asia Conference on Information Systems (PACIS 2013), Jeju Island, South Korea.

Chen, Y., Lee, S. Y. M., Li, S., & Huang, C.-R. (2010). Emotion cause detection with linguistic constructions. In *Proceedings of the 23rd International Conference on Computational Linguistics* (Coling 2010).

Cheung Christy, M. K., & Lee Matthew, K. O. (2010). A theoretical model of intentional social action in online social networks. *Decision Support Systems, 49*(1), 24–30. doi:10.1016/j.dss.2009.12.006

Chiras Daniel, D., & Reganold John, P. (2010). *Natural Resource Conversation Management: Management for a Sustainable Future.* Prentice Hall.

Choi, S. (2013). An empirical study of social network service (SNS) continuance: Incorporating the customer value-satisfaction-loyalty model into the IS continuance model. *Asia Pacific Journal of Information Systems, 23*(4), 1–28. doi:10.14329/apjis.2013.23.4.001

Chorafas Dimitris, N., & Steinmann. (1995). *Virtual Reality Practical Applications in Business and Industry.* Prentice Hall.

Choudhary, P. (2012). *The Unlimited Business Opportunities on the Internet.* Xcess Info store Private Limited

Chris, B. (2010). *Social Media 101 Tactics and Tips to develop your Business online.* John Wiley and Sons Inc.

Chu, Z., Gianvecchio, S., Wang, H., & Jajodia, S. (2010). Who is tweeting on Twitter: Human, bot, or cyborg? In *Proceedings of ACSAC '10.*

Chun Ho Chan, R., Kai Wah, S., Wing Yi Lee, C., Kim To Chan, B., & Kit Leung, C. (2013). Knowledge Management using Social Media: A Comparative Study between Blogs and Facebook. *Proceedings of the American Society for Information Science and Technology, 50*(1), 1–9. doi:10.1002/meet.14505001069

Chung, J. Y., & Buhalis, D. (2008). *A study of online travel community and Web 2.0: Factors affecting participation and attitude*. Paper presented at the ENTER 2008 Conference on eTourism, Innsbruck, Austria. doi:10.1007/978-3-211-77280-5_7

Chung, J. E. (2015). Antismoking campaign videos on YouTube and audience response: Application of social media assessment metrics. *Computers in Human Behavior*, *51*, 114–121. doi:10.1016/j.chb.2015.04.061

Chung, N., & Koo, C. (2015). The use of social media in travel information search. *Telematics and Informatics*, *32*(2), 215–229. doi:10.1016/j.tele.2014.08.005

Chung, N., Lee, S., & Han, H. (2015). Understanding communication types on travel information sharing in social media: A transactive memory systems perspective. *Telematics and Informatics*, *32*(4), 564–575. doi:10.1016/j.tele.2015.02.002

Cialdini, R. B. (1993). *Influence: The psychology of persuasion*. New York, NY: Harper Business.

Cialdini, R. B., Wosinska, W., Barrett, D. W., Butner, J., & Gornik-Durose, M. (1999). Compliance with a request in two cultures: The differential influence of social proof and commitment/consistency on collectivists and individualists. *Personality and Social Psychology Bulletin*, *25*(10), 1242–1253. doi:10.1177/0146167299258006

Cialdini, R., & Golstein, N. (2004). Social influence: Compliance and conformity. *Annual Review of Psychology*, *55*(1), 591–621. doi:10.1146/annurev.psych.55.090902.142015

Clements, M., Serdyukov, P., de Vries, A. P., & Reinders, M. J. T. (2010). Using Flickr geotags to predict user travel behaviour. In *Proceedings of SIGIR '10*. doi:10.1145/1835449.1835648

Clifton, B. (2012). *Advanced web metrics with Google Analytics*. Hoboken, NJ: John Wiley & Sons.

Cognizant. (2014). *Customer Insight Command Center Speeds 'Just-in-Time' Marketing*. Retrieved December 04, 2015, from http://www.cognizant.com/InsightsWhitepapers/customer-insight-command-center-speeds-just-in-time-marketing-codex1015.pdf

Cohen, H. (2011). *What is Social Commerce?* Retrieved December 04, 2015, from http://heidicohen.com/what-is-social-commerce

Colace, F., Casaburi, L., De Santo, M., & Greco, L. (2015). Sentiment detection in social networks and in collaborative learning environments. *Computers in Human Behavior*, *51*, 1061–1067. doi:10.1016/j.chb.2014.11.090

Conroy, M. J., & Paterson, J. T. (2013). *Decision Making in Natural Resource Management: A Structured Adaptive Approach*. Willey-Blackwell.

Cooley, R., Mobasher, B., & Srivastave, J. (1997). Web mining: Information and pattern discovery on the world wide web. In *Proceedings of the 9th IEEE International Conference on Tool with Artificial Intelligence*. doi:10.1109/TAI.1997.632303

Cornard Levinson, J., & Gibson, S. (2010). *Guerrilla social media marketing*. New Delhi: Tata McGraw Hill Education Private Limited.

Cornelissen, J. (2014). *Corporate communication: A guide to theory and practice*. London, UK: Sage Publications, Ltd.

Cox, A. M., Clough, P. D., & Marlow, J. (2008). Flickr: A first look at user behaviour in the context of photography as serious leisure. *Information Research*, *13*(1), 1–19.

Cross, R., & Katzenbach, J. (2012). The right role for top teams. *Strategy & Leadership*. Retrieved November 29, 2015, from http://www.strategy-business.com/article/00103?gko=97c39

Crossan, M. M., Maurer, C. C., & White, R. E. (2011). Reflections on the 2009 AMR decade award: Do we have a theory of organizational learning? *Academy of Management Review, 36*(3), 446–460. doi:10.5465/amr.2010.0544

Cugelman, B., Thelwall, M., & Dawes, P. (2011). Online interventions for social marketing health behavior change campaigns: A meta-analysis of psychological architectures and adherence factors. *Journal of Medical Internet Research, 13*(1), 84–107. doi:10.2196/jmir.1367

Culnan, M., McHugh, P., & Zubillaga, J. (2010). How large US companies can use Twitter and other social media to gain business value. *MIS Quarterly Executive, 9*(4), 243–259.

D'Onfro, J. (2013, Oct. 4). Twitter admits 5% of its 'users' are fake. *Business Insider*. Retrieved from http://www.businessinsider.in/Twitter-Admits-5-Of-Its-Users-Are-Fake/articleshow/23479699.cms

da Silva, N. F. F., Hruschka, E. R., & Hruschka, E. R. Jr. (2014). Tweet sentiment analysis with classifier ensembles. *Decision Support Systems, 66*, 170–179. doi:10.1016/j.dss.2014.07.003

Dalkir, K. (2005). *Knowledge Management in Theory and Practice*. Burlington, MA: Elsevier.

Dashefsky, A., DeAmicis, J., Lazerwitz, B., & Tabory, E. (1992). Americans Abroad: A Comparative Study of Emigrants from the United States. New York: Springer Science + Business Media, LLC. doi:10.1007/978-1-4757-2169-0

Davidow William, H. (2011). *Over connected- The Promise and Threat of the Internet*. London: Headline Publishing Group.

De Mauro, A., Greco, M., & Grimaldi, M. (2015, February). What is big data? A consensual definition and a review of key research topics. In AIP Conference Proceedings (vol. 1644, pp. 97–104). doi:10.1063/1.4907823

De Meo, P., Ferrara, E., Abel, F., Aroyo, L., & Houben, G-J. (2013). Analyzing user behavior across social sharing environments. *ACM Transactions on Intelligent Systems and Technologies, 5*(1), Article 14. DOI:10.1145/2535526

Deans, P. C. (2011). The impact of social media on C-level roles. *MIS Quarterly Executive, 10*(4), 187–200.

Deemter, K. V. (2010). Not Exactly. In *Praise of Vagueness*. Oxford, UK: Oxford University Press.

del Fresno, M. (2012). *El consumidor social: Reputación online y social media*. Barcelona, B: Editorial UOC.

DeLoatch, P. (2014). Predictive social analytics must clear data silo hurdles. *Content Management, TechTarget*. Retrieved from: http://www techtarget.com

Demirhan, K., & Cakır-Demirhan, D. (2015). Gender and politics: Patriarchal discourse on social media. *Public Relations Review, 41*(1), 308–310. doi:10.1016/j.pubrev.2014.11.010

Dentus Social Media Handbook. (2010). Mumbai: Popular Prakashan Private Limited.

Denyer, D., Parry, E., & Flowers, P. (2011). "Social", "open" and "participative"? Exploring personal experiences and organizational effects of Enterprise 2.0 use. *Long Range Planning, 44*(5/6), 375–396. doi:10.1016/j.lrp.2011.09.007

Di Gangi, P. M., & Wasko, M. (2009). Steal my idea! Organizational adoption of user innovations from a user innovation community: A case study of Dell IdeaStorm. *Decision Support Systems, 48*(1), 303–312. doi:10.1016/j.dss.2009.04.004

Di Gangi, P. M., Wasko, M. M., & Hooker, R. E. (2010). Getting customers' ideas to work for you: Learning from Dell how to succeed with online user innovation communities. *MIS Quarterly Executive, 9*(4), 213–228.

Diehl, A., Grabill, J. T., Hart-Davidson, W., & Iyer, V. (2008). Grassroots: Supporting the knowledge work of everyday life. *Technical Communication Quarterly, 17*(4), 413–434. doi:10.1080/10572250802324937

Dispositional Affect. (2014, Feb. 17). In *Wikipedia*. Retrieved Sept. 28, 2015, from https://en.wikipedia.org/wiki/Dispositional_affect

Djelic, M. L., & Ainamo, A. (2005). The telecom industry as cultural industry? The transposition of fashion logics into the field of mobile telephony. *Research in the Sociology of Organizations, 23*(1), 45–82. doi:10.1016/S0733-558X(05)23002-1

Dodds, P. S., Harris, K. D., Kloumann, I. M., Bliss, C. A., & Danforth, C. M. (2011). Temporal patterns of happiness and information in a global social network: Hedonometrics and Twitter. *PLoS ONE, 6*(12), e26752. PMID:22163266

Doney, P. M., & Cannon, J. P. (1997, April). An examination of the nature of trust in buyer-seller relationships. *Journal of Marketing, 61*(2), 35–51. doi:10.2307/1251829

Dong, J. Q., & Wu, W. (2015). Business value of social media technologies: Evidence from online user innovation communities. *The Journal of Strategic Information Systems, 24*(2), 113–127. doi:10.1016/j.jsis.2015.04.003

Dong, J. Q., & Yang, C. H. (2015). Information technology and organizational learning in knowledge alliances and networks: Evidence from U.S. pharmaceutical industry. *Information & Management, 52*(1), 111–122. doi:10.1016/j.im.2014.10.010

Drerup, T. (2015). Diurnal rhythms in investor sentiment. *Journal of Behavioral and Experimental Finance*. .10.1016/j.jbef.2015.07.002

Drucker, P. (1994). *Definition on the "need for Knowledge Management"*. Academic Press.

Drumwright, H. (2014). *How Social CEOs Harness Social Media for Knowledge Management*. Retrieved November 29, 2015, from http://www.kmworld.com/Articles/Editorial/ViewPoints/How-Social-CEOs-Harness-Social-Media-for-Knowledge-Management-99833.aspx

Duggan, M., & Smith, A. (2014). *Social media update 2013*. Washington, DC: Pew Research Center.

Dutta, M. J. (2015). New communication technologies, social media, and public health. In R. Detels, M. Gulliford, Q. Karim, & C. Tan (Eds.), *Oxford textbook of global public health* (pp. 388–399). Oxford, UK: Oxford University Press. doi:10.1093/med/9780199661756.003.0102

Dynel, M. (2014). Participation framework underlying YouTube interaction. *Journal of Pragmatics, 73*, 37–52. doi:10.1016/j.pragma.2014.04.001

Edwards, C., Edwards, A., Spence, P. R., & Shelton, A. K. (2014). Is that a bot running the social media feed? Testing the differences in perceptions of communication quality for a human agent and a bot agent on Twitter. *Computers in Human Behavior, 33*, 372–376. doi:10.1016/j.chb.2013.08.013

Eileen, B. (2011). *Working the Crowd Social Media Marketing for Business*. British Informatics Society Limited.

Eisenberg, N., & Miller, P. A. (1987). The relation of empathy to prosocial and related behaviors. *Psychological Bulletin, 101*(1), 91–119. doi:10.1037/0033-2909.101.1.91 PMID:3562705

Elishar, A., Fire, M., Kagan, D., & Elovici, Y. (2012). Organizational intrusion: Organization mining using socialbots. In *Proceedings of the 2012 International Conference on Social Informatics*.

Elliott, N. (2011), *Which Social Media Marketing Metrics Really Matter? (And To Whom?)*. Retrieved from http://blogs.forrester.com/nate_elliott/11-02-23-which_social_media_marketing_metrics_really_matter_and_to_whom

Elyashar, A., Fire, M., Kagan, D., & Elovici, Y. (2013). Homing socialbots: Intrusion on a specific organization's employee using socialbots. In *Proceedings of 2013 IEEE/ACM International Conference on Advances in Social Networks Analysis and Mining*.

eMarketer. (2014). Social Networking Reaches Nearly One in Four around the World. *eMarketer*. Retrieved October 13, 2015, from http://www.emarketer.com/Article/Social-Networking-Reaches-Nearly-One-Four-Around-World/1009976

Emigration from the United States. (2015, Jan. 27). In Wikipedia. Retrieved Jan. 31, 2015, from http://en.wikipedia.org/wiki/Emigration_from_the_United_States

Esipova, N., Pugliese, A., & Ray, J. (2014, Jan. 17). Potential Net Migration Index declines in many countries: Southern Europe's economic troubles make it less attractive. Gallup. Retrieved April 29, 2015, from http://www.gallup.com/poll/166796/potential-net-migration-index-declines-countries.aspx

Evans, D. (2010). *Social Media Marketing- An Hour a Day*. New Delhi: Wiley India Private Limited.

Expatriation Tax. (2014, June 28). Internal Revenue Services. Retrieved Feb. 22, 2015, at http://www.irs.gov/Individuals/International-Taxpayers/Expatriation-Tax

EY. (2015). *Social Media Marketing: India Trends Study*. Retrieved December 08, 2015, from http://www.ey.com/Publication/vwLUAssets/EY-social-media-marketing-india-trends-study-2014/$FILE/EY-social-media-marketing-india-trends-study-2014.pdf

Facebook. (2015). *New Tools for Managing Communication on Your Page*. Retrieved December 04, 2015, fromhttps://www.facebook.com/business/news/new-tools-for-managing-communication-on-your-page

Faist, T. (2008). Migrants as transnational development agents: An inquiry into the newest round of the migration-development nexus. *Population Space and Place*, *14*(1), 21–42. doi:10.1002/psp.471

Fama, E. F. (1998). Market efficiency, long-term returns, and behavioral finance. *Journal of Financial Economics*, *49*(3), 283–306. doi:10.1016/S0304-405X(98)00026-9

Farashbandi, F. Z., Geraei, E., & Siamaki, S. (2014). Study of co-authorship network of papers in the Journal of Research in Medical Sciences using social network analysis. *Journal of Research in Medical Sciences*, *19*(1), 41–46. PMID:24672564

Fattah, M. A. (2015). New term weighting schemes with combination of multiple classifiers for sentiment analysis. *Neurocomputing*, *167*, 434–442. doi:10.1016/j.neucom.2015.04.051

Fernandez, E. W. (1995, Jan). *Estimation of the Annual Emigration of U.S. Born Persons by Using Foreign Censuses and Selected Administrative Data: Circa 1980*. U.S. Bureau of the Census, Population Division. Working Paper No. 10.

Ferrara, E., Varol, O., Davis, C., Menczer, F., & Flammini, A. (2014). *The rise of social bots*. Retrieved Nov. 17, 2014, from http://arxiv.org/pdf/1407.5225.pdf

Fersini, E., Messina, E., & Pozzi, F. A. (2014). Sentiment analysis: Bayesian ensemble learning. *Decision Support Systems*, *68*, 26–38. doi:10.1016/j.dss.2014.10.004

Filo, K., Lock, D., & Karg, A. (2015). Sport and social media research: A review. *Sport Management Review*, *18*(2), 166–181. doi:10.1016/j.smr.2014.11.001

Fitzgerald, M. (2009). Why social computing aids Knowledge Management. *CIO*, 1-5. Retrieved April 15, 2009, from http://www.cio.com/article/395113/Why_Social_Computing_Aids_Knowledge_Management

Flowers, A. (2015, Dec. 10). Immigration projections rebound with the economy. *DataLab*. Retrieved Jan. 31, 2015, from http://fivethirtyeight.com/datalab/immigration-projections-rebound-along-with-the-economy/

Fonseca, N., & Boutaba, R. (2015). *Cloud Services, Networking, and Management*. John Wiley & Sons. doi:10.1002/9781119042655

Foreign Account Tax Compliance Act. (2015, Feb. 14). In *Wikipedia*. Retrieved Feb. 22, 2015, from http://en.wikipedia.org/wiki/Foreign_Account_Tax_Compliance_Act

Forrester. (2010). *The ROI of social media marketing*. Retrieved from https://frankdiana.files.wordpress.com/2011/04/roi-of-social-marketing-forrester-report.pdf

Francisco, A. (2013). Realizing the Opportunity for Big data in Educatio. *Digital Promise*. Retrieved from http://www.digitalpromise.org

Freeman, D. M. (2013). Using Naïve Bayes to detect spammy names in social networks. In Proceedings of the AISec'13.

Freeman, L. C. (1977). A set of measures of centrality based upon betweenness. *Sociometry*, *40*(1), 35–41. doi:10.2307/3033543

Friedman, D., Steed, A., & Slater, M. (2007). Spatial social behavior in Second Life. In the proceedings of IVA 2007. *LNAI*, *4722*, 252–263.

Fries, S. (1992). *NASA Engineers and the Age of Apollo*. Retrieved from http://ntrs.nasa.gov/archive/nasa/casi.ntrs.nasa.gov/19920019101.pdf

Fu, X., Yang, K., Huang, J. Z., & Cui, L. (2015). Dynamic non-parametric joint sentiment topic mixture model. *Knowledge-Based Systems*, *82*, 102–114. doi:10.1016/j.knosys.2015.02.021

Gallagher, E. (2015, Mar. 18). Tracking the Mexican botnet: Connecting the Twitterbots. *Revolution News*. Retrieved March 25, 2015, from http://revolution-news.com/tracking-the-mexican-botnet-connecting-the-twitterbots/

Gallaugher, J., & Ransbotham, S. (2010). Social media and customer dialog management at Starbucks. *MIS Quarterly Executive*, *9*(4), 197–212.

Gallo, C. (2012). *The Power of Four Square- 7 Innovative Ways to get your customers wherever they are*. New Delhi: Tata McGraw Hill Education Private Limited.

Gangemi, A. (2013). A comparison of knowledge extraction tools for the Semantic Web. In P. Cimiano et al. (Eds.), *ESWC 2013. 361 – 366*. Berlin: Springer-Verlag. doi:10.1007/978-3-642-38288-8_24

Gao, L., Zhang, C., & Sun, L. (2011). RESTful Web of Things API in sharing sensor data. *IEEE Xplore*. Retrieved Nov. 15, 2014, from http://ieeexplore.ieee.org/stamp/stamp.jsp?arnumber=6006157

Gelb, B. D., & Sundaram, S. (2002). Adapting to word of mouse. *Business Horizons*, *45*(4), 21–25. doi:10.1016/S0007-6813(02)00222-7

Georgescu, M., & Popescul, D. (2015). Social media: The new paradigm of collaboration and communication for business environment. *Procedia Economics and Finance*, *20*, 277–282. doi:10.1016/S2212-5671(15)00075-1

Ghiassi, M., Skinner, J., & Zimbra, D. (2013). Twitter brand sentiment analysis: A hybrid system using n-gram analysis and dynamic artificial neural network. *Expert Systems with Applications*, *40*(16), 6266–6282. doi:10.1016/j.eswa.2013.05.057

Gilbert, E., & Karahalios, K. (2009). Predicting tie strength with social media, In *Proceedings of the SIGCHI Conference on Human Factors in Computing Systems* (pp. 211-220). ACM.

Gillin, P. (2009). *The New Influencers- Marketers Guide to New Social Media*. Quill Driver Books

Gillin, P. (2009a). *Secrets of Social Media Marketing*. Quill Driver Books.

Gillin, P. (2009b). *The New Influencers- A Marketers to Social Media*. Quill Driver Books.

Goh, K. Y., Heng, C. S., & Lin, Z. (2013). Social media brand community and consumer behavior: Quantifying the relative impact of user- and marketer-generated content. *Information Systems Research, 24*(1), 88–107. doi:10.1287/isre.1120.0469

Golbeck, J., Koepfler, J., & Emmerling, B. (2011). An experimental study of social tagging behavior and image content. *Journal of the American Society for Information Science and Technology, 62*(9), 1750–1760. doi:10.1002/asi.21522

Golden, M. (2012). *Social Media: Strategies for Professionals and their firms*. Wiley and Sons. doi:10.1002/9781119200352

Goldhaber, M. H. (1997). *The Attention Economy and the Net*. Retrieved from http://firstmonday.org/article/view/519/440

Gomes, O. (2015). Sentiment cycles in discrete-time homogeneous networks. *Physica A, 428*, 224–238. doi:10.1016/j.physa.2015.01.084

Grace, T. P. L. (2009). Wikis as a knowledge management tool. *Journal of Knowledge Management, 13*(4), 64–74. doi:10.1108/13673270910971833

Granados, N., & Gupta, A. (2013). Transparency strategy: Competing with information in a digital world. *Management Information Systems Quarterly, 37*(2), 637–641.

Granovetter, M. S. (1973). The strength of weak ties. *American Journal of Sociology, 78*(6), 1360–1380. doi:10.1086/225469

Gretzel, U. (2001). *Social network analysis: Introduction and resources*. Retrieved from http://lrs.ed.uiuc.edu/tse-portal/analysis/social-network-analysis/#analysis

Griffin, A. (2014, Dec. 19). Instagram's spam account purge leaves accounts shedding millions of followers. *The Independent*. Retrieved Dec. 19, 2014, from http://www.engadget.com/2014/12/19/instagram-purges-spam/

Groves, P., Kayyali, B., Knott, D., & Van Kuiken, S. (2013). The 'big data' revolution in healthcare. *The McKinsey Quarterly*.

Gu, B., Park, J., & Konana, P. (2012). The impact of external word-of-mouth sources on retailer sales of high-involvement products. *Information Systems Research, 23*(1), 182–196. doi:10.1287/isre.1100.0343

Guenard, R., Katz, J., Bruno, S., & Lipa, M. (2013). Enabling a New Way of Working through Inclusion and Social Media. *OD Practitioner, 45*(4).

Gundotra, V. (2011). Introducing the Google+ project: Real-life sharing, rethought for the web. *The Official Google Blog*.

Guo, D., & Chen, C. (2014). Detecting non-personal and spam users on geo-tagged Twitter network. *Transactions in GIS, 18*(3), 370–384. doi:10.1111/tgis.12101

Gutierrez, F. J., & Poblete, B. (2015). Sentiment-based user profiles in microblogging platforms. In *Proceedings of HT '15*. doi:10.1145/2700171.2791027

Haddi, E., Liu, X., & Shi, Y. (2013). The role of text pre-processing in sentiment analysis. In *Proceedings of 2013 Information Technology and Quantitative Management* (ITQM 2013).

Hai-Jew, S. (2009, Sept.) Exploring the immersive parasocial: Is it you or the thought of you? *MERLOT Journal of Online Learning and Teaching, 5*(3). Retrieved Oct. 9, 2015, from http://jolt.merlot.org/vol5no3/hai-jew_0909.htm

Hai-Jew, S. (2014). *Conducting Surface Web-Based Research with Maltego Carbon*. Scalar Platform. Retrieved March 15, 2015, from http://scalar.usc.edu/works/conducting-surface-web-based-research-with-maltego-carbon/index

Hajmohammadi, M. S., Ibrahim, R., Selamat, A., & Fujita, H. (2015). Combination of active learning and self-training for cross-lingual sentiment classification with density analysis of unlabeled samples. *Information Sciences, 317*, 67–77. doi:10.1016/j.ins.2015.04.003

Halatchliyski, I., Moskaliuk, J., Kimmerle, J., & Cress, U. (2013). *Explaining authors' contribution to pivotal artifacts during mass collaboration in the Wikipedia's knowledge base.* New York: Springer Link.

Halfaker, A., & Riedl, J. (2012). Bots and cyborgs: Wikipedia's immune system. IEEE, 79 – 82.

Halo. (2014). The two-minute guide to understanding and selecting the right analytics. *Halo.* Retrieved from https://halobi.com/2014

Hammond, W. E., Bailey, C., Boucher, P., Spohr, M., & Whitaker, P. (2010). Connecting information to improve health. *Health Affairs*, *29*(2), 284–288. doi:10.1377/hlthaff.2009.0903 PMID:20348075

Han, B. M., & Anantatmula, V. (2006). Knowledge management in IT organizations from employee's perspective. In *Proceedings of the 39th Hawaii International Conference on System Sciences.* IEEE Conference Publications

Hanna, R., Rohm, A., & Crittenden, V. (2011). We're all connected: The power of the social media ecosystem. *Business Horizons*, *54*(3), 265–273. doi:10.1016/j.bushor.2011.01.007

Hansen, R., & Birkinshaw, J. (2007). The innovation value chain. *Harvard Business Review*, *85*(6), 121–135.

Harrison, J. S., & Freeman, R. E. (1999). Stakeholders, social responsibility, and performance: Empirical evidence and theoretical perspectives. *Academy of Management Journal*, *42*(5), 479–485. doi:10.2307/256971

Harvey, C. (2012). 50 Top Open Source Tools for Big data. *Datamation, ITBusinessEdge.* Retrieved from: http://www.datamation.com/data-cente

Haryal, V., & Pillai, A. (2011). *Social Media Simplified Twitter; Face Book-Beyond Casual Networking.* New Delhi: Ocean Paper Backs.

Hawn, C. (2009). Take two aspirin and tweet me in the morning: How Twitter, Facebook, and other social media are reshaping health care. *Health Affairs*, *28*(2), 361–368. doi:10.1377/hlthaff.28.2.361

Haydon, J. (2014). *Facebook marketing for dummies.* New Delhi: Wiley India Private Limited.

Heckner, M., Neubauer, T., & Wolff, C. (2008). Tree, funny, to_read, google: What are tags supposed to achieve? In Proceedings of SSM '08.

Heldman, A. B., Schindelar, J., & Weaver, J. B. (2013). Social media engagement and public health communication: Implications for public health organizations being truly "social". *Public Health Reviews*, *35*(1), 1–18.

Hendler, J. (2009). Web 3.0 emerging. *Computer*, *42*(1), 111–113. doi:10.1109/MC.2009.30

Hestres, L. E. (2013). *Preaching to the Choir: Internet-Mediated Advocacy, Issue Public Mobilization and Climate Change: New Media and Society.* Sage Journals.

He, W., Zha, S., & Li, L. (2013). Social media competitive analysis and text mining: A case study in the pizza industry. *International Journal of Information Management*, *33*(3), 464–472. doi:10.1016/j.ijinfomgt.2013.01.001

Hietanen, H., Athukorala, K., & Salovaara, A. (2011). What's with the free images? A study of Flickr's Creative Commons attribution images. In *Proceedings of MindTrek '11.*

Hilbert, M. (2016). Big data for Development: A Review of Promises and Challenges. *Development Policy Review*, *34*(1), 135–174. doi:10.1111/dpr.12142

Hirschman, B. R., St. Charles, J., & Carley, K. M. (2011). Leaving us in tiers: Can homophily be used to generate tiering effects? *Computational & Mathematical Organization Theory*, *17*, 318–343. doi:10.1007/s10588-011-9088-4

Hoeffler, S., & Keller, K. L. (2002). Building brand equity through corporate societal marketing. *Journal of Public Policy & Marketing, 21*(1), 78–89. doi:10.1509/jppm.21.1.78.17600

Hoffman, D. L., & Fodor, M. (2010). Can you measure the ROI of your social media marketing? *MIT Sloan Management Review, 52*(1), 41–49.

Hollsenstein, L., & Purves, R. S. (2010). Exploring place through user-generated content: Using Flickr tags to describe city cores. *Journal of Spatial Information Science, 1*, 21–48. doi:10.5311/JOSIS.2010.1.3

Holtgraves, T. M., Ross, S. J., Weywadt, C. R., & Han, T. L. (2007). Perceiving artificial social agents. *Computers in Human Behavior, 23*(5), 2163–2174. doi:10.1016/j.chb.2006.02.017

Hong, S. (2012). Online news on Twitter: Newspapers' social media adoption and their online readership. *Information Economics and Policy, 24*(1), 69–74. doi:10.1016/j.infoecopol.2012.01.004

Hoornweg, D. (2011). *Cities and Climate Change: Responding to an Urgent Agenda.* World Bank Publication.

Howard, P. N., & Hussain, M. M. (2011). The role of digital media. *Journal of Democracy, 22*(3), 35–48. doi:10.1353/jod.2011.0041

Huang, C. Y., Chou, C. J., & Lin, P. C. (2010). Involvement theory in constructing bloggers' intention to purchase travel products. *Tourism Management, 31*(4), 513–526. doi:10.1016/j.tourman.2009.06.003

Huang, J., Baptista, J., & Newell, S. (2015). Communicational ambidexterity as a new capability to manage social media communication within organizations. *The Journal of Strategic Information Systems, 24*(2), 49–64. doi:10.1016/j.jsis.2015.03.002

Huang, J., Zhang, J., Li, Y., & Lv, Z. (2014). Business value of enterprise micro-blogging: Empirical study from Weibo. com in Sina. *Journal of Global Information Management, 22*(3), 32–56. doi:10.4018/jgim.2014070102

Huang, Y., Basu, C., & Hsu, M. K. (2010). Exploring motivations of travel knowledge sharing on social network sites: An empirical investigation of U.S. college students. *Journal of Hospitality Marketing & Management, 19*(7), 717–734. doi:10.1080/19368623.2010.508002

Huang, Z., Zhao, Z., Liu, Q., & Wang, Z. (2015). An unsupervised method for short-text sentiment analysis based on analysis of massive data. Intelligent Computation in Big Data Era. doi:10.1007/978-3-662-46248-5_21

Huber, M., Kowalski, S., Nohlberg, M., & Tjoa, S. (2009). Towards automating social engineering using social networking sites. In *Proceedings of the 2009 International Conference on Computational Science and Engineering.* IEEE. DOI doi:10.1109/CSE.2009.205

Huiskes, M. J., & Lew, M. S. (2008). The MIR Flickr retrieval evaluation. In *Proceedings of MIR '08.* doi:10.1145/1460096.1460104

Huy, Q., & Shipilov, A. (2012). The key to social media success within organizations. *MIT Sloan Management Review, 54*(1), 73–81.

Hwang, T., Pearce, I., & Nanis, M. (2012). Socialbots: Voices on the fronts. *Interaction, 19*(2), 38–45. doi:10.1145/2090150.2090161

Hwang, Y. H., & Fesenmaier, D. R. (2011). Unplanned tourist attraction visits by travellers. *Tourism Geographies: An International Journal of Tourism Space, Place and Environment, 13*(3), 398–416. doi: 10.1080/14616688.2011.570777

Insel, T. R., Landis, S. C., & Collins, F. S. (2013). The NIH brain initiative. *Science, 340*(6133), 687–688. doi:10.1126/science.1239276 PMID:23661744

Ioanid, A., Militaru, G., & Mihai, P. (2015). Social Media Strategies for Organizations using influencer's power. *European Scientific Journal*. Retrieved from http://eujournal.org/index.php/esj/article/view/6144

Jacobson, J. L. (2012). *42 rules of social media for small business*. Prolibris Publishing Media Private Limited.

Jarche, H. (2013). *The Knowledge Sharing Paradox*. Retrieved from http://jarche.com/2013/03/the-knowledge-sharing-paradox/?goback=.gde_4453809_member_241895872

Jarvenpaa, S. L., & Majchrzak, A. (2010). Vigilant interaction in knowledge collaboration: Challenges of online user participation under ambivalence. *Information Systems Research*, *21*(4), 773–784. doi:10.1287/isre.1100.0320

Jarvenpaa, S. L., & Tuunainen, V. K. (2013). How Finnair socialized customers for service co-creation with social media. *MIS Quarterly Executive*, *12*(3), 125–136.

Jayasingh, S., & Venkatesh, R. (2015). Consumer Engagement Factors in Facebook Brand Pages. *Asian Social Science*, *11*(26), 19–29. doi:10.5539/ass.v11n26p19

Jeffries, A. (2014, Feb. 14). You're not going to read this but you'll probably share it anyway. The Verge. Retrieved Aug. 26, 2016, from http://www.theverge.com/2014/2/14/5411934/youre-not-going-to-read-this

Jensen, P. B., Jensen, L. J., & Brunak, S. (2012). Mining electronic health records: Towards better research applications and clinical care. *Nature Reviews. Genetics*, *13*(6), 395–405. doi:10.1038/nrg3208 PMID:22549152

Jeong, E., & Jang, S. C. (2011). Restaurant experiences triggering positive electronic word-of-mouth (eWOM) motivations. *International Journal of Hospitality Management*, *30*(2), 356–366. doi:10.1016/j.ijhm.2010.08.005

Jett, J., Senseney, M., & Palmer, C. L. (2012). Enhancing cultural heritage collections by supporting and analyzing participation in Flickr. In *Proceedings of ASIST 2012*. doi:10.1002/meet.14504901287

Jin, Y., Matsuo, Y., & Ishizuka, M. (2006). Extracting a social network among entities by web mining. In *Proceedings of ISWC'06 Workshop on Web Content Mining with Human Language Technologies*.

Jones, J., Temperley, B., & Lima, A. (2009). Corporate reputation in the era of Web 2. 0: The case of Primark. *Journal of Marketing Management*, *25*(9/10), 927–939. doi:10.1362/026725709X479309

Judith, Z. (n.d.). *Social Media adds to knowledge sharing*. Retrieved from http://essay.utwente.nl/63098/1/Zande_van_der_Judith_-s_1254235_scriptie.pdf

Justin, H. (1997). Knowing What We Know. *Information Week*, 46.

Kamen, A. (2013, Nov. 12). In the loop: Tina Turner formally 'relinquishes' U.S. citizenship. *The Washington Post*.

Kang, M., & Schuett, M. A. (2013). Determinants of sharing travel experiences in social media. *Journal of Travel & Tourism Marketing*, *30*(1/2), 93–107. doi:10.1080/10548408.2013.751237

Kaplan, A. M., & Haenlein, M. (2010). Users of the world, unite! The challenges and opportunities of social media. *Business Horizons*, *53*(1), 59–68. doi:10.1016/j.bushor.2009.09.003

Kaplan, J. (2015). *Humans Need Not Apply: A Guide to Wealth and Work in the Age of Artificial Intelligence*. New Haven, CT: Yale University Press.

Karagiannopoulos, V. (2012). The role of the internet in political struggles: Some conclusions from Iran and Egypt. *New Political Science*, *34*(2), 151–171. doi:10.1080/07393148.2012.676394

Kartaltepe, E. J., Morales, J. A., Xu, S., & Sandhu, R. (2010). Social network-based botnet command-and-control: Emerging threats and countermeasures. In Proceedings of ACNS 2010, (LNCS), (vol. 6123, pp. 511–528). Berlin: Springer-Verlag.

Kasemsap, K. (2015d). The role of cloud computing in global supply chain. In N. Rao (Ed.), Enterprise management strategies in the era of cloud computing (pp. 192–219). Hershey, PA: IGI Global. doi:10.4018/978-1-4666-8339-6.ch009

Kasemsap, K. (2014a). The role of brand loyalty on CRM performance: An innovative framework for smart manufacturing. In Z. Luo (Ed.), *Smart manufacturing innovation and transformation: Interconnection and intelligence* (pp. 252–284). Hershey, PA: IGI Global. doi:10.4018/978-1-4666-5836-3.ch010

Kasemsap, K. (2014b). The role of social networking in global business environments. In P. Smith & T. Cockburn (Eds.), *Impact of emerging digital technologies on leadership in global business* (pp. 183–201). Hershey, PA: IGI Global. doi:10.4018/978-1-4666-6134-9.ch010

Kasemsap, K. (2014c). The role of social media in the knowledge-based organizations. In I. Lee (Ed.), *Integrating social media into business practice, applications, management, and models* (pp. 254–275). Hershey, PA: IGI Global. doi:10.4018/978-1-4666-6182-0.ch013

Kasemsap, K. (2015a). The role of customer relationship management in the global business environments. In T. Tsiakis (Ed.), *Trends and innovations in marketing information systems* (pp. 130–156). Hershey, PA: IGI Global. doi:10.4018/978-1-4666-8459-1.ch007

Kasemsap, K. (2015b). The role of social media in international advertising. In N. Taşkıran & R. Yılmaz (Eds.), *Handbook of research on effective advertising strategies in the social media age* (pp. 171–196). Hershey, PA: IGI Global. doi:10.4018/978-1-4666-8125-5.ch010

Kasemsap, K. (2015c). The role of cloud computing adoption in global business. In V. Chang, R. Walters, & G. Wills (Eds.), *Delivery and adoption of cloud computing services in contemporary organizations* (pp. 26–55). Hershey, PA: IGI Global. doi:10.4018/978-1-4666-8210-8.ch002

Kasemsap, K. (2016a). Creating product innovation strategies through knowledge management in global business. In A. Goel & P. Singhal (Eds.), *Product innovation through knowledge management and social media strategies* (pp. 330–357). Hershey, PA: IGI Global. doi:10.4018/978-1-4666-9607-5.ch015

Kasemsap, K. (2016b). The roles of knowledge management and organizational innovation in global business. In G. Jamil, J. Poças-Rascão, F. Ribeiro, & A. Malheiro da Silva (Eds.), *Handbook of research on information architecture and management in modern organizations* (pp. 130–153). Hershey, PA: IGI Global. doi:10.4018/978-1-4666-8637-3.ch006

Katz, G., Ofek, N., & Shapira, B. (2015). ConSent: Context-based sentiment analysis. *Knowledge-Based Systems, 84*, 162–178. doi:10.1016/j.knosys.2015.04.009

Katz, L. (1953). A New Status Index Derived from Sociometric Index. *Psychometrika, 18*(1), 39–43. doi:10.1007/BF02289026

Katzmair, H. (2014). Social Network Analysis: The Science of Measuring, Visualizing and Simulating Social Relationships. *FAS Research,* 207-211.

Kaufman, M. B. (2012). Online communities for healthcare professionals can help improve communication, collaboration. *Formulary (Cleveland, Ohio), 47*(4), 161.

Kaushik, A. (2012). Best Social Media Metrics: Conversation, Amplification, Applause, Economic Value. *Vikalpa, 37*(4), 92–97. Retrieved from http://www.vikalpa.com/pdf/articles/2012/Pages-from-Vikalpa374-69-111.pdf

Kawasaki, G.,, & Fitzpatrick, P. (2015). *The Art of Social Media for Power Tips for Power users.* Penguin.

Keegan, B. C., Ceni, A., & Smith, M. A. (2013). Analyzing multi-dimensional networks within MediaWikis. In *WikiSym '13.* doi:10.1145/2491055.2491056

Kennedy, L. S., Chang, S. F., & Kozintsev, V. (2006). To search or to label? Predicting the performance of search-based automatic image classifiers. In *Proceedings of the 8th ACM International Workshop on Multimedia Information Retrieval.*

Kennedy, L., Naaman, M., Ahern, S., Nair, R., & Rattenbury, T. (2007). How Flickr helps us make sense of the world: context and content in community-contributed media collections. In *Proceedings of MM '07*. doi:10.1145/1291233.1291384

Kennedy, J., & Eberhart, R. C. (2001). *Swarm Intelligence*. San Francisco: Morgan Kaufmann Publishers, Academic Press.

Kietzmann, J. H., Hermkens, K., McCarthy, I. P., & Silvestre, B. S. (2011). Social media? Get serious! Understanding the functional building blocks of social media. *Business Horizons*, *54*(3), 241–251. doi:10.1016/j.bushor.2011.01.005

Kim, A. J., & Ko, E. (2012). Do Social Media Marketing Activites Enhance Customer Equity? An Empirical Study of Luxury Fashion Brand. *Journal of Business Research*, *65*(10), 1480–1486. doi:10.1016/j.jbusres.2011.10.014

Kim, D. Y., Lehto, X. Y., & Morrison, A. M. (2007). Gender differences in online travel information search: Implications for marketing communications on the Internet. *Tourism Management*, *28*(2), 423–433. doi:10.1016/j.tourman.2006.04.001

Kim, H., Son, J., & Suh, K. (2012). Following firms on Twitter: Determinants of continuance and word-of-mouth intention. *Asia Pacific Journal of Information Systems*, *22*(3), 1–27. doi:10.5859/KAIS.2012.21.2.1

Kim, S., Koh, Y., Cha, J., & Lee, S. (2015). Effects of social media on firm value for U.S. restaurant companies. *International Journal of Hospitality Management*, *49*, 40–46. doi:10.1016/j.ijhm.2015.05.006

Kim, T., Jung, W. J., & Lee, S. Y. (2014). The analysis on the relationship between firms' exposures to SNS and stock prices in Korea. *Asia Pacific Journal of Information Systems*, *24*(2), 233–253. doi:10.14329/apjis.2014.24.2.233

Kipp, M. E. I., Buchel, O., & Neal, D. R. (2012). Exploring digital information using tags and local knowledge. In *Proceedings of ASIST 2012*. doi:10.1002/meet.14504901318

Kiron, D., Palmer, D., Phillips, A. N., & Kruschwitz, N. (2012). What managers really think about social business. *MIT Sloan Management Review*, *53*(4), 51–60.

Kitayama, S., & Markus, H. R. (2000). The pursuit of happiness and the realization of sympathy: Cultural patterns of self, social relations, and well-being. In *Culture and Subjective Well-Being*. The MIT Press.

Klenner, M., & Petrakis, S. (2012). Polarity preference of verbs: What could verbs reveal about the polarity of their objects? In G. Bouma, A. Ittoo, E. Métais, & H. Wortmann (Eds.), *Natural Language Processing and Information Systems*.

Klien, F., & Strohmaier, M. (2012). Short links under attack: Geographical analysis of spam in a URL shortener network. In *Proceedings of HT '12*.

Knight, K. (2014). How Pinterest is pushing social commerce. *BizReport*. Retrieved December 04, 2015, from http://www.bizreport.com/2014/03/how-pinterest-is-pushing-social-commerce.html

Komaromi, K., & Erickson, S. (2011). Using Social Media to Build Community. *Competition Forum, 9*(2).

Koncz, P., & Paralič, J. (2013). Active learning enhanced document annotation for sentiment analysis. In A. Cuzzocrea, C. Kittl, D.E. Simos, E. Weippl, & L. Xu (Eds.), *Availability, Reliability, and Security in Information Systems and HCI*. Springer. doi:10.1007/978-3-642-40511-2_24

Kontopoulos, E., Berberidis, C., Dergiades, T., & Bassiliades, N. (2013). Ontology-based sentiment analysis of twitter posts. *Expert Systems with Applications*, *40*(10), 4063–4074. doi:10.1016/j.eswa.2013.01.001

Koo, C., Wati, Y., & Jung, J. J. (2011). Examination of how social aspects moderate the relationship between task characteristics and usage of social communication technologies (SCTs) in organizations. *International Journal of Information Management*, *31*(5), 445–459. doi:10.1016/j.ijinfomgt.2011.01.003

Korda, H., & Itani, Z. (2013). Harnessing social media for health promotion and behavior change. *Health Promotion Practice*, *14*(1), 15–23. doi:10.1177/1524839911405850

KPMG Consulting. (2000). *Knowledge Management Research Report 2000*. Retrieved from http://www.providersedge.com/docs/km_articles/KPMG_KM_Research_Report_2000.pdf

KPMG. (2011). *Going Social How businesses are making the most of social media*. Retrieved November 21, 2015, from https://www.kpmg.com/FR/fr/IssuesAndInsights/ArticlesPublications/Documents/Going-social-how-business-are-making-the-most-of-social-media.pdf

Kucuk, S. U., & Krishnamurthy, S. (2007). An analysis of consumer power on the internet. *Technovation*, *27*(1-2), 47–56. doi:10.1016/j.technovation.2006.05.002

Ku, E. (2012). Distributed fascinating knowledge over an online travel community. *International Journal of Tourism Research*, *16*(1), 33–43. doi:10.1002/jtr.1895

Kumar, R. & Rosé, C.P. (2014). Triggering effective social support for online groups. *ACM Trans. Interact. Intell. Syst.*, *3*(4), Article 24. DOI:.10.1145/2499672

Kumar, V., & Mirchandani, R. (2012). Increasing the ROI of social media marketing. *MIT Sloan Management Review*, *54*(1), 55–61.

Lai, L. S. L., & Turban, E. (2008). Groups formation and operations in the Web 2.0 environment and social networks. *Group Decision and Negotiation*, *17*(5), 387–402. doi:10.1007/s10726-008-9113-2

LaMance, K. (2014, Mar. 27). Reinstatement of U.S. citizenship lawyers. *Legal Match*. Retrieved Feb. 22, 2015, from http://www.legalmatch.com/law-library/article/reinstatement-of-us-citizenship-lawyers.html

Laroche, M., Habibi, M. R., & Richard, M. O. (2013). To be or not to be in social media: How brand loyalty is affected by social media? *International Journal of Information Management*, *33*(1), 76–82. doi:10.1016/j.ijinfomgt.2012.07.003

Laroche, M., Habibi, M. R., Richard, M. O., & Sankaranarayanan, R. (2012). The effects of social media based brand communities on brand community markers, value creation practices, brand trust and brand loyalty. *Computers in Human Behavior*, *28*(5), 1755–1767. doi:10.1016/j.chb.2012.04.016

Lauinger, T., Pankakoski, V., Balzarotti, D., & Kirda, E. (2010). Honeybot, your man in the middle for automated social engineering. In *LEET' 10, 3ʳᵈ USENIX Conference on Large-Scale Exploits and Emergent Threats*. Retrieved Nov. 19, 2014, from https://www.sba-research.org/wp-content/uploads/publications/autosoc-leet2010.pdf

Lawson, C., & Cowling, C. (2015). Social media: The next frontier for professional development in radiography. *Radiography*, *21*(2), e74–e80. doi:10.1016/j.radi.2014.11.006

Lee, K. (2014). *Know What's Working on Social Media: 19 Free Social Media Analytics Tools*. Retrieved May 22, 2016 from https://blog.bufferapp.com/social-media-analytics-tools

Lee, H., Reid, E., & Kim, W. G. (2012). Understanding knowledge sharing in online travel communities: Antecedents and the moderating effects of interaction modes. *Journal of Hospitality & Tourism Research (Washington, D.C.)*, *38*(2), 222–242. doi:10.1177/1096348012451454

Lee, J., Lapira, E., Bagheri, B., & Kao, H. A. (2013). Recent advances and trends in predictive manufacturing systems in big data environment. *Manufacturing Letters*, *1*(1), 38–41. doi:10.1016/j.mfglet.2013.09.005

Lee, K., Oh, W. Y., & Kim, N. (2013). Social media for socially responsible firms: Analysis of Fortune 500's Twitter profiles and their CSR/CSIR ratings. *Journal of Business Ethics*, *118*(4), 791–806. doi:10.1007/s10551-013-1961-2

Lee, S. Y. T., & Phang, C. W. (2015). Leveraging social media for electronic commerce in Asia: Research areas and opportunities. *Electronic Commerce Research and Applications*, *14*(3), 145–149. doi:10.1016/j.elerap.2015.02.001

Lee, S., Hwang, T., & Lee, H. H. (2006). Corporate blogging strategies of the Fortune 500 companies. *Management Decision*, *44*(3), 316–334. doi:10.1108/00251740610656232

Lee, W., Xiong, L., & Hu, C. (2012). The effect of Facebook users' arousal and valence on intention to go to the festival: Applying an extension of the technology acceptance model. *International Journal of Hospitality Management*, *31*(3), 819–827. doi:10.1016/j.ijhm.2011.09.018

Lemmerich, F., & Atzmueller, M. (2011). Modeling location-based profiles of social image media using explorative pattern mining. In *Proceedings of the 2011 IEEE International Conference on Privacy, Security, Risk, and Trust, and IEEE International Conference on Social Computing*. doi:10.1109/PASSAT/SocialCom.2011.186

Leonardi, P. M. (2014). Social media, knowledge sharing, and innovation: Toward a theory of communication visibility. *Information Systems Research*, *25*(4), 796–816. doi:10.1287/isre.2014.0536

Lerman, K., & Jones, L. A. (2006). *Social browsing on Flickr*. arXiv:cs/0612047v1

Lerman, K., Plangprasopchok, A., & Wong, C. (2007). Personalizing image search results on Flickr. Association for the Advancement of Artificial Intelligence.

Leung, D., Law, R., van Hoof, H., & Buhalis, D. (2013). Social media in tourism and hospitality: A literature review. *Journal of Travel & Tourism Marketing*, *30*(1/2), 3–22. doi:10.1080/10548408.2013.750919

Levine, R., Locke, C., Searls, D., & Weinberger, D. (1999). *The Cluetrain Manifesto*. Retrieved from http://www.cluetrain.com/book/

Levy, M. (2009). WEB 2.0 implications on knowledge management. *Journal of Knowledge Management*, *13*(1), 120–134. doi:10.1108/13673270910931215

Li, C., & Bernoff, J. (2011). *Groundswell: Winning in a World Transformed by Social Technologies*. Cambridge, MA: Forrester Research, Inc.

Lim, J. S., Hwang, Y. C., Kim, S., & Biocca, F. A. (2015). How social media engagement leads to sports channel loyalty: Mediating roles of social presence and channel commitment. *Computers in Human Behavior*, *46*, 158–167. doi:10.1016/j.chb.2015.01.013

Linke, A., & Oliveira, E. (2015). Quantity or quality? The professionalization of social media communication in Portugal and Germany: A comparison. *Public Relations Review*, *41*(2), 305–307. doi:10.1016/j.pubrev.2014.11.018

List of former United States citizens who relinquished their nationality. (2015, Feb. 18). In *Wikipedia*. Retrieved Feb. 22, 2015, from http://en.wikipedia.org/wiki/List_of_former_United_States_citizens_who_relinquished_their_nationality

Liu, D., Hua, X.-S., Wang, M., & Zhang, H.-J. (2010). Retagging social images based on visual and semantic consistency. In *Proceedings of WWW 2010*. doi:10.1145/1772690.1772848

Liu, D., Hua, X.-S., Yang, L., Wang, M., & Zhang, H.-J. (2009). Tag ranking. In *Proceedings of 18th International Conference on World Wide Web 2009*. doi:10.1145/1526709.1526757

Liu, S. M., & Chen, J.-H. (2015). A multi-label classification based approach for sentiment classification. *Expert Systems with Applications*, *42*(3), 1083–1093. doi:10.1016/j.eswa.2014.08.036

LoginRadius. (2015). *Social Login and Social Sharing*. Retrieved December 04, 2015, fromhttp://cdn2.hubspot.net/hubfs/436275/PDF/LoginRadius-Social-Login-Sharing-Trends-Q1-2015.pdf?t=1433972843555

Loshin, D. (2013). *Big data analytics: from strategic planning to enterprise integration with tools, techniques, NoSQL, and graph*. Elsevier.

Lovejoy, K., & Saxton, G. D. (2012). Information, community, and action: How nonprofit organizations use social media. *Journal of Computer-Mediated Communication*, *17*(3), 337–353. doi:10.1111/j.1083-6101.2012.01576.x

Lovejoy, K., Waters, R. D., & Saxton, G. D. (2012). Engaging stakeholders through Twitter: How nonprofit organizations are getting more out of 140 characters or less. *Public Relations Review*, *38*(2), 313–318. doi:10.1016/j.pubrev.2012.01.005

Lovett, J. (2011). *Social Media Metrics Secrets*. Indianapolis, IN: Wiley Publishing, Inc.

Lucia, W., Akcora, C. G., & Ferrari, E. (2013). Multi-dimensional conversation analysis across online social networks. In *Proceedings of the 2013 IEEE Third International Conference on Cloud and Green Computing*. doi:10.1109/CGC.2013.65

Luo, T., Chen, S., Xu, G., & Zhou, J. (2013). Sentiment Analysis. In T. Lu, S. Chen, G. Xu, & J. Zhou (Eds.), Trust-based Collective View Prediction. Springer. doi:10.1007/978-1-4614-7202-5_4

Luo, N., Zhang, M., & Liu, W. (2015). The effects of value co-creation practices on building harmonious brand community and achieving brand loyalty on social media in China. *Computers in Human Behavior*, *48*, 492–499. doi:10.1016/j.chb.2015.02.020

Luo, X., Zhang, J., & Duan, W. (2013). Social media and firm equity value. *Information Systems Research*, *24*(1), 146–163. doi:10.1287/isre.1120.0462

Luo, Y. L., & Hsu, C. H. (2009). An Empirical Study of Research Collaboration Using Social Network Analysis. In *Proceedings of 2009 IEEE International Conference on Computational Science & Engineering*. doi:10.1109/CSE.2009.253

Lytle, R. (2013). *Google+ Communities: A beginner's guide*. Mashable.

Maass, W., & Kowatsch, T. (2012). *Semantic Technologies in Content Management Systems: Trends, Applications and Evaluations*. Springer Science & Business Media. doi:10.1007/978-3-642-24960-0

Machová, K., & Marhefka, L. (2013). Opinion mining in conversational content within web discussions and commentaries. In A. Cuzzocrea, C. Kittl, D.E. Simos, E. Weippl, & L. Xu (Eds.), *Availability, Reliability, and Security in Information Systems and HCI*. Springer. doi:10.1007/978-3-642-40511-2_11

Mahr, D., & Lievens, A. (2012). Virtual lead user communities: Drivers of knowledge creation for innovation. *Research Policy*, *41*(1), 167–177. doi:10.1016/j.respol.2011.08.006

Majchrzak, A., Wagner, C., & Yates, D. (2013). The impact of shaping on knowledge reuse for organizational improvement with wikis. *Management Information Systems Quarterly*, *37*(2), 455–469.

Malthouse, E. C., Haenlein, M., Skiera, B., Wedge, E., & Zhang, M. (2013). Managing Customer Relationships in the Social Media Era: Introducing the Social CRM House. *Journal of Interactive Marketing*, *27*(4), 270–280. doi:10.1016/j.intmar.2013.09.008

Mangold, W. G., & Faulds, D. J. (2009). Social media: The new hybrid element of the promotion mix. *Business Horizons*, *52*(4), 357–365. doi:10.1016/j.bushor.2009.03.002

Markoff, J. (2015). *Machines of Loving Grace: The Quest for Common Ground between Humans and Robots*. New York: HarperCollins.

Marlow, C., Naaman, M., boyd, d., & Davis, M. (2006). HT06, tagging paper, taxonomy, Flickr, academic article, to read. In *Proceedings of HT'06*.

Marra, G. (2012). Socialbots are robots, too. In Socialbots: Voices on the fronts. Academic Press.

Martin, P., & Ericson, T. (2011). *Social media marketing*. New Delhi: Global Vision Publishing House.

Marx, S. (2010). *Measuring Social Media and Its Impact on Your Brand*. Cisco.

McAfee, A. (2006). Enterprise 2.0: The Dawn of Emergent Collaboration. *MIT Sloan Management Review*. Retrieved from http://adamkcarson.files.wordpress.com/2006/12/enterprise_20_-_the_dawn_of_emergent_collaboration_by_andrew_mcafee.pdf

McAfee, A. (2009). *Enterprise 2.0: New Collaborative Tools for Your Organization's Toughest Challenges*. Boston, MA: McGraw-Hill Professional.

McAfee, A. (2009). *Enterprise 2.0: New collaborative tools for your organization's toughest challenges*. Boston, MA: Harvard Business School Publishing.

McCarthy, J., Rowley, J., Ashworth, C. J., & Pioch, E. (2014). Managing brand presence through social media: The case of UK football clubs. *Internet Research*, *24*(2), 181–204. doi:10.1108/IntR-08-2012-0154

McCoy, S., Everard, A., Polak, P., & Galletta, D. F. (2007). The effects of online advertising. *Communications of the ACM*, *50*(3), 84–88. doi:10.1145/1226736.1226740

McGath, T. (2013, Sept. 17). Get out While You Can: Why Young Americans Should Emigrate. *Alternet*.

McKenna, K. Y., & Bargh, J. A. (2000). Plan 9 from cyberspace: The implications of the Internet for personality and social psychology. *Personality and Social Psychology Review*, *4*(1), 57–75. doi:10.1207/S15327957PSPR0401_6

Measure, S. (2015). *State of Social Media*. Retrieved December 04, 2015, fromhttp://get.simplymeasured.com/rs/801-IXO-022/images/2015StateOfSocialMedia.pdf

Measured, S. (2015). *The State of Social Marketing*. Retrieved December 08, 2015, from www.simplymeasured.com

Meerman, S. D. (2012). *The new rules of marketing and PR*. New Delhi: Wiley India Private Limited. Golden, M. (2011). *Social media: Strategies for professionals and their firms*. Wiley and Sons. Flynn, N. (2012). *The social media handbook*. New Delhi: Wiley India Private Limited.

Meraz, S. (2009). Is there an elite hold? Traditional media to social media agenda setting influence in blog networks. *Journal of Computer-Mediated Communication*, *14*(3), 682–707. doi:10.1111/j.1083-6101.2009.01458.x

Mergel, I. (2013). A framework for interpreting social media interactions in the public sector. *Government Information Quarterly*, *30*(4), 327–334. doi:10.1016/j.giq.2013.05.015

Mersey, R. D., Malthouse, E. C., & Calder, B. J. (2010). Engagement with Online Media. *Journal of Media Business Studies*, *7*(2), 39–56. doi:10.1080/16522354.2010.11073506

Meske, C., & Stieglitz, S. (2013). Adoption and use of social media in small and medium-sized enterprises. In F. Harmsen & H. Proper (Eds.), *Practice-driven research on enterprise transformation* (pp. 61–75). Heidelberg, Germany: Springer–Verlag. doi:10.1007/978-3-642-38774-6_5

Michaels, C. F., & Carello, C. (1981). *Direct Perception*. Englewood Cliffs, NJ: Prentice-Hall, Inc.

Mika, P. (2007). *Social networks and the sematic web.* Springer-Verlag.

Miles, S. J., & Mangold, W. G. (2014). Employee voice: Untapped resource or social media time bomb? *Business Horizons, 57*(3), 401–411. doi:10.1016/j.bushor.2013.12.011

Milgram, S. (1967). The Small World Problem. *Psychology Today, 2*(1), 60–67.

Miller, J. A., Ramaswamy, L., Kochut, K. J., & Fard, A. (2015, June). Research Directions for Big data Graph Analytics. In *Big data (Big Data Congress), 2015 IEEE International Congress on* (pp. 785-794). IEEE. doi:10.1109/BigDataCongress.2015.132

Miller, A. R., & Tucker, C. (2013). Active social media management: The case of health care. *Information Systems Research, 24*(1), 52–70. doi:10.1287/isre.1120.0466

Mislove, A., Koppula, H. S., Gummadi, K. P., Druschel, P., & Bhattacharjee, B. (2008). Growth of the Flickr social network. In Proceedings of the WO SN '08. doi:10.1145/1397735.1397742

Mitter, S., Wagner, C., & Strohmaier, M. (2013). Understanding the impact of socialbot attacks in online social networks. In *WebSci '13.*

Mohajerani, A., Baptista, J., & Nandhakumar, J. (2015). Exploring the role of social media in importing logics across social contexts: The case of IT SMEs in Iran. *Technological Forecasting and Social Change, 95,* 16–31. doi:10.1016/j.techfore.2014.06.008

Mohammad, S. M. (2012). *#Emotional Tweets.* In the First Joint Conference on Lexical and Computational Semantics (*SE$M), Montréal, Canada.

Moreno, A., Navarro, C., Tench, R., & Zerfass, A. (2015). Does social media usage matter? An analysis of online practices and digital media perceptions of communication practitioners in Europe. *Public Relations Review, 41*(2), 242–253. doi:10.1016/j.pubrev.2014.12.006

Morgan, D. (2016, Aug. 21). So you want to move to Canada? CBS News. Retrieved Aug. 21, 2016, from http://www.cbsnews.com/news/so-you-want-to-move-to-canada/

Mosquera, A., & Moreda, P. (2012). The study of informality as a framework for evaluating the normalization of Web 2.0 texts. In G. Bouma, A. Ittoo, E. Métais, & Hans Wortmann (Eds.), *Natural Language Processing and Information Systems.*

Mou, Y., Miller, M., & Fu, H. (2015). Evaluating a target on social media: From the self-categorization perspective. *Computers in Human Behavior, 49,* 451–459. doi:10.1016/j.chb.2015.03.031

Muhammad, I., Carlos, C., & Diaz, F. V. S. (2015, July). Processing Social Media Messages in Mass Emergency A Survey. *ACM Computing Surveys, 47*(5), 67.

Müller-Birn, C., Dobusch, L., & Herbsleb, J. D. (2013). Work-to-rule: The emergence of algorithmic governance in Wikipedia. In *Proceedings of C&T '13.*

Murdough, C. (2009). Social Media Measurement: It's Not Impossible. *Journal of Interactive Advertising, 10*(1), 94–99. doi:10.1080/15252019.2009.10722165

Murthy, D. (2013). *Twitter: Social Communication in the Twitter Age.* Cambridge, MA: Polity.

Mvandermeer. (2012). *Knowledge Sharing Through Social Media Use.* Retrieved from https://www.scanyours.com/knowledge-sharing-through-social-media-use-3/

Nadkarni, A., & Vesset, D. (2014, September). Worldwide Big data Technology and Services 2014–2018 Forecast. *IDC*. Retrieved from http://www.idc.com

Nagaraja, S., Houmansadr, A., Piyawongwisal, P., Singh, V., Agarwal, P., & Borisov, N. (2011). Stegobot: A covert social network botnet. In Proceedings of IH 2011, (LNCS), (vol. 6958, pp. 299 – 313). Berlin: Springer-Verlag.

Nambisan, S. (2002). Designing virtual customer environments for new product development: Toward a theory. *Academy of Management Review*, *27*(3), 392–413. doi: 10.5465/AMR.2002.7389914

Nambisan, S. (2013). Information technology and product/service innovation: A brief assessment and some suggestions for future research. *Journal of the Association for Information Systems*, *14*(4), 215–226.

Nambisan, S., Agarwal, R., & Tanniru, M. (1999). Organizational mechanisms for enhancing user innovation in information technology. *Management Information Systems Quarterly*, *23*(3), 365–395. doi:10.2307/249468

Negoescu, R.-A., & Gatica-Perez, D. (2008). Analyzing Flickr groups. In *Proceedings of CIVR '08*. doi:10.1145/1386352.1386406

Neher, K. (2014). *Visual social media marketing for dummies*. New Delhi: Wiley India Private Limited.

Neiger, B. L., Thackeray, R., Van Wagenen, S. A., Hanson, C. L., West, J. H., Barnes, M. D., & Fagen, M. C. (2012). Use of social media in health promotion purposes, key performance indicators, and evaluation metrics. *Health Promotion Practice*, *13*(2), 159–164. doi:10.1177/1524839911433467 PMID:22382491

Newman, D. (2015). Social media metrics: Using big data and social media to improve retail customer experience. *IBM Big data and Analytics Hub*. Retrieved from: http://www.ibmbigdatahub.com

Newman, E. F., Stem, D. E. Jr, & Sprott, D. E. (2004). Banner advertisement and web site congruity effects on consumer web site perceptions. *Industrial Management & Data Systems*, *104*(3), 273–281. doi:10.1108/02635570410525816

Newman, M. E. (2001). The structure of scientific collaboration networks. *Proceedings of the National Academy of Sciences of the United States of America*, *98*(2), 404–409. doi:10.1073/pnas.98.2.404 PMID:11149952

Newman, M. E. J. (2006). Community centrality. *Physical Review*, *74*.

Newman, M. E. J. (2010). *Networks: An Introduction*. Oxford University Press. doi:10.1093/acprof:oso/9780199206650.001.0001

Nguyen, L. T., Wu, P., Chan, W., Peng, W., & Zhang, Y. (2012). Predicting collective sentiment dynamics from time-series social media. In Proceedings of WISDOM '12.

Niu, Z., Hua, G., Tian, Q., & Gao, X. (2015). Visual topic network: Building better image representations for images in social media. *Computer Vision and Image Understanding*, *136*, 3–13. doi:10.1016/j.cviu.2015.01.010

Nott, C. (2015). A maturity model for big data and analytics. *IBM Big data and Analytics Hub*. Retrieved from http://www.ibmbigdatahub.com

Nov, O., Naaman, M., & Ye, C. (2009). Analysis of participation in an online photo-sharing community: A multidimensional perspective. *Journal of the American Society for Information Science and Technology*, *61*(3), 555–566.

Nov, O., & Ye, C. (2010). Why do people tag? Motivations for photo tagging. *Communications of the ACM*, *53*(7), 128–131. doi:10.1145/1785414.1785450

O'Reilly, T. (2006). *What is Web 2.0. Design patterns and business models for the next generation of software*. Retrieved from http://www.oreilly.com/pub/a/web2/archive/what-is-web-20.html

Oestreicher-Singer, G., & Zalmanson, L. (2013). Content or community? A digital business strategy for content providers in the social age. *Management Information Systems Quarterly, 37*(2), 591–616.

Oh, S. & Syn, S.Y. (2015). Motivations for sharing information and social support in social media: A comparative analysis of Facebook, Twitter, Delicious, YouTube, and Flickr. *Journal of the Association for Information Science and Technology*, 1 - 16.

Olanrewaju, T., & Willmott, P. (2013). Finding your digital sweet spot. *Insights and Publications*. Retrieved from http://www.mckinsey.com/insights/business_technology

Oppong, S. A., Yen, D. C., & Merhout, J. W. (2005). A new strategy for harnessing knowledge management in e-commerce. *Technology in Society, 27*(3), 413–435. doi:10.1016/j.techsoc.2005.04.009

Orlikowski, W. J., & Gash, D. C. (1994). Technological frames: Making sense of information technology in organizations. *ACM Transactions on Information Systems, 12*(2), 174–207. doi:10.1145/196734.196745

Ortigosa, A., Martín, J. M., & Carro, R. M. (2014). Sentiment analysis in Facebook and its application to e-learning. *Computers in Human Behavior, 31*, 527–541. doi:10.1016/j.chb.2013.05.024

Osimo, D. (2005). Web 2.0 in government: Why and how. Institute for Prospective Technological Studies (IPTS), Joint Research Center (JRC), European Commission.

Paek, H. J., Hove, T., & Jeon, J. (2013). Social media for message testing: A multilevel approach to linking favorable viewer responses with message, producer, and viewer influence on YouTube. *Health Communication, 28*(3), 226–236. doi:10.1080/10410236.2012.672912

Paine, K. D. (2011). *Measure what matters: Online tools for understanding customers, social media, engagement, and key relationships*. Hoboken, NJ: John Wiley & Sons.

Palmer, B. (2014). Realizing a return on big data investments—within a year. *IBM Big data and Analytics Hub*. Retrieved from http://www.ibmbigdatahub.com

Panagiotopoulos, P., Shan, L. C., Barnett, J., Regan, A., & McConnon, A. (2015). A framework of social media engagement: Case studies with food and consumer organisations in the UK and Ireland. *International Journal of Information Management, 35*(4), 394–402. doi:10.1016/j.ijinfomgt.2015.02.006

Panahi, S., Watson, J., & Partridge, H. (2012). Social Media and Tacit Knowledge Sharing: Developing a Conceptual Model. World Academy of Science, Engineering and Technology.

Pangaro, P., & Wenzek, H. (2015). Engaging consumers through conversations: A management framework to get it right across converged channels. *Procedia: Social and Behavioral Sciences, 213*, 628–634.

Pang, B., Lee, L., & Vaithyanathan, S. (2002). Thumbs up? Sentiment Classification using Machine Learning Techniques. *Proceedings of the Conference on Empirical Methods in Natural Language Processing (EMNLP)*. doi:10.3115/1118693.1118704

Papadopoulos, T., Stamati, T., & Nopparuch, P. (2013). Exploring the determinants of knowledge sharing via employee weblogs. *International Journal of Information Management, 33*(1), 133–146. doi:10.1016/j.ijinfomgt.2012.08.002

Parise, S. (2009). Social media networks: What do they mean for knowledge management? *Journal of Information Technology Case and Application Research, 11*(2), 1–11. doi:10.1080/15228053.2009.10856156

Park, S., Lee, W., & Moon, I.-C. (2015). Efficient extraction of domain specific sentiment lexicon with active learning. *Pattern Recognition Letters, 56*, 38–44. doi:10.1016/j.patrec.2015.01.004

Passel, J. S., Cohn, D., & Gonzalez-Barrera, A. (2012). *Net migration from Mexico falls to zero—and perhaps less*. Pew Research Center. Retrieved Mar. 5, 2015, from http://www.pewhispanic.org/2012/04/23/net-migration-from-mexico-falls-to-zero-and-perhaps-less/

Patterson, M. (2015). Social Media Demographics to Inform a Better Segmentation Strategy. *Social Media Demographics for Marketers*. Retrieved from http://sproutsocial.com/insights

Paul, C. (2009). *The Digital Hand Shake- Seven Proven Strategies to grow your Business using Social Media*. John Wiley and Sons Inc.

Pavelko, R. L., & Myrick, J. G. (2015). That's so OCD: The effects of disease trivialization via social media on user perceptions and impression formation. *Computers in Human Behavior, 49*, 251–258. doi:10.1016/j.chb.2015.02.061

Pavlik, J. V., & MacIntoch, S. (2015). *Converging Media* (4th ed.). New York, NY: Oxford University Press.

Pawlowski, J., & Pirkkalainen, H. (2013). *The use of social software for Knowledge Management in globally distributed settings*. Retrieved, November 2013, from http://www.slideshare.net/jan.pawlowski/research-issues-in-knowledge-management-and-social-media

Peck, D. (2013, June 19). Why so many Americans are Leaving the U.S. --in 1 Big Chart. Chartist. *The Atlantic.*

Pennebaker, J. W. (2011). *The Secret Life of Pronouns: What our Words Say about Us*. New York Bloomsbury Press.

Pentin, R. (2010). *A new framework for measuring social media activity* [PowerPoint slides]. Retrieved from http://www.slideshare.net/Ifonlyblog/iab-measurement-framework-for-social-media-final4-3

Perez, C., Birregah, B., Layton, R., Lemercier, M., & Watters, P. (2013). REPLOT: Retrieving Profile Links On Twitter for suspicious networks detection. In *Proceedings of the 2013 IEEE / ACM International Conference on Advances in Social Networks Analysis and Mining*.

Perkins, A. (2015). The Evolution of Social Media Recruiting. *Recruiter*. Retrieved December 04, 2015, from https://www.recruiter.com/i/the-evolution-of-social-media-recruiting/

Pervin, N., Takeda, H., & Toriumi, F. (2014). *Factors affecting retweetability: An event-centric analysis on Twitter*. Paper presented at the International Conference on Information Systems (ICIS 2014), Atlanta, GA.

Peters, K., Chen, Y., Kaplan, A. M., Ognibeni, B., & Pauwels, K. (2013). Social Media Metrics —A Framework and Guidelines for Managing Social Media. *Journal of Interactive Marketing, 27*(4), 281–298. doi:10.1016/j.intmar.2013.09.007

Petz, G., Karpowicz, M., Fürschuß, H., Auinger, A., Stříteský, V., & Holzinger, A. (2014). Computational approaches for mining user's opinions on the Web 2.0. *Information Processing & Management, 50*(6), 899–908. doi:10.1016/j.ipm.2014.07.005

Phang, C. W., Zhang, C., & Sutanto, J. (2013). The influence of user interaction and participation in social media on the consumption intention of niche products. *Information & Management, 50*(8), 661–672. doi:10.1016/j.im.2013.07.001

Phosaard, S., & Wiriyapinit, M. (2011). Knowledge Management via Facebook: Building a Framework for Knowledge Management on a Social Network by Aligning Business, IT and Knowledge Management. *Lecture Notes in Engineering and Computer Science, 2192*(1), 1855–1860.

Picchi, A. (2015, Feb. 12). Record number renouncing American citizenship. *CBS News. Moneywatch.*

Ployhart, R. E. (2014). *Social Media in the Workplace: Issues and Strategic Questions*. Retrieved December 03, 2015, from https://www.shrm.org/about/foundation/products/Documents/Social%20Media%20Briefing-%20FINAL.pdf

Popescu, A., & Grefenstette, G. (2010). Mining user home location and gender from Flickr tags. In *Proceedings of the 4th International AAAI Conference on Weblogs and Social Media.*

Poria, S., Cambria, E., Howard, N., Huang, G.-B., & Hussain, A. (2015). Fusing audio, visual and textual clues for sentiment analysis from multimodal context. *Neurocomputing.* doi:10.1016/j.neucom.2015.01.095

Porter, L. V., Sweetser, K. D., & Chung, D. (2009). The blogosphere and public relations: Investigating practitioners' roles and blog use. *Journal of Communication Management, 13*(3), 250–267. doi:10.1108/13632540910976699

Postman, J. (2009). *Social corp: Social media goes corporate.* New Riders.

Poston, L. (2013). *Social media metrics for dummies.* New Delhi: Wiley India Private Limited.

Praude, V., & Skulme, R. (2015). Social Media Campaign Metrics in Lativia. *Procedia: Social and Behavioral Sciences, 213,* 628–634. doi:10.1016/j.sbspro.2015.11.462

Preethi, P. G., Uma, V., & Kumar, A. (2015). Temporal sentiment analysis and causal rules extraction from Tweets for event prediction. *Procedia Computer Science, 48,* 84 – 89. doi:10.1016/j.procs.2015.04.154

Prensky, M. (2004). *The death of command and control.* Retrieved from http://www.marcprensky.com/writing/prensky-sns-01-20-04.pdf

Prieur, C., Cardon, D., Beuscart, J. S., Pissard, N., & Pons, P. (2008). *The strength of weak cooperation.* Retrieved May 30, 2015, from http://arxiv.org/ftp/arxiv/papers/0802/0802.2317.pdf

Qiao, Yu. (2014). *Customer Relationship using Social Media.* Retrieved December 04, 2015, fromhttp://cse.tkk.fi/en/publications/B/1/papers/Qiao_final.pdf

Quazi, S. A. (2009). *Principles of Physical Geography.* APH Publishing Corporation.

Quercia, D., Capra, L., & Crowcroft, J. (2012). The social world of Twitter: Topics, geography, and emotions. In *Proceedings of the Sixth International AAAI Conference on Weblogs and Social Media.* Association for the Advancement of Artificial Intelligence.

Rafferty, P., & Hidderley, R. (2007). Flickr and Democratic indexing: Dialogic approaches to indexing. *New Information Perspectives, 59*(4/5), 397–410.

Rastogi, P. N. (2000). Knowledge management and intellectual capital - The new virtuous reality of competitiveness. *Human Systems Management, 19*(1), 39–48.

Rattenbury, T., Good, N., & Naaman, M. (2007). Towards automatic extraction of event and place semantics from Flickr tags. In *Proceedings of SIGIR 2007.* doi:10.1145/1277741.1277762

Real, J. C., Roldan, J. L., & Leal, A. (2014). From entrepreneurial orientation and learning orientation to business performance: Analysing the mediating role of organizational learning and the moderating effects of organizational size. *British Journal of Management, 25*(2), 186–208. doi:10.1111/j.1467-8551.2012.00848.x

Registered Bots. (n.d.). In *Wikipedia.* Retrieved from http://en.wikipedia.org/wiki/Wikipedia:Bots/Status

Reichental, J. (2013). *Knowledge Management in the age of social media.* Retrieved from, http://radar.oreilly.com/2011/03/knowledge-management-social-media.html

Relinquishment and renunciation guide—RenunciationGuide.com. (2015). Retrieved Mar. 8, 2015, at http://renunciationguide.com/

Renunciation of U.S. Nationality. (n.d.). U.S. Department of State, Bureau of Consular Affairs. Retrieved Feb. 22, 2015, from http://travel.state.gov/content/travel/english/legal-considerations/us-citizenship-laws-policies/renunciation-of-citizenship.html

Rice, M. (2010, June 4). Not Everyone Wants to Live in America. *Forbes Magazine.*

Rich, R. (2014). Big data: It's all about business value. *Big data Analytics, tmforum.* Retrieved from http://inform.tmforum.org/features-and-analysis/featured/2014

Richter, A., & Riemer, K. (2009). *Corporate social networking sites: Modes of use and appropriation through co-evolution.* Paper presented at the 20th Australasian Conference on Information Systems (ACIS 2009), Melbourne, Australia.

Richter, A., Stocker, A., Muller, S., & Avram, G. (2012). Knowledge management goals revisited: A cross-sectional analysis of social software adoption in corporate environments. The Journal of Information and Knowledge Management Systems, 43(2).

Ring, D. (2015). *SHRM survey cites significance of social media in HR.* Retrieved November 29, 2015, from http://searchfinancialapplications.techtarget.com/news/4500253646/SHRM-survey-cites-significance-of-social-media-in-HR

Rishika, R., Kumar, A., Janakiraman, R., & Bezawada, R. (2013). The effect of customers' social media participation on customer visit frequency and profitability: An empirical investigation. *Information Systems Research, 54*(1), 108–127. doi:10.1287/isre.1120.0460

Roberts, M., Wanta, W., & Dzwo, T.-H. (2002). Agenda setting and issue salience online. *Communication Research, 29*(4), 452–465. doi:10.1177/0093650202029004004

Rong, W., Nie, Y., Ouyang, Y., Peng, B., & Xiong, Z. (2014). Auto-encoder based bagging architecture for sentiment analysis. *Journal of Visual Languages and Computing, 25*(6), 840–849. doi:10.1016/j.jvlc.2014.09.005

Ronson, J. (2015). *So You've Been Publicly Shamed.* New York: Riverhead Books.

Rorissa, A. (2010). A comparative study of Flickr tags and index terms in a general image collection. *Journal of the American Society for Information Science and Technology, 61*(11), 2230–2242. doi:10.1002/asi.21401

Roski, J., & McClellan, M. (2011). Measuring health care performance now, not tomorrow: Essential steps to support effective health reform. *Health Affairs, 30*(4), 682–689. doi:10.1377/hlthaff.2011.0137 PMID:21471489

Ross, C., Orr, E. S., Sisic, M., Arseneault, J. M., Simmering, M. G., & Orr, R. R. (2009). Personality and motivations associated with Facebook use. *Computers in Human Behavior, 25*(2), 578–586. doi:10.1016/j.chb.2008.12.024

Ruths, D., & Pfeffer, J. (2014). Social media for large studies of behavior. *Science, 346*(6213), 1063–1064. doi:10.1126/science.346.6213.1063 PMID:25430759

Safer, M. (2015, Apr. 5). Wikimania. 60 Minutes. *CBS News.* Retrieved April 6, 2015, from http://www.cbsnews.com/news/wikipedia-jimmy-wales-morley-safer-60-minutes/

Safko, L., & Brake, D. (2009). *The social media bible.* John Wiley.

Saif, H., He, Y., & Alani, H. (2012). *Semantic sentiment analysis of Twitter. In Proceedings of ISWC 2012.* Springer-Verlag Berlin Heidelberg.

Saif, H., He, Y., Fernandez, M., & Alani, H. (2015). Contextual semantics for sentiment analysis of Twitter. *Information Processing & Management,* 1–15.

Sallot, L. M., Porter, L. V., & Acosta-Alzuru, C. (2004). Practitioners' web use and perceptions of their own roles and power: A qualitative study. *Public Relations Review*, *30*(3), 269–278. doi:10.1016/j.pubrev.2004.05.002

Sandhu, S. (2009). Strategic communication: An institutional perspective. *International Journal of Strategic Communication*, *3*(2), 72–92. doi:10.1080/15531180902805429

Saxenian, A. (2006). *The New Argonauts: Regional Advantage in a Global Economy*. Cambridge, MA: Harvard University Press.

Schachter, J. P. (2006). *Estimation of Emigration from the United States using International Data Sources. United Nations Expert Group Meeting on Measuring International Migration: concepts and Methods*. New York: United Nations Secretariat, Dept. of Economic and Social Affairs, Statistics Division.

Schefren, R. (2015). Find Your Strategic Sweet Spot– Its What Makes a Business Different: Great Companies Always Know Their Sweet Spot. *BizShifts Trends*. Retrieved from http://bizshifts-trends.com/2015/

Schmidt, K., & Ludlow, C. (2002). Inclusive branding: The why and how of a holistic approach to brands. Basingstoke, UK: Palgrave Macmillan. doi:10.1057/9780230513297

Schmitz, P. (2006). Inducing ontology from Flickr tags. In *Proceedings of the WWW 2006*.

Schniederjans, D., Cao, E. S., & Schniederjans, M. (2013). Enhancing financial performance with social media: An impression management perspective. *Decision Support Systems*, *55*(4), 911–918. doi:10.1016/j.dss.2012.12.027

Schouten, E. (2012). *Big data As A Service*. Retrieved from: http://edwinschouten.nl/2012/09/19/bigdata-as-a-service/

Schroeck, M., Shockley, R., Smart, J., Morales, D. R., & Tufano, P. (2014). Analytics: The real-world use of big data. IBM Global Business Services & Saïd Business School at the University of Oxford, IBM Institute for Business Value.

Schroeder H. (2013). The Art of Business Relationships Through Social Media. *Ivey Business Journal*. Retrieved December 06, 2015, from http://iveybusinessjournal.com/publication/the-art-of-business-relationships-through-social-media/

Schroeder, R. (2002). *Copresence and interaction in virtual environments: An overview of the range of issues*. Paper presented at the Fifth International Workshop on Presence, Porto, Portugal.

Schuller, B. W. (2015). Modelling user affect and sentiment in intelligent user interfaces. In *Proceedings of the IUI 2015*. doi:10.1145/2678025.2716265

Schultz, F., Utz, S., & Göritz, A. (2011). Is the medium the message? Perceptions of and reactions to crisis communication via twitter, blogs and traditional media. *Public Relations Review*, *37*(1), 20–27. doi:10.1016/j.pubrev.2010.12.001

Schupak, A. (2015, July 1). Google apologizes for mis-tagging photos of African Americans. *CBS News*. Retrieved July 2, 2015, from http://www.cbsnews.com/news/google-photos-labeled-pics-of-african-americans-as-gorillas/

Schwabish, J. A. (2009). *Identifying Rates of Emigration in the United States Using Administrative Earnings Records*. Congressional Budget Office, Working Paper Series.

Selwyn, N. (2009). The digital native-myth and reality. *Aslib Proceedings*, *61*(4), 364–379. doi:10.1108/00012530910973776

Serdyukov, P., Murdock, V., & Van Zwol, R. (2009). Placing Flickr photos on a map. In *Proceedings of SIGR '09*. doi:10.1145/1571941.1572025

Severyn, A., Moschitti, A., Uryupina, O., Plank, B., & Filippova, K. (2015). Multi-lingual opinion mining on YouTube. *Information Processing & Management*, 1–15.

Shaheen, M. A. (2008). Use of social networks and information seeking behavior of students during political crises in Pakistan: A case study. *The International Information & Library Review, 40*(3), 142–147. doi:10.1080/10572317.200 8.10762774

Shapiro, M. A., & Park, H. W. (2015). More than entertainment: YouTube and public responses to the science of global warming and climate change. *Social Sciences Information. Information Sur les Sciences Sociales, 54*(1), 115–145. doi:10.1177/0539018414554730

Shawar, B. A., & Atwell, E. (2005). Using corpora in machine-learning chatbot systems. *International Journal of Corpus Linguistics, 10*(4), 489–516. doi:10.1075/ijcl.10.4.06sha

Sheth, A. (2009). Citizen sensing, social signals, and enriching human experience. Semantics & Services. *IEEE Internet Computing*, 80–85.

Shi, R., Messaris, P., & Cappella, J. N. (2014). Effects of online comments on smokers' perception of antismoking public service announcements. *Journal of Computer-Mediated Communication, 19*(4), 975–990. doi:10.1111/jcc4.12057

Shirky, C. (2011). The political power of social media technology, the public sphere, and political change. *Foreign Affairs, 90*(1), 28–41.

Siau, K., Ee-Peng, L., & Shen, Z. (2001). Mobile commerce: Promises, challenges, and research agenda. *Journal of Database Management, 12*(3), 4–13. doi:10.4018/jdm.2001070101

Sigala, M., Christou, E., & Gretzel, U. (2011). *Web 2.0 in travel, tourism and hospitality: Theory, practice and cases.* Farnham, UK: Ashgate Publishing.

Sigurbjörnsson, B., & van Zwol, R. (2008). Flickr tag recommendation based on collective knowledge. In *Proceedings of the WWW 2008*. doi:10.1145/1367497.1367542

Sinclaire, J. K., & Vogus, C. E. (2011). Adoption of social networking sites: An exploratory adaptive structuration perspective for global organizations. *Information Technology & Management, 12*(4), 293–314. doi:10.1007/s10799-011-0086-5

Singer, P. W., & Friedman, A. (2014). *Cybersecurity and Cyberwar: What Everyone Needs to Know.* Oxford, UK: Oxford University Press.

Singla, A., & Weber, I. (2009). Camera brand congruence in the Flickr social graph. In *Proceedings of WISDM '09*. Retrieved June 23, 2015, from https://www.flickr.com/groups/api/discuss/72157631682781762/

Sin, S., Nor, K. M., & Al-Agaga, A. M. (2012). Factors Affecting Malaysian young consumers' online purchase intention in social media websites. *Procedia: Social and Behavioral Sciences, 40*, 326–333. doi:10.1016/j.sbspro.2012.03.195

Size of Wikipedia. (2015, Feb. 19). In *Wikipedia*. Retrieved Mar. 5, 2015, from http://en.wikipedia.org/wiki/Wikipedia:Size_of_Wikipedia

Skyrme, D. (2007). *Knowledge networking: Creating the collaborative enterprise.* London, UK: Routledge Publications.

Small, D. A., Loewenstein, G., & Slovic, P. (2007). Sympathy and callousness: The impact of deliberative thought on donations to identifiable and statistical victims. *Organizational Behavior and Human Decision Processes, 102*(2), 143–153. doi:10.1016/j.obhdp.2006.01.005

Smeltzer, S., & Keddy, D. (2010). Won't you be my (political) friend? The changing Face(book) of socio-political contestation in Malaysia. *Canadian Journal of Development Studies, 30*(3/4), 421–440.

Smith, C. (2015). Facebook is leading the way in social commerce. *Business Insider*. Available at: http://www.businessinsider.in/Facebook-is-leading-the-way-in-social-commerce/articleshow/48076273.cms

Smits M. & S. (2014). The impact of social media on business performance. *Proceedings of the 21ˢᵗ European conference on information systems*. Retrieved December 06, 2015, from http://www.staff.science.uu.nl/~vlaan107/ecis/files/ECIS2013-0713-paper.pdf

Souders, S. (2007). *High performance web sites: Essential knowledge for front-end engineers*. Sebastopol, CA: O'Reilly Media, Inc.

Statista. (2015). *Statistics & Facts*. Retrieved December 04, 2015, from http://www.statista.com/topics/1164/social-networks/

Statistics. (2015). In *YouTube*. Retrieved Mar. 8, 2015, at http://www.youtube.com/yt/press/statistics.html

Stawski, S. (2015). *Inflection Point: How the Convergence of Cloud, Mobility, Apps, and Data Will Shape the Future of Business*. Financial Times Press.

Stcherbatcheff, B. (2014, June 28). Why Americans abroad are giving up their citizenship. *Newsweek*. Retrieved Mar. 3, 2015, from http://www.newsweek.com/why-americans-abroad-are-giving-their-citizenship-256447

Steininger, K., Rückel, D., Dannerer, E., & Roithmayr, F. (2010). Healthcare knowledge transfer through a web 2.0 portal: An Austrian approach. *International Journal of Healthcare Technology and Management*, *11*(1/2), 13–30. doi:10.1504/IJHTM.2010.033272

Stephen, A. T., & Toubia, O. (2010). Deriving Value from Social Commerce Networks. *JMR, Journal of Marketing Research*, *47*(2), 215–228. doi:10.1509/jmkr.47.2.215

Sterne, J. (2010). *Social media metrics: How to measure and optimize your marketing investment*. Hoboken, NJ: John Wiley & Sons.

Stockdale, R., Ahmed, A., & Scheepers, H. (2012). *Identifying business value from the use of social media: An SME perspective*. Paper presented at the 16th Pacific Asia Conference on Information Systems (PACIS 2012), Ho Chi Minh City, Vietnam.

Strahilevitz, L. J. (2005). A social networks theory of privacy. *The University of Chicago Law Review*, 919–988.

Strauss, J., & Frost, R. (1999). *Marketing on the Internet. Principles of online marketing*. Upper Saddle River, NJ: Prentice Hall.

Streaming APIs. (2015). *Twitter*. Retrieved March 16, 2015, from https://dev.twitter.com/streaming/overview

Stringhini, G., Kruegel, C., & Vigna, G. (2010). Detecting spammers on social networks. In Proceedings of ACSAC '10. doi:10.1145/1920261.1920263

Stvilia, B., & Jörgensen, C. (2007/2008). End-user collection building behavior in Flickr. In *Proceedings of the American Society for Information Science and Technology*.

Stvilia, B., & Jörgensen, C. (2010). Member activities and quality of tags in a collection of historical photographs in Flickr. *Journal of the American Society for Information Science and Technology*, *61*(12), 2477–2489. doi:10.1002/asi.21432

Subramaniam, N., Nandhakumar, J., & Baptista, J. (2013). Exploring social network interactions in enterprise systems: The role of virtual co-presence. *Information Systems Journal*, *23*(6), 475–499. doi:10.1111/isj.12019

Suh, H., van Hillegersberg, J., Choi, J., & Chung, S. (2013). Effects of strategic alignment on IS success: The mediation role of IS investment in Korea. *Information Technology & Management*, *14*(1), 7–27. doi:10.1007/s10799-012-0144-7

Suh, J. H. (2015). Forecasting the daily outbreak of topic-level political risk from social media using hidden Markov model-based techniques. *Technological Forecasting and Social Change*, *94*(1), 115–132. doi:10.1016/j.techfore.2014.08.014

Sultan, N. A. (2011). Reaching for the "cloud": How SMEs can manage. *International Journal of Information Management, 31*(3), 272–278. doi:10.1016/j.ijinfomgt.2010.08.001

Sun, A., & Bhowmick, S. S. (2010). Quantifying tag representativeness of visual content of social images. In *Proceedings of MM '10*. doi:10.1145/1873951.1874029

Syred, J., Naidoo, C., Woodhall, S. C., & Baraitser, P. (2014). Would you tell everyone this? Facebook conversations as health promotion interventions. *Journal of Medical Internet Research, 16*(4), 148–156. doi:10.2196/jmir.3231

Tang, L., & Sampson, H. (2012). The interaction between mass media and the Internet in non-democratic states: The case of China. *Media Culture & Society, 34*(4), 457–471. doi:10.1177/0163443711436358

Tan, W. K., & Chen, T. H. (2012). The usage of online tourist information sources in tourist information search: An exploratory study. *Service Industries Journal, 32*(3), 451–476. doi:10.1080/02642069.2010.529130

Tata Consultancy Services (TCS). (2013). *Mastering Digital Feedback: How the Best Consumer Companies Use Social Media*. A TCS 2013 Global Trend Study. Retrieved December 03, 2015, from http://www.tcs.com/SiteCollectionDocuments/Trends_Study/mastering-digital-feedback-with-social-media-2013.pdf

Tatai, G., Csordás, A., Kiss, A., Szaló, A., & Laufer, L. (2003). Happy chatbot, happy user. *LNAI, 2792*, 5–12.

Taylor, M., & Perry, D. (2005). Diffusion of traditional and new media tactics in crisis communication. *Public Relations Review, 31*(2), 209–217. doi:10.1016/j.pubrev.2005.02.018

Thackeray, R., Neiger, B. L., Smith, A. K., & van Wagenen, S. B. (2012). Adoption and use of social media among public health. *BMC Public Health, 12*(1), 242–247. doi:10.1186/1471-2458-12-242

Thakor, P., & Sasi, S. (2015). Ontology-based sentiment analysis process for social media content. *Procedia Computer Science, 53*, 199 – 207. doi:10.1016/j.procs.2015.07.295

Thau, B. (2015). Retail product placement: Tapping data to optimize merchandise displays. *IBM Big data and Analytics Hub*. Retrieved from http://www.ibmbigdatahub.com

Thelwall, M., Buckley, K., Paltoglou, G., Cai, D., & Kappas, A. (2010). Sentiment strength detection in short informal text. *Journal of the American Society for Information Science and Technology, 61*(12), 2544–2558. doi:10.1002/asi.21416

Thomas-Jones, A. (2010). *Putting the social in social networks. In The Host in the Machine: Examining the Digital in the Social* (pp. 57–75). Oxford, UK: Chandos.

Tik, J. (2005). Why is Flickr so successful? *Flickr Central*. Retrieved May 30, 2015, from https://www.flickr.com/groups/central/discuss/36512/

Tiwari, A. K. (2010). *Infrastructure for Sustainable Rural Development*. New Delhi: Regal Publications.

Toffler, A. (1980). *The Third Wave*. New York, NY: William Morrow & Company.

Tomer, S., Avishay, G., & Brunia, A. (2015, October). Socializing in Emergencies- A review of the Use of Social Media in Emergency Situations. *International Journal of Information Management, 35*(5), 609–619. doi:10.1016/j.ijinfomgt.2015.07.001

Toni A., Bäck, A., Halonen, M., & Heinonen, S. (2008, December). Social media road maps exploring the futures triggered by social media. *VTT Research Notes*.

Trainor, K. J., Andzulis, J., Rapp, A., & Agnihotri, R. (2014). Social media technology usage and customer relationship performance: A capabilities-based examination of social CRM. *Journal of Business Research, 67*(6), 1201–1208. doi:10.1016/j.jbusres.2013.05.002

Troil. (2010, Mar. 21). In *Urban Dictionary*. Retrieved June 20, 2015, from http://www.urbandictionary.com/define.php?term=troil

Tsolmon, B., Kwon, A.-R., & Lee, K.-S. (2012). Extracting social events based on timeline and sentiment analysis in Twitter corpus. In G. Bouma, A. Ittoo, E. Métais, & H. Wortmann (Eds.), *Natural Language Processing and Information Systems*. doi:10.1007/978-3-642-31178-9_32

Turban, E., Liang, T. P., & Wu, S. P. (2011). A framework for adopting collaboration 2.0 tools for virtual group decision making. *Group Decision and Negotiation, 20*(2), 137–154. doi:10.1007/s10726-010-9215-5

Turkle, S. (2011). *Alone Together: Why We Expect More from Technology and Less from Each Other*. New York: Basic Books.

Turney, P. (2002). Thumbs Up or Thumbs Down? Semantic Orientation Applied to Unsupervised Classification of Reviews. *Proceedings of the Association for Computational Linguistics*. arXiv:cs.LG/0212032

U.S. Citizens and Resident Aliens Abroad. (2015). Internal Revenue Service. Retrieved Mar. 5, 2015, from http://www.irs.gov/Individuals/International-Taxpayers/U.S.-Citizens-and-Resident-Aliens-Abroad

U.S. Embassy Beijing. (n.d.). *Air Quality Monitor*. Embassy of the United States. Retrieved from http://beijing.usembassy-china.org.cn/aqirecent3.html

U.S. International Social Security Agreements. (2015). Social Security Administration. Retrieved Mar. 5, 2015, from http://www.ssa.gov/international/agreements_overview.html

User:AntiVandalBot/FAQ. (2006, Oct. 25). Retrieved Nov. 23, 2014, from http://en.wikipedia.org/wiki/User:AntiVandalBot/FAQ

Valentini, C. (2015). Is using social media "good" for the public relations profession? A critical reflection. *Public Relations Review, 41*(2), 170–177. doi:10.1016/j.pubrev.2014.11.009

van Belleghem, S. (2012). The Conversation Company boost Your Business through Culture. In *People and Culture*. London: Koga Page.

Vander Wal, T. (2007, Feb. 2). *Folksonomy*. Retrieved June 22, 2015, from http://www.vanderwal.net/folksonomy.html

Varvello, M., & Voelker, G. M. (2010). Second Life: A social network of humans and bots. In *Proceedings of NOSSDAV'10*. doi:10.1145/1806565.1806570

Vassallo, J. (2015). Social Media's Impact on the Human Resources Industry. *Business2community*. Retrieved November 23, 2015, from http://www.business2community.com/human-resources/social-medias-impact-on-the-human-resources-industry-01338454#ScJFrY7YSK6CIZ30.99

Venkataraman, S., & Das, R. (2013). The Influence of Corporate Social Media on Firm Level Strategic Decision Making. *International Journal of E-Business Research, 9*(1), 1–20. doi:10.4018/jebr.2013010101

Vijayendra, H., & Pillai, A. (2011). *Social Media Simplified- Twitter, Face Book- Beyond Casual Networking*. New Delhi: Ocean Paper Backs.

Wagner, C., Mitter, S., Körner, C., & Strohmaier, M. (2012). When social bots attack: Modeling susceptibility of users in online social networks. In Proceedings of #MSM2012 workshop.

Wagner, D., & Wagner, H. (2013). *Online communities and dynamic capabilities: Across-case examination of sensing, seizing, and reconfiguration.* Paper presented at the 19th Americas Conference on Information Systems (AMCIS 2013), Chicago, IL.

Wagner, C. S., & Leydesdorff, L. (2005a). Mapping the network of global science: Comparing international co-authorships from 1990 to 2000. *International Journal of Technology and Globalisation, 1*(2), 185–208. doi:10.1504/IJTG.2005.007050

Wagner, C. S., & Leydesdorff, L. (2005b). Network structure, self-organization, and the growth of international collaboration in science. *Research Policy, 34*(10), 1608–1618. doi:10.1016/j.respol.2005.08.002

Wagner, C. S., & Leydesdorff, L. (2008). International collaboration in science and the formation of a core group. *Journal of Informetrics, 2*(4), 317–325. doi:10.1016/j.joi.2008.07.003

Wald, R., Ghoshgoftaar, T. M., Napolitano, A., & Sumner, C. (2013). Predicting susceptibility to social bots on Twitter. *IEEE IRI 2013.* doi:10.1109/IRI.2013.6642447

Walker, J. (2005). Feral hypertext: When hypertext literature escapes control. In Proceedings of HT '05.

Wallsten, K. (2007). Agenda setting and the blogosphere: An analysis of the relationship between mainstream media and political blogs. *Review of Policy Research, 24*(6), 567–587. doi:10.1111/j.1541-1338.2007.00300.x

Wang, A. H. (2010). Detecting spam bots in online social networking sites: A machine learning approach. In Data and Applications Security XXIV, (LNCS), (vol. 6166, pp. 335 – 342). International Federation for Information Processing. doi:10.1007/978-3-642-13739-6_25

Wang, C., Chen, W., & Wang, Y. (2012). Scalable influence maximization for independent cascade model in large-scale social networks. *Data Mining and Knowledge Discovery, 25*(3), 545–576. doi:10.1007/s10618-012-0262-1

Wang, G., Sun, J., Ma, J., Xu, K., & Gu, J. (2014). Sentiment classification: The contribution of ensemble learning. *Decision Support Systems, 57*, 77–93. doi:10.1016/j.dss.2013.08.002

Wang, Y., Chen, Y., & Benitez-Amado, J. (2015). How information technology influences environmental performance: Empirical evidence from China. *International Journal of Information Management, 35*(2), 160–170. doi:10.1016/j.ijinfomgt.2014.11.005

Wasserman, S., & Faust, K. (1994). *Social network analysis: Methods and applications.* New York: Cambridge University Press. doi:10.1017/CBO9780511815478

Waters, R. D., & Jamal, J. Y. (2011). Tweet, tweet, tweet: A content analysis of nonprofit organizations' Twitter updates. *Public Relations Review, 37*(3), 321–324. doi:10.1016/j.pubrev.2011.03.002

Watts, D. J., & Strogatz, S. H. (1998). Collective dynamics of 'small-world' networks. *Nature, 393*(6684), 440–442. doi:10.1038/30918 PMID:9623998

Webb, S., Caverlee, J., & Pu, C. (2008). Social honeypots: Making friends with a spammer near you. In *5th Conference on Email and Anti-Spam (CEAS).* Retrieved Nov. 15, 2014, from http://www.ceas.cc/2008/papers/ceas2008-paper-50.pdf

Weber, L. (2011). *Everywhere: comprehensive digital business strategy for the social media era.* Hoboken, NJ: John Wiley & Sons.

Wending, C., Radisch, J., & Jacobzone, S. (2013). *The use of Social Media in Risk and Crisis Communication.* OECD Working Papers on Public Governance no 25. OECD Publishing.

Wiig, K. (1997). Knowledge Management: Where Did it Come From and Where Will It Go? *Expert Systems with Applications, 13*(1), 1–14. doi:10.1016/S0957-4174(97)00018-3

Wijnhoven, F., & Bloemen, O. (2014). External validity of sentiment mining reports: Can current methods identify demographic biases, event biases, and manipulation of reviews? *Decision Support Systems*, *59*, 262–273. doi:10.1016/j.dss.2013.12.005

Williams, L., Bannister, C., Arribas-Ayllon, M., Preece, A., & Spasić, I. (2015). The role of idioms in sentiment analysis. *Expert Systems with Applications*, *42*(21), 7375–7385. doi:10.1016/j.eswa.2015.05.039

Wilson, C., Boe, B., Sala, A., Puttaswamy, K. P., & Zhao, B. Y. (2009). User interactions in social networks and their implications. In *Proceedings of the 4th ACM European conference on Computer systems* (pp. 205-218). ACM. doi:10.1145/1519065.1519089

Wilson, J. (2009). Social networking: The business case. *Engineering & Technology.*, *4*(10), 54–56. doi:10.1049/et.2009.1010

Wilson, R. K., & Eckel, C. C. (2006). Judging a book by its cover: Beauty and expectations in the trust game. *Political Research Quarterly*, *59*(2), 189–202. doi:10.1177/106591290605900202

Wipro. (2012). *Social Media: Impact and Relevance in Managing Human Resources in India*. Retrieved December 03, 2015, from http://www.wipro.com/documents/Social_Media_Report_Feb_2012.pdf

Wong, E. (2013, Jan. 12). On scale of 0 to 500, Beijing's air quality tops 'crazy bad' at 755. *NY Times Online*. Retrieved Nov. 15, 2014, from http://www.nytimes.com/2013/01/13/science/earth/beijing-air-pollution-off-the-charts.html?_r=1&

Won, S. G. L., Evans, M. A., Carey, C., & Schnittka, C. G. (2015). Youth appropriation of social media for collaborative and facilitated design-based learning. *Computers in Human Behavior*, *50*, 385–391. doi:10.1016/j.chb.2015.04.017

Woo, J., Kang, A. R., & Kim, H. K. (2012). Modeling of bot usage diffusion across social networks in MMORPGs. In *Proceedings of WAS A 2012*. doi:10.1145/2425296.2425299

Wood, R. W. (2014, May 3). Record numbers renounce U.S. citizenship—and many aren't counted. *Forbes Magazine*. Retrieved Feb. 22, 2015, from http://www.forbes.com/sites/robertwood/2014/05/03/americans-are-renouncing-citizenship-at-record-pace-and-many-arent-even-counted/

Wright, D. K., & Hinson, M. D. (2009). An updated look at the impact of social media on public relations practice. *The Public Relations Journal*, *3*(2), 1–33.

Wu, K., Yang, S., & Zhu, K. Q. (2015). *False rumors detection on Sina Weibo by propagation structures*. Paper presented at the International Conference on Data Engineering (ICDE 2015), Seoul, South Korea. doi:10.1109/ICDE.2015.7113322

Wu, L. L., Wang, Y. T., Su, Y. T., & Yeh, M. Y. (2013). *Cultivating social capital through interactivity on social network sites*. Paper presented at the Pacific Asia Conference on Information Systems (PACIS 2013), Jeju Island, South Korea.

Wu, L., Hua, X.-S., Yu, N., Ma, W.-Y., & Li, S. (2008). Flickr distance. In *Proceedings of MM'08*. doi:10.1145/1459359.1459364

Wu, L. (2010). Applicability of the resource-based and dynamic-capability views under environmental volatility. *Journal of Business Research*, *63*(1), 27–31. doi:10.1016/j.jbusres.2009.01.007

Xiang, Z., & Gretzel, U. (2010). Role of social media in online travel information search. *Tourism Management*, *31*(2), 179–188. doi:10.1016/j.tourman.2009.02.016

Xiang, Z., Wober, K., & Fesenmaier, D. R. (2008). Representation of the online tourism domain in search engines. *Journal of Travel Research*, *47*(2), 137–150. doi:10.1177/0047287508321193

Yanai, K., Kawakubo, H., & Barnard, K. (2012). Entropy-based analysis of visual and geolocation concepts in images. In Multimedia Information Extraction: Advances In Video, Audio, And Imagery Analysis For Search, Data Mining, Surveillance, And Authoring. John Wiley & Sons, Inc.

Yan, G., He, W., Shen, J., & Tang, C. (2014). A bilingual approach for conducting Chinese and English social media sentiment analysis. *Computer Networks*, *75*, 491–503. doi:10.1016/j.comnet.2014.08.021

Yang, G. (2009). *The power of the Internet in China: Citizen activism online*. New York, NY: Columbia University Press.

Yang, S. U., & Lim, J. S. (2009). The effects of blog-mediated public relations (BMPR) on relational trust. *Journal of Public Relations Research*, *21*(3), 341–359. doi:10.1080/10627260802640773

Yates, D., Wagner, C., & Majchrzak, A. (2010). Factors affecting shapers of organizational wikis. *Journal of the American Society for Information Science and Technology*, *61*(3), 543–554. doi: 10.1002/asi.21266

Ylagan, A. (2014, July 15). Governments can bridge costs and services gap with sensor networks. *O'Reilly Radar.*

Yoo, K. H., & Gretzel, U. (2011). Influence of personality on travel-related consumer-generated media creation. *Computers in Human Behavior*, *27*(2), 609–621. doi:10.1016/j.chb.2010.05.002

You, S., DesArmo, J., & Joo, S. (2013). Measuring happiness of U.S. cities by mining user-generated text in Flickr.com: A pilot analysis. In *Proceedings of ASIST 2013*.

Yu, Y., Duan, W., & Cao, Q. (2013). The impact of social and conventional media on firm equity value: A sentiment analysis approach. *Decision Support Systems*, *55*(4), 919–926. doi:10.1016/j.dss.2012.12.028

Zanella, S., & Paris, I. (2014). Social Recruiting. *The Adecco*. Retrieved December 08, 2015, from http://www.adecco.com/en-US/Industry-Insights/Documents/social-recruiting/adecco-global-social-recruiting-survey-global-report.pdf

Zangerle, E. & Specht, G. (2014). *'Sorry, I was hacked": A classification of compromised Twitter accounts*. Academic Press.

Zeiller, M., & Schauer, B. (2011). *Adoption, motivation and success factors of social media for team collaboration in SMEs*. Paper presented at the 11th International Conference on Knowledge Management and Knowledge Technologies (i-KNOW 2011), Graz, Austria. doi:10.1145/2024288.2024294

Zervas, P., Tsitmidelli, A., Sampson, D.G., & Chen, N.-S., & Kinshuk. (2014). Studying research collaboration patterns via coauthorship analysis in the field of TeL: The case of Educational Technology & Society journal. *Journal of Educational Technology & Society*, *17*(4), 1–16.

Zhang, D., Prior, K., Levene, M., Mao, R., & van Liere, D. (2012). Leave or stay: The departure dynamics of Wikipedia editors. In Proceedings of ADMA, (LNAI), (vol. 7713, pp. 1 – 14). Berlin: Springer-Verlag.

Zhang, J., Qu, Y., Cody, J., & Wu, Y. (2010). *A case study of micro-blogging in the enterprise: Use, value, and related issues*. Paper presented at the 28th Annual ACM Conference on Human Factors in Computing Systems (CHI 2010), Atlanta, GA.

Zhang, K., Zhao, S. J., & Lee, M. K. O. (2013). *Product attitude formation on online review sites with social networks*. Paper presented at the Pacific Asia Conference on Information Systems (PACIS 2013), Jeju Island, South Korea.

Zhang, J. (2015). Voluntary information disclosure on social media. *Decision Support Systems*, *73*, 28–36. doi:10.1016/j.dss.2015.02.018

Zhang, K., Xie, Y., Yang, Y., Sun, A., Liu, H., & Choudhary, A. (2014). Incorporating conditional random fields and active learning to improve sentiment identification. *Neural Networks*, *58*, 60–67. doi:10.1016/j.neunet.2014.04.005 PMID:24856246

Zhao, L., Lu, Y., Wang, B., Chau, P. Y. K., & Zhang, L. (2012). Cultivating the sense of belonging and motivating user participation in virtual communities: A social capital perspective. *International Journal of Information Management*, *32*(6), 574–588. doi:10.1016/j.ijinfomgt.2012.02.006

Zhao, S. (2003). Toward a taxonomy of copresence. *Presence (Cambridge, Mass.)*, *12*(5), 445–455. doi:10.1162/105474603322761261

Zhu, Y. Q., & Chen, H. G. (2015). Social media and human need satisfaction: Implications for social media marketing. *Business Horizons*, *58*(3), 335–345. doi:10.1016/j.bushor.2015.01.006

Zimmerman, J., & Deborg, N. G. (2014). *Social media marketing all-in-one for dummies*. New Delhi: Wiley India Private Limited.

About the Contributors

N. Raghavendra Rao is an Advisor to FINAIT Consultancy Services India. He has a doctorate in the area of Finance from Pune University India. He has a rare distinction of having experience in the combined areas of Information Technology and Business applications. His rich experience in Industry is matched with a parallel academic experience in Management & IT in Business Schools. He has over two decades of experience in the development of application software related to manufacturing, service oriented organizations, financial institutions and business enterprises. He contributes chapters for books. He presents papers related to Information technology and Knowledge Management at National and International conferences. He contributes articles on Information Technology to main stream news papers and journals. His area of research interest is Mobile Computing, Virtual Technology, and Commerce in Space, Ubiquitous Commerce, Cloud Computing, e-governance, Knowledge Management, and Social Media for Business Applications. He is an independent editor for research reference books.

* * *

Rashid Ali obtained his B.Tech. and M.Tech. from A.M.U. Aligarh, India in 1999 and 2001 respectively. He obtained his PhD in Computer Engineering in February 2010 from A.M.U. Aligarh. His PhD work was on performance evaluation of Web Search Engines. He has authored more than 100 papers in various International Journals and International conference proceedings. He has presented papers in many International conferences and has also chaired sessions in few International conferences. He has reviewed articles for some of the reputed International Journals and International conference proceedings. He has supervised 16 M.Tech Dissertation and one PhD Thesis. Currently, he is supervising four PhD candidates. His research interests include Web-Searching, Web-Mining, soft computing (Rough-Set, Artificial Neural Networks, fuzzy logic etc), and Image Retrieval Techniques.

Tasleem Arif obtained Master's in Computer Applications from University of Jammu and Ph.D. in Computer Science from Baba Ghulam Shah Badshah University Rajouri, Jammu & Kashmir, India. His Ph.D. work was on Academic Social Network Extraction from online sources. He has authored about 30 papers in various International Journals and International conference proceedings and has been organizing secretary of some conferences/seminars. Currently he is working as Sr. Assistant Professor in the Post Graduate Department of Information Technology, Baba Ghulam Shah Badshah University Rajouri, Jammu & Kashmir. His research interests include Web Mining, Soft Computing, Information Retrieval, Data Mining, Recommender systems, cryptography and network security.

Shalin Hai-Jew works as an instructional designer at Kansas State University. She has created online learning for The Boeing Company, Washington Online, and a number of colleges and universities. For years, she worked as a faculty member in the U.S. and in the P.R.C. (1988 – 1990, 1992 – 1994, the latter two years through the UNDP). She conducts data analytics for grant-funded projects. She reviews for a number of publishers and publications. She has edited a number of books and published a number of academic research articles. She has B.A.s in English and psychology, and M.A. in English from the University of Washington, and an Ed.D in Educational Leadership (with a focus on Public Administration) from Seattle University (2005). She has been the recipient of a number of academic awards and scholarships. She is currently editing texts on data analytics in the digital humanities, techniques for coding imagery and multimedia, and selfies.

Sudarsan Jayasingh is a PhD Scholar at VIT Business School Chennai and his research area is Social Media Marketing. He is working as an Assistant Professor at SSN School of Management, Chennai. He has published research papers in reputed journals, book chapters and conferences. He has around 18 years of teaching experience.

Ana Isabel Jimenez-Zarco is an Associate Professor in the Innovation and Marketing Area at the Open University of Catalonia, and a Part-time professor at the Marketing Department of ICADE, Pontificia of Comillas University. She has PhD in Economics and Business Sciences from the University of Castilla-La Mancha, Spain. She has Post degree in Building Models in Ecology and Natural Resources Management from the Polytechnic University of Catalonia. Until 2002 she taught in the Marketing disciple at the University of Castilla-La Mancha, and the East Anglia University of Brighton and Chapingo University of Mexico. From 2003 she has been a Co-Director of the Master's Degree Program in Marketing and Communication Management at the Open University of Catalonia. She served as a Program Director of the Bachelor's Degree in Business Administration. As a researcher, her main areas of interest are innovation and entrepreneurship. She is an author of several books in these areas, and serves as a reviewer and associated editor of several international journals.

Sudarsanam S. K. has PhD in mathematics from IIT Madras. His PhD thesis is in the area of fuzzy equations. He is a Professor at VIT Business School Chennai (under VIT University Vellore). He has more than 14 years of IT industry experience and has managed projects of size more than 5 Million USD and has handled teams of size up to 80 resources. He has good academic experience of 6 years and teaches subjects related to Project Management, Operational Analytics, DB System, and Business Intelligence for MBA students. His research interests are in the area of Fuzzy Systems, Information Systems, Financial Analytics and Social Media analytics. He is currently supervising 6 Ph.D. students in various research areas including Social Media and Knowledge Management. He has several publications in international journals in the area of Fuzzy logic and Information Systems. He also presents papers in several international conferences in the area of Business Analytics. He is currently Dean-in Charge of the VIT Business School Chennai. He also conducts workshops and management development programs for corporate sector.

Kijpokin Kasemsap received his BEng degree in Mechanical Engineering from King Mongkut's University of Technology, Thonburi, his MBA degree from Ramkhamhaeng University, and his DBA degree in Human Resource Management from Suan Sunandha Rajabhat University. Dr. Kasemsap is a Special Lecturer in the Faculty of Management Sciences, Suan Sunandha Rajabhat University, based in Bangkok, Thailand. Dr. Kasemsap is a Member of the International Economics Development and Research Center (IEDRC), the International Foundation for Research and Development (IFRD), and the International Innovative Scientific and Research Organization (IISRO). Dr. Kasemsap also serves on the International Advisory Committee (IAC) for the International Association of Academicians and Researchers (INAAR). Dr. Kasemsap is the sole author of over 250 peer-reviewed international publications and book chapters on business, education, and information technology. Dr. Kasemsap is included in the TOP 100 Professionals–2016 and in the 10th edition of 2000 Outstanding Intellectuals of the 21st Century by the International Biographical Centre, Cambridge, England.

Venkatesh R. is a Professor of Marketing in VIT Business School, VIT University, Chennai. He has a PhD in Services Marketing from IIT Madras with 28 years of work experience (13 in Industry & 15 years in Academics). He has published in many International Journals earlier. Has also presented papers in 15 International Conferences in India & one in USA (May, 2005). At present, he guides 5 PhD scholars at VIT Chennai.

Matilda S. holds B.E. (Hons) Degree from Madurai Kamaraj University, M.S Degree from BITS Pilani and PhD in Computer Networks and Communication from Annamalai University. She was awarded the sixth university rank during her undergraduate study. Her research interest includes 4G Networks, Cross-layer design methods, enhancing QoS, Network Simulation tools, Buffer design and Big data. Matilda.S is dually certified to teach regular and special education in Engineering. She is a Cisco certified instructor for CCNA and is certified by IBM for Rational Rose. She has also obtained the coveted *Cambridge International Certificate for Teachers and Trainers* (CICTT) in Engineering. She is a reviewer of research work has 13 research publications to her credit. She is a life member of ISTE, IAENG and senior member of IACSIT. She has rich experience in teaching and administration at different levels. Currently she is the Vice Principal and Dean- Academics of IFET College of Engineering affiliated to Anna University.

Neus Soler-Labajos is a Digital Marketing Consultant and a Part-time Professor of Marketing and Market Research at the Open University of Catalonia. She has a Degree in Market Research and Techniques at the Open University of Catalonia and Diploma in Business Sciences at the University of Barcelona. She accomplished a Strategic and Operational Marketing Program at the University of Minnesota. She has an Executive MBA and Post degree in Social Media and Community Management. Her career is closely linked to the commercial and business marketing. She has an experience of over twenty years as the Marketing Manager in one of the pioneer corporations of the textile sector in Spain. She currently develops marketing activities as a freelance, focused on market research, brands' implementation and product development. She also develops teaching activities in the area of marketing and is the author of educational materials. She is a lecturer and consultant. Her main focus is on digital marketing, specializing in social media and e-commerce.

Srinivasan Vaidyanathan has been an accomplished and results-driven delivery director in IT industry and has over 20 years of progressive, managerial and leadership experience in high visibility and multifaceted roles in IT majors, Cognizant and Capgemini. He had led large-scale software deliveries for several flagship customers that cut across industrial sectors. He has demonstrated success of delivery management, business development, Resource Planning, Financials, HR and Quality Management in his professional domain. He has hands-on experience in leading Knowledge Management at various capacities of his corporate tenure. He has proven abilities to implement standards, procedures, and processes that improve software delivery quality. He is currently on the pursuit of his doctoral research in Knowledge Management, under the guidance of Dr. Sudarsanam, at VIT Business School, Chennai, with a view to contribute to the literature leveraging his amassed experience and knowledge. His areas of interest include Social Media and Knowledge Sharing. He has published research papers in reputed journals.

Index

Printed in the United States
By Bookmasters